THE
TAIPING
REBELLION

Chin Shunshin

Translated by Joshua A. Fogel

AN EAST GATE BOOK

M.E. Sharpe

Armonk, New York
London, England

An East Gate Book

Cover calligraphy by Harrison X. Tu

Library of Congress Cataloging-in-Publication Data

Chin, Shunshin, 1924–
  [Taihei tengoku. English]
The Taiping rebellion / by Chin Shunshin ; translated by Joshua A. Fogel.
    p. cm.
"An East gate book"
  ISBN 0-7656-0099-04 (alk. paper)—ISBN 0-7656-0100-1 (pbk. : alk. paper)
   1. China—History—Taiping Rebellion, 1850–1864—Fiction. I. Fogel, Joshua A., 1950–
II. Title.

PL847.I5 T27 2000
895.6′35—dc21   99-049758
CIP

Printed in the United States of America

The paper used in this publication meets the minimum requirements of
American National Standard for Information Sciences
Permanence of Paper for Printed Library Materials,
ANSI Z 39.48-1984.

∞

BM (c) 10   9   8   7   6   5   4   3   2   1
BM (p) 10   9   8   7   6   5   4   3   2   1

Contents

Translator's Note

What follows is an English translation of the entire text of Chin Shunshin's long historical novel, *Taihei tengoku*. I have added an occasional word here or there to make the text clearer, but otherwise altered nothing. In addition, I have included the birth and death dates, where known, of a number of major historical personages who populate the pages of this work. I have not done this for the principal historical figures on the Taiping side. Their stories are told below, and I did not want to give away too much of the drama in advance. The connecting fiber tying together the various scenes and battles of the Taiping Rebellion—the Lian family—is entirely fictional.

JAF
February 2000

THE
TAIPING
REBELLION

1

An Evening in Nagasaki

—1—

Waves were breaking in the shadows cast on the water by the circular moon. Undulating, flickering . . . it was as if light and water were at play with one another.

"So, this is good-bye. Take care," urged the voice of a young man.

"How can I ever thank you?" Lian Liwen said slowly in a faltering, unsteady Japanese. The paper lantern held by the young man beside him illuminated a small boat by the shore.

"I really didn't do anything worthy of thanks," said the young man as he lowered his head.

"Masasuke, you're so young and already so busy. That's remarkable."

"Well, Mr. Lian, your Japanese certainly has improved, but so has your ability at flattery." Lian laughed. "Not even a year has passed, has it?"

"Perhaps we shall meet again," said Lian Liwen as he stepped on board the boat. The black shadow of a Chinese vessel floated over the open sea. The boatman silently rowed, and soon the small craft was far from shore. The young man looking on from the shore held the lantern high. He had a long, thin face, that of someone still in his youth. Ōkubo Masasuke was in fact only twenty years old, by Japanese reckoning.

As the boat carrying Lian Liwen approached the Chinese ship, he removed the hood covering his head. The pigtail stuffed into the hood came dangling loosely down his back. Now he could see before him a rope ladder hanging from the ship's deck. There, in the open sea before Bōnotsu in the domain of Satsuma, Lian boarded his vessel bound for Nagasaki.

The year was 1849, second year of the Kaei reign in Japan. In that year, the Qing government in China sent eight trading ships to Nagasaki, though Number Seven had been shipwrecked at Amakusa. Lian was now boarding Number Four in Satsuma bay.

During the years the Tokugawa regime enforced its exclusion policy, trading ships from China had to carry a special piece of identification known as a *shinpai,* or license. The license for vessel Number Four of 1849 was issued in the name of one Li Yisheng, and the shipowner named on it was one Niu Xinyuan. The real owner, though, was Lian Weicai, proprietor of an establishment known as the Jinshunji, which had its main office in Xiamen (Amoy), Fujian province, in China.

At the conclusion of the Opium War seven years earlier, the Treaty of Nanjing had compelled the Chinese to open five ports to foreign trade. Until then the Qing government had allowed only Guangzhou (Canton) as a trading site, much as Japan at that time had made Nagasaki its only window to the outside world.

Following the Opium War, the Jinshunji had spread its commercial ventures principally to Hong Kong and Shanghai, while the main office in Fujian remained in name only. Lian Weicai's fourth son, Liwen, had been in Shanghai, but the previous year he had asked to be allowed to sail to the Ryūkyū Islands.

"I'll take about a year. That should do it," he had said, and his father agreed without hesitation. Liwen wanted to go somewhere unfamiliar and forget about everything. He had been married just over a year when his young bride suddenly died, and her death had painfully wounded him.

The Ryūkyūs were a difficult place to work, and that was precisely what Liwen was looking forward to. The Shimazu domain of Satsuma, located on the island of Kyūshū in southern Japan, held control over the Ryūkyū Islands and engaged in trade with China through them. This "trade" was conducted in a form whereby the Ryūkyūs received a kind of enfeoffment by imperial edict from China, and as a subordinate state they bore tribute to the superior Qing regime in China. The Japanese shogunate in Edo officially authorized this arrangement.

As a matter of principle, the shogunate only permitted the Chinese and the Dutch to trade at Nagasaki. The monopoly agency that saw to this trade for the shogunal authorities was known as the Nagasaki Hall. Shimazu domain was now muscling in on its terrain. Of all the domains throughout Japan, though, only Shimazu was engaging in foreign trade on its own, and only in Chinese goods. In 1810 the shogunate was compelled to permit the sale of these imports at Nagasaki. Although at first restricted to a specified list of articles for sale, Shimazu forcibly expanded the list at will. Shimazu's influence over the shogunate was exceptionally strong because it held a trump card: it supported and preserved the Ryūkyūs, without which the island chain would have ceased to remain part of Japan.

Thus the shogunate had no choice but to be conciliatory. Shimazu, for its part, made full use of the privileges accruing to official authorization to participate in commerce at the Nagasaki Hall—indeed, more than full use.

Recognition of Shimazu's special rights was solely so it could dispose of the items acquired in the Qing–Ryūkyūan "tribute trade" and lay items in stock. Yet Shimazu secretly carried on foreign trade beyond the scope of the tribute trade. The very presence of a large volume of Chinese artifacts in the case of the other domains would have been sufficient to cast suspicion on them, for the disposal of such items would have been exceedingly difficult. Secret trade itself necessitated the elimination of a domain's ruling family.

Shimazu domain, however, got away with calling its private trade "Ryūkyūan tribute trade." That provided the perfect cloak of invisibility. It ensured the legality of the origination points for the commercial products being exchanged and made it possible for the Nagasaki Hall to become an officially recognized sales site.

Because of the secret nature of this trade, there were no official records kept. In the Ryūkyū Islands, however, every staff person knew that trade was being implemented outside the structure of the tribute trade. Chinese vessels came to the Ryūkyūs to sell Chinese products; they purchased marine produce and returned to China. Unlike the trade in Nagasaki, though, no bothersome license was required of the Chinese here.

Soon these Chinese vessels also began appearing in the waters off Satsuma, and Shimazu domain transacted business with them under conditions favorable to the Chinese. Thus even vessels carrying official licenses disposed of a part of their cargoes in the coastal islands off Satsuma before continuing on to Nagasaki. There were, as a result, occasions when Chinese vessels called at Nagasaki with almost nothing left to sell on board.

The principal partner in the secret trade, including that of Shimazu domain, was the Jinshunji. Lian Liwen had gone to the Ryūkyūs to carry on business related to this trade, and to engage in work-related negotiations in Satsuma as well. One of the parties with whom he had contact was Ōkubo Toshiyo, Shimazu's overseer for the Ryūkyū Islands, and Liwen had become close friends with his son, Masasuke.

Ship Number Four, carrying a license, as always, unloaded its cargo bound for Shimazu at Bōnotsu, and from there it headed for Nagasaki. Having business to attend to in Nagasaki, Liwen had taken advantage of the ship's scheduled route and boarded it in the waters off Satsuma. The young Masasuke, who saw Liwen off by the harbor, was later to become known as Ōkubo Toshimichi (1830–78), a major political figure in Japanese history. At this time, Masasuke was listed in the domainal register as an official scribe.

—2—

The clamorous peals of gongs and drums continued for a time on the deck of Chinese vessel Number Four. This animated ceremony had become customary in celebration of a safe arrival. Once the ship dropped anchor outside the harbor, it awaited the appropriate measures to be taken by the office of the Nagasaki Administrator. In due time, several dozen small crafts rowed out from the shore, attached a tow line to the Chinese ship, and drew it into the harbor. Once inside the harbor, it again lowered the anchor it had just raised. The gongs clanged and the drums beat to signal this whole event.

When the instruments of celebration quieted down, an inspector and the interpreters from the office of the Nagasaki Administrator boarded the Chinese vessel. They carried a placard enumerating forbidden items, which they hung from the ship's mast. It was, of course, written in Japanese, and was translated into Chinese by the interpreters for the men on board the ship. The main objects banned were Christian items. When the inspection was completed, immigration procedures commenced. The license was checked, and presentation of the cargo list and the ship's manifest was requested.

Lian Liwen's name appeared on the manifest as someone who had boarded in China, and the cargo list, written before the ship had set sail, excluded the portion of items delivered to Satsuma. Because of this, they had to make arrangements in advance for the quantity of business to be conducted with the domainal authorities in Shimazu. In fact, this had been one of Liwen's tasks.

Once the proper documents were presented, the famous loyalty test known as *fumie* was exacted: to come ashore, the men on board ship had to "step on an image" of Jesus or Mary (the meaning of the term *fumie*) as a visible act of blasphemy against Christianity. This completed, the Chinese were allowed to disembark. Once on shore, they were not permitted to roam at leisure through the city. Like the Dutch, who were confined to Dejima, the Chinese were placed in a "Chinese Compound."

Prior to the Genroku reign, which began in 1688, Chinese mixed with Japanese and lodged within the city of Nagasaki, probably because the authorities felt safe in assuming that there was little chance any Christians were among them. There was always, however, the fear that mixed residence might enable individuals to partake of secret trading. In addition, reports were transmitted to the shogunate to the effect that the Kangxi Emperor (r. 1662–1722) of the Qing dynasty had appointed a Jesuit to head his Directorate of Astronomy and that he had allowed the return of missionaries who had been chased to Macao. Thus the Japanese authorities had become attentive to the possibility of Christian connections among the Chinese.

The Chinese Official Residence was completed in 1689. It was located on the grounds of the shogunate's garden of medicinal plants at Jūzen Temple. It covered an area of 9,373 *tsubo* (over 337,000 square feet), much larger than Dejima, which was not even 4,000 *tsubo* (roughly 144,000 square feet). The Dutch were not allowed one step outside of Dejima, which they referred to as their "Far Eastern Prison." The Chinese, by contrast, were permitted outside their Official Residence at certain specified times for temple visits and the like, if accompanied by Japanese officials.

In compensation for being confined to single spots, both groups were allowed to call in prostitutes to relieve their boredom while away from home. Certain prostitutes, from the Maruyama district of Nagasaki, were picked for Dejima and others for the Chinese Official Residence. After the hard labors aboard ship, this provided the men with an opportunity for some enjoyment. Once they had tread upon the image, merchants and seamen alike turned to more cheerful pursuits. Those who had made the voyage a number of times had their own particular favorites among the women. Higher-ups, like the shipowners, had women who may as well have been called their "Nagasaki wives."

Lian Liwen also headed in a lighthearted step toward the Chinese compound. Since this was his first time in Nagasaki, he had no favorite prostitute picked out. He was elated because he knew that his elder brother Zhewen was already in the compound. Two years Liwen's senior, Zhewen had quietly left the family business to devote his energies to painting. Zhewen had come to Nagasaki from the Chinese port city Ningbo about six months earlier aboard a Chinese vessel licensed in the name of Zheng Langbo. It was the Chinese vessel Number One of the present year.

Though unofficial, there were also Chinese who came to Japan on the invitation from the Nagasaki Administrator. As a rule, since merchants, shipowners, and seamen returned on the ships that had brought them, their stays in Nagasaki lasted only a few months. Invited guests, on the other hand, were allowed longer stays and did not necessarily return to China aboard their ship of arrival. This category included doctors, artists, writers, and Buddhist priests.

Lian Zhewen apparently developed an interest in traveling to Japan after a fellow painter had put the idea in his head. He was endowed with the wanderlust of an artist. Although Zhewen had been in Suzhou for a time, even when Liwen was in nearby Shanghai, he had not been able to contact his peripatetic brother. Now, three years had passed since they had seen one another.

Aboard ship, bound for Nagasaki, Liwen counted the length of time that had transpired and was again appalled at how long it had been. Zhewen was already thirty-one. "And I'm going to be thirty next year," he thought, pondering their respective ages. At that point, the visage of his late wife floated into his mind, her face and figure slender, youthful until the day she died. The contours of her face seemed to resemble Masasuke's, and Liwen realized, as he was about to enter the Chinese compound, that this was one reason he had such positive feelings about Ōkubo Masasuke. In Kagoshima, capital of Shimazu domain, Liwen had known Masasuke's acquaintances, who included a wide assortment of young people. There were, for example, the imposingly heroic types, such as a young fellow by the name of Saigō Kichinosuke (later, the famous Saigō Takamori, 1828–1877). He seemed like a brilliant young man, but Liwen felt no particular fondness for him as he did for Masasuke.

When they had parted company, Liwen presented Masasuke with the gift of a well-known Chinese text of that time, the *Haiguo tuzhi* (Illustrated Gazetteer of the Sea Kingdoms) by the Chinese scholar and official, Wei Yuan (1794–1856). "I'd like Lord Kichinosuke to read this book," he muttered. The *Haiguo tuzhi* was a work written on the basis of documents given Wei Yuan by Lin Zexu (1785–1850), the Chinese commissioner whose actions against Great Britain were said to have elicited the attacks on China that were later known as the Opium War. It described conditions in the world in the immediate aftermath of the Opium War and advocated the need for China to modernize. It was just the sort of book he wanted a young man like Saigō to read, but Liwen was unable to give it directly to him, using Ōkubo rather as a conduit.

The region in Nagasaki where the Chinese Official Residence was located is now named for that structure. It was surrounded by a brick wall over seven feet in height, beyond which had been dug a concentric moat six feet deep and six feet wide. Upon passing through the front gate, one found various buildings, such as a station for officials and a business exchange. Only after passing through the inner gate did one enter the actual residential quarters of the Chinese.

"Hey, over here. Liwen, why are you so absent-minded?" Hearing himself addressed, Liwen looked toward the inner gate.

Three Chinese vessels had already docked in Nagasaki, and between four hundred and five hundred Chinese were then staying at the compound. Maybe an acquaintance was trying to welcome him over by the gate, where some twenty of his fellow countrymen were gathered. Thinking his brother might be among them, Liwen glanced cursorily at the group, but his brother didn't seem to be there. Liwen was about to hurry on when he heard: "Hey, brother . . . " Liwen stared ahead, and extricating himself from the group was none other than his elder brother, Zhewen. And no wonder Liwen had looked right past him a moment earlier, for the whole shape of his brother's head seemed to have changed. During the Qing dynasty of the Manchus, Chinese men shaved their pates, allowing only a queue or pigtail to hang from the back of their heads. During the year he had now spent in Japan, Liwen often hid his queue in a hood, so as not to alter his appearance physically. Zhewen, by contrast, had grown a full head of dark black hair. Observing his brother from the side, Liwen saw that he had no queue.

"What happened to your head?" asked Liwen. The queue was a Manchu custom, and when the Manchu regime established the Qing dynasty to control China, they compelled the Chinese to follow their custom. Failure to wear one's hair in a queue was seen as tantamount to failure to submit allegiance to the Manchus. It was punished with decapitation, so Liwen's shock was fully justified.

"You're not upset that I've become a monk, are you?" said Zhewen laughing. Being Buddhists themselves, the Manchus respected Buddhist monks and recognized their practice of taking the tonsure. Early in the Qing dynasty, which began in 1644, many proud ethnic Chinese who opposed the alien custom of the queue became monks for that reason alone. Having shaved his entire head like a monk, though, Zhewen was now letting all his hair grow back. From the front, a novice monk looked just like someone with a queue, but in Zhewen's case, his entire head already sported three centimeters of hair. He seemed to be concerned about it, because as he walked along, Zhewen would rub his head from time to time.

"You haven't really entered the priesthood, have you?" asked Liwen.

"I really have. You're listening to a genuine monk!" said Zhewen, tapping his own head with a clenched fist. But he was laughing, so Liwen still didn't know the truth.

"So, have you been assigned a Buddhist name?"

"A Buddhist name? Well, yes, I have one. . . . It's Jiuqu." Liwen broke into laughter. It was scarcely possible that such a strange Buddhist name as "Jiuqu" existed. Also, Liwen knew that his elder brother often used the pseudonym of "Jiuqu of the Mountains." Jiuqu was a famous scenic spot in the Wuyi Mountains of their native Fujian province. The great scholar Zhu Xi (1130–1200) had composed a "Ballad of Jiuqu." The Lian brothers often walked with their father to the Linxi Temple in the Wuyi Mountains, and both had had to memorize the "Ballad of Jiuqu."

"It's best that way," said Zhewen as he clapped his brother on the shoulder. "Anyway, let's go. You're probably tired. Dinner's been prepared in my rooms."

Liwen felt the warmth emanating from his brother's palm on his shoulder.

—3—

In one of Zhewen's rooms, a circular, red-lacquered table had been set and three chairs placed around it. The brothers sat facing one another, and behind Zhewen was a large folding screen on which a landscape had been painted.

One glance and Liwen was sure that Zhewen had painted it. Although he had no understanding of art, Liwen did have a desire to be able to give expression to beauty in some fashion. Having no means of expression, though, the sight of Zhewen's paintings aroused an uncannily sympathetic wish in him to be able to paint like his brother.

In the three years since the brothers had last seen each other, so many things to talk about had accumulated. They didn't even know where to start. Liwen was going to ask about their parents, but when he thought about it he realized that, prior to coming to Japan, Zhewen hadn't seen them. Liwen had seen them about a year before and was probably in a better position to answer questions about them. While he remained taciturn, Zhewen asked:

"Who do you think has better Japanese, you or me?"

"I don't know. What do you think?"

"Well, from now on, let's try to speak only Japanese. I've been here half a year, and you've been here for a year."

"So I've been in Japan twice as long."

"But length of time doesn't necessarily mean you're better. Anyway, let's compare our Japanese. The girl can act as referee."

"Girl? What girl?" asked Liwen, and without answering Zhewen turned and said in Japanese:

"Sodewaka, come in here." From behind the screen, a young woman appeared. "This is my younger brother Liwen. What do you think? Does he look like me?" Zhewen addressed her in Japanese.

The young woman answering to the name of Sodewaka sat down and said, smiling: "Yes, indeed. No one could fail to see that you are brothers."

As Zhewen explained to his younger brother, Sodewaka was a prostitute from the Hikidaya section. Liwen had more experience living in Japan than his elder brother, so he knew all about Japanese prostitutes. When he had been in Satsuma, Liwen had heard stories of double suicides involving Nagasaki prostitutes and Chinese merchants. These had occurred much earlier, but the stories were passed from generation to generation. The intimacy between Chinese men and Nagasaki prostitutes actually seemed rather exaggerated to him. The story of how a shipowner by the name of Jiang Yunge, well-known as a scholar in his own right, had produced a child by a prostitute by the name of Sodeōgi had reached Satsuma.

Zhewen pursed his lips and said with admiration:

"You really are knowledgeable. It got all the way to Satsuma?"

Liwen explained: "Jiang Yunge is a famous man, and I have contacts at the Nagasaki Hall. I'm up on events in Nagasaki."

There were Chinese at this time who, although altogether unknown in their own country, were known by virtually everyone in Japan. The painter Yi Fujiu and the literatus Jiang Yunge were two such men. One story was widely known of how the great Japanese scholar and writer Rai San'yō (1780–1832) had come all the way to Nagasaki just to see Jiang Yunge, but Jiang's ship had not yet docked and Rai was ultimately unable to meet him. At that time, Rai and Jiang called on the same prostitute, Sodesaki, and Rai wrote her several poems. Sodesaki was a different woman from Sodeōgi, who had given birth to Jiang's child, but many of the prostitutes from Hikidaya had the element "Sode" in their names. Sodewaka, whom Zhewen had called into the room, was employed in Hikidaya.

Sodewaka began to strum the samisen. Having lived in Japan for nearly a year, Liwen was accustomed to the overall atmosphere this produced. In Satsuma, they had always sat directly on tatami, but inside the Chinese Residence, chairs had been arranged to make it more comfortable. He gazed at Sodewaka's fingertips, radiantly white from plucking the strings of the samisen. He was concentrating his attention on her fingers because he found her face too painful to look at.

Liwen then sadly understood. Having lost his own wife, he could practically feel his brother's pain. Zhewen had once been in love with a woman by the name of Qingqin. After they had parted, she inexplicably committed suicide, together with the great poet and scholar Gong Zizhen (1792–1841). That had taken place eight years earlier. When he first saw Sodewaka's face, the remarkable resemblance to Qingqin had not struck him, but after looking at her for a while he now saw it.

Food and drink were brought in as she played the samisen and sang. A man of some forty years of age entered the room after the waiter and said:

"Today's meal is special. It is guaranteed to meet with your satisfaction." The speaker was the chef from the Chinese compound. When the cooks and young handymen from the Chinese vessels came on shore, they quickly transformed themselves into cooks and waiters at the Chinese compound.

Then the wine arrived, and it served to stimulate conversation. Sodewaka had much to say, perhaps conscious of the fact that it was part of her job.

Rumors were circulating about Sodeōgi and Sodesaki, who were twenty to thirty years her senior, and a variety of stories told by older female entertainers circulated.

"In the past"—this expression seemed to be attached to everything in Nagasaki as a kind of prefatory phrase—Nagasaki had been a site of commercial exchange, but trade per se had seriously declined. When the Chinese compound was constructed 160 years earlier, it could accommodate 5,000 Chinese. In especially cramped times, as many as 10,000 might be in residence there, with about one *tsubo* (36 square feet) of space per person, making it a busy, bustling place. That situation had now changed. Only rarely did the population at the Chinese compound now exceed 500, and when ships departed in the autumn, only a few dozen residents remained. The main reason was the fact that the content of the trade had changed. Even the prostitutes in Nagasaki understood what had happened.

During the golden age of Nagasaki, copper was Japan's principal export item. There was an insufficiency of copper in China for the minting of currency, and a large quantity was imported from Japan. Since the minting of coinage was, of course, the business of government, stocking of raw materials was carried out on a national scale. Importers—known by the rather pretentious name of "official-merchants dealing in copper"—needed a special license from the government, and they generally had close contacts with high-ranking Chinese officials. These "official-merchants" were altogether different from the small businessmen around them.

The representative of the Japanese side exporting the copper was Izumiya, which managed the copper mines in Japan. Izumiya was the store name for the Sumitomo family. The Genroku era (1688–1704) was the peak period for copper exports. There were years during this era when the amount of copper transported by Chinese vessels exceeded seven million catties. Now, though, the figure had dropped to between 500,000 and 600,000 catties.

The value of copper had continued to fall in China of late. Large quantities of silver were flowing out of China with the purchase of opium, and this made the price of silver explode. The value of copper dropped proportionately. For a long time in China, one tael of silver had been worth 800 copper cash. But, with the increased importation of opium, silver was rapidly spent to pay for it. Now, one tael of silver was worth 2,000 copper cash. As the monetary value of copper declined, its luster as a commodity dissipated. Replacing copper now as the principal item of export to China were the three representative marine products of dried abalone, dried sea cucumber, and shark fin. Still, marine products were in no position to completely replace the position once held by copper.

Reduction in the volume of trade became unavoidable, and this state of decline pervaded the atmosphere of Nagasaki. It was most acutely felt in places like the red-light district, and thus the fact that a prostitute would have some small knowledge of economics was not at all odd. In her own feminine way, Sodewaka spoke of the apparent decline of Nagasaki with stories of a time when it had been a flourishing city.

"The knowledge of these things that you have!" said Zhewen, half in jest.

"She really knows what she's talking about," added Liwen in praise. Since she had eliminated details and simplified matters, her account was rather easy to understand.

"I learned it all secondhand from great men," said Sodewaka. "But good days will come again soon. The customers complain all the time that Satsuma is an impediment to accomplishing this or that. They really do."

"Satsuma?" The word slipped out of Liwen's mouth.

"You know, it sounds like my younger brother speaks Japanese with a slight Satsuma accent."

"No, no. It's just that I have a friend from Satsuma . . ." responded Liwen hurriedly.

—4—

Sodewaka left soon thereafter. She was a popular young woman and had another engagement that she was obliged to attend. The music ceased and the room suddenly became silent, though the atmosphere seemed to grow warmer. The two brothers were all alone. Had there been no entertainment, the reunion after three years might not have gone so smoothly. Zhewen for his part appeared to be pondering all of these arrangements and contingencies. The chopsticks had not been applied at all to the food laid out on the table.

"Let's eat a little. Otherwise, the cook will be angry," he said as he picked up his chopsticks.

"Okay. After all, he did come in specially to pay his respects earlier." Liwen put his spoon in the bowl of dried abalone soup.

"Satsuma's reputation is pretty bad, isn't it?"

"It would seem so in Nagasaki."

"It's because they act so high-handedly . . . just like our Jinshunji." Although Zhewen had left the family business, he knew his father and the nature of the Jinshunji well.

"It's not just arrogance," said Liwen defensively, as an employee of the Jinshunji.

"That's true enough. Simple arrogance wouldn't work. Incidentally, will Satsuma be able to push ahead unchallenged?"

"You're a painter. Are you really interested in such things?"

"I'm interested in things of the world, in women and whatnot. If everything disappears, there won't be anything left to paint. I'll never be able to paint really well if I have no more than ordinary human curiosity. At least, that's what I believe."

"Well, shall I tell you what I think then? Satsuma will succeed. All you hear in Nagasaki these days is complaints. No one dares stand in their way."

Everyone knew of Satsuma's secret trade, and not only the purchasing of Chinese items in the Ryūkyū Islands and off Satsuma's waters. Everywhere marine products were being stored. The shogunate had established a monopoly system on trade and was strictly enforcing it to the extent that the so-called "three items" of dried abalone, dried sea cucumber, and shark fin were banned from domestic consumption. As if to mock this ban, though, Shimazu domain carried on business with Hokkaidō and the north districts of Honshū. At times, Shimazu sent vessels disguised as foreign ships to Hokkaidō and carried on a massive secret trade in marine produce. This produce was then shipped to the Ryūkyū Islands and sold by Chinese vessels principally owned by the Jinshunji. Thus, the marine goods that circulated through the Nagasaki Hall had declined in quantity and quality. Since marine goods that moved unlicensed via the Ryūkyūs came on the market more cheaply, even transporting them to Nagasaki was not profitable. This was one of the reasons that the number of Chinese vessels calling at Nagasaki had decreased over the years.

"So, Japan's changing. It sounds like it's really changing a lot. And, if Satsuma has people of genuine ability . . ." said Zhewen.

"Oh, Satsuma has such men," replied Liwen promptly. "All Satsuma has lacked is resources, but it looks like that too may have materialized."

"Thanks again, it would seem, to our Jinshunji."

"No. Even without the Jinshunji, somebody else would be serving as Satsuma's partner."

"Then it's the trend of the times?"

"I think so," said Liwen with a firm nod, as he was reminded of Ōkubo and Saigō.

A lamp was now lighted, lending greater warmth to the atmosphere in the room. Zhewen casually poured some Shaoxing wine into a teacup, and downing it in a single gulp, continued:

"It's not just Japan. China's changing too. From now on, you'll see."

"Didn't it change ten years ago at the time of the Opium War? Only Guangzhou had been an open port before the war, and now there are five open ports for trade."

"No, that was only a superficial change. From now on you can expect an internal transformation. . . . Yes, a change of real substance."

"Really?"

"Before I came to Japan, I traveled to the province of Guangxi," Zhewen said, changing the topic of conversation. This was the first Liwen had heard of his brother's travels. Zhewen was reffering to a time about half a year earlier, a period when Liwen had been busy shuttling between the Ryūkyū Islands and Satsuma. Although instructions from his father on matters of business came frequently, no news had arrived about other family members. As a matter of course, Zhewen was often wandering here and there. So, the fact that he traveled was only natural, even though no one had bothered to inform Liwen.

"To the city of Guilin?" asked Liwen. Guilin was well-known as a scenic spot in Guangxi province. It had been nicknamed the ancestral home of landscape painting. Together with Lushan and Huangshan, it was one of three places painters dreamed of visiting once in their lives. As a painter, it was only natural to expect that Zhewen had gone there.

"I went to Guilin afterward," responded Zhewen.

"Afterward? So, where did you go?"

"To a place called Guiping."

"Guiping? I think I've heard of it. Isn't it near Guilin?"

"I don't know what you mean by 'near.' It's actually rather far."

"Is the scenery nice there?"

"There's a picturesque spot known as Xishan there, but more to the point, that's where Xiling lives. Father sent me there to inquire about her health."

"Is that so?" said Liwen, beginning to understand.

Xiling was a woman whose name was never mentioned aloud among the members of the Lian family, particularly in front of their mother, because their father had once had an affair with her.

Lian Weicai had been able to build the Jinshunji into a major concern within his lifetime, primarily because he received virtually unlimited capital support from a certain "white-headed foreigner." The expression "white-headed foreigner" denoted the Parsi people, many of whom now live in the city of Bombay and have become a considerable force in the world of Indian finance. His family had come originally from Persia, but because they were Zoroastrians who had refused to convert to Islam, they had been compelled to leave their native land. The Parsi people, geniuses in the realm of finance, had been very active in the international economy of the nineteenth century. A large number of them lived in Guangzhou.

Xiling was the daughter of this particular Parsi man and a local Chinese woman. After his death, Lian Weicai became the guardian of his benefactor's daughter, and after a short period of time their relationship developed into an amorous one. Xiling was a sharp woman by nature. She seemed only to be satisfied when she was actively involved in matters. Then, during the Opium War, her younger brother, whom she loved dearly, was killed, and she herself was raped by British troops. For a time, she seemed to have transformed into a different person altogether.

The Lian brothers had met Xiling only rarely, because their father had kept her as far from the family as possible. Liwen could count the few times he had actually seen her. The four Lian brothers all secretly harbored goodwill for this woman with whom their father was involved in such a delicate relationship. When they were young, she was like a glimmering star in the sky. In fact, she was just four years older than the eldest of the four Lian brothers, Tongwen.

She was young, beautiful, frank by nature, and she always seemed vibrantly alive. For the Lian brothers, who had no female siblings, such a woman as Xiling became a kind of object of infatuation. Although none of them dared express it as such, each was able to surmise his brothers' thoughts.

"Xiling is quite well. She's almost forty years old but just as beautiful as ever," reported Zhewen, in a way that revealed he understood what Liwen was feeling without the need for any response.

"I'd heard that she became a Buddhist nun?"

"No, though she did enter a convent. She covered her head, but kept her hair. Apparently, the head of the monastery agreed."

"Then she's just boarding at the convent," said Liwen, with an obvious sense of relief.

"Guiping is way off in the countryside."

"Is that so?"

"Yes, but that part of the hinterland is probably going to become the base for events that will change the world, and I thought I'd go take a look for myself."

"What sort of 'base' are you talking about?" asked Liwen.

"A base for what might as well be called a separate country. It looks like major events are brewing."

"What's going on there?"

"There's a group known as the Society of God Worshippers."

"The Society of God Worshippers?" Liwen seemed to remember having heard of it somewhere or other.

—5—

The "God" in this group's name was a reference to the Judeo-Christian deity who dwelt in heaven. It was apparently a religious organization that worshipped Him. The Chinese expression for "God" was on old term, *Shangdi*, which often appears in the ancient Chinese classical texts. For the Chinese in older times, the term *Shangdi* carried certain Daoist reverberations. However, *Shangdi* in the title of the Society of God Worshippers was altogether different. The leaders of this group publicly announced that the wooden images with their full-grown beards in Chinese Daoist temples were merely scraps of wood. In fact, there were rumors afloat that they were smashing these idols to bits.

"They're Catholics!" explained some people rather simplistically.

"No, they've slightly remodeled Catholicism. It's some sort of money-making scheme," said others, with knowing nods of the head, a theory Liwen had occasion to hear in Shanghai. Following the Opium War, foreign missionaries had become conspicuously active in China. The number of Chinese believers did not rise dramatically, however, in proportion to the fervor of the missionaries' desire to spread the gospel. Some of these converts were not the most scrupulous people, having become Christians as an expedient means for doing business with foreigners. Chinese at that time had developed a distinctly allergic reaction to foreigners, and people who had contacts with missionaries risked the suspicion of their neighbors. When Liwen had been in Shanghai, he often argued with students there about Christianity.

"It'll never capture the minds of the Chinese people. That's hopeless," he would claim.

Liwen well understood the strength of Christianity's appeal. His family had numerous contacts with foreigners, and his knowledge of Christianity was far greater than that of the average Chinese. He knew that despite differences of nationality—be they English, American, French, Dutch, or whatever—Westerners were almost all Christians. When they had come to Japan, they barely surveyed the situation there at all, and yet they had been able to give rise to frequent acts of Christian martyrdom among the Japanese. Despite this, he had a negative opinion about the future of Christianity in China, largely because of the opium trade. The foreigners involved in the questionable activities concerning the selling of opium were all Christians, and that was a serious fact to contend with.

"The Society of God Worshippers in Guangdong province is a little bit different," a young business connection from Guangzhou had once told Liwen. That was probably the first time he'd heard the name of the group. When Liwen asked in what way it was different, his acquaintance responded: "They have no contacts with foreigners at all. It's all Chinese."

Maybe there was a chance they'd become a powerful force, thought Liwen. Although interested at the time, when he was in Shanghai, Guangdong seemed so far away, and there was no need to know all the details about movements at such a distance. Liwen's interest in the Society of God Worshippers remained frozen at that level.

En route to the Ryūkyūs, he stopped in Hong Kong and Guangzhou. There he heard the story that the leader of a mysterious religious group had been apprehended and imprisoned by the authorities. It certainly seemed like a foreign religion, much like Catholicism.

At the time he wondered if it might have been what his business contact had spoken about, but the name "Society of God Worshippers" did not pop into his head at the time. It was hidden somewhere in his memory, an unimportant detail.

Liwen also heard the rumor that the fellow who had been arrested already seemed to have been released. In any event, mysterious and confusing things were going on in the countryside, making it hard to discern the real facts. From his perspective, though, it all seemed utterly irrelevant. Not a single person in Hong Kong or Guangzhou within Liwen's range of contacts had the least interest in this "religious band."

So, he too figured that it could hardly be of much consequence. But now his brother was saying that this group might transform the entire world. While Liwen was fully cognizant of the fact that his brother was an artist, not a man of practical affairs, he still believed that Zhewen was a man of genuine insight. Be it good or bad, his capacity to make a judgment in an instant surpassed that of anyone Liwen had ever known.

"Wasn't there a raid by the authorities on this Society of God Worshippers last year?" Liwen asked. He still lacked hard information that rumors he had picked up in Hong Kong and Guangzhou were ultimately connected to the Society of God Worshippers.

"That's right. They were outsmarted. A man named Feng Yunshan was thrown in jail. But he was soon let out," Zhewen responded.

"So it's the same story I heard."

"You heard about this somewhere?"

"I think it was in Guangzhou. It was before I left for the Ryūkyūs, so it must have been around May."

"In fact, Xiling was involved in the release of Feng Yunshan."

"Really? Xiling?"

"Seem strange to you? Someone who looks like a Buddhist nun helping to get a Christian set free? Well, that's just like Xiling."

According to Zhewen, the two principal figures in the founding of the Society of God Worshippers were Hong Xiuquan and Feng Yunshan. Its headquarters was located in the area of Thistle Mountain in Guiping county. In the foothills of Thistle Mountain was a village known as Jintian. In the eyes of the conservative landed gentry, the religious activities of this group were abominable. For example, they desecrated Chinese religious icons, and in the Ganwang Temple of Xiangzhou, they destroyed images of deities right before onlooking officials. They also wrote and pasted on the walls of temples poems slandering the deities revered there. These actions were all part of their proselytizing work.

A country gentleman by the name of Wang Zuoxin had organized a *tuanlian* in his locality of Guiping county. A *tuanlian* was a form of local self-defense. Realizing that it was best if they protected their own homes with their own hands, local men of influence provided the funding for this *tuanlian*. Soon, however, these organizations began to look more and more like private armies for the local gentry. With a *tuanlian* that operated at his command, Wang Zuoxin had been able to capture Feng Yunshan. One reason he was able to do so were the claims he made that Feng had deceived the people, swearing allegiance to them and then trampling their deities of the soil and grains underfoot.

Be that as it may, the Society of God Worshippers was also well-organized. Two of Feng's cohorts, Zeng Yasun and Lu Liu, recaptured him from the authorities soon thereafter, on December 28, 1847. Wang Zuoxin lodged a protest in Guiping over Feng's release. His written complaint noted that the followers of the Society of God Worshippers had already reached several thousand in number.

Feng Yunshan also submitted a document in Guiping by way of rebuttal, and it noted: "Despite having taught men to revere heaven, I have regrettably been falsely accused. At our temple in Guangdong are displayed memorials to the throne from the highest authority of the provinces of Guangdong and Guangxi. Has not the Emperor offered his imperial rescript upon them?"

Among the many conditions signed in the aftermath of the Opium War was freedom for Christian missionaries, and the Emperor in Beijing accepted this condition, probably with great reluctance. At the temple in Guangdong, they hoisted aloft this document, through the office of the governor-general of Guangdong and Guangxi provinces, indicating official authorization of Christian missionaries. The document was ratified by the Emperor himself, and no one dared breach its conditions. At the temple, it stood as an unparalleled talisman.

Guiping County Magistrate Wang Lie was a bit perplexed. Wang Zuoxin had used the expression "magical writings of the Society of God Worshippers" in his appeal, but these were in fact the very Christian religious texts now recognized by the Emperor. Remembering with aggravation all the riots that had arisen in the otherwise peaceful countryside, Wang Lie rejected Wang Zuoxin's protest: "Your evidence is insufficient. Don't act rashly before carrying out a solid investigation!"

Wang Zuoxin, though, did not give up. He mobilized his *tuanlian* for a second time, captured both Feng Yunshan and Lu Liu, and this time turned them over to the subcounty magistrate. Both were imprisoned.

Hong Xiuquan set out for Guangzhou to organize a movement to gain their release. The office of the local authorities was not about to resolve such a major issue on its own responsibility. The suspicion that he had intended a rebellion had been cast upon Feng, and hence the issue had become a major one. As a result, the local area remained unsettled. So Hong decided that it would be best to head directly for Guangzhou, seat of the governor-general whose authority spanned both Guangdong and Guangxi provinces, and lead the effort for the release of Feng and Lu with the higher authorities themselves.

"It was Xiling who encouraged Hong Xiuquan to do this," said Zhewen. "She explained in detail that it was best for him to proceed to Guangzhou and approach the authorities there from every possible angle."

"Things won't calm down if he doesn't do something."

"It seems he's been acting quietly for a while, but rumors connected to the Society of God Worshippers have been reported from time to time of late."

"So, Father got worried and sent for you?"

"That's right . . . Well, then, what do you say, Liwen, shall we go outside?" Zhewen proposed.

"Fine."

Liwen too wanted to breathe some fresh air outdoors. Perhaps the two brothers did share something in their dispositions.

—6—

"Outside" in this context still meant, of course, within the grounds of the Chinese compound. The evening sky was dense with clouds. Light crept in through the windows of buildings here and there, but it was desolate at best.

Because it had been constructed to accommodate some five thousand Chinese, the Chinese compound initially contained twenty separate buildings. When the number of Chinese there came to exceed ten thousand, every one of those buildings was overcrowded. Now, though, it was rare to find more than five hundred Chinese residing here—only ten percent of the planned number. Buildings in disrepair or no longer in use at the compound were torn down, and there was no new construction to speak of. Only seven buildings now remained, and of them only five were in active use, and the grounds of the Chinese compound had become as shabby as they were spacious.

"It's lonely around here," said Liwen.

Zhewen smiled: "Just today ship Number Four entered port, so it's a little more populated than usual."

The wind blew faintly. It was the sixth month on the lunar calendar, already midsummer. Zhewen stopped short and looked around. A bit of moonlight peered through from rifts in the clouds.

"There's no one here," said Zhewen dejectedly.

"It's true. . . . With the ship having arrived, there are probably more people in the rooms."

"Since there's no one here right now, there's something I want to say to you."

"Something you couldn't say back in your room?"

"However expansive my lodgings may be, there are still several dozen people under the same roof—and probably government spies among them. There may be some people who will pass along secret information concerning others to help them carry on business successfully."

"Spies for which 'government'?"

"For both sides. Both the Japanese and the Chinese governments want all sorts of information, and we've got some information we don't want them to get hold of."

"Do you sense that you've been marked by someone?"

"I think so. . . . It was probably unwise to have cut my queue," said Zhewen, touching his head.

Even when one publicly entered the priesthood, the act of cutting off one's queue rendered one worthy of special attention. For some reason, Zhewen now seemed to regret having removed it. Whatever his subsequent regrets, to his credit Zhewen carried out the act as planned.

Zhewen looked around once more and asked: "Do you plan to return directly to Shanghai on ship Number Four?"

"I don't know yet. I may. Perhaps I'll go on to Satsuma and cross to Fuzhou via the Ryūkyū Islands. I'll have to think about it some more," answered Liwen.

"Either way's all right. But if you return, go to Guangxi. . . . This isn't my wish, but Father's."

"Guangxi? Does this have something to do with the Society of God Worshippers?"

"Earlier I mentioned that the Society of God Worshippers might transform the world as we know it. Father has no doubt about it at all."

"Do you believe it?"

"I'm convinced."

"But if such a Christian association were to take control over the whole country . . ." said Liwen as he looked around himself.

"I don't know if they'll seize the entire country, but I am convinced they'll shake our country from its roots and change our world as we have come to know it."

"Did you see Father before coming to Japan?"

"No. Wen Zhang came to Suzhou to relay Father's wishes to me. He emphasized that he was repeating what Father had said word for word," said Zhewen.

Wen Zhang was the son of Wen Han, chief clerk of the Jinshunji, who had helped their father build that establishment to prominence. Although not yet fifty years of age, Wen Zhang had succeeded his late father in the position of chief clerk. Their trust in him was absolute; when he said he was repeating their father's words exactly, there was no doubt that what he said represented their father's precise wishes.

"Guangxi is a frontier region even in China. . . . Can our nation really be undermined from such a place? In the countryside, a few thousand people may seem like a lot, but throughout the country as a whole. . . . " said Liwen dubiously.

"Satsuma's on the outskirts of Japan, the furthest region south . . . I think Father foresees that the forces that arise in the Japanese periphery and in the Chinese periphery will transform both countries."

"How are they going to change things?"

"Father's idea is that whatever they do will be preferable to the present situation."

"That's for sure," said Liwen, thinking of his father as essentially a destroyer.

"I mentioned before that I'd gone to Guiping to pay my respects to Xiling. That wasn't true. I went there at Father's wish to pass along his plans for the future to Xiling."

"'Plans for the future'?"

"Yes. He was successful in getting Feng Yunshan released, but as a result he'll have to remain quiet for a while. So, things are going to get a bit more complicated. Perhaps it's unfair, but he said that he doesn't want to rely solely on Xiling. He'd like to send you, Liwen, to attach yourself to the Society of God Worshippers so she can separate herself from it for a time."

"I am to join the Society of God Worshippers?"

"Yes. That's why you'll have to proceed to Guangxi. There's no reason to hurry, but there's no time to waste."

"What about Satsuma?"

"I'll take over our business affairs in Satsuma and the Ryūkyūs. That's the main reason I became a Buddhist initiate. . . . Once things settle down, I'll have to take over the business."

"This all sounds just like Father!"

Feelings of content and discontent mingled in Liwen's breast. He was unhappy about being moved about here and there, like a piece on a chessboard, at his father's will. He was twenty-nine years old, a full adult in his own right. Nonetheless, he was happy about being placed in such an apparently important position as this trip to Guangxi portended.

Whether or not this group actually took control over China was beside the point. His father had ordered him to go and attach himself to the Society of God Worshippers, the group his father foresaw shaking up the entire Chinese nation. "Attach" in this context seemed to imply economic support as well as offering advice to the group's leaders.

Liwen conjectured to himself that his father probably wanted Zhewen to undertake this task at first, but it seemed so onerous that he decided to give the job to him, Liwen. The secret trade with Satsuma and the Ryūkyūs was difficult, to be sure, but it was a path he had tread many times. Once he consulted with the responsible parties in Satsuma, even an artist like Zhewen would have none of the troubles he had encountered.

A lovely voice could be heard amid the samisen melodies. The gentle breeze that had been blowing subsided, and Liwen became moist with perspiration. This was not just a consequence of the wind, thought Liwen. The new task before him was kindling a flame within him.

"So, I am to succeed you in the business concerning Guangxi," said Liwen.

"Father should now be in Xiamen. It'd be best if you went there and asked him in person. Also, Xiling is much more up-to-date on circumstances at the scene. Before coming to Japan, I spoke with Wen Zhang, and it seems Father's a little worried."

"What's he worried about?"

"First of all, Mr. Wang Juzhi, who gained national fame for his heroism, took Father into his confidence. He's no longer alive, and Father's links with various adventurist groups have become weaker than they were in the past."

"I see. The idea then is to try to forge a bond between these adventurist groups and the Society of God Worshippers."

"Secondly, in the effort to obtain the release of Feng Yunshan, Hong Xiuquan went to Guangzhou, but he didn't return to Thistle Mountain. . . . Father's worried because Feng followed Hong, and he doesn't know what will happen if both leaders have disappeared."

"The local large landholders and other men of influence hate them that much. So, the group could be wiped out while they're away."

"There is that worry, but there are steadfast, able-bodied men among the leaders that stayed behind at Thistle Mountain. If I remember correctly, one named Yang Xiuqing is a particularly capable man, and the two leaders apparently left him in control. What Father fears is that Yang will overstep his authority in their absence. They've been united until now, but could easily split in two. The work to be done in Guangxi is really important." Zhewen's low voice was interrupted by a high-pitched woman's voice: "Who's out there? Is that you, Zhewen? I'm on my way back to your place now." Accompanied by a young attendant holding a paper lantern, Sodewaka approached them. From the light that shone on her feet, Sodewaka seemed to be walking somewhat dizzily.

Zhewen whispered rapidly into Liwen's ear: "I must say this quickly. The Society of God Worshippers has never been simply a religious organization, but has been quite intent on revolt—at least, that's true of its leaders. Thus, you are going to become a rebel. I want you to be aware of all this from the start."

"I understand. There's nothing for me to be afraid of."

"Good," said Zhewen as he left his younger brother and approached Sodewaka.

"Isn't it early?"

"I had another obligation to appear at, and did I have to drink there!"

"Why don't we go drink some more. It's not that late." Zhewen looked back over his shoulder at his brother. "Let's go back to the rooms and drink to our hearts' content."

And the bits of the moon that had been visible again became completely concealed behind the clouds.

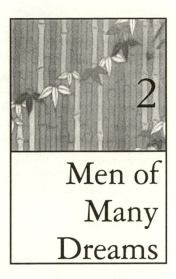

2

Men of Many Dreams

—1—

According to the calendar, autumn had already passed, but in the town of Xishan (Guiping county, Guangxi province) the trees were still lushly verdant. Here and there into the stone face of the mountains tinged with moisture, Chinese scholars had carved literary inscriptions.

Lian Liwen came to a stop before an inscription of three large Chinese characters: "blue, cloudy sky." Beside them in rather small characters one could read the inscription: "An autumn day in the twenty-second year of the Daoguang reign (1842), calligraphy by Li Shaolian of Jingshan."

Seven years ago, murmured Liwen, that very year.

That year, the British Army had attacked at the Yangzi River in the midst of the Opium War, and the Qing government had signed the humiliating Treaty of Nanjing. The Jiangnan Military Commander, Chen Huacheng, a man who had been close to Liwen's father, had died in battle at Wusong just two and one-half months before the treaty. The treaty was signed aboard the British warship *Wellesley* on the twenty-fourth day of the seventh lunar month—already into autumn. At precisely that time, some refined scholar off in the mountains of Guangxi had inscribed in a free and easy manner the characters "blue, cloudy sky."

Liwen shook his head lightly and slowly began walking on. Following the Pearl River upstream from Guangzhou, he had arrived in Guiping. The Pearl River's local water system was known in this area as Xunjiang. Liwen's contacts met and proceeded to carry him in a palanquin as far as the Longhua Temple. Then, once he dropped his baggage at the temple, he decided to walk ahead to the Xishi Monastery with a young priest for a guide.

It took less than ten minutes to walk from the Longhua Temple to the Xishi Monastery. Tucked cozily into the foothills at Xishan, Xishi was a convent set apart from the main temple. Xiling, the unshorn nun, was to be waiting for Liwen at the convent.

At that time the county seat of Guiping was situated at the confluence of the Qian and the Yu Rivers in the Xunjiang system. Until the end of the Song dynasty in the thirteenth century, the county seat had been located in Xishan. The Xishi Monastery had itself been built as a convent late in the Tang dynasty (618–907). Liwen's young guide offered this information by way of introduction.

"Where the road bends to the left there is the gate to the Xishi Monastery," said the bonze, pointing to a spot where the mountain path divided. The stone wall obstructing the left side suddenly broke off there, and altogether different scenery emerged if one turned at this point.

Looking ahead, Liwen realized that the woman standing before the entrance to the convent was in fact Xiling. Her head was covered by a hood, and she was dressed in nun's garb. Although she was still at a considerable distance, Liwen recognized her immediately. It was *that* year, he thought, ever since *that* year.

Seven years earlier, while staying at the Siwentang, a bookstore in Shanghai, Xiling had given birth to a daughter with blue eyes. At the time Liwen had been in Shanghai and frequented the bookstore. Upon reflection he realized that he had not seen her since. That was when the English invaded Ningbo. He remembered the three Chinese characters—"blue, cloudy sky"— that he had just seen.

A framed sign—"Xishi Monastery"—hung over the gate to the convent. On the pillars to either side were carved a long series of gilded Chinese characters:

> The tall building soars magnificently,
> while the cloud banks beyond the heavens
> support the white stone.
> The temple gate is immersed in a flush of freshness,
> while the misty water of the pond
> engulfs the dust of the world.

As Liwen approached the gate so as to be able to read this inscription, Xiling raised her right hand to the height of her face and smiled gently. He was glad to see that she looked well. Liwen heaved a sigh of relief, although his brother had said in Nagasaki that trouble could be in store if she was "too well."

"You look very well," said Xiling to Liwen.

"So do you," said Liwen, looking up toward Xiling from the bottom of the stone steps before the gate.

"You've really grown up. . . . You saw Zhewen in Japan?"

"Yes. . . . He's well and remains in Japan. . . . It's been some time since I've stayed at the Longhua Temple," said Liwen as he ascended the steps.

"I received a communication from your father," said Xiling as she turned her back on him and walked ahead. Liwen followed.

Although it was part of the temple complex, the convent seemed to have a distinctive freshness about it. Compared to the overly grave atmosphere surrounding the Longhua Temple itself, one sensed a lighter air about the Xishi Monastery.

Liwen was led into a room with a magnificent view, and there he sat down opposite Xiling. Beyond her gently sloping shoulders, he could see the dense greenery of Xishan, a lush green whose energy seemed to merge with Xiling. Feeling somewhat suffocated, Liwen decided to break the ice:

"Please tell me in detail about the Society of God Worshippers. That's the reason I've come here after all."

"That's not such a pressing issue, is it? First, tell me about Japan. What sort of a country is it?"

Xiling's bluish eyes sparkled in the light. She had always been curious. Not only did she want to know about strange and rare things, she was actually likely to plunge right into them. She may already have turned forty years of age, but her disposition had not changed at all.

—2—

"Hong Xiuquan is an extremely sensitive man—frighteningly so."

Having heard Liwen speak about Japan at length, Xiling finally began to describe the Society of God Worshippers, looking first at its founder, Hong Xiuquan. Many members apparently called it simply the Society of God.

Hong was not a native of Guangxi, but hailed from Hua county in Guangdong province, not very far from the city of Guangzhou. He was born in Fuyuanshui, close to the Hua county seat. Later, his family moved to the nearby village of Guanlubu.

They were a Hakka family. What did Hakka—literally, "guest family"— mean? It implied that theirs was not an indigenous local family. It was a term applied by residents of the area to immigrants who had left their own home regions because of local conditions, such as civil strife. Although the term carried the literal meaning of "guest," Hakkas were never treated as honored guests. They were more like uninvited guests. The indigenous populations were wary of these people, who were seen as having forced their way into the region, and they became objects of discrimination.

All that remained for those who moved to this new area was barren land that had been abandoned by local farmers by then. Profitable ventures were dominated by the people who had lived for generations on the land, while the newcomers could only take jobs that came with poor conditions. Just finding a job, no matter what sort it was, was considered fortunate.

With such unfavorable circumstances, Hakkas had to work diligently and live frugally in order to survive. The binding of women's feet was a common practice at that time in China. Young girls' feet were tightly wrapped with cloth so as to inhibit growth. When they grew up, they were only able to walk totteringly. Although Hakkas were ethnic Han Chinese just like their neighbors, the practice of footbinding was extraordinarily rare among the Hakka people. Women too had to work, and Hakkas could not afford the luxury of robbing their women of the capacity to move freely because of bound feet.

The Hakkas were a proud people. They no longer knew in detail the circumstances that had compelled their ancestors several hundred years earlier —indeed, well over a thousand years earlier—to migrate. They had principally moved from the north to the south, and it was likely that opposition elements among them had refused to surrender in times of dynastic transition or warfare, preferring instead to flee southward. Their ancestors had been as strong as steel, and would have considered submission an act of cowardice. Stories have it that, at the time of the collapse of the Ming dynasty and with imperial control over China falling to the Qing dynasty of the Manchus in 1644, the most stubborn forces of resistance to the Manchu invaders were groups of Hakkas.

The impact of Hakkas in the creation of modern China has been remarkably large. Hong Xiuquan, leader of the Taipings, Sun Zhongshan (Sun Yatsen), leader of the 1911 Revolution, and other revolutionary leaders were Hakkas. The percentage of Hakkas in the overall Chinese population was infinitesimal, and yet among the leaders of contemporary China one finds many Hakkas, Marshall Ye Jianying being the best known. There is even a theory that Deng Xiaoping is from a Hakka family in Sichuan. Well-known to Japanese was the late Liao Chengzhi (1908–1983) of the Sino-Japanese Friendship Association, who hailed from a Hakka family in Guangdong.

Because they were hard-working and indomitable, Hakkas were feared as well as discriminated against. However, Xiling, who was part Han Chinese and part Parsi, had no prejudice whatsoever with respect to Hakkas.

"I met people in Guangzhou who knew Hong when he was a little boy, and I listened to their stories. They said that, more than anything, he was hot-tempered, and even when playing games he was never happy until he became the general," said Xiling amicably.

"I gather that he failed the civil service examinations a number of times?" asked Liwen. He had obtained a general outline of Hong's life from his brother in Nagasaki.

The Hong family was one of cultivator-farmers, though they only had a small amount of poor land, and life for them had been difficult. When he was a youngster the family had apparently raised cattle. Whether he was a promising lad or not, at age seven (Chinese style), he entered the village school and studied the standard traditional curriculum of the Four Books and Five Classics.

As it turned out, Hong showed a pronounced capacity for study, but his family was growing poorer and was ultimately unable to pay even the low monthly tuition at the village school. He was able to continue his studies only because the school waived the instructional fees for such a talented boy as he, and with the assistance of relatives, he stayed in school until he was sixteen. At age sixteen he sat for the local Guangzhou examinations and failed.

Hong was born on the tenth day of the twelfth month of the eighteenth year of the reign of the Jiaqing Emperor: January 1, 1814, according to the solar calendar. By the lunar calendar, he was already two "years" old in roughly twenty days. Thus, to say he was "sixteen" at the time of these examinations places them in 1828, when he was actually only fourteen full years of age. In 1836, when Hong was twenty-four (Chinese style), he took up the challenge of the local examinations a second time and again was utterly defeated. From the time he was eighteen, Hong had been supporting himself as a teacher in the village school.

On this unsuccessful attempt, Hong had gone to Guangzhou to sit for exams, and at that time he had had two important experiences. He heard that the well-known Guangzhou scholar Zhu Ziqi (1807–1882) was giving public lectures at the Liurong Temple. A native of Nanhai county, Guangdong province, Zhu was living in retirement in the town of Jiujiang in Nanhai county. He was later to be known as the Teacher of Jiujiang. After he subsequently passed the highest level of the imperial examinations, Zhu would work as a county magistrate in Shanxi province. But at the time that Hong Xiuquan was taking the exams for the second time, Zhu was still just a promising, energetic young scholar. Barely thirty years of age, he had already gained considerable popularity among the younger students for his emphasis on the practicality of knowledge.

During these lectures at the Liurong Temple, Hong heard Zhu expound his theory of the "Three Ages." It was a great shock to him. The idea of the

"Three Ages" derived from the ancient Chinese classic, *The Spring and Autumn Annals:*

1. The age of oneself and one's father was the age of things seen, things directly experienced.
2. The age of one's grandfather was the age of things heard.
3. The age of one's great grandfather and one's ancestors was the age of things reported to have been heard.

During the Qing dynasty, scholars of the Gongyang school—namely, a group of scholars who interpreted the text of *The Spring and Autumn Annals* according to another text known as the *Gongyang Commentary,* and were a practical group who stressed politics and economics—explained these "Three Ages" as: Disorder, Ascending Peace, and Great Peace.

With its reverence for antiquity, Confucianism readily accepted the notion that the past was a good era and that the world had gradually degenerated over time. Most Confucians advocated bringing the worsening contemporary world, even just a little bit, into closer proximity to the good times of the past.

Zhu Ziqi's theory of the "Three Ages," however, posited a transition from disorder to ascending peace, and finally, toward great peace. In his view, the past was a bad time that was gradually improving. He argued for the need to examine what was historically necessary to usher in that era of improvement.

For Hong Xiuquan, who had learned this musty old reverence for antiquity in his village school, Zhu's social evolutionism was a startling thesis. Hong later recalled this experience: "It was as if the scales pasted to my eyes suddenly fell to the ground."

Hong realized at this point just how closed his own thought processes had been. "I felt as I had been confined to a dark house and that this was the entire world," he later recounted to Xiling. "I was still unaware, though, of how expansive the world could be if I just opened the door and let the light flood in."

His second important experience occurred in the streets, when he heard the preaching of a Christian missionary. A Westerner would say something, and a Chinese interpreted it for the crowd: "Open your eyes wide and you shall see. What do you all worship now? Don't you just worship any and everything? We pray only to the Lord God Jehovah. We believe in Jesus Christ and pray to God. All the rest are demons. Those things in your temples—aren't they just lumps of wood and copper? Is there a spirit within them? There is not! You don't know this, for your eyes have been covered. . . ."

At the time Hong did not understand the doctrine being preached, but the words, "your eyes have been covered" stuck in his mind. This experience occurred shortly after he had heard Zhu Ziqi expound the theory of "Three Ages," and Hong was feeling the acute need to open his eyes to everything around him. Perhaps something struck a respondent chord in Hong's mind.

The Chinese missionary who was interpreting handed him a book and said: "Please read this book for more detailed matters. By all means, please read it." Hong took the book. On the cover were printed the Chinese characters *Quanshi liangyan*, and along the side the English translation appeared in words Hong, of course, could not read: *Good Words to Admonish the Age*.

Hong searched through his pockets for the money to pay for it: "It's okay," said the Chinese missionary warmly, "it's yours. I happily give it away for free to those who have listened intently. Please do read it."

"But for a number of years Hong did not read it," said Xiling, "and it remained crammed in among other books on his shelf."

"Why was that?"

"I'd rather you heard the answer for that directly from Hong himself."

"Really?"

"Well, I really can't say for sure. If you hear it from someone who doesn't know, then you're not going to know either." Xiling laughed.

Seven years earlier, when they had last met in Shanghai, a certain darkness had hung about Xiling, but that seemed now to have completely lifted. There was no sadness in her laughter, but rather an invigorating clarity. Nor was her language in any way artificial.

—3—

"Be careful. There's been a small disturbance in this area, and . . . before long it may turn into a major uprising throughout the land," Xiling said to Liwen as he left for the village of Jintian to meet Hong Xiuquan.

Public order in Guangxi province was declining precipitously. Neighboring Guangdong, for that matter, was not so secure, but with the governor-general's office in Guangzhou being right there in Guangdong, the presence of the government's military forces had managed to keep things under control. Perhaps it was only the rural situation in Guangxi that was deteriorating.

"There's a shortcut, but you might not want to take such a solitary route to get there," cautioned Xiling.

"It seems as though evil sorts from all over the entire nation have all moved to Guangxi," joked Liwen.

"The thieves who'll stab you on those back roads aren't necessarily bad people."

"Are you saying that bandits might not be evil?"

"That's right. Perhaps it could be a father whose children are crying at home with empty stomachs. He may be a good, hard-working man. There are many destitute people who have nowhere to work. Most of them are that way."

"What a dreadful situation there." Liwen shrugged his shoulders.

Ever since the previous year (1848), incidents large and small had continually arisen throughout Guangxi. In April, a man by the name of Qin Xingwan, who was affiliated with the secret religious organization known as the Heaven and Earth Society (or Triads), had come to Guangxi from Guangdong. He joined forces with one Huang Qizhen of Binzhou, and together they rose in rebellion in the nearby Wuxuan area. They were finally put down in September.

That same April, Huang Weiye and Huang Tiansong of Zhen'an prefecture led a revolt and killed the prefectural magistrate, Shen Yuyin. This too had been a Heaven and Earth Society uprising.

In an incident that December, a Guangdong man named Zhang Yaxiang had confronted the government's troops at Binzhou, and Deng Zongheng, the local brigade commander, had died in the fighting. In this incident, the so-called Guangxi mafia—Sun Jiaxiang of Guiping, Xie Jiangdian of Hengzhou, Li Zichang of Qinzhou, Su Sanxiang of Lingshan, and Xu Yayun of Gui county—participated.

In January of 1849, the forces of Ma Chenglong and Ma Chenghu of Hengzhou had attacked the city of Huaixi in Gui county. Then in April, river pirates known as the "skiff bandits of Guangdong" besieged Wuzhou in Guangxi. This act was perpetrated by a group led by Zhang Zhao, known as "Big-Headed Ram," Tian Fang, known as "Big Carp," and Hou Zhi, known as "dog with the turned-up mouth." In May, Zhang Yaxiang's group invaded the prefectures of Nanning, Liaozhou, and Guilin. They wrapped their heads in red cloth and carried banners on which were written: "Transform the heavens and follow the correct path." It was June when Hong Xiuquan and Feng Yunshan returned from Hua county in Guangdong to Guiping—the base of operations for the Society of God Worshippers—during this period of turmoil. Hong had made his way to Hua county to secure Feng's release from jail, and they returned together.

Six days after Lian Liwen arrived in Guiping, he was finally able to meet Hong. He had wanted to see him immediately, but despite the fact that his message was transmitted by Xiling herself, he received the following answer to his request: "At present, I'm very busy. When I find a moment soon, let's get together. At that time, let me suggest the Xishi Monastery." A bit on the pompous side, thought Liwen.

Shortly after noon that day, a messenger from the Society of God Worshippers came to the Xishi Monastery to convey an oral message: "He arrives in Jintian in the evening, and he'd like you, Mr. Lian Liwen, to come alone, with no escorts. We will send someone to meet you in front of the Sanjie Ancestral Temple. That person will address you with the words: 'Things are a mess because the Litang Bridge collapsed.' You are to respond: 'It was a wooden bridge, so it easily collapsed. Build it with stone next time.' Your escort will recognize you on this signal and guide you to the home of the founder of our religious group."

This all struck Liwen as fine, provided the messenger did in fact come and guide him, though the Society of God Worshippers did seem to have a penchant for the dramatic. The journey from Xishan to Jintian village was somewhat less than 30 kilometers, and that included two river crossings by ferry. While the seat of Guiping county was densely populated, there were isolated spots along the rural roads going there. Xiling was worried that Liwen would be attacked by robbers: "You look like you're someone with lots of money."

"Not a chance!" Nonetheless, Liwen wore the most ordinary clothes he could find. This was to be a trip of 30 kilometers on foot, so he wore light clothes and carried no baggage to speak of.

"In any event, if you run into bandits, be sure to obediently hand over your purse. By no means put up any kind of a fight. No matter how weak they may seem to you, any sort of confrontation is dangerous. Even if it's just one thief, you never know with whom he may be aligned," Xiling warned in great detail.

"Of course. I'm not all that brave in any case. Rest assured that I'll never put up any resistance."

When the time arrived, Liwen left the convent and walked through a tunnel of greenery in Xishan. Soon, he came upon the abundant flow of the Xunjiang. Counting Liwen, there were altogether eight passengers on the ferry. In the interim before it departed, Liwen learned in general terms the identities of his fellow passengers. Two were merchants—one from Liuzhou and one from Xiangzhou—both in the timber business. Each was accompanied by two other men. In such times of disorder, especially in areas known for rebellion, these attendants served effectively as bodyguards.

The two men in the timber business were, in fact, competitors, but traveling at this time there was reassurance in numbers. It seemed from their conversation that the two merchants had just met for the first time on this trip. They had decided to continue together in Gui county because that meant an actual increase in bodyguards from two to four for both.

The last person was a woman about thirty years of age. Since her feet were not bound, he assumed she was Hakka, though she did not speak in the

Hakka dialect. She said that her own family lived in the village of Gucheng in the Wutong Mountains and that she had married into a farming family in Gui county. On her trip home, she had heard of this group of six going in the same general direction, and she decided to take advantage of the opportunity and go with them.

The other passengers on board called her "Asao." It was a general expression for a woman of undetermined age whose name was unknown.

"Asao, isn't Gucheng way back in the sticks? You follow the Peng River upstream to get there, right?" asked one of the bodyguards.

"It's in the mountains," she responded abruptly.

"You're pretty refined for someone raised in the mountains, aren't you, Asao?" said another bodyguard in a teasing tone of voice.

"Who asked you?" she replied boldly.

"Not very friendly, are you?"

"Who said I had to be friendly to you guys?"

"Oh, she barks."

"'Barks'?—How dare you talk to me like that!"

Her beautiful eyebrows seemed to stand on end in anger. Just as the bodyguard had said, she seemed rather elegant for someone raised in the mountains. She had a slender, dark-complexioned face with remarkably thick, long eyebrows that seemed all the lovelier in anger.

"Oh, what do you know, Asao is angry with me . . . and now we're here together . . ."

The merchants intervened at this point.

—4—

Guangxi was teeming with bandits, and traveling with two or three bodyguards would seem to have been little insurance against a gang of several hundred or even several thousand bandits. Yet, that was not the case, for even though it seemed as if all social order had broken down, there were still filiations within the world of banditry. These were what is roughly referred to as "secret societies." If accounts were properly settled in advance with the principal groups among these secret societies, then travel was surprisingly safe. "Settling accounts" meant, of course, giving them money. It was a kind of transit duty, if you will. As proof that a group of travelers had "settled accounts," the secret society would send along a bodyguard with them. Once his face was recognized, no bandit in that secret society's confederation would attack them. Part of this transit duty went to the bodyguards themselves. To prevent a group's passage once this money had been received was seen as a violation of their moral code.

If one were protected by several dozen—even several hundred—armed guards, one was still by no means safe. If those guards had no connection to the secret societies, then bandits affiliated with secret societies showed them no mercy. In fact, if the number of guards was large, that might actually kindle hostilities and incite a large-scale attack.

Such bodyguards were, then, a kind of living, breathing passport, and their faces provided proof that one had paid the transit duty. They were known for their ruthlessness and existed on the peripheries even within the context of the secret organization of the Heaven and Earth Society.

The bodyguards for the timber merchants accompanying Liwen were not men of especially high breeding. To while away the boredom of the trip, they had turned to mocking this married woman returning to her village.

Of the four bodyguards, only one appeared to be the least mild-mannered. He may have been forty years old, perhaps older. In an extremely harsh tone of voice, he berated the others:

"You do anything intolerable and I'll report you!" The others in the group shrugged their shoulders. From this response, it would seem that he meant to report them to someone with considerable authority.

"We didn't say anything so bad. We said she was refined—that's a compliment."

"That's right. Asao got angry all by herself for nothing."

"I don't have the slightest idea what she got so angry about." The three guards spoke in succession, pouting all the while.

"And I don't have the slightest idea why you are all so damned stupid. Are your heads all full of shit or what?" Asao continued her harangue.

This all transpired on board the ferry.

"Hey, all of you, you're on a boat! Arguments are forbidden!" screamed the ferryman, pole in hand.

He was afraid that, if an argument broke out, the small ferryboat might capsize. It was ordinarily the rule to stay calm in ferries.

It stood to reason that the boatman also had his contacts with the secret societies for the very reason that he made a living with his ferry along the Xunjiang. Otherwise, he would have been hounded by skiff bandits and unable to make a go of it. His words carried that much authority, and both the woman and the bodyguards fell silent.

As soon as the boat landed along the northern bank of the river, the two parties reconvened their quarrel. The men were finding this woman, though, beyond their capacities to control. Liwen, as an uninvolved third party, had been listening to their exchanges and felt as though she had been laying it on a little too thickly. The bodyguards had in fact been playing with her, but, in Liwen's judgment, they had yet to exceed acceptable limits.

"All right! We were wrong! It's enough!" said one of the bodyguards at last, but this only seemed to fuel her anger.

"No, it's not! What're you thinking about, you shitheads? Why don't you crawl around on the ground under my feet and think about it some more," she said abrasively.

Having tried to calm her down, the bodyguards now seemed to fly into a rage at these words.

"Who do you think made it possible for this trip to go so smoothly from Gui county? Do you know, you with the vile mouth? You, a woman traveling! You should be more modest!" said a young bodyguard spewing spittle.

The two timber merchants were becoming frightened, but she was not defeated yet. "Who the hell wants to travel with shitheads like you? What were you saying? You were protecting me? Don't make it seem like you've done me any favors!"

"I don't want anything to do with her any more."

"I'm sorry I was traveling with you, too. I'm going with this guy, so you all can get the hell out of here," she said, looking in Liwen's direction.

"So that's what you want. You're an odd one!" spit out the mildest of the four bodyguards.

"Fine, let's go. Come on, let's go." The bodyguards pressed the two merchants and took off. The woman stood her ground. Under the circumstances, Liwen was in no position to budge.

The bodyguards didn't so much as look back. The two merchants turned around every so often, but the six of them soon disappeared as the road bent.

"Well, that's quite a relief. Shall we continue?" she said to Liwen.

This was too much for Liwen, though he didn't know what to do next. Until a moment earlier, they had been a group of eight, but just one man and one woman together now presented Liwen with an ethical dilemma.

"Did you want me to see you as far as Gucheng?" asked Liwen.

"I wouldn't be so bold. As far as Jintian will do. I have relatives there."

"In that case . . ."

Having come this far, there was no turning back now. Any complications arising from their party of two were explainable, and the ferryman on the Xunjiang would substantiate their story. So, Liwen decided to accompany this woman to Jintian.

"Do you have a wife?" she asked.

"Yes, I do." Liwen tried to recall the visage of his late wife to his mind, but his wife, perhaps sulking because of the present circumstances, would not appear to him.

The woman's voice had completely changed from her earlier arguments with the bodyguards.

"Do your parents live in Gucheng?" Liwen said as politely as possible in a reserved manner.

"I've left home for good. I never want to see my husband's face again."

"But . . ." Liwen was at a loss for words.

"Let's go," she beckoned him.

They headed north. The area was rich in water, and the soil was fertile. If public order in the region was good, then no explanations would be necessary.

"The land is well-plowed, isn't it?" There was nothing further to say, so Liwen looked around at the fields before them. However well-plowed the fields, at harvest time, bandits often came and harvested on their own. Taxes and farm rent were heavy. It was an era in which peasants were compelled to abandon land that should have been sowed. The expanse of painstakingly plowed fields was a very moving scene.

"It's because this area is within the control of the Society of God Worshippers."

"Is that right?" Liwen nodded his head. So, there was a strong organization known as the Society of God Worshippers, and it protected the resident population. They had to defend against bandits with force. The Society of God Worshippers was not the only armed group at this time—there were all sorts of them, including the self-defense bands known as *tuanlian*, established by landlords for their own protection.

Before them stood a grove of trees. There were many laurels in the area, and timber merchants came to Guiping to buy them. When they came to the edge of the forest, the woman stopped and let out a piercing laugh. It happened all of a sudden, and Liwen thought for a moment that she had undergone some sort of abnormal spasm. He soon realized that it was no spasm.

Twenty men rushed out of the woods and surrounded Liwen. "Bandits" was his first thought. She laughed shrilly, for they were surrounding only Liwen. Now, everything was beginning to make sense. She was clearly a decoy for this group of thieves.

Liwen stuck his hands in his pockets, pulled out his purse, and thrust it in the face of the man standing in front of him.

"Eight coins of silver. That's all I've got. It's no lie. Strip me and do a body search if you want," said Liwen. The men stayed away from him and said nothing. From behind he heard the woman's voice:

"Eight coins of silver, you say? You think we're interested in such a paltry amount?"

"What do you want, then?" Liwen returned the question.

"Your body!"

"My body?"

"The favorite son of the Jinshunji of Xiamen. They'll pay a lot for you. I think Lian Weicai will be quite free with his money. Ha, ha, ha." She laughed, in a pleasant manner, it seemed.

They grabbed Liwen's arms, and a piece of cloth loosely covered his eyes from behind. The blindfold gave off the aroma of a sweet osmanthus bloom.

—5—

The blindfold was removed and before him stood the same woman. She was sitting on a low bench much like a chopping block, leaning against a wooden wall behind her. Her legs stretched out in front of her.

Although Liwen's hands were tied, the rope had been carelessly knotted. In fact, he was not at all restricted in his movements—something his captors had done on purpose. They were only feigning to constrain him.

"How much do you think your father would fork over?" she asked.

"I couldn't say . . . probably not a single copper," Liwen responded. So it's money, he thought, as he became so calm he surprised even himself. When he realized that it was money they wanted, he saw that for the present his life was not in any immediate danger.

Liwen didn't know what sort of a group was holding him, but they certainly had ties at some level to secret societies. Taking this line of reasoning one step further, perhaps they were tied to the late Wang Juzhi. Wang's name had an uncanny impact in this part of the world, and the one name that was inseparable from that of Wang Juzhi was Lian Weicai, Liwen's father.

They don't know anything about it, thought Liwen. If they had known, then there would have been no reason for them to concoct such plans to take the son of Lian Weicai hostage and extort money.

Very few people knew of the bond between Lian Weicai and secret societies. It was not at all common knowledge, but the leaders would understand. If his father received a demand for ransom, he would surely try to track it down. Rank was very strict in this realm, and the chain of command from superior to inferior was absolute. His father was certain to be able to trace the identity of the leaders of the group holding Liwen. They don't know anything of Lian Weicai's ties to secret societies, so they've got to be just underlings, thought Liwen, without any sense of fear whatsoever. It actually astonished him that they were not profusely apologizing to him.

"If he doesn't fork over even a single piece of copper, you won't live," she said.

"Nothing I can do about that. A human being dies only once."

"You're a brave one!"

"No, I'm rather a coward. I know when to give up. That's a positive trait, wouldn't you say?"

Liwen looked up. A spider's web hung from a dark crossbeam, and a faint, listless sound could be heard. He eventually became aware of the sound. There were no windows in the wall to either side of him.

At about the height of the person standing in front of the wall before him was a small square hole. It was very small—hardly a window at all. Since the room was lit up, there must have been an aperture for admitting light in the wall behind him that he could not see.

"So, we'll just have to wait patiently for your father's answer," said the woman as she stood up.

Liwen had been looking at the ceiling and now turned his eyes to the right.

"What're you looking for? You've been twisting around constantly. You don't know where you are, do you?" she said, looking down at Liwen. Liwen was now looking straight ahead at the spot where she had been sitting just a moment before. She was still leaning against the wall but was now sitting directly on the floor.

"No, I don't recognize the place, but . . . I have a rough idea," said Liwen.

"A rough idea?"

"We're not that far from the laurel forest, are we? . . . It was six hundred thirty-eight paces."

"So, you counted."

"Well, there was nothing else to do." Liwen had been blindfolded in the forest and transported on a litter carried by two men. He had counted their steps.

"There's nothing to do here either. You have something to count?"

"I'll just patiently think about what to do."

"You'll have plenty of time."

She departed by way of the door in the left corner of the wall in front of him. The door closed and he could hear it being bolted shut.

He didn't know how much time had passed, but it seemed like somewhat more than thirty minutes, perhaps less. He surveyed the room. His arms were still bound, but when he squeezed them together, the rope seemed to loosen. He was afraid that they would retie the ropes binding him, after throwing him into this room, but thus far they had failed to do so. With all the strength he could muster in his shoulders, Liwen squeezed his arms together. The gaps in his bindings were larger than he had expected. By wriggling his body, he was able to use his right hand and eventually he removed the rope.

Once free, he examined the room. There was in fact an open window in the wall to which he had had his back. Light shone in, but there was no grating over it, and it looked as though a person could crawl in or out through it. Liwen leaned the bench that looked like a chopping block on which the woman had been sitting against the wall lengthwise, used it as a footstool, and tried to escape through the window.

It was almost too easy. These people really were underlings, he thought. The way they had tied him seemed so amateurish. That fact and the fact that they had not placed a guard to watch the house led him to believe that they were not experts in this line of work at all.

Just as Liwen had supposed, there was a stream in front of the house. The sound he had heard earlier was the monotone of the plying of a boat's oars. He was becoming bolder. They're not much of an adversary, he thought. He was frankly amazed at their slipshod methods. Even more astonishing was the fact that just the right boat was docked on the shore, with poles neatly sitting diagonally inside it. This was Liwen's first trip to this area, so he had examined a map closely until its details were etched in his mind. From its width, he could tell he was looking at the Sipan River. It was less than one-third as wide as the Xunjiang they had crossed earlier.

Liwen was able to steer the boat quite adequately. This is so stupid, he was thinking. When he arrived at the far shore, he gave in to an impulse to laugh out loud to his heart's content, as the tension till that point abated.

Once across the Sipan River, he decided to continue the journey north. There was a pathway there that made it unnecessary for him to consult the map in his mind. It was a direct route to the north.

Jiantian village was over five kilometers from there. Actually, the point where he had crossed the Sipan River was on Jintian territory. The center of the village, where there was a cluster of private homes, was some five kilometers away. The temple was situated in the center of the village as well. During the trek he met an old peasant and asked directions just to be sure, and, as he had expected, the Sanjie Ancestral Temple stood near what appeared to be a row of houses.

This soon became apparent. The homes in the area were all extremely poor, and that made the stone construction of the temple seem almost excessively grand. It was already time for his appointment. No one was standing in front of the temple. Liwen walked over, stopped by the entranceway, and took a deep breath. There was a two-line stanza, something like a magic charm, written on the gatepost.

As he gazed at the stanza and pondered its meaning, a voice addressed him from behind:

"Things are a mess because the Litang Bridge collapsed." Liwen was taken by surprise. As the expression goes, he was frightened out of his wits. The voice was that of the woman from before. And, sure enough, when he turned around, it was she standing before his eyes. In haste, he spoke the passwords: "It was a wooden bridge, so . . . it easily collapsed."

—6—

"We were most discourteous to you. Please accept my apologies. But, we were about to discuss events of the gravest consequence to the entire realm, and I thought that, even though you were the son of Lian Weicai, we needed to ascertain what sort of man you were," said Hong Xiuquan as he stared firmly into the face of Lian Liwen.

Aware that he was curling his lips, Liwen covered his expression with a smile. From the scene at the ferry on the Xunjiang, the whole thing had been an elaborate drama to evaluate his character. Liwen was led by a woman from the Sanjie Temple into a spacious home, and there he saw the timber merchants and their bodyguards.

"Were you looking in from the holes in the wall on the opposite side?" asked Liwen.

Hong Xiuquan frowned and nodded in a dignified manner. Liwen stared back at him. Hong had a strange face. An intrepid expression was eerily mixed with what appeared to be nervousness. One sensed that this mysterious quality went to the core of Hong's personality.

Liwen waited until the smile on his own face subsided, and then said:

"Character evaluations of this sort mustn't be one-sided. Mightn't I have the same opportunity? After all, we shall be discussing important matters. One must be extremely cautious."

"You wish to evaluate me?" asked Hong without changing his expression.

"Yes. That is correct."

"And how do you intend to go about doing that?"

"I would like to ask you a question."

"Go right ahead."

"I have heard the story of your dream. That dream . . . I would very much like to hear it in your own words."

"So that's it?" Hong shut his eyes.

There were just the two of them in the deserted room now: Lian Liwen and Hong Xiuquan. The amateur performers in the bizarre little play who had shown their faces earlier had all disappeared.

"Yes, the story of your dream," repeated Liwen.

In the year after he had heard Zhu Ziqi's public oratory and the Christian street evangelist—1837—Hong had taken the civil service examinations for the third time and again failed them.

From the time he had gone to Guangzhou to sit for the exams, his physical condition had been strange. The shock that came over him when he learned of his failure was the final straw. He ran a high temperature and was unable to do so much as walk.

The distance from Guangzhou to Hua county was not very far—about 30 minutes by cart. Hua county people often walked to and from Guangzhou at that time.

When Hong's medical condition became extremely critical, the doctor diagnosed him as beyond all hope. Family members rushed to Guangzhou. Since it mattered little where he died, they wanted him to be at home. So they placed him unconscious on a litter and carried it back.

In addition to his parents, Hong had two elder brothers, an elder sister, named Xinying, and a younger sister, named Xuanjiao. His two sisters were in constant attendance at his sickbed.

Hong had contracted his illness in Guangzhou in the second lunar month of the year. Later, the Taipings made the second day of the second month "the day of recompense to the Father." That day corresponds to March 8 on the solar calendar. In the Taiping vocabulary, "Father" always implied their God Jehovah. The day Hong became ill was understood as the origin of God's bestowal on Hong of his mission.

In his dream, Hong Xiuquan ascended to heaven at midnight of March 1. He was ordered by God to fight and expel the devils that were leading the men of the world astray.

"But, let me describe this in greater detail for you," said Hong.

In his cloudy state of consciousness at the time, it had seemed to him as though many people had come to pay him their respects, and he thought they had come to fetch him from the world.

"So, I called my parents, my brothers and their wives, and my wife to my bedside, apologized for acts of unfiliality, and bid them farewell. Soon an angel came for me, and put me in a sedan chair, and we soared into the heavens. On either side of the heavenly gates, countless beautiful women appeared. I had entered heaven, and it was full of light. Its glory was brilliant, completely unlike the vulgar world below."

There was scarcely any modulation in Hong's words. He spoke disinterestedly, his eyes remaining closed the entire time. Perhaps the events of the times were being fused together behind his eyelids.

"Next, they dressed me in the imperial robes," Hong continued, "and men wearing hats with peaked crowns arrived. There were many, many of them. They cut open my stomach, slicing it to shreds."

"Your stomach?"

"Yes. They replaced all of my internal organs. The Heavenly Mother then appeared and spoke as follows: 'My son, your body was impure from the time spent in the world below. Your mother shall cleanse you in the river, so that you may then go see your father.' So the Heavenly Mother cleansed me, and then led me before the Heavenly Father, Supreme Lord-on-High."

"What sort of personage is the Heavenly Father, Supreme Lord-on-High?"

"He wore a high-brimmed hat, and his golden beard hung down to his waist. He was attired in the black dragon robe, and placed his hands upon his knees. His was a truly correct bearing. I fell to my knees before him. The Heavenly Father spoke to me sorrowfully: 'There is not a single person on earth whom I have not nourished. I have given every one of them food to eat, clothes to wear, and blessings to enjoy. All the myriad things of heaven and earth are my creations. And yet, in spite of this, they have all lost sight of their true hearts, and no one holds me in reverence. What is worse is that they have been led astray and confused by devils and have offered up to these devils those things that I conferred upon them. It is as though they were raised by demons. They do not even know that these demons have captured them with plans to do them harm. My heart grieves for them and feels compassion.'"

"The Heavenly Father spoke to you in just that way?"

"Yes. Exactly, not a word differently. Even were I to try I could not forget these words."

"What did the Heavenly Father do next?"

"The Heavenly Father, Supreme Lord-on-High presented me with a golden seal and a sword of snow amid clouds. He told me to expel the devils with these. In unison with the angels, I was to fight everywhere for thirty-three days. I was to seize all my brethren who had been followers of these devils and return with them to heaven. However, I was to be merciless with those with wicked minds, leaders among the devils, and the children of the devils. I was ordered to attack every last one of them. The Heavenly Father from his eminent position showed me how the demons were misguiding the people and causing them injury, and he instructed me in methods of warfare. I was also assisted from time to time in these military matters by a middle-aged man who stood at the Heavenly Father's side. Before I was even aware of it, I was calling this man Heavenly Elder Brother."

"That was Jesus Christ, was it not?"

"That is correct. . . . But at the time I still did not know it. All I knew was that the Heavenly Father and the Heavenly Elder Brother were in heaven."

"How did you awake from your dream?"

"I was asked by the Heavenly Father to descend into the world below: 'How will the people in the world below ever become aware of the delusions of the demons and be able to ascend into heaven if you do not go down into their world?' I wanted to remain in heaven, but the Heavenly Father became angry. 'After you have completed your work in the world below, you may return to heaven and enjoy its pleasures one and all.' The Heavenly Father and the Heavenly Elder Brother sent me back to this world. When I was on the verge of departure, the Heavenly Father wrote in seven Chinese characters the name he had selected for me: Heavenly King, Quan of the Great Way."

Hong's family had affixed the character "ren" (meaning benevolence) to the names of all the males in Hong Xiuquan's generation. His two elder brothers were, thus, Hong Renfa and Hong Renda. His first cousins were Hong Ren'gan and Hong Renzheng. Hong Xiuquan himself had been named Renkun by his parents. For spiritual reasons, he also adopted the name Hong Huoxiu. He later called himself Xiuquan, as the Heavenly Father had called him when he ascended into heaven during his dream.

"At that point I awoke from the dream. I looked at my parents and brothers by my bedside and recounted for them how the Heavenly Father had ordered our person to be emperor and to rule over all the people of the realm."

"They were undoubtedly surprised," said Liwen.

The expression "our person" was used by the general populace for the first person during the Spring and Autumn and Warring States periods, from the eighth through the third centuries B.C., with the meaning of "we." Beginning in the reign of China's first emperor in 221 B.C., all persons beneath the emperor himself were forbidden from using the expression.

Hong could see the consternation in his father's eyes when his son awakened from this dream and referred to himself with the term "our person." Should anyone else have heard him, it would have without a doubt been considered an act of *lèse majesté*.

"He was certainly surprised. Thinking that I had become possessed by demons, they brought a witch doctor to me. I was quite a laughingstock."

For the first time a sly smile floated onto Hong's face. Liwen focused all of his energies on Hong's eyes, and Hong stared right back at him.

Liwen was thinking, just as Hong's father had worried twelve years earlier: Has this guy taken leave of his senses? But, as intently as he looked at Hong, he could recognize nothing insane in Hong's facial appearance. Calmly, and to himself, Liwen wondered if maybe Hong had actually flown up to heaven and met the Heavenly Father and the Heavenly Elder Brother there.

"At that point had you already read *Good Words to Admonish the Age,* which you were handed on the street in Guangzhou?" asked Liwen.

"I had flipped through the pages only, but I hadn't actually read it."

"Only flipped through the pages?"

"That's right. I finally read it some six years later. When I was reorganizing the books on my bookshelf, I found this thin volume covered in dust. I read it then, to my great astonishment. The words of the Heavenly Father during my dream were exactly the same as those in this booklet. It was at that point that I discovered that the Heavenly Father was Jehovah and the Heavenly Elder Brother was Jesus Christ."

"This occurred six years later?" Liwen mumbled. Hong said that he had not read it, only flipped through its pages. The images received from the missionary pamphlet, *Good Words to Admonish the Age*, must have slipped into his consciousness though he himself was unaware of it. While suffering from the fever, these images probably floated back up into his mind.

Liwen only pondered these thoughts; he did not verbalize them. *Good Words to Admonish the Age* was an introductory text to Christianity written by an overseas Chinese believer by the name of Liang Afa (1789–1855) who had it printed in Malacca. Liang was a disciple of the English missionary William Milne (1815–1856), a Protestant who had been expelled from the Catholic Church.

In preparation for his meeting with Hong Xiuquan, Liwen had gotten his hands on a copy of Liang's pamphlet in Guangzhou and tried to read it. He was now trying to verify the story Hong had just presented to him. Hong's dream seemed to be more deeply tinged with Daoism than with anything Christian. The golden seal and precious sword with which he was to attack the demons was really a Chinese Daoist conception.

Only the apparent correspondence between the Heavenly Father and the Heavenly Elder Brother with Jehovah and Christ, respectively, provided a slender link to Christianity. Perhaps that was a lingering image from his flipping through the pages of *Good Words to Admonish the Age*.

"Six years. That was just the right space of time. If I had just had the dream and not read the book, then I probably would never have been able to ascertain that it was the Heavenly Father who had commanded me. By the same token, had I just read the book and not had my dream for those forty days, I don't believe that I would ever have been won over to Christianity," said Hong.

A high fever for forty days—all sorts of fantasies must have crept into his mind during that time. Among them were an aged Heavenly Father and a middle-aged Heavenly Elder Brother, whom he now firmly believed were Jehovah and Christ.

Just then the door to the room opened, and a young man entered.

"I thought I said that until my talk with this person was over, no one was to enter this room!" Hong reproached the young man.

"Urgent news has arrived," he said, falling to his knees before Hong.

"What urgent news?"

"It is from Hua county. It was an easy delivery, without any problems."

Hong sat up on the edge of his chair.

"It is a boy."

"Really?" Barely any change had come over Hong's face until that point, but now it loosened up completely. Hong Xiuquan's wife, née Lai, had given birth to a son in Hua county. It was November 23. The son was named Tiangui.

3

A Hero
in the
Setting Sun

—1—

A smile spread over the face of thirty-six-year-old Hong Xiuquan when he heard the news of the birth of his son back in Jintian. At that same time, Lin Zexu was sixty-five years old and spending his waning years in Changsha, Hunan province.

It was late fall, soon to turn to winter.

"The frost causes damage, and the sick tree feels compassion for the autumn leaves"—Lin was ruminating on this poem, which he had composed upon leaving the city of Kunming in Yunnan province. According to the rules of such poems, known as regulated verse, they had to be written in matching couplets. The match Lin chose for "autumn leaves" was "setting sun." The sun was sinking in the West, and so too did Lin Zexu see his own life.

Charged with responsibility for China's defeat in the Opium War, the disciplinary action taken against him was consignment to Xinjiang (Chinese Turkestan). That had transpired eight years earlier. For a time he participated in an interim project as director of public works repairs on the Dong River, and a full year passed before he actually proceeded to Xinjiang. Three years later he succeeded with a reclamation project on the north–south road to Tianshan, and he was pardoned and reinstated as governor of Shaanxi province. One year after that, he set off for Kunming to assume a new post as governor-general of Yunnan and Guizhou provinces. This occurred at a time of serious local fighting between Han Chinese and Muslim Chinese.

Two years or more after coming to Kunming, Lin had virtually resolved the ethnic disputes. While this political work had all gone smoothly, in his personal history Kunming represented a dark era. He had lost his loving, faithful wife Shuqing during this time, and he himself was inclined to ill health.

Many times Lin petitioned the court in Beijing to allow him to retire, but the Daoguang Emperor refused to permit it. The emperor's plan was that, once the ethnic disputes had been solved, he would recall Lin to Beijing and appoint him to the position of Grand Minister of State, in which he would serve as a political advisor.

However, after the emperor became aware of Lin's illness and the loss of his wife, he allowed him to retire and return to his hometown. Lin proceeded from Kunming in Yunnan to his home village of Houguan in Fujian province.

When he had been sent to Xinjiang, Lin's wife, as one would expect, remained behind in his hometown, but she insisted on joining him when he took up his appointment in Kunming. People tried to prevent her from doing so, arguing that Kunming was far in the hinterland, but she said nothing and simply shook her head.

"There's no great hurry. You can come at your leisure," wrote Lin to her when he learned of local conditions for travel. He had gone to Kunming from Xi'an via Chengdu, Sichuan province. He knew well the great pain with which she was living.

Lin also knew that his wife's remaining days were few. He wanted to spend at least her last days together. If she remained in Fujian, then he might not get an opportunity to see her ever again. No matter how well she attended to her health now, this was a fact.

Somewhat over a year after she had arrived in Kunming, October 15 of the previous year, Lin Shuqing passed away. He was at her bedside at the time, as were their three sons, Lin Ruzhou, Lin Congyi, and Lin Gongshu. At the end, the expression on her face, although wracked by illness, indicated her happiness that they had all come to be with her.

After her death, Lin pressed his request for retirement more forcefully. Life was something one devoted to one's country. This was the essential framework with which a bureaucrat in premodern China worked. When he resigned, all of Lin's energies were exhausted, and what remained was little more than a skeleton. This was summed up in the expression that a request for retirement was "to seek the release of one's body." In a poem composed upon leaving Kunming, Lin had written: "Tears abound in the request for a body, the gowns of an old official." In September of the year following Mrs. Lin's death, Lin Zexu had his wishes realized, and his appeal to retire was officially accepted. He and his three sons returned home with the coffin of his late wife. They traveled via Guizhou along the Qingshui River. They followed the course of the Qingshui downstream, and when it entered Hunan province it turned into the mighty Yuan River. The Yuan River system connected to the Xiang River system. The Lin party took the Xiang River and headed toward the big city of Changsha.

They were traveling without urgency, and as the first anniversary of the death of Lin's wife was approaching, Lin wanted to hold the ceremony commemorating that occasion in a lively, bustling place. They had found no such place on the trip from Yunnan to Guizhou. Changsha, the capital of Hunan, was the largest city in that region, and many of Lin's friends lived there. From the time he had left Kunming, Lin had been planning to arrive in Changsha by the appointed date for this ceremony.

He arrived in time, precisely on the anniversary. The Buddhist memorial service took place on a small boat. Not wanting to put anyone out, Lin and his sons decided to remain and sleep on board the boat even after they had arrived in Changsha.

Incense was burning and its smell enveloped the boat. Passing his hand over the coffin of his wife, Lin murmured to himself that he was going to proceed with alacrity. He too was feeling the waning days of life, pondering what to leave behind rather than what was to be done. His physical strength was dissipating. Somehow, though, he still had some energy left as he wondered what could be done for China.

For 30 years Lin Zexu had worked as an official of the Chinese government, and he was thinking that the last piece of work he would leave as a guide to the younger generation was his experience, and the views he had reached on the basis of that experience. Thus, he needed to know the present national situation in great detail.

There was a person in Changsha who could provide him with such information. In addition to performing the ceremony for his wife, Lin also intended to meet this person. As yet, they had never met, but Lin had often heard his name—Zuo Zongtang (1812–1885), from Xiangyin county, Hunan.

—2—

We begin with an examination of a Chinese expression, much in use in the middle of the nineteenth century: *yudi bingfa*. What does it mean?

The first character, *yu*, means something in which one rides, such as a palanquin or cart. Because the earth or ground—*di* in Chinese—was that over which transport for all living things takes place, it became customary to call the world or the globe *yudi*. The term *bingfa* means military strategy.

The comparable expression, "global military strategy," has not gained much currency, perhaps because it is so close to the term "geopolitics," popular in Germany during the Nazi period.

Those Chinese who engaged in *yudi bingfa* studied how best to pursue policies to enhance national wealth and strength by making detailed investigations of their nation's topography, climate, products, human feelings, political conditions, and culture. As a realistic political figure himself, Lin Zexu was interested in such people.

"After all this time I hardly need anyone preaching morality to me," thought Lin, already feeling stingy about his time. "I want to learn what I don't know in the little time that remains."

Ever since he had been a young boy, though, Lin had hated wasting time with discussions of general principles. He recalled his intimacy with the famous Gongyang School of thought and his associations with its adherents, who laid emphasis on practical political and economic issues. This group included the late Gong Zizhen, whose death had been a terrible shock to Lin. It also included Wei Yuan, to whom Lin had entrusted documentary materials he had collected in Guangzhou.

Wei Yuan had passed the highest level of the imperial civil service examinations and was now serving as a department magistrate.

"What a waste," thought Lin, for now that Wei was a magistrate, he probably had no time to pursue his studies. Lin would have given him much more important work to do or had him devote his time to scholarship. Lin had continued his correspondence with Wei Yuan over the years, though Wei always complained that he had no time to pursue his research on *yudi bingfa*, or global strategy.

Now that Wei was a piddling administrator, the first name in *yudi bingfa* was most likely Zuo Zongtang. Lin had first heard Zuo's name some time ago. While governor of Jiangsu province, Lin's superior, the governor-general of Jiangsu and Jiangxi, Tao Zhu (1779–1839), often spoke of Zuo. That was already ten years ago, when Zuo was barely in his late twenties. Tao, also a Hunan man, was very fond of his home region. He frequently would say to Lin, "There's a young fellow in Hunan named Zuo Zongtang. He's young, but brilliant at *yudi bingfa*. He'll distinguish himself before too long." Then, after a short space of time, Tao would add: "He's really quite eccentric, though."

After his return to the fold from Xinjiang, Lin selected two men for positions of responsibility: Zhang Liangji (1807–1871) and Hu Linyi (1812–1861). Hu was actually Tao's son-in-law and also from Hunan province. When he was serving as an assistant examining official during the Jiangnan provincial exams of 1840, he committed some sort of minor infelicity and was demoted.

The next year his father died, and he returned to his native town and remained behind closed doors in private life for the next four years.

When Lin became governor-general of Yunnan and Guizhou, he summoned this Hu Linyi, whose name and talents he had heard often mentioned
by Tao, from Hunan to Yunnan to serve as his "right arm."

"Zuo Zongtang is far more talented than I am," Hu told Lin, "but there
may be a bit of a problem with him in public."

"The late Tao often mentioned him and said he was quite an eccentric.
What sort of a fellow is he, anyway?" asked Lin.

Hu frowned. "Well, let us just say that he is a bit warped. He is someone
of enormous capability—in my view, the most brilliant man alive. He's just
very hard to deal with, but there is no one alive who can compare with him in
the field of *yudi bingfa*."

"Can we get him to come here to Yunnan? How about his serving at the
same rank as you?" Lin suggested.

"I shall write him and see. He will certainly be pleased."

Hu Linyi and Zuo Zongtang were the same age and were related by marriage through Tao Zhu. While Hu had passed the third and highest level of
the civil service examinations, though, Zuo was still only at the second level.
That he was thirty-eight years of age and still had not reached the same level
as Hu did not necessarily mean Zuo's career was lagging far behind. Zuo,
however, thought of himself as a man of unparalleled ability in China, so it
was personally mortifying for him to have been surpassed by others in the
examinations. This was quite a sore spot for Zuo.

Hu wrote him, but Zuo's response was a note of refusal: "For reasons of a
lawsuit concerning the Tao family, I cannot at present leave Hunan." It was
not merely an excuse. Hu Linyi knew of the lawsuit involving the Tao family. Thus, Lin had been unable to appoint Zuo to his staff.

When Lin resigned to return home and Hu came to bid him farewell, Hu
said: "Zuo Zongtang has said that he would like to meet your excellency in
Changsha. If possible, please do grant his request." Hu had made contact
with Zuo in advance.

Changsha was the provincial capital of Hunan. Prominent civil and military officials of Hunan resided there, and many of them were old acquaintances of Lin. In addition, Lin was still popular as the hero of the Opium
War, so when he arrived in Changsha, all sorts of people came to meet him.

The governorship of Hunan was in the process of being reshuffled. Feng
Dexing (1801–1868), former provincial administration commissioner of
Jiangning (present-day Nanjing), had only arrived in August. He had served as
an official in Guizhou about six years earlier, and thus there were many topics
of conversation he shared with Lin. In the midst of their lively chat, Feng said,

"This must be very difficult, meeting people one after the next. It's not good for your health. How about if we gather groups together for you to meet with all at the same time?" He then handed Lin a batch of name cards of those who wished to meet him.

Lin smiled and said: "You're right. I may not be able to deal with them all one at a time."

"Fine, then let's do it in groups, and I'll take over the handling of things. We'll manage somehow."

Feng Dexing decided to set a time at which the guests could come to pay their respects, and Lin would then meet with them in groups. The high provincial officials of Hunan organized themselves into a group and came to pay their respects. The next day, military personnel paid a group visit to Lin. Meetings with people other than Lin's relatives and old friends were turned down.

"It's for your own health," said Feng insistently to Lin, who seemed a bit hesitant about the refusal to meet people.

Although Changsha was a large city, the circle of Lin's acquaintances, including civil and military officials, was not that broad. It soon spread among this group that it was the governor who had made this arrangement.

The first group of high provincial officials, numbering about 30 in all, formally visited Lin on the day after his arrival in Changsha. They included: administrative bureaucrats, such as the provincial governor, the provincial administration commissioner (head of the provincial administration), the surveillance commissioner (head of provincial legal affairs), and prefectural magistrates; financial bureaucrats, such as the tax circuit intendant and the salt control circuit intendant; and certain high military men, such as the provincial military commander and the regional commanders.

Lin had decided to receive his Changsha guests on the boat where he was staying. When he looked at the list given to him of those coming to pay their respects, he wondered if they would all fit on board. Zuo Zongtang's name did not appear on the list.

The offices held by those on the list were not given, but it was filled with the names of those from illustrious local families. Although Zuo held no official post, his name echoed throughout China as a scholar of *yudi bingfa*. And, insofar as he was a well-known scholar, he was far superior to the few nongovernmental persons whose names appeared on the list.

"Is there something wrong?" asked the servant who delivered the list to Lin, noting an expression of doubt on Lin's face.

"I don't see Zuo Zongtang's name," said Lin.

"I know that we informed him, but for some reason no answer was forthcoming," he said hesitantly.

"Makes no difference," said Lin lightly. He had heard from many quarters what an oddball Zuo was. Lin detected it again in the servant's equivocal words: "for some reason."

—3—

The boat was not large, but it could accommodate 30 people. Seating the guests closely together, with their elbows virtually rubbing against their neighbors on either side, might actually encourage familiarity.

The Qing court was then carrying out a reshuffling of high officials bit by bit. Ten years earlier, just before Lin Zexu was sent as imperial commissioner to Guangdong, he had been serving as the governor-general of the Huguang provinces (Hunan and Hubei), stationed in the city of Wuchang, and during that time he had made any number of trips to Changsha. Most of the officials from that era, though, were no longer living in the city. There were three men he remembered having met in Changsha, but when he asked about them, he learned that they had been transferred and had never returned to work in Changsha. These were men he knew primarily from Beijing and Guangzhou.

Lin did not speak in an overly formal manner when receiving his guests. He spoke of present conditions in Yunnan and Guizhou provinces and of recollections from his days in Changsha.

"How would present-day Changsha compare to the Changsha of ten years ago?" asked one person. "Don't you think that it has really fallen into a sad state of decline?"

Lin smiled and answered, shaking his head: "My boat just arrived in Changsha yesterday, and I have yet to go on shore. Since I haven't even touched Changsha soil, I'm in no position to answer your question."

Everyone there laughed out loud. The questioner cast his eyes downward, and Lin felt sorry for him. The fact of the matter was that even though Lin had yet to step on land at Changsha, from the boat he had had time to survey conditions at the wharf at his leisure.

It was an honest impression—Changsha had declined drastically from ten years before, but Lin didn't want to speak solely of sentiments like "decline." If Changsha had truly fallen into decay over the past decade, then he wanted to talk about how to return it to prosperity.

The conversation dampened once the laughter had subsided. At that point, an attendant in the Lin family came forward and said:

"A visitor has arrived."

"Really?" Lin looked over in Feng Dexing's direction. The guests that day had all come through arrangements set up by Governor Feng. He had decided to decline meetings for Lin with any others than those planned for. The governor's subordinates should have been standing guard at the wharf.

"This is strange. All those who applied are already here," said Feng with a dubious look.

"What happened to your troops?" asked Lin.

The soldiers on the wharf were about to turn the intruder away. "The soldiers told me that they wished first to seek your advice," said the attendant, slipping his hand into his pocket and removing a crimson-colored card on which was written in black ink: Zuo Zongtang, Hunan, provincial graduate. The writing on the card was so large that, when the attendant handed it to Lin, the other members of the group could all make out what it said.

A hum of voices erupted, and Lin heard whispers about him:

"Oh, it's Zuo Zongtang . . ."

"What a character! And at such a time!"

"What shall we do?" Lin asked Feng, with a forced smile. Since he had entrusted the entire business of this collective visit to Governor Feng, Lin thought it out of place at this point to express his own views.

In actual fact, Lin had come to Changsha to meet this man. Although he had long anticipated this meeting, Zuo's method of putting in an appearance seemed to rub everyone the wrong way.

"Because of your relationship with Tao Zhu, let's not send him away. Our visit has already taken up a great deal of time. I think it's time for us to go. Master Lin, from now on the time is yours," said Feng. He stood up and the others all rose as well.

"That guy always enters so dramatically."

"That red name card. He wrote it so large and in black so everybody could read it."

"How ostentatious!" All of the guests' low whispers were audible to Lin. In fact, they probably spoke in such a way as to ensure that he would hear them. It was like the echoing of a warning: Master Lin, don't be deceived by this mountebank Zuo Zongtang.

Lin didn't want to hear any of this, shutting his eyes but unable to escape it. Even a person of particular distinction surely must have his share of character flaws too, thought Lin. Just then the sound of a plop into water was immediately followed by someone shouting.

"What's happened?"

"Someone fell into the river."

"Who?"

"Zuo Zongtang."

"Again?"

Lin could hear this flurry of voices on all sides, as he opened his eyes.

Someone had jumped into the river. Someone else threw a rope from the shore. Finally, Zuo was salvaged from the water. "Pull! I can swim!" yelled Zuo as he thrust his head out of the water and shook it vigorously.

Several planks had been laid out from the shore to facilitate getting on and off the boat. Zuo had been about to step on the planks when the governor's soldiers lined up and tried to prevent him from boarding, as they had been ordered to do. This led to trouble, pushing and shoving ensued, and Zuo lost his balance and fell into the water. Waving off the people who tried to help him safely onto land, Zuo found his way under his own strength to the planks and climbed up on them. He was dripping wet from head to toe.

Lin walked over to the planks, and Zuo drew himself up to his full height. This was the first meeting between the two men. Although they had never seen one another before, both knew who the other was.

"Lin Gongbao?" said Zuo. The Qing court had conferred on Lin Zexu the title of "Junior Guardian of the Heir Apparent." This title implied a role in the education of the heir apparent to the Manchu throne, but it was merely a title, with no substance in and of itself. An honorary designation, it was referred to generally as *gongbao*. Within the court, however, this title carried a high degree of respect. The sense it conveyed was of a post far above governors and governor-generals.

Lin smiled broadly and said softly: "Master Zuo?"

"I am very happy to meet you." Zuo bowed with arms folded, his legs planted firmly on the planks.

"Do come on board," said Lin, offering him a hand.

"I am deeply honored." Zuo stood up straight and walked up onto the boat. His clothes were still dripping wet.

"You should change clothes or you'll catch cold. You must take care of your health," said Lin.

"Thank you, I shall."

"Ah, Ruzhou," said Lin, turning to his daughter. "Go get some of my clothes for Master Zuo."

"Of course. Come this way, please," said Ruzhou, showing Zuo the way inside the boat.

"Well, I think then that we shall excuse ourselves. What do you think, gentlemen?" said Governor Feng Dexing, turning to the group of men who had come to pay their respects to Lin.

They all nodded silently, and the group departed. Zuo gazed after them.

—4—

"Until your wet clothes dry out, we can't let you go," said Lin to Zuo when the latter had changed clothes. Evening was fast upon them.

"In which case I shan't be able to return home tonight," said Zuo, as he dried his wet queue with a towel.

"They certainly won't be dry until tomorrow."

"I shall send an attendant home to explain the situation to my family."

"That's best. Otherwise, they'll probably be worried on your behalf. Let us have a leisurely chat this evening."

"It's rather prosaic to have a quiet conversation along this pier. Might we not move the boat to a more elegant setting?"

"I agree. You know Changsha far better than I. Tell the boatman where to go."

"I would suggest a place from which the Yinpen mountain range can be seen," said Zuo.

The Xiang River flowed due south, nestling just to the west of Changsha. There were two islands along this stretch of the river: the longer one to the south was Shuiluzhou; the shorter one to the north was Fujiazhou. They sailed to the west side of Fujiazhou, from where the Yinpen range was visible.

As the luster off the water of the Xiang River was beginning to be obscured by the evening haze, Lin had the dinner table on board set and provisioned with food and drink.

The five men—Lin, his three sons, and Zuo—talked throughout the night. It was actually a conversation between Lin and Zuo, as Lin's three sons were there primarily to listen.

"There is ample time until tomorrow morning. Let us have a full and detailed conversation, and let us begin with a major issue—that of principles. Will that be all right?" proposed Zuo.

"I have no objection."

"Well, then, what country do you think deserves our closest attention as concerns the future of China? It has been eight years since the opening of China, and now even the towel I was using before to dry off with is produced in England. From now on every corner of our daily lives will be invaded by foreign lands. We have got to learn about foreign things. From your personal experience of having confronted foreign countries, Mr. Lin, I would like to hear your frank views on this matter."

Zuo placed his hands on his knees and assumed a stern pose. Perhaps he thought that, if he relaxed this pose, discussion of such a serious matter would be impossible.

"I have not the slightest doubt that Russia will be China's bane in the future. I say that without hesitation," answered Lin promptly. This was an issue he had often considered, and his response was clear.

"I did not expect that answer. At the time of the Opium War, Mr. Lin, you engaged in a variety of negotiations with the English. And, I have heard that it was a time of great bitterness for you. Yet you say that Russia will cause China more troubles than England." As he spoke, Zuo lifted his hands from his knees slowly and placed them on the table.

"Having negotiated with the British, I learned what they wanted," said Lin in a soft voice. "Then I was sent off to Xinjiang where I could hear the beating of Russian hearts at our border. I could smell Russian body odor, and I observed what Russia was aiming at as well."

"How do the two countries differ?" asked Zuo, leaning forward unconsciously.

"England is a mercantile nation. The function of their military capacity is to protect commerce. If you can understand merchant psychology, you can deal appropriately with them. . . . England has taken over India, but in my view the purpose of this was to preserve merchant rights, and now they seem to have more trouble than they bargained for. Yes, England forced the sale of Indian opium on us. India had nothing else to sell us. England is carrying around this heavy burden, and I think she's about to change her ways of doing things."

" 'Ways of doing things'?"

"The way she devoured India causes indigestion. Henceforth, the British will not try to grab huge expanses of land, but just base points. Hong Kong is a good example. Concession areas. These are perfect because they're not large. Merchants have no need for large tracts of territory."

"And smaller stretches of land are easier to take control over. We would be unprepared if they came after a tiny piece of land like this island. Shouldn't we be on guard?"

"Master Zuo." Lin stared at Zuo for a moment and then turned to his three sons. He had been relaxed until then, and all of a sudden his demeanor turned grave. During the short silence that ensued there was a stuffiness in the air.

Then Lin resumed: "I have had considerable experience negotiating with foreign countries and have learned a great deal in the process. I think I have more knowledge about foreign matters than the average person. So I know what there is to fear. I must speak out loudly about these things, but in my present position I am unable to do so. I want to make men of will aware of what I have said here. It's so very sad."

"What is so sad?"

"The foreign powers are so far advanced."

"I too am aware of that much. After all, we lost the Opium War. We did not win because the enemy was so far ahead of us."

"The difference between us is enormous. Desperately so."

"Then we have to strive further, try harder. We are a people with ancient traditions."

"It will take time," said Lin, slowly shaking his head. "It will depend on our efforts, but if things stay as they are, then we may have a few hundred years."

"A few hundred years? That's an immense period of time!" Zuo cried.

"I said 'If things stay as they are.'"

"Yes?"

"If our people can be remade, then perhaps the time can be shortened. Time is closing in on them, though."

"Remake people?"

"Our men, as they presently are, are no good. Half of our adult population is addicted to opium. Our people are servile. This won't do at all."

"I agree."

"I'm really worried about Russia. We share a long border with them. They are not a mercantile country like the British, but an agricultural land. Those who live off agriculture desire land more than anything else. Their yearning for land is extraordinarily fierce. And Russia has only cold land. They may seek to do business with the world, but in the winter their ports are all frozen. Thus, Russia aims instinctively in a southerly direction. We lie to their south, and therein lies the danger."

—5—

"I'm speaking as an individual. I was laying great hope on having this conversation and listening to you today," said Lin Zexu with a forced smile, after his discussion comparing England and Russia and the problem of remolding the Chinese people.

"What I have to say is by no means as large in scope or scale as what you have just spoken of," said Zuo Zongtang, in an atypical gesture of modesty.

"Not at all. My observations aren't large—they're just vague. I'd like to hear what you have to say in more concrete terms. What do you believe most deserves our attention in China today?"

Lin lifted his cup and crossed his legs. He was trying to create for Zuo an atmosphere in which it would be easy to converse.

"Rather than deserving attention, I would phrase it as worthy of our anxiety. I'm speaking of bandit activities, which are especially severe in Guangxi. Among the rebel groups in Guangxi is one in particular, known as the Society of God Worshippers. They are a pernicious band, and perhaps we should concentrate on them," said Zuo.

"From time to time I have heard things about this Society of God Worshippers, and, if I am not mistaken, they seem to follow the teachings of Christ, of all things."

"That's right. It's all foreign produce—even their God. They are unprecedented in China."

"True enough. Though, after all, the Buddha came originally from India."

"The Buddha . . . well, he was in the neighborhood. Christ is from the West."

"Have you collected much in the way of documentation on this Society of God Worshippers?"

"Yes, I have. I have amassed whatever I have been able to get my hands on. This subject, I believe, is the most important of all."

"Please tell me what you think, and I would like to have copies of materials made concerning what you are unable to say."

"Fine. I shall report in as great detail as I can, and have the materials delivered later. Actually, they are already in order, and I would very much like to have you look them over." Zuo spoke as if he were gathering momentum.

Zuo had been invited to participate in the group that had just paid their collective respects to Lin, but he had chosen instead the overly dramatic appearance of earlier that evening. From Lin's perspective, Zuo seemed like a man with a strong desire to show himself off. During their conversation, Lin thought that when Zuo had fallen into the water earlier, maybe, just maybe, it had not been the result of a misstep, but all part of his program; for, once he had fallen into the water, he would draw attention to himself.

Men with egos like Zuo's always were better at making conversation than they were at listening to it. Zuo was much more animated and alive when he was speaking to Lin than when he was listening to Lin speak. To be sure, Zuo was an excellent speaker. Hu Linyi had contacted him to the effect that he would be able to meet with Lin Zexu, and from that time forward Zuo had been thinking about what he would say. It was as if he had gone over and over a draft until it was implanted in his mind.

In his discussion of the Society of God Worshippers, Zuo touched first on its founder, Hong Xiuquan. Zuo did not dwell on the fact that Hong was from a Hakka family in Hua county, Guangdong province. This was an acknowledgment on Zuo's part that Lin knew that much of Hong's background, and he made no explanation at all concerning the Hakkas, inasmuch as such details were perfectly self-evident to a man such as Lin, from Fujian province.

Zuo briefly described Hong's dream of meeting the Heavenly Father and the Heavenly Elder Brother. Lin had actually heard the story of Hong's dream in Kunming. His old friend Lian Weicai had informed him in considerable detail of "something that had recently caught his attention." Perhaps Zuo had gotten wind of the fact that Lin was already in possession of such information.

"He claims that the Heavenly Elder Brother in his dream is Jesus Christ and that the Heavenly Father is Jehovah. What do you think of this dream, Mr. Lin?"

"I've heard that he only became aware that the persons in his dream were

Christ and Jehovah six years after he had his dream. Also, I'm told that, before the dream, he had flipped through the pages of some Christian tract by the name of *Good Words to Admonish the Age*. Perhaps that book served as a stimulus to his dream. Since he sustained a high fever for forty days, he probably had all sorts of dreams that filled up every nook and cranny of his mind." Lin's view was based on common sense.

"But, Mr. Lin, do you trust such a man as Hong Xiuquan?"

"Trust? I haven't met him yet."

"I'm speaking only of his dream. Did he actually have this dream? I think it's highly doubtful. More likely, he concocted this dream, trying to make use of Christianity. It is my view that Hong did not have his purported dream at all. The story is a fabrication—a drama, if you will." Zuo's tone was becoming increasingly heated.

"Oh, a drama, you say." Lin scrutinized Zuo's face. A play: Zuo Zongtang, standing before him, was some sort of actor himself.

"He aims to amass a following of people. Wouldn't you agree?"

"It's not inconceivable. I think it may indeed be possible. If Hong is hatching some sort of plot, then using Christianity is a brilliant scheme."

"Do you really think so, Mr. Lin?" asked Zuo, smiling. "Wouldn't it have been easier to use an established religion—one that has historically proven itself—than to fabricate an altogether new superstition as a way to gather followers?"

"Yes, but Christianity has had considerable results."

Lin was remembering that, at the time of the Opium War, he had wholeheartedly studied conditions in the West. And at the root of those conditions was the Christian religion. Lin had read through the Chinese missionary text, *Good Words to Admonish the Age*. His immediate response after completing it was that with their savage ferocity the Westerners were using Christianity to soften men's minds. He was a Buddhist. He prayed for his wife's happiness in the next world, and every day during this period transcribed sutras by hand. In public he was a Confucian, but in private he was a Buddhist. It was not that he was without a capacity for religious faith.

Good Words to Admonish the Age, though, stirred no religious feeling in him at all. At the time he had read it, he remembered feeling that it was a failure as a proselytizing text. But the depth of an impression gained through reading a piece of writing can differ greatly from person to person. Lin knew this from long experience. Scholars for whom he had the highest respect might be moved to tears by a book he considered worthless. So, although *Good Words to Admonish the Age* may not have stirred Lin's heart, it was still possible that it deeply moved Hong Xiuquan.

Be that as it may, Zuo continued to believe that Hong Xiuquan was acting out a part.

"All Westerners are Christians, are they not? Perhaps, by using Christianity, he's trying to attract Westerners as allies. Insofar as I have been able to investigate the matter, though, thus far there has been no collusion with foreigners. Of the future, who can say?" said Zuo.

"I'd like to hear about Hong Xiuquan's abilities with a crowd of people," said Lin, speaking for the first time in an encouraging manner.

"Certainly." Zuo seemed to reflect momentarily that he had been arguing in an overly prejudicial way on behalf of his theory of Hong Xiuquan as actor.

—6—

Once Hong Xiuquan had read *Good Words to Admonish the Age*, he baptized himself according to a method described in the book. He then demolished the images and tablets of Confucius enshrined in the village school where he was employed.

"Hong understood full well what would happen when he did this," said Zuo.

In the school, where students studied the traditional Confucian curriculum of the Four Books and Five Classics, Confucius was of course worshipped. The village operated the school. Hong was merely a hired teacher, and the images and tablets to Confucius were not his property to dispose of. He must have known perfectly well that by destroying them he would be incurring the wrath of the village elders. Someone like Hong who had studied the Four Books and Five Classics with a vengeance himself, and yet had repeatedly failed the civil service examinations, surely knew what response his action would elicit.

"In short, he wanted to attract people's attention by doing this. No doubt about it," Zuo asserted.

Lin was amused. After all, attracting people's attention by doing bizarre things was Zuo's specialty. He was sorely tempted to lump Hong Xiuquan, whom he had never laid eyes on, together with Zuo Zongtang standing before him.

"The village teacher was fired, wasn't he?" asked Lin emphatically.

"Of course he was. But he was intent on his missionary movement in any case. I don't think he was too regretful about the teaching position."

"Was this Christian 'missionary movement' you speak of really such a simple business? In the West it's a well-established religion, but in China he'd have to start at the very beginning. Also, many people in China are wary of anything foreign."

"I believe that 'religion' has itself become something popular."

Zuo proceeded with a brief discussion of his own unique theory of religion, which was also to suffice for an explanation of the Society of God

Worshippers. While Lin was listening to details about the Society of God Worshippers, he was simultaneously sizing up Zuo Zongtang as a person. In Lin's evaluation, Zuo's judgmental propensities were full of self-righteousness, but his resolution was exceptional and he clearly had the makings of a capable official.

Yet, for any of this to have meaning, Zuo had to be given a position. Lin was thinking that he would have been able to use Zuo well. Lin was becoming very lonely, for he would have no opportunity to hire Zuo and could only hope that others would do so in his stead.

"Popular, you say," said Lin, laughing at Zuo's notion. Zuo was expecting laughter as a response.

"That is correct. Until something becomes popular, no one pays it the least attention. Once it does become popular, though, then everyone jumps on board lest they be later than the next fellow. Religion is no different. It has a difficult time at first, but once it starts to catch on, it moves along more smoothly than we could ever have imagined. But, you cannot simply sit back and wait for popularity. You have to maneuver toward popularity. Hong Xiuquan is an excellent actor and extraordinarily shrewd."

"Are you saying that he's done other things of a dramatic nature?"

"I think so. I cannot point to anything specific, but I believe that someone like him must have done so," said Zuo, again with an assertive tone.

He's probably right, thought Lin to himself. This is a quality of the two men, after all, so if anybody would understand this about Hong, it stands to reason that it would be Zuo.

"He has accomplices," Zuo continued. "He could never have pulled all this off alone. At the very beginning, he had two accomplices. One was a friend from his hometown, Feng Yunshan, and the other was his cousin, Hong Ren'gan. They were both essential to the core of believers who made up the Society of God Worshippers. Among these believers were Hong's parents and his brothers. However, they still lacked the capacity to arouse popularity around them. Eventually, Hong Xiuquan and his colleagues began making trips to various and sundry local sights to proselytize their movement."

"For a hired village teacher, he certainly figured out a clever way to accrue funds to support his travels."

"Not really. They traveled around as peddlers. Hong had been a village teacher, so he sold brushes and ink—with considerable success, it would seem. That was the source of their travel money. Then, in a very short time, the Society of God Worshippers somehow managed to become popular. And now they're quite powerful."

Lin had made a point of demonstrating as little knowledge as possible about the Society of God Worshippers, but from time to time he would interject a question to spur this conversation with Zuo forward: "What I have heard is that their movement flourished not in their native village in Hua county, Guangdong, but in the Guiping region of Guangxi."

"Yes, that's true. It's very suspicious."

"Why suspicious?"

"The reason they did not make Hua county their base of operations is probably that it was too close to Guangzhou. Numerous high government officials—the governor-general, governor, provincial military commander, troop commanders, and the like—all reside there. There are also many soldiers in Guangzhou. Such a place would hardly suit their plans, because their aim from the very start was rebellion."

"You say that without the least reserve."

"Is anything else conceivable? They must have had some plan to have gone to such pains in such a determined manner."

Zuo was a realist. As far as he was concerned, the idea of a selfless religious movement was impossible.

"You mean they chose the area around Guiping as a base for their movement? There were many other places far from Guangzhou, weren't there?"

"True, but there are many Hakkas in Guiping and Gui counties. It was easy for him to establish friendly ties with fellow Hakkas living in such an out-of-the-way place. He had relatives there, too. In the village of Sigu, Gui county, he had a first cousin, and he used this tie in the beginning," explained Zuo.

In Japan, and in the West, generally, there is no linguistic distinction made between first cousins on the mother's side as opposed to the father's side, but in China they had different names. The children of one's father's brothers were called *tang xiongdi* or "paternal male first cousins" and *tang jiemei* or "paternal female first cousins." They all shared the same surname. First cousins with different surnames, the children of a mother's brothers or a father's sisters, naturally had other surnames. The latter first cousins were called *biao xiongdi* or "male first cousins carrying another surname" and *biao jiemei* or "female first cousins carrying another surname." The male first cousin upon whom Hong had depended was Wang Shengjun, on his mother's side.

"So, he went to Gui county with those two cohorts?"

"No, just Hong and Feng Yunshan went. Hong Ren'gan is nine years Xiuquan's junior, and his family was opposed to his going so far from home. Xiuquan only stayed in Gui county for three months, and after a convincing performance he returned to Hua county. That was in 1844. That makes it five years ago."

"You spoke of his 'performance'?" asked Lin, recalling the scene of Zuo's own falling into the water.

"There is an exquisite temple not too far from the village of Sigu, known as Liuwu Temple. There they worship both a man and a woman, singing hymns to this man-woman together. In other words, the ignorant rabble worship and heap praise on their deity for this illicit cohabitation. Well, Hong Xiuquan composed a poem that reprimanded this temple."

"If it really is such an evil deity and illicit temple, then it's perfectly natural for him to have rebuked it."

"I agree completely, but Hong Xiuquan and his comrades pulled a crafty trick. They investigated the place before the fact and discovered that the temple's altar had been gnawed away by termites to the point of near collapse. So, he wrote and distributed a poem in which he claimed that two demons, the male and the female worshipped there, had to be exterminated. It became the talk of the area. Soon, the base of the altar collapsed and the stories of Hong Xiuquan's supernatural powers spread. Everything had gone precisely as planned. He carried out precisely what he had intended."

Zuo frowned exaggeratedly with a look of utter disgust.

—7—

The enshrined androgynous deity of the Liuwu Temple at the base of Liuwu Mountain probably was a semblance of the Buddha of Joy. The openly sexual eulogies of this primitive people were concentrated on this one particular deity, and they had been handed down for generations. It was rare to find that such an "illicit temple" had survived into an era of rigid Confucian morality. Yet it had become customary not to interfere in the internal affairs of the religions of the Zhuang and numerous other minority peoples of Guangxi province.

Those with training in Confucianism at first reviled the obscene androgynous deity at the Liuwu Temple. When Hong Xiuquan attacked the Liuwu Temple—with screams of "Do not fear the deity. To hell with it!"—the local people did not vocally support him. There was, though, quiet applause among a segment of the population. It seemed clear that Hong had taken every eventuality into consideration. Whatever criticism may have been raised against him, he apparently counted on not receiving any sort of life-threatening beating for his actions. Or at least that was Zuo Zongtang's suspicion.

Hong was said to have attracted roughly one hundred followers during his three months there. Again, Zuo emphasized that this was by no means a result of the power of Hong's religious ideas. The nephew of Hong's cousin, Wang Shengjun, was caught up in this affair and imprisoned, and Hong organized the effort that saw to his release. In rural areas, where many were illiterate, even if they went through all the proper formalities, they might still find themselves thrown in jail, with fines levied against them. There were numerous cases in which officials had taken advantage of the local residents' ignorance to do as they wished.

While he was in Sigu village, Hong Xiuquan worked hard to help such people in distress. Those who were released and who were exempted from paying fines in many cases became his followers. Hong's "supernatural powers"—as demonstrated by the collapse of the altar in the Liuwu Temple— also may have played a role in his attracting believers.

"Hong was well aware that he had no particular charisma when it came to attracting followers. They say that only when he returned to his native village did he begin to study in earnest. He was studying Christianity. Then he began publishing all sorts of essays. Members of the Society of God Worshippers carry his writings around. It's utterly ridiculous, but they revere and read his stuff as if they were reading the Chinese classics. He has texts entitled 'Ode on the Origin of Virtue of World Salvation,' 'Proclamation on the Origin of Virtue for the Enlightenment of the Age,' and 'Proclamation on the Origin of Virtue for the Awakening of the Age.' I shall send copies of these materials for you to examine later," said Zuo.

Each of the titles of these pieces by Hong that carried Chinese characters for the expression "Origin of Virtue" were actually already in Lin Zexu's possession. Lian Weicai had expressly sent them to him.

"Thank you. They'll be quite useful, I'm sure," said Lin politely, without noting that he already had them.

"There is also something entitled 'Ode on the Hundred Correct Things,' but it's quite short and I have it with me here." Zuo removed a piece of folded paper from his pocket and handed it to Lin. It was covered with tiny Chinese characters.

"Oh, this?" Lian Weicai had sent this work to Lin as well. It began with the following sentences:

> An ode on the hundred correct things,
> Singing of the hundred correct things.
> The truly correct enjoy heavenly emoluments;
> The truly correct stand in awe of Heaven's decree.

It was not a long piece, but the character for "correct" apparently appeared 100 times within it. Lin thought he might try to count them, but he quit midway as the effort began to seem ever sillier.

"It's one line of nonsense after another, and it's hardly an essay. A rather self-indulgent character to think that he might pass the local examinations by writing such prose," said Zuo.

Lin was thinking that Zuo was better off not speaking about others in this way. But, with his own excess of self-confidence, Zuo attributed his personal failure to pass the highest level of the examinations to the ignorance of the examining officials.

"He conveys his meaning, doesn't he?" said Lin as he glanced through the text.

"He just 'conveys' it. However it may qualify as an essay in prose, it lacks style."

"Really?" Lin disagreed. He thought it a distinctively good piece of writing, but he dared not contradict Zuo's penchant for making such assertions. Prose evaluations were subjective in any event.

"In short, he calls for destroying superstition, worshipping only Jehovah, expelling injustice and replacing it with righteousness, ceasing to do evil and carrying out good, transforming grudges and animosities into mutual love and respect, and creating a world of great unity in which all under heaven will be one family."

"Aside from the worship of Jehovah," said Lin, "I'm prepared to agree with every other point."

"Everyone thinks that way. However, among the superstitions to be destroyed is Confucianism. It includes the destruction of images and tablets to Confucius."

"That would present a problem."

"A big problem," said Zuo forcefully.

"Yes, indeed," muttered Lin. He too was thinking that there were important issues raised by the Society of God Worshippers, but not a movement that attacked Confucius.

Lin was thinking as well that a difficult problem lay in the racialist position taken by the Society of God Worshippers. The Qing dynasty then in power was a regime presided over by a Manchu emperor. Members of the Society of God Worshippers were calling the Manchus "Tatar devils." "Tatar" was a term used by ethnic Han Chinese for the ethnic group living beyond China's northern border. The addition of "devils" was a usage unique to the Society of God Worshippers.

The dual objects of their destruction, then, were superstition and the Tatar devils. That Han Chinese—who comprised the great majority of the population of China—harbored feelings of discontent for the Manchu regime in power would seem to be only natural, and Lin was fearful that racialist thought on the part of the Society of God Worshippers might ignite this discontent.

Once set ablaze, the flame could burn the present system itself to the ground. Lin was apprehensive on behalf of those on the side of the establishment. As a Chinese, though, he realized that China needed some sort of revival and remaking of her people. Perhaps, he thought, the Society of God Worshippers might carry out this human renewal? Perhaps we have to yell out loud for the overthrow of the Tatar devils, he thought, in order to eradicate the base servility of the Chinese people today. He felt uneasy with one aspect of Hong Xiuquan's movement, but had high hopes for another aspect of it.

"The two of them divided the work between them. Hong wrote bizarre essays in Guangdong, and Feng gathered crowds in Guangxi. Feng found the turf in Guiping county more advantageous than in Gui county, so he made the former his base of operations. They had been working apart for almost three years. Hong then traveled to Guangxi to see Feng—that would have been in the seventh month of last year." Zuo was continuing his explanation.

Hong and Feng, in their respective fields, worked tirelessly on behalf of the Society of God Worshippers. Feng was the crowd-pleaser and the organizer. Hong was responsible for making their religious thought systematic and logical.

At that time there were rebel groups all over China. Affiliates of the Heaven and Earth Society and various other secret societies were numerous, but none of them was armed with a system of thought.

It was hard to stay together when a group of conspirators went out and plundered. This had long been the essence of bands of thieves in China. But, what would happen if they were rigidly organized with an ideology? Weren't Hong's followers a collective of people who had been remolded? Maybe, thought Lin, they would be a group worth entrusting China's future to.

"Here is a list of the leaders of the Society of God Worshippers," said Zuo, as he withdrew a piece of paper from his pocket. On it were the following names:

Hong Xiuquan, Hua county, Guangdong
Feng Yunshan, Hua county, Guangdong
Yang Xiuqing, Guiping county, Guangxi
Xiao Chaogui, Guiping county, Guangxi
Wei Changhui, Guiping county, Guangxi
Shi Dakai, Gui county, Guangxi
Qin Rigang, Gui county, Guangxi
Hu Yihuang, Pingnan county, Guangxi
Lu Liu, Guiping county, Guangxi

"Of these, Lu Liu died in prison," said Zuo, pointing to Lu's name on the list. He continued talking through the night, oblivious even when the night sky began to brighten with the morning light.

4

Season of Thieves

While Lin Zexu was in Changsha, a major event erupted elsewhere in Hunan province. When Provincial Governor Feng Dexing returned to his residence after paying his respects to Lin, he received a stunning piece of information:

"The county seat of Xinning has been occupied by a religious sect, and County Magistrate Wan Dingen has been murdered."

Xinning was located in the southwest part of Hunan, along the Fuyi River, close to the border of Guangxi province. From the perspective of Hunan province as a whole, it was a peripheral region, but the seizure of a county seat and the murder of a county magistrate were nonetheless nothing short of astounding incidents.

What was meant by "a religious sect?" In the vocabulary of the day, that invariably referred to the White Lotus Sect.

Tradition had it that the White Lotus Sect was founded by one Mao Ziyuan early in the Southern Song dynasty (early in the twelfth century). It was originally a popular religious organization of believers in Pure Land Buddhism. Many of its initiates were desperately poor, and there was a fear that this group might easily be transformed into a band of peasant rebels. Through the years, successive officials had suppressed their activities, but over time the White Lotus Sect had survived these suppressions and become a stronger organization as a result.

In the late Ming dynasty, from the sixteenth into the seventeenth century, believers in Pure Land Buddhism were joined in the White Lotus Sect by followers of Maitreya Buddhism. The Maitreya was a bodhisattva who was to return to earth at the end of days to save the masses of the people. It was a kind of world-renewing movement. In the present Qing dynasty, the White Lotus Sect had risen in rebellion any number of times, its followers being primarily the poorer peasantry. It was during these uprisings that the doctrine of transforming the world—a revolutionary element—emerged.

A large-scale uprising by the White Lotus Sect was put down at the very beginning of the nineteenth century. Thereafter, groups with no connection whatsoever to religion were often simply labeled "White Lotus" whenever an uprising occurred. Rebel armies themselves apparently practiced this custom as well.

Thus, when Xinning was attacked and the attackers were reported as "a religious sect," the government was using the term in this general way. In fact, there was no link to the White Lotus, as the group that had invaded Xinning was a sect of the Heaven and Earth Society. Under the command of their leader, Li Yuanfa, they held Xinning for one and one-half months; and when the government troops in Hunan were finally mobilized, the rebels abandoned their conquest and moved west.

Rebel disturbances of this sort inevitably produced a chain reaction. With no land to till and no work to do, many poor Chinese were hovering on the brink of starvation. What came into their hunger-tortured minds were the bags of rice piling up in the storehouses of the authorities. There was also the food in the warehouses of the large landlords, who were linked to the officials. If they were going to die of starvation anyway, why not rise in rebellion once and for all? Many people who hesitated before the very thought of "rebellion" were emboldened when they heard that a rebellion had actually erupted, and they then decided to join in.

Once government troops headed toward Xinning to crush Li Yuanfa, that necessarily meant that the government's hold over lands elsewhere would become weaker. As noted, Xinning was in Hunan but close to Guangxi province, and in the region near Hunan—Quanzhou and Lingchuan counties, Guangxi—a chain reaction did occur. All of the elements were affiliates of the Heaven and Earth Society, though dubbed "White Lotus."

Li Yuanfa fled Xinning county, but he had hardly been defeated. At the Hunan–Guangxi border was an area known as Dajuantong or "Great Silk Tube," and there he defeated the government army led by the Provincial Military Commander Ying Jun. The government's losses included the death of Assistant Brigade Commander Xiong Zhao.

Li Yuanfa's rebel army numbered in the thousands—some said in the tens of thousands—and many joined them on the march. A large number of them saw joining the rebel forces as the only remaining way that they might eke out an existence. Needless to say, when they retreated from Xinning, the rebel army removed from official storehouses whatever provisions and supplies they could carry, and their numbers rose as they welcomed new members to increase their fighting strength.

When the rebel forces entered Guangxi, they passed through Xing'an, Lingchuan, and Yongfu before arriving in Huaiyuan. In order to provide for their swollen ranks, they confiscated the estates of landlords and wealthy farmers along the way. The landlord-organized self-defense corps known as *tuanlian* proved powerless before the army of Li Yuanfa. When his forces entered Guangxi from Hunan, they had grown enormously in troop strength and from the amassed goods and materiel seized. Their plan was ultimately to return to Hunan.

The imperial court in Beijing ordered Huguang (Guangdong and Guangxi) Governor-General Yu-tai (1788–1851), who was stationed in Wuchang, to move south into Hunan and crush the rebel army of Li Yuanfa. The edict was issued on February 2, 1850. This whole affair had, in fact, become even more serious for the court, as the emperor's state of illness was worsening.

Lin Zexu had then come to the Yangzi River from Changsha and was residing in Nanchang, capital at that time of Jiangxi province, on his way home to his native province of Fujian. Because his physical health was not encouraging, he decided to spend some time recuperating in Nanchang and wait until the Chinese New Year had passed.

—2—

The province of Guangxi was in a state of tumult. Following the supreme orders of the imperial court, the government forces were concentrating all of their energies in attacks on the rebel army of Li Yuanfa. Other, non–White Lotus rebels were active here and there in Guangxi as well.

River pirates known as "skiff bandits" had unexpectedly attacked the town of Yongan from Nanping. Their leader, a man by the name of Luo Dagang, was associated with a Guangdong affiliate of the Heaven and Earth Society. The assault took place on the fifteenth day following the lunar new year. The rebels seized the auspiciously named site of Changshouxu (literally, "longevity burial grounds") and then vanished like the wind, for the skiff bandits were far more agile in their movements than any land-based rebel troops.

On the day prior to Luo's attack on Changshouxu—namely, the fourteenth day of the new year (1850), or February 25, according to the solar calendar—the Daoguang Emperor died at the detached Shende Palace on the magnificent grounds of the Yuanmingyuan in the suburbs of Beijing.

Ever since the first Qing emperor, Shunzhi, assumed the throne in 1644, the Manchus had made a practice of not publicly installing an heir apparent as long as the emperor remained in good health. The successor to the throne was to be the most capable of all the princes, regardless of age, but the successor's name was not made public. A framed piece of calligraphy bearing the four Chinese characters for "propriety, greatness, public-mindedness, and enlightenment" hung above the throne in the Ganqing Palace, where the emperor carried out his daily political duties; and the name of the heir apparent was sealed behind this plaque. It was referred to as the "sealed treasure," and only the emperor himself knew the identity of the prince whose name was "sealed."

According to the customs of the imperial family of the Qing dynasty, it was expected that all princes would, in the best sense of the word, compete through study to gain the recognition of their father, the reigning emperor. The court feared that, were a successor named early on, hangers-on would appear and try to spoil the heir apparent in the hope of subsequent favors. In addition, such a practice could easily lead to the creation of cliques. Thus, they had tried to prevent such abuses.

On his deathbed, the Daoguang Emperor summoned his high officials and announced before them the "sealed" name of the heir apparent. As they all had expected, it was his fourth son, Yi-zhu. The Daoguang Emperor had had the misfortune of witnessing the early deaths of his first three sons, and hence Yi-zhu was actually now the eldest. He was born in 1831 and was twenty "years" old by Chinese reckoning, although only eighteen years and seven months in fact. Yi-zhu acceded to the dragon throne on the twenty-seventh day of the first lunar month of the new year, having held the position of heir apparent for only thirteen days following Daoguang's death.

The Qing dynasty practiced the custom of having only one reign title for each emperor. The emperor, who had used the reign title "Daoguang," was posthumously known as the Daoguang Emperor. This same institution was adopted in Japan following the Meiji Restoration of 1868. There was one difference: in Japan the reign title changed at the time of the emperor's death, while in the Qing dynasty the reign title remained the same, even after the emperor's death, until the coming of the new year, at which point it then changed. This system followed a Confucian belief that, with the passing of one's father, one should continue to serve as if he were alive and not abruptly change one's filial inheritance. The year 1926 in Japan was, accordingly, both the fifteenth year of the Taishō reign (which began in 1912) and the first year of the Shōwa reign (which ended in 1989). Such a phenomenon would never have arisen in the Qing system. With Yi-zhu's accession, an imperial edict was issued to the effect that the following year would be the first year of the Xianfeng reign period. He was thus to be known as the Xianfeng Emperor.

The thirtieth year of the Daoguang reign, 1850, saw the Daoguang Emperor on the throne for only fourteen days, while for most of the year the Xianfeng Emperor ruled China. Since an urgent governmental communiqué took roughly twenty days to go from Beijing to Guangzhou, the earliest that news of the passing of the Daoguang Emperor could have arrived in Guangxi was at the beginning of the second lunar month.

At about that time, Li Yuanfa's forces, having entered Guangxi with increased strength, changed directions as planned and headed toward Hunan. In the battle with rebel forces, the government armies in Guangxi lost their high-ranking Manchu military official, Assistant Regional Commander Ma-long-a. It was a bitter pill to swallow.

Unable to rely on their armies to crush the rebels, the Beijing government dismissed Hunan Provincial Military Commander Ying Jun and replaced him with a man by the name of Xiang Rong (1801–1856). Also, Feng Dexing was replaced as governor of Hunan because "he was not diligent in bandit suppression," as the official document read.

After returning to his native Fujian province, Lin Zexu learned that the highest civil and the highest military officials in Hunan, who had warmly welcomed him in Changsha, had both lost their positions. Only bad news was coming to Lin's attention, following the death of the emperor. This bad news, as far as the government was concerned, was by no means "bad" news for the rebels. Upon hearing of Daoguang's demise, Hong Xiuquan allegedly said, using the normal terminology of members of the Society of God Worshippers: "The old leader of the Tatar devils has died." Lian Liwen was not a member, but he was among them when this piece of news arrived.

"The Tatar devils' new leader is younger," added Hong. "We must remain vigilant at all times."

"What happened to Li Yuanfa?" asked Liwen.

While the Society of God Worshippers was a religious group formed on the basis of Christian ideals, it was markedly different from the White Lotus Sect with their beliefs in Pure Land Buddhism and the advent of the Maitreya Buddha. Nevertheless, while in Guiping—the headquarters of the Society of God Worshippers—Liwen sensed a sympathy from ordinary members of the organization for Li Yuanfa's "rebel" army. Hong Xiuquan, however, had adopted a much more severe view of things.

"It's no good at all. His military discipline is too relaxed. They fly White Lotus banners but there is no genuine religious faith among the troops he has amassed," responded Hong.

"But they certainly must have accumulated considerable momentum if they were able to kill the assistant regional commander of the Guangxi Army."

"The time was ripe to seize the day. When he loses this momentum, what will he do then? Only the dissolution of his forces will remain. How is Li Yuanfa going to protect his momentum now? He's utterly without a policy of any sort."

"He may have some strategy or policy. After all, he did boldly venture out on this rebellious path. Perhaps our ignorance of his troop strength makes it seem as though he lacks such a program," said Liwen.

"No, I'm well aware of his military capacity. I've got men placed in his army."

"Is that so?"

One group of Li Yuanfa's rebel forces was at that time located in the vicinity of Xiuren, not far from Guiping. Since they were trying to recruit troops to expand the size of their forces, they rejected no one who wished to join them. Thus, it was actually quite simple for members of the Society of God Worshippers to join surreptitiously in order to learn the internal workings of this rebel band.

Hong phrased his response to Liwen in such a way that made it seem strange for the Society of God Worshippers *not* to have placed spies in Li Yuanfa's organization. Probably, Hong had put observant personnel into the rebel army and was receiving a continual stream of reports from them.

"They're reliable people. According to their reports, Li Yuanfa doesn't have the slightest idea what Pure Land Buddhism is or who the Maitreya Buddha is. And, of course, not a single religious ceremony is carried out among the troops. How can such an organization maintain its momentum?" What Hong was alluding to was the fact of the strong religious belief that bound the Society of God Worshippers. Once he and his organization had achieved momentum, he implied, they would be able to maintain it indefinitely.

"In any event, for a small group of people to work in unison is one thing, but I think it would be extremely difficult to forge a single purpose in the hearts of those who comprise a large group. Is there such strength in religious belief? Even if everyone shares the same beliefs, there are sure to be both the highly devout and less religious members even within such an organization." Liwen was honestly expressing his doubts. Maybe Hong was overestimating the depth of religious belief within his own Society of God Worshippers.

"When you say 'a large group,' what size are you referring to?" Hong smiled as he put this question to Liwen.

"Well, . . . I can't really respond in concrete terms to a question of numbers," Liwen was left mumbling.

"I'm thinking about a million. . . . No, about a million units. That's 'a large group.'"

"A million . . ." To seize the realm would require such a massive military organization. Liwen had learned many details about the Society of God Worshippers from Xiling, and he had gathered that they were contemplating a transformation of the state itself.

"Liwen," called Hong solemnly, "at some point I'd like to chat with you about all sorts of things. While we're climbing that hill over there. I'll call for you soon." Hong was pointing to Zijingshan, or Thistle Mountain.

—3—

Three days later, a messenger from Hong Xiuquan came summoning Liwen, informing him that their mountain-climbing day had arrived. It took Liwen a moment before he recalled their conversation three days before, though he still did not know what Hong really wanted to speak of.

He was to meet Hong at a specific farmer's home at the foothills of Thistle Mountain. The mountain pathway was narrow and led deep into the surrounding hills. It served also as a shortcut for freight transport through this mountainous region.

"I've been told that this path has been well-trodden for many years past. It's not as lonely a route as it might seem," said Hong when they neared the narrow path, which meandered along until it was soon out of sight. They were not likely to meet anyone for some time walking along it.

The traders who transported produce from the province of Guangdong and foreign commodities imported into Guangzhou (the great majority of which was, of course, opium) crossed Thistle Mountain and headed north. Word had it that commerce had once thrived in this area.

"Since when have things become so desolate around here?" asked Liwen.

"Over the last seven or eight years. The last two or three seem to have been particularly bad."

"The opening of a port at Shanghai has really had a major effect, then."

There were several routes for transporting freight from the south, centered in Guangzhou, to the Yangzi delta. Crossing Thistle Mountain was but one of them—one for rather small-scale transportation. Now, though, all the routes were declining in prosperity. With the conclusion of the Nanjing Treaty in 1842 as a consequence of the Opium War, China's previous trading situation of a single open port at Guangzhou had been radically altered. Now there were five open ports for foreigners to engage in trade with the Chinese, and Shanghai became the base for supplying merchandise to the Yangzi delta region.

"There's more to it. The people have become poorer and poorer, and their spare money to purchase goods has dried up."

"Why is that so?"

"They have no work. Until just recently, Thistle Mountain was full of wealth. Yang Xiuqing is always bragging about it."

One of the leaders of the Society of God Worshippers, Yang Xiuqing was born near Thistle Mountain. His father died when he was five, his mother when he was nine, and he spent his youth in desperate poverty. Nonetheless, he would still boast about the riches of his native area of Thistle Mountain.

The uncle who raised Yang after he became an orphan worked in the production of charcoal. From the time Yang was a boy, he helped out with his uncle's work. There were numerous petrified trees suitable for conversion to charcoal in the mountains, and the harder the wood the better for making charcoal. In his youth Yang had seen many porters and merchants come and go at Thistle Mountain. Residents of the area could earn small tips by acting as guides for these visitors.

Mountain bandits lived in the area of Thistle Mountain as well. They proudly called themselves "Bandit Heroes of the Forest," but they could hardly live up to such a glamorous name. They were on friendly terms with residents of the region, and the fact that porters and traders who hired local residents as guides were not attacked by these bandits was due largely to the moral code of these heroic forest dwellers of Thistle Mountain. As Yang grew up and had occasion to work as a porter, he became an intermediary in the relationship that was forged between the bandits and the local residents. Soon this intermediary had become a local leader, and through him this bond was strengthened.

Charcoal was the principal industry of the mountain, but indigo—used as a dye for clothing—was also produced there. Its quality was rather high, and at times this product sold very well. The local people also grew bamboo shoots, a kind of mushroom, a kind of ginger known as *shajiang*, and a pollen used by the Chinese as a medicinal herb. Hunters in the area often caught a hornless animal known as the *huangjing,* or muntjac, which resembled a tiger. There were also raccoons, as well as rock hares—known for their speed in racing up steep slopes. There were a number of valley streams—bearing such names as Daping, Daguang, Hualei, and Xiaojiang—in the mountains, and the salamanders there had earned a high reputation as a local delicacy.

This was clearly what people meant by the wealth of the mountain. Local residents were by no means affluent, but they somehow eked out a living, and thus had the leisure to brag about the wealth of the mountain nearby. Now this once rich mountainous region was no longer so wealthy. The decline of Thistle Mountain had begun with the opening of the port at Shanghai, as porters and merchants eventually stopped using the mountain route. The importation of British products made of iron rendered charcoal virtually unsalable.

The Tropic of Cancer cut through Guiping county, which made the region tropical in climate. Thus the charcoal produced there was not needed or used for heating, but rather as fuel for metalworkers and blacksmiths. The more iron implements, such as agricultural tools and the like, were shipped from British factories to China, the more Chinese metalworkers lost their businesses, unable to compete commercially with items produced in post–Industrial Revolution Britain. The loss of work for metalworkers spelled the end of business for charcoal traders as well.

As textiles mass-produced in Manchester flowed into the ports of Guangdong and Shanghai aboard English ships, the small Chinese textile businesses also rapidly lost all their markets. They no longer had the surplus to purchase indigo for dyeing, and thus the indigo of Thistle Mountain would not sell even if it had been produced.

The wealth of the mountain had become utterly worthless.

"We've walked for a rather long stretch now and have yet to run into a soul," said Liwen.

"Aha! As soon as you deprecate the mountain, the master of the mountain shall appear," said Hong with a smile on his face.

The man who appeared was none other than Yang Xiuqing, whom Liwen had already met. Raised in Thistle Mountain, Yang had a dark complexion and penetrating eyes. When he saw Hong and Liwen, he burst into laughter, revealing a mouthful of white teeth. Liwen observed that, although his mouth was laughing, his eyes were not.

"Elder Brother Xiuquan and Master Liwen, are you still having your conversation?" asked Yang abruptly. It appeared as though Yang knew the matters under discussion that day.

"No, not yet, but we were just about to," responded Hong.

"Well, then, let me begin," said Yang.

Liwen had been in the same company with Yang on several occasions. More than anything else, he had noted Yang's aggressiveness. If he felt he could do something himself—even involving other people's affairs—he might try to do so. And yet, he showed no overwhelming penchant to demonstrate his own capacities. He might say this and do that, but strangely enough he did not give one the impression of being a "meddler." When Yang intervened, things went well, and people seemed to anticipate his interference on their behalf when matters became difficult for them.

For his talk with Liwen, Hong Xiuquan had carefully chosen the route along which they would walk, invited Liwen to join him, timed everything appropriately, and then broke the ice at just the right moment. Yang's nature was altogether different. He would discard all of these preparations and dive directly into the core of the business at hand.

"We trust you," said Yang. "Especially Elder Brother Xiuquan—he has absolute faith in you. So, we have a favor to ask of you."

Raised in abject poverty, Yang had never learned to read or write. Despite his illiteracy, from time to time he used difficult expressions with unexpected eloquence. He had probably picked up most of this by ear, and he also certainly had an extraordinary memory.

"What is that?" asked Liwen. Yang fell in step with Hong and Liwen as they walked further along the mountain path.

"We'd like you to go to that woman's place," said Yang.

"What woman?"

"Li Xinmei."

Li Xinmei was the woman he had met aboard the ferry on his way from the village of Jintian to the seat of Guiping county. She had performed her part, together with the members of the Society of God Worshippers, in the drama of Liwen's abduction and evaluation. At that time she had taken refuge with the Society of God Worshippers, but she was not, strictly speaking, a member. She was an extremely proud, independent soul.

Many women in south China were bold-spirited. This was especially true of Hakka women and those who worked in wetland rice cultivation, for whom the custom of footbinding was rare. Many pirate bands operated along the coastal region of Guangdong province. Some continued to carry on their illegal activities into the middle of the twentieth century. There is considerable documentary material concerning their attacks on foreign ships, and among these sources are references to a woman leader of a group of pirates.

Some Hakka women were accomplished in the martial arts. Hong Xiuquan's younger sister, Xuanjiao, was well-known as an expert in the art of swordsmanship. They were not only pirates, either, for some groups of adventurers affiliated with the Heaven and Earth Society on land even had woman leaders. The names of Su Sanniang and Qiu Ersao also appear in the historical record.

Li Xinmei was one such woman. Her mother was reputed to have originally been the leader of a Heaven and Earth Society group with between eight hundred and one thousand subordinates under her command, and Li Xinmei may have carried on her mother's legacy. In Jintian village, Liwen had heard that she had amassed as many as two thousand followers. She had not only received her maternal inheritance but increased it considerably. No doubt she was quite a remarkable woman.

Apparently, this woman of only about thirty years of age was deeply concerned with how to run such a swollen organization. She had heard that the Society of God Worshippers was well-managed and came to see for herself. Her connections to Hong Xiuquan and Feng Yunshan were slight. While in

Guangzhou, she concealed her identity by acting as a servant to a foreign missionary, and there she learned about Christianity. The missionary believed in the necessity of converting his servants first, as an expedient to good proselytizing. She later recalled: "At that time I was about half convinced."

Coming to Guangzhou on this "study trip," she converted to Christianity, although she still maintained her own organization. She became a member of the Society of God Worshippers, though it might be more appropriate to call her an honorary member.

"It's true, I haven't seen Xinmei for a while," said Liwen. Although Li Xinmei occasionally came to visit with Xiling at the Xishi Monastery, he had not seen her since the new year.

"She's returned to her own faction—in order to start a rebellion." Yang spoke in businesslike fashion.

"To start a rebellion?" Liwen unconsciously returned the question, but Yang ignored the emotion in Liwen's query and continued:

"We want you to go to her place. She learned from the Society of God Worshippers here, and she'll probably use what she's learned in her rebellion. We want you to observe the good and bad points of her operation, because in the future it'll serve as a reference point for our own uprising. We've had a communication from her. She wants us to send her someone to take charge of keeping records, and we've decided on you."

—4—

One historical source of the time has the following entry: "A woman bandit of Guangxi province, Li Xinmei, with over 2000 men, plundered Beisi in Qianjiang." It was dated the middle of the third lunar month, 1850—late April or early May. Qianjiang lay in the northwest of Binyang county, midway between the cities of Liuzhou and Nanning, at a point where the Qingshui River flowed into the huge Hongshui River. From here the Hongshui changed its name to the Qian River. It was about 120 to 130 kilometers to the west of Guiping county.

"So, you've arrived. Well, that's fine, because you know how to write." This was the curious manner in which Li Xinmei greeted Liwen.

She had been re-forming the group of followers passed down to her by her mother into something resembling the Society of God Worshippers. Three days after he arrived at her base of operations near Qianjiang, Liwen sent a report back to the Society of God Worshippers in Guiping: "Li Xinmei's group is studying the organization of the Society of God Worshippers, but religious activities are not flourishing. Christianity is exhorted, but no one is engaged in missionary work. More than a scribe like myself, Li Xinmei should find talented people to preach the gospel and enthusiastically pursue the conversion movement."

Although still shrouded in secret, the organization of the Society of God Worshippers was such that all of its members donated all of their property to the group. The property so collected was called the "Sacred Treasury," and all food, clothing, and shelter of the membership were provided from this "Sacred Treasury." Li Xinmei copied this organizational scheme and created something dubbed the "Heavenly Treasury." Her followers were, from the very start, a band of ruffians who had neither homes nor property to donate. Since they survived on quotas from their plunder, that soon left them nothing to contribute to the "Heavenly Treasury."

The Sacred Treasury of the Society of God Worshippers was well-managed largely because those who had some small amount of family property did dispose of it when they joined the group. Their motives for joining were many and varied—some for reasons of fervent religious belief and some because they had no other alternative. This last group within the membership included those who had not paid taxes and were about to have all of their property seized by the government. Under these dire circumstances, they donated their property to the Society of God Worshippers as a means of escape. Low-level officials, landlords, or both were responsible for placing them in these circumstances, and they simply wanted a place where they could live as human beings. In exchange for such a place, they were willing to give up what little money and property they might have accumulated.

Li Xinmei's miscalculation was that, because her group had gained a reputation as "roving bandits," people did not recognize it as a refuge where one might live as a human being. As long as there were no new members, her "Heavenly Treasury" would never materialize. This situation led ultimately to the use of force. There were cases of contributions being coerced at the point of a sword from peasant families who lived in single thatched-roof huts—a practice no different from extortion. Thus, her group's reputation declined steadily until no one any longer sought entry into it.

Realizing the difficult position her organization found itself in, she chose to lead her people in rebellion earlier than initially planned. The man in charge of the Heavenly Treasury was an older cousin of hers by the name of Li Qun.

"How does it stand with the weapons you've collected to this point?" she asked in consultation with Li Qun.

"We still have a ways to go," he said, shaking his head. "We're really lacking in self-confidence, but we do have a means of operation."

"What do you mean?"

"We're not aiming at big cities. Our sights are only on small places. That way we can increase our stockpile of weapons through plunder and then later attack bigger places."

"Where's a good place to start?"

"A spot where we can dispose of our loot rapidly would be great. I'm thinking of Beisi. It's close to the river, so we can flee quickly on boats."

"Several kilometers south of Beisi there's a government warehouse, but there are troops guarding it."

"I've heard that the troops at Beisi are soon to move north, because Li Yuanfa's forces have shown up again to the south of Guiping."

"I've been hearing the same thing. The provincial military commander and his troops came under fire from the boy emperor, and they've got to go after Li Yuanfa. They're all in a flurry because, more than anything else, it's a matter of face to them. Are they mobilizing the troops guarding Beisi?"

"That's what I've heard from a reliable source. I think there's no doubt about it."

"Then it's decided!" Li Xinmei was quick to make a decision, as one might expect when a group has only one leader. "On the third day following the mobilization of the troops at Beisi, we attack it."

Because of Li Yuanfa's seizure and occupation of Xinning, high-level civil and military officials had been reprimanded and dismissed. The august majesty of the great Qing empire had been injured by its inability to handle the rebel forces. It was known that there were small rebel forces in local areas throughout China, but these were not sufficient cause for the state to disperse its limited military might. The government had no choice now but to concentrate all of its forces against Li Yuanfa and his army of several tens of thousands of men.

The timing was right for Li Xinmei. She had at first planned to attack Binyang with its population of 50,000, but her troop strength and weaponry were insufficient. On Li Qun's advice, she now changed the objective to an attack from the south on Beisi, a rural town with a military warehouse.

The majority of the government troops at Beisi began to move north, just as rumors had it, and only eighty of them were left to guard the warehouse. To reinforce the weakened guard, however, the Guangxi authorities mobilized the local *tuanlian*.

When this news arrived, Li Xinmei said coolly: "The *tuanlian*'s no problem for us. Why would they risk their lives to protect the storehouses of the officials? If it were their own towns or villages, that's another story."

Her prediction was right on target. When her armies attacked, the *tuanlian* forces ran away. They actually seemed more to have disappeared. They knew the terrain well and understood that it was much better to extricate themselves by whatever means possible.

The government troops ran about trying to escape, discarding their weapons, and eventually surrendered to the forces of Li Xinmei. The majority of the eighty government soldiers seemed to be old or semi-invalid. The commander of the attack on Li Yuanfa selected their boldest troops and left behind the weakest, who were virtually useless as guards.

Liwen also participated in the attack on Beisi.

"But, this was hardly a war," he said, revealing his feelings to Li Xinmei.

Disappearing in the twilight, they surrounded the Beisi warehouse, fired a warning signal, and screamed en masse from all four sides. Li Xinmei's troops were prepared with a fair amount of firearms, but they really had no need to use them. In command of a vanguard group, one young man called out jokingly from the side: "It's our voices. From now on we've got to practice yelling. Swords and guns are useless."

"Things are not always this way. You can make light of it now, but it's going to be much harder work next time around," said Li Xinmei reprovingly.

—5—

The evening they occupied Beisi, Lian Liwen was especially busy. After rifling through the military warehouse, Li Xinmei decided to beat as hasty a retreat as possible, with all of her followers intact. They were divided into five brigades, each departing along a different route, with plans to regroup at a predetermined spot. With only two thousand members, they were not yet in the same position as Li Yuanfa's large band. They had only guerrilla tactics at their disposal.

The warehouse was stocked with quantities of supplies far beyond what Li Xinmei had ever imagined, and that put her in good humor. "Now we're in a position to attack Binyang next. I'm very excited."

"How many people will we need to lay seige to Binyang?" asked Li Qun.

"I'd like to say ten thousand, but that's impossible. But we need at least five thousand. Once we go through all of this stuff, we ought to have enough in war funds, don't you think?" said Li Xinmei, motioning with her jaw to the mountain of supplies that had been carried out of the warehouse.

"Five thousand is no problem," responded Li Qun.

The goods they had taken in booty were loaded on boats that evening, taken to a town known as Laibin, and sold off to a group similarly affiliated with the Heaven and Earth Society. Responsibility for this venture fell naturally to the man in charge of the Heavenly Treasury, Li Qun.

Li Qun kept Liwen busy checking as closely as possible the supplies taken from the military warehouse to the Heavenly Treasury, and then recording them in a special register. In addition to roughly two thousand bags of grain, there was cooking oil, kerosene, and the like. The boats on hand were over-loaded, so they hurriedly borrowed three more from the local skiff bandits. Heaven and Earth Society groups had this extremely useful form of lateral communication.

Li Qun took charge of loading the vessels. He was an exceedingly shrewd fellow who had already been made responsible for the Heavenly Treasury. He had experience in the transport business and was well-accustomed to moving merchandise.

"But this is the first time I've had so much material to move," he said joyously.

Liwen made two copies of the register, one of which he passed along to Li Xinmei. She made an odd expression upon receiving it, puffing up her cheeks with air. The lamp in the corner of the warehouse gave off little light and from time to time flickered, illuminating this expression on her face. There was a strange amorousness in her at that moment, thought Liwen.

Li Xinmei was full of hope. Five thousand troops. If they could take Binyang with five thousand men, then they would surely reach ten thousand, and with a force of ten thousand troops, she would no longer be leading a restless band of guerrillas but be able to overrun the entire land as a mighty force like that of Li Yuanfa.

The Qing armies had been made fools of by rebel forces everywhere and gradually lost their fighting strength. They seemed incapable of suppressing the bandits. Li Xinmei had predicted to Liwen that an age of competing, locally based military leaders was soon to come, though Liwen doubted at the time that she had any ideas of launching a rebellion to seize the entire country.

From her expression that evening it seemed that until that moment she had had no such ideas. She had no pretensions of remaining the leader of a roving band. That was merely an inheritance from her mother. Liwen answered his own earlier doubts, for something like capturing all of China was the true conception of an initiator, not an inheritor. Li Xinmei was a second-generation bandit, but she was also a woman full of vitality, full of energy—not the sort to sit back and run through her inheritance.

The fact that she had become affiliated with the Society of God Worshippers seemed to be a well-planned maneuver. In the coming age of competing local leaders, the Society of God Worshippers was without the least doubt going to exert great influence, and it seemed to her a good idea to be associated with such an organization.

Liwen stared at her cheeks for a while, until she released the pent up air.

"What're you looking at?" she asked, noting his fixed gaze.

"Your cheeks were all puffed up."

"Huh?" She touched her right cheek with her hand and laughed. "Puffed up, eh? That's strange?"

"No, not strange. You looked very attractive."

"Oh, stop joking with me!" She shrugged her shoulders. It was a very masculine gesture, but Liwen's response was a sense of warmth. Outside, the work of carrying the stolen goods to the Hongshui River was moving along rapidly.

"You know, I'm thinking that, once all this stuff is put in the Heavenly Treasury, none of it'll be ours."

"That's true. Until now we've been dividing everything up equally."

"It's a great blessing to have the Heavenly Treasury full."

"No doubt about it. That's just what Elder Sister says."

This exchange among the men carrying the merchandise was audible to Li Xinmei and Liwen inside the warehouse. As leader of her party, Xinmei was called "Elder Sister" by her followers. A male leader of a Heaven and Earth Society affiliate would have similarly been dubbed "Elder Brother."

"Liwen, I want you to get on board the boat too," she said.

"What? Me? Together with the group from the Heavenly Treasury?"

"Right. They'll dispose of the goods in Laibin, and they'll need a clerk to record the transactions there. We need to cover all of our tracks here." And she rose from the chair in which she had been seated.

—6—

The little fleet of boats sailed down the Hongshui River. There were ten vessels in all, including the boats borrowed from the skiff bandits and a raft that looked as if it were sprouting hair.

Countless waterways flowed around and through Guangxi province, and Li Xinmei now had something on the order of a navy among her forces. These were boatmen, not the professional skiff bandits, but a small group— perhaps as many as fifty altogether. In addition, there were about thirty men, traveling separately, with responsibilities for the Heavenly Treasury. The vessel on which these men sailed, though, was short of hands, and hence they were obliged to help out with a variety of jobs under the direction of the boatmen. Being unaccustomed to this work, it grew late before the boats could set sail—a dangerous hour. Difficulties seemed to arise at every turn, but the specialists dealt with these as they arose.

No one feared that the *tuanlian* might return with reinforcements. Perhaps a complaint would be lodged with the local official, but unarmed local officials were incapable of any action. Had they tried, the rebels would have immediately burned down their offices and killed them. Officials were usually seen as the direct exploiters of the population. So when they heard the news of the arrival of rebel forces, these bureaucrats usually gathered their families together and fled.

Li Xinmei's people had learned from scouting reports that there were scarcely any government troops in the Beisi region, but they remained extremely cautious, with their torches burning at a lower intensity.

Lian Liwen was aboard the same boat as Li Qun. Among this fleet of dilapidated junks, their vessel was more on the order of a real ship, as befit the man in charge of the Heavenly Treasury. Li Qun called it a "salt boat," because it was used to transport salt, one of the government's monopoly items. It was formerly owned either by the government or perhaps a state-designated merchant. Because it was for use on inland waterways, its draft was shallow, but it was designed in such a way as to enable the loading of as much salt as possible.

"The torchlights on the shore are getting smaller and smaller," said Liwen, standing on deck.

"Wouldn't you expect that the further away we get, the smaller they'd appear?" said Li Qun dryly. He was a completely emotionless man. He then added, as if discharging the words: "Now they've entirely disappeared. That flame there and this one . . ."

Liwen could not hear what followed. The wind had not muffled Li's voice, but Li seemed to stop speaking at this point. Liwen was disturbed by the way in which Li Qun had broken off his speech. His voice seemed to have disappeared just like the torches on shore in the distance.

They had boarded ship near Qianjiang, and it was in this region at the border of the town of Laibin that the river changed its name from the Hongshui to the Qian River. The Qian converged with the Yu River in Guiping and became known as the Xun River.

The distance from Qianjiang to the objective of Laibin was not terribly far—between 30 and 40 kilometers—but the vessels were traveling at an almost unbelievably slow pace, and that evening the wind's direction was particularly disadvantageous.

"Damn! We've got to pick up speed. This won't do at all," grumbled the boatmen incessantly.

Late in the night, as Liwen was dozing off, half in a dream, he heard Li Qun's voice:

"Hey, how much further? Are we almost there?"

"Yeah. It's only a few more kilometers, but conditions are terrible."

"When do you think we'll arrive at Dawan?"

"Depends on the wind. Maybe the wind direction will change in the morning," the boatman responded dully.

It seemed rather strange to Liwen in his state of semiconsciousness. The freight was supposed to be sold in Laibin to a group connected to the Heaven and Earth Society. And yet, Li Qun was asking the boatman how much time remained prior to arrival at Dawan. Dawan lay way beyond Laibin—perhaps 70 kilometers from Qianjiang. Once the freight was disposed of at Laibin, was the fleet supposed to proceed to Dawan and disperse? The whole organization had split up with the intention of reassembling at a place called Shanglin. Dawan was in an altogether different direction. Then again, perhaps the owner of the boats was in Dawan. Satisfied with this explanation, Liwen dozed off again.

Some time later, when it was still dark outside, Liwen awoke calling out in pain. He was lying on the ground, and a man astride a horse was above him. Liwen's hands had been trampled upon by the horse's hooves, but in the darkness he was unable to tell who was on horseback. It was a single person, and he had several assistants standing on either side. Before he knew what was happening, Liwen was completely surrounded, and rope was cutting into his skin all over his body.

"Tie that rock to him," said a voice coming from near Liwen's head. It was without a doubt Li Qun's.

Liwen gnashed his teeth as he now realized what had happened. Li Qun, chief of the Heavenly Treasury, planned to seize all of the plundered loot. The crew in charge of the Heavenly Treasure were, obviously, Li Qun's confidants, and the boatmen were probably coconspirators.

They were all betraying Li Xinmei. They were going to throw him, bound tightly hand and foot, a stone fastened to the rope for weight, into the Hongshui River. And he would be disposed of.

"Hurry up and throw him in!" Li Qun said.

It's all over, thought Liwen, as the face of his late wife floated with startling vividness into his mind.

—7—

Lian Liwen had resigned himself to death, but it did not come. The rock that had been tied to his waist to ensure that he would sink to the bottom of the river actually helped save his life. Li Qun and his confederates picked a large rock heavy enough to drown an adult, but in fact it was too heavy. They were operating on the assumption that the heavier the better, but the assumption was false.

The problem lay in the rope that bound the rock to Liwen. It was the ship's rigging, once undoubtedly very firm, but also quite long. To inspect every inch of the rope for a single worn spot here or there was difficult.

Liwen had no way of knowing what sort of rope his adversaries had used to tie him up, though he later reasoned that it must have been a mooring line.

If they always secured boats at the same spot, then they probably also used the same mooring lines. If this particular line was always at this same site along the shoreline, of which there were many along the Hongshui River, then eventually it would be worn down to the point of fragility. The rock was too heavy, and so the already weakened rope could not support it, and it tore apart at its worn point.

This all transpired while Liwen was underwater and unaware of what was happening to him. When he saw that his entire body was suddenly free, he realized what must have happened. The heavy rock had simply shredded the rope binding him, releasing him like an act of sleight of hand.

Li Qun's group had complete confidence in the weight of the stone. It was also dark out, and they made no effort to inspect the fate of their abandoned object. Liwen later recalled that when they dropped him into the water, it seemed that his body became free almost immediately.

Had Li Qun's gang been even slightly more attentive to the water's surface near where Liwen had been thrown in, they would probably have discovered him swimming away and have pursued him. Liwen was lucky this time. After the death of his wife, he was convinced that good fortune had forsaken him altogether, but that was not the case. Having escaped calamity on the Hongshui River, he regained a sense of confidence in his luck.

He came ashore dripping wet and for a few moments just sat, confused about what to do next. Should he return to the west toward Shanglin, where they planned to regroup, and report on Li Qun's treachery? Ultimately, he decided to follow the Qian River back to the Society of God Worshippers in Guiping. Guiping was much closer. Once he reported this incident to the Society of God Worshippers, Li Xinmei would certainly be able to communicate with him. Contact via the Society of God Worshippers would probably also be more rapid than if he proceeded to Shanglin.

The intelligence-gathering capacities of the Society of God Worshippers and its communications network went far beyond Liwen's imagination. By the time he finally made his way to Guiping, the leaders of the Society of God Worshippers already knew of Li Qun's betrayal of Li Xinmei and had reported it to her. Feng Yunshan was in charge of intelligence for the Society of God Worshippers. He handled a wide variety of data and was brilliant at analyzing it.

"What will become of Li Xinmei's organization now?" Liwen asked Feng.

"She braved such troubles to put together a force of two thousand strong, but all to no avail now. They'll disintegrate, fall apart naturally," Feng responded.

"Really?"

Liwen then remembered how, when he boarded the boat, Li Qun had ceased speaking after mentioning that the torchlights had disappeared from the shoreline. It was an intimation of sorts that something besides the light was going to disappear: Li Xinmei's entire organization.

Until that point, the practice among these thieves was to share equally all that had been plundered. Li Xinmei had introduced the institution of the "Heavenly Treasury" from her association with the Society of God Worshippers, and she had worked hard to persuade her people of its importance. The Heavenly Treasury that had finally come into being was now thoroughly depleted. It was unlikely that Li Xinmei's followers would sit by idly when they learned that their portions had vanished. There was no longer any point in staying with her, and her followers would surely leave in dribs and drabs.

"Even with this sudden creation of a Heavenly Treasury, it's useless if the group is not firmly sustained by religious belief," said Feng, though anyone could have foreseen that much. The example of the Society of God Worshippers enabled Liwen to understand the gist of Feng's statement.

"Has it already dissolved?" Liwen again recalled that Li Xinmei was both the leader of a remarkably powerful rebel band and yet extremely naïve.

"The people haven't all left yet, though the organization as such has disintegrated. Maybe they'll attach themselves to another group . . . Sooner or later, some much larger organization will siphon off their strength. As far as this new organization is concerned, the dissolution of other parties and factions will certainly be nothing to grieve over," said Feng. He spoke about this "organization" as if it were comprised of strangers, but clearly he was referring to the Society of God Worshippers.

Liwen was speaking with Feng in a peasant home in Jintian village. At that moment a young man entered to report: "They were defeated at Xiuren. The news has just arrived." Xiuren was located about 80 kilometers east of Liuzhou. In that vicinity, the rebel forces of Li Yuanfa, who had marched all the way from Hunan to Guangxi, were now engaged in a battle with government troops. The young man's report of a "defeat" was a reference to the rebel army. The Society of God Worshippers would never have assumed the side of the government.

Until then, the government's suppression of Li Yuanfa had not been well-handled at all. Compared to the rebels, the fighting spirit of the government's troops was abysmally low. The government armies in Hunan and Guangxi had already lost several high-ranking officers. These officers had led their men into battle, but the troops failed to support them on the field. They just watched their officers being killed.

It was at this point that a stern order was issued in Beijing to the effect that one provincial governor and one provincial military commander, high-level civil and military positions respectively, were being called to task for their failures and were to be cashiered. The next time the government's armies would fight more assiduously. The story was circulating that a large number of firearms were being sent through Changsha and Guilin, and many troops were to be mobilized. For that reason Li Xinmei's group had attacked the weakened military warehouse at Beisi.

"What happened to them?" asked Feng.

"They scattered in all directions."

"Dead?"

"Not very many. Li Yuanfa has apparently already escaped to the north."

"That's good."

Was Feng Yunshan happy that nothing had happened to Li Yuanfa? It seemed to Liwen that Feng was happy because few deaths in the large rebel army meant ever greater military strength when the Society of God Worshippers eventually absorbed them.

"However, Li Zhaogong was captured," said the young man. Li Zhaogong was a deputy commander in the rebel forces.

"He's sure to be murdered by the Manchu devils." Feng shut his eyes and thought about it.

Despite his escape to the north, ultimately Li Yuanfa was not able get away. He proceeded as far as Xinning in Hunan province by himself and hid out nearby in a mountainous area known as Jinzifeng before being captured by a local volunteer brigade. It was just a month following his defeat at Xiuren.

With the capture of Li Yuanfa, Xiang Rong, the man who had replaced Ying Jun as Hunan's provincial military commander, declared that the uprising had been pacified. It had lasted roughly six months from the occupation of Xinning.

5

Assemble at Jintian Village!

—1—

White pus oozed from his ears. His once sharp eyes had lost all sparkle, looking unknowingly about him. His mouth hung open, his voice attempting vague sounds that fell short of actual words: "Ah, ah . . . ah . . . ." Occasionally, these noises grew louder until they resembled something like the howling of an animal. He was walking, staggering like a drunkard. He stumbled and tripped over a rock beside the road. Sluggishly, he got up once more and tried to continue walking, but this time he ran smack into a tree and collapsed on his backside.

Three peasants were sitting along a nearby footpath between ricefields. Looking over at him, one said: "Hey, he's blind. Otherwise, how'd he ever run right into that huge tree?"

"He's out of his mind."

"What mind did he have? . . . He's more like a puppy dog."

"It's like he's possessed by something."

"Maybe. Possessed, eh, by God, probably."

"More like by a fox or a badger."

"He's blind, and looks like he wouldn't hear you even if you yelled. It's hopeless." They were speaking of none other than Yang Xiuqing, "the ablest man of Thistle Mountain" and a leader of the Society of God Worshippers. For some inexplicable reason, this man who was the very essence of vitality had now suddenly fallen into a state of dementia. No, it was worse than dementia; there were actually two men in Jintian village who had gone crazy, always wandering around grumbling incomprehensibly. What they said was meaningless, but at least what issued from their mouths were more or less classifiable as words. It was just that ordinary people had no sense as to the logical connection between these "words." In comparison, Yang Xiuqing was in far worse shape. He no longer seemed at all like a human being, as one of the peasants had intimated.

Yang had fallen into this state shortly after Li Xinmei's attack on Beisi and the defeat of Li Yuanfa's rebel army by the government at Xiuren. It was the fourth lunar month, which meant the weather had already turned quite hot. A complete invalid, Yang was not even wiping the sweat from his brow.

Lian Liwen crossed over by Yang, who was sitting right where he had fallen. Liwen tried to offer Yang a hand to get back on his feet, but he soon realized that it was hopeless. After he had walked two paces past Yang, he whispered: "Not bad at all," and turned around to look at Yang, but the man on the ground made no response whatsoever.

Yang was faking the dementia. Only a few of the highest leaders of the Society of God Worshippers knew this. Liwen, who had received Hong Xiuquan's absolute trust, was occasionally called to meetings of these leaders. The financial assistance of his father, Lian Weicai, undoubtedly lay behind this trust. But Liwen wanted to believe there was a spiritual bond between them as well.

The day of the uprising of the Society of God Worshippers was drawing near. Preparations had to be made for that day, and these had to be hidden from the eyes of the authorities. The method of camouflage was discussed in a secret meeting of the group's highest leaders.

An incident had arisen by chance in Xinyi county, Guangdong province, in which a member of the Society of God Worshippers by the name of Ling Shiba had been subjected to an inquiry by the local county magistrate, Gong Buxiao. Ling had been enthusiastic in his missionary work, going around soliciting membership in the Society of God Worshippers with such slogans as, "A major uprising is at hand. You can avoid danger by joining the Society of God Worshippers." Or, "An epidemic is raging. Only members of the Society of God Worshippers who drink a special potion will not become ill."

He eventually attracted a group of several hundred at a place called Daliao and carried out a group prayer.

Many religious proselytizers circulated exaggerated stories of the extraordinary efficacy of religious belief. When it became too much for the authorities to tolerate, however, they grabbed Ling as "someone who was deceiving the common people." At this point the Society of God Worshippers became involved.

As a result of the official inquiry, Ling received a warning from the county magistrate. Ling avoided a more serious examination because he expressed remorse.

Ling Shiba was not one of the principal figures of the Society of God Worshippers and was thus not privy to the impending plan for an armed uprising. He could hardly testify to what he did not know, so Hong Xiuquan and the other leaders were not overly worried about the outcome of the inquiry into his activities. However, the very fact of being investigated meant that henceforth every action taken by the Society of God Worshippers would be observed.

Religious associations made the authorities very nervous, because, as in the case of the White Lotus Sect, they could easily turn into kernels of peasant uprisings. This was the primary reason the Society of God Worshippers had initially come under scrutiny.

At the secret meeting in Thistle Mountain, Yang Xiuqing had argued: "We have to demonstrate that the Society of God Worshippers is by no means a rebel group."

"What do you mean?"

"For example, there are all sorts of pretenses we can assume for Elder Brother Xiuquan becoming gravely ill or for internal dissension between Elder Brother Xiuquan and Elder Brother Yunshan."

"I might fake a serious illness on behalf of the Society of God Worshippers," said Hong.

"But there's also the danger of falling under suspicion—I mean if the tactic is too obvious," interjected Liwen.

"I'm opposed to any kind of internal dissension, even as a disguise. It'll have an effect on our fighting spirit, and we rely on religious belief and fighting spirit," offered Feng Yunshan frankly.

"That's true. Anyway, the two of you could never put on such a performance," said Yang smiling. Liwen was thinking precisely the same thing.

"Excuse me for saying so, but when it comes to acting the two of you are not terribly persuasive. This is Elder Brother Xiuqing's area of expertise," said Liwen candidly.

"Why not let me put on a show?" said Yang. Whatever the job, Yang always seemed to step forward to volunteer.

"What sort of performance did you have in mind?" asked Feng.

"Since the lot of you are a bunch of amateurs, it'll naturally have to be a one-man show."

Yang described his plan. Although certainly a quick-thinking person, his plan was clearly not concocted on the spur of the moment. He had already considered every angle in advance, and Liwen was highly impressed by this.

"I'll become sick, pull the bedding over my head, moan and groan, and generally carry on. Maybe I can come up with a really elaborate illness. Elder Brothers Xiuquan and Yunshan will be greatly concerned about me as I become completely at the mercy of this illness. It'll make us seem far from ready to revolt."

The elaborate illness Yang mentioned was the wholly unforeseen dementia that he was now enacting. He did not remain in bed, but wandered here and there, so as to catch as many eyes as possible, all of which required enormous skill as a performer, but this was one of Yang's marvelous talents. The verisimilitude of his performance was further conveyed by the fine supporting roles played by Hong and Feng of being "greatly concerned."

"If he plays the part too well, we really should be worried. If he stays like that too long and doesn't return to normal, it could become a problem." Feng quietly expressed this thought to Liwen.

—2—

"I'm getting a little concerned," murmured Liwen to himself as he walked along. After passing Yang Xiuqing, turning around, and speaking to him, he thought it best not to go back a second time. He was concerned about Yang himself.

There were many ways to confuse the authorities, but the important thing was to convince them that the Society of God Worshippers was anything but a rebellious organization. The logic ran as follows: Yang Xiuqing had become completely disabled because of some disease of unknown origin, and thus the Society of God Worshippers could not function as a rebel group. Without Yang, the Society of God Worshippers itself would cease to function.

This was how Yang framed it himself, perhaps an indication of his own self-confidence. In fact, both the actual leader of the Society of God Worshippers, Hong Xiuquan, and his right-hand man, Feng Yunshan, believed it as well. Liwen recalled the story his brother, Lian Zhewen, had told him on the night he left Nagasaki. When Feng had been imprisoned, Hong marched on Guangzhou to secure his release, and Yang was left to watch over the organization at Thistle Mountain in the two leaders' absence. According to Zhewen, their father had expressed the fear that Yang would overstep his authority while Hong and Feng were away: "They were united until then, and Yang wouldn't hesitate to divide them."

After arriving in Guiping, Liwen heard the details of how Yang had prevented the Society of God Worshippers from falling apart in the absence of Hong and Feng. He used superstitions of spirit possession long practiced in the region by professionals in this line of work, which were particularly widespread along the Xunjiang area. It was a state of spirit possession in which the body becomes suddenly stiff. At first one so stricken moves about violently for a long time. This movement then ceases and the rigidity remains, but in this interval a spirit is thought to take possession of the body. Soon the body speaks the "words of the spirit." Sometimes it is the spirit speaking, and sometimes it is deceased persons from the spiritual realm. In response to the requests of those from the nether realm who sought their services, these professionals would then convey the words of spirits or dead persons.

Many of the adherents of the Society of God Worshippers in the Guiping region were restless in the absence of Hong and Feng. Local men of influence, who despised the Society of God Worshippers, were encouraged by Feng's imprisonment and began circulating the rumor that "heathen religions like the Society of God Worshippers were soon to be annihilated."

Hong and Feng were the main pillars of the Society. While Hong absorbed himself in the study of doctrine, Feng was responsible for missionary and organizational work. With the two pillars of the organization gone, the Society in Guiping was inviting a real crisis.

It was during this period of time that Yang tried out his spirit possession at a meeting of adherents of the Society of God Worshippers. It transpired two years earlier, on the third day of the third lunar month of 1848. With his body perfectly rigid, Yang conveyed the words of the Heavenly Father, Supreme Lord-on-High—the name used by the Society for Jehovah—which went roughly as follows:

> We have caused Hong Xiuquan to be born into the world, made him the true sovereign of all the lands of the realm, and have sought to save mankind from falling into depravity. In spite of our efforts, because men have not learned to revere and worship us as the Heavenly Father, they know not wherein lies the true sovereign and continue to turn their backs on us. Originally, we intended to send a massive plague of murrain down to cause the deaths through illness of all mankind. However, we could not bear the thought of all men in the vulgar world below dying from disease. And so we issue forth a great clemency and descend into the vulgar world below through the person of Yang Xiuqing. Yang Xiuqing shall expiate the sins of all mankind.

Thereafter—even after the Society of God Worshippers had become the Taiping Heavenly Kingdom—this divine revelation of Jehovah via Yang was known as "Heavenly Father's Descent to Earth." It came to be celebrated on the third day of the third lunar month every year as the Day of Jehovah's Visitation.

From what he had been told by Xiling, Liwen knew that this "Heavenly Father's Descent to Earth" had been a genuinely moving event. Some of those believers present were brought to tears, as Yang Xiuqing had put on an incomparable performance.

The first "Heavenly Father's Descent to Earth" was profoundly meaning-ful. It both recognized Hong Xiuquan as the true sovereign of all the lands of the world and expiated the sins of all mankind, allotting to Yang a role earlier played by Jesus Christ. Liwen knew only a little about Christianity, but he understood the gravity of this event and his father's anxiety, for a strong possibility existed that such an organization requiring unity could easily be-come bifurcated.

To be sure, the "Heavenly Father's Descent to Earth" was a ruse cooked up to preserve the organization, and it did calm the uneasy minds of believ-ers who were moved by it. Taking advantage of his success, Yang launched a fund-raising campaign for the release of Feng Yunshan. Impoverished char-coal makers pooled as much money as they could and amassed several hun-dred taels of silver to contribute to the cause.

It was unclear whether maneuvering from above or below had proven the more efficacious, but in any event, Feng Yunshan was released from prison and returned to Thistle Mountain. When he learned that Hong Xiuquan had repaired to Guangzhou to obtain his release, Feng left Thistle Mountain for Guangzhou. They crossed paths once and eventually were reunited in Hua county.

Shortly after Feng set off for Guangzhou, Xiao Chaogui underwent a spirit possession. He was not possessed by Jehovah, though, but by God's son, Jesus Christ, the elder brother of Hong Xiuquan. This event was subsequently known as the "Heavenly Elder Brother's Descent to Earth." It occurred on the ninth day of the ninth lunar month, later celebrated as the Day of the Elder Brother's Visitation. Xiling told Liwen that Xiao Chaogui's Heavenly Elder performance as a spirit medium for Jesus Christ was no match at all for the inspiration conveyed by Yang's "Heavenly Father's Descent to Earth": "I was truly stimulated by Yang Xiuqing. Xiao Chaogui's a blockhead, and his 'Heavenly Elder Brother's Descent to Earth' was not a very bright idea."

Xiao Chaogui was from Lulutong, Wuxuan county, Guangxi province. Wuxuan and Guiping were adjoining counties straddled by Thistle Moun-tain. He was thus, importantly, a resident of the Thistle Mountain region. Xiao's late wife was a relative of Yang Xiuqing's, and the two men had been close for some time.

Shortly after the "Heavenly Elder Brother's Descent to Earth," followers of the Society of God Worshippers began a fierce idol-smashing campaign, which seemed to erupt far more spontaneously than any of their prior activi-ties. Even though Hong and Feng were not present, the Society of God Wor-shippers was operating quite smoothly.

Before Hong and Feng returned from Hua county to Thistle Mountain, Yang carried out the second "Heavenly Father's Descent to Earth." During his possession, he said: "Observe the orders!" Did "orders" here mean the orders of God? Since their leader Hong Xiuquan was not present, everyone linked these orders with Yang as the voice of God. And, even if Jehovah did issue orders, they were being conveyed by Yang Xiuqing.

"Now I am concerned," repeated Liwen.

—3—

Liwen was on his way to the Xishi Monastery. He had to persuade Xiling. The previous day a letter had arrived from his father in Shanghai. Liwen's job from the very start was to convince Xiling to leave Guiping, but he had yet to succeed in this task. His father's letter suggested that she might change her mind if Liwen offered "to accompany her to Beijing."

The situation in Guiping had grown tense, and Lian Weicai wanted to move her to a safer place. For her part, Xiling did not want to leave Guiping precisely because it was so unsettled there.

"You will soon witness things that are rarely seen," she had told Liwen with a smile on her face when he last tried to prevail upon her to leave.

Liwen also knew very well that Xiling was not a simple bystander in these events. At the time of the Opium War, she had had contacts with people connected to foreign trading companies who were likely to have been involved in opium smuggling. She had also been on friendly terms with such righteously indignant intellectuals as Qian Jiang and He Dageng. By nature she was incapable of remaining quietly by, but it was unclear just what she was personally searching for. Engulfed in the turmoil of the Opium War, she had undergone extraordinary experiences, but none of it seemed to change her basic character.

Now she was working assiduously to try to forge a bond between the leaders of the Heaven and Earth Society and the Society of God Worshippers. Her old acquaintances, Qian Jiang and He Dageng, were closely tied to the Heaven and Earth Society. By drawing on these relationships, she gained considerable influence within the Heaven and Earth Society. Because of her relationship to Lian Weicai, who was secretly funding the Society of God Worshippers, Xiling was one person who could not be ignored on that front either. As one able to exert influence in both quarters, a sense of mission seemed to motivate her in her work.

"Beijing?" she said, looking up at the ceiling of the Xishi Monastery, after listening to Liwen. The word "Beijing" seemed to elicit a reaction. She truly missed the old capital. There was no particular reason for this response—

which in itself was very much like Xiling. Lian Weicai had known her from childhood and understood this about her.

"Xiling, don't you miss the ancient capital?" asked Liwen.

"Beijing is not the ancient capital. It's the present capital. From inside it, they can see everywhere throughout the country. At the time of the Opium War, I was in Guangzhou, but I wanted to look out at China from Beijing," responded Xiling. This reasoning had the strong ring of something thought up after the fact. "So, will you go to Beijing? You will certainly be able to gain a perspective on events in Guiping from there."

"Well, but . . ." Xiling's line of vision hurriedly ran between the ceiling and Liwen's face before her. She paused momentarily and then continued: "I've got work here that I've begun now. I can't just ignore it, can I?"

"But, Xiling, must this work be done by you?" asked Liwen.

"What?" She seemed to be caught off guard by a question she had never anticipated. "Well, it's work I've started, and . . ."

"I have a general idea of the nature of the work you've started. Is it something I might do?"

"Liwen . . ." She looked intently into his eyes and shook her head softly. It was by no means a gesture of denial.

"I know Big-Headed Ram and Big Carp. I've met Luo Dagang in Guangzhou, and I was with Li Xinmei until just recently."

Big-Headed Ram and Big Carp were nicknames for two Heaven and Earth Society leaders, Zhang Zhao and Tian Fang, respectively. The strength of these links between leaders of Heaven and Earth Society groups and Xiling were, without a doubt, due to Lian Weicai's presence. Lian's son Liwen would thus have considerably stronger ties.

"Our views are the same. It is still impossible for the Society of God Worshippers to arouse the entire nation by itself. But, if we can merge the Heaven and Earth Society with the Society of God Worshippers, then—"

"That's it. Merge the two," said Xiling in great agitation for some reason.

"Then, if we're both motivated by the same idea, it'll be easier for me, being younger, to carry out the work. Look, Xiling, you are only maintaining contacts with people. I can do it too." When he finished speaking, Liwen had the feeling that he had succeeded in persuading her.

Xiling could not sit still. She was always involved in one thing or another, and now it really appeared as though something seldom witnessed was about to erupt right where she was in that part of China. By the same token, though, it was a rare opportunity to go to Beijing.

"It's true. You are young. I'm so envious," she said.

"So, you'll leave soon for Guangzhou? It's easier these days to travel by ship from Guangzhou to Shanghai. Father awaits you in Shanghai. When do you think you'll depart?" Liwen wanted to dispose of this whole business as quickly as possible. If they dilly-dallied, there was the danger that she might change her mind.

"First, I must explain to you all the work I've begun. I want the person who succeeds me in my work to know how far I've already proceeded."

"Of course. I am always at your disposal. We can start right now, if you like."

"Why not? The earlier the better." Xiling leaned forward. She too seemed to fear that she might change her own mind.

To convince Xiling to leave for Beijing, Liwen had decided in advance that he would claim to share her views. In actuality, he had different ideas altogether about dealing with the Heaven and Earth Society.

Xiling's ideas on the matter were twofold. The Society of God Worshippers lived by extremely strict precepts, indeed suffocatingly so. It compensated for this severity by offering a rock-solid organization and an unsurpassed capacity for concerted action. United through religious belief, its members had a vitality burning with idealism that boasted a might beyond what they actually possessed.

By contrast, the Heaven and Earth Society had a more chivalrous spirit. As an association, it was very loosely organized, with many examples one could point to of individuals who had left and sneaked into other groups because they were unhappy for one reason or another. No one was deterred from joining, and no one was pursued for leaving.

The strictness of the Society of God Worshippers kept it firm, but it also made aspects of the organization difficult to penetrate. People who had been forced off the land to become refugees might think of surreptitiously entering the Society, but they would ultimately keep it at arm's length when they learned of all the disciplined training in religious doctrine, precepts, and the like. It was no easy matter to put together the massive force of people needed to arouse an entire nation.

The looseness of the Heaven and Earth Society also presented problems, Xiling felt, and remaining somewhere between the two groups was the best place for her to be. Thus, in her mind, the intermixing of the two organizations was the best policy, and this had become the principal aim of her work.

By contrast, Liwen was of the opinion that Chinese chivalrous fellowships, in the aftermath of Wang Juzhi's death, had all fallen into decay. They lacked the strength of will necessary, and they seemed ever more like roving bands of vagabonds. But, he still had to pay deference to the considerable number of people attracted to affiliated Heaven and Earth Society groups.

Liwen seemed to be contemplating a united front of antiestablishment groups centered around the Society of God Worshippers. Such a simple notion as intermixing the two groups, he thought, would never actually materialize. His hope in the case of the Heaven and Earth Society was that, by cooperating with the Society of God Worshippers, the former would learn from the severity of the latter's regulations, while the latter, he anticipated, might loosen their exclusivity in matters concerning religion.

After Xiling departed, Liwen set to work on the project she had launched, but of course not in the manner in which she had handled it. He first assigned ranks to the various Heaven and Earth Society groups. Even within groups that had degenerated into bands of roving vagabonds, there were differences in quality.

Groups of high quality were to be enticed into a cooperative strategy with the Society of God Worshippers. Groups with whom nothing could be done along these lines might be compelled to start riots in various sites throughout China prior to the uprising of the Society of God Worshippers. They would provide camouflage for that critical insurrection. Everything might not be so conveniently managed, he realized, but at least with this plan in mind he could proceed with the project.

For their part, the Society of God Worshippers was fortifying its basic plan of action aimed at a coming insurrection. They did not reject those who approached them, such as the followers of Li Xinmei, because they keenly felt their insufficiency in numbers, and the Society's leaders were as yet not united in their views. Yang Xiuqing was pondering how best to amalgamate such a rabble force to invest them with vigor. Hong Xiuquan, however, feared that such a ragtag band of troops would dilute the purity of the Society of God Worshippers. At the time of their secret conference, Hong declared: "I am well aware of our insufficient numbers in troop strength. However, I am afraid that if we amass an impure force prior to our uprising, it will transform the nature of our army. If we first obtain one or two military victories, then they will naturally be attracted to us. And, of course, a major voice will not be accorded any force that joins us after we have risen in revolt. In this way we can maintain the purity of our military."

In response, Yang held: "But, even before the uprising, we can educate them and dissolve their organizations and only then allow them to join us."

In the end, they decided that it was impossible to permit the inclusion of such a motley crew because of the numerous secrets that had to be kept prior to insurrection. They would not actively work with such people, but by the same token, neither would they purposely exclude them from participation.

Yang was still a bit dissatisfied. "If they'd just leave the training to me, everything'll be just fine," he mumbled into Liwen's ear. He was an activist, but the conference had decided to restrain him from such strategic maneuvering. It was at that point that he disguised himself as a complete decrepit incapable of any sort of activity whatsoever.

Liwen wondered if he should proceed with such work in Yang's stead, but he was not pleased by these thoughts. Liwen had a physiological repulsion to Yang. He did not enjoy the feeling, and his inability to control the emotion made him feel all the more immature. He resolved this difficulty by reconsidering the issue at hand—he wasn't doing this for Yang Xiuqing but for the Society of God Worshippers.

If liaison work with the leaders and masses of the Heaven and Earth Society was done in a coherent fashion, it was not likely to be that difficult. At least, Liwen felt that it was a respectable line of approach insofar as he understood Wang Juzhi, the legendary figure in that realm. And the first person he had approached to establish access to that channel was Li Xinmei.

Although her attack on Beisi had been successful, she had been subsequently betrayed by Li Qun and was now living in obscurity, her followers dispersed. Forlorn and crestfallen, she had fled the arena of action. Liwen decided he would go visit her in the home where she had taken refuge.

"What do you know! Have you come to pay a sympathy call?" she said to Liwen as soon as they met.

"Well, there's something of a sympathy call involved."

"But you didn't come here solely for that, did you? The quicker the better. Let's get to the point right now." Her tone of voice had a certain recklessness to it.

"Elder Sister, if you were to round up your people, how many could you get?" asked Liwen.

"That's not for me any more. I no longer have any use for that. Oh, right now, maybe two hundred to three hundred, but I'm sick of it. The money's all gone, and so are my friends, as they say. I just can't endure it. I saw that clearly this time. For me that's all finished." Her voice broke off into tears.

Liwen felt sad continuing this discussion. Apparently embarrassed by her tearful voice, Li Xinmei collected herself and asked:

"Is the Society of God Worshippers putting together a rank and file assortment of troops?"

"Yes. It's actually something of my own invention."

"You're doing it by yourself? Then I'm by myself too. I'll join the Society of God Worshippers as an individual. Only as an individual. If that's okay . . ."

"It's fine. Joining as an individual is fine," answered Liwen.

—5—

When Liwen left Guiping for Guangzhou, he traveled in the company of two of Hong Xiuquan's subordinates, Huang Shengjue and Hou Changwang. He lied to them about his reason for making the trip, saying he had business at the Jinshunji office in Guangzhou. Hong's two men were more honest: "We're going to greet the family of Mr. Hong Xiuquan."

As they put it, the family in Hua county, Guangdong, all had been summoned to Guiping. This meant the uprising was near at hand. Once they had risen in armed insurrection, they would become open rebels against the state, and Hong's entire family would surely have been arrested by the authorities. At this time in China, crimes extended to one's fifth generation relatives. If no provision were made for Hong's family members, every one of them would be executed. There were many cases within the Society of God Worshippers where entire family groups took part in the insurrection. It was much safer to move family members than to leave them where they were.

While Liwen remained in Guangzhou, news arrived to the effect that the county of Guangning (about 120 kilometers northwest of Guangzhou) had been surrounded by several thousand bandits, but this group soon relinquished its hold and departed. Rumor had it that the county magistrate had negotiated with the bandits and paid them off with 2,500 taels of silver.

"All officials ever think about is taking bribes," everyone was saying, in thorough disgust. "I guess they pay out bribes sometimes too."

Once the insurgents lifted their siege of Guangning, they crossed the provincial border, invaded Guangxi, and surrounded He county. The government's armed forces in the region were under the command of a Manchu officer by the name of Yi-ling-a, a regional vice-commander, but he did not even attempt to attack them. The wretched He County Magistrate He Nianchou committed suicide.

At the same time in Gui county near Guiping, several dozen followers of a Heaven and Earth Society group pillaged a town known as Longshanxu. Both provinces of Guangdong and Guangxi were becoming more and more embroiled in turmoil.

It seemed to Liwen that conditions were becoming ever more favorable for the Society of God Worshippers. In order to camouflage their movements, he had been thinking about stirring up a Heaven and Earth Society band of inferior quality to cause disturbances in various spots, but as it turned out there was no need for schemes of this sort. The fact was that circumstances were playing into the hands of the Society of God Worshippers. He had come to Guangzhou specifically because of his promise to meet with several leaders from Li Xinmei's organization.

His first appointment was with a man by the name of Li Yongchou, who was none other than the head of the rebel band that had squeezed the 2,500 taels of silver out of the magistrate in Guangning. His followers trained their sights on far-fetched objectives and moved on to attack He county, Guangxi, while Li himself returned to Guangzhou. The leader brazenly enjoyed himself while entrusting such dangerous matters to his subordinates, another indication of the decline of the Heaven and Earth Society.

The greater part of the bribe extorted from the magistrate probably went directly into the pockets of the head of this outfit as well. Having just come into this great windfall of money, Li Yongchou was now living it up in Guangzhou. Of course, Li was in no position to march triumphantly down the main thoroughfare of the city.

He was hiding out in a house near the Hualin Temple, southwest of the central city. It was said that when the great Bodhidharma came to China from India, the first temple at which he resided was the Hualin. There are conflicting opinions concerning the era in which the Bodhidharma arrived in China, and indeed some even doubt his actual existence. People in this part of China believed he arrived during the Putong reign period (520–26) of Emperor Wu of the Liang dynasty.

The present temple dated to the early Qing dynasty, although it boasted an ancient history. The region around the temple was known as Xiajiufu, although locals called it Xilaichudi (literally, "first site of the coming from the West"), a popular reference to the Bodhidharma.

Liwen was blindfolded, placed in a palanquin, and transported to Li's place of hiding. Yet, from the window of the room into which he was ushered, he was able to see certain stone monuments, and he knew it was the Hualin Temple because he was so familiar with Guangzhou. He laughed to himself that there was no purpose whatsoever served by the blindfold. They had him wait for half an hour in this room before a man dressed in black appeared and said without ceremony: "This way, please."

The hallway was poorly lit. The building was constructed of tiles, and repair work appeared to have been scrupulously attended to. The man in black stopped before a green-lacquered door and said to him: "Our leader will not meet you unless you swear an oath of brotherhood. We shall carry out the ceremony right here and now."

Long, thin pieces of red paper hung on either side of the green door, each bearing a line of writing. In sum it carried the meaning that only a loyal heart could swear such a bond of brotherhood and it forbid those without chivalry from entering that place. "What childish nonsense!" thought Liwen, between the blindfold and the bombastic couplet inscribed on the red paper. He had heard from his father, though, that Wang Juzhi began all these practices for purposes of self-defense.

The *Code of Laws of the Great Qing Dynasty* forbid on pain of severe punishment "swearing bonds of loyalty to those of a different surname." The aim of this injunction was to warn that the root of rebellious organizations lay in the forging of fictive fraternal alliances beyond the scope of the family. Because the government's control over this practice was strict, it was only natural that rebels had to be extremely prudent in matters of self-preservation. This prudence was now little more than formal, perhaps another indication of the decline of the Heaven and Earth Society.

The green wooden door opened with a grating sound. Inside it was pitch-black, but when the creaking of the door ceased a light in the back suddenly shot out. At first it seemed as though the light was floating on air, but it was soon clear that there were two candles.

"Come forward please," said a voice, and Liwen slowly moved in the direction of the light. With every step the number of lights increased, so that when he reached the candles in the center, the room was well lit up. A statue of Guanyu, the Chinese god of war, had been erected in the foreground, flanked by images of two great military men of antiquity traditionally at his sides. Guanyu was stroking his long beard. To each side of the image of Guanyu was hanging not just a strip of red paper, as in the case of the green door, but full scrolls. The Chinese characters on them were not inscribed in India ink but in gold paint. They read:

> The loyal heart is chivalrous,
> There is unity in common cause.

Before the statue of Guanyu were placed a variety of red, yellow, and blue banners, each inscribed with various Chinese characters. Some of them looked as though they were composed from elements of characters but in idiosyncratic ways distinctive to the Heaven and Earth Society and not likely to appear in any standard dictionaries.

"Please be seated," said the voice, as Liwen wondered what else there was to do in any event. Liwen turned to the left, facing the statue of Guanyu, where there was a red-lacquered chair. As he sat down, he noticed another red-lacquered chair in front of him.

He heard a cough—not just a simple cough, but clearly some sort of signal. One by one, the lights began going out until only the two candles in front of Guanyu remained illuminated. Another audible cough, and then plodding footsteps followed. Li Yongchou appeared, exaggeratedly waved his hands, and sat down in the chair facing Liwen.

Liwen tried to rub the area in which he was sitting. It was wooden, with nothing spread over the seat. The other chair had a yellowish cushion on it. There was a marked distinction between the two chairs. They may have sworn brotherhood, but it certainly appeared as though Liwen was the younger brother and the man facing him the older brother.

—6—

Compared to the overblown stage equipment, the ceremony of swearing the fraternal oath was extremely simple. He merely had to repeat the salutation of folding his arms at his chest and bowing.

"With each bow, please lower your head three times, fold your arms, and approach the tablets," said a serious, unnaturally affected voice.

Liwen stood in front of his chair, and Li Yongchou stood facing him. With his chin forward, his eyes seemed to be riveted just over Liwen's head. He had an elongated face. It was hard to discern in the poor lighting, but he seemed to have no color whatsoever to his complexion.

From experience Liwen could tell that Li was an opium addict. Since coming to Guangzhou, Liwen had realized just how much the Society of God Worshippers in Thistle Mountain lived in an altogether different world. There were no addicts in Thistle Mountain, because the Society of God Worshippers strictly forbade opium.

The interval after he stood up had grown irritatingly long. Eventually a trembling voice called out, "The first bow recognizes Heaven as the father." Li raised his folded arms and lowered his head. Liwen hurriedly imitated him.

After lowering his head three times in succession, a short space of time ensued before a long, drawn-out, muffled voice said: "The second bow recognizes the Earth as the mother." In precisely the same way, he folded his arms and lowered his head three times, as he would with each bow.

"The third bow recognizes the sun as the elder brother."

"The fourth bow recognizes the moon as the elder brother's wife."

"The fifth bow is for the fifth ancestor."

"The sixth bow is for the Elder Brother Wan Yunlong."

"The seventh bow is for Mr. Chen Jinnan."

"The eighth bow is for harmony among brothers."

With the eighth bow, the ceremony came to an end. The first four bows— for Heaven, Earth, the sun, and the moon—are self-evident. There were many theories, even among members of the Heaven and Earth Society, about the fifth bow. One theory argues that, counting from the founder, the fifth ancestor was venerated because he had established the foundations for the Heaven and Earth Society. The problem with this theory was that it failed to explain why the founding ancestor was not also venerated.

Because the Heaven and Earth Society was a secret society, it left no documents about its organization. Most of the materials now referred to as "documents" concerning it are based on the confessions of members captured by the authorities, and they are altogether unreliable.

There are three theories about the group's origins: a Taiwan theory, a Fujian theory, and a Shaolin Temple theory. The Taiwan theory claims the origins of the Heaven and Earth Society in the following way. The regime established in Taiwan in the mid-seventeenth century by Zheng Chenggong—or Koxinga as he became known in the West—in opposition to the Qing, eventually submitted to the dynasty. But those followers who were too proud to do so created a secret society to continue their resistance. The Shaolin theory claims that, since the Shaolin Temple had been a base for the anti-Qing movement, it was razed to the ground and the fighting men there were massacred early in the dynasty. The story has it that five priests managed to escape by the skin of their teeth, and they went on to organize the Heaven and Earth Society. Some explain that this bow is not for the fifth ancestor but for the five priests. Some even explain it as five founders.

Wan Yunlong and Chen Jinnan were, it would seem, early leaders of the Heaven and Earth Society, but no reliable records substantiating their activities remain extant.

Each bow was accompanied by three lowerings of the head, which made 24 in all. At that point the ceremony of swearing brotherhood came to an end. The affected voice Liwen had heard earlier then intoned: "Thus we happily conclude the ritual of sworn brotherhood."

No sooner was this sentence uttered than another, excited voice called out: "Well, the formalities are over. Let's have some wine, some wine. Go call the girls and bring some opium too." This voice belonged, of course, to Li Yongchou.

Liwen had mistakenly thought that there was a wall behind him, but actually a wooden door made of a number of planks had been fitted between the walls. Before he knew it, it was pulled back.

It was still the middle of the day outside, and brilliant sunshine flowed into the capacious room all at once. Liwen rubbed his eyes, stunned, as uproarious festivities ensued. About ten women wearing heavy make-up like prostitutes suddenly appeared and planted themselves around the chairs. No table had been in the room when Liwen arrived, but now three were lined up. It all happened with incredible speed, and before he knew it the tables were laid out with food and drink.

"Here you are," said a woman next to Liwen as she presented him with a wine cup. As he took the cup, a woman to his other side poured him wine from a large jar.

"Younger brother, you must enjoy yourself to your heart's content." Liwen could hear Li Yongchou's animated voice, but he could not see his face. When he tried to look in the direction of the voice, Li was already sprawled out on a settee concealed behind the tables and could not be seen.

"Drink up! Drink up!" With this prodding from the women smelling strongly of cosmetics, Liwen tasted the wine. It was ferociously strong. The smell of opium began to float into his vicinity, as the odor from the cosmetics seemed to lessen in density.

Whether or not the funding for the wild gala was paid out of the county treasury—the 2,500 taels of silver from Guangning—was beside the point, for in either case there was little doubt in Liwen's mind that it was levied from the impoverished pockets of the resident population. Since the first group of women occupied all the chairs, those who arrived later sat directly on the floor. Some were lying down, and some were squatting with one knee drawn up in quite an unladylike pose. One of them wound her arm around Liwen's leg and said in a saccharine tone of voice: "Some wine, please." She was already drunk, having apparently been drinking in another room before she joined them. A lovely female voice uttered a mild shriek. One of Li Yongchou's subordinates was flirting with her. He was probably one of the leaders' favorites among the underlings who had not gone to Guangxi.

When Li finished his third cup of wine with great effort, he turned to Liwen. "Younger brother, come sit by my side." With his foot the bandit chief then shoved aside the woman seated next to him on the settee where he was lying. She let out a scream, and Liwen had no choice but to sit down where she had just been evicted.

"You seem so modest, younger brother," said Li. Liwen felt worse every time Li used the expression "younger brother."

"I'm not being modest. It's just that I can't drink that much wine," answered Liwen.

"There's no place for modesty here," said Li, sitting up abruptly from his sprawled out position, "because this feast and wine is all from Thistle Mountain, where you used to be."

"What's that? Thistle Mountain? The Society of God Worshippers?"

"That's right. Guangning and He county saw to it. I ordered it, from that guy at Thistle Mountain. Of course, it wasn't free. The reward was enough for about a hundred banquets like this one."

"So, this—" Liwen stopped short.

"So, younger brother, there's no reason whatsoever to be modest, because the wine comes originally from Thistle Mountain."

As Li Yongchou spoke, he tapped the top of his silver cup with his opium pipe.

—7—

While they had decided in advance not to make any active approaches to the Heaven and Earth Society, certain operations were clearly still under way, albeit these were not in the name of the Society of God Worshippers. The engineer of these operations had to have been Yang Xiuqing. After Liwen had met a few leaders other than Li Yongchou, he came to believe this more and more firmly.

Furthermore, the direction these operations were headed was exactly what Liwen had been considering. Yang was apparently allocating funds to encourage localized rioting by rebel forces like those of Li Yongchou. And he was urging groups with even a semblance of discipline to join them at Thistle Mountain. "Wait until the tenth month of the year," Yang had been saying repeatedly. But why then? Yang had spoken confidently of his ability to educate groups affiliated with the Heaven and Earth Society, and now he was out among them, acting out the role of a demented individual. "The tenth month" probably meant that he would demonstrate his miraculous recovery at that time.

Liwen became very nervous as the idea of a "miraculous recovery" dawned on him. By virtue of the Heavenly Father's Descent to Earth, Yang had gained a special position in the religious order, and he seemed to be trying to enhance that position even further now with a "miracle." But why in the world was he posing as such a decrepit character? It was not simply to demonstrate to the authorities that the Society of God Worshippers was anything but a band of rebels.

It must have had something to do with Jesus Christ. During the Heavenly Father's Descent to Earth, he reported that, instead of the Lord God wiping out all mankind through sickness, He would have Yang Xiuqing expiate their sins. Yang's decline into a state of dementia reflected his accepting the encumbrance of illness on behalf of mankind.

Liwen hastily retraced his steps to Guiping county, Guangxi. Neither Hong Xiuquan nor Feng Yunshan were present at that time on Thistle Mountain. They split up the leadership to fool the authorities, and even rather high-level Society leaders were unaware of the location of Hong and Feng. Liwen learned the truth from Xiao Chaogui.

Both Hong and Feng were in hiding in the village of Shanren in Pingnan county, at the home of the local leader of the Society of God Worshippers, Hu Yihuang. Pingnan county was just to the east of Guiping county. Thistle

Mountain (in Guiping county) ran East–West between Wuxuan and Pingnan counties. Shanren was in Penghua Mountain, but generally speaking, these were an extension of Thistle Mountain.

Once the Society of God Worshippers divided its leadership, secret instructions went out to believers in all localities: "Assemble at Jintian village!" Since we have no extant documents, it is unknown just when these instructions were issued. Theories range anywhere from July through November. They probably went out late in July and probably to all locales at the same time because the message was top secret. For a time, adherents were to become conspicuously active in many locales. Since they staggered the times for these actions, there is no fixed theory on precisely when the instructions were issued.

In actual fact, the Society of God Worshippers was not at this time under the observation of the government—not at all. Whereas the activities of the Heaven and Earth Society groups were sufficiently egregious to merit the government's attention, prior to this event the Society of God Worshippers was merely under the watchful eyes of a segment of the local gentry. The Society had not caused any disturbances through plunder up to this point. The Heaven and Earth Society had plundered, taken hostages, received bribes from local magistrates, and forced magistrates to commit suicide. The impression that clung to the Heaven and Earth Society was one of "murderers and thieves."

From the government's perspective, the Heaven and Earth Society was enormously injurious—an object worthy of obliteration. By contrast, the Society of God Worshippers was merely pursuing their destruction of idols. They demolished temple icons, burned Confucian tablets, and wrote poems attacking Confucius, Laozi, and the Buddha on temple walls. But they never went beyond this.

It was the local gentry class that became enraged by the destruction of the images dedicated to Confucius, just as it was locally influential men who had captured Feng Yunshan. That Feng's release had been rather easy to obtain reflected the fact that his crimes were neither "thievery nor murder." Insulting Confucius was not necessarily taken as an act of rebellion.

The rural gentry were the local people of quality. They may have had their own armed self-defense units, the *tuanlian*, but they were not "officials." Once Yang Xiuqing and his followers had collected several hundred taels of silver from the charcoal workers and used it for bribes, the appointed "officials" chose the appropriate moment and released Feng.

Government forces during this period were much too busy suppressing "bandits" of the Heaven and Earth Society who were ravaging sites all over the region. They did not even bother to worry about the idol-breakers of the

Society of God Worshippers. The more spectacular the violent activities of the Heaven and Earth Society, the more beneficial it would be to the Society of God Worshippers.

As the adherents of the Society of God Worshippers gradually converged upon Jintian village, the government was informed for convenience's sake: "They're sending the idol-smashers somewhere en masse. It's certain to cause trouble, but we're too busy right now. We can't control it to that extent."

The actions of the Heaven and Earth Society were not spontaneous. Yang Xiuqing was behind them, and few knew the extent to which he was managing them. Liwen was melancholy despite the fact that Yang was doing for him what he wanted to do himself.

Eventually, the followers of the Society of God Worshippers from other places began to appear in Jintian.

6

Objective: Penghua Mountain

—1—

"What in the world is going on?" That was the question on everyone's mind. Not just the general populace either. Officials too, and members of the Heaven and Earth Society then on the rampage, as well as the bulk of the membership of the Society of God Worshippers then gathering in Jintian village—they were all wondering the same thing. It could only be described as bewilderment.

Rebel bands affiliated with the Heaven and Earth Society were forming into groups one minute and breaking apart the next. There were instances in which rifts over war booty were causing bitter feuds within the Heaven and Earth Society. There were even cases in which such animosities grew so severe that one group secretly informed the authorities of the hiding place of its adversary's leader. And the officials who received such information were, needless to say, more than a little dubious about it.

"What is going on?" The one person who probably had the best handle on this problem was at that moment drooling saliva, and stumbling over stones and into trees: Yang Xiuqing—the man faking dementia. This, at least, was the opinion of Lian Liwen.

The recent pillaging and sacking of towns by the starving, homeless bands of the Heaven and Earth Society appeared to be basically spontaneous acts. However, there was someone pulling the strings from behind as to time and place, and in such a way that would favorably camouflage an uprising by the Society of God Worshippers. This much information Liwen had gleaned from bandit leader Li Yongchou in a fit of drunkenness.

Military training in the village of Jintian had already begun, with Xiao Chaogui principally responsible for it. It was unusual at that time to find ordinary common people engaging in military exercises. Training was being offered in a number of places, especially in Guangxi province, where the ravages of banditry were extreme. No one knew when a given town or village would be subject to attack. Because the government's troops were so unreliable, self-defense was the only recourse to protect life and property. For that reason military exercises had been initiated to confront the common enemy.

Landlords and other local men of influence organized *tuanlian*, and they supported and trained these private armed forces in public. The Society of God Worshippers also initiated military training. In and of itself, this was nothing extraordinary. The Society might also be subject to attack by bandits, and like others, self-defensive measures seemed the best preparation. Beyond its idol-smashing activities, the Society of God Worshippers had not yet committed a single act of despoliation.

It was offensive military training that incurred the displeasure of the authorities, whereas no one found fault with self-defense. At the training ground in Jintian village, known as "the encampment," offensive drilling was indeed being administered. The instructors were training the troops precisely with this in mind. From outside, particularly in the eyes of an amateur, such distinctions were impossible to make.

Given the times, the government was actually encouraging self-defense, but by the same token it was not happy with the amassing of weapons among the populace beyond what was absolutely necessary. The Society of God Worshippers was stockpiling weaponry in preparation for the day of its insurrection. Furthermore, it had to do this without arousing the suspicions of the authorities or their lackeys—spies sniffing around for information.

Wei Changhui and his family had begun raising geese and ducks at their home, and they already had several hundred of them. Wei was the wealthiest man among the leaders of the Society. His family had formerly been large landlords, and thus no one thought it the least bit odd that he had already raised several hundred geese and ducks.

One drawing of Wei Changhui's home actually portrayed a munitions factory. Many families had their forges to produce agricultural tools for their own use. For a large landlord household, this was nothing exceptional. At the Wei forge, though, they were producing weapons for the insurrections— swords and spearheads—and they were working at it day and night.

A large number of people coming and going at such a landlord household, where an entire extended family would ordinarily live together, was not likely to incur official apprehensions. However, the incessant production of farm tools day and night was rather odd. Why were they making so many hoes and ploughs all at once? One or two all-night manufacturing operations were safe, but if it became known that this was an every-night occurrence, that would surely lead to suspicions.

Even if they wanted to work surreptitiously, the metalwork done at forges made noise. To hide this noise, Wei concocted a plan of raising geese because geese squawk loudly. The person placed in charge of the operation had to keep them gobbling continually, and this honking successfully concealed the noise of the weaponry in production.

Wei was a man of strong likes and dislikes, but he never showed them on the surface. Under ordinary circumstances, he could greet someone he absolutely abominated with a smile on his face. However, the hatred he felt within remained unchanged, never weathered no matter how much time elapsed. He was what might commonly be referred to as a highly vindictive man.

Wei had purchased the title of a national university student for his father. In an era when government was so exalted over the people, all commoners could think of was how to obtain an official title. The government then awarded various official ranks to those who had donated money, in accordance with prescribed rates. This practice was called *juanguan* in Chinese, or "the purchase of office." Although a bureaucratic status would then be given to the purchaser, he never really assumed office, but was content to hang a placard bearing his title over his door.

Thus, over the door to Wei Changhui's home hung the sign "Court Gentleman for Promoted Service." A court gentleman for promoted service was a bureaucratic prestige title of rank 9A. Although higher than a noncommissioned officer, this post was below the level of a commissioned officer. Nonetheless, the title of national university student that he had bought for his father was a status of high prestige. Perhaps for a budding high-level official, this was a rank one held prior to receiving an appointment.

Strictly speaking, though, displaying the placard of "Court Gentleman for Promoted Service" was not entirely legal. There was a mark of distinction between a commissioned and a noncommissioned officer, and thus at first there was nothing to find fault with, but in the wide world there were now people prepared to be critical of Wei, no matter how unwarranted their claims. Also resident in Jintian village was a man by the name of Liang Jia who had enticed Police Chief Wang Ji into arresting Wei Changhui for the crime of impersonating an official. To secure his release from jail, the Wei family had to pay several hundred taels of silver.

"You'll pay for this!" Wei swore in vengeance.

The enemy were "officials" and "the gentry," as well as men like Liang Jia, who was allied with them. Liang had passed the first level of the civil service examinations, but he had failed at the next stage held at the provincial level. His ambition was to become a ranked official, but at present he was still unable to do so. That frustration had driven him to anger when he saw the sign hanging over the Wei home.

When Hong Xiuquan and Feng Yunshan came proselytizing on behalf of the Society of God Worshippers, Wei was quickly won over. For their part, Hong and Feng had concentrated their missionary work on people of lower social stations in the area of Thistle Mountain. They had not been actively appealing to large landlord families, like that of Wei Changhui, in Jintian village. After his release from jail, Feng stayed at the Wei home in Jintian on his way back to Thistle Mountain. At the time, lodgings were hard to come by in rural villages, so many travelers boarded at landlords' homes because the latter usually had plenty of extra rooms.

This transpired just after Wei Changhui had paid his huge ransom and been released for "impersonating an official." It was at this time that Wei first became aware of the Society of God Worshippers, despised by the local gentry and officials alike, and thereupon he invited himself into the room where Feng was staying to listen to him discuss his religious principles.

Wei learned that the officials and the local gentry were "devils" whom the Society of God Worshippers argued had to be destroyed. He resolved on the spot to join the Society of God Worshippers and to give everything in his possession to the organization. While this constituted his entrance into the Society of God Worshippers, it's doubtful that it constituted his religious conversion. He was simply a man of violent emotions prepared to take radical action if called upon to do so.

Relinquishing all of his wealth was more than mere lip service. And indeed, he did turn over everything he owned to the Society of God Worshippers. The money Wei contributed to the Society's preparations for insurrection played a critical role. Virtually the entire expense of feeding the people who had gathered in Jintian for military training came from Wei Changhui's pocket. The same was true for the cost of manufacturing weapons. Not only did he contribute a production site, but he also shouldered the entire cost of materials and fuel.

Wei Changhui became the sworn brother of Hong Xiuquan, Feng Yunshan, Yang Xiuqing, and Xiao Chaogui. Together with Shi Dakai and Qin Rigang in neighboring Gui county, these seven men formed the core leadership of the Society of God Worshippers. The weapons manufactured by the secret foundry at the Wei home were furtively transported to a pond known by the name of Xiniu, or Rhinoceros. There was a huge cave there, invisible from the outside, that was near the encampment and just above water level, an ideal spot to conceal the weapons.

—2—

While the Society of God Worshippers did not engage in acts of plunder or rioting, it did destroy icons of various deities and images of Confucius. In the eyes of local officials, it was a group of dangerous elements, but the fact that such light measures as the arrest of Feng Yunshan were adopted to crush them was an indication that they were still preoccupied with the rampages of other rebel groups. The Society of God Worshippers was ever vigilant of being under official surveillance. Thus, as the time for the all-important uprising neared, Hong Xiuquan and Feng Yunshan decided to disappear from Jintian village and lay low in Shanren village, Pingnan county.

Since they expected that the suppression would begin with arrests of the top leadership, the two founders of the Society of God Worshippers vanished from sight, and that event was followed by Yang Xiuqing's decline into dementia. To an outside observer, it appeared as though the Society of God Worshippers had fallen on hard times. Although they did seem to be engaged in some sort of training, this was attributed to their own defense preparations against bandits. After all, even rich people like Wei Changhui were now joining the Society.

Locally, some thought the training at the encampment at Jintian village was more like a private militia armed to protect the household of Wei Changhui. In this sense, the admission of slightly different types into the Society, like Wei, proved to be a genuine advantage to the Society of God Worshippers.

In nearby Gui county was a young leader of the organization, only about twenty years of age at the time, by the name of Shi Dakai. He had not come from roots of grinding poverty, as had Yang Xiuqing or Xiao Chaogui, but had been born into a middle-level landlord home and had received a regular education. Unlike Wei Changhui, Shi entered the Society of God Worshippers when he listened to Feng Yunshan speak of their religious doctrines, which he then embraced. Following his religious conversion, he followed the organization's general direction and became a leader in the rebellion. Unhappy with the policy of gathering the multitudes at Jintian all at the same time, Shi amassed another group of Society followers for the time being at a place known as Baishaxu in Gui county. His group alone numbered over one thousand.

This size for a group was not sufficient to warrant the least suspicions in Gui county. One of the mountains within Gui county was known as Silver Mountain, indicating that the area had once been a silver mining region. When the value of silver rose, the government would order the opening of the mine. Silver was thus mined there intermittently, and at such times miners would come to the area from other regions. The mine had just been re-opened at this time, and miners from the nearby area were living in temporary huts at Silver Mountain.

The majority of the miners were Hakkas, as was Shi. After propagandizing the cause of the Society of God Worshippers among them, he had gained over one thousand new adherents. He then summoned these new recruits to Baishaxu, and their camp looked at a glance just like the temporary quarters built for the miners at Silver Mountain. To be sure, for temporary quarters there were some oddities here. At other such sites, gambling was an inevitable and ubiquitous accessory, but there was no gambling at Baishaxu. In its place, from time to time, group prayers were conducted. Although not a curiosity of the sort one might want to see firsthand, a huge tree had been felled and used to make a gate-like structure at the east–west crossroad at Baishaxu.

Clouds of smoke rose from their camp—too black to be solely from cooking. Ovens had been built, and everyone was convinced that these were for the miners. In fact, Shi Dakai was casting artillery pieces there, work to which his followers were well-accustomed.

After remaining at Baishaxu for some thirty days, they dispersed in different directions. Departing in unobtrusive, small groups, they all had the same preselected place to reassemble: Jintian village. Though they themselves were careful not to act at all conspicuously, the continued pillaging raids of groups within the Heaven and Earth Society proved fortunate as cover for their movements at this time. In just the few short weeks they had been at Baishaxu alone, the following string of incidents transpired:

1. Zhang Zhao sacked Xiangzhou.
2. Chen Yagui captured Xiuren and was moving in the direction of Guilin.
3. Pan Da attacked Longzhou, and with the death of Department Vice-Magistrate Wang Shuyuan, the brigade vice-commander fled without a fight.
4. Zhang Yazhen and his followers of the Revive Righteousness Lodge (many groups within the Heaven and Earth Society took names with the suffix "Lodge") captured Qianjiang.
5. Lu Yaxiang invaded Jiaojianpo.

These incidents all took place in the province of Guangxi alone. A similar list might be compiled for the neighboring province of Guangdong as well.

Even with all this activity going on, there were still people focused on the movements of the Society of God Worshippers.

"Just because they haven't fomented riots lately doesn't mean we can relax our vigilance one little bit. It's just the rabble causing the present troubles, the sort of bandits found in every era, but those guys in the Society of God Worshippers are intent on overthrowing the moral and social order of our times. This makes them far more dangerous. If we fail to nip them in the bud, then we're likely to have a huge problem on our hands in the future." These were arguments with which gentrymen, such as Wang Zuoxin (who had arrested Feng Yunshan) and Liang Jia (who had informed on Wei Changhui), used in trying to persuade local officials.

"But if they don't do anything, I can't just go arrest them," responded Ni Tao, the Guiping county magistrate at the time.

"They're destroying images of deities," said Wang with his jaw clenched.

"Even more outrageous things are being done by brigands closer to home. If I send troops there, . . . well, I might be severely reprimanded," replied Ni.

One group that had sacked their town and murdered some officials was still prowling the vicinity. The central government had ordered Ni Tao in no uncertain terms to use all force necessary to crush this group. If he were to have, in spite of this order, turned his troops on a band of idol-smashers, he might have been reprimanded with language such as: "Have you completely failed to understand the importance of the events around you? Despite the report that a group from the Great Victory Lodge had murdered Wang Shuyuan at Longzhou and escaped in your direction, you arbitrarily moved your forces somewhere else!"

"The Society of God Worshippers is linked to the bandits here. I've heard that their leader was seen at Thistle Mountain," said Liang Jia. The gentry had their own intelligence networks.

"Really? How so?"

"One of my spies claims to have caught sight of Luo Dagang there."

"Luo Dagang?"

"Wei Changhui's home is being used for something highly secretive. He is clearly harboring bandits there."

"If that's true, then it certainly changes things," said Ni, nodding in agreement. If the Society of God Worshippers was sheltering bandit leaders, then he had an excuse to dispatch troops there. Ni consulted with the military authorities in Taozhou prefecture. The local military man in charge was Li Dianyuan.

"Okay, let's send Police Chief Zhang Yong there," said Li. After having thought it over, he decided to send Zhang Yong with 150 troops on a mission to investigate the activities of the Society of God Worshippers.

The Society of God Worshippers had also penetrated the officialdom with spies of their own, and the government's operation was soon reported. The weaponry being manufactured at Wei Changhui's home was immediately hidden in the cave at Xiniu pond, and anything else that might invite suspicion was removed.

Zhang Yong was a typical low-level official who acted arrogantly on the authority of his superiors. With his 150 soldiers, swaggering with gross exaggeration, he carried out his investigation and turned up nothing.

"Where are Hong Xiuquan and Feng Yunshan?" Zhang asked angrily.

"They're away on a trip."

"Where are they now?"

"I don't know. They are doing missionary work with no particular destination."

"If you get word from them, contact a local official immediately. Great . . . those two guys are out carrying on their filthy activities." And with an unnecessarily overblown flourish of his hand, Zhang and his troops withdrew.

Three days later, Zhang was found dead behind his home. It was a sight that effectively said: "Anyone who lays hands on the Society of God Worshippers will end up this way." A great stir ensued among the landed gentry, but the local officials made no subsequent effort to meddle in the affairs of the Society.

"Things are not what they seem. We again received a report that one company of bandits is headed our way. We've got countless things that must be done. If we could only get our hands on Hong Xiuquan somehow," said Ni Tao, shaking his head. No officials had come, let alone inspected Jintian village or Thistle Mountain. On the day that Zhang Yong's body was found, Lian Liwen witnessed the supposedly "demented" Yang Xiuqing washing his coat in the Hualei River by Thistle Mountain. At the time, Liwen thought: "Such a filthy, sweaty coat. . . . He must be washing it for a reason, but does he really want it clean?" Liwen later learned of Zhang's death, and the suspicion arose in him that maybe Yang had been washing blood out of his jacket.

—3—

After Shi Dakai and his 1,000 miners had left Baishaxu, a "latecomer feud" erupted in Gui county, almost as if it had been waiting for Shi's departure. "Latecomer" was a term that referred to people who had come to a particular area relatively later than others. In Guangxi it was often employed in reference to the Hakka people. "Feuds" were literally armed conflicts.

"Latecomer feuds" occurred not only in Guangxi; they were a phenomenon seen throughout neighboring Guangdong, Fujian, and in Taiwan as well. The earlier indigenous population sought to protect its preexisting rights, and the "latecomers" were seen as trying to wedge their way into local society somehow. Local trouble usually compounded these perceptions and led to emotional conflicts.

A feud of this sort erupted in Gui county late in the eighth lunar month. It was actually more an emotional confrontation than a conflict of interests. It came about as a result of a "latecomer" by the name of Wen taking as his bride an indigenous local woman. Had she been his legal wife, the problem would not have been so serious. An indigenous man made some deprecatory remark to Wen, calling him a "newcomer." "Newcomer" did not mean the man had just arrived that day or the day before. Many such families had taken up residence in that area generations before. Some claimed descent from men and women who had fled south when the capital of the Northern Song dynasty fell in the twelfth century. If their claims were accurate, then the migration had occurred 700 years earlier.

People clung to this mode of discrimination. Marriages between the two groups were rare. Latecomer men tended to marry latecomer women. It was in fact more common for them to marry women of the Tong minority ethnic group (now called the Zhuang people) than to marry indigenous women.

Shi Dakai was a latecomer—that is to say, he was a Hakka—and his mother was a Zhuang woman surnamed Xiong. Also, Wei Changhui, the great landlord of Jintian village, had become Sinified, though he was originally a Zhuang. This may in part help explain the level of prejudice contained in Liang Jia's anger when he observed the placard over Wei's door that read "Court Gentleman for Promoted Service."

Even though the marriage was not between equals, the newcomer had taken a native as his wife, and that was sufficient to rile the native men. Off they went to attack the Wen home, beating every latecomer they ran into along the way. The latecomers were not about to stand by and accept such abuse, and they gave as well as they received. The result was an immense feud in which a number of men were killed. Officials intervened in the trouble, but because they sided with the indigenous population, their intercession was wholly unfair. It was a form of collusion between the authorities and the locals.

One theory argues that the armed feuds of this era were struggles between Zhuang and Hakka. However, bonds between Zhuang and the Han Chinese officials were never very strong. Troubles arose from emotional conflicts between the earlier-settled Han Chinese and those who came to the region later.

—We can't live here. All the officials are on their side!

—That's right. Everything's against us. We can't even breathe!

—Maybe, but is there any other place where we can live?

—Just over in neighboring Guiping. There're Hakkas like us living in Thistle Mountain there.

—Jintian village in the foothills is the same way.

—Members of the Society of God Worshippers live there.

—That Society was created by Hakkas like us, you know.

—Then let's go there, to Jintian village!

Gui county was the first place in which Hong Xiuquan and Feng Yunshan had carried on their evangelical work, though only a tiny portion of the Hakka community of Gui county had joined the Society of God Worshippers. They had in fact moved to Thistle Mountain because of the paltry results of their earlier missionary work. Though small in number, in such times the voices of the adherents of the Society of God Worshippers carried considerable influence. When people worried that they might have nowhere to go, Thistle Mountain and Jintian village became designated as safe havens.

With the lead of the Society of God Worshippers, great masses of Hakka families from Gui county flocked to Jintian village. Young and old, men and women formed a long line as they trudged along the route northeast, carrying all they owned with them in carts or on poles across their shoulders.

"Go on! Get out! Be quick about it!" Such were the voices they heard from behind as they departed.

"And don't ever come back!" Occasionally a stone was thrown in their direction.

"Be patient, just be patient. Just a little more patience." A Hakka leader strenuously counseled and soothed them.

One official record has the following note concerning the outcome of an armed feud in 1850: "Over three thousand old and weak men and women uprooted themselves from their land and fled." These people arrived in Jintian about the same time the thousand miners came to Thistle Mountain. Although the latter claimed that they had escaped after losing a local armed conflict, this mass immigration sought to conceal the mysterious activities surrounding the mine. Nonetheless, they could not continue to hide such a massive operation forever. Gradually, too, the military training at the Jintian encampment was becoming more and more emboldened.

Many families had joined the Society as units, and all young people—even the women—were receiving military training. The sexes were rigidly segregated at the encampment into a "male barracks" and a "female barracks." As a result, husbands and wives could not live together.

"Until that day comes . . ." One often heard this expression at the encampment. Everyone had their own personal ideas about the meaning of "that day," and no one was too far off.

—4—

A small river—the Zi River—flowed to the east of Jintian village. It converged with the Daping, Daguang, Hualei, Xiaojiang, and other rivers of the Thistle Mountain area and emptied into the Sipan River.

Across the Zi River and facing Jintian village was a village by the name of Xinyu. Wang Zuoxin, mortal enemy of the Society of God Worshippers, was the principal landlord in Xinyu village and a Confucian absolutist. He was also the leader of the local *tuanlian* self-defense corps in the vicinity. Two years earlier, Wang had mobilized a *tuanlian* unit, captured Feng Yunshan, and thrown him into the Guiping county jail, and he was not at all satisfied with the reason for Feng's subsequent release. Practically every day, he boarded his sedan chair and headed for the Guiping county seat.

Whenever County Magistrate Ni Tao saw Wang coming, he thought to himself: "Not again . . ." Still, since Wang had proven helpful to Ni in the past and since he had given Ni countless presents, Ni had no choice but to listen to him. What Wang had to say never varied: Why were the authorities not seizing control over the Society of God Worshippers?

"If Hong Xiuquan or Feng Yunshan show up, we shall certainly arrest them," responded Ni Tao.

"Oh, really? Then, let's not make the same mistake twice."

Two years earlier, no sooner had Ni placed Feng in jail than he was compelled to release him on orders of the governor-general. One of the consequences of China's defeat in the Opium War was the formal acceptance of Christian missionary activities, and it seemed that the authorities in Guangzhou ordered Feng's release in Guiping out of fear of claims to that effect from foreign powers. "Don't worry, because next time they won't just be involved in Christian missionary activity," said the county magistrate.

The Guiping authorities were attentive to the fact that military training at the Society of God Worshippers' encampment in Jintian village went well beyond the ordinary scope of *tuanlian,* and that the mass immigration of Hakkas there was raising the Society's numbers at an alarming rate.

"They are the ones who murdered Zhang Yong," said Wang urgently.

"There's that too" muttered Ni.

Although the stabbing of Zhang Yong was clearly a case of homicide, the magistrate had reported it to his superiors as an accidental death. An actual murder would have necessitated his arresting the perpetrator, and that would only add one more impossible task to Ni's list. He was already too busy and was not the least bit interested in loading himself down with more official business.

"Even their women go around brandishing spears. They're intent on rebellion. No doubt about it!" said Wang impatiently.

"In any event, we shall find those two." Even as he spoke these words, Ni prayed in his heart that Hong Xiuquan and Feng Yunshan would never return to Guiping county. He hoped that Hong and his followers would make their next move outside of Guiping, even if the training at the Jintian encampment was for the purpose of rebellion. "Feng Yunshan isn't far away at all. He's close by. He's in easy contact with Jintian village," said Wang.

Wang detested Feng even more than he did Hong. Hong shut himself up indoors and devoted his time to theoretical research, while Feng was principally in charge of idol-smashing and missionary work. Precisely at this time, the Guiping county magistrate changed. Ni Tao was, to his great relief, transferred to neighboring Pingnan county, and Li Mengqun assumed the post in Guiping.

The county of Guiping, which had jurisdiction over both Jintian village and Thistle Mountain, was known even at the highest levels of the Qing government as one of the most troublesome of all counties. Such a place required the services of a more energetic man, and Li Mengqun had been chosen with this in mind. Li hailed from the town of Guangzhou in Henan province (not to be confused with the similarly named, much more famous city in Guangdong). He had reached the top rung of the imperial civil service examinations in 1847, and that promised him entrance into the elite course for bureaucrats. He was soon appointed to the post of Lingchuan county magistrate, Guangxi province, and when Li Yuanfa's forces invaded his area from Hunan, he led troops onto the field of battle with impressive results.

His appointment was not a simple county magistracy. By virtue of his achievements against Li Yuanfa, he was accorded the station of a subprefectural magistrate. A county magistrate was rank 7A, but a subprefectural magistrate enjoyed the higher rank of 5A. In other words, he was considered a man of high caliber. The dispatching of such a person to Guiping county indicated a stance on the part of the central government that it would now settle down and crush the Society of God Worshippers of Jintian village and Thistle Mountain.

Ni Tao may have been trying to deceive his superiors, but they had alternate sources of information. Those reports indicated that Police Chief Zhang Yong appeared in fact to have been murdered and that the Society of God Worshippers was responsible. Murdering an official was an act of rebellion, and rebellion had to be confronted as such.

When they heard the news of Li Mengqun's appointment to the post of Guiping county magistrate, even the leaders of the Society of God Worshippers realized that what they had long awaited was indeed finally soon to come.

Heaving a sigh of enormous relief, Ni Tao moved to neighboring Pingnan county, but within three days of his transfer he again received a visit from Wang Zuoxin. Perhaps he has come merely to pay his respects, thought Ni.

"I have come today on a matter of grave urgency," said Wang, with a rather abbreviated greeting.

"What? What business? You live in Guiping county, and I'm no longer magistrate there," said Ni.

"I understand that. You are the county magistrate of Pingnan. A grave matter has arisen in Pingnan county."

"What 'grave matter'?"

"Is not Penghua Mountain in Pingnan county?"

"Of course it is."

"There's a place called Shanren village by Penghua Mountain. Are you acquainted with it?"

"I was just appointed here and haven't traveled around the county yet, but I know of it from the map."

"A man by the name of Hu Yihuang lives in Shanren village, and I've learned that he is hiding Hong Xiuquan and Feng Yunshan there."

"What? Those two guys? Are you sure? Is that what this is all about?"

"Yes. There is no doubting the seriousness of this matter. I've checked it over and over. I've mobilized the *tuanlian* and we're surrounding them at a distance, but I'd like the government troops to be sent in as soon as possible," said Wang.

"You're absolutely sure?" asked Ni to make sure.

"We have surrounded them, so there is no escape possible. The merit earned will be all yours."

"I see." The magistrate rose and breathed heavily.

Only the leaders of the Society of God Worshippers knew that Hong and Feng were hiding in Shanren village. The only other person who may have known was the contact man between Shanren and Jintian. The liaison man sent from Shanren village had argued with a group of *tuanlian* en route and carelessly blurted out: "You'll pay for this when our leaders in Shanren village seize the realm."

The man was arrested, and under torture he confessed everything. It was soon apparent in Shanren village that they were surrounded. This information had to be delivered to Jintian posthaste. Just at this time Li Xinmei arrived in Shanren village. She had received word from Lian Liwen to proceed to Jintian village for military training at the women's barracks. She came by water from Guangzhou, upstream along the Datong River into Penghua Mountain to Shanren.

"Shall I report the situation to Jintian?" she offered.

"We're completely surrounded," said Hu Yihuang dejectedly.

"I can break through. Don't worry. I'm sure of it," she responded.

She was quite adept at dressing up like an itinerant actress, and she was an exceptionally fine juggler. When she neared the point of the *tuanlian* encirclement, she began to put on her show, and while cursing the troops for the piddling change they gave her for her performances, she did manage successfully to break through their surrounding web.

—5—

A mass prayer meeting was being conducted in Jintian village. The slightly elevated plateau at the encampment ordinarily seemed quite extensive, but when as many as ten thousand gathered there it was crowded.

The young Shi Dakai led the group in prayers. His voice was full of life as he intoned a verse from "Ode on the Origin of Virtue of World Salvation." The group repeated after him, and when they finished, a tense moment ensued.

It was time.

Teetering this way and that, a man ascended the platform of packed earth that had been constructed for leading the prayers. A commotion arose among the crowd. The man was clad entirely in rags—it was Yang Xiuqing. His face was utterly filthy, sweat on top of dirt. Only one corner of his jaw appeared less grimy, where saliva was dribbling down from his mouth. Yang stooped and looked around at his surroundings, just like an enormous monkey. Those nearest could see the expression on his face, his eyes moving but empty.

What a magnificent performance, thought Lian Liwen in wonderment from the very last row.

Those on the platform were visible to all no matter how far away. The entire crowd of ten thousand kept their eyes fixed on this figure. Unconscious of their own breathing, a stir in the crowd was followed by strained silence. It had been roughly half a year since Yang had begun acting strangely. Since then many people had come from Gui county, and they had heard stories of Yang Xiuqing from his quick-witted days. People from the area had actually seen Yang almost every day and knew him to be an extremely shrewd, intelligent man.

What a shame, thought the many people who averted their eyes when they happened to run into him along the road.

Slow in his movements, Yang finally reached the top of the platform, and slowly his body began to tremble. To give him room, Shi Dakai leapt from the platform to the ground. Swaying from side to side, Yang's body then began to shake. He remained stooped over, and the slow trembling gradually grew more and more rapid.

A second commotion arose among the crowd, as the scene before them grew more bizarre. Through the last half year, people had only seen Yang move about sluggishly. Now before their very eyes they found it hard to believe that this was the same Yang Xiuqing trembling violently. It appeared to all as though a tremendous force was shaking him. Yang held out both his arms before him. They were moving wildly. His hands actually appeared to be moving even more agitatedly and more rapidly than his body.

A third stir in the mass of onlookers was the greatest thus far. Yang's body, shaken by this tremendous force—everyone was already beginning to believe it was the power of the Heavenly Father Jehovah—suddenly collapsed on the platform. He lay flat on his face for a moment, his hands on top of one another and his face placed on them. He was not moving. A few seconds passed. A few seconds later and voices from the crowd shouted:

"Is he dead?"

"Help him!"

Then, instantly Yang Xiuqing stood up. The agility with which he did so matched the violence that had only moments before wracked his entire body. Now his face was no longer as wretchedly filthy as it had just been. The former Yang Xiuqing now stood before them. Rags draped his body, but his face was gleaming. The people stood in disbelief, some even rubbing their eyes with their fists.

While he was laying face to the ground on the platform, Yang had furtively wiped his face with an already dampened sleeve. It was a masterful performance right down to the finest detail. He raised his hands to shoulder height and uttered a sound.

Earlier residents of Jintian village in the crowd must have recognized his pose, for someone shouted: "It's the Heavenly Father's Descent to Earth!" When the shout faded, though, dead silence reigned throughout the encampment.

And, then, the Heavenly Father conferred a message to his believers through the mouth of Yang Xiuqing: "Heaven's second oldest brother Hong Xiuquan and Heaven's third oldest brother Feng Yunshan are now surrounded by devils in the village of Shanren by Penghua Mountain. You my followers must go there immediately and save them! Raise your troops! The objective is Penghua Mountain!"

When he had finished speaking, Yang stood still, his appearance unchanged. After a moment, as if waking from a dream, he added: "Where am I? How in the world did I ever get here?"

Among the documents of the Taiping Rebellion is one describing this incident. It reads in part: "It was then the first day of the tenth [lunar] month when the Heavenly Father revealed his great power. He again opened the golden mouth of the Eastern King [Yang Xiuqing] and made him quick of hearing, sharp in sight, intelligent, and deeply spiritual."

"Penghua Mountain!"

"Let's go!"

"The objective's Penghua Mountain!"

A great chorus of voices rose like a storm. Shi Dakai pulled out his weapon during this interval. No one had the least suspicion of the intensive preparations under way.

"Just the young men. The women remain here!"

"People of Gui county, other than the miners, stay here too. Jintian village must be protected against devils too!"

"To war!" So spoke Shi Dakai, Xiao Chaogui, and Wei Changhui in succession.

The men scrambled to grab their weapons, and they began to march toward Penghua Mountain. Once they crossed the river, it was a distance of some 50 kilometers from Jintian village to Shanren. The chorus of "Objective: Penghua Mountain" continued throughout the march.

When the *tuanlian* surrounding Shanren village and the several hundred government troops dispatched by Ni Tao saw the armed multitudes from Jintian coming at them, they scattered in all directions without a fight. Hong Xiuquan and Feng Yunshan were rescued from the home of Hu Yihuang and returned triumphantly to Jintian village.

This incident, however, was a clear manifesto of rebellion on the part of the Society of God Worshippers. There was no longer any road back. Only forward.

7

The Men with Long Hair

—1—

"Cut off your queues and let your hair grow!" The order came down from Yang Xiuqing. He had already shorn and discarded his own pigtail and was growing a full head of hair tied in a knot at the crown. First, a word on the queue or pigtail. Originally a common Manchu hairstyle, it required that a man shave his pate, leaving only an area on the back of the head unshorn. He then grew the hair in this spot on the back of his head long, braided it, and allowed it to hang down his back.

From about the time of the Ōnin Wars in fifteenth-century Japan, too, men shaved the tops of their heads, tied up the hair at the back of their heads into a topknot, and wore it rolled over their pates. This practice was said to have begun as a result of the extreme heat and stuffiness when wearing a helmet in battle, causing men often to feel faint from the heat. The custom may thus have derived on the mainland as well from the wearing of armor.

The common Chinese hairstyle through the end of the Ming dynasty in the mid-seventeenth century was the knobbed fashion. The hair was tied at the back with a piece of cloth so that it would not appear disheveled. When the Manchus conquered China in the middle of the seventeenth century, they forced the custom of the queue on Chinese men as visible proof of submission. This was no tepid ruling from on high, for the saying went that he who relinquishes his hair will not relinquish his head. Those who did not shave their heads and wear the queue were executed. Those who refused to submit to the Manchu custom were seen as enemies of the Qing dynasty and were mercilessly liquidated.

Han Chinese thus despised the queue as an alien custom of an alien race, but they were in no position to alter the decree and therefore had to wear pigtails. Nonetheless, those who really hated it had no choice but to enter the Buddhist priesthood and become monks. Monks shaved their entire heads and thus had no hair to braid and wear in the back as a queue. In the early Qing period, many Chinese were said to have entered the priesthood for this reason alone.

Over the subsequent 200 years, the queue had become thoroughly acculturated in China. No one had ever seen anyone who wore their hair from the forehead to the top of the scalp. Two hundred years before, the queue had seemed bizarre, but now it was bizarre not to wear a queue. Yet, despite this, men who wore their hair in the Chinese topknot were certainly not eccentrics following bizarre customs, for they faced decapitation as rebels for their actions.

Thus, Yang Xiuqing's order carried a great deal of weight. Cutting off their queues and letting their hair grow was nothing short of announcing that they were all rebels. The fervent adherents of the Society of God Worshippers—especially those Hakkas who had fled after being defeated in armed feuds with the local indigenous populace—may have hesitated in severing their queues. But, when Yang Xiuqing's order came down, the leadership all removed theirs, and without a moment's hesitation, the rank-and-file members of the Society of God Worshippers followed suit. The miners aligned with Shi Dakai cut and discarded their pigtails to a man.

In Jintian village, the custom of wearing a queue became the exception. Had it become known that a single person had cut off his queue, the authorities would have come to arrest him. However, when such an enormous number had done so as a group, the officials stayed away. A number of lower-level followers in Jintian village simply disappeared at this point in fear of becoming scapegoats for the entire rebel band.

Now, Jintian village was "rebel terrain," and it had already become widely known that the people there had risen in revolt. And not just Jintian village and Thistle Mountain. The Penghua Mountain area around Shanren village where Hong Xiuquan and Feng Yunshan had been hiding was also within the sphere of influence of the Society of God Worshippers.

Yang Xiuqing, who had miraculously recovered from his dementia, raised a massive group of men and led them to rescue Hong and Feng. Though it was more than just a rescue operation, they routed the Qing Army surrounding Penghua Mountain and brought that area under the control of the Society of God Worshippers.

It was here that the Taiping Heavenly Kingdom (a name not formally in use until even later) effectively rose in rebellion. Hong Xiuquan performed a

ceremony for the raising of an army here on his thirty-eighth birthday—
January 11, 1851 (January 10, according to another theory)—but this was no
more than a ceremony. The Society of God Worshippers of Jintian village,
Thistle Mountain, and Shanren village by Penghua Mountain in Huazhou
had entered a state of war with the Qing dynasty. Its military forces were
divided into two branches: a Jintian Army and a Huazhou Army.

The Qing armies were less concerned with the Jintian village area, long
within the sphere of the Society of God Worshippers, than with the Huazhou
region, which until only recently had been completely under the control of
the Pingnan county authorities. To have had that area taken without even a
fight constituted a complete loss of face for the government.

"This is really bad. Finally, I thought I had come to a quiet area," sighed
Ni Tao at his own bad luck. He had transferred from Guiping county to
Pingnan county to avoid any further trouble with the Society of God Worshippers. The orders from the Guangxi provincial authorities were specific:
"Use all possible effort to recover Huazhou at Penghua Mountain!" It was a
peremptory order—no matter what happened, Penghua Mountain had to be
recovered. Ni Tao requested the mobilization of *tuanlian* in the nearby areas.

"It's got nothing to do with our village." Every *tuanlian* leader in every
village was reluctant to call out their troops. If their own village were attacked, then the young men would surely take up arms, but to risk their lives
to back up forces elsewhere seemed genuinely stupid.

There was a rumor circulating in public at that time that the Society of
God Worshippers would take revenge by any means necessary on those who
cooperated with the officialdom. Most of the *tuanlian* were balking at their
marching orders.

"They're a bunch of youngsters who've been left in our charge by their
parents. I can't make them go fight for nothing," said a *tuanlian* commander.

"Now it's only the Huazhou region, but they'll soon be attacking your villages, too. If you don't want your villages burnt to the ground, we've got to
exterminate the Huazhou bandits right now!" pleaded Ni Tao in a hoarse voice.

"Well, that may be, but . . ."

Ultimately he gained their consent to mobilize the *tuanlian* of two villages near Huazhou: Hualiang and Luojian. Local men of influence in the
area near the base of the Society of God Worshippers had become aware of
the great crisis facing them.

—2—

What was going on in Guangxi could not be simply left to run its course. In
the capital in Beijing, countermeasures were being seriously considered. The

reports coming in from the localities were loaded down with embellishments. If ten men had been killed, the report would read: "The number of enemy slain exceeded one hundred." Reports from the field were not simply diluted; more often than not a losing battle would be transformed into a great victory.

Such exaggerated reports were bound to be detected at some point. Different sources were relaying to Beijing that masses of bandits were gathering in one locale where they were supposed to have been defeated and completely exterminated. Only upon comparison of the two memorials could something approaching the truth be gleaned.

The central government already knew full well that the situation in Guangxi had become critical. Not just the reports of high-level local officials were arriving at court. Nonofficial local gentrymen could appeal to the Censorate, even though they lacked the qualifications necessary to present memorials to the throne.

"Bandit infestation has become extreme. Please order the Governor-General of Guangdong and Guangxi, Xu Guangjin, to take firm hold of the situation."

So ran a petition to the Censorate from three gentrymen within Guangxi province. The governor-general named here was the man with the highest level of responsibility, whose jurisdiction covered the two provinces of Guangdong and Guangxi. High-level officials tended to have lateral contacts, and such sources soon brought to Xu Guangjin's attention that men of importance in Guangxi had petitioned Beijing. He immediately penned the following memorial: "Inasmuch as banditry has become widespread as well in Shaozhou and Lianzhou in Guangdong province, I have been unable to concentrate my military forces solely in Guangxi. Please dispatch a high official specially charged with encouraging bandit suppression." Translation: I'm too busy to attend to everything. And Beijing had no choice but to recognize that this was true.

The Xianfeng Emperor, who in subsequent years would always be indisposed, completely abandoned to a life of debauchery, had just ascended the throne at age twenty and was still vigorous.

"So, the problem is personnel. Well, there is no one. Send a high official, he says," said the Xianfeng Emperor, as if trying to preserve his emperor-like majesty before the grand councilors.

"Yes, your majesty, precisely."

The mention of a lack of qualified personnel included, of course, members of the Grand Council, which made the emperor's response exceedingly humiliating. Every morning, the several grand councilors called on the emperor to assist him in important matters of state. At these sessions they decided on the plans of action to be forwarded to administrative offices for enactment.

"What do you think about sending some high official to whom I can delegate plenipotentiary powers to handle the problems in Guangxi? Who would be right for the job? I'd like to know whom each of you have in mind," said the Xianfeng Emperor.

At that time there were five grand councilors: Mu-zhang-a (1782–1856), Qi Junzao (1793–1866), Sai-shang-a (d. 1875), He Rulin (1781–1853), and Ji Zhichang (1791–1861). Mu-zhang-a was a Manchu, Sai-shang-a a Mongol, and the other three Han Chinese. Pan Shien (1770–1854), a Han Chinese grand councilor who had served the Daoguang Emperor over a period of fifteen years, had resigned the previous year due to old age. Chen Fuen (d. 1866), a Han Chinese in his fourth year as a grand councilor, had resigned due to poor health in the fifth month of the current year. Pan and Chen had not been replaced, so that the Grand Council had been reduced from seven members to five.

In the first month of the present year, when the Daoguang Emperor had died and the young Xianfeng Emperor succeeded him on the throne, everyone thought that the new emperor would change the roster of grand councilors. The grand councilors were themselves of this opinion and were rather unsettled about it. Close associates of a former emperor often put the new emperor ill at ease. A new emperor would have his own aspirations and would want his own people in place to see them to fruition. In fact, four years hence, every single member of the current Grand Council would no longer be there. To be sure, there was little exuberance in the advice proffered by the grand councilors.

"Ji Zhichang, whom do you propose?" demanded the emperor.

Of the five grand councilors, Mu-zhang-a was the oldest, having served for twenty-three years and for the past thirteen at the post of chief grand councilor. Although Pan Shien, who had just retired the previous year, was ten years his senior, he had always contented himself with a secondary position to that of Mu-zhang-a. The former emperor had had extraordinary confidence in Mu-zhang-a.

Ji Zhichang had just joined the Grand Council the previous year and occupied the lowest seat on it. He was from Jiangyin, Jiangsu province, a brilliant scholar who ranked third in the capital examinations of 1832, for which he was awarded the prestigious title "Seeker of the Garland." Despite his low position on the council, he was already sixty years of age and served also as the left censor-in-chief. Upon receipt of this imperial inquiry, Ji fell to his knees and responded: "If we do not soon obliterate the bandit uprising in Guangxi, the root of the troubles will survive into the future. The high official to be dispatched as imperial commissioner must be a man who can take bold steps. No one that I know of is more worthy of this task than Lin Zexu, who is now living in retirement in the province of Fujian."

The emperor mumbled something quietly. He shook his head slightly, but inside he heartily agreed. Lin Zexu had headed the list of grand councilors the Xianfeng Emperor had conceived for himself. When Pan Shien announced his retirement the previous year at the advanced age of eighty, he suggested that the appointment of Lin would prove highly felicitous.

Chief Grand Councilor Mu-zhang-a, however, was opposed, and offered the view that he had heard Lin to be wracked by enervating illness, making him unfit for appointment. At the time of the Opium War, Lin represented the hard-liners on the scene, and Mu-zhang-a the compromisers in Beijing. They had ferociously opposed one another. Now, some ten years later, this rivalry had not abated.

In the fifth month of the year, the Xianfeng Emperor issued the following order to Liu Yunke, governor-general of Fujian and Zhejiang provinces: "Investigate Lin Zexu's state of health. If he is able to come to the capital, have him do so immediately. If his illness remains uncured, tell him to repair here after his complete recovery."

Liu Yunke left at once for Fuzhou, met with Lin, and sent the following report to Beijing: "Lin Zexu's health is frail, although at present he only suffers from lumbago. Yet his legs are so swollen that he is unable to kneel down to perform obeisance. His face is rather worn and haggard, though his speech and spirits still seem quite healthy. I conveyed to him that, as soon as he recovers fully, he is to repair to the capital promptly."

Liu was probably conveying Lin's own inclinations. He had every intention of going to Beijing to assume a position of importance, but it could not be soon. His health had, in fact, much improved of late. Claiming that his swollen legs made it impossible for him to kneel down was merely an excuse for refusing to come to court at that very moment.

Though six months had not even passed since the death of the previous emperor, Lin was already troubled over changes in the political realm in Beijing in that short time. Although he had been apprised in detail of conditions in Beijing by Lian Weicai, there was no sign that Mu-zhang-a, his old political enemy, had lost his position at court.

"I think it would be best to watch the situation at a distance for a little while longer," advised Lian Weicai.

By the same token, Lin had just left the office of governor-general of Yunnan and Guizhou provinces in the seventh month of the previous year for reasons of illness. He judged it wisest to wait just a bit longer. It was about this time that the subject of dispatching an imperial commissioner to Guangxi with plenipotentiary powers came up for discussion between the emperor and his grand councilors.

"When all is said and done, there's nobody better than Lin Zexu. What do you think, Mu-zhang-a?" said the emperor to his chief grand councilor, after first querying the lowest-ranking member of the council.

"May I humbly submit that I have learned that Lin Zexu is presently at his original place of domicile, convalescing from illness. If the imperial commissioner we speak of now is to assume a high military position, I am wondering if a man who is sick is fit for the job," responded Mu-zhang-a.

"This illness of his is already six months old. He's probably recovered by now."

"If he has indeed fully recovered, then he should come to the capital at once. That was your order. Seeing that he has yet to arrive in Beijing can only mean that he has yet to have fully recovered."

"No, he's fine. I've heard he's just being extra careful," said the emperor. It appeared as though the emperor was receiving reports on the state of Lin Zexu's health from channels other than those used by the grand councilors— a further demonstration of his profound attachment to Lin Zexu.

Mu-zhang-a fell prostrate before the emperor, gnawing his lips furtively in frustration.

"Send a courier to him!" The appointment of Lin Zexu was put into effect.

—3—

"Former Governor-General of Yunnan and Guizhou, Lin Zexu shall be appointed imperial commissioner. He shall proceed to Guangxi immediately, confer there with Zheng Zuchen, Xiang Rong, and Zhang Bilu, and devote himself entirely to the eradication of the bandit scourge." This decision was reached on the seventeenth day of the tenth lunar month. Fifteen days later, on the first of the following month, Lin received the imperial edict in Fujian.

Although the news came by an express courier traveling day and night, Lin Zexu knew of the edict two days before the official government messenger arrived. Lian Weicai was in possession of the information, and he visited Lin in his home in Fuzhou. On the day following his acceptance of the official edict, Lin departed for Guangxi directly.

On the eve of his departure, Lin sat across a table from Lian, as they quietly drank a cup of wine together. This was the first opportunity they had had to do so for some time.

"It's already been ten years since you first received the imperial commissioner's seal," said Lian.

"Twelve years to be exact. I felt so refreshed back then. I envy having been twelve years younger then, but I envy the feeling of freshness back then even more," said Lin, his wine cup before his mouth.

"You do not feel that way now?"

"Isn't that something you should know better than anyone?" Lin then finally poured his wine into his mouth. The expression on his face seemed one of genuine bitterness.

They had often discussed the possibility that the uprising of the Society of God Worshippers in Guangxi might actually save China. They had exchanged views as well on the Heaven and Earth Society. Lin had met with the late Wang Juzhi and was sympathetic to the Heaven and Earth Society group that followed Wang. He was of the view that, once the Heaven and Earth Society lost such fine leaders as Wang, the group would be reduced to bands of local bandits. Yet he retained his hope that, if they could find leaders of excellence, they might become a force for the future of China.

Every corner of Lin Zexu's mind was imbued with a Confucian education, and a sense of antipathy on his part for the Society of God Worshippers was inevitable. Even if such a group could delude the common people and become a major force for a time, Lin believed they would eventually wither away without laying down roots throughout the land of China. It was the Heaven and Earth Society, he felt by contrast, that might present a serious threat to the Qing dynasty and that might be entrusted with the future of China.

Lin sensed the inconsistency here, for one like himself, who lived off a stipend given by the Qing government. It was this internal conflict that was responsible for his lack of a feeling of vitality, compared to the time of the Opium War, of which he had spoken to Lian. As far as Lian Weicai was concerned, the Society of God Worshippers was the organization worthy of their attention. He had repeatedly offered this explanation to Lin, but this had only led to irritation, as he was unable to get Lin to appreciate the central points he was trying to make.

"In any event, I'm off for Guangxi, and maybe I'll understand—when I see it with my own eyes—whether or not this Society of God Worshippers is a stronger organization than the Heaven and Earth Society, as you say," said Lin.

"Please do go observe them. After an appropriate time, when you return to the capital, I will help out in any way that I can. It's a waste of time for you to try to fight this group in Guangxi," said Lian, shaking his head.

"You have such hopes for them?"

"In this harsh world where people can't so much as raise their fists in anger, yes, I think they're truly a remarkable group."

"And they're going to create a new world?"

"I think they may have the power to do so. The problem is the extent to which they are able to concentrate that power. If I may speak frankly, I would like to see them build their microcosm in Guangxi or Hunan."

"You mean a state within the state?"

"That's right. Then everyone will be able to compare the two. Which is better? Knowing which is inferior can only enrich our lives. It's competition. Without competition, there's no progress."

"Ha, ha, ha. The words of a merchant, indeed. But we can't allow a second state to emerge within China."

"I understand that, but neither do I want you to destroy that state within," said Lian.

"We are in no position to choose what we like or dislike in our work. As for myself, I have little energy left. This is not like fighting the British."

"Well then, at least do not overstrain yourself. The fatigue is showing."

"Does my face look that worn and tired to you?" asked Lin, passing his hand across his face.

"It is not just your face. Your whole body shows its exhaustion. Please do take care of yourself," said Lian, frowning.

Lin Zexu's departure from Fuzhou roughly coincided with Yang Xiuqing's miraculous recovery, and his transmitting the words of the Heavenly Father at the encampment in Jintian village, as well as the rescue of Hong Xiuquan and Feng Yunshan from the encirclement at Huazhou. At the same time, Qi-ying (1790–1858) and Mu-zhang-a were holding a secret meeting at Qi-ying's second home on Cuihua Lane in Beijing. At first, Qi-ying reproached Mu-zhang-a: "Why didn't you prevent the appointment of Lin Zexu?"

"I'm not the only member of the Grand Council. Also, before the emperor even queried me, he asked another grand councilor's views. There was nothing I could do."

"Lin Zexu will throw the imperial court into utter confusion. He's a real danger!"

"I know. In his eyes, there's only the country, not the dynasty."

"If you understood that, then why were you incapable of dissuading his appointment?"

"When the time comes, I'll do everything I can. But at that time it won't require as much of a fight."

"Why is that?"

"Lin Zexu is a dangerous but extremely capable man. There are ways to make use of such people. He mustn't be appointed to sensitive posts. That much I fully understand. If he were being appointed in a situation such as the war with Britain, it wouldn't have been that hard for him to destroy the imperial court on behalf of the hard-liners. But, from what I've been told, the bandit suppression in Guangxi is not such a major problem," explained Mu-zhang-a.

Lin Zexu's patriotism was profound, but Mu-zhang-a's suspicion was that Lin loved the "country" of China, not the Qing "dynasty" founded by the Manchus some two hundred years before. In other words, he was arguing that Lin might take the extraordinary stance that the future prosperity of China might require or eventuate the fall of the Qing dynasty. Perhaps Lin would adopt such a measure without hesitation.

For Mu-zhang-a, being a Manchu, the Qing dynasty was everything. Without the dynasty he was nothing by himself. For a Han Chinese such as Lin Zexu, by way of comparison, the Qing was just one in a long sequence of dynasties. Dynasties came and went, disappeared and reappeared. If the Qing perished, the subsequent dynasty would inherit sovereignty over China. Lin was thus not necessarily glued to the fate of the Qing. He and others like him could never articulate such thoughts, of course, but Mu-zhang-a judged this to be true from what he knew of Lin's personal history.

"You say there's no danger?"

"The Guangxi bandits must be crushed. The stronger the attackers, the better. Even if we attack to excess, the basis of our dynasty will not be undermined. This is different from the war with Britain. If we loosen the grip in this instance, the bandits will expand their influence, and that will endanger the imperial court. Putting down the bandits requires a man of resolution. Someone like Lin Zexu," explained Mu-zhang-a.

"Naturally. Lin Zexu's poison is also the cure," muttered Qi-ying.

—4—

Foreigners often called the queue a "pigtail" because of its appearance, and took it as a symbol of the Chinese people. The male members of the Society of God Worshippers in Jintian village and Huazhou, though, severed theirs, and soon hair began to cover the tops of their heads. There were individual differences in how men grew their hair, but the fact that the entire head was now black was something that had not been seen in China for the past 200 years. It was as if a new Chinese people were beginning to be born.

"Why haven't you cut your queue?" asked Li Xinmei abruptly, upon seeing Lian Liwen's freshly shaved head and his queue hanging down his back.

Although virtually everyone in Jintian village had removed their queues, men who had special responsibilities that necessitated their entering "devil" zones (namely, areas under the control of the Qing government) retained their queues. They would be unable to continue their work otherwise. Liwen, a guest of the Society of God Worshippers, was one such person.

"No, no," said Liwen bashfully, putting his hand to his head.

"It's strange. Everybody's head is black, so that a pale-colored one really stands out. It's like the world's been turned upside down," said Li Xinmei.

Indeed it was a topsy-turvy world. In one corner of Guangxi, a separate universe had come into existence, what Lian Weicai had called a state within a state. It was a situation the Qing dynasty could not allow to continue. Spirits were high in this separate universe where men lived with long hair. They would rub their heads and tell each other: "We're not ordinary living human beings. We've been chosen to create something altogether new."

They lived with a sense of mission that they were building an unprecedented, thoroughly new world. At first this notion circulated only among the leaders, but it had spread with amazing rapidity. Once they had severed their queues, at that moment when they all adopted this "deviant" appearance, group solidarity grew that much stronger.

"The Heavenly Father Jehovah is watching over us."

"The Heavenly Father will take care of everything for us. Those who have given their lives for the creation of the new heavenly kingdom will be beckoned to the Heavenly Father's side and will be shrouded in glory."

"Those who defy us are demons, the enemies of heaven."

Countless times they repeated these lines until their minds were inculcated with them, and more than anything else they came to believe that their pitch-black heads were symbolic of the idea that they were the chosen ones. Training at the encampment grew more and more intense. The training was divided between the male and female barracks, and Hong Xiuquan's younger sister, Xuanjiao, ran the entire operation on the women's side. She had been chosen for this highest position of responsibility in the women's barracks by no means solely because of her relationship to the group's leader, for she had genuine capabilities of her own.

In the fifth month of the year, Hong Xiuquan sent Huang Shengjue and others to summon his family members in Hua county, Guangdong to Guangxi. At that time, Xuanjiao happened to be in Guangzhou on a matter of urgency, and was unable to join the rest of her family. Shortly thereafter, she arrived in Guangxi by herself. Along the way, she had displayed her martial prowess to collect money and use it for her traveling expenses. From her youth, Xuanjiao had practiced martial arts. Women in Hakka society did not bind their feet and were treated much more on a par with men. Many Hakka women studied the martial arts, although Xuanjiao truly excelled by virtue of her passion for them. Martial arts were one of the media practiced by street performers of the time, similar to Li Xinmei's talent at sleight of hand. The Hakkas had the custom of teaching women such a practice so that they could help make ends meet in times of emergency.

Hong Xuanjiao was an expert in the use of swords and spears as well as in the use of the limbs. As a result, she actually led the women's forces on the exercise field with her hands and feet. Oftentimes, Li Xinmei worked as Xuanjiao's assistant.

"Tell me," said Xinmei, changing the subject of conversation, "do you think the Society of God Worshippers will succeed? Liwen, come on, tell me what you think honestly. You can see that I've already taken a liking to the organization, so my eyes no longer see things clearly."

"Whether it will succeed or not depends on the extent to which it can resolve certain problems."

"What sort of problems?"

"There is one Society of God Worshippers. The reason things are going well now is that it is divided between Jintian and Huazhou. Hong Xiuquan is in Huazhou, and Yang Xiuqing's in Jintian."

"True, I've had similar thoughts. There's no question that Hong is the head of the organization, and until now the line of succession following him was Feng Yunshan, Yang Xiuqing, Xiao Chaogui, Wei Changhui, and Shi Dakai. Now, it looks to me like Yang has risen and outpaced Feng Yunshan," said Xinmei.

Within the Society of God Worshippers, the eldest son of the Heavenly Father was Jesus Christ, while Hong Xiuquan and the other major leaders were all younger brothers. Christ was referred to as the Heavenly Elder Brother, with Hong as the Heavenly Second Brother. Feng was the Heavenly Third Brother, and Yang the Heavenly Fourth Brother. Even within the leadership, these appellations were used, although in terms of real strength, Yang far outpaced Feng. Hong and Feng had been absent from the base area of the movement for some time now, and gaining control over the masses, which Yang had achieved by virtue of his feat of divine possession, had become his preeminent talent.

"There's a danger that it'll divide in two. If that happens, the movement will go nowhere."

This was the locus of all the problems, as Liwen saw it. His father Lian Weicai also regarded the success or failure of the Society of God Worshippers as dependent on its ability to remain unified.

"Yang will probably soon replace Hong. In any event, Hong is a bookworm. Yang is very strongly allied with the charcoal workers and the porters. Also, Hong's not from this area. It's like he's renting on Yang's land."

Despite the claim to having lost her objectivity due to a fondness for the Society of God Worshippers, Li Xinmei had clearly seen everything she ought to have.

"Among the old boys from Thistle Mountain, Xiao Chaogui is really strong, and Yang's getting stronger every day. They've been able to make good use of the Heavenly Father's Descent to Earth and the Heavenly Elder Brother's Descent to Earth."

Xinmei and Liwen were carrying on this exchange in a house overlooking the Sipan River.

"There is one thing I might be useful at, I mean, as far as keeping the Society of God Worshippers from falling apart. I'd like your advice on this," said Xinmei.

"What is it?" asked Liwen.

"Cutting Yang Xiuqing's power down just a little bit. Let me put it another way: strengthening Hong Xiuquan's hand a bit."

"Is this something you can do?"

"If there's some sort of intermediary, I can."

"Intermediary?"

"That's right. Isn't Xiao Chaogui a widower? Hong's sister Xuanjiao is also single, isn't she?"

"I think I see what you mean."

If Xiao Chaogui and Hong Xuanjiao were married, it would strengthen Xiao's bond with Hong Xiuquan, and to that extent it would probably weaken his ties with Yang Xiuqing. As far as the future unity of the Society of God Worshippers was concerned, it was an excellent idea.

"But, if the parties concerned aren't interested, there's nothing you can do about it, is there?" Liwen said, smiling.

"That's my particular talent. I've been watching, and both of them are interested. In matters involving men and women, I'm never wrong!"

Xinmei's self-confidence was astounding. Despite her mature age, she too was still single, and yet she made a point of knowing everything there was to know about male–female relations.

—5—

The Society of God Worshippers was also thriving in Yulin, Guangxi province, where its leader there was a man by the name of Lai Jiu. Now that the Society had openly demonstrated its rebellious intent, it had to make preparations in a variety of locations to confront the efforts by the authorities at suppression. Lai Jiu stole a march on them by attacking the county administrative offices, routing the government's troops, and then leading his followers to Thistle Mountain. The Society of God Worshippers of Yulin was immense, numbering in the thousands of households.

As the number of people increased, so too did their vitality, but the rapid population increase led to problems of provisioning. Xiao Chaogui spoke before the masses of the Society:

"In order to test the spirits of our younger brothers and sisters, the Heavenly Father has temporarily limited the amount of provisions to the Society of God Worshippers. My friends, we must be patient for a short time."

Precisely at times like these it was essential that morale remain high. The extent to which one or two military victories would raise morale remained unknown. In Huazhou, Hong Xiuquan decided to attack the village to which *tuanlian* troops had been dispatched on the orders of Pingnan County Magistrate Ni Tao. Hong's first purpose was to raise morale; his second was to demonstrate to the entire realm that heaven's retribution was being visited upon the enemies of the Society of God Worshippers. Thereafter, when the Society began its military activities, this served as an effective object lesson: it was not absolutely necessary to be an ally of the Society of God Worshippers, but never oppose it!

The villages of Hualiang and Luojian provided the authorities with *tuanlian* forces at Penghua Mountain.

"This is heaven's retribution!"

"Know the wrath of the Heavenly Father!"

"The Heavenly Elder Brother has ordered us to raze these villages!"

"Now, have you felt His vengeance?"

Hong Xiuquan and Hu Yihuang led the Huazhou armies in their attacks on Hualiang and Luojian. At the sight of sudden attacks by the troops of the Society of God Worshippers with their gongs ringing loudly, the residents of Hualiang village ran off to the nearby mountains without a fight.

"Burn the home of Chen Jiahuai to the ground!" ordered Hu Yihuang.

Chen Jiahuai was the leader of the Hualiang *tuanlian*. He had no official position whatsoever, but was merely a local person of influence comparable to a fire chief. Until this point, Hu Yihuang had been on rather good terms with Chen, as someone whom he recognized from a neighboring village. To himself, Hu was actually relieved that Chen had managed to make his escape.

Once Hualiang had come under attack, it was clear that Luojian village was next. This afforded the innocent residents an opportunity to gather together their belongings and flee. The forces of the Society of God Worshippers could then enter the uninhabited village of Luojian and destroy all the homes of the local gentrymen. There was indeed not a single human visage to be seen when they entered the village, as all the residents had apparently fled.

The Luojian *tuanlian* commander was Tan Zhancheng. When the army of the Society of God Worshippers came storming in to burn down his home, Tan was standing with five young men in the courtyard. They had spears in their hands.

"Bandits! To rebel against the dynasty is an outrageous act of treason! You shall be punished by heaven!" So saying, Tan thrust his spear forward and came running with his head bent as if in prayer. The members of the Society of God Worshippers were caught thoroughly unprepared for a fight and scurried away to avoid Tan's thrust. However, Tan had not taken aim at anyone, as if prepared to fight to the death before his own home.

Quickly recovering from their initial confusion, the soldiers of the Society of God Worshippers surrounded the six men. If they had been ragged, undisciplined government troops, even numbering in the hundreds, they would probably have fled the desperate resistance of these six men, but these were men imbued with the ideals of the Society of God Worshippers. Even if beaten temporarily, they were sure to regroup rapidly. The struggle ensued, and Tan and his five young followers were all slain.

"What a bunch of idiots! We'll never drink together again, eh?" Hu Yihuang said softly, stooping over next to the corpse. He and Tan Zhancheng had been drinking buddies, and when he heard about what was going on he raced over to the scene of action.

Having completed their retaliation at Penghua Mountain, the Huazhou Army of the Society of God Worshippers withdrew to Jintian village. Hong Xiuquan was feeling somewhat uneasy having left his base area in the hands of Yang Xiuqing for such a long period of time. En route they came upon Lian Liwen along the banks of the Penghua River. He was wearing a bamboo hat. Although the season when fierce sunshine would necessitate such a broad-brimmed hat was past, the atmosphere was such in this region that men with queues had to hide them.

"You've finally returned," said Hong as he lowered a bundle from his shoulders. This had been Hong's first experience at leading his troops into actual battle.

"I'm relieved it's still so early, because there's so much work waiting to be done," said Liwen.

"The leaders of the Heaven and Earth Society are coming, aren't they?" Hong knew this in advance. Liwen mumbled:

"You already knew this, but there is something you may not have expected."

"What's that? What didn't I expect?"

"Miss Xuanjiao's wedding."

"Really?" Hong Xiuquan was understandably astonished, and indeed it was something he had not in the least expected. After momentarily losing his train of thought, he cleared his mind and asked:

"To whom?"

"Xiao Chaogui," responded Liwen.

Hong turned around, leaving only his back to Liwen's view, his way of not allowing Liwen to see the expression on his face. In his mind, he was calculating the power relations within the Society of God Worshippers. He should quickly have reckoned that the balance was now tipped in his favor. Eventually, he turned back toward Liwen and said, shaking his head:

"I'm surprised . . . stunned actually." His eyes, opened wide and thus giving him the expression of astonishment, were smiling.

8

Hoist
the Flag!

—1—

The Han River flowed to the east of the city of Shantou (Swatow). In bygone times it was known by a bizarre name meaning "foul stream." Administratively, it belonged to Guangdong province, but people generally thought of it as the frontier between Fujian and Guangdong. Travelers approaching the Guangji Bridge spanning it had a sense that, finally, they had made progress on their journey, and their mood would change.

Just before crossing the bridge, Lin Zexu said to his son Lin Ruzhou:

"I wonder if I'll cross this bridge on my way back."

"What?" Ruzhou thought it an ill omen for the day. He worried that his father's health was rapidly declining. Lin Zexu knew better than anyone the weak state of his own physical condition. To Ruzhou, it sounded as though his father was not sure he would live to make the return crossing over this bridge.

"If we can get to Guilin, then perhaps we can take the Xiang River by way of Changsha," said Lin Zexu.

He had received orders that he was to quell the uprising in Guangxi. If he chased the bandits to the north from the south, he would have to go from Guilin to Hunan province. Continuing this scenario, he could then go from Changsha, capital of Hunan, to Wuhan, and return along the Yangzi River. No, better yet, when he achieved victory, he would have to head for the capital to make his report, and then he would take the Yangzi route home.

"Oh, of course, I see," said Ruzhou, relieved.

"Either way, I certainly shan't be crossing this bridge on my return." Lin Zexu shut his eyes tightly, as if to stifle the pain. Since they had left home, Lin had had a touch of diarrhea, and Ruzhou knew of it.

"Does your stomach hurt?" asked Ruzhou.

"Oh, from time to time it rumbles, but the pain's nothing to speak of." Lin tried to smile, but the look of pain failed to disappear.

He got down from the sedan chair before crossing the Guangji Bridge and paid his respects at the temple next to it. The Han River often overflowed its banks, and the bridge had sustained major damage eight years earlier at the time of a serious flood. So as to calm the deities of the waves, the temple here, dedicated to the eighteen Luohan, or personal disciples of the Buddha, and to the twenty-four deities who buttressed bridges, had originally been built during the reign of the Xuande Emperor (r. 1426–35) of the Ming dynasty. Although destroyed by fire in 1663, it was immediately rebuilt the next year.

> "Water beside the Guangji Bridge,
> "Flowing far, far into the distance and returning still . . ."

Lin softly chanted these words after lifting an incense stick. A scholar senior to Lin had once presented him with a poetry collection that included poems about the Guangji Bridge, written in a style of five Chinese characters to a line. He began to chant, but only these first two lines came to mind. It was a poem he had liked, but try as he might, he could not remember the lines that followed. Lin took his loss of memory as a sign of the rigidity of the aging human mind.

He was on his way now to Guangxi, site of a rebellion, with a great task to perform, and he wondered if he was really up to it in his present physical state. The thought made him uneasy. He knew he was not well physically, but to himself he prayed for a return to good health. The apprehension nonetheless remained, for what worried him was not simply the present bout of diarrhea.

"Shall we take a rest at Chaozhou? Father, I think it would be best for you to convalesce there for two or three days," said Ruzhou.

"No, I'm in a big hurry. This is no ordinary situation. We haven't even time for a minute's delay," answered Lin.

He leaned over the railing of the bridge and stared momentarily at the flow of the Han River. Its waters were calm, and the sky had been clear for some time.

"Let's cross the bridge," said Lin, returning to the sedan chair. His steps were unsteady, and he staggered a bit before bending down to get inside.

Ruzhou noticed how sluggishly his father moved, how heavy his body seemed.

Lin had actually crossed this bridge once before, two years earlier, just after it had been repaired and was effectively new. It was made of stone and had pontoon portions where boats were lined up for crossings. When they reached the west bank, Lin stopped the sedan chair and once again got out.

"I want to see Fujian soil again," he said by way of explanation.

It seemed only natural to feel some sort of sentimentality whenever one left the land connected to one's birthplace, but Lin was not a man who by nature would have allowed his sentimentality to come to the surface. Ruzhou noticed how out of character it was for his father.

His hands on the railing, Lin said: "In olden days, men took it for granted that the South was an area of miasma. They even believed poisonous fish lived in this river, and hence dubbed it 'foul stream.' Until Lord Han came here, this river had no choice but to endure such an unpleasant name."

This day found Lin Zexu loquacious. Ruzhou, concerned as he was for his father's health, sought to avoid as much as he could being his father's conversational partner. Despite this, Lin continued to chat at length. Even without a partner to make perfunctory responses, he continued to speak on his own, as if there were a danger of some sort in keeping silent.

The famous poet of the Tang dynasty, Han Yu (768–824), whom Lin had just mentioned, once offered up to his emperor an essay—entitled "On a Bone of the Buddha"—encouraging the repression of the Buddhist religion. Because of it, he was demoted to the post of Chaozhou prefect in the year 819. Tradition held that when he went to take up his new position in Chaozhou, Han Yu exterminated the poisonous fish infesting the waters of the "foul stream," and thereafter the name of the river was changed to carry his surname: the Han River.

This was a famous legend, certainly known to Lin Ruzhou, who lived in neighboring Fujian. Lin Zexu made it a practice not to speak about what his partner in conversation clearly already knew. That too made his present behavior all the more out of the ordinary.

Ruzhou felt a sense of gloomy foreboding. It was right on the mark. Having spent just a single night in Chaozhou (present-day Chao'an), Lin Zexu arrived in Puning and immediately collapsed. Until just prior to his collapse, he had supported himself entirely by force of will, but when he could no longer do so, he abruptly lost consciousness.

Lin breathed his last on November 22, 1850 in a lodging in Puning. He was sixty-six years of age. On his deathbed, he called out the words: "South of the star." Nobody knew what this meant. When his casket returned eastward, several thousand Chaozhou residents came out in mourning garb to send him off. Ruzhou stopped the hearse for a long time, smack in the middle of the Guangji Bridge.

"Well, Father. You did, after all, return across this bridge," said Ruzhou quietly to the casket.

—2—

"When Hong Xiuquan and his men learned that Lin Zexu was on his way to suppress them, they trembled with fear before his famous name and sought to split up into small groups and flee, their courage in shambles. News of his death, though, revived their spirits, and their forces again grew stronger."

That was the story circulating in the outside world at the time. Several scholars of the day wrote essays to that effect. Such stories were, of course, aimed at discrediting the rebels.

Regardless of whether Imperial Commissioner Lin Zexu lived or died, the Society of God Worshippers had reached a point from which there was no return. Far from breaking up into small groups and dissolving, one leader after another of Heaven and Earth Society sects was applying for admission into the Society of God Worshippers. Military training at the Jintian encampment was growing more feverish, and military preparations were also well under way. Hong Xiuquan continued to command all of the military forces of the Society of God Worshippers. Beneath him were placed five army corps: the central army, the front army, the rear army, the left army, and the right army. Each army was led by a commander, and under his control were placed six levels of official positions. Young and old, male and female, everyone was incorporated into this structure, with no distinctions between military and civil posts. However, the male and female barracks remained strictly segregated.

Feng Yunshan put this organizational scheme into effect. Although spiritually grounded in Hong Xiuquan's philosophical ideas, actual organizational matters fell to Feng.

"Isn't this a bit severe?" asked Liwen with a dubious look when Feng first showed him the draft of documents on discipline.

Many had joined the Society of God Worshippers as entire family units, and then husbands and wives were segregated into their respective barracks. They saw each other once each week at Sunday prayers. And, they literally "saw" each other only.

"We're doing what has never been done since the dawn of history. Even if it's a bit on the strict side, it's not overly strict," responded Feng tranquilly. He had a gentle face that belied the content of his words. Should husbands and wives who lived separately secretly rendezvous, they were to be executed without mercy.

"What about basic human feelings?" said Liwen, thinking that the Society of God Worshippers had to be flexible if it was to succeed in its movement to transform the world.

"Are human feelings absolute?"

"Well, at least, human beings do always try to circumvent disciplinary restrictions."

"I'm anticipating that. If we forbid something on pain of execution, there will surely be violators."

"So, why have you constructed such an unnatural discipline?"

"A great enterprise requires the unnatural."

"I understand, but—"

"This strict discipline may, in actual fact, be loosened up. Say . . . in the area of operations. But, in extraordinary times, we have to get back to our roots. Thus, initially, discipline will be strictly enforced. And, it may not be continued as such for very long, until the Manchu devils are overthrown. Everyone will be made aware of this in advance. If a husband and wife wish to live happily under the same roof, then they will surely be prepared at the earliest possible date to destroy the demons," said Feng, smiling as usual.

To be sure, what the Society of God Worshippers was attempting to do was an unprecedented, great enterprise—to bring down the Manchu dynasty and create a kingdom on earth devoted to the praise of the Heavenly Father. To carry out this task, there was no room whatsoever for self-indulgence. It was in this sense that a rigid discipline was necessary. As Liwen walked from Feng's to Yang's residence, he sensed a change in the atmosphere.

"Eight leaders, . . . all big shots," said Yang suddenly as soon as his eyes caught Liwen's. This was Yang's way of saying that these were the eight leaders of the Heaven and Earth Society who, in concert with the Society of God Worshippers, had come to keep contacts alive for the fight with government forces.

Liwen was reminded of his conversations with Feng over the issue of strict disciplinary rules, and he wondered if these bigshots from the Heaven and Earth Society were prepared to tolerate such restricted behavior. Many members of secret societies had extricated themselves from "honest" society precisely because they hated its strictures. Were they likely now to submit to the far more constricting discipline of the Society of God Worshippers? As much as he considered this problem, only pessimistic responses came to Liwen.

"They have no religious belief," said Liwen.

"If they're willing to act in concert with us, then sooner or later they'll gain religious belief. You'll see how they become believers." Yang spoke with extraordinary self-confidence. His confidence was buttressed by his manifold accomplishments gained through manipulating members of the Society of God Worshippers gathered at Jintian village: his technique of the Heavenly Father's Descent to Earth, his self-imposed state of dementia, and his own "miraculous recovery" from it.

Sure, thought Liwen, he'd been able to manipulate good men and women who had already devoted themselves to religious life, but would he be able to sway secret society adherents who were by no means so virtuous.

"Have they handed everything they owned over to the Sacred Treasury?" asked Liwen.

New initiates into the Society of God Worshippers were required to relinquish all of their wealth and property to the Sacred Treasury. Hence, all the necessities of life were supplied by the Society of God Worshippers. Feng Yunshan had initially conceived this plan from a notion of Christian communal living. Would they now be able to compel the same behavior on the Heaven and Earth Society members who had swung over to their cause? Li Xinmei's attempt to implement such a policy with her rebel band had proven to be a spectacular failure.

"They can come empty-handed," said Yang nonchalantly.

If they did join the Society of God Worshippers empty-handed, after secreting their plundered booty somewhere in advance, then they would be receiving food and shelter without having had to give a thing to the Sacred Treasury. Not a promising beginning at all, but Yang seemed to have dispensed with the problem of the Sacred Treasury quite simply. The disciplinary regulation read: "Anyone who possesses private property will be executed without mercy." Showing up empty-handed may just have been an expediency. If their consciousness did not undergo a change, though, there would soon be a proliferation of cases entangled in these disciplinary rules.

"It will surely take time to inculcate so rigid a discipline on these guys," said Liwen, offering his own opinion.

"Time? We haven't got any just now, do we? The officials have clearly become our enemies. They're sending their soldiers to wipe us out. Countless numbers of troops. We've got to amass just as many soldiers too, and soon we'll have enough. There's no time for dawdling. We're massing enough men to fight. Nothing's more important right now. What do you think? I've worked very hard to open contacts, and finally things are beginning to take shape."

So saying, Yang unhesitatingly read off the names of the eight leaders. Although illiterate, his memory was phenomenal. He might have continued with a list of twenty or even thirty names.

—3—

1. Luo Dagang, of the skiff bandits
2. Zhang Zhao, "Big-Headed Ram"
3. Tian Fang, "Big Carp"
4. Hou Zhi, "Curly-Mouth Dog"
5. Guan Ju, "Big Double Shells"
6. Wang Yong, "Bean Skin"
7. Li Donggou, from Guangdong province
8. Dan Yande, also from Guangdong.

Liwen listened as Yang Xiuqing ran off the list of the eight leaders, although it was not an overly inspiring group. To the contrary, he thought they would probably bring with them an assortment of knotty problems to the Society of God Worshippers, for since the death of Wang Juzhi, the various cliques within the Heaven and Earth Society had rapidly fallen into decay.

Liwen walked over by the encampment. At the women's barracks, military training was under way in a hilly area. At the men's barracks on level ground nearby, they were repeating the lesson on the deployment of units at the sergeants' level. The smallest fighting unit of the Society of God Worshippers was a group of five in which one squad commander led four "holy soldiers." Five of these squads—twenty-five troops in all—and were led by a sergeant.

The sound of horses' hoofs could be heard.

"Hey, young master!" yelled a loud voice drowning out the horses. A horse came right up to Liwen's side and stopped, and a young man dismounted with a swing. He seemed much smaller after reaching the ground, shorter than the far from grand horse he had just been riding.

"Tan Qi, what's the hurry?" said Liwen, addressing him. The young man, Tan Qi, was wearing a red bandanna around his head. He was one of Hong Xiuquan's bodyguards. Although small in stature, he had unusual muscular strength and extraordinary agility. Like his friend Liwen, he was a frank man by nature.

"Always on the go," said Tan Qi, smiling. He had such a long, thin face that he had been given the nickname "Horseface." He was also the finest horseman, bar none, in the Society of God Worshippers. No one knew his age, and Tan would reveal it to no one. He was a native of Hua county, Guangdong, as was Hong Xiuquan.

"So, you're riding horses right out in the open now."

"That's something to be thankful for. Ha, ha, thanks to you, my work is much easier to do."

Now that the Society of God Worshippers was openly in rebellion, there was no longer any need to hide that fact. While they had sought to hide their true intentions from the authorities, they had had to abstain from galloping around on horses. Now that the regions of Penghua Mountain and Thistle Mountain fell within the sphere of influence of the Society of God Worshippers, all semblance of the officialdom had vanished.

"It's dangerous to let yourself go too much and wander far away," said Liwen, smiling. He always enjoyed chatting with Tan Qi.

"What do you mean? It's safe to go as far as the Dahuang River area." The upper part of the Xun River—that portion running from the Pingnan county seat to the Guiping county seat—was called the Dahuang River.

"You've been to the Dahuang River?"

"Yes, I have, on some liaison work," Tan blurted out. He well knew what to tell Liwen. It seemed that several Heaven and Earth Society leaders had gathered at the Dahuang River to request entrance into the Society of God Worshippers. The group, which included Luo Dagang, Zhang Zhao, and Tian Fang, was among those river pirates often dubbed "skiff bandits," and as long as they remained on water, the authorities could do nothing to stop them.

"Are the leaders coming to Jintian?" asked Liwen.

"Immediately, with underlings carrying presents. And then, after that, we go over there."

"Did you go along with that plan of action?"

"Uh-huh . . . and it went well. In any case, I've got to make my report."

Tan Qi nimbly remounted his steed and headed toward the Sanjie Temple, the hoofbeats leaving a pleasant sound in his wake. Hong Xiuquan had turned Sanjie Temple into his personal headquarters.

The secret societies that these eight leaders controlled had ten thousand members at the very least. Such numbers were eagerly sought, for the confrontation with the government's armies that was awaiting the Society of God Worshippers was no longer avoidable. However, it might also become the toxin that would bring on the Society's decay. Liwen had often related his personal view to Hong Xiuquan, that in cooperating with the Heaven and Earth Society, they had to choose from their counterparts carefully.

"I know, I know. When they join the Society of God Worshippers, we shall make them vow to abide by our principles," said Hong quite candidly.

A verbal promise was simple, thought Liwen, but wouldn't it be better to investigate and select first those who would stand by what they promised? The Society of God Worshippers lacked sufficient time to do this. Eventually, the eight leaders sent a delegation of sixteen men to Jintian village, a purely formal gesture. In response, the Society of God Worshippers sent a like number to the Dahuang River, although the latter sixteen had more than ceremonial tasks to carry out.

As Hong Xiuquan had been saying, those who joined the Society of God Worshippers had to abide by its practices. The sixteen representatives of the Society of God Worshippers sent to meet the eight leaders of the Heaven and Earth Society were responsible for explaining those practices to them.

Among those dispatched to the Dahuang River was one man by the name of Bo Yafu. He was the most eloquent speaker in the delegation from the Society of God Worshippers. Initially, all sixteen members were at the same status level, but Bo achieved a kind of leader status when it came to explaining his group's principles.

"You guys are incredibly strict," said Big Carp after listening to the explanation.

"Aren't you strict as well? You stick a dagger at people when they join the Heaven and Earth Society. That's really frightening," said Bo.

New entrants into the Heaven and Earth Society had a dagger at their throats at the time they swore their vows. It was this initiation ceremony to which Bo was referring.

"Yeah, I guess that is rather severe."

"Hasn't anyone ever had their throat slit when they're entering your organization?" Bo looked around in sequence at the faces of the leaders to whom he was speaking, Big Carp and Big-Headed Ram.

The initiation ceremony into the Heaven and Earth Society was truly a frightening experience, and the dagger placed at the neck lent a gruesomeness to it. But, it was merely a ceremony, for the dagger never drew blood, and new entrants knew this.

"Nobody's ever gotten killed."

"It's the same thing with us."

"Yeah, but no alcohol and no opium. That's awfully rigid. You smoke opium, and it's all over, right?" said Big Carp as he drew his index finger across his throat in the manner of an execution.

"Well, that's a rule. But, I drink a little wine every now and then, and I do this too," said Bo, holding the thumb and pinky of his left hand erect and the other fingers bent, a gesture indicating opium-smoking.

"Really? So you drink . . ."

"As much as I please. I've been doing it for some time, and as you can see, my neck is still firmly attached," said Bo, bending his head forward in jest. Big Carp and his associates laughed.

—4—

The leaders of the Heaven and Earth Society wanted to join forces with the Society of God Worshippers because the Qing government was becoming more serious about bandit suppression. The news that Lin Zexu had been appointed imperial commissioner and was being sent to Guangxi had no influence at all on the Society of God Worshippers, but it had a major impact on the Heaven and Earth Society groups. Lin had attained a kind of god-like status in Guangdong and Guangxi. That Lin Zexu was on his way in person indicated in no uncertain terms that the government was really getting down to business. The army of suppression would probably be reinforced, and the Heaven and Earth Society groups feared that one by one they would be individually crushed. The very fact that eight of the leaders of these groups, who ordinarily dealt with each other only reservedly, had assembled at the Dahuang River indicated the attenuation of their sense of crisis.

On occasion, they had cooperated in the past. When engaged in a particular operation, if one group thought its numbers too low, it might rely on hired helpers. Two or three groups had previously come together, and the record until then for concerted group action was five. The assemblage of eight of these groups now was, to say the least, an extraordinary event. For their part, they were still insecure that there were only eight of them.

The government was in a position to mobilize an immense fighting force of several tens of thousands—perhaps as many as one hundred thousand—troops. Guangxi Provincial Military Commander Min Zhengfeng had been dismissed, and Hunan Provincial Military Commander Xiang Rong was on his way to Guangxi—yet another indication that the government was pouring all of its energies into crushing the rebel forces in Guangxi.

"The Society of God Worshippers seems to be training intensively."

"But they're not affiliated with the Heaven and Earth Society."

"You can't talk like that now!"

"But they're different from us."

"It's okay if they're a little different, isn't it? Soon they'll be just like us."

"But they outnumber us. They may be planning to turn us into them!"

"We can pretend we're becoming like them, and all the time work on changing them."

"That's it! Let's fight it out. We're more experienced than they are. Anyway, our voice will get stronger in time."

The eight leaders parried arguments of this sort and then made application for entrance into the Society of God Worshippers. Their aim was to act with extreme humility at first and then try to seize control over the organization. The Society was probably aware of their new initiates' intentions and set to work from the very start with a strategy aimed at transforming them.

Each with roughly half of their followers in tow, the eight rebel leaders marched into Jintian village. There was a bit of trouble among them en route.

"Look here, Dagang, you're the closest of us to the Society of God Worshippers. Things will surely work out fine for you," said Big-Headed Ram first.

"What about me resembles them?" asked Luo Dagang in response.

"When you and I did some business together earlier, weren't you really angry when we killed that old lady?"

"Oh, not that. It makes me sick to my stomach just thinking about it."

When Luo and Zhang had once joined forces to attack the town of Yanjiang in the eastern part of Guangxi, an old lady in a home being plundered began screaming loudly at them, all the time pointing a finger directly at Zhang:

"You bastards! Heaven's wrath will catch up with you soon enough and hand you your heads severed at the neck! Your time will come soon."

"What!" screamed Zhang back at her. "To hell with you, you old bag!" And so saying he softly raised the sword in his hand and killed her with a blow through the shoulder blades.

Luo Dagang was indignant. He clung to a principle of not committing murder even in the course of pillaging raids. "If you want to do business with me, then do it my way!"

"What's that? You asked me to help you."

"It's just like you. I never want to see your huge head of a ram again!"

This exchange had caused a rupture between the two men. After dividing the spoils of their raid, Zhang Zhao hastily withdrew with his men. This incident had taken place one year earlier, and during that interval the two men had not seen one another, but they had now agreed to come to a reconciliation because of the six other leaders present at the Dahuang River. Also, because self-defense against the government's forces was increasingly becoming a critical problem, the two men agreed to come and not mention the affair of the previous year. In spite of this, Big-Headed Ram, a man of no discretion whatsoever, had broached the subject en route to Jintian. Big Carp (Tian Fang) stepped in at this point and calmed the two of them down, and somehow or other they made their way to Jintian.

When the eight leaders and their followers arrived at Jintian village, they were stunned by the scene confronting them—an execution. A simple scaffold for a hanging had been constructed at the encampment, and for some reason the rope dangling from it was yellow in color. The man to be executed was Bo Yafu, someone well-known to the eight Heaven and Earth Society leaders. Xiao Chaogui explained the details concerning the execution to them: "We gave him many opportunities to reconsider his ways. He did not, however, attempt to put a stop to his evil behavior. There are limits to our patience too. He is a man full of poison. The brethren of the Society of God Worshippers are all full of sin, but they are capable of knowing their sins and struggling to neutralize the poison in their bodies. Whether or not it is neutralized, the effort to do so is worthy of our esteem. This is the basis of the teachings of the Society of God Worshippers. Those who are unable to put forth the effort are those who cannot accept the teachings of the Society. They can no longer be considered our brethren. Hence, we must consider means of preventing the spread of the poison. What you witness now is the final means we take." His tone was one of bitterness.

As Yang Xiuqing had transmitted the words of God during the Heavenly Father's Descent to Earth, so too had Xiao Chaogui played the role of transmitting the words of Jesus Christ during the Heavenly Elder Brother's Descent to Earth. Xiao was not as accomplished a performer as Yang, but he nonetheless moved people through his powers of speech.

"What evil behavior?" asked Luo Dagang.

"He drank alcohol, smoked opium, and coveted personal gain," replied Xiao promptly, as though he had been waiting for precisely this question.

"What personal gain?"

"Recently, sixteen men went to meet you gentlemen at Dahuang River. You presented them with many gifts. The Society of God Worshippers requires that all property be placed in the Sacred Treasury. Private property is not allowed. The sixteen men explained this to you at the Dahuang River. Bo Yafu was among them. After returning, fifteen of them delivered the gifts they had received from you into the Sacred Treasury. Only one, Bo Yafu, retained his gifts as his personal possessions. We can no longer endure the poison of Bo Yafu, and he is incapable of neutralizing the poison within himself. On behalf of the brethren of the Society of God Worshippers, we must execute him. It's a terrible shame."

"It sure is," said Luo Dagang, as if moaning.

Bo was brought out blindfolded, his hands tied behind his back. He was being supported on either side so that he could walk, for it appeared as though all strength had left his body. The hanging was carried out in silence, in a thoroughly business-like manner. Bo no longer had sufficient energy to raise his voice. It was as if a doll were swinging from the scaffold.

—5—

Needless to say, the execution of Bo Yafu was a tremendous shock to the leaders of the Heaven and Earth Society. It served as an object lesson that the severe discipline of the Society of God Worshippers was not there for form's sake alone, like the initiation ceremony of the Heaven and Earth Society. One of the eight leaders was moved by the experience, but the other seven were terrified.

"We can't work with bastards like these!" said Big-Headed Ram, his mouth quivering in a highly atypical manner.

The seven leaders, himself included, and their underlings departed Jintian village. The man who had been moved was Luo Dagang.

"I can see that your claim to save mankind is not empty talk. I shall enter the Society of God Worshippers," he said, his mouth trembling.

A gloomy look spread across Yang Xiuqing's face. After all his efforts to lay down foundations and attract allies to their cause, he had summoned these men to Jintian village only to see them part company so soon. He had not opposed the execution of Bo Yafu itself. Bo had been a problem since childhood, and his execution had been postponed only because of his ability with words. What Yang opposed was letting the men of the Heaven and Earth Society see Bo's execution.

"The poison must first be expunged"—this was Hong Xiuquan's point of view, and it had won the day. Hong had become unusually obstinate in holding to this basic principle. He really was not a practical, but a theoretical, man after all.

"Well, it just means we're going to have to go back out and rally more people to our cause," said Yang, standing alone.

Li Xinmei happened to be standing near him and heard this offhand remark.

"Fourth Elder Brother, don't be so downhearted. I'm working on getting Su Sanniang and Qiu Ersao to join us, and it's going very well. Just leave it to me," she said.

"Is that so? The women leaders are probably better than the men," Yang grumbled.

Many groups in Guangdong and Guangxi were led by women. Li Xinmei had been a rebel leader, and Su Sanniang and Qiu Ersao were leaders of considerable influence.

Because emotions are enough for women, thought Yang.

With the exception of Luo Dagang, the male rebel leaders could only get by on monetary profit. When they learned that they could hold no property privately, the leaders of the Heaven and Earth Society could not abide this practice and withdrew from Jintian.

"I'm going soon." Li Xinmei seemed incapable of sitting still. In order to convince these influential women leaders, she left Jintian village in pursuit of the seven leaders of Heaven and Earth Society groupings.

"Not only are our allies declining, but these guys will now join our enemies," said Yang.

"Join our enemies?" asked Liwen.

"To protect themselves from attack by forces of the government, we tried to get them to align with us. But it failed. So, now what do they do? How do they protect themselves?" Yang had returned a question rather than given Liwen an answer.

"Well, I guess they'll flee?" said Liwen dubiously.

"They can't run away, because the government troops will soon come flooding into Guangxi. If they can't escape, then they'll have no alternative but to surrender. They'll just say: 'Spare our lives, please, and we'll help you crush the Society of God Worshippers.' And before long we'll have to fight these same guys," said Yang, biting his lips.

"It'll be good if Xinmei returns with some people," said Liwen.

"It would. . . . But, you can't expect anything, because the disappointment is too great when your hopes and expectations are dashed. Ha, ha," Yang laughed. It was not a fabricated laugh. Being a practical man, Yang was undoubtedly considering many different sorts of situations and hammering out countermeasures in his head. His laugh was by no means one of despair.

Tan Qi came riding up on horseback just as Xinmei was leaving. He was, of course, heading for Hong Xiuquan at the Sanjie Temple, but upon seeing that Yang Xiuqing was nearby at the encampment, he slowed up and called out, "The imperial commissioner died in Chaozhou!"

"Imperial commissioner? You mean Lin Zexu?" asked Liwen, but the question failed to reach Tan Qi on horseback, as he galloped off.

The question really required no answer. The only man appointed imperial commissioner and sent to Guangxi was Lin Zexu. He would have had to have passed through Chaozhou en route to Guangxi from his native Houguan in Fujian province.

"Lord Lin." Liwen looked up at the sky. He had revered Lin, a close friend of his father's, and had heard that Lin was being sent to crush the "bandits" in Guangxi. Liwen found himself in a complicated frame of mind because he had placed himself within the Society of God Worshippers, which was among these "bandits." Perhaps, he had thought, he could stand between the Society of God Worshippers and Lin Zexu and perform a certain important function from that position, but with Lin's death that hope now dissolved.

Upon receiving the news of Lin Zexu's death, the imperial court in Beijing conferred on him the posthumous title of "Literary Patriot." At the same time, the court appointed Li Xingyuan, former governor-general of Jiangsu, Jiangsi, and Anhui, to replace Lin. Guangxi Governor Zheng Zuchen, who had allowed the bandits to run rampant, was dismissed together with Guangxi Provincial Military Commander Min Zhengfeng, and Zhou Tianjue (1772–1853), former director-general of grain transport, took over as the governor of Guangxi.

Two thousand reinforcements from Hunan and three thousand more troops from Guizhou had already entered Guangxi province. Soon after hearing of

Lin's death, the court received a report that former Yunnan Provincial Military Commander Zhang Bilu, at the head of the three thousand Guizhou troops, had died from illness at Xunzhou, Guangxi.

"Did he really die from illness?" asked the young Xianfeng Emperor to his grand councilors. Leading Grand Councilor Mu-zhang-a was not in attendance. The emperor had dismissed him. Mu-zhang-a's staunch ally, Grand Secretary Qi-ying, had also been relieved of his post. The highly motivated new emperor was attempting to create his own system.

"So it has been reported," responded Sai-shang-a, the Mongol grand councilor.

"You believe all those reports? Haven't most of the reports been completely unfounded until now? Xunzhou has been the scene of incessant fighting," said the emperor.

Perhaps Zhang Bilu had actually not died on the battlefield. If that were true, then a defeat was being covered up. If it had been a victory, a commander's death on the battlefield would surely have been reported as a glorious deed. Death from illness always seemed to be a lie covering a military defeat.

The grand councilors could not respond to him. For the time being, command of Zhang's Guizhou Army, it was decided, would be entrusted to Zhou Fengqi, the regional commander of Zhenyuan.

—6—

Zhou Fengqi proceeded with his forces to Guiping county. His advance troops arrived in Cai village, close to Jintian, but they were unable to achieve their objective. From the state's perspective, bandits, be they of the Society of God Worshippers or the Heaven and Earth Society, were still just bandits. The spies the army loosed among them reported on the two meetings between the leaders of the Heaven and Earth Society and representatives of the Society of God Worshippers.

The judgment of the commanders of the government forces was that the two groups had aligned, and the enemy was now everywhere in this area.

From the viewpoint of the Society of God Worshippers, the occupation of Cai village by Qing forces reflected the government's aim of ultimately seizing Jintian. As Yang Xiuqing had anticipated, the leaders of the Heaven and Earth Society at the Dahuang River, under pressure from the government's army, would surrender and probably take up arms against the Society of God Worshippers in exchange for a pardon. Although the Society was prepared for this eventuality, the mood in Jintian village became considerably gloomier.

With the approach of the Qing Army, the Heaven and Earth Society leaders did in fact lay their weapons down and throw their hands in their air, and the army went right ahead and proceeded to occupy Cai village. To the secret society people, it thus seemed as though the army was principally after the Society of God Worshippers, and they decided to stand back and remain observers for the time being.

Jintian village, needless to say, was in a state of general mobilization. Hakkas driven out of Gui county by local armed feuds, coal miners led by Shi Dakai, and others who had come to join the Society from Pingnan, Wuxuan, Xiangzhou, and elsewhere, massed their collective forces at the bases in Thistle Mountain and Jintian village, and swore mutual loyalty against the enemy. For those who had been driven from their homes, Jintian would be their final stand. They had nowhere else to go and were prepared to defend it to the death.

Burning with the spirit of battle, they had no regard whatsoever for their own lives. No one feared that his family might be left with no food or shelter in the eventuality of death, because the communal structure of life established through the Sacred Treasury ensured against that worry.

Prayers were held before the battles began. Hong Xiuquan led the prayers and announced that those who died in battle would be summoned by God to live in heaven.

"Destroy the devils!"

"Defend Jintian village!"

"Glory to the Society of God Worshippers!"

With these shouts, the forces of the Society of God Worshippers took up their weapons. Tears filled the eyes of their newest member, Luo Dagang. He had been planning various strategies with his followers from the Heaven and Earth Society, and with a sense of unsurpassed freshness he took took up arms as well, fully prepared to lay down his life if need be. A great battle cry rose.

Although they had troops in Xunzhou, the bulk of the government's forces came from Guizhou. They were strangers in their present locale. Although stationed in Cai village, most of their leaders did not even know in which direction Jintian village—the base of the Society of God Worshippers—was to be found, and in what areas the skiff bandits of the Heaven and Earth Society operated. Their morale was very low.

All manner of rumors were circulating among the government's forces concerning the death of the provincial military commander. The story was spreading that, because he had spoken disparagingly of the Society of God Worshippers, an assassin had ambushed him to settle the score. The troops spoke among themselves in suppressed tones: "It's frightening. Don't say anything bad about the Society of God Worshippers, even if they split open your mouth. Those guys must be crazy."

"You really think so—that they're crazy? What would you do if they overheard you?"

"Shake like a leaf!"

They were about to join battle with the Society of God Worshippers, but their fighting spirit remained low. The two armies had fought once before—on New Years Day, 1851—and that battle had ended in a major defeat for the government.

In addition to the immediate threat of the Qing Army, the Society of God Worshippers also had to take into account the secret society forces at the Dahuang River under Big-Headed Ram, Big Carp, and the others. But, they remained silent about these secret society groups and focused solely on the government's forces.

The death-defying forces of the Society of God Worshippers swept down on the government's army. The battle was entirely one-sided, as the Qing troops fled and the Society of God Worshippers followed in pursuit. The Society sustained virtually no casualties, while the government lost some three hundred men. Regional Vice-Commander Yi-ke-bu-tan, seeing that the battle was lost, lashed his horse in an effort to escape. However, his horse stumbled and fell at the bridge spanning the river at Cai village, and Yi-ke-bu-tan was thrown tumbling to the ground beneath the bridge. There soldiers of the Society of God Worshippers pursued him to administer the *coup de grâce*.

In the ranking system for military officials of the Qing dynasty, a provincial military commander was rank 1B, a regional commander was rank 2A, and a regional vice-commander was rank 2B. The comparable rankings for civil officials were held by provincial governors and their subordinates, provincial administrative commissioners. When someone at the level of a general died in battle, it spelled a crushing defeat.

The entire advance force at Cai village was annihilated. In the rear, Regional Commander Zhou Fengqi rode ahead at top speed and was able to save the remnant troops from that defeat on the following day. Zhou then sent them all back to the rear.

The Heaven and Earth Society leaders watched this fighting from the sidelines. Even after witnessing the impressive strength of the Society of God Worshippers, they assumed it was merely a temporary phenomenon. When all was said and done, the Heaven and Earth Society leaders showed no interest in returning to Jintian village. In fact, they saw the moment as an auspicious one for themselves.

"Now, it'll be easier to break the ice," said Big-Headed Ram. Although it was he who had proposed the alliance with the Society of God Worshippers, it was always better to negotiate with a counterpart who was in more difficult straits. The wholesale defeat of the Qing's forces meant that the secret society leaders at the Dahuang River were now in a good position to sell their services to the state and at a high price.

—7—

The hills near Xiniu pond where the Society of God Worshippers had hidden their weapons were known as the Xiniu Range. They effectively formed a part of the encampment. Despite being called hills, their slope was in fact very gentle. From the top one could see far into the distance, making it a highly convenient point before which the Society could mass its followers and carry out ceremonies.

The ritual of raising the banner was carried out there on the tenth day following the great victory at Cai village; the tenth day of the twelfth lunar month in the thirtieth year of the (deceased) Daoguang reign, the day corresponding to Hong Xiuquan's birthday. The leader of the Society of God Worshippers was thirty-eight on this day—January 11, 1851. Later, when the Society of God Worshippers became the Taiping Heavenly Kingdom, and created its own calendar, this day was designated, "ninth day, twelfth month, first year prior to the establishment of the Heavenly Calendar of the Taiping Heavenly Kingdom," in the same way we now use "B.C."

On the rectangular banner, in red against a yellow background, was written: "Heavenly Father, Heavenly Elder Brother, Heavenly King, Taiping Heavenly Kingdom." From beneath the earth it seemed to spring high into the sky. The banner was ritually installed in a hole previously dug for it, and when Hong Xiuquan intoned some sort of incantation, a device calmly drew in the ends of the cords fastened to the flagstaff on all sides, and accordingly the banner receded back into the ground. The success of this performance was the brainchild of Yang Xiuqing.

It was difficult to follow all of Hong Xiuquan's incantation, but everyone knew the first sentence well: "The yellow banner, wafting this way and that, has leapt over Fire Mountain."

The flag flying over the Xiniu Range was supported at the base by a rock. Dubbed the "flagpole rock," to this day it is stored at the site where it was cut. It formed the shape of a three-dimensional triangle or pyramid, a kind of large rice ball 50 centimeters high.

People fell to their knees in reverence before it in the belief that they were looking at the product of a miracle. Many bowed their foreheads all the way to the ground, though a few did keep their heads raised. Those who kept their heads up were the most devout of believers. For it was a strict teaching of the Society of God Worshippers that one was never to bow down before anything save the Heavenly Father himself.

It was at this point that the term "Taiping Heavenly Kingdom" was established as the name for their nation. This is what they were doing—establishing a nation. Nothing could have more clearly announced their intentions to overthrow the present regime. A solemn prayer ceremony followed, led by Hong Xiuquan. When the prayers concluded, Yang announced loudly:

"We shall dub the new year as the first year of the Heavenly Calendar of the Taiping Heavenly Kingdom."

Use of the Qing dynasty's current reign title during celebrations of the lunar New Year were seen as indications of submission to the throne, but the Society of God Worshippers viewed the present Qing regime as devils they aimed at overthrowing—so much so that they had now fixed a name for their own state: the "Taiping Heavenly Kingdom." Taking the next step of assigning a new reign title was natural. Their army was called the "Taiping Army," and the core of the regime, centering around Hong Xiuquan, was called the "Heavenly Dynasty." Hong assumed the title "Heavenly King," and his son Hong Tiangui came to be called the "young monarch."

Why did they not adopt the title of emperor? In China, the emperor was the most exalted person on earth, while princes and other imperial relatives were designated as "kings." It was common knowledge among the Chinese people that kings were beneath the emperor. Why then did the highest leaders of the forces that sought to overthrow the Qing emperor and become the new rulers of China only assume the name "king," one step below that of emperor?

There were reasons for this, of course. The state policy of the Taiping Heavenly Kingdom followed the Christian religion, and the object of their reverence was God alone. In the Society of God Worshippers, God was referred to as the "Heavenly Father" or "Supreme Lord." The Chinese term for "emperor" (*huangdi*) contained one element of the Chinese term for Supreme Lord (*shangdi*), and this suggested something on a par with the one, absolute God. Thus, the Taiping Heavenly Kingdom went to pains to abjure use of this element (*di*) and settled on "king" (*wang*) instead.

From the perspective of the Society of God Worshippers, the eldest son of the Supreme Lord Jehovah was Jesus Christ, and his next son was Hong Xiuquan. Christ became as a "prince" to the Lord, so the term for "prince" also had to be avoided. For this reason, Hong's son was instead called the "young monarch."

Commanders for the five Taiping armies were assigned orally by Hong Xiuquan as follows:

1. Central Army Commander   Yang Xiuqing
2. Front Army Commander   Xiao Chaogui
3. Rear Army Commander   Feng Yunshan

4. Right Army Commander   Wei Changhui
5. Left Army Commander   Shi Dakai

When these commands had been delegated, Central Army Commander Yang Xiuqing rose to the platform and said: "I shall now declare the five rules of military discipline. These constitute the essence of our army. Because they are extremely simple, see that each and every one of them are engraved on your minds."

With this introduction, Yang took a deep breath and raised his voice to say: "Rule Number One: Obey the regulations!" The specific term used for "regulations" was well-known within the Society of God Worshippers. It combined the idea of both a religious prescription and an extrareligious order of the Society. This rule then stressed the unity of religion with politics and the military.

"Rule Number Two: Men and women are to be kept separate!" Many people had joined the Society of God Worshippers—it would now be best to call it the Taiping Army—as family units and had then been separated into men's and women's dormitories or barracks. This principle was adhered to even when they set out on military expeditions.

"Rule Number Three: Never commit a transgression!" The Taiping Army was qualitatively different from the debased Qing military forces. They were not a ragtag band of thieves. During military campaigns, they were not allowed to take a single item from the resident population. Confiscation, rape, and the like were promptly punished by execution.

"Rule Number Four: Be public-minded, delicate, and obey the promises made by each leader!" "Public-mindedness" here meant the Society of God Worshippers' principle of no personal wealth. "Delicate" came from a Guangxi regional expression that actually carried the meaning of "conciliatory." "Promises" referred here to specific orders to abide by the "regulations" of Rule Number One. It pointed to the commands that lower-level military officers were to carry out on the scene.

"Rule Number Five: Be cooperative, and when on the verge of battle, do not withdraw!" From here the fight to capture the realm ensued. Cowardice and irresolution were not permitted.

The transformation of the reign title and Yang's proclamation of the five rules of military discipline made an impression on each and every member of the Taiping Army.

The order of the sons of the Supreme Lord Jehovah had, of course, Christ as the eldest brother, with Hong as the next brother. The third and fourth brothers were, respectively, Feng Yunshan and Yang Xiuqing. This ranking was known to every member of the Society of God Worshippers. The first of the five armies beneath the Heavenly King was the central army and should naturally have been assigned to Feng Yunshan, but Yang was given this position. Changes were under way in the relationship between position and power.

Much of Yang's speech at the banner-raising ceremony was to make it crystal clear to the masses of the Society of God Worshippers that he was the number one advisor to Hong Xiuquan.

"We must advance our army now as rapidly as possible," continued Yang.

The government's troops under Zhou Fengqi retreated after their major defeat. Examining the situation some ten days later, they apparently had adopted a strategy of trying to cut the Taipings' supply lines. If the Taiping forces remained motionless, they would effectively starve themselves to death. Thus, Yang called for a quick military advance. But where should they head?

"We're heading for Jiangkou and shall depart in two days' time. All posts make necessary preparations," said Yang.

9

Advances
and
Retreats

Jiangkou faced directly onto the wide Dahuang River. There was a small settlement there with a population of roughly ten thousand. On their way to Guiping, the residents of Jintian village had to cross the Dahuang River, and so they stopped to buy provisions in Jiangkou. They knew this area better than they did Guiping

The surrounding land was very rich, and merchants from nearby often assembled at the wharf. The prosperity and wealth of Jiangkou was said to far surpass Xunzhou, Guiping, and even Pingnan. For a rural town, it had quite a row of impressive merchant houses, and by the banks of the river was an immense storehouse of grain.

Next door to it stood the warehouse of a pawnshop in which all manner of goods were stored. All of these possessions belonged to Wang Zuoxin. Members of the Society of God Worshippers instinctively associated the name Jiangkou with that of Wang, the sworn enemy of the Society. Both the arrest of Feng Yunshan and the death in prison of Lu Liu were Wang's doing. This local gentryman continually and obstinately complained to the county authorities about the Society of God Worshippers. For their part, the local officials—who lived by a policy of peace at any price—stayed away from the Society to avoid trouble. As far as Wang was concerned, belief in Christianity was synonymous with treason.

Wang's constant prodding was a great nuisance to the county authorities. In 1844, the Qing court relinquished the interdiction against Christianity. A proclamation lifting the ban was issued to the churches in Guangzhou by the governor-general of Guangdong and Guangxi, and to it the imperial vermilion seal was affixed. Thus, one could no longer be apprehended solely for believing in Christianity, and the county authorities had no choice but to release Feng Yunshan after his arrest by the *tuanlian*.

Wang Zuoxin nonetheless mobilized his *tuanlian* forces a second time, seized Feng and others, and charged them then on suspicion of "rebelliousness." It was at that time that Hong Xiuquan led a movement to Guangzhou to secure their release. Wang was enraged when Feng was released again. He burst into the offices of the county authorities and demanded:

"The Society of God Worshippers is plotting rebellion! What in the world is the county doing about it?"

Although the activities of the Society of God Worshippers did indeed appear to be rebellious, the authorities claimed that the Society had no leader, and were thus reluctant to get involved. Wang ascertained that their leader was in fact at Penghua Mountain, and he requested that the county send troops after him there. His anger had become so intense and persistent that it defied imagination.

While Wang abhorred the Society of God Worshippers, for their part, Society members detested Wang as well. They dubbed him "the enemy of Heaven." Every member of the Society of God Worshippers who heard Yang's instructions "We're heading for Jiangkou," knew immediately this meant a reprisal against Wang.

No sooner had they heard the toponym "Jiangkou" emerge from Yang's lips, than a commotion arose within the Society of God Worshippers. The call went out from everyone in a great chorus: "It's Jiangkou! To Jiangkou!" And the chorus clearly had Wang's name in mind.

At roughly the same time, Wang Zuoxin was seated across from Pingnan County Magistrate Ni Tao, beating the table in exasperation. They were in a back room of Wang's granary.

"Is the Society of God Worshippers that much to be feared? They're just a bunch of ignorant, illiterate peasants and charcoal makers who believe in foreign devils! Why must our army with the great authority of our august court cross the river? I cannot abide this!"

"Don't speak in that manner. It was not I who made this determination. After careful investigation, military specialists reached this decision," said Ni Tao, in an effort to placate Wang. The government army had decided to withdraw from Jiangkou and cross the Dahuang River. This marked a step in retreat from the Society of God Worshippers. With the defeat at Cai village, the leaders of the Qing forces had become much more cautious.

"Do you intend to forsake our people living in Jiangkou?" asked Wang Zuoxin.

"No, that is not my intention. Once I've withdrawn the Guizhou troops who do not know the local terrain to the opposite shore of the river, I'll turn Jiangkou over to prefectural troops who do know the area well."

"But aren't these 'prefectural troops' really bandits by another name?"

"Don't say that! They may once have been bandits, but now they have been pacified by us. If they heard you, it would arouse them. Do you think it would be a good idea to start trouble at this point?"

Ni Tao's situation was gloomy indeed, but he regained his composure after Wang's incisive point.

Once the local government troops, with their main force in Guizhou, re-treated to the southern shore, a group affiliated with the Heaven and Earth Society that had submitted to the government came in to hold the Jiangkou area. This was the group of seven led by Big-Headed Ram, who had earlier considered forging an alliance with the Society of God Worshippers. As Wang Zuoxin had said, this group of Heaven and Earth Society leaders had been bandits through and through until that moment, and now they had surren-dered to the magistrate of Xunzhou prefecture and been renamed "prefec-tural troops."

"Well, I guess I can accept them as prefectural troops for now," muttered Wang under his breath.

"I believe the recent military defeat was due to the fact that the Guizhou forces knew nothing whatsoever of their surroundings. By comparison, didn't that Big-Headed Ram's army know every nook and cranny of the area? Who knows what might have happened if that bunch had surrendered *before* the battle at Cai village," suggested Ni Tao.

"In any event, I would like the government's forces to be more strong-willed, more strong-minded."

"I know what you have in mind. Soon, the newly appointed imperial com-missioner will be arriving at the head of a large army. I know little of military matters, but according to the officers I have heard that they're going to de-ploy a large force and spread a net around Jintian village. I have to take an overall approach and ignore minor mistakes for now."

"That's true enough," said Wang, still dissatisfied nonetheless.

Even if they lost one or two towns in the process of forming an immense surrounding web at Jintian, those could still be recouped after the fact. This was certainly not the sort of instance in which each and every detail had to be fastidiously scrutinized. That was how Wang understood Ni's main point.

However true this may have been, one town that could not fall into the hands of the Society of God Worshippers and be recovered afterward was Jiangkou. From his own speech and actions to that point, it was clear that Wang knew just how much he was detested by the Society of God Worshippers. Were Jiangkou actually to fall into their hands, his life would surely be forfeit. Even if the town were later recaptured, he was not likely to survive.

"So long as you understand my position. Well, I'll soon be returning to Pingnan," said Ni Tao, rising.

"Oh, you're going to Pingnan? Actually, I have some business in the Pingnan county seat, too. Would it be appropriate for us to travel together?" said Wang, affecting a smile.

—2—

The magistrate of Xunzhou prefecture, which covered Guiping and Pingnan counties, was a man by the name of Liu Jizu. Acting as representative for the seven leaders who had abandoned the idea of entering the Society of God Worshippers, Zhang Zhao had sounded Liu out about their surrender. The government's military forces learned from their crushing defeat at Cai village that in the future, they needed to have much better knowledge of local geography.

The Guizhou troops under the command of Zhou Fengqi had sustained considerable casualties, and supplementary forces were needed in preparation for the next battle. The surrender of the seven Heaven and Earth Society leaders came at just the right time, and their troops were incorporated into the government forces in the capacity of "prefectural troops." The Jiangkou region was placed in the hands of these new "prefectural troops," since the Dahuang River was familiar terrain to them, and they thus became the trusted mercenaries of the government's military.

Wang Zuoxin, however, refused to invest any trust in these former bandits. Wang was a man of considerable insight. Before he left for Pingnan in the company of Magistrate Ni Tao, he said to himself in the confines of his own room, "They really do know the local terrain. That means that when they're defeated, they're certain to beat a hasty retreat."

His premonition was borne out superbly. The reason he left for Pingnan was that he foresaw the seizure of Jiangkou. His hatred for the Society of God Worshippers was matched by his knowledge of them. Although he spoke of them as "ignorant peasants and charcoal workers," he still marveled at their stunning capacities when they gathered their forces together—something of which genuinely ignorant people, he well knew, were incapable.

The Society of God Worshippers clearly had some wise leaders of their own, and they hardly failed to surmise the government's plan to surround them. Encirclement meant that their supply lines would be cut. To mount an effective resistance, they first had to preserve their food supplies carefully.

Where were they keeping their provisions? There was no place in the vicinity of Jintian that was better stocked with provisions than Jiangkou. Everyone in the area knew that much. Wherever they may have sought a point at which to break through the encircling web, the Society would certainly first attack Jiangkou to protect their provisions. This, at least, was Wang's reading of the situation and his reason for escaping to Pingnan.

The Taiping Army began its charge to the east on the twelfth day of the twelfth lunar month. The entire army was heading for Jiangkou. The women's brigade was mobilized as well. In all they numbered 20,000. In actual fact, they had already begun to deplete their provisions in Jintian village.

"Once we get to Jiangkou, we can eat to our hearts' content," said Yang Xiuqing prior to their departure. In that sense, the mass movement of troops on Jiangkou was aimed at securing food. When they later learned that the "prefectural troops" under the Heaven and Earth Society leaders were waiting in Jiangkou, the leaders of the Society of God Worshippers decided to mobilize as large a fighting force as possible.

Although the Heaven and Earth Society troops had raided and plundered countless sites, they had no experience in sustaining an assault on a position they were defending. When attacked by the government troops, they had always run away. Once they decided on a spot to regroup later, they spread out in all directions with the wind.

Luo Dagang, the only Heaven and Earth Society leader to remain and actually join the Society of God Worshippers, knew the weaknesses of the secret societies well. It was he who suggested raising as massive an army as possible for the assault.

"They've never defended any specific piece of land. If their opponents are small in number, perhaps they may be able to bring themselves to offer a vigorous defense, but if they're threatened with a real fighting force, they'll give up immediately and run away as fast as their feet will take them. Even if we don't have sufficient weaponry, that's no problem. The women's brigade is terrific. With numbers of people we'll make them lose heart," said Luo.

When the Taiping Army of 20,000 strong pressed forward to Jiangkou, Zhang Zhao and the other leaders and rank-and-file troops under them fled upriver without engaging in a single battle. The majority of their men were "skiff bandits," and thus they first took to hiding out on water. Having held this kind of final trump card in reserve, they never had to face the Taiping forces in battle. Even if there was a way they might have worked as an auxiliary battalion, they were not about to so much as cross a dangerous bridge to that end.

"The Society of God Worshippers has come to attack. Their numbers are huge!"

"Really? Are there really so many of them?"

"It's a human wave. An enormous number."

Uttering shrieks of this sort, people hurriedly leapt into boats along the Dahuang River. Their fears were not merely of the numbers of Society members headed their way but of the Society itself. It was beyond their comprehension how these people could place everything they had once owned into the communal Sacred Treasury and devote themselves thoroughly, in body and soul, to the cause of their organization. We all tend to be frightened by that which we do not understand. It was precisely because the rebel leaders had recognized the extraordinary strengths of the Society of God Worshippers—even though they were unable to understand its source—that they had earlier sought an alliance with the Society.

Such a terrifying opponent was now approaching in great numbers. Why fight such an opponent when a perfectly good avenue of escape lay before them? The former bandits fled to a man, and the Taiping Army occupied Jiangkou without bloodshed.

"Find Wang Zuoxin and drag him over here!" commanded Hong Xiuquan

Hong was a man who far preferred absorbing himself in the study of doctrine and religious meditation than he did the affairs of the world around him. Only rarely did he issue such commands to take action. Nonetheless, in Jiangkou he roared out the demand that Wang be brought before him. It was not overly surprising in view of all the attacks the Society of God Worshippers had incurred because of Wang Zuoxin. But, for all their searching, Wang was nowhere to be found.

"His son, Wang Jiyuan, said he left for Pingnan."

"It seems likely that Wang has in fact left for Pingnan."

"According to an eyewitness, he accompanied the local magistrate."

As these reports came to Hong one after the next, he bit his lip in anger.

"Drag Wang Zuoxin's entire family here! Empty out his warehouses and stores now, and put everything into the Sacred Treasury!"

Hong ordinarily took council with Yang Xiuqing before deciding on important matters, but in this instance he was unilaterally issuing orders.

—3—

The homes and shops in Jiangkou were built closely together, and a short distance away was the residence of an elite family named Chen in a place called Shitoujiao. Hong turned this place into the base for the Taiping Army. The biggest home in the area was that of Wang Zuoxin, and the Taipings had decided to destroy it as a matter of revenge. For that reason, they had made the second largest home, the Chen mansion, their headquarters. Word had it that the residents of the Chen mansion had been shipwrecked, escaping along the Dahuang River together with Zhang Zhao's forces.

"We don't have any boats," said Feng Yunshan.

The Taipings' one deficiency was the lack of a naval force. Their core was made up of mountain people—peasants, charcoal-makers, miners, and the like—people with no relationship to the waterways whatsoever. In this instance, the participation of the Heaven and Earth Society's skiff bandits might have provided an opportunity for the Taiping military to improve itself. However, aside from Luo Dagang's group, these people had all deserted the cause, and Yang Xiuqing for one deeply regretted it.

Before leaving Jintian village, two points of view were raised among the leadership concerning plans following the occupation of Jiangkou. The first called for moving south down the Xunjiang, attacking the city of Guangzhou, and setting up there a base for the Taiping Heavenly Kingdom. The second view called for collecting their resources in Jiangkou, and then returning north with them as far as Hunan province, with an eye on its provincial capital at Changsha. These were dubbed, respectively, the Southern Advance and the Northern Advance positions.

The Northern Advance view won the day, but the final decision was to be made in a conference of the leaders at the Chen mansion. Leaders from Guangdong, such as Hong Xiuquan and Feng Yunshan, were actually opposed to moving on Guangzhou. Yang Xiuqing and Xiao Chaogui, raised in the mountainous region around Thistle Mountain, pressed for a Southern Advance.

As far as the latter were concerned, Guangzhou was the center of everything. Once a central base near it had been secured, they reasoned, the Taiping Heavenly Kingdom could expand its national might in all directions. Feng Yunshan, who opposed this view, argued that, insofar as the Taipings lacked a strong navy, a move south along sea lanes was impossible for them at this point in time.

Lian Liwen was sitting in a room in the Chen mansion, reading a book, when Tan Qi called in to him: "They want you in the meeting. I think they want to hear your views."

"I wonder what they want?" said Liwen, rather puzzled, although he had guessed the general contours of what was going on. When he entered the room in which the meeting was taking place, Yang Xiuqing said:

"Our plans are set. We apologize for seeking your views only after having already decided, but since your responsibility does not run to that level, we'd like to hear what you have to say." They were seeking his views on the question of proceeding north or south.

"I do not believe that occupying Guangzhou would be impossible, though it will require certain conditions. We'll have to attract an even larger group of skiff bandits as allies than Big-Headed Ram had. But, even if we succeed in taking Guangzhou, we won't be able to extend our influence in all directions from there," explained Liwen.

"Why is that?" asked the young Shi Dakai. Because he was young and not well-trained in such matters, Shi Dakai had not earlier expressed his views for or against. He was now eager to absorb everything he could.

"The area around Guangzhou is known as Lingnan because of the mountain range behind it. It's a lot easier to come down a mountain than to climb it. To attack on the heels of descending a mountain is very easy, but to attack after an ascent is much more difficult. Guangzhou is not the sort of place from which one commands the realm. Historically, the kingdom of Nanyue became self-sufficient in the tumultuous years at the end of the Qin dynasty two thousand years ago, but in the succeeding era of the Han dynasty, it was compelled to submit. During the reign of Emperor Wu of the Han, a great minister of Nanyue sought autonomy for his state, but he was attacked and destroyed by the Han. Centuries later, the Southern Song court escaped here as well, but ultimately perished in the mountains. Throughout China as a whole, there is an excessive bias in favor of the south."

Knowing that his point of view would in no way bear on the council's decision, Liwen felt quite at ease expressing what he believed. At the time of the Opium War, Lin Zexu called for and organized armed bands of naval volunteers. These bands had long since been disbanded, but their weapons remained hidden among the populace. Should some event come up, they were in a position to grab the weapons and rise up without delay. The Qing government was now worried about public order in Guangdong province, because, in addition to the proverbial hotheadedness of Guangdong Chinese, many of them were now armed. It was an area ripe for an uprising, and there were numerous problems in trying to keep the region under control. Since the Taiping forces aimed at establishing their own political regime, they too had to consider matters from the perspective of control.

"I have said that we must first make the skiff bandits our allies, but they're full of men of very low quality, and they are widely despised by the resident populace. If popular sentiment becomes unruly, then we might have to work hard to maintain public order," predicted Liwen.

"At the same time as occupying Guangzhou, we could sever our ties to these bad elements among the skiff bandits. At least, keep them away from the center of action. The Taiping Heavenly Kingdom will establish a pure and proper government. What do you think of that?" asked Shi Dakai.

"We can hardly expect a group that's cut off or kept at arm's length to act obediently." This time Yang Xiuqing stepped in to respond in place of Liwen.

From Yang's tone Liwen was confident that they had decided to advance north, because Yang had been the most influential support of the Southern Advance.

Hong Xiuquan rose from his chair and said politely: "Thank you for your views, Mr. Lian. Although we had already decided to move north, you have now convinced the members of the council further."

As he absorbed these words, Yang Xiuqing, still sitting, said: "Well, let's move on to the next matter before us. We must decide quickly on a battle array for our move north."

At that point, Tan Qi entered the room. He was not a member of the council, but someone who could come and go freely at such meetings. He had gathered intelligence on various matters.

"Qiu Ersao and Su Sanniang have arrived," reported Tan, and Yang immediately asked:

"How many people?"

"They've each got about two thousand."

"That means four thousand all together, eh," said Yang with an intense nod of his head.

Li Xinmei, who had disappeared for a time from Jintian village, had succeeded in enticing these two woman leaders to join their cause.

—4—

"It was wise to come. I only wish I could have gotten here sooner," said Su Sanniang several times. She seemed to enjoy the austere atmosphere of the Taipings.

"If you put it that way, it was worth the trouble to entice you here. Compared to that . . ."

Li Xinmei—the person who had brought her—seemed happy, but Xinmei became silent after addressing Su. The other person she had invited, Qiu Ersao, did not seem as though she was becoming accustomed to the prevailing Taiping atmosphere, thrusting one condition after another before them.

Each of the two of them, Su and Qiu, commanded a force of about two thousand, stationed to the right and the left extremities, respectively, of Jiangkou. The Taiping armies had already taken up positions before the Dahuang River, and the two newly incorporated armies served as extensions of this troop alignment. With these reinforcements, the Taiping Army did not deepen its forces, but lengthened them.

Su Sanniang's troops were positioned at the far left wing, well to the East of Shitoujiao. Among the soldiers under her command were some three hundred women who, according to Taiping custom, were placed in women's barracks.

Though Su Sanniang was a woman herself, her position in command of a force comprised entirely of men was extraordinary. This unit had become a kind of private reserve, responding only to her orders.

Of the troops under the command of Qiu Ersao, some five hundred were women, but she refused to allow them to be placed in the women's barracks. She was afraid that it would weaken her overall fighting capacity. The Taiping military leaders decided to allow her this exceptional practice.

To acquaint himself with the state of things, Liwen—together with Li Xinmei—paid visits to the two camps of Su and Qiu. Qiu did not even try to hide her discontent.

"This idea of launching an attack on Guangzhou is crazy. What'll we do about boats? Luo Dagang's got a few, but far from enough. Big-Headed Ram and Big Carp are hidden all along the Dahuang River. They'll grab us as soon as we get near the water. You may not be able to see this, but I sure can," she said.

Secret society military forces, such as those of the Heaven and Earth Society, were unlike the Society of God Worshippers. They had not been defeated in battle at Jiangkou, but had simply moved from land onto water, and they had not lost a single man in battle there. Liwen could see that, in the Jiangkou area, the Dahuang River described a huge, languorous curve. Qiu could apparently see that there were secret society troops hidden all across the area.

"Big-Headed Ram may be stronger when it comes to war, but Big Carp is better at concealing his men," she said. Qiu concealed her age well, but she was long past fifty. Her face was flat with taut cheeks, and her entire body was muscle-toned. To Liwen there was nothing in the least feminine about her.

"To delude the enemies, first delude your allies," as the old strategic adage ran. Thus, the Taiping military leaders, having decided on a northern advance, let it be known among their followers that they were set on moving south. They did not even make the truth known to the newly incorporated rebel leaders. Thus, when Qiu Ersao called it a crazy idea, Liwen could not deny the story of a southern campaign, which placed him in a difficult position. He was much relieved when he left her camp for that of Su Sanniang.

Su Sanniang was thirty-five years of age, and she indeed reminded Liwen of his idea of a woman. She had a dark complexion with a charming round face. Although she was about the same height as Qiu, Su lacked the stature of a larger person, and she was as happy as she could be to have joined the Taiping Army. While there were a fair number of women among the troops in the right wing encampment of Qiu Ersao, a gloomy mood hovered about it. The left wing encampment under Su Sanniang's command was entirely male except for the leader, and remained in high spirits.

There was a certain femininity in Su Sanniang's manner of speaking as well. "Lingshan is a really marvelous place. If we didn't have this business to attend to, I could probably live there forever." She had a way of mixing pride in her native place into the discussion. Her hometown of Lingshan was along the coast of Guangdong province. Today, it is an area that has been incorporated into the Zhuang Autonomous Region of Guangxi province.

Unlike Li Xinmei and Qiu Ersao, Su had not inherited her band of followers from a parent. She was originally an ordinary housewife. Her husband had been a member of the Heaven and Earth Society, but he had never engaged in any secret society military or bandit activities. He owned a few boats and ran a transport business.

"If we didn't have this business to attend to." This was her way of noting that her husband had been murdered. He had become involved in a business rivalry and was killed in the city of Nanning. It was a safe guess that the culprit was a Guangxi native in the same line of work. And this ordinary housewife Su Sanniang now found her life completely transformed.

She knew the name and address of her husband's murderer, but she was unable to have him apprehended. It was futile to appeal to the police, because the culprit was closely tied to bureaucrats in the Nanning region. Incapable of having the authorities punish the murderer, there was nothing she could do. The situation was mortifying for her, so painful at times, that she would knit her brow and gnash her teeth. Then, one day, she regained a gleaming countenance and said to herself, "If the authorities can't do it, then I suppose I'll have to."

Because of the family transport business, a large number of young men worked for her, and they were all outraged at the underhanded tactics of their competitor.

"I have decided to punish him. One person could do it alone, but who'll follow me?" No sooner had she spoken, than several dozen young men who worked for her stepped forward. They were porters and other transport workers and thus had traveled to many places. To ensure their own safety while traveling, they had forged close ties with many local figures of importance. As a small token of goodwill, whenever they passed nearby, they made a point of bringing presents from home for these people. Furthermore, because Su Sanniang's late husband had been a member of the Heaven and Earth Society, these local bosses sympathized with her plight.

"Why not hire a number of these men?" She couldn't reject such a well-meant suggestion. She hired men—several hundred in all—from various locales under her command. They then attacked and killed the man who had murdered her husband near Nanning, and they burned his home to the ground.

Naturally, she then became a wanted criminal, and she found that she was a splendid bandit. Thereafter, she had two mottoes:

Stand up against the powerful and help the weak.

Take from the rich to aid the poor. She was also a good-natured person and thus established an instant rapport with her followers. The men who had hired out to her the large number of followers said, "The young people put in your hands can stay where they are if you want." When she insisted that they return home, many specially requested that they be allowed to remain in her service.

"With my husband dead, my first life is over," she often said. "This is a second life, as far as I'm concerned—a bonus, an extra—and I will use it generously on your behalf."

Three days after the Taiping Army set forth from Jintian village—on the fifteenth day of the twelfth lunar month—Imperial Commissioner Li Xingyuan (1797–1851) arrived in Liuzhou from Guilin. The following day, Guangxi Provincial Military Commander Xiang Rong arrived at the Guizhou county seat. Li Xingyuan was a native of Hunan province. After serving in the important position of governor-general of the three provinces of Jiangxi, Jiangsu, and Anhui, he had retired to his home village to recover from an illness.

The Qing court had earlier appointed Lin Zexu as imperial commissioner, but he had died en route to taking up his post. His replacement, Li Xingyuan, was similarly recovering from an illness (in Hunan) when the summons arrived. Perhaps the court thought it important that Li was then in Hunan, much closer to the trouble spots in Guangxi province than if he had to be dispatched from the capital. For his part, Li was rather an opportunist, but, his illness aside, he was only fifty-five years old, hardly Lin Zexu's advanced age. And, he had successfully quelled a Muslim uprising while serving as governor-general of Yunnan and Guizhou.

In the fourth lunar month of the present year, Li appeared in Beijing to pay his respects before the coffin of the Daoguang Emperor, who had passed away three months earlier. At that time, there was discussion of his possibly assuming a more strategic position in the government.

"My mother is quite old and in failing health," he had said, declining any such offer at the time.

Lin Zexu had been unable even to pay his respects to the late emperor. By comparison, Li's own illness seems not to have been serious. His mother's poor health, even more than his own, provided a sounder reason for his retirement. At least, the court thought as much.

Appointment to the position of imperial commissioner under such emergency circumstances could not be declined, and Li departed Hunan for Guangxi despite having not recovered full bodily strength. After reaching Guangxi, Li finally learned something of the general contours of the activities of the Society of God Worshippers. He had not been receiving reliable reports, even in neighboring Hunan province to the immediate north. At the time he had sent the following error-ridden memorial to the court in Beijing: "The leader of the bandits in Jintian village, Guiping county, Wei Zheng, along with Hong Xiuquan and others, have organized the Society to Honor Younger Brothers . . ."

Wei Changhui's former name had, in fact, been Wei Zheng, although written with a different Chinese character from the one used by Li, and Li took him to be the leader of the group. He also incorrectly wrote the character for "quan" in Hong's given name, and took him to be a subordinate of Wei's within the organization. By the same token, Li completely misunderstood the name of the group itself, for which he had the correct pronunciation—Shangdihui—but two of the three Chinese characters were wrong, indicating that reports received in Hunan had not been written documents, but oral communications, as the four errors were each exact homonyms.

Having spent his days at home in an easy, carefree retirement, Li was now being drawn by force into the fray, and he didn't like it one bit. He claimed to be physically weak still, but alcohol poisoning was in fact the cause. Maintaining his dignified manner throughout the morning hours, he would soon begin to drink when the afternoon arrived. Before drinking he would become nervous and impatient, and after drinking he would no longer be capable of normal judgment. That such a person was selected as imperial commissioner was a clear indication that the court lacked the personnel it desperately needed at the time.

"These bureaucrats are worthless. Years of accomplishment are completely wiped out by one solitary mistake. What can you do about it?" complained Li, as was his wont, when he arrived in Guangxi. Li made this statement, fully conscious of the fact that his predecessor in the region, Guangxi Governor Zheng Zuchen, had been blamed and subsequently dismissed for being unable to suppress a bandit uprising in Guangxi.

It usually did not end simply with dismissal. Exile to Xinjiang as an example to others was an oft-heard rumor. Zheng had attained the highest degree in the civil service examinations in 1805, and his official record spanned forty-five years. He was over seventy years of age, so that banishment to the desert would be an extraordinarily cruel form of punishment. Although the court would ultimately decide on what punishment to mete out, Li had to file the necessary documents. One of the responsibilities of an imperial commissioner was to make an on-site investigation and report accordingly to Beijing.

What an awful business, thought Li. Reflections of this sort upset Li so much that alcohol became his only consolation. In spite of his weak physical state, his intake of alcohol increased after arriving in Guangxi. "I hate it. I hate this detestable business and all the abhorrent people involved!" he said to himself, wine cup in hand. By "abhorrent people," Li had Guangxi Provincial Military Governor Xiang Rong—a man several years his junior—in mind. Xiang hailed from Guyuan, Gansu province, although his family was originally from the province of Sichuan. With a background entirely in the military, he had risen to the high position of a military governor. Although clearly someone of considerable talent, Xiang knew no life outside of military encampments, and that made his vision rather myopic.

"I'm the brightest guy around."

"This is war, and it's war that I know best."

"He may be an imperial commissioner, but when it comes to war, he'll have to listen to what I say."

Such thoughts frequently came to Xiang's mind, and he never tried to hide them.

Li Xingyuan had never wanted to meet Xiang Rong. When he stayed over in Liuzhou, he contacted him by letter. That way he was more at ease, not having to worry himself too much about actually seeing the man.

Li was disgusted by the virtually unimaginable force attained by the Society of God Worshippers in Guangxi. The strength of the government's troops at the scene was simply insufficient to attack and defeat the Society with its more than twenty thousand soldiers amassed at Jiangkou. His efforts to obtain reinforcements from the Chaozhou Army of the governor-general of Guangdong and Guangxi were rejected. He had even requested of Beijing the mobilization of the Guizhou forces.

It often rained at this time of the year—another source of discouragement to Imperial Commissioner Li. Finally, some 2,000 troops from Yunnan, 800 volunteers from Fujian, and 600 able-bodied young men of the ethnic Yao people recruited on the spot in Guangxi, arrived in Xunzhou.

"We shall attack this very day." Though he penned this message in a letter to Li in Liuzhou, Xiang Rong did not pursue the attack. The war was, in effect, postponed due to rainy weather.

The additional troops arrived on the twelfth day of the first lunar month, which meant that a full month had passed since the day of the Taiping assault on Jiangkou. The irritated imperial commissioner wrote in a letter to Xiang Rong: "For several weeks now, over ten thousand troops have been waiting in Pingnan at a cost of well over one hundred thousand taels of silver per day. If [the attack] is called off again and no mopping up is carried out, how can we comfort the emperor's mind? [To ease the emperor's worries] is like cauterizing the intestines, like sitting in continual fear."

"He's practically lost his mind, the damned imperial commissioner," yelled Xiang Rong in the direction of this letter after reading it. He then turned his head to the side and spit. "It's best to burn out the sores on such intestines. Leave matters of war to me—that's what I say." What Xiang wanted to say was that his insides were burning even hotter, and he had fallen into a state of despair after observing the encampment along the southern bank of the Dahuang River. The government's forces had no fighting spirit, and they feared the Society of God Worshippers.

The superstition was being circulated in whispers among the government's soldiers that "the enemy uses magic and sorcery, and we have no hope of winning."

The 2,000 Yunnanese troops who arrived on the twelfth day of the first lunar month had run into bandits en route. They had engaged them in battle, lost, and fled the scene. They were in effect a remnant force, completely unreliable. Then, the Guizhou Regional Commander Zhou Fengqi arrived. Ever since the defeat at Cai village, he had looked particularly glum, but for whatever reason his face was now covered with a smile.

"I finally prevailed upon Qiu Ersao. The enemy's right flank has been torn off."

"What? That's great," said Xiang Rong, a smile slowly appearing on his face as well. "Because tomorrow's finally the day. It came just in time."

The government's forces had resorted to fomenting internal dissension within the Taiping Army. The leaders of the Society of God Worshippers were held together by belief, and none of them could have been enticed into treachery by the authorities, but a new entrant like Qiu Ersao bearing some sort of dissatisfaction might turn her allegiance to the Qing's armed forces.

"The main force of the eastern route army will soon depart. Advance troops should already be crossing the river," reported Zhou Fengqi.

—6—

The sixteenth day of the first lunar month in the first year of the reign of the Xianfeng Emperor—February 18, 1851. Soldiers from six different provinces—Guangxi, Guangdong, Guizhou, Yunnan, Hunan, and Fujian—under Xiang Rong's command were divided into Eastern Route and Western Route Armies. The eastern route army had taken a detour to ford the Dahuang River along its lower reaches and approach to the rear of the Taiping Army.

The western route army reached the river further up from the point where the Taiping forces were camped. It would attempt a head-on assault. They had already engaged the right flank of the Taipings, but the forces of Qiu Ersao that defended that flank had already negotiated a switch of allegiances and submitted to the Qing authorities.

After crossing the river, the eastern route army further subdivided into three detachments. To the north of the Chen mansion ran a small string of mountains known as the Niupai range. Once they crossed these mountains, they would try to storm the Taipings. Although it was a secret operation, the movements of such a large force became known to the Taipings through the local villagers, whose support they held.

Taiping forces immediately took countermeasures. They set an ambush at Panshi village to the east of Jiangkou, facing the pass through which the enemy would have to come, and buried land mines before them. Many of the troops in the Taiping Army were miners, and many of them specialists in digging tunnels and planting explosives.

The Taiping strategy was to feign defeat and lure the enemy in even deeper. The government troops were taken completely unawares. They had expected a surprise attack. A small detachment of Taipings with whom they had come in contact ran off in a state of utter confusion, and they chased after the rebels, yelling: "Don't let them get away! Seize them!"

Needless to say, this detachment of Taipings was merely a decoy, and the bait lured the Qing Army to the area where the land mines were buried. The noise from the explosions and the signal guns announcing the attack of the Taiping ambush came at the same time. It was as if the earth split apart and spewed the enemy troops in all directions. When the Qing forces realized that they had been ensnared in a trap, an officer screamed for calm and quiet, but the soldiers had already fallen into a state of panic, able only at that point to run from where they were to the farthest spot their legs would carry them.

It was a major defeat for the dynastic forces. The eastern route army was dealt a crushing blow in this battle, in which the Qing armies lost over ten officers and over three hundred troops. Among the officers killed was Assistant Brigade Commander Wang Chongshan, whose rank (5A in the Chinese military system) was comparable to a field officer.

As for the western route army, it too was drawn in by a decoy detachment. Having won over Qiu Ersao, the Qing military leaders had expected an easy victory for the western route army. On the assumption that Qiu's forces would protect them on the far right wing, the Taiping army would never have so much as dreamt of a sudden attack from the government troops. This was what the government troops were counting on, so that they could then abruptly rout the decoy detachment.

The Taipings, though, had long known of Qiu Ersao's defection. The Qing forces pursued the rebel decoy and tried all at once to penetrate the rebel base camp. Once they got as far as Jiangkou, they realized that there was a large enemy force to their rear. At that point, another enemy force before them rushed directly at the Qing Army.

"This is impossible!" screamed Liu Jizu, a local magistrate and commander of the western route army, smacking himself on the forehead. Because of the betrayal of Qiu's forces, the Taipings were being overly watchful, extremely cautious. Attacked from both front and rear, the Qing Army found its escape route shut off, and many of its troops sought refuge by jumping into the Dahuang River. At this time, the boats of Zhang Zhao's force of skiff bandits did not appear on the river as planned. Fearful that Taiping forces, who were adept at the use of gunpowder, would set their vessels on fire, they had stayed away from the shore.

The western route army suffered casualties in excess of five hundred—more than the eastern route army. It was a major defeat for the Qing government.

While his two armies went into battle at Jiangkou, Imperial Commissioner Li Xingyuan did not even budge from Liuzhou. As usual, he sent orders to his generals at the front in the form of documents. Furthermore, he reported to Beijing, "We have won. Though our forces did incur casualties."

Although Li Xingyuan and Xiang Rong had never gotten along, their interests were identical when it came to this embellished report. If they did not report it as a difficult fight but a victory nonetheless, then things would go badly as well for Xiang Rong as a military commander.

Since it was a reported victory, the account balance had now to be put right. They wanted to retaliate against the Taipings, and Xiang Rong was overzealous. Li Xingyuan understood Xiang's hastiness well, but they could not respond too rashly and take even greater numbers of casualties. In a letter to Xiang, Li wrote: "It is better to wait for action with calm." This was his way of saying that sometimes you can better see the scene of action when you are actually separated from it, as was his own case off in Liuzhou. There is a certain objectivity this way that is not imperiled by the feverishness of the immediate situation.

Although a great defeat for the government's forces, the victory produced a contemptuous attitude among the Taiping Army that the government's army was hopelessly weak. Taiping military leaders even began thinking about moving from defensive to offensive strategies.

By the same token, among the government troops there was an overwhelming wariness of the Taiping Army's might. They had at first considered it a ragtag force of farmers and charcoal workers of no importance whatsoever, but the latter turned out to be unexpectedly strong on the field of battle.

The Taipings now began to mobilize troops in rapid succession to attack Qing military camps. The Qing Army, for its part, was disappointed in its expectations of reinforcements, but weaponry, ammunition, and supplies were gradually replenished. An order went out from Beijing to the Customs Authority in Guangzhou to send 300,000 taels of silver posthaste for military expenditures. Also, artillery was to be sent—foreign-made pieces stocked in large numbers in Guangzhou.

From the third through the fifth day of the second lunar month, the Taipings besieged Qing military encampments, but this action ended in defeat for the attackers. Half a month had transpired since the defeat at Jiangkou, and in that time artillery and shells were supplied to the government troops, without the knowledge of the Taipings. In the fighting on the fifth, the rebels sustained a particularly large number of casualties.

The following day, the Qing Army attacked Taiping positions, just at a time when the Taiping forces were exhausted by several consecutive days of fighting.

"We've already decided to move north," said Yang Xiuqing. "In accordance with this plan, it would seem that the time has come to abandon Jiangkou and somehow beat a graceful retreat. We should be thinking about this right now."

"We can't accept this defeat without fighting just one more major battle," said the young Shi Dakai with his eyes glued solely to the outcome of the present fighting.

"Emotions play no role here. The calmer the better in war," said Yang aloofly.

—7—

Yet another detestable person has arrived, thought Li Xingyuan. He had been drinking wine since that morning. It was the only way he was going to remain the least bit conciliatory. About ten days after the defeat at Jiangkou, Zhou Tianjue, provincial governor of Guangxi, had come to Liuzhou from Guilin. Although he was nearly eighty years of age, he still paraded around in a maddeningly arrogant way. He had come as the replacement for the dismissed Zheng Zuchen.

"A man of great loyalty and integrity" was his reputation. Loyalty and integrity were certainly fine qualities, but he seemed to have an excess of both. There was also the view circulating that he was "crude."

He was an honest man with a perfectly clean conscience concerning himself. He would, by the same token, unhesitatingly say unpleasant things directly to others, and he had an excess of frills about him as well. While governor-general of grain transport, Zhou had been implicated in a case involving the forging of an official seal and had been demoted. Afterward, he retired on the pretext of illness. That was seven years earlier, and in those seven years he had led an itinerant life. With the accession of the new emperor, Zhou was given the opportunity for a comeback as Guangxi governor at the recommendation of Du Shoutian.

Du Shoutian had served as both an assistant grand secretary and minister of works in the Qing government. More than anything else, his record shone as the man personally in charge of the new emperor's education. He had not instructed the emperor solely in reading and writing, but rather he introduced the young man to the responsibilities of his new job, how to go about being emperor.

The imperial succession in the Qing dynasty at this time was not governed by a rule of primogeniture. The reigning emperor picked his successor, and the order of the sons' ages played no role in the choice. The Xianfeng Emperor had received his father's recognition and was thus named heir apparent. All of this, he well knew, was due to the coaching of Du Shoutian. After the new emperor's accession to the throne, Du's powers grew even greater.

Insofar as he was a man of integrity, Zhou's attitude was perfectly clear: "There's nothing for me to fear, because the emperor's teacher, Du Shoutian, will always be behind me."

Zhou never verbalized it, but written all over his face were the lines: "What is it with youngsters like Li Xingyuan? When he passed the highest level of the civil service exams, I had already risen from prefect to surveillance commissioner. He's maneuvered well and become very successful, but he's on an altogether different level from me."

Upon arriving at his new post, Li Xingyuan's first job was to carry out an investigation into the affairs of Zheng Zuchen prior to the latter's dismissal as governor of Guangxi. Li was sympathetic to Zheng and wanted to write as favorable a report for the court as he could. Yet the report would not be authored solely by Li, as it was to be a joint report with Zhou Tianjue.

"He was caught up in a complex web of circumstances," said Li. "Whoever had been governor at the time would probably have been unable to prevent these bandits from appearing."

Zhou's complexion changed as he approached Li. "What's that? Are you saying that the same fate would have befallen anyone who would have been governor? Aren't you being a bit presumptuous? Are you saying that even if I, Zhou Tianjue, had been governor of Guangxi at the time, the same thing would have happened? If it had been me, I'd have crushed this, this Society of God Worshippers in its infancy. What in the world do you mean that it would have been the same for anyone?"

The more Zhou intoned, the more Li became angry:

"That is my personal point of view. Is it forbidden to express one's views?"

"I'm not saying it's forbidden to express your views, but I am saying that it is improper to express improper views," lashed out Zhou the octogenarian, grinning all the while.

In the overflow of anger he was now feeling, Li's desire for wine grew accordingly. "I have business to attend to. We'll talk about this matter again at a later date. Excuse me," he said, rising from his seat and returning to his room. He then removed a flask of white wine from the shelf and poured himself a cupful. It emitted a powerful aroma, and Li closed his eyes and gulped it down. His hand holding the cup was quivering. "Even if he's well over twenty years older than me, I'm the commander of bandit suppression in Guangxi! I'm the imperial commissioner, and that old man's no more than an assistant. And yet he speaks to me like this! I say you're an inhuman brute! Hmm, well put."

From time to time, Li took a drink while muttering to himself. After draining another cup of wine, his hands would cease shaking.

Some twenty or more years earlier, when Zhou was a county magistrate, he had inflicted on a criminal the punishment of severing the sinews of the leg, and ever since he had been accused of being an "inhuman brute." Li Xingyuan remembered that his superiors at the time protected Zhou's excesses by citing the latter part of the traditional saying: "Love the people like a child, and despise evil like an enemy."

While the imperial commissioner and the governor sent to Liuzhou to assist him found themselves at odds, the Taiping Army at the front in Jiangkou had begun a stealthy retreat to the West. The Qing forces had taken control of the Niupai mountains and the southern shore of the river, while the Taipings camped to the east.

There were skirmishes but no major battles fought that day. At the Taiping encampment the drums continued beating, as they had since the previous day.

"We crushed them with large artillery, so they're trying to rouse the troops with their drums. They can beat their drums all day long and never be a match for our artillery," scornfully laughed the regional commander of Linyuan, who had been rushed to the scene from Yunnan province.

The drums continued without stop into the evening of the eighth day of the second lunar month, straight through until daybreak.

"They've been banging on those drums all night long," said Xiang Rong, rubbing his eyes the next morning. "They probably didn't want us to sleep."

"What a bizarre thing to do!" As the regional commander uttered this statement in a somewhat subdued voice, he was looking over at Xiang Rong's room.

"What's so bizarre?"

"There's not a single flag flying."

"What? A flag? What flag?"

"Over the camp of the Society of God Worshippers. Early this morning there was a whole row of flags in a line over there."

"Damn it! We may have been fooled!"

Xiang Rong dressed quickly and dispatched a reconnaissance detail. The Chen mansion at Shitoujiao was completely empty, with no trace of the Taiping Army. The Qing forces crossed the river, scaled the Niupai mountains, and occupied Jiangkou, now emptied of the enemy. The local residents were dragged from their homes here and there. During the nearly two months of confrontation, the Qing military sensed that the Taipings enjoyed the support of the resident populace. Now, it was time to investigate. The local elder was tied up and beaten with rods.

"You've been consorting with the bandits!" said Xiang Rong with a menacing glare.

"No, that's absurd. They were armed, and we're just simple farmers. We had no choice but to obey what they told us," said the elder, his forehead rubbing the ground in prostration.

"There's no question that you were involved with the enemy. Even if they forced you to beat the drums all night long, you couldn't have done it unless your minds were in concert with the rebels."

"We were being watched. Until just a little while ago, this woman leader of theirs was holding a dagger before us. She said she'd kill us if we stopped beating the drums."

"What's that? A woman leader? Su Sanniang?"

Xiang Rong ordered a search through every corner of Jiangkou, but not a single Taiping soldier, let alone a woman leader, was discovered.

"For the crime of consorting with the enemy, we shall burn Jiangkou to the ground. It will serve as a warning to others."

So saying, Xiang Rong set the punishment for Jiangkou, and the government forces reduced Jiangkou to ashes. This only infuriated many local young people, who took off in pursuit of the Taiping Army to join the rebels. Xiang Rong's actions had the effect of actually increasing the enemy's numbers.

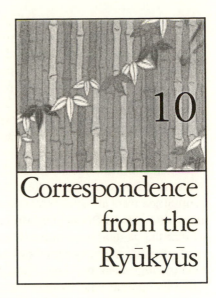

10

Correspondence from the Ryūkyūs

—1—

There is a place called Naminoue, or "above the waves," by the city of Naha on Okinawa island. As the name implies, Naminoue is located at a point where the shore juts out over the sea, and a Buddhist temple there is known as the Gokokuji. Originally a temple of the Shingon or Esoteric Buddhist sect, for many years it had gone without a resident priest. For some five years now, a remarkable and strange man had moved in with his family and taken up residence.

His name was Bernard Jean Bettelheim, a Christian missionary, forty years of age. Although born in Hungary, he had married a woman from England and become a naturalized Englishman. His wife's name was Elizabeth. In addition to the two of them, Bettelheim had brought a Chinese cook with them from Hong Kong. There were also two huge dogs that formed part of the household.

Lian Zhewen often strolled over to Gokokuji. Prior to his arrival in Okinawa, Bettelheim had mastered Chinese during his time in Hong Kong. For his own part, Zhewen could speak English, so the two men made excellent partners for conversation.

Bettelheim was quite a talkative character—a man who in fact spoke incessantly. He was always involved in his missionary work whenever he went into town, and he always performed this work in the Okinawa dialect. His language abilities were such that after just a year in Naha, he could speak with virtually native fluency.

Strange indeed, thought Zhewen, as he gazed over at Bettelheim in the chief priest's chambers of the Gokokuji, which was now a reception room. The ordinarily loquacious Bettelheim had been silent for some time. It was unprecedented that he would sit opposite a guest for a full ten minutes and have nothing to say. Zhewen had brought with him and shown to Bettelheim three pamphlets written by Hong Xiuquan: "Ode on the Origin of Virtue for World Salvation," "Proclamation on the Origin of Virtue for the Enlightenment of the Age," and "Proclamation on the Origin of Virtue for the Awakening of the Age."

Bettelheim, who often went by the Chinese name Bo Deling, could read and write Chinese well. The documents he presented to the Ryūkyū government office were always composed in Chinese, and he signed them: Personally written by Bo Deling, English subject. Since Hong Xiuquan had written so that the general population would be able to read and understand him easily, these pamphlets presented no problem for Bettelheim. He took his time reading them and then reread them when he had finished. Then, just when one would have expected his ordinary flood of eloquence to come gushing forth, he did not so much as open his mouth.

"What do you think?" asked Zhewen, and Bettelheim finally responded:

"It's very difficult. . . . Very, very difficult."

"You mean the written style?"

"No, no. The content."

"I think it's written rather simply."

"What I mean by difficult is to determine whether this is genuine Christianity or not. It's really very hard to say."

Zhewen wanted to ask what particular points in the texts he had found dubious, but Bettelheim then changed the subject:

"By the way, Jiuqu, weren't you going to draw something for me?" "Jiuqu" was Zhewen's pen name as an artist. Some time back, Bettelheim had asked Zhewen to add some illustrations to certain Christian missionary writings he had composed himself.

"What sort of drawings did you have in mind? Let me know specifically what you'd like, and I'd be happy to do it," said Zhewen.

The Ryūkyūs, or Liuqiu Islands in Chinese, were a dually subordinate state, falling simultaneously under the control of Shimazu domain in Kyushu, Japan's southernmost island, and having received investiture by the Qing dynasty in China. The Ryūkyū king possessed credentials from China, going back to the Ming dynasty (1368–1644), to the effect: "We invest you as king of the Ryūkyūs."

Investiture meant that the Ryūkyū Islands would be allowed to bring tribute to the Chinese court, namely, that trade relations could proceed. In order to continue trade with China, the Ryūkyūs established a relationship of sub-servience to China, though in fact they were controlled by Shimazu. This was the essence of "dual subordination." To secure a profit from the China trade via the Ryūkyūs, Shimazu domain accepted the fact of Ryūkyūan investiture by the Qing dynasty. When the Chinese emissary of investiture came to the Ryūkyūs, the Shimazu official resident there simply disappeared for a period of time.

Lian Weicai had sent his fourth son Liwen to further his trading transactions with Japan, mainly by way of Satsuma and the Ryūkyūs. Liwen had set the foundation when his elder brother Zhewen took over for him. Although Zhewen was also an artist, Liwen had established sufficiently strong personal ties and bonds that Zhewen was able to keep a close watch on the family business on the side.

Initially, Liwen had established a relationship with Bettelheim, which Zhewen carried over. It was from his younger brother that Zhewen had received the written material and learned of Hong Xiuquan's movement.

By cutting off his queue, Zhewen had publicly expressed his lack of any intention for the time being of returning to China. For now, he was enjoying the life he spent between Satsuma and the Ryūkyūs. A painter in Nagasaki once said to him that, "The southern lands were unsuited to art," but Zhewen disagreed. The colors and contours were too clear, he had said, but Zhewen believed that they had their own beauty. Even more than the scenery in the Ryūkyūs, Zhewen loved the simple human feelings of the local populace.

Because of the nature of control over the Ryūkyūs, the ban on Christianity was not as severe as it was in Japan proper. Indeed, a missionary such as Bettelheim was able to reside there, as he had for the past five years. Before Bettelheim, a French missionary by the name of Theodore A. Forcade had lived for a short time in Naha. Yet, no matter how fervid these missionaries may have been, their efforts at gaining converts could point to few or no results. They were always tailed, and even when the local residents received pamphlets from Bettelheim, they delivered them to the government office, and the pamphlets were then returned to him.

Bettelheim apparently did not learn from experience, as he continued to distribute pamphlets on behalf of his missionary work. He disseminated them widely, as if throwing them away, and then they were collected by the authorities and returned to him. For several years now, Bettelheim had been doing precisely the same thing. Some of the pamphlets were written in Chinese characters and some in the Japanese syllabary. The former he had brought with him from Hong Kong, while the latter he had prepared himself. Now he thought that maybe he would be able to attract a little human interest if pictures were added to the text.

Despite such fervent Christian proselytizing, Bettelheim had demonstrated nothing of the response Zhewen expected to the religious activities of Hong Xiuquan. Perhaps silence on the part of this ordinarily talkative missionary was a particularly significant response in and of itself. One could clearly sense no good will in Bettelheim's quiet.

"Do you mean to say that what Hong Xiuquan is espousing in Guangxi is not genuine Christianity? Only what Europeans espouse is true, but not that of the Chinese? Is it that only Europeans can expound Christian beliefs?" Zhewen persisted despite Bettelheim's having changed subjects. Bettelheim looked befuddled.

"That is not what I mean. Yet, when I was reading those pamphlets, I couldn't help but think that there was an awfully strong and pervasive flavor of Confucianism," the missionary responded earnestly.

"For a long time, Confucianism has been scholarly orthodoxy in China. It has permeated the very Chinese language. Therefore, there may often be a Confucian coloring when using Chinese. However, I have heard stories of how Hong and his followers have been destroying Confucian temples and burning images of Confucius."

"I wonder how reliable those reports are?" said Bettelheim dubiously. Reports of Hong Xiuquan and the Society of God Worshippers had been conveyed to Hong Kong only dimly, which was even more the case in the distant Ryūkyū Islands.

"They're accurate. No doubt about that, if only because I've heard them from Liwen. Liwen is now in Guangxi."

Just at that moment, Mrs. Bettelheim brought out some tea for them.

—2—

Lian Weicai's sixtieth birthday was already past, and in the first year of the reign of the Xianfeng Emperor, 1851, he was sixty-three by Chinese counting. After attending the funeral of Lin Zexu in the town of Houguan in Fujian province, Lian proceeded immediately to Shanghai. The plan was then to go on to Beijing together with Xiling, who was to arrive from Guangxi. However, some urgent business arose in Xiamen (Amoy), and he was compelled to return alone to the south by sea.

The Lian family had a villa, called Hongyuan, or Wild Swan Garden, in the eastern suburbs of Xiamen. Although it had been burnt to the ground during the Opium War, a roughly similar structure had been built in its place. However, the Tide-Gazing Mountain Chamber, located at the highest point of the original villa grounds, was moved and constructed anew on Gulangxu, an islet to the west of Xiamen. It was there that Lian usually spent his nights.

It was the fourth month on the lunar calendar, and summer had already descended on subtropical Xiamen. Lian unfolded the letter from Zhewen that had been forwarded to him from the Ryūkyū official residence in Fuzhou. Fuzhou served as a kind of window for the Ryūkyū Islands in their trade with the Qing dynasty. The Ryūkyū state had set up a branch office in Fuzhou, which was called the "Ryūkyū official residence." It was, needless to say, supported by Satsuma.

Under the *sakoku* ban on foreign intercourse of the Tokugawa government, Japan had lost contact with the outside world for a considerable period of time. Nagasaki was Japan's only outlet. In time, though, Satsuma alone was able to spread its antennae through the "Ryūkyū official residence" in Fuzhou.

So-called "Crown Ships" carrying an emissary of investiture were later sent from Fuzhou to the Ryūkyūs by the Qing court. Trading ships also plied the sea-lanes between Naha and Fuzhou. Zhewen's letter to his father had similarly been sent via the "Ryūkyū official residence" in Fuzhou. Lian had very much wanted to learn about conditions in Japan, and Zhewen reported to him from the Ryūkyūs and Satsuma. Zhewen often illustrated his letters, which pleased his father enormously.

Developments in Japan are becoming very serious indeed, said Lian to himself, as he read the letter. He then opened up his inkstone case and began rubbing the ink and water in preparation for writing. The hand movements served to calm his mind a bit, for there had been several points in Zhewen's letter that had shaken him up. The sad fate was described here of a man who stood at the vanguard of his times. Over ten years earlier in Japan, the case of "Bansha jail" had arisen. The year was 1839, just before the outbreak of the Opium War. The shogunal authorities themselves had been stunned by the uprising of Ōshio Heihachirō (1793–1837) in Ōsaka some two years before, and were still quite nervous about Japanese interested in Dutch learning and other intellectuals as well. As it so happened, a man by the name of Torii Yōzō (1796–1873), an eccentric opposed to Dutch learning, charged the three famous Dutch learning scholars, Watanabe Kazan (1793–1841), Takano Chōei (1804–1850), and Koseki San'ei (1787–1839), with a crime he had cooked up, and they were arrested. Koseki committed suicide, and Kazan was captured and killed himself while under house arrest.

In his fifth year of life in prison, Takano Chōei was released because of a fire in the jailhouse. He was supposed to return once the fire was brought under control, but Chōei chose to remain underground. As a wanted man, he was compelled to do virtually everything for himself. Lian Weicai could fully understand Chōei's attitude of: "If I don't do it, who will?"

When Lian's fourth son, Liwen, was in Japan, he sent his father a detailed report of the story of Chōei's underground life. Secretly, Lian prayed that nothing ill would befall this pioneer in the neighboring land. In the previous year (1850), though, he heard that Chōei, having in vain burned his face with poisons in an effort to disguise himself, was captured in a raid on his home and met his end at this point in suicide. He was only forty-six years old, with such a talented future before him.

Despite his suicide, it soon became apparent in Japan that men like Chōei who had gained European learning were becoming more and more necessary for Japan itself. Foreign vessels and gunboats were approaching Japanese shores with increasing frequency all the time. Just two years before, the English warship *Marina* had magnificently stood at sea and surveyed the port of Tokyo. One year later, a Dutch trading ship had entered Nagasaki, and presented a written account—based on hearsay—that the Americans intended to open Japan to commercial trade.

The shogunate began to build fortifications at strategic points along the seacoast. Orders came down to the chief magistrate of Nirayama, Egawa Tarōzaemon (1801–1855), to construct a reverberating furnace, which made large-scale iron manufacture possible. This measure was taken with attention to national defense, as cannons made largely from copper were now replaced with the stronger iron cannons.

According to Zhewen's letter, this was not undertaken solely at the shogunate's behest, for plans had been drawn up in both Satsuma and Saga domains for the building of reverberating furnaces. It was a form of encouragement, insofar as it was permitted, of iron artillery manufacturing, which had until that point been restricted by the authorities. This represented a major change.

"This is really a severe turn of events," muttered Lian. The hand grinding the inkstone was moving rapidly. He removed it from the ink, sat up straight, and then turned the page. Letters at this time were written on special Chinese letter paper. Zhewen did not write letters as frequently as his brother Liwen, so the length of each one was greater.

As he turned the page, Lian involuntarily smiled. Half of the new page was a drawing. It bore the likeness of a Westerner wearing glasses, whose eyes seemed dazzled by the light. Although the Westerner appeared gaunt, one sensed a tenacity in the figure portrayed. Beneath the drawing, Zhewen had written: "This is a man by the name of Bo Deling. He is an extremely stubborn man, a missionary of English nationality. For the past five years, he has continually been digging up the earth and then covering the hole with the dug soil, only to once again dig where he just covered."

Occasional mention of Bettelheim had appeared in letters from Liwen as well. For his own part, Lian had tried to imagine the pastor's appearance from Liwen's written descriptions, but the image he had conjured up was far from the drawing by Zhewen. Lian had pictured a more energetic, stouter man.

In 1816, two English ships, the *Lyra* and the *Alceste,* docked in the Ryūkyūs. The captain of the former was Basil Hall (1788–1844), grandfather of B. H. Chamberlain (1850–1935), who later became professor of Japanese philology at Tokyo Imperial University. Basil Hall subsequently wrote several works on his travels to the Ryūkyūs and elsewhere in East Asia, including *Account of a Voyage of Discovery to the West Coast of Corea and the Great Loo-Choo Island,* and Hall's party seemed to find great enjoyment in the Ryūkyūs. After returning home, one enthusiastic officer aboard formed an association known as the Loo Choo Naval Mission, and raised contributions for a monetary fund, with an eye toward eventually sending missionaries to the Ryūkyūs.

Bettelheim was the first missionary sent by the Mission, arriving in the Ryūkyūs in 1846. Some twenty-seven years elapsed following the return of Basil Hall and his men before the Ryūkyū Naval Mission realized its goal. Although this goal of posting a missionary was achieved, Christian proselytizing did not proceed at all well. Bettelheim's labors, as Zhewen had spoofed them, were much like covering a hole one had just dug, only to dig it once again.

"But despite this fellow's stubbornness, you can have a friendly relationship with him," continued Zhewen. "It's actually quite a fortuitous friendship, because he may prove to be very advantageous. So, for now, I see him every day. He can't remain here that much longer, so I've got to get to know him well before it gets to be too late."

—3—

His name was Nakahama Manjirō (1827–1898), known best by the name of John Mung. He was a fisherman from the Tosa domain on the Japanese island of Shikoku. Shipwrecked, he was picked up by an American whaling vessel and taken to the United States, where he received an education. The shipwreck occurred when he was fourteen years old, and he then spent ten years in the United States, so that he forgot most of his Japanese. Even when he did occasionally remember something, it was in Tosa dialect, which was of little use in the Ryūkyūs.

In the United States, John Mung studied navigation and the science of surveying. He had returned to Japan with the expectation that his studies in America would be useful to his native land. The American vessel dropped him off in the Ryūkyūs in January 1851.

Despite being a shipwreck victim, once someone had been overseas, returning to Japan could be dangerous. For John Mung, unable to communicate in Japanese, Bettelheim was sure to be an excellent partner in conversation, but the two did not hit it off well at all. To Bettelheim, this English-speaking Japanese seemed like a shady character. To John Mung, the missionary's excessive religiosity was an utter nuisance.

Occasionally Lian Zhewen, who also spoke English, would be present. Zhewen was thirty-two years old and seemed closer in terms of age to the twenty-four-year-old Manjirō than was the forty-year-old Bettelheim. Zhewen listened avidly to John Mung's stories of the United States, and the latter was favorably impressed by Zhewen's enthusiasm. Zhewen knew the world of artists, of which Mung was ignorant, and Mung absorbed much from Zhewen about art and China. John Mung already knew full well about Bettelheim's world.

There was one more person with whom John Mung did have contact: Itarashiki Chōchū, the official interpreter for the Ryūkyūan authorities. Itarashiki later took the surname Makishi, and played a very important role in the history of the Ryūkyūs. Being a talented man, he was chosen for study in China, but upon seeing Qing China after the Opium War, and for reasons of his own, he decided to study English.

For these reasons, Itarashiki Chōchū was able to speak Chinese as well. The Ryūkyū government authorities had entrusted him in dealings with Bettelheim, and when John Mung arrived, Itarashiki was sent to handle the case. When Commodore Perry later called at the Ryūkyūs, Itarashiki entered into negotiations with him as well.

Perhaps it was only natural that Zhewen and Itarashiki would hit it off so well. Zhewen described in great detail conditions in China, in which both Itarashiki and John Mung were deeply interested. Zhewen knew of recent events in his homeland despite having been away for a period of time, from letters he had received from Liwen. Liwen was a faithful correspondent, and, despite being among the armed forces of the Taiping rebels, often wrote his elder brother. It was his responsibility as well to report to his father on developments concerning the Taipings. On occasion, Lian Weicai simply sent Zhewen (in the Ryūkyūs) Liwen's letters about the Taipings without comment. There were also times when Liwen wrote Zhewen directly via the Ryūkyū official residence in Fuzhou.

While Lian Weicai sat in his Tide-Gazing Mountain Chamber at Gulangxu, reading the letter from Zhewen in the Ryūkyūs, Zhewen sat in his own rooms in Naha, reading a letter from Liwen.

"Oh, so closely written," he said to himself as he unfolded the letter. "And there must be ten pages here, and such small characters. This'll make quite a piece of substantial reading." Liwen's communication described in detail circumstances surrounding the Taipings after the withdrawal from Jiangkou.

It is often said that no matter how difficult or complex an offensive strategy might be, none is more so than one of planned withdrawal. It was not a rout, but the dispersed withdrawal of the Taiping forces might have appeared as a defeat when viewed from one side only. Especially for those people who retained an animosity for the Society of God Worshippers, their wishful thinking seemed to have come true. When they saw the troops of the Society of God Worshippers running as fast as their feet would take them to the West, it seemed beyond a doubt that the Taipings had been routed.

Liu Xingxuan, a leader of the local defense forces in the village of Wangmoxiang, which lay between Jiangkou and Jintian village, had been thinking of a way to succeed in getting his superiors to recognize him by performing some remarkable feat. When the Taiping forces advanced on Jiangkou from Jintian village, he yielded to pressure and did not try to interfere. Then reports indicated that the Taipings had sustained several consecutive days of military defeats. They would probably escape in utter confusion to the West, he thought, and this was an opportunity he could not pass up.

Liu hurriedly called out the *tuanlian*. It was pitch black out, but the *tuanlian* were familiar with the local terrain. They captured a dozen or more Taiping troops who had been separated from their main force and tied them to trees.

The Taiping Army had just reorganized their fighting units, and they functioned with great vigor. During their planned retreat, there were occasional contacts between units and there were troop roll calls. Thus, the youthful organization would promptly know when troops were unaccounted for and when local *tuanlian* were moving about.

A patrol spotted the Taiping forces tied to trees, and a separate detachment that had encountered the *tuanlian* learned of the situation in confessions gathered from *tuanlian* forces they had captured.

"What do we do?" asked subordinates in the army, and Yang Xiuqing, general of the central army, immediately responded:

"Attack Wangmoxiang and massacre the *tuanlian*! Those who help the devils are our enemies, and heaven will reveal what fate will catch up with them."

Three thousand troops of the Taiping Army surrounded Wangmoxiang, a village of no more than one hundred households.

"If you don't hand over the men whom we are about to call out by name, we shall burn this village to the ground and kill everyone, regardless of age or sex. We are at war. This is no idle threat, as you may soon see," the Taiping commander shouted loudly in front of the homes of the village elders.

Several men who hailed from this village were now troops in the Taiping Army, so they knew the names of the *tuanlian* leaders.

"Liu Xingxuan, Liu Shangzhen, . . ." Eventually, thirteen names were called out, and they gave the village thirty minutes.

A torch burned brightly, just enough to illuminate the evening sky. The entire army was out for revenge, as hell itself was about to appear before their eyes. No one had the least doubt about this.

There was frantic movement within the surrounded village. The lives of the thirteen *tuanlian* leaders or the lives of several hundred local villagers? It was one or the other. Wangmoxiang chose to give up the thirteen men in a human sacrifice. None of the villagers wanted to be present at the time of execution.

"Forgive us for such a heartless thing, but what choice . . ." implored one of the village elders.

This story soon spread throughout the land, and, in its depiction of the brutality of the Taiping Army, it gave rise to an antipathetic response. Yang Xiuqing recognized this negative side to the action, but went ahead with the executions of the village *tuanlian* leaders, nonetheless.

In the subsequent fighting, there would be victories and defeats. Although this instance was not a defeat, it marked a significant step backward. By virtue of these executions, though, even when the fortunes of the Taiping Army looked bad, the local resident populace was not likely to become informants for the government's forces. It was this "positive" side that Yang stressed.

—4—

Liwen's letter described this bloody incident in dispassionate terms. Not being present at the place of execution, Liwen heard the story from others. Despite this, his report described the scene so vividly and with such detail, that it made those who read it feel as though they were observing it firsthand. As he was reading his younger brother's letter, Zhewen thought, "This Liwen has a remarkable flare. To be able to convey this scene to others so splendidly takes quite a talent." As an artist, Zhewen was always concerned with and endeavoring to reproduce a given scene or set of circumstances. Painting was not the sole mode of reproduction, for writing was an important means as well. When it came to "expression," painting and writing were at the same level. Thus, Zhewen was also capable of distinguishing quality of expression in writing.

"Such talent! What a waste for a merchant! Liwen has the ability of a Cao Xueqin," sighed Zhewen, invoking the name of the author of the great novel *Dream of the Red Chamber*, as he looked at Liwen's letter.

Two days after its withdrawal from Jiangkou, the Taiping Army entered the familiar Thistle Mountain area and reached Dongxiang in the county of Wuxuan. Two days after that, on the twelfth day of the second lunar month,

Guangxi Governor Zhou Tianjue passed through Xunzhou and entered the Wuxuan county seat. Provincial Military Commander Xiang Rong, having recovered Jiangkou, arrived there on the fourteenth day of the second month.

Fighting broke out between the Qing and Taiping forces in Wuxuan on the seventeenth day of the second lunar month. The Taipings led the attack this time, and held the superior position throughout. Xiang Rong was surrounded in the battle before he knew what had happened. He was saved by a prefect named Zhang Jingxiu, who was under the command of Zhou Tianjue. Zhang's troops rushed to the scene, and, aware of the formidable reinforcements they represented, the Taiping Army raised their siege.

The Qing forces, which were scraped together from military units in various places, were not controlled as a military organization per se, though discord at the top was especially severe. The disharmony between Imperial Commissioner Li Xingyuan and Guangxi Governor Zhou Tianjue involved a question of personalities as well as something beyond the powers even of the two men concerned.

"In particular, we request selection of a regional commander." The date attached to this memorial, signed jointly by Li, Zhou, and Xiang, was the twenty-first day of the second month.

Because bandit activity in Guangxi had reached unimaginable proportions, they were requesting that someone with the highest responsibility and absolute powers be dispatched, who could spur the troop commanders on, as well as provide leadership. In actual fact, Li Xingyuan had come to Guangxi, entrusted with plenipotentiary powers, to attain just those aims. In effect, the fact that Li affixed his name to this memorial, implied that he had thrown up his hands in despair.

On the very same day, Hong Xiuquan performed his official enthronement ceremony in the vicinity of Dongling in Wuxuan. Liwen was not present at the ceremony. He was still, more or less, seen as an outsider. Only a few members of the Taiping elite were present at the coronation. The great majority of Taiping adherents learned the following day, "Yesterday, the Heavenly King ascended the throne." And no one was told of the details concerning the actual ceremony itself.

Liwen questioned Yang Xiuqing, Feng Yunshan, and others of the highest Taiping echelon, but the only response he received was: "The accession is a secret ritual, and we shall not be publicizing its shape and form."

From the early days in Jintian village, Hong Xiuquan had been using the title, Heavenly King. The ceremony of accession was merely formal ratification. This was not, though, simply a self-styled title, for there was a perceived need to announce to the entire realm that there was substance to this claim, through the ceremony of enthronement.

Perhaps, thought Liwen, with doubts on his mind, no real ceremony at all was carried out. It was strange that such a major event as the ceremony of Hong's accession to the throne would be restricted, while performers such as Yang Xiuqing were available.

It was understood that a ritual for the purposes of confirmation was necessary. Not one member of the Taiping Army, however, knew what exactly had transpired during the ceremony. The army was comprised of peasants, charcoal workers, and failed examination students. It was a band without so much as a hint of a connection to such things as imperial courts and the like.

The troops talked the matter over among themselves. "It would be strange, wouldn't it, if they didn't have an accession ceremony, since he is, after all, the 'Heavenly King'?"

"So one day they went and carried it out, and the next day they announce it to everybody. That's fine, isn't it?"

"No objection here."

When Liwen asked the young and sincere Shi Dakai about the nature of the accession ceremony, Shi's answer was precisely the same as that of the other Taiping leaders, as if some previous agreement had been reached. But the image was all confused, and there was a sense of fear that children would create rumors around it, and stories would leak out.

After the battle of the seventeenth, there were no large-scale hostilities, and a stalemate ensued. The Taiping Army held the mountainous region to the southwest of Thistle Mountain, covering some 40 kilometers east to west. Sixty to seventy villages fell under their control. That meant that the Taipings were effectively on home ground, because this was not far from the original base of the Society of God Worshippers. Replacements of provisions and the like were therefore relatively easy.

Pitted against the Taiping forces, the Qing military lacked the capacity to surround the enemy, and their morale was extremely low as well. The Qing adopted a policy of "sit and fight." They built strong, immense, pillbox-like structures, and were prepared to fight from them should the Taipings attack. This was not an activist, offensive strategy, but an effort to tire out the opponent by dragging out the conflict as long as possible. Indeed, the Qing had no other effective means of fighting.

"There are numerous groups of bandits, and the military power of the official armies is insufficient. Please send reinforcements." So went the repeated requests of the commander of the Qing forces in Guangxi to the central government. Beijing ordered bannerman Wu-lan-tai (1792–1852), vice-commander-in-chief of Guangzhou, to provide military assistance to Guangxi. This order went out on the twenty-second day of the second lunar month, but Wu-lan-tai did not leave Guangzhou until the twelfth day of the third lunar month, for preparations were still needed if he was planning military engagements. Wu-lan-tai led a group of 1,000 Manchu soldiers into the province of Guangxi. Despite this small number of troops, they brought along a large number of weapons: 100 small artillery pieces and 200 small arms.

Later, historians have asked why, when Qing military capacity was weak and there was discord among its generals, did the Taipings just settle down in Wuxuan; and why they did not forcibly break through and attack Guilin? The Qing forces remained just outside Wuxuan. Troops were mobilized from Liuzhou to Guilin, with scarcely any remaining resident in these places. Had the government's troops been defeated at Wuxuan, it is questionable whether they could have made the long trek across uninhabited terrain to Guilin.

The Taipings in Wuxuan, though, had no means of knowing Qing troop strength and troop disposition, nor did they have information about internal division among the Qing military leaders.

Although the present situation was unclear in many ways to Liwen, it seemed likely that Qing reinforcements were to arrive sooner or later. The more they sat back and remained quiet, the more anxiety it aroused. It was during this period of deadlock that he wrote to Zhewen in the Ryūkyūs: "They've gone so far as to have an enthronement ceremony, so perhaps the Taipings will be more resolute about fighting. The plan was to move north and attack the heart of the country. I sense that there is a desire for greater activism. Maybe even these courageous men of the Taiping Army, who for so long did not venture far from the familiar environs of Thistle Mountain, are becoming uneasy."

—5—

On the day Zhewen read his brother's letter, he had already written one of his own. The very experience of encountering such extraordinarily exquisite prose as that of Liwen, two years his junior, stimulated Zhewen to no end— an artistic impulse, no doubt.

What Zhewen had written was half letter and half drawing. He was trying to convey recent events in his personal life in prose and picture. It arrived in Liwen's hands at the beginning of the sixth lunar month.

Everyday affairs continued in the very area where the Taipings and the Qing forces were fighting. Porters came and went, carrying not only food and clothing, but even letters. In the mountains of Wuxuan, what was most lacking for the Taiping Army was not food provisions, but salt and the saltpeter used in the production of gunpowder. The shrewd porters joined with merchants and transported salt and saltpeter to the Taipings, and payment was always forthcoming for the goods that the

Taiping Army—following a strict military discipline—purchased, rather than commandeered.

When Zhewen's letter reached Wuxuan, the Taipings had already designated porters for this transport. It was limited to those with long-time associations with, or family relations among, the Taiping troops. This was because of the "poison salt case." Zhou Tianjue had paid off some porters to carry salt that had been mixed with poison to the Taipings. Perhaps the mixing had been done improperly, for the "poison salt" did not have excessive toxicity. The worst that occurred was an outbreak of diarrhea among a few dozen soldiers. A doctor versed in pharmacology ascertained that the root cause of the group diarrhea lay in the salt. At about the same time, a Taiping spy who had infiltrated the Qing Army submitted this report: "Be careful with the salt! Zhou Tianjue announced that he will completely wipe out the Taiping Army with poison salt."

Thereafter, only reliable porters were used. The man who brought Zhewen's letter was a member of the Society of God Worshippers and was so designated.

Eventually, the deadlock in the tide of war began to break up. After Liwen sent his letter to the Ryūkyūs from Dongling, Imperial Commissioner Li Xingyuan died at the Wuxuan county seat. There was alcohol poisoning as well as blockages throughout his body; there was more than one cause of death.

The spy also reported that there was a widely entertained theory circulating among the Qing forces that Li Xingyuan had committed suicide. Yet the truth remained unclear. While the suicide theory could not be denied, if it was true, what had motivated the imperial commissioner?

Suicide obviously is preceded by despair, but what was he despairing over? He had failed to achieve victory in his battles with the Taipings. Things were not going well for him among the Qing military commanders under Zhou Tianjue. Vice-Commander-in-Chief Wu-lan-tai, recently arrived from Guangzhou, soon found himself in opposition to Provincial Military Commander Xiang Rong over strategy. It may have looked as though there was no hope of victory over the Taipings. The former Guangxi Military Commander Min Zhengfeng had been incapable of suppressing rampant bandit activity, and for that reason he was banished to the deserts of Xinjiang. What sort of punishment awaited Li if he failed to suppress the Taipings? Perhaps despair had set in as he pondered this dilemma.

Rumors of the imperial commissioner's suicide stimulated the morale of the Taiping forces.

Li died on the twelfth day of the fourth lunar month. Shortly before this, the court in Beijing had decided to dispatch Grand Secretary Sai-shang-a to Guangzhou in response to the special joint memorial for a regional commander. Sai-shang-a was a Mongol, the Wenhuadian (Palace of Cultural Efflorescence) Grand Secretary, or, first name on the list of seven regular members of the Grand Secretariat. He was also minister of revenue and grand minister of state. He was a big shot with virtually no peer.

However, to send a major figure was an acknowledgment that the uprising in Guangxi was becoming a serious situation. Any regime would want to see rebellion on its territory as something as insignificant as possible. For the Beijing government, the Taiping uprising was usually belittled as the "wriggling of petty bandits," at least on the surface.

Publicly, the assignment of Sai-shang-a read, "We direct you to proceed to Hunan." En route to Guangxi from Beijing, he would have to pass through Hunan. His mission was to take over all military affairs in Guangxi.

The lineup of important figures who accompanied Sai-shang-a included: Ba-qing-de, a Mongol banner commander-in-chief; Da-hong-a, a Manchu banner vice-commander-in-chief; and Chang-rui, regional commander of the Tianjin garrison. They were all, including Sai-shang-a, important Manchus or Mongols; not one was Han Chinese. By the same token, all of the leaders at the front lines—Li Xingyuan, Zhou Tianjue, and Xiang Rong—were Han Chinese. Also, Wu-lan-tai—who was directed to Guangxi from Guangzhou—was a Manchu commander. This new personnel revealed the Qing court's strong sense of distrust toward Han Chinese.

Misgivings were circulating at the Qing court too: If the Qing dynasty of the Manchus collapses, Han Chinese probably won't be overly troubled. Rebel forces all over the land, including the Taipings, are all raising the standard: "Destroy the Manchus and revive the Han." When it comes to it, will Han troops fight wholeheartedly against such rebel units?

The participation of Manchu generals, however, only served to confuse the situation at the scene of action. The 1,000 men under Wu-lan-tai's command were Manchu soldiers, imperial guards who had been stationed in various places. They often boasted: "We're the army under the Son of Heaven's direct control!" Wu-lan-tai himself was a Manchu of the Plain Red Banner, a military man by origin. His accomplishments in that vein began in campaigns when Zungaria gained the support of Kokand (a Muslim state presently in the Republic of Uzbekistan) and rose in rebellion in Xinjiang in 1826. For his meritorious deeds, he was made head of the junior guardsmen, a position that carried a 9A rank, comparable to a noncommissioned officer. In 1835, he rose to the position of protector lieutenant, rank 6A, indisputably a commissioned officer. At the time of the Opium War, he was already a brigade commander, rank 3A, the equivalent of a general.

Wu-lan-tai's character was perhaps most apparent during an incident involving a powder magazine explosion. The explosion killed a number of soldiers, and he was the sole person responsible for it. The sanction against him was a loss of position, but he was to remain at his post, it was argued, to afford him the opportunity to redeem himself. For a man who had achieved so much so rapidly, this was an unexpected setback. At that point, he dug in his heels. Through a thorough investigation of the causes of the powder magazine explosion, he ascertained that it transpired during the production process, and he then proceeded to change the production method.

His "contribution to the reform of the production method" proved sufficient for him to recover his former position. His enthusiasm concerning gunpowder production was motivated by his effort to establish that the fault was not his as supervisor, but lay with the producers, and accordingly, the sanction taken against him was unjust. This episode also revealed his belief in himself as a virtually flawless human being. His implacability was extraordinary. He was a man of frightening self-righteousness.

Perhaps it was inevitable that soon after his arrival in Wuxuan, a conflict of opinion emerged with Xiang Rong. A vice-commander-in-chief of a provincial bannerman army was comparable to a regional commander in the Green Standard forces (a Han banner regiment). A commander-in-chief was at the same level as a provincial military commander. Provincial Military Commander Xiang Rong was, from the perspective of rank, Wu-lan-tai's superior. Wu-lan-tai, however, had no regard whatsoever for such things.

His self-esteem came to the surface in his conceit that he was, after all, the imperial court's designated general. Xiang Rong was not amused. This younger man arrived in Guangxi with no knowledge of local conditions and then suddenly sounded off loudly to the following effect: "What is this? This lineup just won't do. Strategy and planning have been handled perfunctorily, I'd say."

"Then do as you please," said Xiang Rong, ignoring him.

At the time of the Zungar Rebellion in 1826, Wu-lan-tai was a low-level soldier in the Qing Army, but Xiang Rong led an entire army unit as brigade vice-commander, rank 4A, during the same military engagement.

"Different sorts of people altogether, that guy and me," said Xiang Rong, loudly enough to be audible to a group of men.

Leaders of the Qing forces were gathered in the Wuxuan county seat. Li Xingyuan had died on the ninth day following Wu-lan-tai's arrival. Four days after that, the Taipings advanced their troops to Xiangzhou. This action meant that the Taiping Army had moved out of their base in Thistle Mountain.

Hearing the news that "the bandits are entering Xiangzhou," the Guizhou Provincial Army took the field. The Guizhou Army was led by Regional Commanders Qin Dingsan and Zhou Fengqi, but even among the low-quality government troops, they had the lowest fighting morale. The forces so badly defeated by the Taipings at Cai village were none other than this Guizhou Army. Among the officers and men, a morbid fear of the Taiping Army was widespread. Given that, the Guizhou Army now effectively took the attitude of an onlooker or bystander when the Taipings invaded a place called Miaowang in Xiangzhou.

"The devils' armies have no will for a fight!" Using their momentum, the Taiping Army moved to occupied locales within Xiangzhou: Gucheng, Sicun, Zhongping, Bozhang, and Dayuexu. They set up encampments at Dubieshan and Ma'anshan, and then attacked the Guizhou Army. The latter was hit with Taiping artillery and retreated.

On the twenty-ninth day of the fourth lunar month, Wu-lan-tai arrived at the Luoxiu military encampment in Xiangzhou to reorganize the remnants of the Guizhou forces into his army. A war of accusations then began. Zhou Tianjue, Xiang Rong, and Wu-lan-tai sent a memorial to Beijing that condemned Qin Dingsan and Zhou Fengqi of the Guizhou Army, for allegedly avoiding a battle with the Taiping Army. Zhou Tianjue then submitted a separate memorial censuring Xiang Rong.

Xiang Rong always brought his son Xiang Jixiong along with the army, and despite the large number of formal officers and staff with the troops, he relinquished full authority in the area of strategy to his son. For that reason, he was accused of "having lost his martial spirit."

Like Wu-lan-tai, Xiang Rong came from a military family, and he was a man of extraordinary self-confidence and, indeed, self-flattery. The similarities between the two men may actually have been responsible for their mutual repulsion. Xiang Rong's conceit involved a mixture of public and private matters.

As for Wu-lan-tai, he made his accusations directly to Beijing: "As to the matter of the bandits having taken refuge in Xiangzhou, I would like my crimes investigated." The court in Beijing responded as follows.

Zhou Tianjue was deprived of the brevet rank of governor-general, and his position as imperial commissioner, which he had assumed upon the death of Li Xingyuan, was discontinued. The brevet rank was not a substantive post, but implied the salary he received. Zhou was the governor of Guangxi province, not a governor-general, but he received a governor-general's salary. He now retained his original post as governor, relinquishing only the brevet rank—not at all a severe punishment.

Xiang Rong and Qin Dingsan were divested of their peacock plumes. The peacock plumes were attached as badges to their official's caps, which they were permitted to wear by virtue of certain accomplishments. Now they were no longer allowed to wear their signs of achievement as before. It was a punishment that forbade them from wearing their medals.

The case of Wu-lan-tai, who had brought impeachment upon himself, was ignored. It was felt that he had just arrived in Guangxi, and that his responsibility was lighter than that of other military leaders on the scene. However, before news of this judgment arrived from Beijing, the Qing forces were once again stricken by a stinging military defeat at the hands of the Taiping Army.

Wu-lan-tai had led detachments of the newly reorganized Guizhou Army to attack the Taipings at Dubieshan and Ma'anshan. They were counterattacked, however, and it ended in complete defeat for the 1000 men of this Qing force. Encountering an ambush, the government's army suffered some 200 deaths, including such high-level military officials as Ma Shanbao (assistant regional commander, rank 3A), Bo-le-guo-bu (brigade commander, rank 3B), and Liu Dingtai (also a brigade commander).

Ironically, the news from Beijing that Wu-lan-tai's "crimes were ignored" was delivered in the aftermath of a gruesome defeat. Perhaps Wu-lan-tai sought to recover his honor, but this time he had handled himself just as badly as he had at the time of the gunpowder magazine explosion. The entire Qing encampment was utterly discouraged.

—6—

"The bespectacled Dr. Bo Deling (Bernard Bettelheim) is the same as always. I unconsciously burst out laughing reading your letter, elder brother. When I was in the Ryūkyūs, the Christian interdiction was still in operation, and so, when Bettelheim would start his street preaching, the authorities would come and chase the people away. Bettelheim would obstinately raise his voice, and even if not a single person was standing before him listening, he continued his incessant sermons. I could hear him even inside the house, and he'd go on for three quarters of an hour or more.

"Bettelheim's a decent man. Only when he acts like a big shot do I want to shrink away.

"There are uninvited big shots in the Qing Army, too. I've heard tell that the Manchu Wu-lan-tai is earnestly concerned that, in his absence, the entire state structure of the Qing dynasty might collapse. These 'uninvited big shots' are wrapped up in themselves, and thus fail to perceive their opponents properly. Wu-lan-tai has no understanding of the Taipings. As far as he's concerned, they're just bandits—a mob, no more. Last month, he was beaten very badly by Taiping forces at Dubieshan. Perhaps it brought him out of his self-intoxication a bit.

"Such self-important sorts aren't limited to the Qing military forces. You'll find them among the Taipings as well.

"After the Taipings entered Wuxuan, different sorts of men from the Jintian days gathered in their camps, a self-impressed military man among them. His surname is Jiao, and he took the given name Liang, which was not his real name, but which he took from the famous Chinese general of the Three Kingdoms period, Zhuge Liang (181–234). They didn't really investigate his background closely, but he himself revealed—in a soft voice so you would think this was a very important matter—that his real given name was Da: Jiao Da, or Jiao 'the Great.'

"He thinks of himself as the reincarnation of Zhuge Liang. He's so completely self-absorbed that it's very difficult to have any kind of interaction with him. He's a lot like Bettelheim, in that, when he opens his mouth, you never know just when he'll close it. Whenever I'm talking to him, I'm reminded of Bettelheim. Jiao Liang's not a bad guy, but he's much more pretentious than Bettelheim, and unbearably vulgar at times.

"Jiao is from Hunan province. Like Heavenly King Hong Xiuquan, he started as an examination student and, like Hong as well, he took the examinations many times and always failed them. There's a kind of charm in the fact that he never hides these failures when speaking of the subject, but quickly he'll arrogantly say: 'That examination official in rural Hunan didn't know anything about refinement in prose, so there was no way I'd ever pass.'

"Jiao is a member of the Heaven and Earth Society, but he doesn't seem to get along at all with Luo Dagang or Su Sanniang, both members of Heaven and Earth sects who are now in the Taiping military forces. Nonetheless, Luo is a fair man and evaluated Jiao as a 'man with considerable clout among the secret societies of Hunan.'

"He's also a gossip and thoroughly full of himself, but what he has to say is interesting. So, the various group leaders ought to be curious about what he says. It's sort of like a feeling that we might want to read an interesting novel. So when I say that he's well-known, it's this sense that I have in mind.

"Since Hong Xiuquan and Yang Xiuqing are planning to proceed north from Guangxi to Hunan, I think they're going to have to enlist the help of the Heaven and Earth Society in Hunan, because there's still no Society of God Worshippers there. They'll have to rely on the Heaven and Earth Society outside of Guangxi.

"Oral evaluations of character are often less than candid. For the purposes of peacefully getting along together, people frequently are prepared to praise one another in public. However, Luo Dagang, who was himself a member of a Heaven and Earth sect and despised Jiao to no end, recognized his 'considerable clout,' and he was certainly not wrong in that regard.

"Yang Xiuqing and others took into account the fact that Luo was an honest and sincere man, and Jiao was accordingly treated with extraordinary courtesy. This seemed to give Jiao even more cause for self-inflation.

"'If I pull some sort of ruse on you, the Taiping Army will be in big trouble, won't it?' said Jiao Liang before the assembled Taiping leaders. 'The Taiping Army has been lucky, because you've hooked up with me and my immense forces. Really, if I weren't around, you'd all die a bunch of beggars in no time.' They all laughed out loud, and actually did seem good-spirited about it.

"Yesterday, this big shot was summoned by Yang Xiuqing. He had a question for Jiao about the best route to take from Guilin into Hunan. It seems reasonable to me that he'd want as much information as possible about the leaders of Heaven and Earth sects along the way, and about the nature and influence of each. I don't know what Yang actually spoke about, but I certainly know Yang's character well. When Jiao returned after meeting with Yang, he said, 'Yang turned the position of commander of the central army over to me. He wants me to take over supervision of the Taiping military forces, but I turned him down. I'm a Zhuge Liang to the end. I have no need for the realm. I'm content to be a military leader within the realm. If requested, I'll offer advice, but leading an army into battle does not accord with my principles,' he concluded, with a broad smile beaming across his face.

"Yang has had nothing to say about offering Jiao the position of commander of the central army. Jiao is a good talker, but he has a habit of fabricating these stories. Early this morning, Jiao went to visit Heavenly King Hong Xiuquan. As he was leaving, he said: 'I've decided to meet with the Heavenly King, because he earnestly requested a meeting to ask me my views on things.'

"In fact, Jiao had applied for this meeting earlier through Hong's staff men. This I knew for sure, and Jiao should have been aware that I knew. Still, he shamelessly said what he said. This kind of audacity would probably even be too much for Dr. Bettelheim.

"When Jiao returned from his recent meeting with Hong, he said: 'Wow, we've got a complete mutual understanding. . . . He wanted me to become a leader of the Taipings, but I, of course, declined. But when the conversation turned to becoming sworn brothers, I couldn't turn him down. . . . I changed my given name from Da to Liang, but from now on the Heavenly King decided that I shall now be called Hong Daquan. Da was part of my original name after all. . . . Since brothers usually share an ideograph in their names, the Heavenly King decided to give me the ideograph, Quan, from his name.'

"I was utterly dumbfounded. He wasn't the least bit shy before Hong, carrying out this remarkable event just as he conceived it. People like Jiao need third parties to hear their tales. He probably thought I'd make a good listener in this case. I didn't show my displeasure, just echoed his mood, and he probably thought I was the perfect sucker. It's true, though, that I gave in to his big mouth.

"I think that Bettelheim is much easier to get along with because he has no particular worldly ambitions. I almost feel as though it'll do Jiao Liang good if you show some distaste for him.

"There is the expression that 'friends and acquaintances are bequeathed by heaven,' but it can be a risky business.

"The young man mentioned in your letter by the name of Nakahama Manjirō seems an extremely fascinating fellow. If you have been bequeathed a good friend, I'm very happy for you."

Lian Liwen completed his letter, which was getting to be quite long. He sipped his tea, took a moment's rest, and then decided to continue writing.

The night was still as death in the environs of the Taiping command at Ma'anshan, Xiangzhou. Late at night, no wind, hot and humid.

11

Escape from the Jaws of Death

—1—

In a dignified, stately manner, Imperial Commissioner Sai-shang-a entered the city of Guilin on the fourth day of the sixth lunar month, 1851. The political and administrative center of Guangxi province is now the city of Nanning, but in the Qing dynasty, the capital of Guangxi was Guilin. The provincial governor resided there, and his office was situated where a soccer field behind the Li River Hotel now stands. The city walls were built facing the Li River.

Until the eleventh month of the previous year, the governor had been Zheng Zuchen, but he was dismissed for having allowed rampant "bandit" activity—the Society of God Worshippers and the Heaven and Earth Society—in Guangxi, and the newly appointed Imperial Commissioner, Lin Zexu, was to take up this post. When Lin died at Chaozhou en route from Fujian to Guangxi, Beijing selected the near octogenarian Zhou Tianjue, as his replacement, which proved to be a personnel error.

Zhou Tianjue was both an old man and obstinate. Seven years earlier, he had left the bureaucracy after being dismissed for an accident that occurred while he was director-general of grain transport, and he still harbored a grudge. He was dismissed because someone had forged his official seal, but there was nothing he was able to do at the time to prevent it.

What did I do wrong, he often thought. It wasn't my responsibility, but they made me take the blame, and it cost me several years of my life.

From his perspective, men like Imperial Commissioner Li Xingyuan were just errand boys. He came into conflict with everyone and argued over everything. It was soon clear to people even in Beijing that this appointment was a mistake. So, by virtue of his age, Zhou was recalled to the capital. Zou Minghe, prefect of the metropolitan prefecture, was appointed as his replacement.

It was Guangxi Governor Zou Minghe who welcomed Imperial Commissioner Sai-shang-a at Guilin, though Zou had just arrived himself.

"Has Jiang Zhongyuan not yet arrived?" asked the imperial commissioner. These were his first words once the prescribed salutations involved in assuming a post were concluded.

"Not as yet, although we have received communication from him. He reports that he is recruiting troops and will be several days late," responded the governor.

"I see." The color of despair rose onto the imperial commissioner's face.

Before he had left Beijing, Sai-shang-a had conducted a study of his own of the new duties involved in attacking and destroying the armies of the Society of God Worshippers. To that end, he had sought out the opinions of many people, and every single person had said that the government's troops were thoroughly useless. The only countermeasure left was to rely on an army of volunteers. There were *tuanlian* forces in various parts of the country to protect their respective local terrain. They were local self-defense forces and had no desire to fight outside of the areas of their homes. If he could only train a fighting corps of men one level of consciousness higher than the *tuanlian* troops, they were sure to be of use in battles against the Society of God Worshippers. And everyone would realize it.

It was too late to start training such a force now. A private army of any genuine utility was not likely to come into existence very soon. Bandits held sway in many places, and the *tuanlian* were resisting, but it was highly doubtful that many *tuanlian* or comparable groups were reliable.

There was, however, an official from Hunan province who had managed to capture some bandits in Xinning, Hunan. Sai-shang-a proceeded to look into this case. His name was Jiang Zhongyuan (1812–1854). He had passed the second level of the imperial examinations in 1837, received the rank of *juren*, and become a teacher. In 1847, when Lei Zaihao of the Heaven and Earth Society attacked and plundered Xinning, Jiang Zhongyuan led local troops in a counterattack, and, marching into the enemy's base, he took the bandit leader captive. He said it was easy to lead local forces, but, if he had not enjoyed considerable popularity, the younger men would never have followed him into battle. Jiang's success was not attributable to the personnel he had rounded up, but to his leadership of this group of young men, who considered themselves his followers. He had not been a teacher for appearance's sake alone.

It was known to Sai-shang-a that Jiang had been recommended for office by Zeng Guofan (1811–1872), but that he was still in Xinning because of the death of his father. When the Xianfeng Emperor ascended the throne in the previous year, he issued an edict calling for each of his high officials to recommend a talented man to the court. Zeng Guofan, a vice-minister in the Ministry of Rites, sent forward the name of Jiang Zhongyuan. By virtue of his distinction of having captured Lei Zaihao, Jiang had been appointed county magistrate. Despite Zeng's recommendation, though, Jiang returned to Xinning to observe mourning for his father.

Xinning was in the province of Hunan, close to the Guangxi border. It was also close to the lair of a bandit group, and after the seizure of Lei Zaihao, Li Yuanfa, along with the remnants of that group, rose in rebellion and killed the county magistrate. The number of bandits was numerous, but the *tuanlian* to resist them was growing as well. Steeled and tempered in battle, the local *tuanlian* towered above forces from other locales, reaching the level of a volunteer corps who were known as the "local militia." The man who trained them was this former schoolteacher, Jiang Zhongyuan.

Since the government's armies were useless, they had no choice but to form new military units. The model for this new military organization would, not surprisingly, be this local militia, and the fact that much was expected of the men who trained them at this time was also not surprising. Sai-shang-a had hoped to meet Jiang Zhongyuan in Guilin, but Jiang was going to be arriving a bit later than planned. The look of disappointment that Sai-shang-a revealed indicated just how great his expectations were.

"Yes, Jiang Zhongyuan has yet to arrive, but there are many well-known local men, such as Mr. Zhu Qi and Mr. Long Qirui, who have devoted considerable energy to training *tuanlian*," said Zou Minghe.

Zou hailed from Jiangsu province, and did not much feel that Hunan could hold a candle to it. Having now become governor of Guangxi, he wanted to lend his support to that province. It seemed to him that the imperial commissioner was investing considerable hope in this Jiang Zhongyuan from Hunan, but he implied that there were talented people involved in *tuanlian* activities in Guangxi as well.

Take Zhu Qi (1803–1861), for example. Having passed the highest level of the imperial examinations and received the *jinshi* degree, he was appointed to the critical post of investigating censor in the central government. Then, due to illness, he returned to his hometown of Lingui in Guangxi. Long Qirui (1814–1868) was the sun in Guangxi's skies. In the metropolitan examinations of 1841, he had ranked first nationwide. Appointed an "expositor in waiting" (namely, someone particularly skilled at explaining classical texts), he entered service in the Forbidden City, having supervised the educational administration of Hubei province until the previous year. He then returned home to observe mourning following the death of his father.

"Yes, he ranked first." Sai-shang-a knew the name of Long Qirui and was trying to help Zou save face. In his heart, though, he knew that war had no relationship whatsoever to examinations.

Jiang Zhongyuan may not have passed the highest level of examinations, but he had successfully captured the bandit ringleader, Lei Zaihao, alive. All the brilliance of official or examination records in the world was no advantage when it came to attacking the Society of God Worshippers.

Sai-shang-a realized that he needed to clarify the critical nature of the current situation. Turning to an attendant, he ordered, "Bring that sword over here." And then, to Zou, "Let me show you the sword of Ebilun," he said, in a serious tone of voice.

"What's that? Ebilun's sword?" Zou turned pale. Ebilun was an elder statesman from the founding generation of the Qing dynasty. He had made for him a treasured sword with a sheath and hilt of pure silver inlaid with precious stones. It was a well-tempered, fine blade that could cut through steel, it was said, as if it were mud. It was later stored in the palace treasury. In 1748 (the thirteenth year of the Qianlong reign), Ebilun's eldest son's heir, Nochin, was named commander general in the Jinchuan expedition. After a series of defeats in battle, the Qianlong Emperor sent this treasured sword to the front with the order, "With the sword of his grandfather Ebilun, kill this unworthy grandson!" And so, poor Nochin was beheaded with the celebrated sword his grandfather had had forged. This action struck fear into the hearts of the entire army, heightening its tension in battle, and ultimately the army pacified Jinchuan. Jinchuan was in Sichuan province, and the rebellion was the work of Tibetans there.

It was not without reason then that Zou Minghe turned pale upon hearing of Ebilun's sword. The fact that the emperor had given this sword to Sai-shang-a meant that he had allowed the imperial commissioner extraordinary means and extraordinary resolution in crushing the rebellion in Guangxi.

"First kill, then memorialize!" This sword was the symbol of authority, offering he who possessed it the right to kill, without receiving imperial sanction first, and only then proceeding to memorialize the throne.

Zou may have been the governor of Guangxi, but heads could roll solely at the discretion of the imperial commissioner. The officer, upon entering, reverently presented the precious sword of dazzling silver. Zou fell quickly to his knees, and Sai-shang-a also turned pale.

—2—

The Taiping Army was about to move. Their movements at this time resembled blotting paper in the sense that there were members of the Society of God Worshippers in many locations, and those who had been unable to join the cause in Jintian village participated in the movement when the Taiping Army approached the area in which they resided. It was as if they were absorbed into the army as it entered these local areas.

They amassed troops as far as Xiangzhou, but their desired course to the north proved to be not at all hospitable. For several successive days the leaders spread out their maps and pondered their strategy.

"We return to Guilin," decided Yang Xiuqing with finality. Turning completely around gave them the sense of making a new start. Still, the advance into Xiangzhou was by no means a waste of time. They learned that there was no adequate way to launch a campaign to the north from there, and they had been able to increase troop strength along the way. Every time the Taiping forces moved, their troop strength increased, so that no movement was ever in vain.

From Xiangzhou they returned to Wuxuan, and following their original course, reentered Thistle Mountain.

"We return to be surrounded," explained Feng Yunshan to the leaders.

"Why return to be surrounded without offering any resistance?"

"So as to break through the encirclement."

"I just don't understand."

"You'll soon see. Wouldn't it be easier to break through the same encirclement if you knew the lay of the land well? We know every inch of terrain around Thistle Mountain and the Guilin area. There will be an opportunity to escape and proceed to the north," expounded Feng, full of self-confidence.

This self-confidence was supported by observations. Lian Liwen and Li Xinmei had scouted it out. It was a pathway that cut through Wudong Mountain to Guangcun via Siwang, Pingnan county, and from there headed north toward Yongan. North of Guangcun lay the village of Huazhou, and this was well-known terrain to the Taiping Army.

Tuanlian troops, let alone the Qing army, would never show their faces in these areas. Huazhou lay within the Penghua Mountain region, where Hong Xiuquan and Feng Yunshan waited in ambush. The region had a special connection with the Society of God Worshippers. The entire strength of their organization, though, had moved in the altogether different direction of Wuxuan and Xiangzhou. As far as the government's troops were concerned, they were convinced that the Huazhou area had been abandoned by the Society of God Worshippers. So, the *tuanlian,* with their obligation to protect their hometowns, were assembled by their superiors and sent off to Wuxuan and Xiangzhou.

It was a blind spot.

"We don't much look like a married couple, do we?" said Li Xinmei.

The two of them moved along separately, occasionally meeting to exchange information.

"It is a waste of effort of sorts," said Liwen with a forced smile.

"Most of the young girls around here are older than their husbands."

"Xinmei, would you like to become a wife?"

"Times were terrible when I was born. . . . And, if I could just make the world a little better . . . what do you think? That's why we're doing all this, isn't it?"

Xinmei sidled up to him. Her eyes glistened, and for some reason those eyes reminded Liwen of his father. Was it because the shine in their eyes was similar? Or, was it because they shared a desire to pass on a slightly better world to the next generation?

Xinmei could easily assume an actress's role, perform tricks, and gather people around her. From such a group she would then be able to gather all manner of information. The local mountain people were a simple, honest folk, who would rarely pass along lies.

"The youngsters have all been lured far away. . . . So, it's gotten real lonely around here. . . . It used to be a little more lively. But without the young people, all the energy in the village is gone. It's really bad," said an old villager as he knocked the ashes out of his long-stemmed pipe.

Assuming the identity of a timber merchant, Liwen had a tree cut down. When he came to pay the security money, he worked out an arrangement for paying off the balance. He asked that trees be cut as close to the roadway as possible.

"That way it'll be easier to haul them off," he said.

In actual fact, when the Taiping Army marched north along this route, in order to impede the Qing army's pursuit of them, they planned to place these trees as obstructions on this road. Liwen's arrangements were to create the materials for this action.

"Many thanks," said Liwen. "I've got a little drinking money. Do you think you could split it between you?"

Liwen wanted the timber in place so that it could be used as soon as possible. By way of precaution, the two men conveyed the rumor to Liwen that the military forces of the Society of God Worshippers had already passed Xiangzhou and were heading toward Guilin from Liuzhou. It seemed as though the storm caused by the rebellion of the Society of God Worshippers had already blown through this area once before.

The Society of God Worshippers—namely, the Taiping Army—had actually returned home from Xiangzhou. Having observed this, Provincial Military Commander Xiang Rong and Vice-Commander-in-Chief Wu-lan-tai were in hot pursuit with their entire armies.

"Wouldn't you know it, they're going back to take refuge in their old haunts in Thistle Mountain. Go after them!" Wu-lan-tai had screamed in a hoarse voice. He was fully aware of the military forces that were following his own troops. These were the Hunan volunteer corps led by Jiang Zhongyuan. Jiang arrived in Guilin from Hunan about five days after the imperial commissioner.

Jiang had been ordered to turn over the command of his forces to Wu-lan-tai. For his part, Wu-lan-tai struck a purposefully innocent pose. Nonetheless, as ordered, the Hunan volunteer corps followed behind Wu-lan-tai's rear.

It's a peasant brigade, thought Wu-lan-tai dissatisfied. If anything, he was overly conscious of the fact that he was in command of an Imperial Army directly subordinate to the emperor himself. His fanatically biased nature played a role in this judgment, for he was a man of extremely deep prejudices. As he saw it, the participation of peasant troops was humiliating to his imperial guard. What bothered him most was that Imperial Commissioner Sai-shang-a seemed to be particularly attentive to Jiang Zhongyuan, the commander of this Hunan volunteer corps.

"I have made a special request of his majesty that Jiang Zhongyuan's troops be put under my command. His majesty has graciously favored me with his permission. Keep that in mind. As for operations for Jiang's forces, I expect soon to seek counsel from his majesty," said the imperial commissioner to Wu-lan-tai.

(If they're put under my command, they will be my troops. Won't their operations be the operations of my troops? Jiang Zhongyuan will then be one of my subordinates. It will not be good for military discipline to single Jiang out for this or that.)

Under ordinary circumstances, Wu-lan-tai might have responded in this way. But, it was on this very day that the imperial commissioner had pulled out Ebilun's sword and referred to the matter concerning Jiang Zhongyuan in the context of an imperial order. However annoying it may have been, Wu-lan-tai kept these thoughts to himself, though resolving in his own mind just to ignore this band of peasant troops.

Though the more he thought about ignoring them, the more it weighed on his mind. He became aware of Jiang's military forces to the same extent that he was himself angry about the whole business. Wu-lan-tai's army had caught the tail of the Taiping forces at Dongxiang, Wuxuan county, and crushed them in battle. The Taipings' advance guard had already by this time reached Xinxu in Guiping county.

—3—

The Taiping Army purposefully took up a long position. The forces under Wei Changhui tried to ford the river at Sipan (Guiping county), and were repulsed by a detachment under the command of County Magistrate Li Mengqun. The Taipings seemed to be carrying out this sort of action needlessly. However, that was by no means the case, for this was clearly part of Yang Xiuqing's strategy. The river-crossing tactic was in preparation for defeat.

The Qing Army was trying to encircle the Taiping forces, which had now returned to their old haunts. The government's numerical troop strength was not high. To carry out an encirclement with an insufficient number of men necessitated contracting the size of the ring as much as possible. The Taipings had detected this weakness and adopted a strategy to force the enemy to expand the ring. An expanded ring naturally became thinner.

As the advance guard tried to ford the river at Sipan, the rear guard was in Dongxiang. The Taipings consciously stretched their forces over this lengthy distance. If the Taipings elongated their military position, then the Qing Army would have to station its men over this same long distance.

Here and there, the two armies ran into each other. It was hardly possible for them not to meet somewhere along the terrain in which both armies were now positioning troops. The Qing had a slightly stronger position. To be sure, the Taiping commanders had been inculcated with Yang Xiuqing's idea that: "There is no need to win a victory. Our aim is to make a fool of the enemy."

Wu-lan-tai had defeated the Taipings at Xinxu (Guiping county) on several occasions, but never decisively because these "advance guards" were never the main force of the Taiping Army. It was like striking at air.

The Taiping rear guard forces fought hard. They had vigorously defended the encampment at Shuangjishan in Thistle Mountain. The Qing army pressed its attack from the end of the sixth lunar month, until Provincial Military Commander Xiang Rong and Bannerman Commander-in-Chief Ba-qing-de forced a surrender on the fifteenth day of the seventh month.

The forces under Yang Xiuqing and Feng Yunshan had already by this time planned their escape from Guiping to Pingnan, and from there in the direction of Yongan. In order to extricate themselves skillfully, though, they had to hold up the battle front as long as possible. For that reason, they might be crushed and have all their plans go for naught before they could ever escape.

Genuine fears of this sort indeed existed. To overcome it, Yang Xiuqing had enacted the "Heavenly Father's Descent to Earth," and Xiao Chaogui had performed the "Heavenly Elder Brother's Descent to Earth." In doing so, they conveyed to the masses revelations from Jehovah and Jesus Christ, respectively.

"Do away with the self and work for the public good!"

"Together we advance as one mind and one fighting force to eradicate the demons."

These had had the ring of a manifesto until that point, but now they rang clearly with the tone of a rebuke. Expanding as it moved, the Taiping Army had to fortify its hold on the region.

As commander of the front army, Xiao Chaogui was with his troops in Mocun near Xinxu, and it was there that he conveyed his revelation. Yang Xiuqing, commander of the central army, was with the main force of the Taiping Army in a place called Chadi in Thistle Mountain. His revelation from Jehovah went as follows: "There is nothing to be sad about and nothing to be afraid of. Life and death are the decisions of Heaven." A sense of despondence seemed to be current among a certain segment of the Taiping troops at the time.

On the day after this oracular presentation, the Taiping camp at Shuangjishan fell. They were defending that area so as to hide their real intentions, and by diligently protecting it, they hoped to convey the notion that they would try to escape via the rear of Thistle Mountain. The Qing Army split up its military forces on the basis of a counterplan. This is just what the Taipings were aiming for.

After the salt poisoning incident, the Taipings were beset with a shortage of salt. Merchants who worked with the military sidestepped the issue of dealing in salt, because it had to be so strictly supervised now. Needless to say, the scarcity of salt had a deleterious effect on the health of the mass of troops, and a large number of men became ill.

The Qing Army, for its part, was also diligent. If they failed to annihilate the Taiping Army here and now, the responsible parties would certainly be punished. There was the sword of Ebilun, the sword that carried the imperial injunction: "First kill, then memorialize!" Indeed, if the imperial commissioner, who had been given this treasured sword, were himself to fail in pacifying the Taipings, he would probably be decapitated with this very sword.

The more experienced members of the Taiping military all felt that the response of the Qing Army was different than it had ever been before. The Hunan volunteers under Jiang Zhongyuan, who had joined the government forces later, were particularly strong. Also, the "Xiang braves" led by Li Mengqun, Guiping county magistrate, were exceedingly courageous. Their name derived from ties to Xiangshang county in Guangdong province. Although the Taipings increased in number as they were on the move, so too did the enemy's troop strength. In addition, sickness was rampant among the Taiping Army. Provisions and salt were in short supply, but greater troop strength was still desired. When he had been in Xiangzhou, Yang Xiuqing had sent home a man by the name of Zhou Xineng from Bobai, a county in the southeastern corner of Guangxi province, close to the border with Guangdong. A man by the name of Ling Shiba, who belonged to a wing of the Society of God Worshippers in Bobai, had forged an alliance with the Heaven and Earth Society and become extremely powerful. Zhou tried to convince Ling to send reinforcements to the front.

Originally, the Society of God Worshippers in Bobai had been of a somewhat different orientation than the puritanical Society of God Worshippers in Jintian village. The alliance between the Heaven and Earth Society and the Bobai group had caused a marked moral erosion in the latter. For example, they had on occasion awarded women to those who had achieved success on the battlefield. This practice was wholly unthinkable in the Jintian Society of God Worshippers. Although talk of calling members of the Bobai Society to Jintian had been going on for some time, Hong Xiuquan, who himself despised their heretical behavior, had not actively taken this tack. Now, though, no one was talking about heresy or like matters. They wanted more troops—even one more.

No communication had yet arrived from Zhou Xineng. According to information Lian Liwen gathered from business clients, Ling Shiba had advanced into Guangdong province and fought the Qing forces in Xinyi and Luoding counties.

The main force of the Taiping military in Thistle Mountain began to move south from Chadi four days after the fall of Shuangjishan, namely the nineteenth day of the seventh lunar month, or August 15 according to the solar calendar. For a mountainous area, Thistle Mountain—which lay virtually adjacent to the Tropic of Cancer—was extremely hot and humid, and it was an especially difficult time for the sick and wounded. If they failed to move now, however, their escape route was certain to disappear.

The Taipings most feared a decline in morale among the troops, and they had to put a stop to the spread of pessimism. As they were set to leave Chadi, Heavenly King Hong Xiuquan issued the following order to the assembled troops: "Fearlessly, gladly, and joyously, let us preserve the moral obligations of the Heavenly Father and the Heavenly Elder Brother. We must never panic. Every single thing has already been decided by the Heavenly Father and the Heavenly Elder Brother. Through innumerable difficulties, the Heavenly Father and the Heavenly Elder Brother will try our minds. We shall all gladly respond to the Heavenly Father and the Heavenly Elder Brother with herbs of sincerity, firmness, and patience. . . . The sick and wounded are many. Let us protect our siblings. If we are unable to defend even one single person, the shame will certainly become known to the Heavenly Father and the Heavenly Elder Brother!"

In the distinctive vocabulary of the Taiping military, the word "herb" was often used in place of "mind." The meaning in this context would be "sincere, firm, and patient minds." Thus began the great mobilization of some one hundred thousand Taiping soldiers, with the first priority of protecting the elderly, the infants, the sick, and the wounded.

—4—

"I've heard that Hong Xiuquan has escaped into Guangdong province aboard a boat on the Wujing River." Lian Liwen scattered this rumor about the area from the towns of Siwang and Guangcun in Pingnan county to Huazhou village. This was the course taken by the escaping Taiping Army.

At other places, Li Xinmei hinted that Hong and others were heading toward Guangzhou: "I heard from one of my friends who's a woman in the Society of God Worshippers that the top guy had run off to Guangzhou. I really don't know if he was traveling there in disguise."

When these two rumors with their different sources coincided, together they exercised far more than double the persuasive power. "Why just the leaders?"

Xinmei frowned at being asked this question, and then responded, "The Society of God Worshippers has got one hundred thousand men. . . . Such a large number would be attacked if they all went by river. First of all, they couldn't get enough boats. Once before, they tried to go to Guangzhou and got as far as Jiangkou, but that was a mess. They finally had to return to Thistle Mountain. There's no alternative but to quietly sneak off to Guangzhou, as a small group."

"And the other guys, they were just left behind? How sad, to be killed by the government troops."

"I'm told the others went to Bobai. They've scattered."

"Of course, there's a Society of God Worshippers in Bobai. So, they've taken off in that direction. About a third of them ought to be able to find their way."

Bobai lay about 170 kilometers to the south of Jintian village. There was a string of mountains—the Darong and Liuwan Mountains—en route, though without any major detour it was not terribly far away.

"No, not at all. I'm sure most of them will make it without incident. All the soldiers from around there have been called up to serve the government, but they should still be able to make it through easily," said Xinmei.

"True enough. If they aren't overtaken, they may be able to escape. The government's troops aren't going to want to fight so badly, because if the enemy escapes, they'll consider it a victory."

Upon hearing this, a white-haired old man who had sawed through a tree near the road snorted. It seemed a gesture indicating a complete lack of friendliness for the government troops.

"Some guy named Zhou said they first went to Bobai and made contact with the local Society of God Worshippers. This woman I know is this guy Zhou's next-door neighbor and knows him real well. . . . If the fighting is over quickly, I hope we entertainers can safely start traveling around again," Xinmei sighed.

"Yeah, my son was taken into the military. I'm an old man and I've got to use my saw. . . . It'd be better not to fight at all." The old man did not stop his sawing hand, slowly pulling it back and forth. It hardly seemed like work for an old man to be doing.

"So, you mean old people are working here and there?"

"Not just me. . . . All the young people are gone from this village. If the Society of God Worshippers were to run off soon, my son could return home."

"I see your point."

"On the rare occasion when you see a young person around here, they're always merchants like you or officials." The old man finally stopped his work and carefully wiped the perspiration from his brow and cheeks with the back of his hand.

Lian Liwen was probably among those tradesmen who had appeared in the area. Officials, after collecting taxes, reported to the authorities on local conditions and offered a variety of other kinds of information. Clearly they had transported along this route the kernel of a rumor planted by Xinmei and Liwen.

Liwen and Xinmei wanted to convey the impression to the superiors of these officials that the Taiping Army seemed to be heading south.

Liwen had heard something to the effect that the Qing Army had espied Zhou Xineng's movement in the direction of Bobai. Zhou was responsible for troop reinforcements, but he was contriving to make it seem as though he was in escape. He was now working as hard as possible to turn the concerns of the Qing Army toward the south.

Even as plans for the actual escape of the Taipings did move forward, the possible destruction of the bulk of the Taiping forces was not something to ignore. The possibility of that happening was very real. Their existence hung in the balance. The Taiping Army was nearing desperation. They could not let down their guard for even a moment. They were now strained to the point of virtual suffocation.

Scattering through the villages centering about Xinxu, the Taiping forces made preparations for the Qing Army's attack. Not only defensive preparations, for if the enemy revealed any cracks in its façade, the Taipings were readying themselves for attack.

"If we do not make our efforts now, then when shall we be able to do so? The time is now to fight to the death!"

The descents to earth of the Heavenly Father and the Heavenly Elder Brother were indications of desperation. There was an almost tragic rhythm to the revelations of the Heavenly Father now. The lines of his speech rhymed, and their rhythm touched the people's minds and hearts directly.

Although the Taiping Army had abandoned the base in Chadi and retreated to the southeast, they wanted to preserve as long a battle array as possible. They outnumbered the government's forces in personnel, but they were protecting the old people and children and they had fewer weapons. The enemy had small artillery, which Wu-lan-tai had transported from Guangdong. These would be useful in mountainous warfare, and they were cause for worry among the Taipings. Nonetheless, the government's forces were a motley crew, and owing to their irregular behavior of attacking one day and assuming a defensive posture the next, the Taipings hoped to find deliverance. They were a group bonded by religious beliefs, and accordingly their interactive network was something remarkable to behold. The Qing Army's fighting stance was thoroughly incoherent, indeed spectacularly so.

The armies of Provincial Military Commander Xiang Rong and Commander-in-Chief Ba-qing-de, who arrived together with the imperial commissioner, were working in cooperation to attack the Taiping forces. A provincial military commander and a commander-in-chief held the same official rank of 1B. The former was the division commander in the Green Standards (Han Chinese who served the Manchus throughout China in provincial units), while the latter was the division commander in the Eight Banners (the organization for Manchus and Mongols [and later Chinese] stationed in military units along the borders and at strategic sites).

Xiang Rong commenced a fire attack on the Taipings. The fires frightened them into trying to flee, but Ba-qing-de's forces were waiting for them. This was essentially a pincer attack. However, Ba-qing-de's forces saw the Taipings before them and got it into their heads that the Taiping Army was coming toward them, setting fires, and intending a surprise attack. A ferocious Taiping assault ensued.

In utter confusion, the officers in Ba-qing-de's army galloped away on horseback, and the foot soldiers followed them. Ba-qing-de was running away before the Taiping Army, which had itself effectively just fled attack. Fooled by this scene, the army of Xiang Rong made no effort to chase after the Taipings.

And what was the result of all this? The Taipings seized massive amounts of weapons and provisions, which Ba-qing-de's forces left in the wake of their hurried escape.

—5—

There were cases of this sort as well in which escape was the result of chance, but this was a rout pure and simple. Further, there were routs and then there were routs, each distinctive in its own way. To be sure, victory at this stage of the battle was not always or necessarily the objective, as the Taiping leaders had pointed out. It was more important now to toy with the enemy, to mock them. A rout that exhausted them was something to be proud of. What was unacceptable, however, was to be caught off guard and flee in complete defeat.

After the retreat from Chadi, the mood changed. Now it was one of advance —no more tarrying in battle. The Taiping Army had been driven to the point that it was no longer able to dally with strategies of simply irking the enemy. Late in the seventh month, when Mocun, close to Xinxu, was attacked by the Qing Army, a man by the name of Huang Yizhen fled in abject fear. It was a particularly ugly reminder of the earlier skulking in the face of the enemy.

A revelation from the Heavenly Father Jehovah was conveyed through the person of Yang Xiuqing: "Huang Yizhen's violation of the law is especially heavy. His crimes are difficult to forgive beneath the snow in the clouds." He was to receive the death sentence. The reference to the "snow in the clouds" was a Taiping military usage and referred to the sword. Hence, this commandment from God was to decapitate Huang, and no one dared oppose an order issued via a descent to earth of the Heavenly Father. A horrifying turn of event, thought Feng Yunshan to himself, though daring not even to show the least expression on his face, let alone utter a word to that effect.

The Society of God Worshippers had faced crises on many occasions before this, but this time they had overcome their difficulties with a descent to earth of the Heavenly Father. When morale hit bottom, when the future was filled with pessimism, when despair had taken hold, a revelation from God would reverberate through the people's souls and arouse their spirits.

The Society of God Worshippers' greatest crisis up to this point was when Feng Yunshan was thrown in jail and Hong Xiuquan left Jintian to lead a movement for his release in Guangzhou. It was at just that critical moment that Yang Xiuqing concocted this stunning technique of God's descent to earth. It was an act of genius on Yang's part. Surrounded as they were now by the Qing armies, a similar earthly descent by Jehovah was a means of resuscitating the Taiping forces now poised at the brink of death. Feng Yunshan was certainly aware of this fact.

But, wasn't the execution of Huang Yizhen overdoing it? There was the idea that by killing one, many would be forewarned. If, by killing one man as an object lesson, the entire Taiping Army could be stirred to action, then it was necessary to proceed and carry out this decision to execute the man.

I'm opposed to this, thought Feng, but I'm going to go along with it and not press my opposition. Still, this is shameless behavior.

The misgivings Feng felt did not have to do with Huang's execution itself, but with the use of a revelation from the Heavenly Father as a medium for carrying it out. This was an issue of the sort that ought to have been decided only after a meeting of the leadership.

When the execution was carried out, Feng turned his back toward Yang Xiuqing and knit his brow in worry. Before long, he thought, they were going to have to change how they performed this divine descent. Whether it was to encourage the rank-and-file troops or to arouse the people's hearts, the earthly descent of the Heavenly Father could only be used to instruct and admonish the group en masse. When it came to a concrete problem, such as the execution of a specific individual, need they worry about a revelation from the Lord God? This really was overdoing it, and excess of this sort had to be curtailed.

The Qing forces, trying to capture the head as well as the tail of the Taiping Army, divided into front and rear armies. Wu-lan-tai led the front army, while Xiang Rong and Ba-qing-de shared leadership of the rear army.

The head of the Taiping forces was drawn out in a fierce attack by the Qing's rear army. Xiang Rong and Ba-qing-de pressed the assault at Fengmenyao Pass, which faced the entranceway into Thistle Mountain. Right Army Corps Commander Wei Changhui's younger brother, Wei Zhixian, was charged with protecting the area. In this battle as well, the cannons held by the Qing forces demonstrated remarkable force. Wei Zhixian was hit by a cannon shell and died in battle.

Fengmenyao Pass was nestled between two mountains just to the north of the dam in present-day Jintian village. During construction of the dam, they cut through the mountains, so that Fengmenyao is now not such a narrow defile. At 9:00 in the morning the wind suddenly shifts direction from north to south. Back in the nineteenth century, when the mountains were closer to each other, the change in winds was considerably more severe than it is today. Hence, the name Fengmenyao: "fengmen" meaning the gateway of the winds, and "yao" referring to a spot where the land was depressed.

Facing this assault, the Taiping forces were driven from Thistle Mountain, and like a surging tempest, poured into the Guilin area near Jintian village. As the Qing Army occupied Fengmenyao Pass, the path into Thistle Mountain was effectively shut off, and the Taiping military now faced its greatest crisis. They were on the brink of annihilation.

The Qing forces' rear army seized Fengmenyao, made the necessary preparations, and was about to lunge into an attack on Jintian village. The front army set up headquarters at Sipan, along the southern banks of the Wujing River, and took up its side of a pincer operation.

The Taiping Army was trapped between the front and rear armies of the enemy. If the Qing armies pressed an all-out attack on both fronts, the Taipings' fate was unsure at best. Although a route of escape to the north was in place, it was a kind of secret passageway through which they might flee only when the right opportunity was provided by an enemy lapse. If they fled along this road before the enemy's eyes, they could be overtaken and mauled, and they would probably even lose their main force before getting away.

It was a desperate situation. But then something altogether unexpected occurred. The front army of the government's forces showed no will whatsoever to pursue the fight. This turn of events was just as unexpected for the rear route army defending Fengmenyao Pass.

"It's all out of whack again!" spit out Xiang Rong.

He thought they were following up a victory and about to administer the *coup de grâce*. Even those in Sipan should have realized that they had been victorious. Following the success, he had sent a messenger off with the report, "We have attained victory, and we are about to commence mopping up the scattered remnants of the enemy."

Thinking only that the enemy, naturally poised to run away, was to be attacked from the front, he did not so much as budge.

"What's the matter with the front route army? What in the world happened?" It was said with a tone of someone whose spirit had just been destroyed. The commanders of the rear route army, which was about to move in pursuit of the enemy, looked dumbfounded, as did the troops.

What in the world *had* taken place?

The mood was almost as if they had been struck by fatigue and just collapsed to the ground.

"Well, now what?" Xiang Rong eventually understood what had happened, and somehow perceived what it was Wu-lan-tai had been planning. Although late, he hadn't failed to understand.

At the base camp of the Qing's front route army in Sipan, Wu-lan-tai was smiling, strangely without so much as altering the curve of his lips.

"Idiot!" he said in a soft voice, facing the door of the room after the staff person who had arrived with the proposal for the attack had left.

Xiang Rong assumed the front route army had launched the attack and annihilated the Taiping forces. What sort of report would Imperial Commissioner Sai-shang-a forward to Beijing?

"Military Commander Xiang Rong attacked the bandit troops with a violent force, seized Fengmenyao Pass, the gateway into Thistle Mountain, and demolished the base of the bandit army at Jintian village." Victory reverted to Xiang Rong as commander of the rear route army, while the name of the front route army was only mentioned as an accessory. Only out of the goodness of his heart had they been granted the opportunity to get some credit for this meritorious deed.

This is disgusting, thought Wu-lan-tai, the professional military man. I won't be somebody else's foil! He may want to share the acclaim, but it's fine if I do all the fighting till the bitter end.

Wu-lan-tai realized that the rear route army was exhausted as a military unit after the ferocious battle to take Fengmenyao Pass. It was surely beyond their capacity to quell the 100,000 Taiping troops single-handedly, but with the help of the front route army, they would be able to annihilate the rebels once and for all. Furthermore, as a result, the front route army would appear just as supplementary, as support.

"The low-level commanders were sickened by Xiang Rong's achievements and refused to work in cooperation with him. In the end, he proved unable to overcome them." So wrote the brilliant poet and scholar Long Qirui, mentioned earlier. He was stunned by the severity of the jealousies of these military men. Wu-lan-tai was not alone in this regard. The generals under his command were all of the same mind: Da-hong-a, Kai-long-a, Li Nengchen, and Wang Jinxiu.

Standing at the precipice between life and death, the Taiping Army arduously strengthened their defenses. Soon after, they most certainly knew that the Qing armies had forfeited the chance to attack.

"So, that's what happened . . ." said the imperial commissioner, as he received a report from the front and understood the truth of the situation there. Of course, on the surface the report said many things designed specifically to hide the truth. But Sai-shang-a inhabited the same universe as the authors of the report, and he was able to make out what had transpired and why.

"The future does not look good," said Sai-shang-a with his lower lip jutting forward in a look of displeasure.

—6—

"If that's what he's planning to do, then we ought to check things out with this in mind . . ."

The front route and rear route armies of the Qing forces were deadlocked in a state of emotional opposition. The Taiping Army was like a fresh fish on the chopping block, wriggling and twisting, trying desperately to leap into a pond and escape with its life. Meanwhile, the Qing military commanders earnestly worked to constrain each other in the fear that anyone other than they themselves would accrue credit for performing meritorious deeds.

A week after the battle at Fengmenyao Pass, Wu-lan-tai attacked Xinxu, but it was a halfhearted effort on his part. Xiang Rong then sent troops into the region of Thistle Mountain, and just at that time the Taipings launched an attack on Xiang's base camp. Neither side could claim a decisive victory.

As much as it could, the Taiping Army tried to seem as though their own movements were in a southerly direction. If they overdid it and seemed too open or straightforward about it, they would probably have inspired skepticism. Moderation was essential.

In proceeding south, the Taiping Army had to cross the Wujing River, and the army had begun to pull down the private residences in Xinxu. In order to conceal any trace of their activities, they tore them down one at a time. The timber taken from the homes was then used to build rafts, and this construction was also not done in the public view. However, observers from across the shore of the river noticed that something was under way.

"Rafts? Where and how do they expect to cross the river? We'll see just how skillful they are at it," said Wu-lan-tai jeeringly.

Wu-lan-tai seemed overly aware of the fact that he was a specialist in military affairs. He had uncommon self-confidence, and it often turned into arrogance with respect to others.

"They're a bunch of amateurs when it comes to warfare," he said, looking across at the other bank of the river and revealing his haughty attitude. Perhaps if they had his expertise in the military arts, they would have exerted more effort in building and hiding their rafts. They were demonstrating just how ridiculous they in fact were; hiding their heads while leaving their tails exposed.

What Wu-lan-tai did not realize until the bitter end was that the Taipings had done this on purpose.

"Keep your eyes on the river," Wu-lan-tai reminded his subordinates.

Eventually, the main Taiping base in Xinxu recovered its animated appearance. Both Lian Liwen and Li Xinmei were already on their way back. It had been reported that all preparations were in order along the northern route. The plan steadily progressing was for "furtive movement of the encampment."

The date was fixed, an easy one to remember: the day following the harvest moon, or the sixteenth day of the eighth lunar month. By the moonlight of the evening of the sixteenth, they planned to move. At first the fifteenth was proposed, because on that evening there would be moon-viewing parties at the Qing camp and the enemy was not likely to be so watchful.

Then the opposing position was put forward with considerable persuasive power: precisely because it was the evening of the harvest moon, they would probably be especially attentive and watchful. No matter how inebriated they became during these parties, they would get up in the middle of the night. It was not just to view the moon in the sky, but to look across the river at the Taiping camp. It seemed that the night of the harvest moon was too "public" for their likings.

So they picked the next night. That year, according to the Chinese calendar, was an intercalary year, which meant there would be two eighth months. It was a custom with respect to this very day that the period of intercalation would be completed in the first of these two months.

It seemed almost unnatural that people cast no shadows whatsoever. In order to camouflage the movement of their base camp, the Taipings left 1,000 of their crack troops till the very end, with orders to show their faces from time to time.

The "supreme directive" to the Qing Army from the imperial commissioner arrived: "Prepare for a southern escape by the bandits of the Society of God Worshippers!" The commander-in-chief of the Qing forces had examined reports compiled on the basis of spying and other intelligence activities, and his judgment was that the armed forces of the Taipings were planning to flee to the south.

While the government forces were especially attentive to the southern movement of the enemy, they were equally negligent about any movement toward the north. The large base of the Society of God Worshippers at Bobai lay to the south. To the north, they had scarcely a toehold.

"When moving forward in victory," explained Li Mengqun—who was well-acquainted with the local area—at a meeting of staff officers, "we might be able to head to the north to expand authority in the region. However, when retreating in defeat, we shall have to head to the basin in the south to preserve what power we have." After he offered this explanation, the other military leaders in attendance all nodded their heads in approval.

The road to the north followed the main course of crossing Thistle Mountain and then on to Wuxuan and Xiangzhou. The Taiping troops had been unable to escape along that route and had been repulsed. It appeared that they had thus abandoned their plan for an extensive march to the north.

Subsequently, the Qing Army obtained information that Zhou Xineng, a Taiping military leader, was secretly heading to Bobai. That seemed to indicate that the Taipings were making preparations to flee to the south.

Also, once the government analysts had examined in great detail the activities of the Taipings centered about Xinxu, nothing but a southern escape route made any sense. Stealthily, the Taipings continued to pull down homes and quietly construct a fair number of rafts, for when it came time to move south, they would have to cross the river.

The quality of the hearsay elicited from the nearby resident populace also indicated in no uncertain terms that the Taiping Army intended to march to the south. The road to the north from Xinxu was a pathway through the mountains. Under no circumstances could an army of 100,000 fit through it all at once. Thus, the possibility of such an escape was considered for the time being to be irrelevant.

On nightfall of the day following the mid-autumn moon, the movement of old men and women, children, and the sick and injured commenced. The officers and men of the front and left armies, separately stationed in the various villages around Jintian, under the command of Xiao Chaogui and Shi Dakai, quietly entered the mountain pass along the Guilin route. Even after they were well into the mountains, there seemed to be no activity out of the ordinary from the Qing base camp across the Wujing River. The path was narrow, but the light of the moon on the evening of the sixteenth was bright and enabled them to proceed more rapidly than expected.

The central army in the Xinxu area began to move to the north about an hour later. It was under the command of Yang Xiuqing and was guarding Hong Xiuquan. At thirty-minute intervals thereafter, the right army under Wei Changhui and the rear army under Feng Yunshan followed. By then it was the dead of night.

After the rear army had departed, a thousand specially selected troops stayed on for about four hours in Xinxu and continued to observe the movements of the Qing troops. The government's armed forces still had not become aware of what was taking place right under their noses. The escape had succeeded.

—7—

Serving as a guide to the advance party of the Taipings was Li Xinmei. Lian Liwen remained behind to work in concert with the final 1,000 selected troops. The two people who had done the preparatory work along the escape route to the north were now with the front and rear, with responsibilities for guidance at the front and for concluding affairs in the rear, respectively.

In the early dawn, the Qing Army realized that the Taipings had evacuated their military base. Wu-lan-tai crossed the Wujing River, entered Mocun and Xinxu, and after plundering them set fire to all the remaining homes.

The historical records of the Qing dynasty report that the Taiping Army set fire to the Xinxu region of Guiping county late at night and then fled, but such a story makes no sense. The Taiping Army escaped undetected. If they had set fires, the Qing forces would surely have become aware of them. Indeed, the homes of Xinxu were burned to the ground, but it was not the Taipings who were responsible. It was the government soldiers.

After pillaging and incinerating the village to vent his rage, Wu-lan-tai began the pursuit to the north in the direction of Guilin. The pathway was narrow, and at points along the way, lumber and other obstructions had been placed. His troops had to remove the obstructions as they moved on, so the going was slow. There were places as well where the road had collapsed. No sooner would they descend into a valley, than they would have to climb a steep precipice in order to continue along the path.

Xiang Rong of the rear route army entrusted the chase to Wu-lan-tai, while he and Ba-qing-de hurried on to Jiangkou. Although he knew that the Taipings' escape route was a mountain pathway to the north toward Guilin, Xiang Rong did not believe that the Taipings really planned to head to the north.

"They were surrounded," said Xiang, "so they took a mountain route to the north, but they'll circle back and head south. Really! It's true. We've got to prevent them from going south." Ba-qing-de agreed with Xiang Rong.

The Wujing River flowed into the Qian River. It then curved at Guiping city and flowed northerly, where it turned into the Dahuang River. The portion of the river that flowed north came to Jiangkou, again described a curb turning to the southeast, and there became the Xun River. The Xun flowed easterly, passing through Wuzhou, and entering Guangdong province. Its name changed to the West River in Guangdong, where it was the largest waterway of the entire province.

If a huge army of 100,000 were to get into such an important area as the city of Guangzhou along the lower reaches of the West River, then they would become a major problem. That had to be prevented at all cost. Xiang Rong was thus hurrying to Jiangkou. "They'll have to try and come ashore and that's where we'll cut them off." The army under Xiang Rong and Ba-qing-de entered Pingnan county from Jiangkou, and from there they headed north. Before them lay the villages of Siwang and Guancun. The Qing Army entered the Guancun Temple. They had come on forced march, so Xiang Rong allowed them all a short respite.

The Taipings learned in reports from the local populace where the government forces would move next. In whatever area this Qing force heading north appeared, most of its operations were under surveillance, and an ambush had been prepared. This was the responsibility of part of the rear army under the command of Feng Yunshan. The Taiping forces sat crouched, holding their breath, as they waited in great anticipation for the signal from their commander.

On their escape to the north this time, luck seemed to revert to the side of the Taipings. On the evening they fled, together with their old, children, and infirm, they were aided by the light of the moon. And, just prior to their encounter with the Qing forces under Xiang Rong four days later, it started to rain violently.

The government's troops were well-provisioned with ammunition. Their guns, however, were flintlocks, and once dampened by the rain, they were no longer serviceable. New guns fixed with percussion caps were expensive and had yet to be bought in large quantities. Thus, despite its superior fire-power, the Qing Army was unable to use any of it.

"This is assistance from Heaven," murmured Feng Yunshan under his breath deep in the thicket in the rear. Lian Liwen was at his side.

"It was just like this at the time of Sanyuanli too," said Liwen in a low voice.

At the time of the Opium War, when the Chinese and British soldiers were locked in battle outside the city of Guangzhou, a heavy rain with thunder came pouring down. Early in the Opium War, the British were still using flintlock weapons, though by the end of the war the new guns from India had replaced the older guns. In the village of Sanyuanli, the Qing prefect burst upon the scene and convinced the Chinese troops that the British army was unable to use its guns and was on the verge of total destruction.

"They should be thoroughly drenched by now," said Feng, leaning forward in the bushes and stretching out his hand to ascertain the force of the rain.

"The government troops haven't been resting for that long. . . . Now would be the right time," said Liwen.

"So be it! Now!" Feng leapt to his feet, raised his hands, and waved them about his head.

Suddenly, a resounding battle cry was raised, and piercing shots followed. This was, of course, gunfire from the Taipings. Although the Taiping troops were also outfitted with older style weapons, they had few of them and those were valued possessions. Before using such prized objects, they were covered to prevent them from getting wet in the rain. Even when fired, they were kept dry by umbrellas held above them.

"We've won," Liwen said to Feng only about ten minutes after the war cry had sounded.

From their position in the bushes, they could only see a small part of the area around the Guancun Temple, but from the atmosphere being conveyed from the battlefield, they could easily see who was winning and who was losing.

"When we placed the troops in ambush, for all intents and purposes, the victory was already decided," responded Feng.

"Well, but don't you think that victory really became ours when the local people gave us all those detailed reports on Qing troop movements?"

"That's true. The way the local populace cooperated with our troops, who wouldn't take a thing from them, not even touch a string of their thread, was altogether different from the way they dealt with troops that burned down their homes."

"When we fight together with the peasantry, the Taiping Army will not be defeated!"

For a while the rain came down with great force. The sound of Taiping weaponry had already ceased to be heard. Perhaps everything was completely drenched. The fighting had now turned to hand-to-hand combat, and this proved disadvantageous, needless to say, to the side that had been the victim of the surprise attack.

Eventually, open reports of one victory after another were conveyed to the commander in the bush.

"We have killed Company Commander Yang Chenggui of the Guzhou Defense Command," reported a messenger.

"Well, a company commander?"

The official post of company commander was a 6A ranking. The report mentioned the Guzhou Defense Command, which meant an officer of troops mobilized from neighboring Hunan province.

"The regional commander of Guzhou should have been Li Fu." A regional commander was the commanding officer, rank 2A, comparable to a major general. The Taipings were intimately acquainted with the command structure and names of commanders in the Qing Army. The local populace and merchants in contact with the government forces informed the Taipings of such matters.

Standing at the front of Xiang Rong's rear route army had been the Hunan troops under the command of Guzhou Regional Commander Li Fu. They were the first to be wiped out.

"Retreat! Retreat!" Xiang Rong had screamed in tears.

The Qing soldiers abandoned everything from their weapons to their provisions and pots and pans and fled to the south. Xiang Rong gathered up the remaining troops and haphazardly escaped as far as Pingnan. Thereafter, he confined himself indoors with the excuse of "having become ill."

On the following day, the front route army under Wu-lan-tai arrived in Longmen, Pingnan county. Claiming they were "searching for remaining bandits to destroy," they stayed for two days. When he heard of Xiang Rong's great defeat, Wu-lan-tai was surely fearful of continuing.

Although heavily burdened with their aged and their young, the Taipings continued with forced marches. Had the Qing Army assiduously pursued them, they might have been able to catch the Taipings. The group of old, young, sick, and injured that had been at the head of the troops had already been outpaced by the front and left armies and was now to the rear of the central army. This group was under the protection of Luo Dagang and Su Sanniang.

The Taipings entered Tengxian, cutting through a secret pathway from Hepingxu, and limped into the village of Dali. Upon their arrival, Hong Xiuquan announced:

"We have escaped from the jaws of death."

12

Attack the Rivers and the Mountains

— 1 —

Their wooden-tipped spears were moving hurriedly, drawing lines here and there in the sand, and then all of a sudden something like a map emerged. Other sticks pointed out specific points in the map in the sand.

"You mean the mountain east of the river?" It was Yang Xiuqing speaking.

"It's called Butterfly Mountain," responded a young man.

"What about east of Butterfly Mountain?"

"The Pingchong River flows there."

"And to the north?"

"That would be Liuhe Mountain. The mountain range runs along this direction." The young man drew another line in the sand as he crouched down.

"Okay, I get the general picture. You can go now, Yiwen," said Yang.

"Yes, thank you." The young man by the name of Yiwen had something more to say, but thinking better of it, he bowed and left. Yang Xiuqing was left alone with Lian Liwen.

"He certainly knows his details," said Liwen.

"He's extremely prompt in his work, a real asset to us," said Yang, shuffling his feet about. He was beginning to erase the map in the sand with his feet. Liwen forced a smile, thinking just how poorly the two of them would get along.

The Taiping Army had pushed north from Pingnan, divided into land and maritime route forces, and had now reached the city of Yongan. While they were contemplating the attack on Yongan, Luo Dagang said with a sour expression, "You'll have to turn this place over to me." When he had been a leader in the Heaven and Earth Society, Luo had once laid siege to Yongan. He had swept in like the wind to plunder the city and then swept out like the wind—a typical strategy for roving bandits. Bandit methods aside, he had acquired invaluable experience attacking the city. Since he was going to be risking his life in that attack, Luo had made a detailed investigation of conditions in the area before the attack on Yongan. That investigation covered as thoroughly as possible the local topography, the resident population, the character of locally influential families, and the disposition of *tuanlian* troops. The primary objective of this earlier investigation was, of course, the whereabouts of goods to be seized.

"That should be useful," Luo Dagang had suggested.

"Will you draw me a map centering on the city of Yongan?" No sooner had Yang Xiuqing spoken than he had Luo sketch a topographical map and give a supplementary explanation. Before doing so, he called in another fellow who was well-acquainted with the local terrain there, and had him trace a rough sketch on the sand.

"Was this prudent?" wondered Liwen, a little discouraged—or was it distrustful?

There was surely a difference between paper and sand, but the maps drawn by the two men were perfect matches. There, on the spot, with his stunning powers of memory, Yang Xiuqing took the map drawn by Luo into his head completely. He checked it against the sketch in the sand, knowing full well that there ought to be no errors in it.

For some reason, though, Liwen seemed to have felt some misapprehension. Yang had never doubted for a moment the accuracy of Luo's map. This was a test for the person he had called in afterward.

Liwen had been through the same experience several times before. Yang had the habit of questioning anyone he felt he had to have thorough knowledge of. The objective was to screen the gist of the concerned party's answers as well as his attitude.

"Didn't he just join the movement at Tengxian?" inquired Liwen.

"Sure, he's a newcomer, but he's a member of the Society of God Worshippers. . . . He even came to Jintian village. I remember it now. I met him on the road. It was odd. . . . He didn't shy away from me, but called out very politely. He was just setting out to return to Tengxian from Jintian, it seemed. . . . I guess he didn't remember. . . . No wonder." An expression of sentimentality, entirely atypical of Yang, spread across his face for a brief instant, and then just as quickly vanished. Liwen knew what was going on in Yang's mind.

He was recalling the time when, as part of a scheme to deceive both foes and allies alike, Yang Xiuqing had assumed the guise of someone suffering dementia. Covered in filth, his body dressed in rags, and with saliva dribbling from his mouth, he was tramping about the Jintian area, tripping over stones and bumping into trees. Everyone seemed to look at him in horror. With words, such as "He's crazy" and "A madman!," people were revolted at the sight of him. Those whom he met were disgusted, and many simply avoided him altogether. Rare indeed were those who addressed him kindly without revulsion. Yang had not forgotten those who had acted gently toward him during this period of feigned insanity.

When the Taiping forces, having escaped by the skin of their teeth, headed north in the direction of Yongan, they passed through Tengxian. Many of the locals from Tengxian joined their army, and among them was that kind man whom Yang had remembered from Jintian earlier.

He was Li Yiwen, later to receive from Hong Xiuquan the Chinese character "Xiu" from his own name and to take the given name Xiucheng. Known to history by the name Li Xiucheng, appraisals of him as a person would be many and varied. At this time, though, he was merely a new recruit into the Taiping Army. Li had for some time been a member of the Society of God Worshippers, and when the Taipings passed through his hometown, he burned down his house, broke off any lingering attachments to the region, and, together with his mother and younger brother, joined the Taiping forces. Although he had been raised in utter poverty, his maternal uncle had opened a village school, and there, Li was able to study while doing an assortment of odd jobs. This was still a time when it was much more usual to find men who were born to destitution also unable to read or write, but illiteracy was not to be Li's fate.

Although a man of peasant origins, Li's appearance was that of a man of elegant lines. His eyes radiated a strange kindness.

"And he's literate too," Liwen began to say, and then stopped himself short. Li Yiwen had inserted a few Chinese characters here and there in his sketch in the sand. To find someone who could read and write in this group was a striking phenomenon, almost worthy of verbal expression. Liwen had nearly forgotten, however, that the man with whom he was speaking, Yang Xiuqing, was illiterate.

Yang was a man of alarming intelligence. Anyone who spent even a short period of time with him would never in the least imagine him to be illiterate. Most people were, in fact, surprised to learn that he was unable to write. Intelligence itself seemed to have no connection with an ability to recognize Chinese characters.

"He's a sympathetic fellow, isn't he?" said Liwen, verbalizing his thoughts about Li Yiwen.

"More than sympathetic—he's a man who understands other people's frames of mind. He may have the capacity to draw the masses in."

"Perhaps so."

Liwen was thinking that Yang could very well have been speaking about himself. Yang had the extraordinary talent of reading other people's feelings. He could rapidly espy what his counterparts were thinking about. However, "sympathy" was something else. When he looked into another's frame of mind, Yang was the sort of man who thought of how he could best make use of it for his own benefit.

"Determination will come later. We'll have to implant that in him with training," said Yang.

More than anything else, Yang considered determination of surpassing importance. In sharpening this determination, "sympathy" might become an impediment.

"The human talent pool is coming together, isn't it?"

"No, not yet, it's still insufficient . . . because we not only have to gather capable men. We have to create them, too. That's right. I have a request for you, Mr. Lian."

"Yes?"

"I'd like to entrust one young man to your care. Actually, he could work at your side, helping you out with various tasks. I think the lad would mature just by listening to your stories from around the world—those from Guangzhou and Shanghai, as well as from Hong Kong and Japan."

"Is he a promising young man?"

"Very much so," Yang said, bowing thankfully. "He's still shy of fourteen years of age—steel to be tempered . . . ."

— 2 —

The Taiping Army claimed to be one hundred thousand strong, but in fact it was estimated that only half that number made the trek to Yongan, and many of them were actually noncombatants. The Qing Army recorded its view of the Taipings' military force at the time: "They number thirty-seven thousand in all. Those that can actually carry out a battle number only five thousand or six thousand." This claim is certainly open to the charge of underestimation. More accurate figures would be fifty thousand men and women overall, and twenty thousand combatants.

Even fifty thousand, though, is a remarkable figure. Just supplying everyone with enough to eat was an immense task. The job of replenishing supplies was no less significant than that of fighting, and there were few people capable of such work. The Taipings were finding that talented men were becoming more and more needed. Yang Xiuqing had been furiously searching for able men, because he realized that the Taipings' very existence depended upon it.

Not just the present, but the future also had to be taken into account. Li Yiwen might soon become a valuable asset. A fourteen-year-old youth by the name of Chen Picheng, whom Yang had entrusted to the care of Lian Liwen, was one for whom anticipations of his future accomplishments ran high.

Chen and Li were from the same village in Tengxian, but unlike Li, Chen had not joined the Taipings when they happened by the village. Accompanying his uncle Chen Chengrong, Picheng had traveled to Jintian village. Although still a youngster, he was a familiar face ever since his arrival in Jintian, and he struck Yang as someone with considerable promise.

"What an adorable child," was Liwen's first impression of Chen. Chen Picheng later changed his name to Chen Yucheng, and we have a contemporaneous record of him that reads: "A man with a face of extraordinary beauty, he has not the least bloodthirstiness." At age fourteen, he was of slight build and looked to be no more than twelve.

Yang's expectations for this young man were not, it seemed, a future in the military. He was entrusted to Liwen to learn about providing the Taiping Army with supplies. He wanted Chen trained to become an expert in this area.

"Thank you very much," said Chen, lowering his head. Just then, Li Xinmei and Su Sanniang appeared before Liwen. With their eyes half shut, evoking a dubious look, they said in succession, "Hey, he's a trustworthy kid, isn't he!"

"Liwen, I'll take the kid in my place."

Chen blushed. Li and Su had come to the peasant hut where Liwen was living to make contact with Luo Dagang. Precisely as Luo had proposed, Yang was entrusting the attack on Yongan city to him. The Heaven and Earth Society group was liable to be seen within the Taiping Army as bad elements, and this was Yang's way of testing their strength. Now, they would have to cooperate with the Taipings.

Luo Dagang eventually arrived. The first task for the young Chen Picheng was to serve this guest some tea.

"Can't we forge some kind of alliance with the remnants of He Hongji's group?" Luo had wanted to ask Li Xinmei about this matter, and they decided to meet at Liwen's place. Su Sanniang had come as Li Xinmei's second.

"Word has it that they've been killed off one after another, but some of them are living quietly in hiding in the city," responded Xinmei.

He Hongji was the leader of a Heaven and Earth Society affiliate that had risen in rebellion in Yongan. Xinmei had worked with him on occasion. Indeed, they had pillaged together. Several months earlier, He had been murdered by Wu Jiang, the proxy department magistrate of Yongan. Wu hailed from the city of Wuhan in Hubei province. He had risen from the position of a petty official to his present status. He was already resigned to the fact that he was not destined to rise through the elite route in China's imperial bureaucracy. He had only just recently arrived in the Yongan area when he began a rigorous house-to-house search in an effort to smoke out rebellious elements of the population, and those he managed to capture were subjected to grueling torture, culminating in the arrest of their leader, He Hongji.

"You worthless dog, you won't live another day." Wu Jiang believed in meting out severe punishments. He Hongji was quickly dispatched, and a group of his followers who were arrested one by one thereafter were also mercilessly punished. As if that were not sufficient, he also saw to it that anyone who gave shelter to the "bandits" would be executed.

"I'll clean this local area up," said Wu.

There was a proprietor of a pawnshop who, for a reward from the authorities, secretly informed on someone lurking in the barn of the house next to his. The very next day, this pawnshop owner was discovered dead in his own home. This was presented as proof that the "bandits" still survived. And with fresh zeal, Wu intensified his house-to-house investigation.

"Xinmei, if you walked around the city of Yongan, wouldn't your supporters secretly address you?" asked Luo Dagang.

"I think so, but—" she said, her eyebrows twitching.

"But, isn't that awfully dangerous?" said Su Sanniang, knitting her brow.

"We've all crossed dangerous bridges. What's dangerous is what exceeds our preparations, isn't it?" Luo folded his hands in his lap with perfect deportment.

"I'll check it out. I'll go make secret contact with them," said Su.

"Many thanks."

"But I'm not going to be able to do this if the attack doesn't materialize. Wu Jiang is making an inhuman object lesson out of Yongan and the whole city is trembling with fear. If you fail to attack at the right time, I can't advise my people who are now lying low to rise in rebellion."

"I see your point. This invasion is on. The time is right." Luo slowly tapped his right knee three times. He certainly seemed full of self-confidence.

Since they worked in unison, He Hongji's subordinates were sure to know Li Xinmei's face. She was quietly to walk about the streets of Yongan, while the remnants of He Hongji's group would devise a way to try to establish contact with her.

If they then rose in rebellion within the city through this secret communication at the same time as the Taipings invaded Yongan, then victory was a surety. This plan also would keep Taiping sacrifices to a minimum.

"Let's give it a try. . . . Or else, . . ." said Xinmei.

"Or else what? Do you have conditions?"

"It would probably be better for two people to enter the city than for one to go alone. Those already in Yongan are mostly in family groups, so wouldn't I be better off as part of a family grouping?"

"A family group?" threw back Su.

"You know, with a child," said Xinmei, looking over in the direction of the youthful Chen Picheng.

— 3 —

As the Taiping Army pressed close, many nearby farming families, particularly landlord households, fled madly into the city of Yongan. They felt they were much safer enveloped by the city walls of Yongan than in their homes surrounded only by bamboo trees. According to records of the time, over four hundred refugees sought the shelter of Yongan. And they did not come empty-handed. Each brought whatever baggage they could carry with them, and food more often than furniture. Were they to become confined to Yongan city, even the most elegant furniture would be altogether useless, whereas food provided sustenance for life. A phenomenal amount of food was transported into Yongan over a few days' time, including several hundred thousand bushels of rice alone.

The Qing court dispatched Regional Vice-Commander A-er-jing-a to defend Yongan. At the head of an army, he took up a station at a place known as Xiushui to the southeast of Yongan. The forces of the approaching Taiping Army, however, proved far beyond his expectations. Recognizing that his troops were outnumbered, he withdrew them from Yongan, while offering Wu Jiang advice on defensive strategies.

Thus the Taipings made no contact with the government armies all the way until their arrival in Yongan. Regional *tuanlian* militias resisted them, but they hardly posed any sort of threat. One *tuanlian* unit led by a man by the name of Su Baode was surrounded and annihilated by the Taipings at Jindai Bridge, outside the southern city gate of Yongan. Abandoned corpses were said to number several hundred.

Xinmei was pulling a wagon loaded with a straw rice bag and various pots and pans. Chen Picheng pushed from behind. There was no mistaking them for anything save a refugee mother and her son. The refugees gathering in Yongan came from all directions far and wide. Xinmei consulted someone familiar with the area and concocted a life story for herself.

"We were on our way back to my parents' home in Longdingli from Yinjiang when we ran into this rebellion," she said. "I'm taking my son along, and need a safe place of refuge." She had crammed enough information into her head about Yinjiang and Longdingli to be able to respond to inquiries.

When she entered the city, however, the troops guarding the gate asked her nothing. Xinmei looked just like a wife of a peasant household. Chen cried out continuously for his mother: "Mama, mama!" They passed through the city gate without incident. A little while, later Xinmei decided to rest momentarily.

"Picheng, you're quite an actor yourself!" she said. They hadn't made fine, detailed plans in advance for Chen to break out in tears and call repeatedly for his mother. This was purely impromptu on the young man's part.

"I had no intention of acting a part. That particular voice just came out naturally. I guess I really felt as though I was fleeing with my mother," said Chen, in apparent embarrassment.

"Really? You thought I was like your real mother? That's funny . . . your mother."

Xinmei patted the young man on the shoulder and with a piece of cloth daubed his face. Between the heat and the tension, he had been perspiring profusely. She dried his face because she wanted its youthfulness to shine forth as genuinely as possible.

"Well, Picheng, let's go. No more resting now. We can do that later. From now on we walk around the streets of the inner city." And she grabbed the wagon.

All those guys Wu Jiang did in, she thought, none of them knew me, did they? Although pressed by this sense of unease, Xinmei would only allow herself optimism now. At least the man who had murdered the informant pawnbroker was certain to be a follower of a Heaven and Earth Society affiliate. So, there was at least one person.

In actual fact, Xinmei played her role with extraordinary skill, far beyond simple optimism. After resting, she drew up the cart, and before she had walked ten paces, a man carrying baskets full of charcoal on shoulder poles approached her from behind and addressed her as he walked by. "Elder sister, did you come here to do something?"

"How many survivors are there in the city?" she asked quickly.

"Only about thirty of He Hongji's followers. They're being sheltered by brethren of the Heaven and Earth Society."

"I want to see them."

"Follow me," said the man with the shoulder poles, who, having slackened his pace a bit, again quickened his step and turned the corner at an ashen-colored wall.

Xinmei was following behind him, and at just about the same moment that he turned the corner, he faltered and fell to the ground on his backside. The basket of charcoal he was carrying toppled sideways. Hurriedly he began gathering up the charcoal scattered alongside the road and putting it back into the basket.

"Ma'am, please, could I stick this load on your cart? Not for free. How about it? I'll give you these five fat pieces of coal as rental," he said.

"What? What are you talking about? Where in the world are you going?" inquired Xinmei.

"It's next to the temple of Guandi. Not too far."

"The Guandi Temple, eh? . . . That'll cost you ten pieces."

"Let's make it eight. And better yet, I'll pull the wagon to the Guandi Temple."

"You'll pull it, eh? . . . Okay, eight's fine."

"Thank you, that will really help. I wasn't all that used to those poles, and my shoulders were aching like they were on fire. Pulling this cart is so much easier!" Having said this much, the man then lowered his voice and went on: "You're going to take revenge for us on the enemies of elder brother, right?"

For a time, they traveled together, but it was only for a short time. Although Xinmei remembered the faces of some of the followers of He Hongji's group, she certainly did not know each and every face of the several thousand adherents, and this man had not lodged in her memory. Nonetheless, most of He's people were certain to know her face as one of the local leaders.

The man's use of the expression "elder brother" referred without a doubt to He Hongji. Since he hadn't used "boss" or "leader," but "elder brother," then it was a good bet that he was an underling in the group.

"That's the plan. There are people who'll work with us. I'm working in contact with the Taipings."

"What do we do?"

"Have you ever eaten crow meat?" asked Xinmei out of nowhere. At her side, Chen Picheng looked up into the sky unconsciously and then surveyed the surroundings. No trace of any crows to be found.

"No, never had crow. But, my cat did. Spit all of it up, too. Most disgusting thing I've ever seen," he said.

"What about the dog?"

"The dog wouldn't eat it. But instead of eating it, the dog will play around with the crow meat. Ha, ha, that'd be great, eh?"

"Sure. If the Taipings attack, they'll burn it down. The yamen office, the military barracks, the homes of rich people, whatever."

"When?"

"Tonight. They say they'll set off firecrackers on a huge scale and attack. They'll fling them together with bamboo pipes filled with gunpowder."

"Good idea, firecrackers, because, you know, the walls in this poor city were built low. Also, the sound of the firecrackers will be heard all over this little town."

"Well then, tell your people quickly, please."

"Anyway, let's go on to the Guandi Temple."

Lifting his shoulders, the man put all of his strength into his arms to lift the wagon.

The question and answer about crow meat were in fact the password between Heaven and Earth Society cohorts. Also, you had to be above a certain level to know the proper words. It was now certain, from his response to the inquiry about crow meat—that the cat spit it up and that the dog played with it—that he was a member of the group. Before revealing the nature of the operation about to unfold, Xinmei had reassured herself just to be on the safe side.

The administrative structure of the Qing dynasty followed the regional hierarchy of prefecture, department, and county. Yongan was a department, which meant it was above a county. The department seat (Yongan city) should have been bigger than a county seat, but the Yongan department seat was in a mountainous area, and was only on the scale of an ordinary county seat on level ground.

With the addition now of some four hundred refugees into the city, it probably felt as though it was bulging. The Guandi Temple area was particularly animated. The open space in front of the temple had become an open-air market. Inside, the temple ground had been turned into a temporary shelter for the refugees.

— 4 —

Relying on its locale up a steep path deep into the mountains, the city walls around Yongan had not been constructed with any height whatsoever. They might have been five meters at the highest point. There would be no problem flinging the bamboo filled with explosives over it.

Among the troops of the Taiping Army, there were several thousand miners who had worked in mines, and they knew how to make gunpowder. The materials were available. En route north, they had made these bamboo pipes during their rest periods.

Preparations for the assault on Yongan city continued even during forced marches. Whatever village they might come upon had a store in which they purchased daily necessities. Every store stocked incense sticks, candles, and firecrackers. The Taipings bought up every single firecracker in every store along their path. The government forces commandeered whatever they wanted, but the Taipings always paid the normal prices.

"When the time is right, we'll attack." When Luo Dagang had said this, he was referring to the concerted throwing of firecrackers and gunpowder-filled pipes of bamboo into the city. The latter would explode, catch fire, and demonstrate the Taipings' fierceness, but they were still incapable of producing too resounding a noise.

To keep the number of casualties low, the Taipings had to reduce the enemies' resistance as much as possible. Ideally, the enemy would put up no fight at all and just run away in the face of the attack. To that end, the Taipings had to make their opponents believe that fighting would be futile. If, through secret, coordinated communications, fires could be set inside the city so that all at once it would burst into flames, the military headquarters of the Qing Army in Yongan might lose its fighting will. That was Luo Dagang's motive in sending Li Xinmei into Yongan to establish contacts.

Now they needed a signal for the uprising to commence within the city. Coordinated timing was of the essence. The easiest signal to communicate would be the sound of the firecrackers exploding.

The Taipings had successfully silenced the *tuanlian* in the vicinity of Yongan city. They were now building ladders to scale the city walls. Though these walls were low, one could hardly just leap over them. They would have to place ladders against the walls and climb them.

For his part Luo Dagang had been collecting something strange—coffins. This region of China was a timber producing area, and it was well-known that there were conveyances for transport along the riverways that were used for the very best of the local timber. The best known of these collection centers was at Liuzhou.

A Chinese expression went: "Eat in Guangzhou, marry in Suzhou, and die in Liuzhou." In other words, when it came to eating, the best restaurants with the richest array of foods were to be found in Guangzhou; when it came to marriage, the most beautiful women were to found in Suzhou; and when it came to dying, the finest coffins in the land were produced in Liuzhou. Originally, they just cut down the trees locally, but more recently, the local people had begun producing caskets for export. Though they were unable to apply lacquer to the wood, they were able to produce semiprocessed goods. It was these items that Luo Dagang was amassing. The wood in a Chinese coffin was extremely thick. Since the coffins produced in this region were top quality, they were especially thick, and they looked tremendously sturdy.

"What are you doing?" inquired Liwen. Luo smiled and responded:

"I'm about to apply a little craftsmanship. You'll soon see."

What he was doing was rather simple to be called "craftsmanship." First, they would make a rounded cavity in both ends of the coffin. Since there were carpenters as well as cabinetmakers among the Taiping troops, this presented no technical problems whatsoever. Into the cavities were thrust the ends of bamboo poles. Then, a test to lift the coffin with the poles was carried out several times. The cavities remained firm, so there was no chance that a coffin held up in this way would become dislocated and fall to the ground.

"You see now?" asked Luo.

"Yes, it's a brilliant idea," Liwen responded, smiling.

Yongan, surrounded by the Taiping military now, would soon rain down a hail of gunfire on the invaders trying to scale the city walls. Thick, firm coffins would provide effective shields. They would raise the coffins onto the walls with the firecrackers inside. Taiping soldiers would then climb the ladders onto the walls. This was the most dangerous time, but with the coffins as shields they would be protected.

"Soldiers who've climbed onto the walls will then pull up the ladders behind them and rest them on the inside of the walls. There'll be no jumping off the walls inside. Using the coffins as shields, they will climb down on the inside and proceed that way," explained Luo.

Since the caskets had originally been intended for human beings, each was just the right size shield for one person. They stood the coffins up and discarded the bottom half in advance. A handle of sorts was attached to each side of the inside. They would then move forward inside the coffin with it straight up, holding it by handles in both hands.

To be able to see in either direction, they also planned to make peepholes in the coffins, but since their lateral vision was unimpaired, they never did carve these holes. Of course, there were not to be that many troops moving forward holding these coffins. The strategy was for those who scaled the wall to continue behind this protection against bullets.

"The idea is not that this tactic will actually be so useful in combat, but that it'll make the troops less intimidated and act somewhat like a charm," Luo explained to Liwen. Soldiers of Heaven and Earth Society affiliates in the Taiping military had a rather low fighting morale. They had risen from lives as bandits, and were not morally gripped by religious belief and armed spiritually, as were the soldiers of the Society of God Worshippers. But, once the incantation "no one will die" was sounded, the troops would probably relax and fight bravely. Luo had lived a long time and had developed quite a knack for it. In fact, he had pinned his hopes more on Li Xinmei's operation to make secret contacts inside the city than he had on the coffins-as-shields scheme.

Ultimately, Yongan fell into Taiping hands, through Xinmei's coordinated efforts, with scarcely a single casualty on their side. The Taiping Army invaded Yongan during the evening of the first day of the intercalary eighth month—September 25, 1851.

When the firecrackers went off, within five minutes, fires were set all over the city. The conflagration that evening could be seen far and wide. The flames had clearly been set in a joint action with the Taipings by their accomplices within the city. The government troops stationed in Yongan undoubtedly imagined that the enemy was attacking from both front and rear simultaneously. The scene was one of great panic.

Gunfire was audible, but it was sporadic, and the coffins being used as shields were scarcely necessary. However, the psychological effect was immense. The very fact that soldiers from the Heaven and Earth Society had fought in the forefront of this battle was without precedent. To the extent that using the coffins as shields in battle set a new standard, this strategy was a great success.

Department Magistrate Wu Jiang, who had brought such ferociously oppressive measures to Yongan, fled into the Guandi Temple with Regional Vice-Commander A-er-jing-a. There, the Taipings attacked and killed them.

Ma Rongsheng, the company commander who was actually in charge of the government's troops, abandoned his post as soon as he heard the firecrackers go off. Almost all of the Qing troops stationed in Yongan city retreated with Ma.

The Taipings had finally become masters of a true city.

— 5 —

For the very first time, the Taipings held a base of operations surrounded by walls. Although not particularly tall, the walls were made of piled bricks and appeared sturdy. Still, once they had taken and occupied Yongan, the Taipings now became a fixed target for their enemies. Without a doubt, they had been more capable of evasive action back in Thistle Mountain. Now, they found their freedom of movement more constricted within the Yongan city walls.

In any event, the Qing Army was sure to try to encircle those city walls thick and fast, with the Taipings inside. The Taipings were well aware of this, but for a short while they needed the time as a group to stop and rest on land surrounded by walls. Until this point, they had been on the move relentlessly. Hong Xiuquan and Yang Xiuqing had no confidence that orders from the commanders were even reaching the rank and file.

Overhaul the organization.

Reorganize the framework.

There was no time to think the matter over in great detail, but they did need some time. Although the city walls would not guarantee them perpetual security, the time needed to put the machinery of the organization into working order might afford a means for the Taiping regime to enjoy some longevity.

The framework for the "Taiping Heavenly Kingdom"— the official name of the movement now—was built during the time spent in Yongan city. In this sense as well, the occupation of Yongan was an extremely important event in Taiping history.

Needless to say, the Taiping military did not simply stay cooped up within the city. They placed guards at strategic sites outside the walls and prepared for the eventual attack by the armies of the Qing. The day after the Taiping first seized Yongan, a Qing force under the command of Wu-lan-tai rapidly advanced to a point some five kilometers from Yongan city. There were some new-style troops among his men: namely, a volunteer corps under the command of Jiang Zhongyuan.

For a time, the paramount leader of the Taiping forces, Hong Xiuquan, held back from entering the city. When he would enter Yongan, the event had to have some special significance. The leaders outside the city were in the process of considering future plans.

The Taiping Army set up three bases outside Yongan: Shuidou village, Mojia village, and Weilong village. General headquarters were set up in the Weilong village temple. All the images and plaques of deities inside were removed, and the altar was also taken outside and burned to the ground. Inside the temple now were a table and chairs only.

"The assault on this city was a splendid piece of work. We killed that demon official Wu Jiang and many of his demonic men, and our own casualties were extremely light. I earnestly believe that this was due to the magnificent leadership of Luo Dagang."

Hong Xiuquan was distributing honors for the victory at Yongan. Luo was sitting erect in a chair across from Hong.

"The demon armies lost the will to fight because of the existence of informants within the city. On this point, I believe the strength exhibited by Li Xinmei in her work establishing contacts there was immense," said Luo. He surely did not believe that he had earned such merit all by himself.

"Yet . . ." Hong Xiuquan sat up straight, his back erect. "It is too bad that, after the demons were compelled to flee, military discipline became rather chaotic. Henceforth, pay more strict attention to this."

"Yes, sir," said Luo, his eyes cast downward. He felt as though his body had become a size smaller.

"So, for now, return to the city, and command your troops with prime emphasis on rigorous discipline."

"Certainly, sir. I shall now take my leave." Luo rose from his chair, bowed, and left the temple.

"That was just the right amount, wasn't it?" asked Hong, taking note of Yang Xiuqing's presence.

"Yes, it was just fine, because you were addressing Luo Dagang," responded Yang.

Even within the Taiping military, troops originally from Heaven and Earth Society groupings still retained characteristics from their days as bandits.

Plundering had taken place after the attack and seizure of Yongan city. At the time, Luo Dagang had gone around shouting himself hoarse: "Put it in the Sacred Treasury! The Sacred Treasury!"

They confiscated the "devils' property"—from bureaucratic offices, from rich families cooperating with the Manchu dynasty, and from Buddhist and Daoist temples. Plundering these items was routine and accepted behavior on the part of the Taiping troops, but they were not allowed to pocket the booty for themselves. Everything was to go to the Sacred Treasury, and not a single thing were they allowed to keep privately. The spoils of war resulting from the fall of Yongan were, of course, stored in the Taiping Sacred Treasury. There was, however, a problem with the amount. The amount that it was estimated they had taken, and the amount that actually was deposited in the Sacred Treasury, were widely divergent.

Before the attack, Luo had sternly expressed to the men under his command, "You have to overcome your former bad habits here and now. You are now troops of the Lord God. Continuing to behave like thieves is simply unacceptable! I'll beat you to death myself!"

After the raid, a physical inspection was carried out, but the scoundrels who appropriated war booty for themselves were not about to do something so foolish as to store the goods on their persons. They stashed it somewhere else. Suspicions about private caches of plunder among the forces of Luo Dagang ran extremely high, and a difference of opinion among the leadership emerged over how to deal with the problem.

Hong Xiuquan was a believer in severe punishment. "Hunt down the culprits and execute them. Whatever you have to do, hunt down ten of them, and imprison Luo Dagang for about ten days. Stick him in a cage so that he'll be exposed to public attention." What Hong considered more important than anything else was the moral purity of the Taiping forces, for this, he firmly believed, was the source of everything.

The opposing point of view was that of Yang Xiuqing, the practical realist. Hong Xiuquan's proposal of executing no fewer than ten offenders looked to offer up a neat, round number of them, even if they had to fabricate the people involved. He had enunciated the view without regard to its efficacy as an object lesson to others. Yang said, "The real culprits aren't going to oppose the executions. They're not about to be picky about the number ten. Three would be fine, and so would thirty."

Hong responded, "Luo will select the ten men. Even if they're not really guilty, the men he'll pick out are bound to be the worst elements in the army. And that too will purify the Taiping Army."

Yang retorted in an unusually severe tone of voice, "If we compel him to single out ten men about whom he has no proof of guilt, Luo will probably leave the Taipings. Making an example of Luo by throwing him in a cage is out of the question. Far from purifying the Taiping Army, it will appear that we have descended into grave chaos. I stand absolutely opposed to taking such action."

Hong remained quiet. He realized that his view would not win out. Yang always had the trump card of the Heavenly Father's Descent to Earth. Hong may have held the highest position in the Taiping military, but he was unable to win this one.

"Mr. Lian, what are your thoughts on this matter?" asked Hong of Liwen.

"I am in agreement with Commander-in-Chief Yang. Is not celebrating the military victory in the attack on Yongan the primary thing here? If we are to turn the heroes of the siege into publicly exposed criminals, then troop morale will undoubtedly atrophy and die," responded Liwen.

A meeting of top Taiping leaders resolved the matter by punishing only those whom it could be proven, on the basis of an investigation, had taken for themselves goods seized in the attack on Yongan. Luo Dagang was not held responsible, and attention was henceforth to be paid to stricter military discipline.

Hong Xiuquan, the Taiping Heavenly King, entered the city of Yongan on the seventh day of the intercalary eighth month, or October 1, 1851. On that day, he issued an edict to the following effect: "All gold and precious metals, all silk cloth, and all precious items that are obtained in the killing of devils and the taking of cities cannot be kept privately but must be deposited in the Sacred Treasury of the Heavenly Dynasty. Violations will be considered criminal."

— 6 —

Zhou Xineng hailed from Bobai in the southern part of Guangxi province.

Bobai was home to many members of the Society of God Worshippers, although few of them joined the uprising in Jintian village. One possible reason for this was that Bobai was quite far from Jintian. Whereas Gui county was virtually the next village over from Jintian, such was not the case by any means for Bobai. Furthermore, the local Society of God Worshippers there, under the leader, Ling Shiba, was too proud to submit to the authority of the group in Jintian. The Society of God Worshippers in Bobai was not as puritanical as in Jintian, either. The adventurism of the Heaven and Earth Society held much greater sway there. The two groups did not get along well, and thus Bobai did not participate en masse when Jintian village raised an army.

Zhou Xineng had come to Thistle Mountain early in the movement. He had been told to go take a look at what was going on there and return. Full-fledged war then broke out with the armies of the Qing dynasty, and he returned to try to convince his comrades in Bobai that they could no longer afford to remain on bad terms with the Jintian group, and that they should literally join forces with the Taiping Army.

It was at this time that Hong Xiuquan, worried that the purity of the Society of God Worshippers might become sullied, had his disagreement with the more practical Yang Xiuqing. In principle, though, Hong was not opposed to appealing to their fellow Society members in Bobai, just not as forcefully as Yang. When he was in Wuxuan, Zhou decided to proceed to Bobai. In addition to the idea of his returning with friends from Bobai, Zhou's return home was an operation aimed at hiding the Taipings' intention of heading north, and making it look as if they planned to move south.

So, it was actually preferable for Zhou's trip to Bobai to become known to the Qing authorities, and little effort was made to shroud it in secrecy. The government side made contact with Zhou near Bobai. At the request of a local official, Zhou's old teacher, Zhong Yiyuan, began to try to persuade him to switch sides.

"Xineng, do you really think that group will capture the whole realm?" asked Zhong of his former pupil, as he stroked his white beard.

"There are many people now involved in this effort to transform the world, and with their cooperation—" began Zhou.

Zhong cut him off. "You think they'll cooperate with you? Those over-cautious peasants? Just look them square in the face. If they rebel, who knows what'll come of it? Don't confuse what you're seeing for cooperation."

"That's true. That may be so."

"To seize the entire realm, you'll need a million troops. How many men did you and the others running around Jintian gather together there? And in the batch you amassed, I'll bet half of them aren't ready to fight. You're carrying along with you crowds of old people and women and children who aren't fit to go anywhere. Do you really think such a group is going to conquer China?"

"We shall try from this point forward to do what we can, and I've come here to collect local allies to the cause."

"Most of your supporters from Bobai have left for Guangdong. Even if they were all here, there would only be about ten thousand of them. And, as you well know, they're all but worthless as fighting troops. Think about it. You're old enough to know better. Get married, have some children. Why not relax and settle down?"

"Oh, how I would like to settle down! But the world won't let me do so. Am I wrong? If I have no land to till, then I have no work. How can I eat? It's the world about us. I would love nothing more than to have some honest job and bring some stability into my life. For that, I'd give up my support for the rebellion of the Society of God Worshippers."

"Are you sincere about this?"

"What do you mean by 'sincere'?"

"An honest job, some stable livelihood, and you'll wash your hands of this rebellion?"

"Of course I'm sincere about that. That's what is at the bottom of my heart."

"You're certain?"

"Let me be the one to stress this point. No doubt about it."

"Good. So, how about if I help you find an occupation?"

"What? Really?"

"I make my living as a teacher. I'm very proud of the fact that, as an educator, I never have to tell lies. When did I ever take advantage or trick anyone?"

Old Zhong Yiyuan shook his head back and forth from left to right. He was full of dignity, his white beard trembling slightly. Without thinking, Zhou lowered his head and said, "Never, not once."

"Good, and you too must refrain from any sort of deception."

"Yes, but . . . you don't mean for this 'honest job' that I should become a schoolteacher. It's true that, when I was studying with you, I was a little bit better than the other kids, but now I've probably forgotten half of what you taught me. . . . I have no faith in my capacities as a local schoolteacher."

"Who asked you to be a schoolteacher? I've got eyes in my head. I know you well enough to know what suits you and what doesn't."

"So, what sort of work would suit me?"

"How about a *dingzi* button rank six?"

"What?" Zhou stared wide-eyed at the face of his old teacher.

The *dingzi* button was a special adornment worn at the top of officials' caps. They differed depending on the wearer's rank in the official Chinese bureaucracy. There were detailed rules and regulations such that the ornamentally engraved gold button on the cap of a rank-one official had a ruby attached, and a rank-six official had a quartz stone affixed.

"Of course, you're not going to become a rank-six bureaucrat tomorrow, but the button will be allowed. We can probably make it official very soon," said Zhong.

This was not, properly speaking, a rank-six official, but treatment commensurate with such a position. For a large amount of money or for some special reason, the Qing government had on occasion conferred such a status. It came with neither authority nor stipend, but was considered a great honor. Zhou's astonishment was fully warranted. The highest local official in the area, the county magistrate, was of rank seven only, and his button was not quartz but a small sapphire of one grade lower.

"No falsehood," continued Zhong, as Zhou stared fixedly at his former teacher dumbfounded. "Until this year, I'd taken the official examinations any number of times and failed them. A *dingzi* button has been my lifelong dream, but now I know the dream will never be realized. By comparison, you're really a lucky man, and precisely because you joined the rebellion of the Society of God Worshippers, too. When I was young, rebellions were few and far between. If I had known all this, I'd have wanted to join up."

A kind of shriek was being wrenched from the heart of the former student. Zhou said, "Of course, there's no way to continue with the rebellion and still get the rank-six button, is there?" He was not that ignorant.

"If you hadn't joined the rebels, you'd never have achieved such remarkable success as this. It's okay, success is success."

Old Zhong Yiyuan's lips, half hidden by his white beard, trembled ever so slightly. Zhou Xineng gulped and leaned forward.

"Is this coming from a reliable source?"

"Absolutely," Zhong nodded in assent.

A look of disquiet floated over Zhou's eyes.

— 7 —

The mission assigned to Zhou Xineng by the Qing dynasty via his former teacher was to accompany a few of his Bobai cohorts, as he had originally planned, and return to the Taiping Army with them. The government needed an informant inside the Taipings, and such an informant had not only to get into the Taiping military itself, but it would be even better if he held a post in the Taiping inner circle. Zhou had been a Taiping leader since the Jintian days, and he was already on the outskirts of the Taiping core. Sending in someone altogether new would have been extraordinarily difficult, because the Society of God Worshippers was an idiosyncratic religious organization. A new entrant would have his actions closely observed and would not be able to get near the Taiping inner circle.

The Qing seemed to have invested considerable energies in the operation of getting Zhou to turn traitor. Indeed, it was apparently worth a rank six in the officialdom. Zhou was dizzy with the thought of a quartz stone affixed to his cap. As a special service agent of the Qing now, he returned to the Taipings.

His position in the Taiping military was army commander. In principle, a commander commanded 13,155 troops. Subordinate to an army commander were five division commanders, each of whom had 2,625 troops under them. Given this structure, Zhou was not just close to the Taiping core—he was a part of it. To be such a central part of the Taiping military structure was much more than any dynastic official of the sixth rank could claim.

"Army commander," thought Zhou. "It's of no practical use whatsoever."

Rather than something big that was useless, he would settle for anything small, so long as it was real. The level of his religious commitment to the Society of God Worshippers had undoubtedly been weak to begin with, and he was probably not too optimistic about the future.

He returned to Yongan on October 10, in the company of 190 young men from Bobai.

"To avoid dangers en route, I have decided to dress my brothers from Bobai in the uniforms of Qing soldiers." He communicated this secret message to Taiping headquarters in Yongan prior to leaving Bobai. Not only were the men dressed in Qing uniforms, but the majority of this group had actually been in a Qing military encampment.

Several days after Zhou returned to Yongan, an important event in the history of the Taiping Heavenly Kingdom transpired. It involved the issuance of an edict concerning the "bestowal of honors."

"Attack the rivers and the mountains." For the Taiping Army, this simple expression implied the conquest of the entire realm—all of China. Those who distinguished themselves to a greater or lesser degree in battle received one of a variety of Taiping hereditary titles.

The next step was the actual taking of the realm. At present they had to continue the hard work on behalf of their descendants. The happiness of their future children, grandchildren, and beyond hung on their next operation.

Another ten days passed, and an edict for the "bestowal of kingship" was issued. Until that point, the title of king had been reserved for the Heavenly King, Hong Xiuquan, but on October 25, he bestowed the title of king on his five highest leaders.

Yang Xiuqing, commander of the central army, became the Eastern King; Xiao Chaogui, commander of the front army, became the Western King; Feng Yunshan, commander of the rear army, became the Southern King; Wei Changhui, commander of the right army, became the Northern King; and Shi Dakai, commander of the left army, became the Assistant King.

On the day when the "attack the rivers and the mountains" succeeded, then the realm was to be divided in such a manner that the Eastern King would govern the eastern sector of China, the Western King would govern in the West, and the Southern and Northern Kings would rule, respectively, in the south and north. The Assistant King was to support the Heavenly Dynasty.

The plan had already become one of gaining hegemony over the entirety of China, and a kind of magnanimity extended down to the rank-and-file troops. News of the "bestowal of kingships" filled the entire army with a joyous sense of buoyancy. Noteworthy was the fact that Feng Yunshan had been lowered in the order. Feng had, after all, founded the Society of God Worshippers with Hong. He had always been regarded as the number two man only to Hong, but now he had fallen to number four.

Because Yang possessed the weapon of the "Heavenly Father's Descent to Earth" and Xiao had demonstrated a similar weapon in the person of Jesus, Feng had been placed beneath them. Furthermore, it was enunciated that "each of the kings shall fall under the control of the Eastern King." What this meant in fact was that Yang Xiuqing was really higher than number two. At this time, an epidemic was raging among the Qing's troops, and the attack to recapture Yongan was being considerably eased. Between that and the bestowal of kingships, the Taiping military was itself apt to fall into a lack of vigilance.

As soon as he arrived back in Yongan, Zhou had already begun his activities.

13

Escape from Yongan

—1—

Fall in Beijing was invigorating. The first day of the intercalary eighth month, the day on which the Taipings occupied the city of Yongan, corresponded to September 25 on the solar calendar, and the autumn chill had yet to be felt. A balmy atmosphere drifted through the capital city.

News of the fall of Yongan had not yet arrived. To be sure, the court in Beijing was not sitting around idly. High-level officials in the Qing government were becoming aware of the bizarre fact that somehow the rebellion of the Society of God Worshippers was different from all other local uprisings throughout Chinese history. It was in this context that the young Xianfeng Emperor had conferred upon Imperial Commissioner Sai-shang-a the treasured sword of Ebilun. An unprecedented sense of crisis enveloped the army raised by the Society of God Worshippers in Guangxi.

Even ordinary city dwellers in the capital were generally aware of the fact that far off in the south, a group of Christians had risen in rebellion. They seemed to think of it as some occurrence in a distant realm altogether. They were much more concerned with the Nian rebels who had risen in Anhui province, because Anhui was much closer to Beijing than Guangxi.

From the government's perspective, the Nian were "bandits," though the rebels saw themselves as the Nian Army or Society. The word *nian* means "to twist," and the current theory about the group's name was that it was an association that found its strength in the way a piece of paper grows firmer when it is twisted. The main feature that differentiated it from the Taiping

Army was the effective absence of any religious component to its foundation. The Nian had contacts with salt smugglers, and its nature, if anything, was more strongly that of a secret society.

Nor were they solely a landed force, for they had bold, undaunted rebel might at sea, as well. Two months before the Taipings took Yongan, there had been an incident in which warships of the Qing navy were attacked by pirates at sea off the Shandong peninsula, and a military adjutant had been killed in the fray.

"The government's really taking it on the head, don't you think?"

"What'd you expect? Their troops don't have a chance."

"Then, I guess they'd better just keep their spirits up."

"For whom?"

"Doesn't matter."

This was the level of response of Beijing's residents to local rebellions.

"What does it mean to be a patriot?" wondered Lian Weicai as he walked through the market area of Beijing. For some reason, this thought had kept recurring to him for a period of years now. The Taiping Army was trying to build a new country; the government forces were trying to suppress them. True patriots aligned with which side?

He was heading toward Cotton Lane outside the city walls of Beijing to make his appointment with Shen Baozhen (1820–1879), Lin Zexu's son-in-law. Shen had passed the highest level of the imperial civil service examinations four years earlier in 1847, and was now working as a compiler in the Hall of Military Glory. Although he was the husband of Lin's second daughter Puqing, he was also the son of Lin's younger sister. Even when there was no blood connection between a couple, they could not marry if they shared the same surname in China. However, a marriage was acceptable for a couple with this sort of blood link so long as they had different surnames.

Shen and Lian had agreed to meet at a home bearing the name Zhaoyuan, or Welcome Garden. It was neither a restaurant nor an inn, nor, for that matter, was it someone's private villa. Lian owned it and he ordinarily kept it vacant.

Cotton Lane, where this empty home was to be found, was generally considered an inauspicious place. Locals referred to Zhaoyuan as the "unlucky house of Yan city." "Yan city" was an old name for Beijing. The story went that, if someone were to construct a residence within this area of the capital, the owner of it was doomed to ruin.

At the end of the Ming dynasty in the early seventeenth century there lived a woman general by the name of Qin Liangyu. Woman commanders were extremely rare in Chinese history. She was the wife of the pacification commissioner of Shizhu, Sichuan province, and when her husband died, she was appointed the local military leader. She was the head or chieftain of what is now called an "ethnic minority," and her troops fought with great valor and were highly effective in battle. When the Ming Army was at the end of its tether in battle with the Manchu armies in the northeast, the forces of Qin Liangyu were a great source of strength. The secret of their military might was strict martial discipline. To retire on the battlefield as one wished, or to violate the orders of a superior, or to confiscate the possessions of the local resident populace, were relentlessly punished by decapitation. The execution ground of Qin's army while they were resident in Beijing was said to have been on Cotton Lane.

As the story was told: "The departed spirits, having no place to which they can return, have gone astray and haunt contemporary men." Since no one wanted to live in such an area, land prices were naturally low. Lian bought the land, most of which was a garden, and built a summerhouse on the grounds, which he named Zhaoyuan. The name carried with it the sense that, if there were spirits confused for over 200 years, then he was enjoining them to come and enter Nirvana.

Lian invited not only departed spirits, however. When he arrived in Beijing, he often invited capital officials to this retreat. In contrast to the "outer officials," those who served in posts in the localities outside the imperial capital, the bureaucrats who worked in the offices of the central government were known as "capital officials." These "capital officials" were the elite, although their salaries were rather low. The local officials earned the same stipends, but had many sources of miscellaneous income, including various forms of what would appear to be "corruption." However, these apparently illicit sources of revenue became customary over time, and were seen as perfectly legitimate forms of income.

Capital officials had to live on their salaries, and they had no choice but to maintain a lavish circle of acquaintances. Those without assets of their own were always in debt. They hoped for transfer to a local post. No matter how much they borrowed, once their local service was decided upon, all their debts could be paid off at once. Thus, although it was best to begin with an official position outside the capital, it was thought that, without the experience of serving in the capital, there was no chance for future success.

Among those who passed the very highest level of the civil service examinations and became metropolitan graduates, those with the highest marks remained at the center and were assigned something on the order of research and training posts. The customary practice was for those with medium or lower scores to be assigned as county magistrates of rank 7A, and begin their bureaucratic careers with a local post.

Capital officials barely eked out a living in the red, but the future was promised to them. When they moved from the capital to a locality, they were abruptly elevated to the position of prefect, rank 4B, or circuit intendant, rank 4A. Sources of income beyond their stipends were numerous, and every financier lent them money unhesitatingly.

Lian Weicai had no special expertise in banking or finance. The reason he offered Shen Baozhen financial help had nothing to do with making money. Nor did it have to do with the connection to Lin Zexu. The assistance had been proffered because, in Lian's estimation, Shen was a man of talent and ability who would serve the entire nation.

The Hall of Military Glory was effectively a state-run publishing house, located in the southwest corner of Beijing's Forbidden City. With government funds, they printed a wide variety of classical texts and rare books. To that end, they had to collect many kinds of books, edit and revise them, and prepare definitive editions. Shen was involved in this sort of work. It was the kind of training for someone who was to become a future national leader. He, of course, had no other sources of income. But, since in due course he would become a high official, he had to maintain friendly contacts with men in positions of authority. And creating personal, human networks cost a great deal of money.

—2—

At the same time that Lian Weicai was supporting Shen Baozhen, he was helping the Taipings. It was clearly some kind of contradiction to be looking after the needs of both the established authorities and those opposed to it. Double-dealing or not, there was probably no better way to go. Yet Lian Weicai had not yet ascertained what China's future would look like. It was still unclear to him. His standard for judgment was the well-being of the people.

All that could be said with certainty now was that hope was gone. Circumstances at present had to be changed, reformed. Should he expect this from talented men on the side of the regime? Or should he expect it from the group that sought to overthrow the regime?

He had placed his son Lian Liwen among the Taipings because he wanted accurate information about them. Were Liwen able to enter the rebels' inner circles, he would be able to gain a true-to-life sense of them, and Liwen had been sending back detailed reports.

Observations of the authorities, on the other hand, Lian Weicai had been carrying out himself. Shen Baozhen was not the only one invited to Zhaoyuan. There was as well another metropolitan graduate of Shen's year, 1847. This was Zhang Zhiwan (1811–1897), who passed with the highest examination paper that year, and he was thus known as the "principal graduate." Zhang, though, was on his way to a position as the principal provincial-level examiner in Henan province, and hence was not then in the capital. Among the metropolitan graduates, those who did especially well remained in the center for research and training, but customarily would be sent to serve as local examination officials. Being the highest graduate of his class, it was expected that Zhang's appointment would be made quickly. The following year Shen Baozhen was sent to serve as the provincial examination official in Shuntian.

One of those who visited Zhaoyuan was a man by the name of Li Hongzhang (1823–1901). Li hailed from Hefei, Anhui province, and like Shen Baozhen, he worked in the Hanlin Academy as an editorial official at the time. He Jing, from Xiangshan in Guangdong province, was also an editor-compiler. Another man bearing the same surname as Shen Baozhen, Shen Guifen (1817–1881), came from Wujiang in Jiangsu province, and was then on an official trip as an examiner in Zhejiang, but he was soon to return to Beijing.

Only one person not from this class of graduates was invited by Lian. He was a metropolitan graduate of 1838, and thus, the senior by nine years of Shen Baozhen and the others. His name was Zeng Guofan, from Xiangshan, Hunan province, age forty, and then serving as left vice-minister in the Ministry of Justice of the Qing dynasty.

Why would someone outside of their class have been invited? In fact, Lin Zexu's eldest son, Lin Ruzhou (b. 1814), was supposed to occupy this particular seat, but he was still observing the mourning ritual in Fujian for his father. Individuals in mourning were supposed to restrain themselves from making long trips. Lin Ruzhou was a metropolitan graduate of the class of 1838, the same year as Zeng Guofan.

On his way to the capital, Lian Weicai had stopped in Fuzhou, capital of Fujian province. Lin Ruzhou said to him, "Zeng Guofan stands above everyone in our class. When you go to Beijing, by all means, make a point of meeting him. I'll write you a letter of introduction to that end."

That year of 1838, Lin Ru'nan passed the metropolitan level of the civil service examinations with the fine place of sixth on the roster. While he was at work in research and compilations, his father, Lin Zexu, was exiled and Ruzhou accompanied him to Xinjiang, where he passed his time without entering government service. Having spent roughly two years at the Hanlin Academy in Beijing, he had observed others at work there at the time. If he were to pick the one person of special talent from all those of his class then in residence in Beijing, he would have unhesitatingly named Zeng Guofan.

It was decided that those assembled at Zhaoyuan would, "Listen to Mr.

Zeng speak about current affairs." In this way, Zeng's attendance would in no way appear unnatural. The men who assembled there that day later became the leading government figures in the turmoil at the end of the Qing period.

"It's been quite a while since I've seen Yuqian. How is he?" asked Zeng Guofan of Li Hongzhang. Li Hongzhang's father, Li Wenan (also known as Li Yuqian), was a metropolitan graduate of 1838. Though he was of the same class as Zeng and Lin Ruzhou, he had ranked 120th among the 194 who passed the examinations that year. He had not gone to work in the Hanlin Academy, but held a string of positions primarily in the judicial field, such as secretary and later director in the Ministry of Justice. Although they were in the city of Beijing, there had been no opportunity for him to meet Zeng Guofan, who had moved rapidly along the road to success. Although it was not entirely true, as some said, that graduation ranking was everything, it did carry considerable weight and influenced men's lives. Zeng had ranked 38th.

The topic of the evening was, needless to say, the matter of the Taiping Army in Guangxi. The conversation moved as follows: "Haoren is a subprefectural magistrate and is now in Guiping, the problem area we're speaking about, and fighting with great bravery I should add."

"He's not just a civil official either, but a man of extraordinary courage."

"In any event, I want to praise the great fight he's putting up."

"Haoren" was the style of Li Mengqun, a fellow graduate of the class of 1838. Ranking low on the list of metropolitan graduates that year, he was abruptly dispatched to take up the post of a local county magistrate. When he transferred to Guiping county—which had jurisdiction over Jintian village, the cradle of the Taiping forces—he was promoted to subprefectural magistrate.

As mentioned earlier, a county magistrate was a 7A rank position, while a subprefectural magistracy ranked 5A. While brilliant men of the same class were working on editorial and compilation projects, as senior compiler of rank 6B in the Hanlin Academy, the much lower-ranked Li Mengqun had already achieved the status of a subprefectural magistrate.

Concerns over the bureaucratic ladder were often so potent as to defy imagination. When the conversation turned to this topic, the expressions on their faces all changed.

"No, just the other day, Li Mengqun was promoted to prefect," said Zeng Guofan. Information of this sort came quickly into the hands of these young compilers.

"Huh? . . ." Sighs mixed in with voices of surprise. A prefect held the rank of 4B.

The times were such that unprecedented promotions were possible irrespective of one's place in the examination rankings. Clearest in everyone's eyes was success on the military front. It looked suspiciously as though an era of disorder was at hand. The times were changing, thought these talented men, some unconsciously rubbing their hands.

It did not escape Lian Weicai's notice that Li Hongzhang's eyes were glistening. Li was probably even more ambitious—let alone talented—than even Shen Baozhen.

"If Haoren can keep up the fight, then he'll surely defeat the bandits one day soon," said He Jing. Among the men in this group, He, a native of Guangdong, was the most interested in the Taipings.

"It hasn't been all that long since they formed their band, so their unity can't be terribly strong. I think a strategy aimed at disrupting them internally might be efficacious," said Li.

"Such a plan has already been put in motion," said Zeng.

"Really, have you, Mr. Zeng?" said Li Hongzhang, his eyes blinking. There was latent strength to Zeng's tone of voice. It appeared as though he had not simply heard that preparations were under way to disrupt the Taipings internally. It was as if he himself had devised the plan. Zeng nodded and responded, "I have recommended Jiang Zhongyuan of Hunan. This fellow has distinguished himself in defeating bandits in the past. He is brave, and at the same time, an excellent strategist. I have instructed in detail by letter how to go about causing disorder among the Taipings. Jiang Zhongyuan has already begun his operations under the staff of an imperial commissioner."

"That is a hopeful development indeed." The young capital officials looked at the face of their senior colleague with expressions of hope. The left vice-minister in the Ministry of Justice was a position that enabled Zeng to participate in the council of state. The young capital officials probably saw in Zeng Guofan their own visages ten years hence.

Lian felt a genuine enthusiasm present. A feeling of sorrow for the current state of the nation, and an agitation over the dazzling brilliance of the promised path to success in the world, were all mixed together.

—3—

In compliance with the instructions of Zeng Guofan, Jiang Zhongyuan was attempting to disrupt the internal workings of the Taipings, then in the city of Yongan. For the time being, the Qing forces would not lay siege to occupied Yongan. There were a number of reasons for this, though particularly emphasized was the fact that "an epidemic was raging within the army," as noted in a report to the capital.

This epidemic was malaria, and indeed malaria was rampant, with the front route army especially afflicted. Even generals at the levels of Xiang

Rong and Ba-qing-de had come down with the disease. The real reason, however, that the Qing Army stood before Yongan and did nothing can be found in a letter penned by Jiang Zhongyuan:

> It is not that the bandits are numerous and our forces are few in number, but that the bandits are strong and we are weak. The soldiers do not obey orders, and the officers do not know their men. The troops and their commanders do not get along well, and relations among the officers are poor.

A basic plan of attack on Yongan was not decided upon for a long time. Wu-lan-tai advocated aggressive warfare. His view was that the enemy was comprised of a bunch of inexperienced peasants. Though government forces had previously failed to capture the enemy, the Taipings were now within a walled city and could be crushed all at once. Xiang Rong took a much more cautious stance. He knew the inner workings of the Taipings far better than Wu-lan-tai and thus knew they were not an enemy that was easily subdued.

Jiang Zhongyuan also advocated war, but he differed from Wu-lan-tai. Where Wu-lan-tai called for an immediate and wholesale attack and destruction, Jiang realized that an all-out assault would not destroy the enemy. Perhaps they could recover the city of Yongan, but the Taipings had considerable numbers, and those that escaped the city would just head elsewhere. And the government's forces would have no choice but to pursue them. Until such time as the Qing Army had confidence that it could wipe the Taipings out, it had to refrain from a general attack. Such was Jiang's point of view.

"When will we acquire this confidence?" asked Wu-lan-tai by way of rebuttal. "It would seem that supplies within the city are rather plentiful."

"We need to wait until the enemy's morale drops."

"And when will that happen? Our morale is likely to decline before theirs."

"We won't just wait around for it to happen doing nothing. We'll maneuver to help make it happen," responded Jiang.

The strategy was to agitate disorder and cause internal rifts among the enemy. The key was to entice discontented elements from within the enemy's camp.

"We sent Zhou Xineng in and he failed, didn't he?" said Wu-lan-tai.

Persuaded by his former teacher to throw in with the Qing forces, Zhou Xineng had entered Yongan and lured his friends Zhu Xikun and Huang Wenan to their side. They were sure to receive some sort of reward, argued Zhou, if they surrendered to the Qing Army—but Zhu and Huang ultimately did not submit.

Yang Xiuqing learned of the defection of Zhou Xineng, and he handled the affair with one of his spirit possessions, speaking in God's name. Intoning aloud the revelation of the Heavenly Father Jehovah, Yang said before a mass audience: "There is a rebellious devil within the city. His name is Zhou Xineng. The devils who have joined with him are Zhu Ba and Chen Wu!" It was October 29. Northern King Wei Changhui examined Zhou Xineng and secured testimony from Zhu Xikun and Huang Wenan.

People were saying to one another, "If you do something evil, the Heavenly Father will see through to it."

"The all-powerful Heavenly Father is watching over us. The enemy won't be able to lay a hand on us."

The following day, the execution was carried out. Zhou, his wife Cai Wanmei, and their son Zhou Lizhen, as well as Zhu Ba and Chen Wu, who had both followed him from Bobai—five people in all—were beheaded.

Wu-lan-tai raised this failure of Zhou Xineng to point up the difficulties of agitational efforts.

"Zhou's failure was to be expected," said Jiang. "It's extremely difficult to succeed in such an operation against the Society of God Worshippers."

"How so? If not against the Society of God Worshippers, then where?" asked Wu-lan-tai.

"The followers of the Society of God Worshippers have very powerful beliefs, so it's a waste of time to try to demolish that. Those inside Yongan city now are not all members of the Society of God Worshippers. Take Luo Dagang, the man who brought the city down. He's not a member. He belongs to the Heaven and Earth Society. Didn't he capture the city through secret communications and the assistance of remnants of the Heaven and Earth Society laying low there? The objective of this operation has to be aimed at the Heaven and Earth Society."

"I see what you're saying. . . . Luo Dagang, eh?"

"No, it's too dangerous near Luo Dagang, and we don't have any good connections to him."

"So, whom do we broach the subject with? A woman? There are a couple of Heaven and Earth Society females there, Li Xinmei and Su Sanniang."

"No, they seem a little too distant. There's someone a bit more within our reach, a man from Hunan by the name of Jiao Liang. If he works out, we'll have our link."

"Jiao Liang? I've never heard of him." Having been sent from Guangdong, Wu-lan-tai knew nothing of the scene in Hunan.

"He's from the town of Xinning, in Hunan, and has made a small name for himself there."

"Hmm, Xinning, eh?" Wu-lan-tai nodded understandingly. Four years earlier, a man by the name of Lei Zaihao had risen in rebellion in Xinning, and Jiang Zhongyuan had raised an army to crush the rebels. Jiang was a native of Xinning, and it was reasonable to expect that he was well-informed about the Heaven and Earth Society there. Lei Zaihao had also been connected to a Heaven and Earth affiliate. Although Jiao Liang was later mildly involved in their activities, when Jiang Zhongyuan, as county magistrate, began exercising local authority, Jiao disappeared. Soon thereafter it was ascertained that he had shown up among the forces of the Taiping Army. Since he was also from Xinning, Jiang Zhongyuan had been able to investigate in great detail Jiao's personal connections among family and friends alike. In fact, Jiang's investigation became so severe that Jiao apparently had decided to lie low for a time.

Abundantly self-confident, Jiao had allegedly told friends in the Heaven and Earth Society, "I'm returning to Xinning now at the head of a huge army. Wait for me!"

Jiao Liang had his eye on the Society of God Worshippers. If possible, he planned to try to take over their entire organization. That, however, was simply expecting too much. He had made no inroads into the leadership. While he kept up his usual bragging and exaggeration, inside he appeared to be growing highly impatient.

This information now reached Jiang Zhongyuan. If Jiao Liang was becoming impatient, then this seemed the best time to try to lure him in. This, then, might provide the best means to effect the operation mentioned in Zeng Guofan's letter of reeking internal discord among the Taipings. Jiang called for a man by the name of Xie Liu, a peddler through various regions in Guangxi province and, as it turned out, an elder cousin of Jiao's wife. Xie and Jiao had been childhood buddies, and Xie was one of the very few people Jiao genuinely trusted.

Through Xie, Jiang attempted a ploy for enticing Jiao into switching sides. He was to amass as many followers as possible within the city of Yongan. At the least, he was to nurture his might to the extent that he could engage in secret contacts when the Qing Army was ready to attack the city. And, Xie was to discuss with Jiao the topic of the reward he would receive.

Jiao was not a man to lay much trust solely on words. Even in a society where acts of heroism had become standard fare, money was still the final arbiter. If he put together a group of followers, he would have to feed them. For funding, Jiang settled at first on an offer of 800 taels of silver—in cash.

—4—

"For the time being, I think it's useless," said Lian Liwen, shaking his head.

"You think so? Not yet, eh?" said Jiao Liang, with his thumb placed firmly on his forehead.

"The others won't permit it."

"Just a small number would be fine. Like ten men from here and twenty from there. I'm not talking about taking everyone out. They just don't understand the extent of my power." Jiao began rubbing his jaw with his thumb.

"Well, well . . .," laughed Liwen. He couldn't really articulate his own point of view, which had led to this incidence of rudeness.

Jiao Liang often came to visit Liwen. The two of them enjoyed a kind of exalted "guest" status among the Taipings. However, compared to Liwen's close ties to the highest leadership of the Taiping military, Jiao was not so highly honored, occasionally being asked to draft documents. And they were not important documents. With his pretensions as the second coming of Zhuge Liang, Jiao Liang was not happy at all.

This time, when he arrived at Liwen's residence, he asked: "I want some troops to serve under me. If I could have some troops to command, wouldn't the leaders come asking my advice?"

The Taiping military had already taken shape as a well-ordered military organization. Luo Dagang and Su Sanniang, leaders of Heaven and Earth affiliates like Jiao, had joined the Taipings at the head of a band of their own followers. Jiao Liang had come to the Taiping camp all by himself, so this demand for troops of his own was a useless, unreasonable proposal. His request for a command put together from small numbers of troops removed from this or that brigade was purely self-serving.

Jiao had joined the Taipings on his own in Wuxuan, and up to that point in time his contribution to the cause had been nil. There were many men from among the core members of the Society of God Worshippers from the days in Jintian village who had yet to receive a military command. Liwen did not want to pass Jiao's request on to the Taiping leaders. It seemed absurd to him. "You'll soon regret it!" said Jiao by way of a parting shot, and then left Liwen.

After a time, Su Sanniang and Li Xinmei arrived. They were both now in command of a small number of women troops in the Taiping Army.

"Did I just see Jiao Liang here?" asked Xinmei, having passed him as she approached Liwen's lodging.

"He was just here. He wants troops all his own to command," responded Liwen.

"He wants a lot of troops. He seems to have had a few adherents crop up recently, but he's making too much of it," said Su Sanniang dubiously.

"I've heard that rumor, too. He's the kind of guy that won't be happy until he's made a general."

"It's not just two or three followers. It's more like a dozen or so? Like the handful of followers of He Hongji in the city," said Li Xinmei.

After the Taipings occupied Yongan, He Hongji's followers, who had earlier escaped to various places, returned to the city. Their numbers were not known with any precision, but estimates ran from one hundred fifty to two hundred, the majority of whom were still not formally under the command structure of the Taiping Army. It was this group that made Jiao want a force under his own command.

"I heard from one of the younger people that Jiao Liang had recently amassed a group of only thirty men for a banquet," said Su Sanniang.

"A banquet?" said Liwen, shrugging his shoulders. This was all but unthinkable in Yongan, which was in a state of war.

"That's what he said—a banquet," Su restated. "And quite a feast as well. If you can find a place sufficiently big and can rely on someone to make the necessary arrangements, even a party is not impossible."

"You can get your hands on the provisions if you fork out enough money."

As if carrying on Liwen's thought here, Xinmei said, "There's something I'm a bit anxious about in this connection. Jiao Liang spent some money, but where did that money come from?"

"Good question. He's had it ever since Wuxuan. He never treated anyone to anything before. The money . . . the money *is* a problem," said Su in a somewhat subdued tone of voice.

The Taipings allowed no private property. All assets had to be placed in the Sacred Treasury, though one could argue that Taiping discipline did not extend to guests. Liwen was in charge of accounting, so he always carried a large amount of personal funds with him. When he, for example, made purchases on behalf of the Taipings, he used this money. All the Taiping leaders were aware that this was going on, but no one knew that Jiao Liang, a guest just like Liwen, had a store of his own money. Everyone thought of Jiao as a poor country bumpkin, and looked on him no differently from other regular members of the Taiping forces.

This really is a serious problem, thought Liwen. Jiao hadn't stolen the money. That would have been impossible, and thieves were beheaded. The disciplinary regulations governing the Taipings were not only for the officers and their troops. They applied as well to the general civilian populace.

If he hadn't stolen the money, perhaps he received it from somewhere. But from whom? If there was someone who had given it to him, then surely there must have been certain conditions attached.

Jiao Liang is someone who bears close observation, thought Liwen, but shall I pass this information along to the Eastern King?

Liwen was confused. Yang Xiuqing, the Eastern King, was in possession of that final weapon, the Heavenly Father's Descent to Earth. And he would use it mercilessly, if necessary, as seen in the Zhou Xineng incident.

"Well, a number of businessmen did recently pay Jiao Liang a visit, didn't they?" said Su, as she thought back to this matter.

"That's right, apparently also from Xinning," said Liwen, also remembering something. In order to enhance their store of supplies, the Taipings in occupied Yongan welcomed merchant travelers to the city. For a while, the Qing Army was incapable of sealing off access to Yongan. For the merchants, the Taipings were always meticulous in paying for goods and were a perfectly safe bet for commercial transactions. It would be safe to assume that, mixed in among these merchants, were a number of Qing collaborators.

"People from Xinning," said Xinmei, seeming also to recall something. "Among the enemy forces was a volunteer army from Hunan. Wasn't the general of that army also from Xinning?"

"Yes, he was. I'm told that Jiang Zhongyuan is from Xinning," said Liwen, and then in a quieter tone he continued: "I really think Jiao Liang is a suspicious character, and we've got to keep an eye on him for a while. I also think it's better for now not to tell the Eastern King."

"Fine." The woman leaders nodded in accord at the same time. Liwen's words seemed reasonable to anyone familiar with Yang Xiuqing's temperament.

Liwen looked around the room they were in. The young man, Chen Picheng, placed in Liwen's service by Yang, had still not returned from the errand on which he had been sent.

—5—

For all their efforts, the Taipings inside Yongan city had not been able to increase their troop strength. The Qing forces surrounding them had amassed reinforcements. At first the Qing Army was unable to blockade the city completely, but once troop strength had improved, it was able to do so.

The Taipings would soon have to find a route of escape and abandon Yongan. They could not go on living in the city indefinitely. But when would they make their escape, wondered the leaders of the Taiping Army—perhaps it was better now to refer to them as the government of the Taiping Heavenly Kingdom.

Although the Taiping military had engaged in a number of missions, they were usually beaten back by the Qing. Since they had to leave the city to commence a fight and then return to the city, regardless of the outcome of the battle, from the perspective of the Qing forces, the Taipings were always retreating.

On November 15, two weeks after the execution of Zhou Xineng, the Taipings fought their way out, but were rebuked by Qing troops under the command of Xiang Rong and Chang-rui.

On November 22, they again massed an army and sallied out, but were attacked by the forces of Xiang Rong and Li Mengqun, and returned to the city. Wu-lan-tai also won a victory after attacking the Taiping base at Mojia village.

Early in December, Huang Man, commander of the advance guard of Luo Dagang's army, was taken prisoner in battle.

On December 17, Xiang Rong returned to his former position as provincial military commander in Guangxi. Responsible for earlier defeats, he had been removed from office and stripped of all bureaucratic positions. A positive reevaluation as a result of his successful string of military victories over the Taipings had clearly led to rehabilitation to his former office.

On December 18, Imperial Commissioner Sai-shang-a, then in Yangshuo (a county to the south of Guilin), called his encampment together and offered the following threatening words of encouragement to his men: "Put forth a united effort, fight strenuously, and plan for victory. I have in my possession the sword of Ebilun, bequeathed by my superiors, and anyone who does not obey orders will be beheaded with it on the spot!"

Sai-shang-a and his men arrived in the Yongan area on December 26. The forces of the Qing Army were fortifying their will for an eventual all-out assault on the city. Between Wu-lan-tai's call for a speedy commencement of that assault, and Xiang Rong's more prudent stance, Sai-shang-a, who had hesitated to take a position, finally decided in favor of an aggressive attack.

"Do you have a point of view?" asked Sai-shang-a, looking at each of the leaders of the Qing Army one by one. When his line of vision came toward Jiang Zhongyuan, Jiang nodded softly and averted his gaze. It was an indication that he agreed with the imperial commissioner.

However, he was still harboring a major difference of opinion. If they were to continue the blockade of Yongan city with another full month of encirclement, then the morale of the Taiping troops was certain to deteriorate precipitously. At that time, the Taipings would lack the capacity even to attempt an escape.

The Jiao Liang operation's in trouble now, thought Jiang, but if the blockade can be kept up, the number of discontented will increase and the operation may be easier to execute. If we could only establish a channel of inside communication, the Taiping Army would surely dissipate. It would be exceedingly difficult, Jiang realized, for the Taipings to repulse an all-out assault.

An urgent request arrived from Beijing. "Has Yongan still not been recovered? What in the world is going on there?"

The high officials in the capital had no idea of conditions at the scene. Many times Sai-shang-a had dreamt that the grand ministers of state had spoken ill of him before the throne at an imperial audience in the Qianqing Palace within the Forbidden City.

"With their repeated sorties, the bandits' fighting strength must have weakened. If our armies are freshly reinforced and are at full strength, there is no reason why we can't recapture Yongan. What could be clearer?"

Hearing Sai-shang-a speak, Jiang thought to himself, Yongan really can be retaken, but the long-haired bandits will be able to escape.

The Taipings cut the queues at the back of their heads and allowed hair to grow in the areas they had regularly shaved previously. Thus, Taiping officers and troops had the appearance of full heads of hair, and were called "long-haired" by the Qing military. The name "bandits" was a vague appellation. Eventually, the name "long-haired bandits" stuck.

Movements by the Qing Army were rapidly conveyed to the Taipings, as ordinary residents of the region acted as the eyes and ears of the Taiping Army. In conferences attended only by high-level officials of state, the servants who prepared tea and the like, frequently overheard things expressed in casual conversation and passed along reports to the Taipings.

Plans for the escape from Yongan were being debated more and more within the Taiping camp. Battles were fought at the end of the year and at the beginning of the next, and it was now the second lunar month of the year, equivalent to mid-March into April. Rain was plentiful at this time of year in Guangxi.

"Use the rain to escape." It was decided that they would pick a day on which the rain was particularly fierce in the middle of the second lunar month.

"The entire army will advance along the eastern road, heading north from Zhaoping and Pingle toward Guilin."

Spies had reported to the Taipings that the government's eastern route army was its least prepared force. Although the Qing Army planned to spread an unsurpassable encirclement around the Taipings, the latter was better informed of the actual state of affairs among the government's forces than those forces themselves.

A small stream known as Guzu Brook ran to the east of Yongan city. The Qing forces guarding that area were troops from the Shouchun defense command in Anhui province, and they were known to be quite weak as a fighting force. They were the army service corps, stationed by Gusu Brook to facilitate transporting supplies and ammunition in relay fashion. They were not battle-ready troops, but at Qing military headquarters, the Shouchun forces were counted as part of the government's military strength.

It was the twenty-fifth day of the second month. According to the calendar newly established by the Taipings, it was the first of the third month, April 4 on the solar calendar, corresponding that year to Qingming. By proclamation of the Heavenly King, the entire army was to escape under cover of rain.

The advance guard was the army of Luo Dagang, which had posted a significant victory in the initial assault on Yongan. The Qing forces at Gusu

Brook were stunned. Unprepared for battle, when these government troops realized that the enemy appearing in the rain was a large army, they dispersed in all directions.

Having defeated this army quickly, the Taipings crossed the Qing encampment and headed for Longliao peak. The mountain paths in this area were extremely narrow, and they had to proceed in single file, thus consuming precious time. For this reason, they suffered their greatest casualties to date.

Wu-lan-tai was at the southern road when he learned that the Taipings were escaping along the eastern road. He then rapidly led his troops toward Gusu Brook. The mountain path at Gusu Brook was at least twice as wide, and the Taipings thought they could not be overtaken by now. However, they could only proceed single file, and the rain made the roadway slippery. They had no choice but to march with care, which in turn decreased their speed. Wu-lan-tai's forces arrived in a hurry to find the rear guard of the Taipings.

Some two thousand aged and young followers of the Taipings were massacred on the spot. Among them was an old man by the name of Wei Yuanguang, uncle of the Northern King, Wei Changhui.

"Kill them! Kill them!" screamed the frontline officers at the top of their lungs.

"Idiots!" yelled Wu-lan-tai. "Don't kill the big shots! Capture them. Take them alive!"

Both sides were covered with mud.

—6—

"You've caught the leader!" said Wu-lan-tai in a highly agitated voice.

"Who's the leader?" he asked an aide. "You mean Hong Xiuquan?"

"Well, I'm not really sure."

"Go find out right now." The aide left.

Jiang Zhongyuan was also at the temporary headquarters set up at Gusu Brook. With him were Feng Jingni, a survivor of the Shouchun Army, and Zhang Jingxiu, both military officers. It was a great victory after crushing defeats, and headquarters was all astir.

"It looks like Yang Xiuqing," came back one report. "According to those who live in this area, it is none other than Yang Xiuqing."

"Anyway, bring him here at once. Whether it's Hong Xiuquan or Yang Xiuqing, either one is a big catch," said Wu-lan-tai, a bit exasperated.

Soon a man with his hands tied behind his back was marched before Wu-lan-tai. He looked to be in his mid-thirties. He of course had long hair, and there were chains tied around his neck. His large eyes glistened as if they were floating in oil, and a pitch black mustache adorned his upper lip.

When he saw the prisoner, Jiang Zhongyuan was momentarily taken aback. It was his fellow townsman Jiao Liang, the man he had tried to recruit into a plan to stir up internal disorder among the Taipings. Several years earlier, Jiang had once seen Jiao. For his part, Jiao should have recognized Jiang, who for some time had been a famous man in their native Xinning. The soldiers holding him on either side threw Jiao about violently. When he came before Wu-lan-tai, Jiao sat down with his legs crossed.

"Are you Yang Xiuqing?" asked Wu-lan-tai.

"Ha, ha," guffawed Jiao. "What's this about Yang Xiuqing? If you've mistaken me for him, then you're in big trouble. Yang Xiuqing's my servant."

"Then, who are you?"

"Me? Ha, ha, my name's Hong Daquan."

"What? Hong Daquan? I've heard of Hong Xiuquan, but never of any Hong Daquan."

"As expected. I've got another name, but after joining the Society of God Worshippers, I abandoned the name I'd used till then. I swore an oath of brotherhood with Hong Xiuquan, and my name was changed to Hong Daquan."

"Sworn brothers, eh? Who was the elder brother?"

"He was older, so I'm the younger brother."

"Are you just like brothers?" asked Wu-lan-tai.

"No, I like alcohol. What's worse, he likes women. Our tastes are different," responded Jiao, looking over in Jiang's direction.

"Why do you have these chains around your neck?"

"A little sibling disagreement. I said he was overdoing it with the women, and Hong Xiuquan ordered Yang Xiuqing to grab me and tie me up in chains." Jiao shrugged his shoulders, rattling the chains about his neck.

Following the battle at Gusu Brook, an officer of the Qing Army had assembled over one hundred prisoners of war. They were asked if anyone among them was of importance, but no one so much as feigned an answer. The interrogating officer, though, watched the prisoners' attitude and line of sight closely. His gaze fixed on this suspicious-looking man with the chains around his neck.

"Hey, you," he called out, approaching. "You're somebody important, aren't you?"

The man responded unabashedly: "You got me. They say if you stick a drill in your bag the tip of it will poke a hole in the bag. That's just what happened. I sure couldn't keep a secret from you. Yeah, I'm a general, commander-in-chief, in fact."

Nor did he speak without shame. His attitude was one of great pride. Probably because he had said he was the commander-in-chief, the word went to headquarters that this man was Yang Xiuqing. At the time, the Qing Army believed that Hong Xiuquan was the overall leader of the long-haired bandits, while his second in command, Yang Xiuqing, was on the rise and practically on a par with Hong. In practical matters, they believed that Yang was actually more important.

While the interrogation was going on, Jiang Zhongyuan was wondering to himself why Jiao was saying such things. Was he teasing the Qing military forces? Perhaps he thought that, because there were witnesses to the fact that he was involved in an operation to disrupt the internal workings of the Taipings on behalf of the government, they would clear this up. Since his life was not in jeopardy, he could afford to make light of the situation and engage in such banter with his captors.

In fact, though, there were no witnesses. Xie Liu had returned to Hunan. That Jiang had asked Jiao to take part in the operation were but words spoken to Jiao by Xie Liu. If Jiang were to assert that he had no memory of such a request, the matter would end then and there.

The operation had made no progress at all, and Jiang was feeling considerable dissatisfaction with Jiao Liang for all the money allocated to him. He regretted having relied on someone like Jiao, who talked through his hat, with absolutely nothing to substantiate his claims. It was embarrassing, thought Jiang, to have to atone for such an error.

"I'll repudiate him," Jiang decided. "I'll say I have no memory of asking him for anything. He's nothing to me."

Jiang then became aware of the chains around Jiao Liang's neck. Probably, the Taipings had also discovered his role in a plot to cause dissension in their ranks. So they had taken him prisoner and thrown him in irons. In their escape from Yongan, the Taipings had probably either opened their prison doors and released the inmates or the prisoners had broken down the doors themselves.

This was what Jiang surmised at the sight of Jiao in chains. All talk of a fraternal quarrel with Hong Xiuquan and the like was pure claptrap, typical of Jiao. As if drunk, Jiang felt his anger mounting as he pondered this ruse by Jiao.

It wasn't worth it to help Jiao. Jiao Liang knew that his fate was to be decided here.

"Send me on to Beijing under armed guard. That's what I'd choose," said this comedic prisoner, his head held high, to Wu-lan-tai's face.

"You say what you want. Whether I cut your head off here or they behead you in Beijing, the fate of the bandits is all the same." Wu-lan-tai rose from his chair, raised his foot, and kicked Jiao in the face. He didn't care for his adversary's attitude.

"You'll pay for this in time!" said Jiao proudly, after being kicked, and a wry smile floated onto his face.

—7—

Wu-lan-tai had killed 2,000 of the Taipings at Gusu Brook. He sent a large number of prisoners, including the man who called himself Hong Daquan, back to the rear, and continued in his pursuit of the Taiping forces. Jiang Zhongyuan concurred in this move.

The 2,000 losses were, of course, very painful to the Taipings, but they constituted only one part of the overall Taiping armed forces. If over half or even one-third of their troops had been massacred, that would have been sufficient reason to cease activity for a while. However, 2,000 was about one-tenth of the Taiping Army. Their main strength remained healthy.

That's not so good at all, thought Jiang.

It had been quite easy to take aim at a target like the walled city of Yongan, but now they had let the enemy loose into a wide open space. Jiang understood that the strategy this time was more to annihilate the Taipings than to recapture Yongan. Thus, if they failed to pursue the Taipings speedily and wipe out their main core strength, the Yongan battle would turn to defeat.

Xiang Rong, restored to his post as provincial military governor of Guangxi, arrived at the head of a huge army. Jiang doubted his personal intentions. Xiang's troops arrived in Zhaoping along the mountain path by Fuyu Brook, and stood there prepared to confront the advancing Taiping Army. With a pincer formation—Xiang Rong's army in front and Wu-lan-tai's army behind—they should have destroyed the Taiping forces.

"The mountain path at Fuyu Brook is impassable," said Xiang Rong. "We have received a report to the effect that, because of the rain, the road has caved in." They learned only later that the road by Fuyu Brook had at no point collapsed, and that, in fact, no such report seems to have ever been received. The truth was that Xiang Rong on his own simply changed the direction along which the troops would march.

Xiang knew only too well how strict Taiping military discipline was, and he knew the ferocity of their troops in battle. Any number of times, their fearlessness had penetrated him to the bone with awe.

This path by Fuyu Brook was a shortcut, and by taking it they could get to Zhaoping more quickly than by the Gusu Brook route. The Taipings had chosen not to take the Fuyu route simply because they were so heavily outnumbered by the government forces.

When they arrived before the Taipings, the Qing forces expected to wait for them. The Taipings would probably send into battle a select group of brave vanguard troops. Ordinarily they were strong, but they had been seriously hurt, leaving open the question of whether they would risk a desperate confrontation and try to cut their way through the government's men. It was a terrible idea to try to face the Taipings flying directly ahead full force. With this in mind, Xiang Rong brought his army around to Gusu Brook on the pretext of the false rumor of a collapsed mountain pass.

It would be much better to pursue a fleeing enemy from the rear, and it certainly seemed like a much safer bet. "If the road's impassable, there's nothing we can do about it. Anyway, let's take the mountain pass by Gusu Brook," said Wu-lan-tai.

"I agree, but shouldn't we send a scouting party ahead to spy on the bandits' movements?" said Xiang, with typical prudence.

"What?" Wu-lan-tai blanched. "The enemy's movements? We know more about the enemy's movements than we need to. Right now is the time to destroy the enemy's rear guard. The conquered bandits are now trying vainly to escape. What other enemy movements are even conceivable? We have no option but to pursue them. And there's no time to lose."

Considering any further discussion a waste of time, Wu-lan-tai leapt on his horse. Taking a deep breath, he thought to himself, "This character Xiang Rong is jealous of my military success. . . . But I saw right through him, right through him."

The great victory at Gusu Brook was truly Wu-lan-tai's military success alone. On the pretext that the road was impassable, Xiang Rong had loitered around, showed up late, and not taken part in the fighting. Wu-lan-tai's distinguished feats in the battles pursuing the Taipings were effectively crushing to Xiang Rong's sense of dignity. Furthermore, through various hints, Xiang Rong seemed to be trying to downplay as much as possible the victory at Gusu Brook. Spying on enemy movements belied the fact that he did not believe that the Taipings had been badly beaten by Wu-lan-tai's pursuing forces. The enemy still had a modicum of fighting strength, and for the first time the government was using the tactic of reconnoitering.

Wu-lan-tai was furious.

"Forward! March on!" he roared from horseback with his whip in hand.

That's dangerous, thought Jiang Zhongyuan, but there's no way to stop Wu-lan-tai. The entire army was trailing behind him. The four brigades of Chang-rui, Chang-shou, Dong Guangjia, and Shao Heling were following Wu-lan-tai's army, and Xiang Rong had no choice but to march ahead with his troops as well.

The Taipings had advanced by forced march as far as Xianhui peak, and there the entire army had stopped to rest. They anticipated the pursuit of the

Qing forces and had thus chosen a place to fight rather than continue to flee. Learning of the local mountainous topography from Li Yiwen, Yang Xiuqing set in place a large ambushing party in the Dadong Mountains.

"We have to fight them." This was all Yang said. He offered no reason why, but Lian Liwen understood the reasoning perfectly well. The Taiping army was a military group with a fighting spirit based in its religious beliefs. If being routed meant that morale had seriously deteriorated, then there was the danger that the whole group would disintegrate. More than anything, they needed one victory here. It was very important.

Everyone felt that the present situation was a rout of the Taipings. That was perfect natural. However, if the Taipings fought and were victorious, then that impression would change completely and thoroughly reorder the two sides' field positions. Furthermore, the Qing forces were thinking only that the Taipings were continuing a desperate effort to escape their clutches. They most certainly did not expect a direct military confrontation. This was the enemy's strategy of surprise.

When the Taipings overran the Shouchun Army's position at Gusu Brook, artillery and ammunition in the process of transport fell into their hands. There were, among the Taiping forces, a fair number of coal miners who were experienced at using this ammunition. Guns emplaced above, troops lying in ambush below, the Taipings quietly awaited the Qing Army.

The government forces were thrown into confusion by the noise of a cannon blast. For all intents and purposes, the Qing troops were defeated at that point without so much as a fight when the battle cry by the Taiping troops lying in wait was sounded. The result was a lopsided victory.

The Qing suffered an immense defeat, 4,000 casualties, and were thoroughly routed. Those that were able to escape with their lives were happy for it. In the battle, the government lost four regional commanders: Tianjin Regional Commander Chang-rui, Liangzhou Regional Commander Chang-shou, Hebei Regional Commander Dong Guangjia, and Yunyang Regional Commander Shao Heling.

Other important figures who died on the battlefield included Adjutants Cheng Lin and Tian Xuetao, Brigade Commander Wang Rui, and Department Magistrate Lin Guangqian. Military Governor Xiang Rong was in the rear, but he escaped at full speed and was saved. Wu-lan-tai fell at a precipice. It was not rocky but he fell into a mountain stream and was thus saved from the brink of death.

Swimming with all his strength, Wu-lan-tai eventually made his way to the rocks. At a grassy area by the river bank, a male figure was sitting in a daze.

"Jiang Zhongyuan," called out Wu-lan-tai, in a hoarse voice.

Jiang grimaced, perhaps trying to smile, and then moved his lips. Nearby a swift stream dashed against the rocks with a resounding boom. Wu-lan-tai could not make out what Jiang had said.

"I should have sent a scouting party ahead." That was what he thought Jiang was saying, but he was wrong.

Jiang had said, "We let them loose, and they're only going to become a bigger and bigger problem."

The Battle at Guilin

14

—1—

Xiang Rong, the commander of this devastated army, was in a foul mood, needless to say. He was burning with indignation. Four regional commanders had died on the battlefield.

Why didn't they open an escape route and save us? he grumbled to himself over and over again. He was less deeply pained by the deaths of four regional commanders in the field, than he was exasperated by the fact that these deaths made it impossible for him to hide this military defeat in the Dadong Mountains.

No matter how many rank-and-file troops had fallen in battle, their numbers could be artfully doctored by means however dubious. The same was not true for regional commanders. When it was necessary for there to be formal contacts between the Qing Army and the Japanese military forces during the Meiji period (1868–1912), a Chinese provincial military commander was paired with a Japanese lieutenant general, and a regional commander with a Japanese major general. It was an extraordinarily rare event for four regional commanders to fall on the same battlefield at the same time.

The death of a high-level commander, rank 2A, was impossible to conceal. Informing the central government of the deaths of four regional commanders was tantamount to reporting, "We have suffered an immense defeat." There was no way to embellish such an event.

The majority of the government's troops that had been crushingly defeated in the mountains withdrew for the time being to the walled city of

Yongan. Yongan had been recovered. The Taipings had abandoned it and were heading north. If they hadn't pursued the Taipings and run into the ambush in the Dadong Mountains, Xiang Rong could have reported to Beijing, "We have recaptured Yongan. The bandits are in flight to the north in utter confusion."

Xiang's anger was also focused on Wu-lan-tai, who had pressured them into a hurried pursuit. At the time, Xiang Rong had proposed that it would be best to send a scouting party ahead, and Wu-lan-tai simply ignored the suggestion.

There were different classification designations within the Qing military for the Eight Banner brigades, which were comprised of direct vassals of the throne and those Han troops who made up the Green Standards brigade. Wu-lan-tai was a vice-commander-in-charge of a banner, comparable to a regional commander in the Green Standards forces. As a provincial military commander, Xiang Rong was thus at a higher station. However, the trend of the times was such that he was unable to check Wu-lan-tai's recklessness.

"I've got to write this up clearly in a memorial to the throne. It's something the imperial commissioner must know," said Xiang Rong to himself.

A few members of his staff were in the room, but he was not about to verbalize this thought to anyone. It was a monologue, a soliloquy, and as long as he didn't put it into spoken words, it would not be dangerous. The "it" here was Xiang Rong's advocacy of caution in pursuit of the enemy and Wu-lan-tai's disregard of his appeal.

Although he took up his brush any number of times, Xiang Rong's fingers trembled, perhaps because he was still so incensed. He was unable to write anything. Rising from his chair, he decided to walk around the room to calm his mood. The staff members stared at him, expressionless.

A loud noise was heard. A deafening crash sounded, and the room creaked slightly.

"Not again!" spit out the provincial military commander.

The Taipings had systematically withdrawn from Yongan, and there was no reason to expect that they would not leave behind devices within the city, which had now passed into the government's hands. In fact, they had buried land mines here and there. Anyone who stepped on a mine was blown to bits, without trace. Some victim of a mine had just set off an earsplitting noise.

Jiang Zhongyuan, who had been commanding a force of brave men from Hunan province, claimed he had taken ill and was returning to his home village. Since he was not a regular in the Qing Army, he was relatively free in his actions. At his point of departure, he allegedly said, "You can't fight with troops like this." The intimation may have been that he was returning to Hunan to enlist new recruits who could fight.

The Qing armies were unreliable.

Ba-qing-de, a commander-in-chief of a banner, which put him at a comparable rank to Xiang Rong, also failed to appear because of illness. He actually was suffering from malaria; it was a severe case, from which he eventually died.

Although their recovery of the city should have recouped their spirits, the Qing encampment within Yongan was thoroughly subdued. Occasionally, a liaison officer would arrive, but since these were primarily casualty reports from the Dadong Mountains, they were not the least encouraging to Xiang Rong.

"What did he say? Did he say that the number of stripped corpses on the battlefield exceeded five hundred? Damned sneak thieves!" railed Xiang Rong, and when the next report arrived, he hurled the teacup in his hand to the floor.

"This is unbearable!" The liaison officer had reported that the banner, which had been abandoned on the battlefield, had apparently disappeared, carried off no doubt by the Taipings.

Although driven to distraction by anger, Xiang Rong still did not lose the intuition of a professional military man. One could read on his face concern for both the fact that the uniforms of the dead on the field had been stripped from the bodies, and that the abandoned banner had been stolen.

Doubtless the Taipings were now planning to dress up as troops of the Qing Army and carry out some operation. There were said to be on the order of five hundred government army uniforms seized from corpses. With these, five hundred Taiping troops could appear in Qing military disguise, and the Qing field banner was an ideal part of this arrangement. Five hundred troops wearing Qing uniforms and raising the Qing flag high would surely be ushered into every city currently defended by the government's armed forces with great ease. And following these five hundred would come tens of thousands of troops of the Taiping Army.

"It's Guilin!" shouted Xiang Rong as he ferociously kicked the fragments of the teacup laying broken on the floor.

Guilin, the capital of Guangxi province, lay before the Taiping Army, then marching to the north. Provincial Governor Zou Minghe was in Guilin, but he had yet to hear news of the defeat in the Dadong Mountains. The tattered forces of Xiang Rong had yet to report their embarrassing decimation to anyone. If possible, he would try to hide it as much as he could.

"Call a woodcutter over here. A woodcutter! Make it someone who knows the mountain trails. Get anyone who's well-acquainted with shortcuts to Guilin," ordered Xiang Rong to his staff.

Although the members of his staff had no idea what he was getting at, these were the orders of a provincial military commander, and the appropriate parties hurried to carry them out.

The wall encircling Guilin was high and strong. The entire city, including Duxiu peak, was well-guarded by the city walls. But even an especially strong fortress is nothing if its gates are opened to an enemy clad in the garb of one's allies.

If Guilin fell, it could be personally disastrous for Xiang Rong. He was provincial military commander of Guangxi, the man with the highest military responsibility in the province. Were the provincial seat to fall effortlessly into the hands of the enemy, he would probably face execution.

If, after a hard fight, the city had surrendered, his punishment would probably have been light, or he might not even be punished at all. If, however, it surrendered without the least resistance, all responsibility would fall squarely on his shoulders. Even if he could hide the defeat in the Dadong Mountains for a while, it would be bound up with the collapse of Guilin.

His life hung in the balance. He had to march immediately to Guilin and get there before the Taipings, and there was no need to lead a large armed force there. He had only one thing to inform the authorities of in Guilin: "They're not our allies!"

—2—

Xiang Rong selected twenty men under his command. He carefully chose all men of proven valor. Where they could ride swiftly by horse, they would use horses, and steep mountain paths would require their walking on foot. Of necessity, these men would have to be able to withstand forced marches day and night without rest. It was not sufficient that they be in robust health, for if they were not also highly agile, they were simply not fit for the job at hand.

After the defeat in the Dadong Mountains, the reckless military commander Wu-lan-tai took a decisive step, and immediately attempted to pursue the Taipings. He cut his own arm, and dripped his blood into the wine.

"The man who drinks this will share life and death with me. Men dedicated to saving our country are closer to me than relatives. Won't anyone drink it?" he said as he pushed the cup before a group of his men.

A pathetic feeling was hovering over the battlefield where the humiliating defeat had taken place. The death of comrades had seriously shaken the men's morale. Those who survived had escaped the jaws of death. Having eluded death's grasp once, the second time would be no different.

"I'll drink it!"

"Me too."

"I'll take three cups."

"I'll drink it up all by myself!"

Wu-lan-tai's men wrangled over drinking the wine—700 men in all. The troops directly under his command that had accompanied him from Guangzhou had served with him for a long period of time, and were imbued with his temperament. Many were ferocious troops of the reckless variety, like their commanding officer.

Wu-lan-tai's army was heading north to confront the Taipings. To that end, they had to be outfitted. Having learned from their bitter experience in the Dadong Mountains, they prudently sent a scouting party ahead as they marched forward.

Xiang Rong, by contrast, had a force of only twenty men, lightly outfitted. They were not planning a military confrontation, but aimed at arriving at the city of Guilin before the Taipings, to which end full military equipment would have been an impediment. The course they chose was also different. Wu-lan-tai's army went to search out the enemy, while Xiang Rong opted for the shortest route possible. Led by a woodcutter familiar with the local terrain, Xiang Rong's force took a shortcut to the north.

The course taken by the Taiping Army was also characteristic. As Xiang Rong had clearly seen, the Taipings had dressed up as Qing troops and were intent upon capturing the city of Guilin. They would have to appear suddenly and enter the city. If a report to the effect that "the Taiping Army is pressing near" were sent to Guilin, the probability was great that the Taiping Army's plans would come to naught. When Guilin, upon hearing of the approaching Taipings, took the necessary precautions, any force flying a Qing banner would not so easily be allowed to enter the city gate.

Thus, the Taipings chose a course of action that called for as little contact as possible with government forces. Virtually all Qing military forces within Guangxi province were mobilized for confrontation with the Taipings. Garrison forces were placed in strategic spots, but the number of troops was smaller than it had been in peacetime. At bases where several hundred troops had once been stationed, now there were only several dozen.

The fact that their troop strength was minimal meant that the scope of their defenses was narrow. Through scouting activities, the Taipings were able to ascertain where the Qing military was placing its men, and hence was able to evade them. The journey from Yongan to Guilin covered some 150 kilometers through such counties as Lipu, Pingle, and Yangshuo. Naturally, there were garrison troops at each of these county seats.

Advancing on the heels of their victory in the Dadong Mountains, it looked as if the Taipings would be able to march right through and trample underfoot the county seat of Lipu, but they avoided it, and when they learned that the Qing had troops stationed at a place known as Maling, the Taipings circumvented it as well. They headed north along a zigzag course, which consumed considerable time, arriving finally at Guilin only thirty days after escaping from Yongan.

When, having made a detour around Maling, the Taipings arrived at the town of Gaotian in Yangshuo county, Lian Liwen was summoned to a meeting of Taiping leaders.

"Mr. Lian, do you plan to continue working in concert with us?" asked Hong Xiuquan.

After assuming the title of Heavenly King, Hong's voice had taken on an added depth. He enunciated his words slowly. Though he had always spoken slowly, he now spoke even more so. At times, this tendency could be irritating.

"Of course I do. That is my intention," responded Liwen.

"Actually," spoke up Yang Xiuquan from the side, "we were thinking of sending you to Hong Kong or Shanghai." Since having become the Eastern King, he showed no signs of change whatsoever.

"Hong Kong or Shanghai?"

"Through our actions we have been able to teach the farmers of this land what we are thinking and what our aims are. But we have not been able to do this for the foreigners."

Perhaps because he spoke directly after Hong Xiuquan, Yang's words had the force of jumping right into Liwen's pocket.

"The foreigners?" Squeezing these words in enabled Liwen to interrupt Yang's flow.

"That's right. We have already established a country known as the Heavenly Kingdom of Great Peace. In the distant future, it shall become one of the many nations of the world, and this must be understood by those countries. Inasmuch as we cannot demonstrate this to them by our actions, we must explain it to them. Since the period of our occupation of Yongan, this matter has become a concern of ours."

"So, you would like me to clarify the Taiping position to the foreign nations?"

"Exactly," said Yang with a nod.

For a moment Liwen remained silent, and then, shaking his head, he said, "The content of what is to be explained to the foreign nations must be made ever so clear. At present I still do not fully understand, myself, and thus I lack the necessary self-confidence to represent you."

"Even to you?" said Feng Yunshan with a sigh. Feng seemed to belie a disappointment that, having lived for such a lengthy period among the core of the leadership of the Taipings, Liwen still did not understand what they were about.

"I do have a general conception, certainly, but the question is whether I am sufficiently capable of explaining the case to the foreigners," said Liwen.

"If you can't, you can't," said Yang frankly. Compared to Feng Yunshan, who still acted timidly, Yang Xiuqing was a decisive man of resolution. Perhaps it was Feng who most ardently placed his hopes in relying on Liwen for this propaganda work with the foreign powers, while Yang remained less moved by this proposal.

"Also, I would not like to leave just now, and I hope you'll be understanding. I really can't leave at this point in time," said Liwen, thinking to himself that he would be present at a certain birth. It wasn't exactly clear just what was to be born. A new society. A new order. He would be there at the center of the force that gave birth to it. He couldn't leave it. That force drew him to it and would not let him leave.

Aside from the highest leaders of the Taipings standing before him, Li Xinmei, Su Sanniang, and perhaps Luo Dagang, had all shared their labors, and all seemed to be captives of this force. They were bonded in a way that made separation difficult.

"It's all right," said Hong Xiuquan very slowly, as if passing final judgment. "One way or another, Ren'gan will do it for us by himself, I'm sure."

It had already been decided that Hong Xiuquan's cousin, Hong Ren'gan, would go to Hong Kong. Undoubtedly apprehensive of Ren'gan's traveling alone, they wanted Liwen to accompany him.

I wonder, thought Liwen, looking up into the nighttime sky. Have they already become one nation among the many of the world? One country on the verge of birth.

—3—

The vanguard forces of the Taiping Army reached Guilin toward the evening of April 17, 1852. Their total troop strength was now 70,000. Over the roughly 150 kilometers from Yongan to Guilin, Taiping troop numbers had grown once again. Every time they were on the move, they clearly increased their numbers.

The Taipings seemed to have a mighty drawing power of sorts. They had as well a small number of men separated from the main body of the army. In addition to stragglers, there were also a small number of troops detached from the army with special responsibilities, such as Hong Ren'gan, who was on his way to Hong Kong.

When Hong Xiuquan had decided that they would rise in rebellion, fearful of repression by the authorities, he assembled his family in Jintian village, which was then in their ancestral home of Hua county, Guangdong province. Hong Ren'gan did not at that time come to Jintian. He only joined the Taipings at a later date, when they entered Xiangzhou. Thus, he had not been with them for a very long time, and Lian Liwen, for one, was worried that he still lacked a full understanding of the nature of the Taiping movement. Although he was to propagate the Taiping cause among foreigners in Hong Kong, Liwen feared that his proselytizing would be rather shallow at best.

Lightly dressed, Xiang Rong's division reached Guilin on the afternoon of the same day. Riding as quickly as they were able through the shortcut, they arrived half a day before the Taipings, even though they set off several days after them.

"Great! The long-haired bandits haven't arrived yet," said Xiang Rong, as he entered the city, raising his shoulders with excessive pride and then lowering them abruptly. He showed every sign of being purposefully at ease, and there was no exaggeration whatsoever in his calm. He was relieved to see that Guilin had not simply been captured by the enemy, and the fear that responsibility for the fall of the provincial capital at Guilin would be placed on him dissipated.

There was, however, something that caused him despair as he entered the city. The military emplacements guarding Guilin had not fully been set up. "50,000 *tuanlian* troops" Guilin had reported to the court. The *tuanlian* militia was under the commander of provincial governor Zou Minghe, but their numbers had clearly been inflated.

"Fine, I'm taking complete command!" said Xiang Rong. He certainly couldn't entrust the troops to a civil official like Zou. It was now time for a professional military man with experience. Also, his life as the Guangdong military commander depended on the defense of Guilin.

The Taiping Army, having purposely reduced their speed, arrived during the evening, about half a day after Xiang Rong. The difference of a half day was decisive, for the Taiping force did not know of Xiang Rong's hasty arrival by a shortcut.

They would wait until nightfall and then, dressed in Qing Army uniforms, they would have the city gate opened. No matter how well-conceived their plans, had they appeared in the light of day, somewhere they might have exposed themselves. The Taipings' plan was to arrive in the evening, and just after dark, marshal several hundred troops disguised as government soldiers before the city gate. Qing military banners were lined up in a row.

A large man wearing the resplendent uniform of a high Qing military official stepped forward before a line of men in Qing troop uniforms. The scene was just outside the Wenchang Gate, the southwest entrance point into the city of Guilin. He shouted, "His Excellency Xiang Rong has returned. Open the gate now for his excellency, the provincial military commander! He has important business to attend to. Open up!"

On the inside of the gate, it was as quiet as death. The man's voice outside had been too loud, so the silence that followed it was ominous. Misgivings began to spread among the troops and commanders of the disguised Taipings. If the city's troops in fact understood that the Guangxi military commander had returned to the Guangxi provincial capital, then they had no choice but to open the gate before doing anything else. Suddenly, gunfire rang out. Then, arrows flew through the air.

"Withdraw!" ordered Yang Xiuqing alertly, as he observed the scene of action from the rear. He realized that the Taiping ruse had been unmasked.

The ability to adapt to changing circumstances was Yang Xiuqing's true strength. He changed his mind and switched positions with resolution. If he lost in an effort to take a city through one strategy, there was always another strategy. Yang was taking stock of cases in which he had failed.

An encirclement campaign. An army of 70,000 was a sufficient number to surround the city of Guilin. It was doubtful that the fighting men within the city could match the Taipings in numbers. The main strength of the Qing forces in Guangxi had been deployed for the siege of Yongan, and many had been lost in the fighting in the Dadong Mountains. So, it seemed to Yang, the Taipings stood a good chance of winning such an engagement.

For a time gunfire continued and a hail of arrows flowed down, but afterward a stentorian voice could be heard from the castle tower.

"You fraudulent thieves! You say you're His Excellency Xiang Rong? His Excellency entered the city some time ago and has been waiting for you. Did you think this was some place far out in the countryside? You imposters will never get into this provincial capital!" The Taipings retreated and made camps at Elephant Nose Hill and Bull Hill. Both were located at slightly elevated sites with commanding overhead views of Guilin.

The men of Wu-lan-tai's army, which had gone through the ceremony of a pathetic oath by drinking from a goblet of wine into which their commander had spilled some of his own blood, were heading for Guilin, one day behind the Taipings.

Xiang Rong's arrival half a day prior to the Taiping forces had a major impact on the military situation. Had he come later, the Taipings in their Qing military disguises would bloodlessly have entered the city and easily taken control of Guilin.

During this half day, Xiang Rong had been active, burning to the ground the more prominent, valuable homes outside the city walls. When the Taipings arrived, anything that might have been of use to them had either been burned or brought inside the city. Rice and other grains held in the granaries outside the city were moved into the city by 3,000 mobilized *tuanlian* troops.

"I should have noticed the burning smell," reflected Yang Xiuqing as he entered camp at Elephant Nose Hill.

Since the private homes outside the city were not close together, the fire did not spread after the flame was set, and by nightfall, when the Taipings arrived, the fires had been put out. Perhaps because of the twilight, not one of the Taiping leaders had noticed the burnt-out homes. When they thought about it later, though, the burning smell had still been in the air. The bullets and arrows from the city killed eight of their men and injured over fifty, and these casualties could have been avoided.

—4—

It was said that in ancient times Guilin was beneath the sea, which was why so many bizarre limestone peaks now sprung from the ground there. Elephant Nose Hill was one of them. There was a large cavern known as Cave of the Moon's Reflection, and the part of the hill straddling it looked just like the nose of an elephant.

The Bodhisattva Samantabhadra (or Puxian, in Chinese) had ridden an elephant, so when the name Elephant Nose Hill was affixed to the place, it seemed only natural that Puxian would be apotheosized at its peak. In the Ming dynasty, a style of pagoda fashioned after a revered vessel that the Buddha had used for spiritual waters was constructed there, and people called it, the Puxian pagoda.

On its first and second stories, the Puxian pagoda was octagonal in shape, and from that point up it was cylindrical. At the top, it was covered by a circular umbrella with two round pagoda finials. Etched into the green stone inlaid in the northern wall was an image of the Puxian Bodhisattva. Although Elephant Nose Hill was not very high, it had over sxity stone carvings from the Tang and Song periods on its face, and literati interested in calligraphy often came to visit this celebrated sight.

At a spot slightly removed from the thirteen-meter Puxian pagoda, the Taiping Army was installing its cannons. From that point, they could bombard the inner city. From Elephant Nose Hill, one could see Bull Hill on the other side of the Wenchang Bridge, and a fortification had been there as well. The Li River ran in front of the hills, and it served also as a moat for the city of Guilin.

Chinese city walls of that time were, for the most part, constructed with brick tiles. However, in Guilin, which was rich in limestone, they built the walls by piling up stones cut from limestone. It certainly looked to be a solid city wall.

"Not bad at all, really." Liwen ladled water from the bottom of the Cave of the Moon's Reflection and drank it down in a tea cup. The body of water was known as the Elephant Nose pool, and it was celebrated for its marvelous taste. The region also boasted a famous liquor known as *Sanhuajiu* or Three-Flower Liquor, and allegedly its preparation required use of the water from the Elephant Nose pool. It simply could not be brewed with water from the Latent Wave Hill area upstream or from the Cockfighting pool further downriver.

Since the extent to which the coming battle would be one of encirclement remained unknown, the Taipings used their food and ammunition frugally. Only on water were there no limitations placed. Although water was everywhere around them, in their efforts to locate particularly savory water, the soldiers time and again lined up at the Elephant Nose pool.

Life continued apace there. One of the Taipings' special qualities was the capacity to carry on life to its fullest, even in the midst of battle.

"Liwen, this is a real inconvenience—one male soldier at a time gaining access to the delicious water here." The voice came from behind him, and there stood Li Xinmei.

"That's true," said Liwen, looking over his shoulder.

What gave the Taiping Army an even more genuine sense of life was the presence of women among the troops. Ever since their days in Jintian village, men and women had been strictly separated, and even husbands and brothers were forbidden from entering the women's barracks. When the male troops lined up at the Elephant Nose pool to scoop up its tasty waters, women could not break into the line.

"Wouldn't it be fairer of we alternated mornings and afternoons?"

"It certainly would. Let's propose that idea."

"It's just a trifling thing, but I think things like that are important."

"I completely agree."

"It would be so great to get control over the city!" Xinmei said, her eyes focused on the city walls beyond the water.

Yongan was the first city that fell into the hands of the Taipings. The whole object of taking a city was to use it as a base and draw on its power to work in concert with the rebellion.

Although a department seat, Yongan city was located in the mountains, not likely to attract the attention of the entire country. By comparison, Guilin was a provincial capital. What's more, Guilin had a reputation as a place of unparalleled beauty—"the scenery of Guilin is the finest in the realm," as the saying went. Its fame in China was preeminent, and if the Taipings were able to seize it, shock waves would resound throughout the empire.

"A new world will be born that much sooner."

There was a radiance in Li Xinmei's eyes as she stared at the city walls.

Born and raised among bandits, it was rare to find someone of such pure idealism. She had failed in the bold experiment of making the organization that she controlled resemble that of the Society of God Worshippers. Yet this failure in no way crushed her idealism. Any number of times, Liwen wondered where this earnestness on her part had come from, but he had no answer. Ultimately, the only answer was the vague supposition that it was part of her nature.

There was something else about Xinmei that Liwen founding intriguing. It had been more than a year since she had risen in rebellion, and in the dust of battle she had actually, for some inexplicable reason, become even more beautiful. At least, so it seemed to Liwen.

The sound of cannon shells exploding could be heard in the distance. A small cloud of dust rose near Bull Hill. The Taipings had the city within the range of their weapons, but that meant as well that the Taiping artillery was within the range of weaponry from the city. In any event, the reply to the cannonade was not particularly vigorous. Neither side had an excess of ammunition. To run out of ammunition at a crucial juncture would be disastrous, and so both sides were being frugal with it.

"I don't like this siege warfare at all," said Liwen. "It has such a gloominess about it."

"It's no fun," said Xinmei, nodding, "to fight an enemy when you can't see their faces. That's why it's odd . . . you can't see their eyes and their noses."

While this exchange took place, the clack of horses' hooves became audible.

"The enemy's here!" screamed a voice.

"The enemy?" said Xinmei, standing on her tiptoes, looking in the direction of the city gate. The Guilin gate had been shut tight, and there was no sign that enemy soldiers inside the city had come out.

"The enemy that chased us here from Yongan! Under the commander of Wu-lan-tai." The voice became fainter in the distance.

"So Wu-lan-tai himself came after us." Liwen was continuing this conversation with Xinmei.

"What an impetuous fool."

"Well, but if we actually fight him, at least it won't be so melancholy. It'll be head-on, face-to-face combat."

There was commotion here and there. The orders to assume battle positions were being executed near and far. Under these tense circumstances, Liwen suddenly shook off his drowsiness. He had said that there was life among the Taipings even in times of battle, but for some reason it now seemed as though fighting had itself become life there. Liwen yawned widely.

"Ha, yawning are you?" said Xinmei, laughing.

—5—

Wu-lan-tai's army appeared near the South Gate of Guilin, and Commander Wu-lan-tai stood at the forefront of the advance guard. He would surely have regretted not being up front.

The General's Bridge connected an ordinary hill known as Big Head Mountain and an isolated mountain range full of caves known as the White Dragon caves. Today the General's Bridge has a roof covering, but at the time it was a plain, open-air bridge.

White Dragon was a general name for a large number of caverns big and small. The biggest was in fact called White Dragon Cave, and a White Dragon Temple had been constructed there. Below it was a crystal spring known as White Dragon Well, and to this day, city dwellers come to draw its waters. Together with Elephant Nose pool, it was well-known for its waters' tastiness.

Among the other nearby caves were Xuanyan Cave, Mahuang Cave, and Longbei Cave. The Taipings were camped here. Since the private houses outside the city walls had been burned to the ground, the caves became suitable barracks for the troops.

Inside the immense White Dragon Cave, famous calligraphers had inscribed the stone facades. Those of the Ming dynasty were most numerous, but there was also a poem inscribed by Li Ge of the Tang dynasty. For the Taiping troops, who hailed from peasant villages in Guangxi, this was like casting pearls before swine, but the story of the inscriptions was passed along to the troops. Few of them were genuinely interested, but one who showed some interest was Shi Dakai, the Assistant King. After seeing the stone inscriptions at Elephant Nose Hill, he had come around to White Dragon cave.

"Hmm, there are some beautifully written characters here, with a stroke of hand different from calligraphers nowadays," stated the young Shi mildly. Opinions varied within the Taiping military about the literary pursuits of the young commander.

One rather chilly view essentially went, "Don't you think it's a little suspicious that he's got some learning."

This opinion was complemented by the laudatory view, which essentially went, "It's only fitting. Assistant King Shi Dakai is not an ordinary military man. He's an extraordinary fellow who combines both the military and the civil." Many of his troops were unconditionally devoted to him. Shi had a certain charisma all his own, such that those who fought under his command were best thought of as the Shi Dakai army rather than the Taiping Army.

Just as Shi was in the midst of appreciating the stone inscription at White

Dragon cave, Wu-lan-tai's impending attack was announced. Shi was instantly transformed from a man of letters to a man of military might.

"Don't leave the cave! You mustn't show the enemy your faces!"

As the order rang out, he suddenly recalled a matter long, long past. Shi was fascinated by history. In fact, he may have been the most learned in history of all who participated in the Taiping movement. He had heard the story from old people in the area of the General's Bridge, which stood in front of the White Dragon caves. However, its origins differed, depending on whom one consulted. Some argued that the General's Bridge was the site where General Peng Yanhui of the Later Liang dynasty (early Tenth Century) during the Five Dynasties period stationed his troops there. Other old timers claimed that it was the spot where the famous General Di Qing (1008–1057) of the Northern Song Dynasty stationed his men.

Generals of the Five Dynasties era like Peng Yanhui were virtually unknown to history, but Di Qing was a military commander who lit up the pages of history. Shi Dakai simply assumed that the bridge was linked with Di Qing.

In the fifth year of the Huangyou reign (1053) under Emperor Renzong, the barbarian bandit Nong Zhigao and his men captured the two prefectures of Guangnan, and the Northern Song court sent Di Qing at the head of 200,000 troops to suppress them. Having pacified the bandits, Di Qing proceeded to Guilin, where, in commemoration of the victory, he erected the "Stele to the Three Generals Who Pacified the Barbarians" at Longyin Cave.

Since the Later Liang had ultimately been unable to protect this terrain, despite the strengths of the story associated with it, ultimately it is best to opt for the story tied to the victorious General Di Qing. Furthermore, Di Qing was one of the historical figures Shi Dakai most admired.

Di Qing had risen from among the rank-and-file to become a commander. He shared hunger, cold, and hard labor with his men, and he was known as a man who rewarded meritorious service and punished errors, who acted with caution and bravery. Shi Dakai was fond of Di Qing's career as well. What strategy would Di Qing have adopted under these circumstances? he wondered to himself.

These thoughts passed through Shi's head as he surveyed the area from the White Dragon caves. Di Qing had not fought any battles here, but had returned here from successful military engagements elsewhere. Nonetheless, Shi fashioned himself plotting strategy with the eyes and ears of General Di.

Since his adversaries did not know the troop strength of the Taipings, the best initial policy was to conceal his troops within the caves. Wu-lan-tai's army was marching directly from the direction of Big Head Mountain. The White Dragon caves were about 1.5 kilometers beyond the South Gate of Guilin. They reached a topographical depression to which the local people had given the vague appellation, Nanqi, or South Valley. When he arrived at this point, Wu-lan-tai probably realized the Taipings were in a weak position.

The main force of the Taipings was centered at the fortresses of Elephant Nose Hill and Bull Hill. South Valley was more or less between these two hills. Perhaps Wu-lan-tai was trying to make out the two fortresses.

"The bridge . . . ," murmured Shi Dakai, still inside the caves. If the Qing Army were to enter South Valley, it had to cross the General's Bridge.

If the Taipings destroyed the bridge, the Qing troops would not be able to move in the direction of South Valley. If the Qing troops did move in that direction, they had to enter the valley, and the Taipings would be able to shoot at them from their position in the caves above. Just as Shi Dakai was about to give the order to destroy the General's Bridge, a second report arrived from a reconnaissance party.

"The commander of the demons' army is Wu-lan-tai!"

Upon hearing this piece of information, Shi Dakai decided to issue new orders. His plan had been to have the bridge destroyed by the time the enemy arrived there, but then he heard that Wu-lan-tai was riding with the advance guard. Now he could destroy the bridge together with Wu-lan-tai.

"The cannons. Withdraw the cannons!" ordered Shi Dakai.

Among the spoils of war from the Dadong Mountains, the Taipings had acquired several small-scale cannons that Wu-lan-tai had transported from Guangzhou. Because of their relatively small size, they were easy to move, and two of them were installed at South Valley. They were rapidly moved to a site from which it would be easy to take out the bridge.

Riding his horse at the head of the vanguard force, Wu-lan-tai called out: "We're fighting the enemy from the Dadong Mountains! The shame must be washed away. Remember the events of that time! Everyone ready?!"

The troops responded in a roaring voice. The advance force, though, numbered only thirty men. Their general was a very impetuous man. Unconsciously, he furiously whipped his riding crop in his hand, and his horse galloped off rapidly. Subordinates in the infantry could not keep up with him, and many on horseback likewise fell behind.

From the cave in which he was hiding, Shi Dakai stuck out a pole with a red flag attached. When he brought the flag down sharply, it was a signal to fire the cannons.

"The general is approaching the General's Bridge!" said Shi, holding the pole tightly with both hands.

—6—

Shi Daikai was struck by how long it took Wu-lan-tai and his men to reach the General's Bridge, thinking to himself that such cannons as he now possessed had not existed in the days of General Di Qing. They may not have had such cannons, but if he had had them, Di Qing would doubtless have employed the same strategy.

For a commanding officer to stand at the head of his advance force was truly an extraordinary event. Wu-lan-tai boldly took this extraordinary measure, exposing his visage to the enemy as he moved forward. Some twenty or more years earlier, Wu-lan-tai had ridden at the head of his troops when he went into Kashgar in Xinjiang in pursuit of the Muslim rebels of Zungaria. At that time, though, he had been a low-level officer. Conditions were different now that he was a general.

Since the campaign to suppress Zungaria, Wu-lan-tai had had no actual battle experience. Having become all but useless as a person, he retained fond feelings for those battles when he was younger. He ate with his subordinates and drank with them the wine into which he had poured drops of his own blood. The present campaign was to be a return match of sorts. Perhaps he had become intoxicated by the position in which he had mentally placed himself.

"Hold up, please hold up! You're going too fast. Wait for the rear guard to catch up," his attendant Li Dengchao called out in a hoarse voice, but the words did not seem to reach the ears of their intended object. Li Dengchao was actually a company commander, a post of grade six, a high-level officer just below a field officer. It went without saying that he had a basic knowledge of military affairs.

It was extremely dangerous in the disposition of troops for the highest commanding officer to ride at the head of his army and for the distance between a small number of advance forces and the troops bringing up the rear to grow far apart. It did not take an expert in military matters to realize this. Wu-lan-tai had become, at best, stuporous, and at worst, utterly deranged.

The General's Bridge had been constructed with quarried limestone at its pier and frame. Its railing, part of the bridge girder, and its planking were made of wood.

When Li Dengchao attempted in a loud voice to call Wu-lan-tai back, the latter actually rode on more rapidly than before. The commander's horse eventually stepped onto the General's Bridge.

"One . . . two . . . three!" Shi Dakai counted slowly to three and then vehemently swung the rod in his hand toward the ground. The red flag fastened to the rod emitted a sharp, swishing sound as it cut through the air, followed by a dry sound as the tip of the rod hit the rock below.

Then, after a single breath, the piercing sound of artillery exploded. The two cannons opened fire at about the same time. Someone with especially good hearing would have been able to discern a succession of cannon fire, but to the ordinary ear it all sounded like one single round. One of the cannonballs had missed and exploded in the rocks off the water's edge. The other cannonball hit the bridge squarely.

The horse Wu-lan-tai was riding bucked its front legs high and neighed in great pain. In the split second that followed, the horse collapsed onto the bridge flooring.

They watched as the nearby railing was blown into the air. The projectile seemed to have grazed the railing and hit both man and horse on the bridge, though the sound of the explosion was not terribly forceful. Cannonballs at that time were not of uniform quality. Many were duds, and the force of explosions varied widely.

The actions on the bridge that followed transpired with great rapidity. Li Dengchao rode up on horseback, lifted onto his own horse Wu-lan-tai, who was sprawled out on the planks of the bridge, and retreated at full speed. The thirty or so members of the advance party followed suit. Had the Taipings had a large store of cannonballs, then the second or third shot would probably have been sufficient to annihilate this advance group. Unfortunately, there were only two cannonballs, and Shi Dakai had ordered them fired at the same time. These were old-fashioned cannons that necessitated a fair amount of time between loading the next shell and firing it.

By the same token, had there been a large number of Taiping troops in the many caves of South Valley, Shi Dakai might have given the order to pursue the enemy, but the Taipings lacked the military manpower to do so.

The Taipings were unable to discern whether Wu-lan-tai had actually been killed. They could make out bloodstains on the planking of the General's Bridge, so it was clear that he had been wounded. A considerable amount of blood had been lost in this one instance, so even if Wu-lan-tai was not dead, he was certainly badly injured.

"Well done," said Shi Dakai in praise of the South Valley unit.

Wu-lan-tai had not died instantly. Badly wounded, he was carried to a place called Liutang, some 30 kilometers south of the Guilin city wall. In this village of Liutang, though, he was not able to receive adequate medical care, and he had to be moved further south to the county seat of Yangshuo.

Then as now, the highlight of a trip to Guilin was the cruise along the Li River from Guilin south to Yangshuo. In the past, one traveled by raft or small boat, nowadays by motorized excursion boat. The scenery along the route down the Li River is breathtaking, and the vista from Yangshuo is spectacular.

"I've got no regrets. I did only what I was able to." Wu-lan-tai kept repeating these words while his injuries were being attended to. He had tried to make up for the defeat at the Dadong Mountains with his own life. In the final analysis, Wu-lan-tai would die without ever learning of the decision reached by the court in Beijing.

He was wounded at the General's Bridge on the first day of the third lunar month, 1852. He died in Yangshuo on the twentieth day of that month. The round of Taiping artillery at South Valley had smashed Commander Wu-lan-tai's knee.

Having withdrawn from Yongan en masse, the Taipings had now inflicted a stinging defeat on the pursuing Qing forces and surrounded the walled city of Guilin. Reports of these events reached the court in the capital about the tenth day of the third month (3/10).

3/13: It was decided that Former Hunan Provincial Military Commander Yu Wanqing be ordered to march to the front in Guangxi.

3/18: An order was issued to Hu-Guang Governor-General Xu Guangjin to lead an army in the direction of Guilin.

3/19: Imperial Commission Sai-shang-a was called to account for these events, and it was decided that he would remain in his position at the demoted rank of four. At the same time, both Wu-lan-tai and Xiang Rong were both punished with: "removal from office and remaining at their posts." In other words, while stripped of all civil bureaucratic position, they were to retain their military commands.

The sentences were delivered on the day before Wu-lan-tai died. By the time word of these decisions was delivered to the scene of the fighting, roughly another twenty days had passed.

When news of Wu-lan-tai's death on the battlefield reached Beijing, the court issued the following: "All demotions heretofore are revoked." Not only was his honor restored, but 1,000 taels of silver were presented to his survivors, and he was awarded the posthumous title of "martial and strong." In addition, he was given the special privilege of the hereditary post of imperial guardsman.

If the government did not bestow special honors on those who went into battle and privileges for their survivors, it might influence the morale of troops in the field. However, since Wu-lan-tai had no children, the one chosen heir among his descendants was awarded with the post of third-class imperial guardsman.

Qin Dingsan, regional commander of Guizhou, took over command of Wu-lan-tai's troops. At the time of the battle of Wuxuan, Qin was the commander who had finally arrived on the scene from Guizhou. He attacked the Taipings at Wuxuan and was defeated by them. One would be hard-pressed to call him a capable commander. The *Draft History of the Qing Dynasty* claims that, although the loyalty and bravery of Wu-lan-tai were the very highest, he was not successful in battle because he failed to get along with Xiang Rong. The overall evaluation was of "a man foolishly loyal and foolishly brave." Wu-lan-tai never did seem to understand what the Taipings were all about.

—7—

The siege of Guilin was ferocious. Although the inner city was within Taiping rifle range, that was only one part of the story. They could bombard the provincial governor's office from Elephant Nose Hill, but the Qing forces had evacuated the office, retreated to the rear, and set up a provisional office. Bombarding a handful of vacant houses was not going to change the situation in any way whatsoever.

"If the ammunition would only carry just a little further," sighed both Taiping officers and men. And so, the once precious cannons were rapidly becoming useless white elephants.

The last hope to which the Taipings were clinging was of collusion with confederates within the city, as had occurred at Yongan. However, the experiences at Yongan had been a lesson for the Qing as well. To prevent collusion, government spies had been sent undercover into Guilin. They numbered no more than a dozen or so, and the Qing Army issued a proclamation to the effect that "anyone who captures a bandit spy will receive one hundred taels of silver, per person."

How many people were falsely accused and killed for this money remains unknown. Ordinarily, anyone who even remotely opposed the authorities and was regarded as a ringleader, was taken right off to the gallows and executed. The plan was that, even if 100 people were killed on the basis of false charges, that was enough to ensure that not a single spy would escape.

Curiously, among the leaders within Guilin, Xiang Rong, the military man, advocated a "strong defensive stance," while Zou Minghe, the civil bureaucrat, was calling for "offensive warfare." Although a provincial governor was a civil post, he actually had direct control over a unit of troops known as the Governor's Command. And he held the power to issue commands. Early in the siege, Zou had ordered his troops to attack, but the result had been a great defeat. He had lost 300 soldiers from Jiangxi province, and there were no subsequent attacks from within the city.

"We've still got enough in the way of provisions. If we can keep our defenses strong, we'll be in good shape. A protracted war surely works to the disadvantage of the long-haired bandits." This was Xiang Rong's point of view, and Zou Minghe had to concur.

Orders were issued to reinforce troop strength in Hunan and Guangdong. Forces from various parts of the country would probably be sent to Guilin eventually. Based on their experience up to that point, the Taipings knew that whenever they moved, their numbers rose, but if they remained stationary, their forces would remain unchanged. In addition, provisions in the outskirts of Guilin were almost completely spent.

The entire Taiping military leadership was well aware of the fact that a protracted war was to be avoided. Judging from conditions within the city, it seemed that any possibility of collaboration was now gone.

The view was put forward that, because there were so many miners in the army, they could dig tunnels, destroy the city walls with explosions, and then try to storm the inner city. Guilin, however, was surrounded by rivers, which rendered this plan extremely difficult.

On 3/20, the day Wu-lan-tai died in action, Yang Xiuqing revealed the overriding plan of action to the leadership: "If we cannot take Guilin within ten days, we should move to the northwest, toward Xing'an and Quanzhou." So far as military matters were concerned, all powers rested with Yang Xiuqing. In matters of tactics or strategy, Hong Xiuquan would not say so much as a single word.

When the explosive-filled tunnels failed to destroy the city wall, old-style "cloud ladders" were employed. These ladders bore this rather high-sounding name because they appeared to "rise into the clouds." Just when the Taiping soldiers were about to reach the top of the wall, though, boiling oil was poured on them, and this effort to breach the wall ended in failure.

Next, they built "Lügong" vehicles, which were more secure than "cloud ladders." These were tall towers constructed of bamboo, which stood at a height equal to the city walls and with wheels attached at the bottom. A suicide corps of a dozen or so men climbed onto the Lügong vehicles, and the mass of remaining troops pushed them up close to the walls.

The strategy was to raid the inner city from these tower-like contraptions, but this too ended in failure. The government troops defending the city poured boiling oil on the towers and set them ablaze, and their bamboo structure was no match for fire.

Morale among the Qing troops within the city rose further when some twenty or more cannons from the Ming dynasty were dug up on the grounds of the Zhaozhong ancestral temple, a shrine erected for the war dead in various wars over the years. Surprisingly, these 300-year-old cannons, which had been buried 200 years prior to their discovery, could still sustain use. Since the defenders of Guilin had few artillery pieces, this finding was like the welcome rain after a long drought.

"Although those soldiers who've given their lives for their country may have perished, they still sought to defend their land," intoned Xiang Rong in a solemn ceremony at the Zhaozhong temple.

With each passing hour, more and more Qing troops from various quarters pressed closer to Guilin. Jiang Zhongyuan had no sooner returned to Hunan than he raised a group of crack troops, and set off once again for the scene of the fighting in Guangxi. The troops under Qin Dingsan, who had absorbed Wu-lan-tai's forces, made contact with Jiang Zhongyuan's men and began to exert pressure on the Taipings' flank.

On lunar 4/1 (May 19), Yang Xiuqing ordered a shift of position for the entire Taiping Army. News of the order first went out to the leadership. If the Taiping Army were to release its encirclement of Guilin and retreat, the Qing Army would doubtless immediately move to pursue the rebels. In order to open up as wide a distance as possible between themselves and the pursuing force, it was best to let the enemy know of the retreat as late as conceivably possible. Thus, they had to withdraw under cover of great secrecy.

For several days, boats of various sizes were assembled, and rafts were built. On both sides of the Li River, a plant known as Phoenix Tail bamboo was growing in abundance. This variety of bamboo had leaves like the feathery fur on the tail of a phoenix, and it was ideal for concealing the boats and rafts on the river's banks.

Ten soldiers remained at each of the two fortresses, one on Elephant Nose Hill and one at Bull Hill. The guns were removed, but one was left at each battery. A total of twenty soldiers were left behind to open fire from time to time on the city.

This ploy was aimed at leaving the impression that the Taiping forces were still in place. It was out of the ordinary for there to be not a single human form in sight. For several days, the Taipings built straw effigies and placed them here and there.

That night, 70,000 Taiping troops, divided into land and water corps, left the Guilin area. The Li River before Elephant Nose Hill was a stream so peaceful that it was dubious whether it actually flowed in any particular direction.

The night was moonless. Only the silhouette of the Douji Hills could be seen in outline. The two hills faced one another and gave the appearance of two chickens in a cockfight (*douji* in Chinese), staring each other down.

Sacred Pagoda Hill could be made out. The pagoda on the hill could barely be discerned. It looked serene. The entire army moved without making a sound.

The water route force went upstream on the Li River, while the land route force took a huge detour to the west. The two forces planned to meet up in Xing'an county, about 60 kilometers to the northwest of Guilin.

From time to time, gunfire was audible in the night. It was coming from the camouflaged guns that had been abandoned by the main force of the Taipings. "Next will be Changsha," murmured Yang Xiuqing.

"Pretty soon, we won't be able to understand anything said to us. We may miss in our objectives there, too," said Feng Yunshan.

While the Taipings had been fighting in Guangxi, the locals spoke the same dialect as they did, as if they were relatives, and they even received information—though sometimes unreliable—on the enemy from the locals.

This was no longer going to be the case, however. When they passed through Xing'an to Quanzhou, they would be entering Hunan province. Hunanese were renowned for their antipathy toward outsiders. The Taipings were probably not going to be treated like relatives from that point on.

"No, no. They've all been equally persecuted by the demons' government, in Guangxi and Hunan both. Their minds . . . we'll win over their minds. Words may be important, but words aren't everything by themselves." Yang's voice was full of self-confidence.

"Whatever happened to Jiao Liang?" asked Xiao Chaogui, as if he had just recalled the subject.

Ever since the escape from Yongan, no one had brought up the subject of Jiao Liang, the man who had assumed the role of a second Zhuge Liang. He had boasted of himself that he was a major figure in the Heaven and Earth Society of Hunan.

Many of even the leaders of the Taipings had had high expectations of Jiao, should they have ever found themselves in Hunan. Although a member of the Heaven and Earth Society, it soon became clear that Jiao enjoyed none of the great stature within it that he had bragged of. It was equally clear that he was using money of unknown origins in an effort to build his own personal faction.

He had been hauled off in chains and thrown in prison, though the jail had been liberated at the time of the escape from Yongan, so he was sure to have been freed.

"He was getting money from the demons' army to try to cause discord among us. He was probably rescued by them," said Feng Yunshan.

"No, I heard that the demons captured him and sent him back to Beijing," said Yang, repeating a piece of information heard from many sources. There was a high probability that this story was accurate.

"The demons will use him as much as they can, and when he's no longer of any use to them, they'll discard him. How pitiful," said Feng, shaking his head.

They were now far from Guilin. The fleet of Taiping boats moved along as quietly as before, although gradually the voices of those on board them were making less and less of an effort to hide their presence.

"He wouldn't have been of any use to us, even in Hunan. He was insignificant," said Yang in an assertive tone of voice.

15

Aftermath of a Massacre

—1—

As she turned around, Li Xinmei's eyes seemed faintly reddish, as if they had been clouded over. They were clearing up now to their normal azure color. Lian Liwen entered the room she was in, and her eyes were asking Liwen a question.

Liwen remained silent, shaking his head from side to side.

"So, it really is true. . . . It's not just some superficial gloss," she said almost muttering.

Liwen nodded. Xinmei turned her face once again toward the wall.

"Can't he somehow be stopped?" Her voice was so low as to be just barely audible. Her sadness had sapped all strength from her voice.

"Yang Xiuqing's gone somewhere, and Hong Xiuquan won't give the army orders. I've asked any number of times, but it's useless," said Liwen.

They were presently within the city of Quanzhou. All windows and doors were shut tight, but the reeking stench of blood wafted through the air. A slaughter was now being carried out within the city walls. The order had been: "Massacre the city." Yang Xiuqing, commander of the central army of the Taiping military, had given it. No discrimination by age or sex—everyone was to be put to death.

Were not the Taipings a legitimate army? "Kill the demons" was among their watchwords. Those who stood with the Manchu Qing government and worked to prevent the realization of the ideals of the Taiping Heavenly Kingdom were dubbed "demons." From the time that Hong Xiuquan had ascended to heaven in his illness, they had been speaking of marching forward, slaying these demons. However, did "demon" apply to the entire general populace of Quanzhou? It couldn't have. And yet, what was presently under way certainly looked like a violation of the teachings of the Heavenly Father Jehovah: "Do not arbitrarily kill brothers and sisters."

The Taipings may have been a legitimate army, but what they were doing was unjustified. Xinmei was troubled by these deep thoughts.

Liwen had tried to persuade the Taiping leadership to rescind the "massacre order." But Yang Xuiqing, who had issued the order, was not present at that time. Hong Xiuquan, who ought to have been the highest leader, did not dare try and alter an order delivered by Yang. Yang possessed the absolute weapon of the "Heavenly Father's Descent to Earth," and even the Heavenly King Hong Xiuquan had reason to fear this.

"I can't abide by this any longer. I'm thinking of pulling out," said Xinmei.

"If you pull out, where will you go? They call themselves the Taiping Heavenly Kingdom here, but the heavenly kingdom is only a goal they're stubbornly aimed at. It's so mundane. It's a far preferable mundane existence, but it's no heaven on earth." Liwen was trying to soothe her, and there was no force behind his words. The massacre at Quanzhou had been a great shock to him, as well. I'd like to bolt from here too, he thought.

When he looked at the faces of the old people, women, and children who had fallen, covered in blood, on the streets, Liwen looked into the sky, wanting to scream with all his might.

Turning her back on Liwen, Xinmei raised her right arm and tried to shake it all away, twisting her body in the effort. Then she turned around to face Liwen directly.

"Honestly, I'm speaking the truth," she said. From both her movements and her tone of voice, it seemed that she was shaking herself free of something. "I'm here with the Taipings because you're here. But when I see all this, I don't think I can stay any longer, even if you remain. It's no good, even if you're here."

Liwen could feel a lump rising in his throat. Xinmei was making her own form of a declaration of love. Liwen understood. Finally, they should be coming to this meeting of minds, just as she was announcing an intention to leave. Perhaps, precisely because this was a time of leave-taking, their hearts could not have been closer.

Xinmei's face was a bit distorted. He could see that she was on the verge of bursting into tears. Liwen took two steps toward her and put his hands on her shoulders, and Xinmei leapt into his arms.

"Come on now, tears don't become you. It's just not like you," he said as he embraced her. He felt a dampness on his shoulder, and her body trembled ever so slightly.

"I'm leaving the Taipings, but I won't be going that far away. One way or another, I'll always be near the Taipings. So I'll see you, come what may. I will see you," she said, sobbing.

"Don't be downhearted, you the queen of the bandits!" said Liwen, shaking her softly.

Another female leader in the Heaven and Earth Society, Su Sanniang, had left her life as an ordinary housewife to join the Taiping Heavenly Kingdom. By comparison, Li Xinmei was born to this world. Her parents were bandit leaders, and she had never lived outside of that realm. Despite this background, she was an idealist of the purist sort. She had tried to incorporate the men under her command into the Taiping military structure, and she now felt betrayed.

She felt most grieved by the massacre at Quanzhou. In the world of banditry, this was the sort of scene she should have been used to seeing.

"Thanks," she said, expressing gratitude for his encouragement.

"If you'll be close by, then I'll see you again."

"That'll depend on what happens to the Taipings. But, once you join the Taipings, there's no time for regrets. I'm happy that you're here and that I'm in your arms."

Her body again began to quiver markedly.

—2—

Quanzhou was a department seat located about 130 kilometers northeast of Guilin. The county seat of Xing'an was located in the middle of Quanzhou. Once they had given up their assault on Guilin, the Taiping military divided into land and sea routes and proceeded to the north with the plan of meeting and reassembling at Xing'an.

There was no battle at Xing'an. County Magistrate Shang Chang abandoned his walled town and fled. With a force of several tens of thousands, the Taipings were rushing forward to a tiny county seat surrounded by countryside. Had the town resisted, it would surely have been an easy victory for the rebels, and a futile resistance for the local county forces. Shang Chang was clearly a wise man.

The Taipings stayed only one night in Xing'an before hurrying on, and not a single drop of blood was spilt there. But, as was Taiping custom, they set fire to the government official's office where the demons nested, the county magistrate's public residence.

When it was learned at the provincial capital of Guilin that the Taipings had lifted their siege and headed north, great joy ensued, though no chase was attempted. Before anything else, Guangxi Governor Zou Minghe sent a messenger to Beijing to report: "We have repulsed the bandit army."

Learning that the governor had dispatched a messenger to the capital in Beijing, a crowd of people gathered before his door, each trying to outdo the next. "I have performed such and such a meritorious deed," they claimed. "Please write down just a few lines about it," they requested. They were all recommending themselves, and the governor rashly agreed to prepare a long list in his report to Beijing. Even bribery was openly talked about.

The highest rank of military exploit was designated "especially meritorious," and following it were four levels comparable to A, B, C, and D. For 100 taels of silver, you could become a "man of military exploits." Everyone knew about this market. Reminiscences from the time concerning it remain extant.

The court in Beijing ordered the imperial commissioner to reexamine the list of those with alleged military exploits to their credit submitted by the governor. Imperial Commissioner Sai-shang-a had entered Guilin seven days after the siege of that city had been lifted, and hence did not know about the actual war situation. He was, however, able to get his hands on information from various quarters, and the utter nonsense of the governor's report became widely and publicly known, indicating that his gaining access to the truth had not proven to be the least bit difficult. It soon became clear that virtually every military deed on the governor's list had no basis in fact, and Sai-shang-a so reported it to the throne. As a result, Governor Zou Minghe was relieved of his office.

Despite the fact that the higher officials of the Qing dynasty usually took care of each other, why had the imperial commissioner's investigative report elicited such a stringent response? Rather than "stringent," it was simply "the truth," though behind this incident were troubles between Sai-shang-a and Zou Minghe.

As imperial commissioner, Sai-shang-a had to eradicate the Taiping forces completely. It was his responsibility. Yet, Zou Minghe was governor of Guangxi, and his responsibilities were limited to defending Guangxi province. Although the imperial commissioner had called for the dispatching of troops in pursuit of the enemy, the governor of Guangxi had, on whatever pretext, not complied. Aside from the Taipings, there were a variety of bandit armies making trouble throughout Guangxi.

As a reason given for his refusal to send troops, the Guangxi governor had said: "I have to place my crack troops and fiercest officers inside the province for purposes of self-defense." Having already departed for the northeast, the Taipings seemed to be heading into Hunan from Guangxi. Once they were all within the provincial boundaries of Hunan, they would no longer be the concern of Guangxi. To chase after them purposefully, battle them within Guangxi, and incur troop losses seemed the height of foolishness. This was Zou Minghe's thinking from his position as governor.

Imperial Commissioner Sai-shang-a was furious with the Guangxi governor for not cooperating, and he retaliated in his investigative report on military deeds.

The commanding officer of the reinforcements from Guangdong, Wulan-tai, had died in battle, and the battalion leader from Guangxi, Provincial Military Commander Xiang Rong, had not put in an appearance by reason of illness. Commanders Xu Wanqing and Liu Changqing, for one reason or another dilatory in their movements, left Guilin at the head of 7,000 troops only after several days had already passed.

The Taipings were ignorant of these goings-on among the government forces. Spies had been sent out, but they had failed to get near the leaders. Numerous reports detailed the mood and activities of the general populace, but what the authorities were up to remained largely unknown.

Pursuit was on its way immediately, and the Taipings could think only of that. It was common sense to think as much. The reason they rested only one day at Xing'an, where they had penetrated the city walls effortlessly, was out of fear of the pursuing Qing Army.

Had there been no resistance at Quanzhou either, the Taipings had had no plan to attack it. They had been marching hurriedly forward. It was a departmental seat and hence was somewhat larger than a county city. With a population of some several tens of thousands, it would have been difficult to dig themselves in and entrench their forces there.

As a group, the leaders of the Taipings' inner councils at the time set their sights on Changsha, capital of the province of Hunan. There was a strong feeling that, if they made it to Changsha, they would survive, and hence they wanted to avoid fighting en route as much as possible. They simply did not have the leisure to fight and take each walled city one after the next.

At Xing'an, the Taipings had entered the city when the county magistrate and officials beneath him had all fled. However, had these officials remained confined to the city, the Taipings would surely have passed through without so much as stopping.

Cao Xiepei, department magistrate of Quanzhou, was a man of serious mettle from Zhejiang. He was not about to abandon his city, like the county magistrate at Xing'an had done. Although the garrison troops within Quanzhou numbered only 500, the magistrate hurriedly gathered the ablest men.

At precisely this time, Brigadier Vice-Commander Wu Changxian, leading an army of reinforcements 400 strong, was heading south from Hunan and entered the walled city of Quanzhou. When the department magistrate requested his cooperation in defending Quanzhou, Wu Changxian consented and placed his troops within the city walls. Quanzhou was then packed with fighting men and the sense of tragedy was palpable. The approaching Taipings had forged a massive military force of several tens of thousands of troops, while the government regulars in Quanzhou, even counting the reinforcements, numbered barely a thousand.

For their part, the Taipings had no plans to take on their adversaries in such a tiny city. They had been marching casually in the foothills of Willow Mountain in the western suburbs outside the city walls. The Taipings' advance troops did not even see Quanzhou as they marched right by.

Several cannons were placed on the walls of Quanzhou. The magistrate, his officials, and Wu Changxian climbed the wall and gazed intently with great anxiety at the Taiping armies.

"They seem to be marching right by."

"It's too bad. I was thinking we might just try our hand with them."

"They seem to be intimidated by our military defenses."

While these words were being exchanged, at the bottom of their hearts they were all relieved.

Taiping troop strength was immense, so the lines of soldiers continued endlessly before their eyes. There were cavalrymen as well, but they were few in number. Most were infantry. Occasionally a palanquin passed by.

"The guys in the sedan chairs are probably the bandits' leaders."

"If I were a commander, I'd try to attack and wipe them out right now."

"No, we can't be sure about it. There've been a lot of sedan chairs going by for some time now. Probably the Society of God Worshippers put their old people, women, and children in those chairs."

The conversation atop the wall of the city ceased about this time. Unlike those that had passed before, now a magnificently lacquered palanquin passed before them. The troops who appeared to be escorting this one were marching in groups before and behind it.

"There's a big shot in there!" said someone, breaking the momentary silence.

"What should we do?" said a voice.

—3—

Department Magistrate Cao Xiepei shut his eyes. He thought he had seen something he shouldn't have. Although a man of firm character, he was the highest official in the department and he had to think of the safety of the resident populace within his jurisdiction. He had made up his mind that, were the enemy to attack, he would then without question vigorously resist and await reinforcements from the Guilin area. However, in his heart he prayed that the Taipings would just pass him by.

Perhaps his prayers would be heard, as the Taipings hurried north into the foothills of Willow Mountain. They were ignoring Quanzhou. But then came the spectacular yellow palanquin, guarded in front and rear. The uniforms of the convoying troops were of far better quality than those of the other soldiers. The person inside the sedan chair was clearly one of the leaders of the Taipings.

"That's probably, uh, Hong Xiuquan. Look at how pompous all that is!"

"Either Hong Xiuquan or maybe Yang Xiuqing. They're supposed to be the two big commanders of the bandit army."

"If I kill a commander, . . . that'd be worth a special military merit. Probably even higher."

The magistrate now wanted to cover his ears. Was it acceptable for a commander of the enemy to pass before him, and for him to merely overlook it? Here was this bandit army comprised of several tens of thousands of men, calling itself the army of "Great Peace" (the meaning of "Taiping"), defying the state. Bring down their commander and they would doubtless scatter to the four winds. That eventuality would certainly ensure an era of "great peace" for the entire realm. As a bureaucrat of the state, charged with responsibility for one regional department, what was the best decision to come to?

"What should we do?" said someone, clearly urging action in a loud voice.

The expectation that the bandits would scatter in all directions was merely wishful thinking. The magistrate had been informed of the Taiping Army's fighting record. They were not to be compared to the local bandits endemic to China, having already demonstrated a vigorous fighting spirit. Although the magistrate knew nothing whatsoever of Christianity, he understood full well the strength of religious belief. Were their leader ever killed, this was not the sort of group that would vanish like the mist.

On the contrary, it would only make them angrier. Troops burning with anger were frightening. If they were to swoop down and launch a savage attack, the walled city of Quanzhou was utterly helpless. A scene in which the residents of the city were fleeing hither and yon in the conflagrations of warfare floated through the mind of the magistrate. Next came a sea of blood and a mountain of corpses.

We'll just let them pass untouched this time, he thought. He had heard tell that they were not the usual run of soldiers. The magistrate let his decision be known, as he rose and conveyed it to his staff.

"Refrain from artillery attack. If they don't attack us, there won't be any fire initiated from this end."

However, the last of his words were lost in the deafening roar of bombardment. Without waiting for the order, someone had fired the large cannon in the middle of the three perched atop the city wall. A huge cloud of dust rose in the foothills of Willow Mountain.

"We hit them!" shouted the gunner.

Something yellow was visible amid the black cloud of dust. It was a piece of the palanquin. If there had been a direct hit, the palanquin would probably have been smashed to bits. The fact that a sizable piece of it had been thrown into the air seemed to indicate a partial hit.

The movements of Taiping troops were clearly visible from the city walls. Everyone was hurriedly rushing for cover. Wu Changxian was surveying the scene with a telescope:

"We hit him! He's probably dead . . . They're carrying him on a wooden stretcher. . . . Even if he's not dead, he's seriously wounded. Maybe it's Hong Xiuquan, or maybe Yang Xiuqing. . . . I'd really like to know who that is," he said.

"You idiot!" screamed the magistrate, but this was drowned out by the battle cry and reached no one's ears.

"They're in complete confusion," said Wu Changxian gleefully. "They can't get away fast enough. Soldiers who've lost their commander dissolve into utter disorder."

Wu Changxian's prediction did not prove to be accurate. The Taiping military forces did not flee in total chaos. Quite to the contrary, troops that had already passed by began to retrace their steps.

A flurry of activity was visible, but it was not the result of a retreat. It soon became clear that the activity on the field was the Taipings assuming a position to launch an assault on Quanzhou. The magistrate could feel the animosity in this activity. We've made the enemy angry, he thought, and now they've become enraged. He was resigned to the fact that there was nothing more to be done.

The man inside the yellow sedan chair had been the Southern King, Feng Yunshan, commander-in-chief of the rear army, and the original organizer of the Society of God Worshippers. A man of composure and dignity, Feng was a man of great popularity among the Taipings. As a result of the cannon attack from the walls of Quanzhou, Feng received serious injuries, which left him on the brink of death.

"Punish the foes of the Southern King!" ordered the Eastern King, Yang Xiuqing. The hatred burned in his eyes as he scowled intently at Quanzhou. The Taiping attack on Quanzhou commenced on the seventh day of the fourth lunar month (May 25 according to the solar calendar). Unlike the fighting up to that point, the war now became one of malice and retribution. The defenders of Quanzhou were slated for certain death. They had cut down an enemy commander and were not prepared for a ferocious retaliation.

The magistrate had been counting on reinforcements arriving from Guilin. If they could just hold out for those reinforcements, it might be sufficient to forestall devastation by the enemy.

The soldiers were on their way from Guilin—7,000 troops under the command of Yu Wanqing and Liu Changqing. They were not coming to rescue Quanzhou, but with the aim of pursuing and attacking the Taipings. However, they allowed an appropriate space between themselves and the enemy, for if they overtook the Taipings too rapidly, that only meant war.

Get out of Guangxi quickly, thought Regimental Commander Liu Changqing. "We have pursued them to the best of our ability, but they somehow beat an extremely hasty retreat—" would run his report, and that should bring the matter to an end.

The cannon attack from Quanzhou on the Taiping Army, then hurriedly on its way to Hunan, led to the latter's assuming a troop position for a siege. When he heard the report, Liu Changqing unconsciously thundered, "Have they gone mad?"

Yu Wanqing had a different notion. He actually was of a mind to welcome the reckless offer of combat from Quanzhou.

"Well done," he said with a meaningful pause after hearing the report.

Yu Wanqing was the provincial military governor of Hunan, and had been sent to Guangxi on orders from Beijing. He had now followed the Taipings to a region that fell under his jurisdiction. Liu Changqing had wanted to drive the Taipings out of Guangxi. However, Yu felt that this merely moved the trouble into territory under his control.

Inasmuch as Yu was the one with full responsibility for military matters in the province of Hunan, he knew only too well that the Hunan defenses were still unprepared for a Taiping attack, so he welcomed the postponement of Taiping movement in that direction and the time it afforded him.

For Yu Wanqing, the Taiping decision to remain in Quanzhou was a favorable turn of events.

—4—

The siege of Quanzhou continued for ten days.

"We must take the city of Quanzhou while the Southern King is alive!" This was the stern order issued by the Taiping Eastern King Yang Xiuqing. The severely wounded Feng Yunshan lay on his back in a house somewhat removed from Taiping headquarters.

"Let's abandon Quanzhou now . . . and move quickly toward Hunan. . . . What happens to me is irrelevant. We must lose no time . . . in getting the Taiping banner. . . . to Hunan," repeated Feng from his sickbed.

"Your body is not in its normal state," said Hong Xiuquan to his old staunch ally. "It will recuperate before you know it. We shall fight. I have entrusted that to others. Rest calmly and sleep."

Hong Xiuquan knew full well that the attack on Quanzhou was wasting precious time. However, he could not rest until punishment had been administered to those who had injured his old and close friend. Yang Xiuqing put in appearances at Feng's bedside from time to time and offered comforting words similar to those of Hong, although he never thought of the attack on Quanzhou as a waste of time.

He had already decided on a "slaughter of the city." After the city fell, a massacre would ensue.

The road ahead for the Taiping Army to follow was long. Were they to take the decisive and horrifying action of a wholesale slaughter, those who might have thought of interfering with the Taiping advances in the small cities en route would surely disappear. So, what seemed like a time-consuming digression most assuredly was not. On the contrary, it would enhance the marching speed of the army. Yang was not just a romantic who outdid himself in the interest of revenge. His decisions were supported by calculations. The 7,000 troops under the command of Yu Wanqing and Liu Changqing came as far as twenty kilometers away from Quanzhou city but made no subsequent effort to advance further. The reason given for their failure to march forward was that "the bridge was destroyed."

After the entire Taiping Army had traversed the Feiluan Bridge to the northwest of the city, they demolished it. Hypothetically, a new bridge might have been constructed, since the government forces did number in the thousands, but in spite of that fact, Yu and Liu left their troops in the region of Luban Bridge, which commanded a view of the city from a distance. Messengers from Quanzhou in search of the reinforcements were repeatedly sent to the command post at Luban Bridge, but the two commanders Yu and Liu ignored them.

"If Quanzhou can hold out for just one more day, the defense preparation in Hunan will be complete. They've got to hang on," said Yu Wanqing.

The Taipings had attacked in anger, and that enmity was conveyed to the defenders. Magistrate Cao Xiepei could only imagine the sorrowful situation that would follow the fall of the city, or perhaps he was prepared for something that would transcend his imagination. Had he known that the government troops due to arrive any moment soon had no intention of supplying reinforcements, he would have abandoned all hope. Since the north gate of the city had still not been surrounded by Taiping soldiers, it had been left open for city residents to flee.

"Anybody who wants to leave, leave now!" said the magistrate. "I will stay here till the bitter end. My fate is now tied to the city, but I don't expect that all residents will choose to risk their fate along with me. Their general toppled, the enemy has been driven to a frenzy. It seems to me that they shall exhaust the limits of brutality. By all means, evacuate the city, please."

Several tens of thousands of city residents fled through the north gate. A fair number volunteered to remain by the side of the magistrate. Of course, the 1000 soldiers were not allowed to desert. Many people did not leave because they had nowhere to go, and then there were the old and infirm who could not be moved.

The Taipings constructed an advance base at the Jiangxi Landsmannschaft Hall outside the city. This was a residence for fellow provincials from Jiangxi province. In China at this time, consciousness of place of origin was still quite strong, and halls of this sort existed even in small, out-of-the-way towns. Quanzhou had played host to many men who hailed from Jiangxi. To every such landsmannschaft hall was attached a "charitable estate." Chinese earnestly wished to be buried after they died in cemeteries in their hometowns. If they died while away from home, their remains would be returned to the hometown. Until appropriate arrangements were made for transporting the corpse, the charitable estate took responsibility for the coffin, and it might arrange a temporary funeral and burial service on the spot.

Taiping soldiers proceeded to dig a tunnel beneath the floor of the Jiangxi Landsmannschaft Hall. Inasmuch as there were a large number of coal miners among the Taipings, tunnel construction was one of their strengths. Since they were inside the building, they could not be observed even from atop the city walls.

With this tunnel digging so camouflaged, the Taipings began to build a tall platform in the courtyard of the Jiangxi Landsmannschaft Hall. A great quantity of earth was produced in the process of digging, and it was used to construct a foundation upon which was set a wooden frame. If this platform was taller than the city wall, then they would be able to command a view inside the city.

They let everyone in the city believe that they were building an observation deck, when in fact the tunnel was their main project. The tunnel ran as far as the wall, and the coal miners dug more widely along the base of the wall. They then planted gunpowder in it. There were a number of still unused coffins in the charitable estate, and they packed the gunpowder into them, carried them down into the tunnel, and placed them at the base of the wall, underground.

On the sixteenth day of the fourth lunar month—the tenth day following the initial attack on the city—the tunnel was completed, and the fuses to the gunpowder were lit. In a feat of remarkable skill, one part of the city wall that rose to a height of seven meters was blown off. Prepared for this eventuality, vanguard Taiping troops climbed over the rubble and rushed into the city, took the unit assigned to guard the gates by surprise, and threw open the main city gate. The immense army of the Taipings then flooded into the city in a great surging mass.

These events transpired in an instant's time, and already the order to slaughter the city's population had been circulated among the officers and men. The massacre was carried out. The Taipings, so clearly a religious band till this point, now seemed transformed into a pack of wild beasts.

"Punish the foes of the Southern King!" yelled Yang Xiuqing here and there in the city, as he called for out-and-out revenge. He was thus absent from the command headquarters.

Hong Xiuquan was sitting in the Taiping headquarters with a discouraged look on his face. Lian Liwen entered and proposed rescinding the order to massacre the populace, but Hong responded:

"It's already been decided. Even I cannot stop it now." The Heavenly King's eyes were half vacant.

"You can say this because you haven't seen what's going on inside the city," said Liwen, pressing Hong. "Please, just go take a look for yourself."

"I must remain here. The Eastern King has gone out. Should the Heavenly King depart this place as well, there would be no one here to respond in an emergency situation. In addition, . . ." At that point, Hong cut himself short, but Liwen thought he understood what Hong was about to say: In addition, I don't want to see what's out there.

No doubt about it, that's just what the Heavenly King had tried to say. Liwen gave up and returned to where Li Xinmei was waiting. For the first time, he embraced her.

War was war. She never expected that everything would be fine and dainty. She understood that much. Xinmei was used to bloody scenes from her years among bandits. However, she had believed that the Taipings were different. That belief had been betrayed, and now she was about to leave.

Liwen did not stop her, for he knew that if he did detain her it would be against her will.

—5—

The arson and the slaughter continued for three days. Though the city of Quanzhou was ablaze, the Qing Army less than fifteen miles away was not about to budge. Feiluan Bridge remained destroyed.

Needless to say, Magistrate Cao Xiepei died at his post. Assistant Regional Commander Yang Yinghe, commander of the Quanzhou garrison force, died in battle. Brigadier Vice-Commander Wu Changxian, who just happened to be passing the area and decided to lend assistance, also died.

Of the one thousand men of the garrison force, some one hundred or more were said to have successfully escaped. The gunner who had not waited for orders, but gone ahead and fired on the passing golden palanquin from atop the city wall, was one of these one hundred.

According to the records of the Qing government, the number of those who died at this time exceeded four thousand. One theory posits that the provincial authorities in Guangxi reported fewer than the actual number. The basic principle of embellishing a report to the court dictated that many casualties were sustained by the enemy and few on one's own side.

Local rumors had it that the number of lives lost as a result of the massacre actually exceeded ten thousand. Slaughter in the city went on for three days.

On 4/18, the Taipings withdrew from Quanzhou, which had been reduced to ruins. Here and there embers smoldered, and the putrid smell of death pervaded the city. Despite the victory they had achieved, gloomy expressions covered the faces of the Taiping troops.

"Okay? From now on, not a single peasant gets killed! You understand? You don't even wound them, let alone kill anyone. Anyone who puts a hand on a peasant will be beheaded on the spot!" Yang Xiuqing repeated this order to the troops and their commanders as they left the city. Having transformed a religious group into a band of wild animals, he was now trying to return them to a religious group at war.

He didn't have much respect for religious belief. He knew well that those bound by religious faith would make a powerful army, and he had to have a mighty army under his command.

Among the rows of troops pulling out of Quanzhou was a sedan chair built much larger than the ordinary size, being borne on the shoulders of eight men. Feng Yunshan was inside on his back. Severely wounded, he had nonetheless seen the fall of Quanzhou city, though not the massacre that ensued. True to his nature, Yang Xiuqing balked at showing Feng the carnage.

Following the flow of the Xiang River from Quanzhou, they traveled by boat for about 35 miles before reaching Hunan province. The Taiping forces maintained over two hundred vessels.

There they found fertile land. Those Taiping rank and file born and raised in the poor province of Guangxi longed with a kind of envy for Hunan. They were full of anticipation. If possible, they wanted to drown their unsavory memories of Quanzhou in the waters of the Xiang River.

The Xiang flowed north from Quanzhou and changed direction toward the east after crossing the provincial frontier into Hunan. As it flowed easterly, the Xiang combined with the Xiao River in the vicinity of Yongzhou, and from there it began flowing to the north once again. Yongzhou was a department seat lying precisely on the present-day site of Lingling. The Taipings were heading at full speed for Yongzhou.

Between Quanzhou and Yongzhou was a ferry crossing known as Suoyi Ford. The two Chinese characters for "Suo-yi" mean "straw raincoat," which indicate that the area received considerable rainfall. When the Taiping forces happened to pass there, though, it was already into the month of June and the spring rainy season had passed.

The Qing Army at Luban Bridge, less than fifteen miles from Quanzhou, had been visually—and only visually—following the withdrawal of Taiping forces, having made no effort to reform into an attack posture. They seemed to be waiting for the appropriate crevice to open and then planned to make their assault.

Meanwhile, the Taiping soldiers were belittling the enemy. "Those guys don't want to fight a war."

"Yeah, they're afraid of it. Life's too precious."

"The troops at Quanzhou were heroic compared to them, don't you think?"

"Yeah, they're worthless. Can't do a thing."

To be sure, the Qing force at Luban Bridge was, for all intents and purposes, cowardly. Called upon for help and reinforcements, they hadn't delivered a single soldier. They sat back watching as the city of Quanzhou was butchered. It might not be too farfetched to imagine that, as they were dying in battle, the Quanzhou garrison troops despised the government's army at Luban Bridge even more than they did the enemy.

"You damned cowards!" screamed someone in the direction of Luban Bridge, though no one there could hear him. They were bold in the face of the enemy, but they also underestimated the enemy.

While fearing an adversary may prove disadvantageous, it is dangerous to underestimate the opponent's strength. As hatred grows, there is a tendency for vigilance in the face of the opposition to diminish. For their part, what became of the Taiping's belittling of the enemy was to be a lesson taught them at Suoyi Ford, and it was an expensive lesson.

Dismissing the enemy out of hand, the Taipings neglected to send out a scouting patrol. They proceeded down the Xiang River by boat, designated some ten vessels as the advance forces, and assigned them the additional task of reconnoitering. However, the men on board those boats became overly impressed with themselves as the advance army, serving at the head of the entire Taiping fighting force, and for one reason or another they ignored their duty as scouts.

Simultaneously acting as scouts and vanguards was itself contradictory within the army's organization. If a scouting party came into contact with the enemy, it had to inform the troops behind it immediately of this fact, but under the same circumstances, a vanguard force was compelled to act valiantly and take on the enemy in battle.

Awaiting the arrival of the Taipings at Suoyi Ford was not the Qing Army, but the army of Hunan volunteers or braves under the command of Jiang

Zhongyuan. When Jiang had seen so clearly that the government's troops were incapable of pursuing a war, he had withdrawn from Yongan to his native Hunan and recruited an army of local braves. It was altogether different from the state's military forces. Furthermore, the men were all natives of Hunan and well-versed in local geography.

Knowing that the Taipings were advancing by sea, even the lowliest foot soldier knew best where to wait in ambush: Suoyi Ford. Jiang selected it as the place to lie in waiting, and all of his subordinates complied.

The area had numerous shoals, and the water rushed through. Jiang had timber collected and placed as obstructions in the river. The Hunan braves lay in waiting on the western bank.

Early on, Jiang sent an urgent document to He-chun, who was in Guilin. It read, "We shall attack the Taipings at Suoyi Ford, though the army of Hunan braves is few in number. We have taken charge of the western bank of the river, but I should like you to dispatch troops to see to the eastern bank. This is a fine opportunity for a pincer operation."

An imperial commissioner had a wing commander under his direct control, and this person was He-chun, the regimental commander of the Suijing garrison. It was he who would devise a plan for attacking the Taipings and who would mobilize the troops.

The Xiang River made a huge curve at this point, and when the boats carrying the advance forces of the Taiping Army completed the turn, they discovered obstacles blocking their passage further on the river.

"It's the enemy! They're somewhere around here!" shouted the commander of the advance forces.

—6—

It was common knowledge that, if some contrivance was found in the river, then an ambush was waiting nearby. Though the Taiping commander was attentive to an ambush, as the commander of an advance force, he was only attentive to fighting under the most extreme circumstances. Since he was doubling as the commander of a scouting force as well, he had to devise a means of informing the troop vessels following them that something was wrong. He should have ordered one of his men to shore with instructions to gallop off at full speed and warn of the impending ambush.

He neglected to do this, however. Actually, he had never even considered doing so, though there would have been plenty of time. Because of the obstructions in the river, the Taipings were unable to move forward, and for a moment an ominous silence hovered about them. Jiang Zhongyuan had placed cannons at selected sites, and his gunners were just waiting for the signal to commence firing. His troops were prepared at any moment to rush out at the enemy. Jiang, though, was trying to wait as long as possible. That way he could draw in the main body of the Taiping Army as close as possible. That main body would certainly go ashore as soon as they heard cannon fire and probably change their planned course.

"We shall draw them in just as much as is necessary," said Jiang, as he watched the unfolding situation from the window of a home that had been turned into his headquarters.

There was no sign that an urgent message had been sent from the advance forces to the main body of the army. Had there been any such indication, whatever it might have been, it would have had to have been suppressed en route, and preparations were in place for just such an eventuality.

The advance troops were no longer able to move forward just at the point where the river made a large turn, and hence they could not be seen by their own troops following behind them.

"The main body of their troops has now passed the line of the Guanyin cedar," reported a scout.

Once the main body of the Taiping Army traversed the point called the "Guanyin cedar," the bombardment was to begin. That meant they had reached a point where they could be drawn in no further. Still, for caution's sake, Jiang Zhongyuan waited. The advance troops of the Taipings were all staring in every direction, trying to locate where the enemy was hiding. Seated in a chair, Jiang cleared his throat and stood up. At last he was going to give the signal to commence firing. Before delivering the order, he said, as if trying to convince himself, "Now should be the right time."

Stepping outside, he waved the red flag in his hands broadly back and forth several times. Eventually, the first cannon thundered, and since they had waited for the right moment and set their targets, they made a direct hit on the boat carrying the commander of the advance forces. People fell, the sail broke in two, and the boat sank.

Then a second and a third volley struck. A column of water spouted up, and the color of the river began to be tinged with red. The main body of the Taiping forces, unable to be of any assistance, turned the bend in the river and confronted the dilemma.

"Abandon ship!"

"Take cover ashore!"

Even in times like these, Yang Xiuqing was able to retain his composure. People were jumping from the boats into the water in an effort to swim to shore. They were picked off by rifle fire, and the overwhelming majority of Taiping soldiers lost their lives there. The enemy remained hidden. Lian Liwen had been aboard the same vessel with the seriously wounded Feng Yunshan. Because of his wounds, Feng was unable to swim.

"Let's go for it and ram the boat into the riverbank," suggested Liwen.

"Nothing else we can do," agreed the other troops aboard.

When the sedan chair carrying Feng was lowered down to the shore, a loud battle cry arose in front of them from the forest, and for the first time the enemy showed its face.

"It can't be!" said Liwen, looking all around him.

It was useless to try to retrace their steps back to the boats that they had run aground. To jostle and force the boats back into the water again would require an immense amount of human strength. And now that the enemy had appeared before them, they had no intention of doing so. Every man devoted his energy solely to saving his own life.

From a distance, Liwen heard a voice call out:

"The eastern shore! The eastern shore!" The voice emanated from a boat in the river, and it was familiar to his ear, unmistakably that of Yang Xiuqing.

The enemy troops emerged from the forest under cover of a bamboo grove. For a moment it seemed as though a brief lull had occurred. Liwen became aware of an irregularity on the battlefield, and Yang's calling out to him was a hint of it.

The resounding roar of the cannons, the gunfire, and the battle cries were all on the western shore, where Liwen and the others had alighted. Some of the Taiping troops who scattered into the Xiang River swam to the western shore, while others struggled to make their way to the eastern shore. The chaos on the eastern bank was considerably less fierce. Perhaps the ambush force was only on the western shore.

"It's the Hunan braves, and there aren't many of them!" Yang continued his shouting from before.

He was certainly trying to calm his men, but it was by no means baseless, irresponsible talk. The order to go to the eastern shore seemed perfectly correct.

The uniforms worn by the enemy when they emerged were different from official government issue. These were surely the Hunan braves organized by Jiang Zhongyuan, whom he had met on a number of occasions at Yongan. There was no question that his forces were strong, but their numbers were few. Liwen was trying to make sense of all the many things that had just popped into his head. Jiang's Hunan braves had taken a large number of casualties at Yongan, and he had reportedly returned to Hunan to raise more men. That report now seemed accurate. Yet for all his efforts, only a short time had elapsed, so that he couldn't have raised that many men.

The ambush seemed just too efficacious a strategy for it to have originated with the commanding officers of the Qing Army. These were not the average good-for-nothing government troops. Slowly but surely, Liwen came to understand the situation at hand.

"There's nothing to be afraid of!" he shouted. He was addressing his allies in the immediate vicinity.

"The enemy is few in number, and they're not on the eastern bank of the river. They must have been prepared for us, but the bombardment won't go on. You can relax now." Liwen was rapidly relating what had taken shape in his mind.

The way the enemy had appeared was to stay crouched, out of sight and catch their prey in a trap, for their numbers were insufficient to win a military victory.

For his own part, Li was still wondering what he should do. Before him was the palanquin of the Southern King, Feng Yunshan, knocked over on its side. Pushing his way through the reed screen, Liwen said:

"Southern King!" Only a groan was audible by way of an answer.

"He's alive!" He tried to turn the sedan chair back up. As a number of the troops recovered themselves, they helped Liwen turn the sedan chair.

"Let's hold it aloft," said Liwen, in the tone of an order.

"What are we going to do with it?"

"Go look for some large wooden planks that washed up on shore. We will put it on them and carry him. We'll swim ahead and protect the Southern King."

—7—

From time to time, the sound of cannon fire could be heard, though not as it had been when the battle began. Gunfire was now also mixed in. Those Taiping troops who made it to the eastern shore of the river, where there were no government soldiers, eventually regained their composure and began returning fire on the Hunan braves across the river on the western shore.

The Southern King was transported across the river on wooden planks with unexpected skill because, it seemed, among the Taiping troops were men who had earlier in their careers been skiff bandits. Although just a piece of wood from a ship that had been destroyed in the cannonade, the plank carrying the Southern King was round in shape and perfect in size to transport a single person. Roughly ten men were placed around it, and they swam through the water while holding the plank aloft.

When we're having tough times, so is the opponent. This was a piece of wartime common sense, but it was also true in the present instance. Jiang Zhongyuan had dispatched an urgent communication to He-chun, requesting troops to be sent to the eastern shore of Suoyi Ford. He-chun, for his part, did not respond.

"I'm taking over supreme command of the fighting. Me and no one else!" He-chun had shouted, cracking his whip on the table with Jiang's urgent communication before him. It was entirely within his power to decide where and if to send troops. He would receive instructions on the matter from no one else. Jiang's request struck He-chun as an impertinence, and Jiang's men were, after all, not a regular part of the government's armed forces.

"Can I send such valued troop strength to such a place? As it is, we have limited troop strength here and have been working under makeshift conditions," screamed He-chun, as he hurled his whip against the wall.

So they thought he should send troops to the eastern bank of Suoyi Ford. And if by doing so a great blow were struck against the Taipings, whose victory would it be? Whose plan would it have been? How would Beijing adjudge the matter?

He-chun quickly calculated the pros and cons, and an answer emerged. Ultimately, no troops were sent. Jiang Zhongyuan waited and waited wearily, but for all his patience no soldiers from Guilin arrived. Just as Jiang began considering sending what few men he could spare over to the eastern bank of the river, however futile it might have been, the Taipings arrived.

Their military genius, Yang Xiuqing, saw the government forces poised for an ambush attack and detected what the enemy was up to. As always, he responded to the situation calmly. Soon after landing on the eastern bank, he took command of an assault on the enemy on the western bank. Nonetheless, Taiping casualties at Suoyi Ford were huge—probably the greatest number of losses since they first raised an army.

Liwen swam assiduously. Large and small columns of water rose here and there on the surface of the river, but the aim of the enemy's rifle fire seemed to be zeroing in on him. The small spouts of water, accompanied by a sharp sound, were becoming all too close. And then he could see the shore in front of him.

As he raised his head, the banner of the Heavenly King fluttering in the wind entered his line of vision. Hong Xiuquan had also arrived unharmed on the eastern bank of the river. He peered strenuously at the litter carrying Feng Yunshan, but from his vantage point he could only make out the Southern King's feet. With all the violent shuttling of the litter, Liwen was worried that Feng might have been further harmed.

It was at that point that his memory suddenly broke off. He remembered only a sharp pain on his right shoulder, and that was all. Dreams followed—strange dreams, to be sure, in which he was soaring into the sky. But how could that be, for human beings can't fly—the thoughts of a rational person wedged themselves into his dreams.

Something was definitely wrong, and it had nothing to do with his apparent flying in the air. He had been swimming in the river. There was a big difference between the sky and the river.

The stars were twinkling in the sky. Could something this ridiculous really be happening? It wasn't stars. But what, then, was it? Something? Something indistinct? Maybe it was because he was in the water . . . that was it—the columns of water making that light sound as bullets glanced off the surface. It wasn't stars at all, and that mistaken impression had to be corrected.

But for all his efforts, he couldn't rectify it. His body was flying through the sky, and here and there he could see the stars. Where was the river running? And what about the spouts of water? Where was this all occurring?

He tried to shout, but he couldn't find his voice. Yet he continued strenuously to raise his voice.

It seemed like he was flying through a dark night sky filled with stars, but he sensed that one corner of that sky was becoming brighter. Still no voice. What was becoming brighter, though, was not a bad omen. The river and water columns would soon emerge. Good. If he could just wait a bit, his voice was sure to return.

He regained consciousness later.

"You've been moaning for some time. Are you okay?" said a female voice. Liwen knew to whom it belonged.

Wouldn't you know it, he thought. Returning to his senses, Liwen muttered vacantly. Softly he opened his eyes. It was all bright now. Actually, it was not such a bright place at all, as he would later recognize. But at the time it seemed blindingly so.

"So, you've awakened, have you?" The woman looked as though she was peeking in on him. Having just returned to consciousness, Liwen could vividly smell women near him.

"Xinmei . . ." his voice said.

"Well, you understood me. You definitely understood me. You were calling me," she said, in an unsteady, trembling voice.

Another woman approached, but Liwen did not know who she was. Following consciousness, he next regained his memory. Its recovery overcame him like an avalanche.

"What happened to the Southern King? And the Taiping Army? Where am I?" Liwen had intended to shout these words loudly, but, as he later learned, his voice was so weak he was barely audible. Xinmei put her face next to his and tried to glean what he was attempting to say.

"The Taiping Army headed south three days ago. That included the Heavenly King, the Eastern King, the Western King, and the Northern King." She said nothing of the Southern King.

When Liwen recovered his strength, she would tell him that the Southern King had been shot and killed while crossing the river.

"So, do you intend to follow the Taiping Army?" asked Xinmei, stroking Liwen's face two days after he had regained consciousness.

"Yes, I shall," responded Liwen, in a strong voice.

Movement North and South

—1—

Ding Shoucun gave the appearance of being mortified by the length of his own jaw, as he rubbed it with his fingers. However, what he was appalled at was not in fact his jaw. He had been ordered to escort under guard a criminal allegedly of considerable import who, for some reason, hardly cut an imposing figure. That was the cause of his disgust. Ding was responsible for accompanying to Beijing the man named Hong Daquan, who had been taken prisoner at Yongan. After departing from Guilin, but prior to his arrival in Changsha, this man's full story finally came out.

"Well, isn't this interesting," said Ding with delight, after having overcome his horror. He surveyed the man, looking for something curious, as if licking his lips in the process. Now, though, he was confronting something of extraordinary interest, so that despite his amazement he was in a good mood.

Ding came from Rizhao county in Shandong province. He had attained the degree of metropolitan graduate in 1835, and served for a time as a secretary in the Council of State, a sort of adviser to the grand ministers of state. When Sai-shang-a was dispatched to Guangxi as imperial commissioner, Ding accompanied him as an attendant.

When he departed from Beijing, Ding told his family and friends: "I shall return after enjoying the natural scenery of Guilin, finest in all the land." He made it seem as though he were leaving on a pleasure trip.

The imperial court anticipated that he would produce a new kind of ordnance that would destroy the insurgents once and for all. Ding had become rather bored with his assignment as the highest attendant to the imperial commissioner. Together with Directors Wen-kang and Xu Youren, he began tests and production of a machine to make mines in Tianjin, but, capricious man that he was, Ding soon began to lose interest even in this as well.

It was rare to find an official who had risen to the status of a metropolitan graduate and who was so well-versed in physics and chemistry. Ding's biography in the *Draft History of the Qing Dynasty* is included in the section on biographies of craftsmen. The highest position he attained in the civil service bureaucracy was as a surveillance commissioner and no further. Thus he was not someone who earned a place in the historical records as an official or a politician. The Chinese expression for craftsman apparently included academic pursuits other than Confucian studies. His biography in the *Draft History of the Qing Dynasty* reads, in part: "He was learned in the arts of astronomy, calendrical science, *fengjue*, and *rendun*, and he produced implements well."

Astronomy and calendrical science are self-explanatory, but *fengjue* and *rendun* are unfamiliar areas. *Fengjue* was an ancient divination practice through which good or bad fortunes were foretold through examination of the four winds. Although little is now known of *rendun*, like other occult arts it probably sought to conceal its true identity. In short, from the perspective of science, these were still in the realm of the mysterious.

To break the monotony, Ding Shoucun enjoyed shocking people. Or, to put it another way, he was always thinking to himself of ways to surprise people with things out of the ordinary. Thus he was forever saying, "You have anything interesting?"

Having already tired of producing a machine to make mines, he wanted to go observe the scenery near Guilin, and was hence concerned about the "long-haired bandits" in Guangxi. What had driven them, he wanted to know, to rise in rebellion? That mystery, however, was solved before he departed for Guangxi. In the light of hindsight, there was no mystery about it at all. It was perfectly normal.

Simply by observing while a member of the great procession accompanying the imperial commissioner, he well understood the sufferings of the common people. On the basis of logical considerations, he had long understood that an increase in the price of silver meant an effective tax increase. This trip made him genuinely feel the sufferings of the people, and not by virtue of logical reasoning. To his way of thinking, they would have had to have been almost unbelievably submissive not to rise in rebellion.

Ding was a member of the establishment, but spiritually he was a bystander. His fidelity to the Qing dynasty was not terribly strong. He had, on occasion, needed money to carry on what he termed "interesting things." In order to finance his laboratory expenses, he had worked as secretary in the Council of State and passed on information about the imperial court that he obtained at work to a merchant.

The man who purchased this information was Wu Zhongshi, who, as Ding was well aware, was connected to Lian Weicai. With his own formidable insight, Ding was able to glean just how much power Lian Weicai really wielded.

Though enjoying the scenery around Guilin to his heart's content, Ding was again becoming bored. He remembered fondly all the laboratory tools left behind at his home in Beijing. Now he wanted to return to the capital, and he wrote Wu Zhongshi: "Please set the wheels in motion so that I can return to Beijing."

It required money to get the court to move personnel. Given the nature of his contacts, however, he fully expected that cooperation through the good offices of Wu and Lian. And that was precisely what happened.

Captured at the time of the fall of Yongan was a principal bandit leader by the name of Hong Daquan, and in Beijing, the decision was reached to "transport him under guard to the metropolitan area." Two high officials, one civil and one military, were authorized to escort him under guard. The military official was Lian-fang, director of the commander-general's office of the metropolitan infantry, and Ding Shoucun was chosen as the civil official.

"Send him to the capital and be very careful, because he seems to be some sort of a big shot. He's a big shot. He concluded a bond of sworn blood brotherhood with Hong Xiuquan and has control over a group of the bandits. No doubt about it. So, I'm relying on you!" said Sai-shang-a at the time of Ding's departure. He used the expression "big shot" rather indiscriminately. Ding's suspicion was that Hong was a much shadier character, but the imperial commissioner's true intentions soon became clear enough.

"Since there are people trying to recapture him, I'd like him executed as quickly as possible, and I'd like that information conveyed." Not only did Imperial Commissioner Sai-shang-a say this to Ding Shoucun, but he had reported his views to Beijing in the form of a document.

The humiliating defeat of having lost four regimental commanders in battle had to be compensated for, even if only somewhat. The imperial commissioner's responsibility in it would be rather light if the bandits also sustained heavy losses and if their leaders were captured.

Hong Daquan was in fact, Jiao Liang, merely a hanger-on living among the Taipings. The fact that he was by no means the big shot he claimed himself to be was only learned after a subsequent investigation. As far as the imperial commissioner was concerned, however, the more important the man he had taken prisoner was, the better. Fortunately, the man bragged continuously about how important he had been in the Taipings.

"Just give me ten thousand men and I'll show you I can annihilate the Taiping Army right away. I know the Taipings' strengths and weaknesses well," he boasted.

The imperial commissioner responded invitingly: "Wiping out the bandits is the most important affair of state. Thus I won't stand in the way of using surrendered commanders who already know the internal conditions among the bandits. I have reported this matter to my superiors. Whether they adopt what you have to say or not depends on their recognition of your talent."

It was, in fact, in opposition to this that the imperial commissioner's appended statement of opinion called for the immediate beheading of this dangerous personage.

Had the man acknowledged, begging for his life, that he was but a simple parasite, that would have occasioned a loss of face for the imperial commissioner. It was thus necessary for him to flatter the man into never losing hope, right up to the bitter end. The bigger a big shot he was, the greater his hope of being awarded a government army to command. This braggart, Jiao Liang, going by the name Hong Daquan, certainly seemed to believe as much, and continued his boasting.

Ding Shoucun was merely on an excursion in Guilin, with no concerns for military matters at all. Though he had scarcely even heard of the Hong Daquan affair, he came to understand the gimmick being utilized by the imperial commissioner while traveling with the prisoner's cart.

"What a pathetic buffoon," he murmured, shaking his head from side to side.

—2—

Ding Shoucun and the others in the party reached Beijing in the middle of the fourth lunar month. On the twenty-third of that month, the Taiping Army, following the massacre at Quanzhou, had been ambushed by the forces under Jiang Zhongyuan and sustained heavy casualties at Suoyi Ford.

The Taiping had planned a long march to attack the city of Changsha, capital of Hunan province, but with the losses at Suoyi Ford these plans would now have to be changed. If they failed to replenish their personnel and supplies, they would never be able to lay siege to Changsha, which was reputed to be even more strongly fortified than Guilin. Not heading in the direction of Changsha to the north, the Taiping forces set out south from Yongzhou (Lingling) for Daozhou. Daozhou was a stronghold surrounded on four sides by mountains and approachable by only one steep road. With such a stronghold, the Taipings would rest their troops, refurbish supplies, and raise more troops. It became known as the Expanded Hunan Army, because they were building up their military forces in the southern part of Hunan.

Southern Hunan had once been a site of powerful Heaven and Earth Society influence, and there were people affiliated with Heaven and Earth Society organizations among the Taipings, as represented by Luo Dagang. Some fifty thousand men had already responded to the call and joined the movement.

Two written appeals were distributed widely: "Edict to Praise Heaven, Punish the Devils, Save the World, and Pacify the Populace"; and "Edict to Praise Heaven and Punish the Barbarians, with Orders to Distribute It Widely." With unbelievable speed, these Taiping appeals spread in all directions, reportedly even being posted on walls in the distant city of Wuchang in Hubei province.

The Heaven and Earth Society in southern Hunan had in fact risen in rebellion any number of times, and thus there were experienced rebels to be found there. The fact that their uprisings had never spread and were usually frustrated midstream was due to organizational weaknesses and a lack of strict military discipline. They took one look at the rigid military discipline of the Taiping Army and thought, "If we had an organization like theirs, our rebellion would surely succeed." Only after the Taipings obtained written pledges from them to abide by military discipline were these rebels incorporated into the army.

The Qing Army, by contrast, had no way to provide for itself. Provincial Military Commander Yu Wanqing was in the Daozhou area, but when the Taipings pressed close, he and local magistrate Wang Kuiyi abandoned the city and fled to Hengzhou. One month later, on a charge of having relinquished his command to the enemy, Yu was dismissed, arrested, and brought before a hearing.

Sai-shang-a roused himself, left Guilin, entered Hunan, and on the first day of the sixth lunar month he arrived at Yongzhou. Since the Taipings had left Guilin on the first day of the fourth month, two months had already passed. The Taipings had replenished manpower and supplies, and the troops were well-rested. On the twenty-fifth day of the sixth month, they departed Daozhou and began to march eastward.

The historical records tell us that they passed through such places as Ningyuan, Jiahe, Lanshan, and Guiyangzhou, and that they occupied Chenzhou on the third day of the seventh month. In distant antiquity, after the fall of the Qin dynasty, Chenzhou was the capital where Xiang Yu (232–202 B.C.) installed the puppet ruler, Emperor Yi of Chu. Numerous Heaven and Earth Society groupings were active in the region, and between twenty thousand and thirty thousand of them joined the Taipings. There were also coal mines in the area, and over one thousand coal miners joined the Taiping military forces. The Taipings established what was effectively an army corps of engineers after occupying Chenzhou.

Of course, the Qing armies did not fail to put up a resistance. County Magistrate Li Qizhao fought to his death at his post in Guiyang, and the Hunan braves under the command of Jiang Zhongyuan were incessantly attacking the Taipings. Generally speaking, though, the Qing government's regular armies commanded by Regimental Commanders He-chun and Chang-lu pursued the Taipings lethargically, while the Hunan braves fought them valiantly.

This was all appropriately camouflaged in the reports sent to Beijing, but at some point the truth was conveyed. The braves were a mighty fighting force. It was about this time that such a voice was heard at the imperial court in the capital. The military victory at Suoyi Ford caused the authorities in Beijing great concern and worry.

Four regimental commanders had died in battle following the retaking of Yongan, and although they had captured the bandit leader Hong Daquan, even in the most favorable light, this was clearly not a military victory. Although they had fought and dislodged the enemy at Guilin, the siege had continued for a month. The enemy had simply broken through the encirclement and continued its forward movement. Had they retreated in defeat, they surely would have headed south for Jintian village, the hometown of the rebellion. Yet they were now moving to the north. This revealed that the reports of the governor of Guangxi concerning military merit on the battlefield were generally without foundation.

Although an apparent military victory, mightn't it just have been a battle at Suoyi Ford? Furthermore, it was now confirmed that the government's regular armies had not participated in the battle there.

—Despite Jiang Zhongyuan's call for reinforcements to the eastern bank of the river, He-chun hadn't dispatched any troops.

—If He-chun had sent him soldiers at that time, they could have joined in a pincer operation and wiped the Taipings out.

—Jiang did send a succession of emergency dispatches, but He-chun ignored them. Jiang was apparently in tears.

—They killed the bandits' big boss, Feng Yunshan, at Suoyi Ford.

—With just a little more effort, they could have put an end to Hong Xiuquan and Yang Xiuqing.

—Hong Daquan was taken prisoner by the imperial commissioner at Yongan, and word is that he isn't at all as important a character as he claims to be.

—That's right. His name hasn't appeared once on a single report that's been submitted.

Conversations of this sort were being exchanged among the men with influential positions in the capital.

Before the carriage transporting the prisoner Hong Daquan passed through Anhui, Supervising Censor Chen Tan submitted the following memorial to the throne:

> Concerning the matter of the arrest of the bandits' bogus military commander Hong Daquan, who has been brought to Beijing under escort, I have heard the following. Hong Daquan was merely being used in the service of the bandits and was by no means an important leader. We have examined materials concerning the names of the rebel leaders heretofore memorialized to the throne, and this man's name is absent. When the bandits had no choice but to flee from Yongan, it seems that the men tried to veil their personal defeat by speaking in exaggerated terms of the glory of the nation. Concealing the truth from those in the metropolitan region was rather easy, but it is much more difficult to deceive the eyes and ears of the entire realm. This shall become especially clear when an imperial edict is issued to the effect that there is no purpose to be served in bringing Hong Daquan to the capital and that the governor-general and governor should inflict punishment en route upon the aforementioned criminal in their locale.

Although Chen Tan was in Beijing, he could see through all the trickery surrounding Hong Daquan. Perhaps Chen feared that by entrapping these underlings, he would cause a big commotion and later cause him to become a laughingstock. The order to execute Hong Daquan en route to the capital was never issued, however.

Wishful thinking ran to such an extent that maybe, by some strange chance, the man really was someone important. Another strong point of view held that, after he was interrogated in Beijing, the internal workings of the enemy might become better known.

—3—

"You're certainly an interesting character, aren't you?" Ding Shoucun said over and over again as he looked into Hong Daquan's face. To be sure, there was nothing the least bit interesting about Hong Daquan.

Hong had been expounding the cause of the Taiping Heavenly Kingdom from within the prisoner's cart en route. In general, his sources were *The Art of War* by the ancient Chinese military strategist Sunzi and the theories of the ancient Legalist philosopher Hanfeizi (ca. 280–233 B.C.). His arguments covered everything from strategy to tactics. Perhaps it would please them, he thought, if they came to admire his extraordinary knowledge or the wealth of his learning. However, just being interesting wasn't sufficient for Hong Daquan.

"I could preach to you all day long, but it won't do you any good, will it?" said Hong.

"I guess not. It's just not enough," laughed Ding pleasantly.

"There'll be better judges of character in the capital, better judges of my character."

"Is my eye for such things so poor?"

"Grand ministers from the Council of State or the ministers of the Six Ministries—men of that caliber will surely be better able to judge character."

"Well, I think you're overestimating them by far. There's nobody among that group with any eye for quality in men. They reserve their keenest insight for the old ladies in the rural villages."

"You're always making jokes. You're not sufficiently serious."

"I'm quite earnest about this. Believe me, I'm telling you the truth."

"Fine, I won't talk with you any longer. It's a waste of time. I'm just moving my lips in vain. Henceforth, I shall just discipline my mind so that, when we get to the capital, I can explain myself to an important official of the Council of State. Please don't interrupt me."

"Perish the thought. I won't get in your way," said Ding, shrugging his shoulders. In fact, Ding was disappointed in Hong.

Were Ding a man with aspirations and administrative experience, he would have tried to transcribe everything he had heard from Hong. For some reason, though, no one en route to Beijing seemed inclined to listen to what Hong was saying. Since such special desires and experiences were precious, Ding thought at least of preserving them for posterity by keeping a chronicle.

The one thing Hong had to excess was ambition. Sunzi and Hanfeizi merely served to embellish that ambition. They lacked any substance with him.

This is no good, thought Ding, if he has no more substance to him. The man's completely empty, except for some odd sort of courage.

Another operation came into Ding's head. Although he was looking at it with the level-headedness of a disinterested party, even Ding was not without worry for the future of the nation. Yet he distinguished the "nation" and the "dynasty" as separate entities. The dynasty was but a short-term attachment stuck onto the surface of the nation, which was eternal.

He was pondering the thought that, if things really got bad, they would have to replace the present dynasty. Entertaining such thoughts was an indication of the low level of his loyalty to the Qing dynasty. If the irreplaceable core was in critical danger, then he had to consider matters more seriously, and it seemed to him as though just such a time for serious thinking had arrived.

The Taipings had been thinking very seriously about this essential "core" and they had resorted to rebellion. They had reached the point at which they had no choice any longer but to rise up. Ding recorded their views and their thoughts in his own words. With this in mind, he tried to elicit more and more in this vein from Hong Daquan, but became disappointed to discover nothing beyond the surface.

Ding's evaluation was that Hong had been discarded by the Taipings. One could not hear the voice of the Taiping Heavenly Kingdom through this fellow, for Hong was outside the mainstream of the Taipings.

Ding's plan was to draw up in his own mind the "voice of the Taiping Heavenly Kingdom" and record it. It would be a literary work. Using the name Hong Daquan, he would bequeath this work to the future. Nor would it be at all difficult to do.

He decided simply to fill it up with his own thoughts. To write up just what he had wanted to say without any restraint ensured that offensive and even criminal statements would appear here and there. However, if these were the words of Hong Daquan, then Ding would have no need to fear punishment. He fully expected that Hong would be executed soon after arriving in the capital, and, as they say, dead men tell no tales.

Ding began to put his plan into operation. Everything he had long locked up in his heart he now began spewing out. Out it all came in succession, as Ding became absorbed in his work.

They were now nearing Beijing, and Ding regretted that he had not decided on his plan a little earlier. When they arrived at the capital, Hong Daquan was handed over in person to the Ministry of Justice. Far from an interview concerning the Taipings with an important official from the Council of State, nothing unusual was said, and an investigative official grilled him. This too was all mechanical. They merely looked to see that the new testimony jibed with the deposition taken at the scene.

Not one investigator so much as asked Hong about his political beliefs or wishes. On the contrary, the investigators themselves seemed to be in a state of panic, having been ordered by their superiors to deliver him to the gallows as soon as possible.

"Were you a sworn brother of Hong Xiuquan? No mistake about it?"

"Were you on intimate terms with Feng Yunshan and the others?"

These were merely confirmations of information already stated. They were questioning him in the form of the "preliminary memorandum." It was purely mechanical.

The sentence, which had been decided from the very start, was now handed down. He was to be executed in the cruelest manner. He was to be flayed alive, carrying the pain out for a long time until he finally died. He would then be decapitated and his head be put on public display.

The question of Hong Daquan's position in the Taiping organization became obscured. Sai-shang-a's dignity was barely preserved. Nothing was white or black. Everything was painted in shades of gray.

—4—

It would be an exaggeration to call it an official send-off party. It was something more like an ordinary gathering, what in today's parlance would be a social gathering to discuss the contemporary situation. On the twenty-second day of the sixth lunar month (July 28), Zeng Guofan, vice-minister in the Ministry of Rites, was ordered to make an official trip to Nanchang, Jiangxi province, in the capacity of principal examiner at the Jiangxi provincial civil service examinations.

Principal examiner was a short-term assignment, but Zeng had already received permission to return to his hometown after completion of business. Thirteen years had passed since he had left his home in Xiangxiang, Hunan province, and not once had he returned there in all these years. Having reached the position of a vice-minister by the age of forty (counting Chinese style), he wanted to make his journey home a triumphant one. His father, Zeng Linshu, had traveled to Beijing some ten years before, but since then they had not seen one another.

Ordinarily the business part of his trip would take two months, but he had received an additional three-month leave to return home. That meant that he would be out of the capital for nearly half a year, and naturally talk of a send-off party began to circulate among his friends.

Zeng himself firmly rejected the idea of overdoing it with a lavish send-off, so their get-together took its present form of a gathering to discuss contemporary politics. Lian Weicai was still in Beijing at the time, and it was decided that the gathering would take place under Lian's good offices.

"Wouldn't it be good to hear from Master Xinzhai?" suggested Zeng Guofan. Xinzhai was Ding Shoucun's style.

Master Xinzhai had gone to the heartland of the uprising in Guangxi as senior attendant to the imperial commissioner dispatched to suppress the Taipings. He had been in the whirlpool of the rebellion. He had also returned to the capital, escorting Hong Daquan, the alleged leader of the rebel army. Everyone wanted to hear what he had to say. Although he was receiving invitations from many quarters, Ding Shoucun suddenly disappeared. If the situation in Guangxi were to become widely known, it would probably aggravate matters.

Zeng and Ding had never gotten along very well. Ding had passed the metropolitan civil service examinations to become a metropolitan graduate two classes ahead of Zeng. As a rule, the capital examination that produced new metropolitan graduates was held once every three years. That was the regularly scheduled official examination. However, from time to time irregular examinations were held "at the gracious will" of the court, and these were hence known as "willed examinations." Through the 269 years of the Qing dynasty, metropolitan examinations were administered 112 times, of which 24 were of this "willed" variety.

Ding was a metropolitan graduate of 1835, the fifteenth year of the reign of the Daoguang emperor. Zeng attained the same degree three years later in 1838. However, since there was an intervening irregular examination in 1836, two classes of graduates separated the two men.

Zeng had achieved a successful career more rapidly than Ding, having become a vice-minister in the fourteenth year following attainment of the metropolitan graduate's degree. Ding had digressed from the main bureaucratic pathway, working on the production of land mines and the like. And he continued to steer clear of that main path.

Zeng was a stern, steadfast man. Every day he searched his heart and recorded his thoughts in his diary. He grieved that his scrupulousness and reflections were insufficient. By contrast, Ding was a man who earnestly sought out enjoyment. If he had gone astray from bureaucratic success, it was because of this search for enjoyment, and he had no regrets at all about it. It was not likely that two such polar opposites would get along.

As a statesman worried about national affairs, Zeng wanted to hear from Ding, who had been at the scene of trouble, about the true situation in Guangxi. He inquired, but Ding's whereabouts remained unknown. Even if he had known where Ding was residing, had Zeng gone there to question him, Ding would likely not have answered him directly.

The gathering now was a fortuitous opportunity. Even the stern Zeng Guofan knew the internal workings of the world of high officialdom in which he lived and operated. Zeng had surmised that Ding was receiving financial support from Lian Weicai. Perhaps the home in which Ding was now concealing himself had been provided to him by Lian.

Zeng guessed correctly that, if he relied on Lian Weicai, then perhaps Ding would appear. Ding did in fact attend the social gathering send-off for Zeng. The party was held at one of the two large restaurants within the city. At the time, high-level bureaucrats often made use of two such immense, high-class establishments, the Longfutang, or Hall of Abundant Happiness, and the Jubaotang, or Hall of Assembled Treasures. At Lian's wish, they selected the Hall of Assembled Treasures to meet.

Lian had come to like the place because, as he put it, "they don't flatter themselves in matters of taste." The great majority of famous restaurateurs had such self-importance as to find no value at all in the cuisine of any restaurant other than their own. The head chef as well as the proprietor of the Hall of Assembled Treasures, however, had the attitude that their restaurant had its distinctive tastes, as did other restaurants.

Thus, when dining at the Hall of Assembled Treasures, one could order particularly delectable dishes from other establishments as well. In addition to the course of dishes served that night at the Hall of Assembled Treasures, the following dishes from other restaurants were ordered:

1. Sea cucumber cooked in onion flavor, from the Fuxingju, or Residence of Flourishing Fortune

2. Boiled redfish, from the Zhimeizhai, or Villa of Enhanced Beauty

3. Cooked Duck, from the Bianyifang, or Store of Advantageousness

The Bianyifang was famous for its duck and chicken cuisine. Inasmuch as it only began serving its renowned Beijing Roast Duck from about 1855, it still was not on the menu at the time of Zeng Guofan's party. Something close to it in taste, however, seems to have been served.

Nearly twenty men comprised this assemblage—more than had been expected. When it was learned that Ding Shoucun was coming, those who ordinarily would not have shown up responded that they would be in attendance.

"You have asked me to recount for you the true state of affairs, but the true state of affairs requires but a word. At present, the dynastic forces are not defeating the Taiping rebels. Any talk of victory at this point would be unreasonable," began Ding. The whole company fell silent.

"When I planned to say this," continued Ding, "I was wondering whether the response would be commotion or dead silence. If it was commotion, then you would all have found my words completely unexpected. If silence, that would have meant you all agreed with me. And thus I addressed you. Hence, even without my detailing the true state of affairs, you all seem to have gleaned it for yourselves. That being the case, my description is beside the point. The actual situation of the dynastic armies is exactly as you know it to be, though there is no reason to expect you to know the state of the Taiping bandits. Probably you have asked me here today, then, to hear from me the state of affairs primarily of the Taipings."

Silence followed this speech. And of course, it was precisely as Ding has stated.

—5—

From the perspective of an impartial observer, it was more than clear. Wishful thinking impinged on Ding Shoucun's judgment not a whit. Standing at the side of the imperial commissioner, he was not in the forefront, but his description of the "enemy" had captured the uninterrupted attention of his audience. Unlike the embellished accounts of the war scene sent to Beijing, what they were hearing from Ding was a live report from someone who had been there. He had acquired a variety of intelligence from the local populace living on land through which the Taipings had passed. People who had come into direct contact with the Taiping Army, while keeping their distance from those serving the government, praised the uprightness of the Taipings' military discipline. Merchants who had sold them goods recounted that they paid fair prices for everything purchased.

Ding had also heard many of the voices of the government troops who had actually fought the Taipings in the field. They revealed some interesting information. They were uniformly stunned to find that the troops that the Taipings fielded existed anywhere in the world, and this sense of surprise was intriguing to Ding.

Ding's manner of describing the Taipings was inclined neither toward the government nor toward the Taipings. It was full neither of regret nor of contemplation. Spoken in a tone of disinterestedness, it had an almost ghastly uncanniness about it.

Yet, for all his dispassionate tone, he was not without emotion. As was his wont, Ding did have something on the order of the feelings of a third party. When he was speaking, however, he did everything he could to suppress those feelings. Ding had other places at which he could express his own feelings and intentions clearly. Thus, he had not mixed them into his discussion the night of Zeng Guofan's farewell party.

A gloomy atmosphere seemed to hover over the assemblage. Ding was thinking to himself that he had to transform this melancholy at the earliest possible juncture.

"As you all know, I have escorted back to Beijing the Taiping leader who calls himself Hong Daquan. He underwent a formal interrogation at the Ministry of Justice, though one would have expected he would not volunteer information and that he would hide as much as he could so as not to act to his own disadvantage. This was my thinking on the matter, so I soothed and comforted him en route to Beijing, firmly promising him that I would absolutely never publicly reveal anything he said to me, and offering him the opportunity to open his mind frankly to me. Even this Hong Daquan seemed to have something about which he wanted to appeal very strongly. After all, rebellion is itself a form of appeal. When I inquired of him if there were someone to whom he wanted to appeal, he responded graciously that he would like to appeal to his majesty the emperor. . . . So, I told him to spit out everything on his mind in the form of a memorial to the emperor, and he wrote it down meticulously as we traveled to the capital. Of course, his sentences are clumsy. And, since there are Hunanese colloquialisms mixed into the text, it was rather difficult, so I have touched it up here and there. Nonetheless, the content reveals what has accumulated in his heart, and hence it reveals what has accumulated in the minds of the long-haired bandits who have extended their rebellion from Guangxi into Hunan. Although I made this firm promise to Hong Daquan, he has now been executed, and there is no longer anything which can be of further disadvantage to him. Thus I have brought this text with me today to present it to you learned gentlemen and encourage you to read it. I have preserved the original. This is but a copy, although I wanted to be sure that Mr. Zeng Guofan would have a chance, before his departure, to be able to look it over. Please feel free to circulate it later."

Ding then pulled out an envelope from the package he was carrying under his arm.

Zeng left Beijing on the twenty-fourth day of the sixth lunar month—September 9 according to the solar calendar—in the midst of a fierce heat wave. The very next day, the Taipings abandoned Daozhou and began their march to the east, but Zeng, of course, did not know this.

Hong Daquan's memorial to the throne, which Zeng read prior to his departure, shocked him greatly. He had been well aware of the fact that they were a serious foe, but in contemplating matters as a high official he had not expected that the Taipings would overrun Hunan with such apparent ease. Upon hearing that they had moved south from Yongzhou, like others of his colleagues, he had anticipated that they would return to Guangxi.

In point of fact, there were voices within the Taiping Army that wanted to return to their homes in Guangxi. Yang Xiuqing, the Taipings' real military commander, curbed such voices and pressed ahead with his original plan to march northward. When Zeng entered Suzhou in Anhui province from Xuzhou, he met with the elderly Zhou Tianjue, who had been relieved of his post as governor of Guangxi.

"It's no good," said Zhou. "We couldn't suppress them even when Xiang Rong was around. It's out of the question with you."

When Zhou was in Guilin, he had censured Guangxi Provincial Military Commander Xiang Rong. However, it was Xiang Rong who had remained in Guangxi, while Zhou lived to a ripe old age relieved of his position. Zhou was an eloquent man for eighty years of age, but he was just attacking the provincial military commander. He didn't so much as touch on the nature of the enemy they were now facing. Zeng was disgruntled by how such old men just got in the way.

Due to an unforeseen incident in which an official seal was stolen, Zhou had been relieved of his post as director-general of grain transport, and for seven years he had been deprived of his livelihood. At this point, it was his deep-seated bitterness that kept him going. As far as Zhou was concerned, the enemy was his colleagues who struggled for meritorious distinctions, and he was startlingly unconcerned about the Taiping rebels, who were on the march his way and were armed. To Zeng Guofan's questions, he offered answers that were not the least pertinent. He was even dubious about any differentiation between the Society of God Worshippers and the Heaven and Earth Society. As governor of Guangxi, and even simultaneously as imperial commissioner, he had made not a single honest inquiry into the nature of the enemy. Although Zhou had been appointed as a result of the death of Lin Zexu, the court had admittedly been uncertain in this personnel matter.

When the Guangxi discussion came to an end, the old man began meandering his way through old stories.

"More than twenty years ago, I worked for a time as departmental magistrate of Suzhou here in Anhui. That place really brings back memories." At an appropriate moment during Zhou's reminiscences, Zeng departed.

Zeng's present business was taking him to Jiangxi province, and hence he traveled from southeastern Anhui, across the Yangzi River, and into Jiujiang. He then proceeded south as far as Nanchang. From that point, had he discontinued his southern movement and gone due west, he would have come to Hubei province. To the south was Zeng's native Hunan. His taking up this new appointment in Jiangxi had the added attraction of being close to his home.

About 80 kilometers to the west of Anqing was a county by the name of Taihu. Twelve days following his departure from Suzhou and Zhou Tianjue, Zeng arrived at the small city of Xiaochi, just to the east of Taihu. The county magistrate of Taihu came out to greet him.

As vice-minister in the Ministry of Rites, Zeng was a high-ranking official of the central government. For the local county magistrate, Zeng seemed almost a court noble. Zeng had been courteously received at various locales throughout his travels. Often, county magistrates had come to the entrance of the county seat to welcome him personally. However, this was the first time that a county magistrate had purposefully traveled for as long as a full day to a specific spot to meet him.

Zeng felt immediately uneasy and wondered what had caused such behavior. The welcoming was altogether out of the ordinary, and the magistrate of Taihu had a pained, sad look upon his face. With his head bent, he approached Zeng, lowered his head deeply, and said, "I must convey bad news to you. . . . Your mother has passed away. Yesterday this news was delivered to Taihu, and I must now convey it to you, sir."

Tears welled up in Zeng's eyes, and several times one could make out efforts to hold back the sobs at the back of his throat.

"Thank you for bringing this information from such a great distance."

Zeng and the county magistrate traveled together to Taihu, and there they commenced the necessary procedures with respect to Beijing. He would have to excuse himself from serving as the provincial principal examiner, inasmuch as any official who lost a parent had to immediately begin a period of mourning in his hometown.

He would have to alter his present status to one defined by the loss of his mother and the necessity of repairing to his hometown for, in principle, a period of twenty-seven months in which he could assume no official business whatsoever. The death of his mother, née Jiang, occurred on the twelfth day of the sixth lunar month—exactly the same day he was to begin his assignment as local examiner.

In the notices from his hometown to that point, there had been no mention that her health had become particularly bad. She was an old woman, but she did not seem to have been bedridden long.

He left Taihu for Jiujiang, just as planned, but then where he should have headed south from Jiujiang, he decided to travel by boat west along the Yangzi. Traveling upstream, he went on land at Huangzhou and set out for Wuchang. Wuchang was on the southern shore of the Yangzi, across the river from Hanyang and Hankou to the north. Together they formed the three Wuhan cities, today simply called, Wuhan.

Hubei Governor Chang Dachun welcomed Zeng at the governor's office, and, after conveying his condolences, said, "I can readily appreciate your desire to pay your respects before your late mother's coffin as quickly as possible, but it seems you shall have to remain here for a short time."

"Why is that?"

"Changsha has been surrounded by the Taiping rebels."

"What?" said Zeng in surprise. He had learned before leaving the capital that the Taiping forces had taken refuge in the frontier regions of Hunan. It had subsequently come to his attention that Jiang Zhongyuan's army of Hunan braves had inflicted a stinging defeat on the Taipings at Suoyi Ford. Jiang had been recommended by Zeng, and Zeng had exulted at news of Jiang's activities.

He later got word that the Taipings were moving toward southern Hunan. It was still unclear when he left Beijing whether they intended to return to Guangxi along byroads or head to the north for a respite.

Perhaps it had all been wishful thinking, but the central government's perspective was that the Taipings, having lost Feng Yunshan at Suoyi Ford, seemed to have lost the momentum they had gathered to that point. In every rebellion there were waves of movement. The encirclement of Guilin was the Taiping bandits' high point, and thereafter they had been on the decline. The battle at Suoyi Ford was ample proof of this. Clearly, they were running out of strength.

At the time of the gathering at the Hall of Assembled Treasures, Ding Shoucun had stressed the power of the Taipings. The capital officials in attendance that evening, including Zeng Guofan, were stunned at what he had to say, but those who knew Ding later discounted much of this, because they knew just how much he enjoyed shocking people.

Zeng arrived in Wuchang on 8/13 (September 26), the forty-eighth day after leaving Beijing. During that time, the Taipings had implemented plans to expand their forces in southern Hunan, invigorating their troops sufficiently to strike north, en masse.

"The Taipings closed in on the South Gate of Changsha fifteen days ago," said Chang Dachun. "They've attacked from the direction of Liling to the southeast. They came in a straight line—no detours."

Zeng's hometown of Xiangxiang was to the southwest of Changsha. It had not been on the pathway of the Taipings. Chang Dachun intended to reassure Zeng that his hometown had not been occupied by the rebels.

"So, I'll continue my trip as planned," said Zeng.

"The sea route has already been blocked by the bandits. That would be exceedingly dangerous."

"I shall take a roundabout route, from Yuezhou by land, and I'll worry about other matters after returning to Xiangxiang."

"I see . . . I can understand your feelings in this matter. Since you speak with such determination, I most certainly shall not detain you further. I shall place a military guard at your disposal, and please be very careful."

"Thank you. You too, Master Chang, be very careful. For the country as well," said Zeng, offering his senior colleague this highest expression of honor and respect.

Chang Dachun was a man of Hengzhou in Hunan province, a metropolitan graduate of 1823, and thus, from Zeng's perspective, a fellow Hunanese fifteen years his senior. He had been transferred from the governorship of Zhejiang to that of Hubei, though he had just received word of his reassignment as governor of Shanxi.

Be that as it may, the Taipings were encircling Changsha, the capital city of Hunan, and the governorship in the neighboring province of Hubei could hardly be changed at such a time. At present he remained in Wuchang with the strange status of "Hubei governor transferred to Shanxi governor."

With an armed guard of two men, Zeng avoided the waterways, and taking a circuitous route through the mountains, headed for Xiangxiang. Chang

Dachun saw him off as far as the gate of Wuchang, there bidding him fare-well. That this might be the final parting between these two men was as distant a thought as a dream for either man. The Taipings attacked Wuchang four months later, and Chang died at his post in defense of the city.

Zeng reached Xiangxiang some ten days later. His father had aged con-siderably, and a gloomy atmosphere permeated the entire family home. His mother had died, and now the Taipings had attacked the provincial capital.

17

Changsha Summer

—1—

Lian Liwen had been recuperating in Changsha. Although the wounds he had received at Suoyi Ford were not terribly serious, he was well-advised not to overtax his remaining strength. This, at least, was his own thinking on the matter. Compared to his wounds, those inflicted at Suoyi Ford on the entire Taiping military were considerably more acute. They had had to alter their plans to attack Changsha after leaving Yongzhou and passing through Hengzhou. In order to replenish personnel and supplies, they abandoned efforts to move north and headed south from Yongzhou toward Daozhou.

While the Taipings were replenishing supplies, Liwen convalesced. If they were able to preserve sufficient strength, the Taipings intended to move on Changsha next. That much had been clear from the start. Thus, as Liwen recuperated in Changsha, he was in effect waiting for the Taiping Army.

Li Xinmei had come to Changsha with Liwen. The massacre of the populace at Quanzhou by the Taipings having left her in despair, she had parted company with the armed forces and hence had not been injured on the battlefield. However, the injury to her heart at Quanzhou was indescribably profound.

Liwen and Xinmei, he with his physical wound and she with her spiritual wound, were each in their own way healing in Changsha. Beside the walled city of Changsha to the west flowed the Xiang River. Liwen and Xinmei often took a boat out on the water. There they relaxed, read books, or hung a fishing line over the side.

The battle at Suoyi Ford had taken place on June 10. Afterward they had slowly come down the Xiang River to Changsha, where it was already the height of summer. There were so many rivers and lakes in the region that Changsha was often dubbed, "the water realm." Its summers were very hot, and boat excursions were aimed at cooling things off a bit.

There were two islands in the river—Shuiluzhou and Fujiazhou—nearby.

"Go to the west of Fujiazhou," Liwen directed the boatman each time they went out on the Xiang River.

"Liwen, you really like it there, don't you? You told the boatman to go west of Fujiazhou the last time we came here too," said Xinmei.

"Yes, I do like it. It's really the best place because you can see the Yinpen Mountains," responded Liwen.

"But always the same place. You are the sort of person who sticks to things he likes the first time. Just like with the Taipings. Once you came to like the Taipings, even what occurred at Quanzhou couldn't alter your feelings about them."

"True enough, true enough . . ."

"It is true. You have a strong sense of duty. You're the kind of person who would be loyal even to people not of this world."

"Ha, ha." Liwen was distracted by his own laughter.

Although they were on very good terms, Xinmei nonetheless sensed that there was a small door into Liwen's mind that remained unopened. On the other side of that door, his late wife still lived. Perhaps it was woman's intuition that enabled Xinmei to understand this.

"In fact, here," Liwen said, tapping the side of the boat, after laughing, "is the place where Lin Gongbao set sail en route from Yunnan back to Fujian province. I've heard the story from my father and wanted to come here."

Lin Gongbao was, of course, none other than Lin Zexu. When he lost his aged wife, while serving as governor-general of Yunnan province, Lin was permitted to resign the following year by reason of his advanced age. He returned to his hometown via Hunan, commemorating the first anniversary of her death in Changsha. He brought her coffin directly from Yunnan, and the Buddhist ceremony of commemorating her death was said to have been carried out on board a boat.

That was just like Master Lin, Liwen's father had said at the time.

Liwen had heard from his father that Lin Zexu had talked all through the night with a man by the name of Zuo Zongtang, at a point on the Xiang River to the west of Fujiazhou, from which the Yinpen Mountains could be seen.

Liwen's father had also met Zuo Zongtang and offered this evaluation of his character: "Master Zuo is also a man of great ability, but he is far from

Master Lin in terms of being a well-rounded person. It's regrettable, but perhaps irreparable."

When Zuo first visited Lin in person aboard Lin's boat, he reportedly lost his footing and fell into the water. This wasn't the only such story concerning him, for there were any number of stories in which he seemed prone to some sort of performance. Liwen had found it interesting to try to imagine just what sort of man Zuo really was, but he was ultimately drawn to this spot to the west of Fujiazhou island by the attraction of Lin Zexu.

"I've heard a lot from you about Lin Gongbao. There it is again. Once you've gained esteem for someone, you follow them to the end. Didn't Lin die recently?" said Xinmei.

"That's right. He died the year before last. It happened en route to his post in Guangxi as imperial commissioner. He was replaced by Li Xingyuan and later by Sai-shang-a, both of whom we've now faced in battle."

"So, you would have had to face Master Lin in battle too."

"Maybe. Death is certainly not a happy event, but . . . frankly, though, it was fortunate as far as I am concerned."

"They say sailing often brings back memories of the dead." Xinmei was adhering to the subject of the deceased, and her adherence was right on the mark. Although captivated by Lin Zexu, what Liwen recalled of his hero on the Xiang River was the transporting of the coffin of his late wife. His humanity was genuinely endearing.

Standing by his side, Xinmei well knew that the visage of Liwen's own late wife had not grown the least bit faint. A woman unaware of this probably could have not been drawn to Liwen.

"I remember the living well, too. I remember now what sort of man it was who came to visit Master Lin on that boat on the Xiang River," said Liwen.

"What kind of man?"

"He tried to leave an indelible impression on Master Lin at their first meeting. And what do you think he did?"

"Well, something so that he would always be remembered? Something really crazy?"

"He tripped on a plank on the boat and fell into the river."

"That's perfect. Never to be forgotten, ha, ha," laughed Xinmei.

"He resides around here, so we'll probably meet him soon. He's quite a famous man."

"Is he an official?"

"No. He passed the provincial level of the civil service examinations, but he hasn't gone into public service. He's famous as a scholar. His name if Zuo Zongtang."

—2—

As mentioned earlier, what the Chinese called *yudi bingfa* entailed a branch of learning concerned with geography, history, politics, military strategy, and tactics. It was an area of scholarship of considerable utility in the practice of Realpolitik, and although he was considered the greatest authority on the subject, Zuo Zongtang had never held a bureaucratic post. Zuo came from a celebrated family in Xiangyin in Hunan province. Due to a familial tie with Tao Zhu, governor-general of Jiangsu and Zhejiang, he had lived as a guest of the Tao family and spent his life in leisure away from the political realm. That was, at least, how it seemed to outside observers.

His own sensibility, however, was not necessarily at ease. Perhaps it was because of an inflated sense of personal importance, but no matter how many times he sat for the metropolitan examinations, he had always failed. He thus remained stuck, unable to reach that pinnacle of becoming a metropolitan graduate.

The bureaucratic world stressed above all else qualifications and a seniority system, and it was exceedingly difficult to succeed in that environment without having passed the metropolitan examination. That would have been fine for a man who was content with a moderate position in life, but Zuo Zongtang was a man whose pride could envelop the entire length and breadth of China. In Lian Weicai's estimation as well, Zuo was a man with whom it might be problematic to live in harmony.

"A man of outstanding capacities in times of chaos"—this was Lian's assessment.

In a time of peace, such a man would find it difficult to distinguish himself, but in troubled times his pride and overweening individuality might be just enough to elicit great deeds. In such times, no one would quibble about qualifications and seniority, and there would be opportunities for the likes of Zuo Zongtang, even without his having attained the metropolitan graduate's degree.

Times were headed directly for chaos. In fact, they were already smack in the middle of such times, and an era of the sort Zuo had eagerly awaited, in which genuine competence would become the standard.

There had been a preliminary announcement, a harbinger. When Lin Zexu was serving as governor-general of Yunnan and Guizhou, he had once sought Zuo to join his staff. Lin appointed two men to the important positions as prefectural magistrates, to serve as his left- and right-hand men. These two men were Zhang Liangji and Hu Linyi. Hu was the son-in-law of Tao Zhu, and a metropolitan graduate in his own right. However, he had been demoted for a small impropriety while serving as assistant examiner at the

Jiangnan provincial examinations. Thereafter, his father passed away, and he was unable to serve in any official capacity because he was in ceremonial mourning. Lin Zexu nonetheless forcibly summoned him from Hunan and made him a prefect in Guizhou province.

Hu recommended Zuo Zongtang as far more talented than himself, having gotten to know him well during the time both men spent in the circle around Tao Zhu. Lin then tried to invite Zuo to join him as well. At the time, though, the family of Tao Zhu was entangled in a lawsuit, and Zuo was charged with resolving it and was thus unable to leave Hunan.

Zhang Liangji had served, along with Hu Linyi, as an assistant to the governor-general of Yunnan and Guizhou. He hailed from Tongshan in Jiangsu province, and had also only passed the provincial level of the imperial examinations. He was, however, a man of remarkable talents, and Lin Zexu promoted him from prefect to surveillance commissioner, and subsequently to provincial administration commissioner.

After Lin left Yunnan, Zhang was promoted to Yunnan provincial governor because of the great success he had in resolving the disputes that had arisen between ethnic Han Chinese and the local Muslim population. Lin had offered him a chance, and Zhang had secured the station of governor on the basis of his competence.

During the period when the Taipings occupied Daozhou en route from Guangxi to Hunan, an attempt was made in Beijing to recall Hunan Governor Luo Bingzhang (1793–1867), whom Sai-shang-a had censured. But who would replace the governor of Hunan? Zhang Liangji was selected for the job.

Hunan had become a perennial battle zone, and high-ranking administrative officials could not be incompetents. No matter how brilliant a career he may have had to that point, an incompetent was useless now. One's ranking by achievement in the civil service examinations was, of course, of no help in the least. They needed someone who had genuine work experience, someone who had faced difficult problems and solved them. It seemed only natural that Zhang Liangji's name came up at the court in Beijing at this time. He was the governor who was credited with resolving the local troubles in Yunnan.

"Hunan Governor Luo Bingzhang is recalled to Beijing, and Yunnan Governor Zhang Liangji is assigned the governorship of Hunan. Gansu Provincial Administration Commissioner Huang Zonghan is assigned the governorship of Yunnan." This personnel order was issued on June 21, just eleven days following the battle at Suoyi Ford.

In this personnel turnover, the abrupt summoning of Luo to the capital was quashed, and it was changed to the effect that he see to increased defense preparations in advance of the new governor's arrival. It was a long way from Yunnan to Hunan, and a certain amount of time would pass before Zhang could take up his new post. Reinforcing defenses was a burning necessity at the time. It seemed appropriate that Luo Bingzhang remain behind. He not only knew Hunan well, but it was expected that he probably knew the enemy well too. He was, after all, a fellow provincial—from Huaxian, Guangdong province—of Hong Xiuquan, Heavenly King of the Taipings.

All sorts of stories were concocted about these two men from the same home province who now found themselves enemies on the field of battle. One tale that circulated widely told of a time when the two of them as boys were studying at the same school, and they exchanged stories of their future ambitions. Hong was reported to have said, "I'm gonna be emperor." And Luo responded, "I'm gonna crush anyone who rises in rebellion and tries to be emperor."

In that year Hong Xiuquan, Heavenly King of the Taipings, who marched into Hunan, turned thirty-eight; Luo Bingzhang, the dismissed governor of Hunan, was about to celebrate his sixtieth birthday the next year. Because of the age difference of over twenty years, it was hardly possible that the two men, despite the fact that they hailed from the same locality, were schoolmates. Even though the story was an obvious fabrication, it seemed to be a little too much so.

Over the next ten or more years, Luo became fatally linked to the Taipings in battle. When Taiping general Shi Dakai invaded Sichuan some years later, Luo, as governor-general of that province, subdued his forces. He was one of the most important people in the history of the Taiping movement, though his first connection with it came as a result of the abrogation of his being recalled to the capital, and hence, he almost missed contact with the Taipings altogether.

Censure from Imperial Commissioner Sai-shang-a was the cause of his being summoned to Beijing. The supposed reason for the censure was responsibility for allowing the Taipings to march into Hunan. In his entry in the famous work *Biographies from the History of the Qing Dynasty*, there is a sentence that declares that the fall of Daozhou was due to errors in his defense of it. The official announcement of his recall, however, was issued nine days after the fall of Daozhou, when news of that defeat had surely not reached the capital.

"The administration in Hunan is slackening." This accusation by the imperial commissioner reached Beijing first. As noted earlier, he had been given the sword of Ebilun, and when he was imperial commissioner heading toward Guangxi, he had publicly ordered an official expedition to Hunan. There was no more than a peasant uprising in Guangxi, and he apparently believed that sending an imperial commissioner such as himself there was beneath his dignity. Thus, Sai-shang-a sent in observational reports on Hunan as well, such as his censure of the governor of the province for responsibility in a lax administration.

En route to Guangxi from Beijing, Sai-shang-a was in a state of extreme ill humor upon entering Hunan. None of the receptions there by local officials were pleasing to him. First and foremost, he was not offered a single good meal. There was no evidence of improvements in housing and other facilities to accommodate the passage of the imperial commissioner. When he queried a local official on this account, he was told, "I have received no special orders concerning the welcoming of the imperial commissioner."

Sai-shang-a smacked the table with his hand and became indignant.

"So, you say you received no special orders. Don't you know that an imperial commissioner carries out the emperor's designs?"

His animosity left a trail.

Shocked by the alarming situation in Hunan, the imperial court in Beijing hurriedly considered a counterplan. After studying the reports of the imperial commissioner, it was decided, "We must change the governor, the man responsible for the loosening of provincial administration."

Later the recall was reconsidered. Luo Bingzhang remained in office for over two years in Hunan, perhaps on account of his considerable knowledge of local provincial circumstances and his common origin with the leader of the Taiping forces. Perhaps as well his cooperation was sought with his compatriot from Yunnan days, Zhang Liangji, the man who was to succeed him as governor.

When Luo had served as provincial administration commissioner for Yunnan, the number two post in the province, Zhang had been serving as surveillance commissioner there, the number three post (a position comparable to a chief of police and head prosecutor). After Luo was promoted to governor of Hunan, Zhang was promoted to provincial administration commissioner. Upon investigation, it was learned that the two men had worked well together in Yunnan. Thus, when Luo was demoted by three grades, he remained on in Changsha.

By the same token, as Zhang was to take up his new appointment as governor of Hunan, he requested of Beijing that "Hu Linyi be transferred to Hunan." Hu was born in Yiyang, Hunan, and he was well-versed in the ways of his native province. Hu Linyi was then prefect of Liping prefecture in Guizhou province, however, and the governor of Guizhou refused to release him, not wanting to lose such an able man as Hu from among his subordinates. Because of the Guizhou governor's resistance, Hu's transfer was held up for over a year before it could be realized.

Although unable to proceed to Hunan together with Zhang Liangji, Hu suggested that Zhang "by all means employ Zuo Zongtang in Hunan. He's a very useful fellow."

The court in Beijing decided to send one more governor-level official to Hunan, Luo Raodian. Three years previously, Luo had been promoted from the position of Guizhou provincial administration commissioner to the governorship of Hubei, but he had resigned to take up mourning upon the death of his father. His mourning now completed, he was of a status necessitating his reinstatement as a governor somewhere. He came from Anhua in the province of Hunan and thus, it was expected, knew local conditions well. In addition, he had been Guizhou provincial administration commissioner at the same time that Lin Zexu was serving as the governor-general of Yunnan and Guizhou, and he had experience as well in dealing with disputes with the local Muslim population.

As the court saw it, "there's no reason to let such a man remain idle." While Imperial Commissioner Sai-shang-a remained in Guilin, capital of Guangxi province, there would be no movement on this front. The imperial court in Beijing ordered him "to proceed to Hunan with no further delay." Luo Raodian was then ordered "to proceed to Hunan and assist the imperial commissioner." People at the time noted that "there were three governors in Hunan."

We have described the personalities on the side of the Qing government in such detail because it is crucial to the history of the Taiping movement. With the inclusion of Zeng Guofan, who was then at home in mourning, all of the important Qing personages who would be responsible for the "subjugation" of the Taipings were all present and accounted for at this stage of the drama.

—3—

The administrative official with highest responsibility for the provinces of Hunan and Hubei was known as the Huguang governor-general. The "guang" element in the title had nothing to do with either Guangdong or Guangxi. When this person, on occasion, also had jurisdiction over Sichuan, he was called the Chuanhu governor-general, but such periods were always extremely short.

The Huguang governor-general at the time that the government was under attack by Taiping forces was, unfortunately for the Qing dynasty, an incompetent, cowardly man by the name of Cheng Yucai (d. 1858). Following Lin Zexu's retirement, Cheng succeeded him as the governor-general of Yunnan and Guizhou. Later, two years prior to the events at hand, Cheng was transferred to the position of Huguang governor-general. Oddly enough, many of those connected with Hunanese affairs at this time had held positions in Yunnan and Guizhou, and Cheng Yucai was among them.

The Huguang governor-general had been in Hengzhou, and begrudgingly so. Originally, the governor-general's residence was located in Wuhan, Hubei province. Ordered to Hunan, he was nearer to the war zone, which caused him no end of worry.

The governor-general's procession moved from the Hunan provincial capital of Changsha to Hengzhou in the south. He assumed the pose of a commander leading his forces into battle. His staff told him to do so, and he had no choice but to follow their direction. And, so, he had remained in Hengzhou since the previous year.

On the day following the arrival in Hengzhou of the news of the fall of Quanzhou, the staff became panicked as the governor-general seemed to have disappeared. Eventually, a letter was discovered in the documents box upon his desk. A subordinate read its content, all the time with a dubious look on his face: "I have been suffering from a chronic ailment, but I did not want to make my staff members worry over this situation. Thus, I have not divulged the information. Since yesterday, the pain of my illness has become difficult to bear, and I decided to have a trustworthy doctor secretly examine me. After hearing the doctor's diagnosis, I plan to return soon. I should like things to be left as they are."

One of the staff members who had known the governor-general for a long, long time said, "Since yesterday? Aside from the fact that at mealtime he ate more than he ever has, there was nothing the least unusual. This is very strange." He was shaking his head.

"Nothing's changed about that, has it?" He was referring to the governor-general's penchant for cowardice.

The governor-general had fled from Hengzhou in ordinary clothing under cover of night and headed for Changsha by river. He wasn't the least bit sick. When he heard news of the defeat of the Taipings at Suoyi Ford and their march further to the south, he returned to Hengzhou from Changsha.

"I'm sorry, very sorry, but I didn't want to exaggerate matters. You see, I needed some quiet recuperation. My work as governor-general is quite afflicting," he said with an air of perfect nonchalance.

Around the time of the Taipings' withdrawal from Guilin, the court in Beijing ordered Xu Guangjin, governor-general of Guangdong and Guangxi, to repair to Guangxi and cooperate with the imperial commissioner. Although only for a few months, six years ago Xu Guangjin had also served as the governor of Yunnan.

Xu had considerable success in Guangdong in the suppression of a group within the Society of God Worshippers under the command of Ling Shiba.

This had won him high praise, and in addition, he simultaneously gained a certain success as the official responsible for commerce in negotiations with the British. Clearly, he was a talented individual.

The atmosphere at the imperial court in Beijing—that "this was a man who could, come what may, get things done"—became relentlessly critical of the dilatory Imperial Commissioner Sai-shang-a, and calls were heard for the latter's dismissal. Eventually, Sai-shang-a was removed from office and replaced by Xu Guangjin.

The chaotic situation among the Qing authorities was communicated to the Taipings in Chenzhou. The majority of the government's troops in Hunan had been moved to Guangxi, but they had yet to return. This information too, it was learned, was generally corroborated.

Taiping commanders and soldiers both had come, as a result of battle, to see the government's armies as being far from a formidable force. Only Jiang Zhongyuan's army of braves was tough and unyielding on the field, and it had been they who had inflicted the heavy losses on the Taipings at Suoyi Ford. However, the braves were limited in number.

"If their numbers increase, then that could be a problem for us," said Yang Xiuqing.

Hong Xiuquan continued reading books and writing documents, while entrusting practical military affairs to Yang. Through the collection of intelligence, something at which Yang was especially proficient, he learned that there was movement on the part of the Qing authorities to increase the size of the brave armies. That was a problem.

"What should we do?" asked the Western King, Xiao Chaogui, impatiently. His wife, Xuanjiao, was the younger sister of Hong Xiuquan. Xiao looked at the increasing power of Yang Xiuqing and felt that balance had to be maintained on behalf of Hong Xiuquan. Otherwise, Hong Xiuquan would pay no attention at all to military matters.

Power grew out of the army. Xiao Chaogui was thinking that he was well-advised to accrue to himself as much power within the military as he could. To that end, he had to distinguish himself on the field of battle. How would he be able to do so? In order to apprise himself of the present situation, he had no choice but to ask Yang Xiuqing.

"There is the means of a surprise attack," said Yang, with a serious look on his face. "The larger Jiang Zhongyuan's army gets, the more trouble for us. I've heard reports of reinforcements coming from Henan, Hubei, and Shaanxi. It behooves us to move quickly on this."

"The faster the better," said Xiao, with arms folded.

"Changsha's just an empty mouth."

"What do you mean?"

"They're not doing anything there. Just having meetings from morning till night."

"Meetings of officials?"

It was self-evident that he was evading both explanations and responsibility. But, Yang Xiuqing was speaking the truth.

With his period of mourning completed, former Hubei Governor Luo Raodian had come to Changsha, but all they seemed to be doing was gathering a group of youngsters together and holding debating sessions. Luo himself enjoyed giving speeches. As soon as he arrived in Changsha, a group of gabbers emerged, and he apparently was happy to serve as the group's leader.

Rumor had it that there were no troops in Changsha, just conversationalists. Wouldn't this be the perfect time for a surprise attack?

"Let's do it," said Xiao in a shrill, nervous voice.

To proceed with the surprise raid on Changsha, Western King Xiao Chaogui departed Chenzhou on August 26. It was only the ninth day following their occupation of Chenzhou, an indication of the speed at which the Taipings were now moving. With a local rebel force that knew the terrain well as their guide, they headed first for Yongxing, and there killed the local county magistrate, Wen Dexuan.

Because of the surprise nature of the attack, they did not mobilize the entire army en masse. To march with such a large force would slow them down considerably, and they had to move with as little equipment and as lightly as possible. Two deputy commanders, Li Kaifang and Lin Fengxiang, served under the Western King, with a total force of roughly two thousand men.

Following the river north from Yongxing, they moved directly toward Hengzhou. The Taipings had learned that the main force of the Qing military, from the governor on down, was in Hengzhou. Thus, they avoided that course altogether, advanced to the northeast, occupied Anren county, and took control of Chaling. The region was one of intense Heaven and Earth Society activity, and the Taipings were able to recruit several thousand new members in Chaling.

Even without planning to build a large military force, their troop strength grew as they marched. They then proceeded further north and occupied Liling, a town that had become famous at this time for its pottery. Their aim was to march on to Changsha, and the reason for occupying terrain was simply so that they could gain a foothold for their advancing forces.

The next day, they abandoned Liling, without regrets. It was the thirteenth day after their departure from Chenzhou. On that very day, Zeng Guofan learned in Xiaochi (Anhui province) of the death of his mother.

Having arrived this close to the city, they gained much intelligence about conditions in Changsha, and not a single home in the southern environs of the city had yet been destroyed. It was common practice in warfare at that time to prepare for an enemy attack by destroying the homes outside a city's walls, thus depriving the enemy of a base of operations. However, that could not be done in Changsha.

Luo Raodian, the man receiving a governor's stipend, did nothing but carry on with his "debating groups," offering countless opinions and never reaching any conclusions. Needless to say, the local residents were opposed to the practice of tearing down the homes outside the city. Since there was an opposition point of view on this issue, the evacuation from those homes had never been carried out.

The real governor had yet to arrive to take up his post. Luo Bingzhang, sacked but remaining on the scene, refrained from interfering in the discussions in which his equally ranked colleague Luo Raodian was engaged. Indeed, there were too many leaders and not enough followers.

Unlike the question of the evacuation of local homes, there was no opposition to the plan of reinforcing the city walls, for no one wished to sustain injuries because of breaches in the walls. The walls around Changsha had suffered considerable damage. There were also spots too weak to sustain attacks. Luo Bingzhang worked assiduously to reinforce the walls at these points. One day, a letter from Governor-General Cheng arrived. "I have heard that you are engaged in reinforcing and extending the city walls. Although I am not opposed to this effort, is it true that the expenditures for construction laborers runs to a twenty percent increase? The times are extraordinary, and it's okay to requisition coolie labor, but I shall not assume responsibility for recruiting labor through increased wages. Please be apprised of this position."

Luo read the letter and laughed out loud: "Again, as usual. . ." He knew full well how Governor-General Cheng Yucai operated. The governor-general was most nervous about the possibility of an audit by the central government. If accounting were on a firm foundation and expenditures were brought under control, then the status of a high official would never come into question. To be sure, he was exacting to the point of fastidiousness when it came to public funds. His reduced budgeting had once actually received high praise from the central government. In an era when featherbedding was the rule rather than the exception, he never padded an account.

The reason for the governor-general's opposition to labor conscription through increased wages was his fear that, at the time of an audit, he would be suspected of padding accounts. It was nothing but a means of self-protection. Under the circumstances in Changsha, forced labor was impossible. There were numerous elements within the city apparently working in collusion with the Taipings, and they were just waiting for a voice of disquiet to be raised among the general populace. Forced labor might provide a suitable opportunity for them.

The governor-general certainly knew all this. Yet, in spite of it, he sent off the letter cited above to serve as a document on file should there ever be an audit. Inasmuch as he was the governor-general of Hunan and Hubei, should Changsha, the provincial capital of Hunan, fall, the grave responsibility for that would devolve upon him. Changsha had to be firmly protected. Far from opposing strengthening it as a fortress, he actively wanted that to happen. He also knew full well that he would not be able to secure labor without increasing wages. It was not that he was opposed to the man responsible on the scene in Changsha for conscripting labor with the bait of enhanced wages.

In his mind, he wanted as much done as possible, but there was also the audit that would transpire in the future. If increased wages for labor became an issue, he would have to justify himself by saying, I opposed it, but it seemed necessary given the extraordinary circumstances. To create proof of this "opposition," he wrote the above letter to Luo Bingzhang. Luo knew the governor-general well and smiled bitterly, thinking that this was just another evidence of his character.

Eventually news of the fall of cities in eastern Hunan, such as Yongxing and Chaling, reached Hengzhou. Cheng Yucai was relieved that they were apparently going to attack Changsha from the east. He, of course, showed no such expression before his subordinates.

The shortest distance charging north from Chenzhou toward Changsha was via Hengzhou, which linked up with the local river system. With news of the Taiping assault northward, the governor-general said, "I've got to get to Changsha to defend the provincial capital."

Once he found refuge in Changsha, he planned to escape on some pretext from there to Wuchang in Hubei province. "I have to be attuned to the general situation in Huguang, which means both Hunan and Hubei." The city in which the Huguang governor-general permanently resided had been fixed as Wuchang, so this was not that grotesque a distortion. Were Wuchang ever to be attacked, he would have to bring an illness into the picture. As a precautionary measure, he covered his chest and abdomen on occasion, faking a look of worry.

Though the Taipings were coming north, it was clear they were making a detour to the east. They were not going to pass through Hengzhou en route to attacking Changsha.

"The bandits intend to lay seige to Changsha from the east. Will you not repair to Changsha to defend the provincial capital?" asked a staff officer.

"Idiot!" shouted the governor-general, obviously thinking, "The enemy has left us alone, and it'd be crazy to leave the security of Hengzhou for Changsha where war awaited."

"Don't you remember the orders from Beijing? I have to greet the arrival of the imperial commissioner."

Indeed, orders had arrived from the capital to the effect that he was to meet with the imperial commissioner and destroy the bandits. No place for this meeting was named, but Sai-shang-a had only just arisen at long last to depart from Guilin, and was not yet in Hunan. It was a perfect excuse: having to greet his arrival.

"Oh, yes, of course." The staff officer left the room, puzzled. Until just then he had said that, if the bandits demonstrated intentions to move northward, then they had to hurry to the defense of Changsha. Well, then . . .

This particular staff man was brand new on the job, but he saw right through the governor-general. No matter how well-adorned the excuse, most people could see it for what it was.

Perhaps it's his age, thought the staff man, in sympathy with the governor-general after all. Cheng Yucai was from Jiangxi, a metropolitan graduate of 1811, in the same class as Lin Zexu. He already had over forty years of service on his bureaucratic record. Zhou Tianjue, who was also of the 1811 class, had been relieved of his job as governor of Jiangxi by reason of old age.

"Our governor-general would probably be best off quitting his post as soon as possible," said the staff officer to himself.

It may have been the right time to do so, but Cheng Yucai was not about to resign his position. He had plans to nurture many more men under the influence of his own important office. He thought about retirement as absolutely little as possible.

—5—

"Please don't speak about the Taipings in front of me any more, whether it's good or bad news," said Xinmei.

Liwen was well aware of her feelings. She had been deeply sympathetic to the ideals of the Taipings. Born into banditry, she was more enthusiastic than anyone to their aspirations for a utopia. Many of those in the Taiping movement, it seemed, had become disillusioned after the slaughter at Quanzhou. The more idealistic the person, the greater the disillusionment. For people far from their homes, however, it was impossible to imagine life apart from the military.

The massacre was done on the orders of the Eastern King; the Heavenly King played no role in it and knew nothing of it. With this thought in mind, there were those as well who attached their hopes to Hong Xiuquan, who was now less and less frequently appearing in public.

Xinmei had been close to the leadership, and she now felt that Hong Xiuquan was no longer reliable. Hailing from a background in the Heaven and Earth Society, and with control over an organization of her own since her parents' generation, Xinmei was a woman of great pride. She retained contacts with Heaven and Earth affiliates even in Hunan, so that she had the confidence to make it on her own, separated from the Taipings.

After meeting up again with Lian Liwen, who had been wounded in the battle at Suoyi Ford, she was no longer alone. These were perhaps the best days of her entire life. Because she was unwilling to listen, Liwen was unable to explain to her why he pinned his hopes on the Taipings. Yet she seemed to sense it, and said nothing to Liwen that found fault with the rebel movement.

In his heart of hearts, Liwen was operating on the premise that, if things continued as they were, the country was headed for disaster, a view he may have inherited from his father. There were numerous rebels opposed to the established order, but most of them were merely groups of thieves and bandits. In the era of Wang Juzhi, the Heaven and Earth Society also lived by strong ideals, but recently they had shelved those ideals for the time being. Ideals were, for them, like so much excess baggage.

At some point in the past, Lian Weicai had told his sons, "Wang Juzhi conceived of ideals as the source of strength. But he didn't try to organize the strength born of those ideals. That wasn't his mission as he understood it. If, at the same time, a person such as Yang Xiuqing should have appeared in the world . . ." Rather than try to cleanse the now decrepit Heaven and Earth Society once again, an altogether new organization had to be built.

The task Liwen's father had assigned him was the exceedingly important one of creating a window from within the Taiping community to the outside world with financial support. Those people who had come from Guangzhou, and had a sniff of the outside world, were now in a minority within the Taipings. The great majority, from Yang Xiuqing on down, were those who knew only the mountain villages of Guangxi.

To create one or more windows into their narrow universe was good for ventilation. Liwen was aware full well of the great importance of his work. For the time being, it was something only he could do, and thus it was impossible for him to leave the Taipings. Even now, as he was recuperating, he retained his contacts with them.

His liaison to the Taipings was a young man by the name of Tan Qi. Far from being either bold or shrewd, Tan was both young and strong, sufficiently so that Hong Xiuquan had selected him as a bodyguard.

Liwen had taken up temporary residence on the second story of a confectionery factory in Changsha. Xinmei was there as well. The manager of the establishment had been a member of the Heaven and Earth Society since her parents' generation.

At that moment a whistling sound could be heard from the crating area in front of the factory storehouse.

"Qi's arrived," said Xinmei. He was an envoy from the world that she had abandoned. Once Tan Qi appeared and made his whistling signal, she displayed no particularly unpleasant facial gesture. When Liwen left Xinmei, and went downstairs to meet Tan Qi, her face showed not a trace of unhappiness. A remarkable woman, thought Liwen.

Tan Qi had been carrying a pole on his shoulder, and hanging from it fore and aft were numerous boxes. Tan was young, but his body seemed to stagger under the great weight. Yet this was all by design, and he was a lad of immense physical strength. Liwen walked along by Tan Qi's side. He felt like the manager's clerk accompanying a porter who was laying in stock. In fact, he walked with Tan as far as the confectionery factory bearing the name Zhaoji.

"There's too few," said Liwen as they walked. "We've grown, gathering people from the Heaven and Earth Society along the road, but there's still far too few of us. Three thousand, it's not enough for a raid on Changsha."

As they spoke, the Western King Xiao Chaogui was advancing troops on the road to Liling. A total force of 3,000 was just too small.

"It seems to me that they're underrating the might of the enemy a little," said Tan Qi.

"At least in the case of the provincial capital! Changsha's much bigger than Guilin. They didn't take Guilin, and now they're aiming at Changsha with only three thousand men." It bordered on recklessness.

"I can see it's futile, but for some reason, the Western King begged wholeheartedly for a chance to take an army into the field."

"The Western King begged?"

"I heard that the Eastern King wasn't willing to support a surprise attack, with Jiang Zhongyuan's army in the field right in front of him, unless they could send enough troops to meet Jiang."

"He wasn't against it, but he wasn't for it either, right?"

"Something like that."

"Any collaborators?"

"They can't be used well either. Yongan was a small town, so that strategy worked well there, but Changsha's ten to twenty times the size of Yongan."

"What'll happen afterward?"

"I'm not really sure. That probably depends on Jiang Zhongyuan."

"Really. This is a tough one. The Eastern King wasn't opposed?"

Yang Xiuqing, the Eastern King, was becoming more an autocrat with each passing day. Had he opposed the idea of a raid on Changsha, then the Western King might have impetuously screamed out some curse without thinking.

Surface appearances notwithstanding, the Eastern King was baiting the Western King. After the death of the Southern King Feng Yunshan at Suoyi Ford, the Eastern King's influence had grown. Were he to reduce the power of the Western King now, the Taiping Heavenly Kingdom would effectively become Yang Xiuqing's.

Western King Xiao Chaogui was a sworn younger brother of Hong Xiuquan and a steadfast follower, but he was something less than a practically resourceful man. The "Heavenly Elder Brother's Descent to Earth" had been a heavy burden on his shoulders. Perhaps, for his part, Xiao was contemplating the suppression of the Eastern King, and to that end, he had to become a successful commander in battle. Hence his desire to launch an attack on Changsha.

Had such a confidence been revealed to Xinmei, she might have responded, "That's why I have no more need for these people, that whole world of hypocrites!"

"Send a courier off to Liling, saying that the walls of Changsha are being reinforced for all to see, and that this can't be taken lightly. Then, demand the necessity of backup support forces. It seemed that in a previous communication, the Western King thought Changsha was without heavy cannon fire, but they've got huge three thousand–catty cannons. This has to be taken very seriously."

Liwen conveyed these instructions to Tan Qi rapidly.

—6—

Qing reinforcements continued to arrive. Troops from Shaanxi were due in Changsha the following day. The local commanding officer was the regional commander of the Xi'an garrison, Fu-cheng.

Liwen conveyed to Tan Qi detailed information he had been able to gather on the Shaanxi Army. The Shaanxi forces would probably arrive before the Taiping troops and station themselves within the city walls. This supposition proved to be correct when it was observed that arrangements were rapidly being made at a place known as Shimapu, or Stone Horse Shop. Liwen dispatched intelligence, to which he added a rough map.

Apprised of the information sent by Liwen, the Taiping force under the command of Xiao Chaogui was readying itself, prior to the actual assault on the city, for battle against a powerful enemy army. Preparations were being made not just in weaponry, but mentally as well.

By contrast, morale among the soldiers of the Shaanxi Army, who had traveled a great distance to Hunan, was low. The climate and topography of Shaanxi were altogether different from those of Hunan. Shaanxi had the customs typical of the loess country in north China of eating food made with wheat. Hunan, which was known as water country, was of course, a rice-eating region.

The Shaanxi troops simply couldn't eat boiled rice, having not eaten until that point. In China today, rice consumption has increased in the north. At least, no one can say they have never eaten boiled rice. It's virtually impossible to imagine from our present perspective, but the Shaanxi soldiers became deeply depressed over the food they received.

Hubei was a rice-consuming region, and for however many days it had taken them to pass through that province, these men had not eaten anything resembling food. This problem is recorded in government documents of the time as a justification of sorts for their behavior. For that reason, they arrived later than expected at Changsha. They entered the prepared garrisoning site at Stone Horse Shop just prior to the arrival of the Taiping forces.

The group of Taipings that had come from Guangxi was keenly aware of the great wealth of Hunan. The rice was far better than in Guangxi. They were full of energy. On September 11, 1852, the Taiping Army made its camp at Miaogao peak, which commanded a view of the walled city of Changsha.

Now, the Qing Army at Stone Horse Shop and the Taipings at Miaogao peak had to fight, whether they wanted to or not. If the Taipings were to advance on Changsha, there would soon be open-field warfare. They knew in advance that their opponents in the field were troops from Shaanxi. However, the commanders of the Shaanxi Army were dreaming of relaxing leisurely and eating their fill of noodles and steamed bread. No one informed them that they would have to fight so soon after their arrival in Changsha.

Under these circumstances, troop strength would not be an issue. Within the city, there were a total of 6,000 soldiers: 3,000 braves and 3,000 from Jiangxi and Sichuan. Local Hunanese forces were spread through various regions of Guangxi and elsewhere, with none of them in Changsha. On the understanding that fighting outside the city walls was the job of the Shaanxi forces, the 6,000 men within the city were not about to rush outside and come to their support.

Needless to say, the battle ended in a one-sided fashion. Out of some sort of sense of duty, artillery was fired from with the city from time to time.

Outside of the city, but away from Stone Horse Shop, Adjutant Zhu Han was stationed at Yinpanling. The Yinpanling Army sallied forth to reinforce the Shaanxi forces, but there seems to have been some secret intrigue apart from the relief troops. Even if they were to confront the Taiping forces and suffer a crushing defeat, they would be able to make their escape back into the inner city. Like the occasional shells fired from within the city, the forces under Zhu Han met the Taipings on the field in a purely perfunctory fashion.

The Shaanxi Army was obliterated. Regional Commander Fu-cheng, Adjutant Yi Peili, Assistant Regional Commander Sa Bao, Brigade Vice-Commander Ta-le, and other high-ranking military men, all died on the field of battle. It was a devastating defeat.

The backup forces commanded by Zhu Han knew the local terrain and were thus able to escape into the city. Having just arrived from a distance, the Shaanxi forces did not even know a route of escape.

The Taipings took control over the southern suburbs of Changsha. After crushing the Shaanxi Army on the field, the Western King Xiao Chaogui ordered his men, "We shall take advantage of this victory and all at once lay siege to the city. All at once!" He wouldn't allow them to relax their grip one bit.

He learned from Liwen's messenger that there were reinforcements coming to Changsha from various places within Hunan, as well as outside the province. If they put it off one more day, it might prove disadvantageous to them. There was a school by the name of the Chengnan Academy at Miaogao peak. With this as their base of operations, they placed a cannon there and converted the warehouse of a pawnbroker on Bixiang Street into an artillery battery.

A small cannon of bronze had been installed in a building known as the Kuixinglou in the city, and government forces were using it to bombard the Taipings. The entire night of the first day of the confrontation was an artillery war.

The range of the Taipings' cannon was limited, and the confectionery factory within Changsha was safe from potential bombardment. Liwen had been impatient waiting there. He wanted to contact his people outside the city and let them know that they were about to make a mistake, but that means was now shut off to him. Tan Qi had left to reach the Taiping forces outside the city walls, but he still had not returned.

The Taipings had missed the objective of their assault. Taiping shellfire was being concentrated on the Kuixinglou, where the Qing Army had installed a cannon. The strength of the small bronze cannon was by no means extraordinary. It was almost a waste of ammunition to use an artillery shell sufficiently powerful to silence it. For some reason, the Taipings had mistaken the city gate tower for Kuixinglou when they eagerly began the artillery attack. Destroy the city gate and storm the city—this was the urgent Taiping strategy now. A multistoreyed edifice was attached to the city gate, but this edifice was not necessarily the gate itself. The Kuixinglou was right next to the wall, and it could easily be taken to be a gate tower. Throughout the night, the Taipings bombarded the Kuixinglou. In the interim, the seven gates into Changsha were firmly shut, reinforced, and took not a single hit.

"They should have scouted the situation out in advance. They'd have a better map of the local geography that way," said Liwen to himself, as he listened to sounds of artillery.

Liwen had drawn a rough map, but it only indicated the site at which the Shaanxi troops had been stationed. It didn't note the locations of the city gates. He fully expected that such things would have been known. Actually, it never dawned on him that there might be a need to indicate the placement of the city gates.

"Don't forget the basics! That's the essence of the matter now," said Liwen as he closed his eyes.

"For all your worrying, there's nothing you can do from here. You're not fighting. Come on, go to bed," said Xinmei.

—7—

The shelling continued into the next day. Luo Bingzhang's wall refortification project produced genuine results. Had he been overly frugal in expenses, the Changsha wall might have been breached by the Taipings' ferocious attack. There were, after all, only 6,000 troops inside the city itself. The order to continue the bombardment, the disposition of troops, and similar military responsibilities all fell under the command of civil official Luo Bingzhang. During the shelling, Luo Raodian assembled the officials in a safe area and convened a meeting.

The man who held the highest military responsibility there was Hunan Provincial Military Commander Bao Qibao. As a matter of course, this military man with his extraordinarily military-sounding name ("Qibao" literally means "aroused panther") made camp by the tower at the southern gate of the city, facing the enemy head on. In his room he had placed an image of a deity transported from the temple of the city god.

"Crush the bandit army with the power of the god," prayed Bao out loud, while making an incense offering.

His military guards whispered stealthily in the shadows among themselves.

"He's calling on the power of the city god."

"He's not praying for the god's might. He's praying for himself."

"He always does that."

"He's useless as a commander."

As these guards saw at a glance, the provincial military commander expected that the enemy's shells would not hit them as long as he carried the image of the city god around with him all day and night. During the first night, the Taiping confused the Kuixinglou for the gate tower and shelled the former. Without a doubt, Bao Qibao believed that this was due to the power of the city god.

Outside the southern gate, Western King Xiao Chaogui personally took command of his troops to lead them into battle.

"Please leave this to us here. The Western King must retire further to the rear, please. Beyond the point where the shells from the bronze cannon are falling." Repeatedly, Deputy Commander Lin Fengxiang admonished Xiao Chaogui in this manner, but the Western King ignored him.

"Morale is the number one issue now. It won't last that long. We're taking a pause now. I can't possibly retreat at this point. Pass me my standard." Xiao took the banner of the Western King in his hand.

Wearing a simple but stunning uniform, and carrying his banner of burning crimson, he cut a conspicuous figure on the field. It was only natural then that he became the target for cannon fire. The fact that Lin Fengxiang and others were fearful became evident to him. The shells began falling closer to the Western King.

"Retreat! Retreat! Quickly!" Lin Fengxiang screamed in a hoarse voice. The Western King didn't listen, but just called back, laughing, "Don't I give the orders around here?"

In the next instant, a red cloud of dust arose at the feet of the Western King. In the Hunan region, nearly all the soil is a reddish clay. The dust off the ground was also red, as was the banner of the Western King.

The banner flew into the air amid the dust and danced about in the sky. Though the dust was thin, the towering figure of the Western King was no longer to be seen. A body lay stretched across the ground, and from it could be heard groans.

"The Western King!" Lin Fengxiang, himself covered with dust, raced over to the spot.

"It's nothing . . . nothing at all," said the Western King.

Xiao was still alive, but when Lin saw his left shoulder he wanted to cry. The white bone was visible, poking through an area drenched in blood, and the bone was shattered.

The next artillery shell fell about a yard from where they were. The red soil whirled up into the air with a whooshing sound and fell back down to the ground.

Lin lifted the Western King onto his back quickly. "Forget the king's standard and come on!" he yelled, as if barking at the sky.

Xiao Chaogui had sustained a serious wound. Li Kaifang and Lin Fengxiang immediately dispatched a messenger to Chenzhou to inform the Taiping forces there of what had just transpired.

"Shall we continue the attack?" asked a staff officer.

"The attack?" Lin Fengxiang stared angrily at the city of Changsha.

"We'll take a brief respite," said Li Kaifang.

Summer was coming to an end in this watery region of Hunan. There was a group of horsemen galloping through an irrigated field. They comprised the urgent courier to Chenzhou. Although they raced along at a good clip, one somehow sensed that they lacked strength.

18

Departure on a Rainswept Night

Xiao Chaogui, the Western King of the Taiping Heavenly Kingdom, had been gravely wounded. Upon hearing this news, Heavenly King Hong Xiuquan momentarily turned pale. Yang Xiuqing, the Eastern King, bit his lip, his eyes cast downward. He was clenching his fists tightly. With knitted brow, Northern King Wei Changhui glanced over in the direction of the Eastern King.

Doubts arose like a cloudy mist in Wei's mind: Yang's expression is all pathos, but does it tell his real feelings? In his heart of hearts, wouldn't he actually be happiest if Xiao died? Wasn't it he who had persuaded Xiao to proceed with the attack on Changsha? I've got to keep my guard up and not repeat the error of the Western King.

Wei drew a lesson from the death of Xiao Chaogui. The Taiping encampment at Chenzhou, though, was enveloped in a gloomy atmosphere.

"We head for Changsha with the entire army," ordered Hong Xiuquan. Although Yang Xiuqing had for the most part taken over military leadership of the Taiping Army, on this rare occasion Hong issued an order. "We shall proceed along the route set out by the Western King," added Yang to Hong's command.

Hong then departed, entrusting what followed to Yang. He knew he had no talent in matters concerning military organization and troop stationing, nor had he tried studying such things. His obligation to study was to the teachings of God and nothing else.

Hong walked with a heavy gait. The door to his sister's room was open. This younger sister, Hong Xuanjiao, was married to Xiao Chaogui. When she recognized her brother's face, she spoke up first.

"I've heard what just went on," she said, looking up, with no trace of tears in her eyes.

"The report said he was badly wounded."

"They probably won't be able to save him, will they? I could tell from the manner in which the emergency messenger was speaking. I'm prepared."

"We still don't know . . ."

"It is best to be prepared for such things in advance."

"That's true." Hong felt his own voice quivering, though his sister's remained the same as always. Ever since childhood, he thought, she had been such a strong-willed young woman. She was not one to need pity.

"I will now begin preparations for departure," she said, her white teeth gleaming—extraordinarily beautiful teeth. She never wore any form of make-up or powder on her face, well aware of her own natural beauty. As he gazed at the expression on his sister's face, a mouthful of white teeth protruding from between her lips, Hong felt pity for her.

As a youngster, Xuanjiao had studied the martial arts and had become particularly adept at the use of a sword. Comparing her to her older brother, who was much more drawn to his books, their relatives would often say, "Imagine if Xuanjiao had been born a boy."

When her brother summoned the family to join him in Jintian village, she was not in their home area of Huaxian at the time. She later proceeded by herself to Guangxi province with scarcely any money for expenses incurred during the trip. To allay such expenses, she earned money by performing demonstrations of swordplay en route.

After arriving in Jintian village, she married Xiao Chaogui, who had lost his first wife, Yang Yunjiao. Of all the women in the Society of God Worshippers, Yang had been a member the longest. She had been a devout Christian, to such an extent that the Taipings had a laudatory expression, "two Yuns"—referring to Feng Yunshan among the men, and Yang Yunjiao among the women.

As far as Hong Xiuquan, whose position all the while seemed to be threatened by the likes of Yang Xiuqing, was concerned, Xuanjiao's marriage to Xiao Chaogui meant that a reassuring support had been put into place. The death of Xiao Chaogui was going to have a subtle influence on power relations within the Taiping Heavenly Kingdom. Such was the feeling among those fighting in the Taiping military. The Taiping Army at Chenzhou suddenly arose in a commotion as the troops set off on the march of over 300 kilometers toward Changsha. The day of their departure en masse was roughly the twelfth day of the eighth lunar month.

At about this time, the government's army of braves under the command of Jiang Zhongyuan arrived in Changsha, where they remained outside the Xiaowu Gate to the city.

It had been during the siege of Changsha that Xiao Chaogui had fallen, and the Taiping Army was not in high spirits. When the bright harvest moon of the fifteenth day of the eighth lunar month shone in the sky, Jiang's forces had broken the siege, moved on the offensive, and inflicted heavy casualties on the Taipings. The newly appointed governor of Hunan, Zhang Liangji, arrived outside the walls of Changsha several days later, accompanied at the time by Zuo Zongtang.

The Taipings had never, in fact, surrounded Changsha. Xiao Chaogui had tried to stage a surprise attack on the city, and thus had not brought a large number of troops with him. He had nowhere near the troop strength necessary to surround the immense city walls of Changsha. The Taiping forces had only blockaded the southern gate to the city, while passage through the other gates to the outside remained open. If troops could get inside, so too could provisions and munitions. When Governor Zhang entered the city, the main force of the Taiping Army, burning with the thought of revenge, had advanced along the route from Chenzhou to Liling. After being wounded, Xiao Chaogui only had a few days to live.

"Dig . . . dig," he kept repeating deliriously.

"Yes. We shall have them dig. We are making preparations at present," said Li Kaifang and Lin Fengxiang at Xiao's bedside, though in his murky consciousness, it is doubtful that he caught what they said.

In his delirium, the Western King was ordering his men to plant explosives in tunnels dug beneath the city walls. In addition to the silver miners from Guangxi, there were some one thousand or more coal miners from southern Hunan among the Taipings, and Xiao had commanded over three hundred of them. He had been pondering the tactic of digging shafts to lay land mines ever since he and his troops had departed Chenzhou.

Xiao had formulated a two-line strategy. He had planned a sudden attack in which Changsha would be taken by storm in one fell swoop. This was the best tactic at his disposal, but if the defense of the city was secure, then he would shift to planting land mines.

Xiao had barely reached thirty years of age, though the precise date of his birth still remains unknown. His assistants, Li and Lin, were both still in their twenties. The first task for the fighting miners in the Taiping Army was not to dig tunnels and plant explosives, but to dig a grave for Xiao Chaogui, the Western King. He was buried at a place known as Old Dragon Pond.

They could not perform an elaborate funeral for him, because they didn't want the enemy to know that one of their generals had died. Old Dragon Pond was chosen because it was difficult to see from the city.

"At the dawn of our victory," announced Li Kaifang and Lin Fengxiang, at his grave, "we shall hold a proper funeral."

—2—

"I wonder if it was this that Master Yunshan was speaking about in Jintian village. Everyone helping those in need. Even the poor are able to eat. Was that it?" asked Xinmei.

Until this point, she had always referred to Feng Yunshan as the Southern King. Having left the Taiping movement, she no longer made such distinctions and ceased using such nomenclature. She still employed terms of respect: Elder Brother Xiuquan for the Heavenly King (Hong Xiuquan), Master Yunshan for the Southern King, and Elder Brother Chaogui for the Western King (Xiao Chaogui), but she dropped all respectful language for the Eastern King and the Northern King. This was only natural, for the former, Yang Xiuqing, had given the order for the massacre at Quanzhou. As for the latter, Wei Changhui, she had apparently just taken a disliking to him.

"That's it. But, it may not continue. It's only a temporary thing," replied Liwen.

They were on the second floor of the confectionery factory in Changsha. Having returned from a walk around the city, Xinmei seemed a bit excited. Within her heart there dwelt the soul of a gallant knight-errant. It was always astir, driving her to the Society of God Worshippers and compelling her to join the Taiping Army. A world in which the poor and the weak could live without enduring humiliation and never go hungry—this is what Feng Yunshan, the first missionary of the Society of God Worshippers, had called for: "We shall rise up to build such a world." In making this appeal, Feng had stirred the adventurer in her.

However, now within the walled confines of Changsha, besieged by the very Taipings who held up this ideal, there was emerging a state of affairs close to the ideal realm posed by the Taipings themselves.

Large quantities of supplies were being transported, and foodstuffs were allocated free of charge to the poor of the city. When officials and government troops purchased goods in stores, they had to pay in cash. Since the government was buying supplies from ordinary shops and paying in cash, a commercial boom of sorts was bringing prosperity to the city. Every evening night stalls lined up, and the local theaters were packed. People were enjoying their lives. Part of the objective toward which the Taipings were focused, as depicted by Feng Yunshan in his missionary speeches, seemed as though it was being realized in Changsha then.

"It may only be temporary, but everybody's happy," said Xinmei, shutting her eyes. The present state of affairs in the marketplace reappeared between her closing eyes just at that instant as she seemed to be trying to scrutinize it.

Eventually, he opened her eyes and said to Liwen, as she moved closer to him, "Don't you think so?"

"The vital point of Master Yunshan's sermons is missing here."

"What vital point?"

"A world in which there are no rich and poor. Do you see that coming into existence?"

"No, I see what you mean." No doubt about it, the highest pitch in Feng Yunshan's sermons was this notion of equality. It had the power to move men's hearts.

A whistle was heard, and Tan Qi, who had been gone for a while, appeared. Liwen walked down the stairs.

"This place is full of soldiers," said Tan, looking from side to side. His job was to convey to the Taiping Army the present situation within the walled city of Changsha. Of the city's seven gates, the Taipings had only blocked off the Southern Gate. The other six were open as usual. In fact, traffic through them was more bustling and busy than ever. Reinforcements from various places had entered the city without the least difficulty.

"Looks like about fifty thousand, wouldn't you say?" said Liwen.

"Probably more," responded Tan, again looking to each side. "I'm thinking of checking it out, but we don't have the men to spare right now."

"How far have they come?" Liwen's question concerned the Taipings' movements.

"The advance forces have reached Liling, and they're hungry for action."

"You can't let what happened at Quanzhou happen again." Because of the serious injuries sustained by the Southern King, the battle at Quanzhou had been fought under extraordinary circumstances, and a massacre had taken place there. It was the one blot on the Taiping record.

That time the Western King had been seriously wounded and had subsequently died. Tan Qi was saying that the Taiping troops at Liling were thirsty for blood, and Liwen was extremely concerned.

With his responsibilities for intelligence gathering, Tan Qi found it difficult to locate people who would cooperate with him, and people who were moved only by money were not reliable. Thus far, collaborators in Taiping military intelligence activities included those who despised local politicians, those who were discontented with their present circumstances, or at least those who thought the contemporary situation ought to be changed. Changsha was terrain where the Heaven and Earth Society held considerable strength. This secret society should have had numerous men of an antiestablishment disposition. Nonetheless, Tan Qi was tortured by the fact that he had been able to contact only a very few collaborators there.

The great majority of the population of Changsha was perfectly happy with things as they presently were and did not approve of a change in present circumstances. Were there a force trying to overturn the prosperous conditions then prevailing in Changsha, it would probably turn on the urban populace as the enemy.

"It's impossible . . . can't be done," Liwen murmured as he approached Tan Qi. "You've got to let the Heavenly King and the Eastern King know about the state of affairs here in Changsha. The city population say they're happy with the authorities. You won't be able to find any conspirators at all here. My opinion is that it would be best not to invade Changsha and to continue the forward advance. Whether you agree with me or not, please convey my views."

"I'll convey them properly," said Tan Qi, nodding in assent.

Liwen began to say that their opposite number here was Zuo Zongtang, but he thought better of it, as he realized that no one in the Taiping leadership knew Zuo's name.

With 50,000 troops having entered Changsha, public order was not being maintained. The authorities thus decided to issue an order to maintain strict military discipline, with severe punishment for offenders. Relief rice was distributed to the poor, using monies saved in the provincial treasury. Purchases from the populace as well were made with provincial government funds.

Zuo Zongtang was only a member of someone else's staff, but he was in a position to influence Governor Zhang Liangji strongly. He thus offered proposals on matters of military discipline and the disbursement of treasury funds. A "governor" was the highest civil official in a province, but the vice-governor or "provincial administration commissioner" by the name of Pan Duo—among a batch of high-level bureaucrats of the time who were all excessively concerned not to rock the boat—was a remarkably capable man, prepared to take drastic steps if necessary. The Chinese bureaucratic system had become such that the consciousness of spheres of jurisdiction was extremely strong. Even if a governor listened to a member of his staff and tried to make use of the provincial treasury, it would all have come to naught if the provincial administration commissioner opposed the idea.

Even if only for a short period of time, from the perspective of the general urban populace, the situation in Changsha had improved radically, and the cause was the joint efforts of capable government leaders: Zhang Liangji, Pan Duo, and Zuo Zongtang.

Public order was restored, and women and children could go out-of-doors in safety. Crowds of people in the streets became larger than usual. Troops were well-treated. Foodstuffs were plentiful, and there was wine as well. Under such conditions, the troops were not going to raise havoc in the streets of the city.

A text of that time, *Chronicle of the Hunan Army,* described the appearance of Changsha: "They forgot that it was a walled city under siege."

Monetary rewards were proffered to those who killed enemy soldiers. Compared to the Taiping Army, then in the throes of despondency over the death of the Western King, morale was high within the walls of Changsha.

—3—

Yes, morale was high. Yet it was probably an artificial morale. As one government army after another entered the city, it looked at the size of the friendly forces and sensed an indestructibility of numbers. In addition, they were all well-treated, so it allowed them a kind of ease of mind. This added margin enabled the Qing soldiers to enjoy some genuine relaxation after considerable tension.

Since they held control over six of the city's seven gates, they had no sense of being surrounded. Military discipline remained strict, though special allowances were issued to the troops so that there would be no instances of trouble between them and the urban dwellers. With the power of money, conditions perked up again, or so it seemed from the rise in morale.

The uniforms worn by the military patrols within the city were splendid. This was an age in which soldiers were thought of as so much human refuse, and the government had to shatter this commonly held notion. To that end, they sought to dress their men as well as possible. This was particularly true, as Zuo Zongtang saw it, for the patrols, who were often seen by the residents of the city.

Zuo had a special skill of which even he himself was ignorant. It entailed that the views he took were for some reason always adopted in full by his superiors. Even in cases when these ideas were less than brilliant, his words carried just the right weight, the needed weight to gain smooth acceptance. He was not, however, the kind of man who assessed his counterparts and tempered his words accordingly.

While dressing up his patrolling troops in all their finery for their appearance in public, behind the scenes, decidedly unclean activities were widely going on. It was Zuo Zongtang's view that, in this way, a marvelous balance could be maintained. It was something that people came to understand and accept.

The uniforms would bear the Chinese character for "heroic" in crimson embroidery within a green circle. Had this been the extent of his proposal, it surely would have elicited opposition, but while tendering this proposition, Zuo Zongtang offered a piece of advice.

"Since the nature of the terrain in Hunan is such that there are numerous secret societies in that province, we must bring them under strict control. The leaders of the secret societies whose whereabouts are known should be arrested immediately. Furthermore, if any sort of spy at all is being used, there remains the danger of collusion so long as those who oppose the government continue unexposed."

By "any sort of spy at all," Zuo was referring to the state's practice of secretly using people with criminal records. Many were, in fact, genuine human refuse. Elite social elements did their best to avoid all contact with such loathsome business. They had ordinary affairs handled by lower strata and awaited reports on how they turned out. There were, however, frequently problems that reached the ears of those in leadership positions.

Requests arose from the quarters of those assigned these unpleasant tasks: "We know where their big shot is hiding, and we are quietly keeping an eye on this person now. To let this opportunity slip through our fingers at this point would be horrendous, and so we are requesting support from government troops."

"Who is this 'big shot' they refer to?" asked Zuo Zongtang of the staff officer who had transmitted the request to him. In terms of status, Zuo was the same level as this man, who worked on the staff of a provincial governor, but he was regarded as occupying a special rank. He himself freely spoke and acted as though he enjoyed some privileged status as well. He spoke to all staff officers in crude language, occasionally as if he were giving them orders.

"I am told that it's a woman."

"A woman? Really? A leader of the Heaven and Earth Society?"

"Yes. She's with the Heaven and Earth Society, but she has apparently also joined the long-haired bandits."

"You say this is a woman leader, a big shot who has joined the long-haired bandits, eh? Then it must be either Su Sanniang or Li Xinmei."

Zuo Zongtang's intelligence network was spread widely, and its meshing was fine. It was also accurate. Zuo himself had an astounding memory. The staff officer stared at him in amazement.

"Uh, yes, it's Li Xinmei," he said, while muttering to himself, What an overbearing attitude this guy assumes, but that seems to be the worst of it.

Over a period of time a clique of devoted followers of this sort had assembled around Zuo Zongtang.

"Is Li Xinmei in Changsha? We knew for certain that she was among the long-haired bandits at the seige of Guilin, but when did she separate herself from the military?" Zuo looked up at the ceiling, while amusing himself with his fingertip in the teacup on the table before him.

"Is she really such a big-shot?" asked the staff officer who had brought Zuo the report.

"For some reason, she let her adherents go and joined the long-haired bandits. I doubt she relinquished much of a heavy burden."

"Do you mean, then, that if she has in fact sneaked into Changsha, she surely must carry a special responsibility?"

"That would stand to reason. Nothing else seems to make sense, does it? What else can it be than an operation aimed at secret communication," said Zuo, with a tone of reproval.

"Yes, of course. For it would seem that the great army of the long-haired bandits will soon reach the city walls."

"We have to deal with this quickly."

"Of course."

"If we capture her, I will personally carry out the interrogation," said Zuo.

When the main body of the Taiping military under the leadership of Hong Xiuquan and Yang Xiuqing received the news of Xiao Chaogui's serious wounds, the encampment had immediately gone into action and departed Chenzhou. They headed north, effectively along the same route taken by Xiao Chaogui's forces earlier.

Only two days later, the Taipings had occupied the city of Liling. Before then, though, news of Xiao Xhaogui's death had reached them. An eerie atmosphere overtook the armed forces, and with eyes looking in anger at Changsha, the entire army marched forward.

Hong Xiuquan reached an area to the south of Changsha's walls on the first day of the ninth lunar month. The Taiping military force under the command of Xiao Chaogui numbered less than five thousand and fought the government's forces well for over a month, despite having lost their commander.

During this interval, Provincial Military Commander Xiang Rong finally arrived at Changsha. He had been at Guilin and had not pursued the Taiping forces, but remained for a time immobile. For this lack of action, Xu Guangjin, the governor-general of Guangdong and Guangxi, denounced him to Beijing: "Xiang Rong prevaricates but does not move forward." Beijing responded with a harsh punishment: "Banishment to Xinjiang."

At the time he entered Changsha, Xiang Rong already knew of the decision reached in the capital. In order to avoid exile to Xinjiang in the far northwest, he was going to have to fight with every conceivable effort then and there. Like a man completely transformed, he began to attend to his military duties with great diligence.

Because they had no batteries, Xiang's forces would not have been able to use their large artillery pieces, so he had them carried to the top of towers, and from there a fierce barrage came raining down on the Taiping forces. The latter had no choice but to discontinue their forward movement.

—4—

Xinmei dashed into an alleyway to the left, but from the corner of the alley before her three men appeared as though they had been eagerly awaiting her. When she looked back over her shoulder, three other men apparently pursuing her appeared.

Strange, she thought. But by the time she had become aware of the tail, it was already too late.

"What do you want? Do you have some business with me?" said Xinmei, assuming a posture. As the leader of this gang of toughs then walked up to her, she did not even flinch, all nerves of steel. The other men approached without answering her.

"Hmm, you had spies," said Xinmei. To the left and right were the walls of private homes, and the men stood in front and behind her. There was no escape. She had rushed, it seemed, headlong into a fatal position. Had she not entered the alley, they would have shot at her. So, either way would have turned out the same. Xinmei spoke to them as she had, though not one of the six men looked familiar to her.

There's no use putting up a fight now, she thought. I've got to think about what I'm going to do next. With this decision in hand, Xinmei could sense from her considerable experience of carnage on the battlefield that this was not to be the place where she would be murdered.

"It doesn't matter where you take me," she said, all the time thinking of her means of communication with Liwen.

It was not far from her present location to the confectionery factory. Liwen would probably come to her if she whistled. But she couldn't do that, because she didn't want to involve him. Yet she did want to inform him that she was being taken somewhere.

She just couldn't think of anything to do. She sorely missed Liwen now. What have I done? she wondered.

The men pressed in on her from both sides and tied her up. She put up no resistance, allowing them to do as they wished.

"What's this? You're just a mouth?" said one of the men. They had apparently expected a fiercer resistance on her part. The others said nothing until she was completely bound.

They tied her hands behind her back and pushed her forward until she came to the end of the alley. She couldn't see from the alley, but at the end where it turned, a sedan chair was waiting.

"I'd love to go in there," she said as she climbed still bound into it.

The route they followed after that was unknown to her, for she was still unfamiliar with the streets of Changsha. She could sense, though, an atmosphere of being outside the city. The sounds of street vendors faded into the distance, and the smells of life gradually disappeared from her surroundings. She was able to tell that the sedan chair was passing through a quiet, inactive area.

Probably a local government office, she thought. By the same token, though, it wasn't a filthy, squalid place like a prison. Eventually the aroma of incense floated back into the air. The entire sedan chair with her inside was carried into a building and set down, after this rather long trip, on the floor. An exchange of voices outside was audible.

"Should we keep her tied up?"

"No, that's probably unadvisable."

"And if she tries to run away?"

"You think she can escape from here? The room is locked, and there are several guard stations outside."

"So, should I untie her?"

"I think that's best."

"Won't she lash out at Master Jigao?"

"What? Why, she'll cower before the left hand of Provincial Graduate Zuo."

"Ha, ha. The left hand of Master Zuo?"

"I know, it's a terrible pun"—the surname Zuo employs the same Chinese character as that meaning "left."

Though Xinmei had received no formal education, she was an exceedingly quick-witted person. She wondered if the person just named might be the very Zuo Zongtang about whom Liwen had spoken.

She was reminded of the happy time she had spent with Liwen as they rowed their boat down the Xiang River. With his reverence for Lin Zexu, Liwen often spoke of the people who surrounded Lin. One episode among them that had really made Xinmei laugh concerned a man by the name of Zuo Zongtang. She had a vague recollection that he used the pen name of Jigao. He was the man who, in order to strongly impress Lin Zexu on their first meeting, fell into a river and crawled out dripping wet.

Liwen had mentioned that since Zuo hailed from this area, they would probably soon meet him.

Xinmei was taken out of the sedan chair, and the rope was removed from her hands.

"The rope wasn't tied very well, you know. You need some more practice at it, because this just won't do," she said.

"Listen to that mouth," said the voice she had heard in the alley. They were now in a corridor to an inner courtyard. The building before them appeared to be a temple, but it lacked the atmosphere of a religious site.

It's an academy, conjectured Xinmei. During this period, schools were often referred to as academies, and there was always a place within such academies to worship Confucius. As the Taipings had marched forward, they had made a point of destroying all plaques to Confucius and all wooden images of him in both temples and academies. Academies were also the places where high-level officials often conducted business. When Lin Zexu had traveled to Guangzhou just prior to the Opium War, he used the Yuehua Academy both for his lodgings and for his business affairs.

Where the corridor turned, a door painted in green stood half open.

"Come in here," said a voice. Xinmei turned in the direction of the voice, gave a scowl, and entered the room. Inside were a red table and four chairs, nothing else. Not even any people.

A door closed behind her, and she could hear the sound of the bolt falling into place.

"A female bandit, no less!" spit out a voice resounding with malice after the door shut.

Xinmei sat down in a chair, wondering what was going on. To be sure, she had been the leader of a group of bandits. Had the government been looking for her, she would have been captured and executed. For that reason she had always been very careful. Whenever she saw someone she didn't know, she thought it was an official or an agent of an official, and often persuaded herself to that effect.

Her vigilance had completely dissipated after joining the Taipings, because she no longer viewed herself as a bandit. Also, Changsha was a place far removed from the region in which she had been active during her bandit days. Perhaps there was a sense of security in the fact that no one was likely to recognize her. Yet she was walking about the city without precaution because she had ceased being aware of the men following her.

I've become honest before I even realized it, she thought, as a forced smile appeared on her face.

Still, there was something strange about all this. If they kill me now, she thought, I have no regrets whatsoever, for I can die an honest person.

—5—

The day after the advance guard of the main force of the Taiping Army reached the outskirts of Changsha, it was quickly drawn into battle. Its opponents were the Hunan braves commanded by the Taipings' formidable enemy, Jiang Zhongyuan, and the Guizhou corps under the leadership of Regional Commander, Qin Dingsan.

Actually, a far more ferocious battle had transpired ten days earlier, and Jiang had been wounded, though not severely. Assistant Regional Commander Ren Dagui had actually been killed on the field of battle there, and to that extent it had been a defeat for the Qing forces. Jiang and Ding were seething with a desire for revenge as they greeted the arrival of the Taiping military. It was just outside the Liuyang Gate that a fierce battle unfolded. The Liuyang River flowed around from the east to the north of Changsha and emptied into the Xiang River. The gate took its name from the river, which faced directly onto it.

Until that point, the Taiping Army had been small in number, and thus had been unable to disperse its troop strength. They wanted to attack the eastern section of the wall, but to do so they would have had to move their troops stationed outside the southern gate, who had been expressly sent there to form a blockade. If the blockade were broken through, it would mean a total loss.

With the reinforcements from the main body of the Taiping Army, they tried to besiege the Liuyang Gate, on the eastern side of the city. It was at that place 120 years later that a grave dating to the Former Han dynasty (206 B.C.–220 A.D.) was discovered—the famous Mawangdui site, where the lifelike remains of a woman were unearthed.

The Taiping Army lost that battle. Jiang Zhongyuan's forces had defeated the Taipings earlier at Suoyi Ford and gained a measure of self-esteem as a result. Because of the setback ten days earlier, they had been burning with renewed martial spirit.

For their part, the Taipings effectively fought for the first time in a new military formation, save for more localized battles. They had incorporated a large number of Hunanese secret society members into their fighting forces. These were new entrants into the Taiping Army, men unused to the fighting style of the Taipings. Furthermore, these men indeed hailed from Hunan, but they were more accurately from the southern part of the province, and hence knew little of the geography in the Changsha region.

The day was lost and the Taipings went into retreat, with 500 men lost on the field. It was a great defeat.

When the Taipings abandoned the front on the eastern part of the city, they decided to build a base to the west. They crossed to the western bank of the Xiang River and established a position there. The famous Yuelu (sometimes known as Lilu) Mountains rose above the western shore of the Xiang. With the separation of the Xiang River, the Taipings' western base was able to exert considerable pressure on the city of Chansha.

Imperial Commissioner Sai-shang-a entered Changsha on the ninth day of the ninth lunar month. Although he had yet to be informed of it, Sai-shang-a was no longer in fact an imperial commissioner. Seven days before his arrival at Changsha, the court in Beijing had divested him of his position and recalled him to the capital—the second of that month, the day Taiping forces had been crushed outside Liuyang Gate.

At the same time, Huguang Governor-General Cheng Yucai was relieved of his post. Cheng, though, was not recalled to Beijing, but was ordered to remain at the scene and take over command of the local military headquarters.

Xu Guangjin (1797–1876), governor-general of Guangdong and Guangxi, succeeded Cheng as imperial commissioner and also took over the post of Huguang governor-general. All necessary government personnel, civil and military alike, would fall under his direction. Xu Guangjin had yet to arrive in Changsha.

South of the city had still not become a primary battle scene in the fighting, as the height of the action moved to the western area. As in the past, though, the tide of the war was still one of advance and retreat, with no truly decisive victory. While the Taiping forces did not lack for military supplies, they were beginning to worry about shortages of salt and oil. These items should have been supplied from the rear, but government troops had already overtaken them.

Newly appointed Imperial Commissioner Xu Guangjin was at the head of over ten thousand soldiers, and after proceeding to Xiangtan from Hengzhou, he did not attempt to move any further. He gave as the official reason that "they would cut off the Taipings' route of retreat." The Taipings, for their part, had had no intention of withdrawing at all. What was cut off was the replenishing of their salt and oil.

The digging of tunnels, which was effectively the last request of the Western King, was not making the kind of progress needed for military purposes. With the arrival of the main force of the Taiping military came the remaining miners as well, and eventually this construction work improved. The fact that the fighting had moved over to the western part of the city proved advantageous to the digging of tunnels. Since the digging had begun from south of the city, the less fighting in that area the better.

Zeng Guofan, who was at this time en route to his hometown to take up a period of mourning, learned of the siege of Changsha while in Wuchang. Rather than take a sea route, he chose to make his way through the mountains to get to Xiangyin. It was the twenty-third day of the eighth lunar month. His hometown was already in a state of uproar.

Xiangyin was only about 60 kilometers removed from Changsha. Zeng learned that Jiang Zhongyuan, whom he had recommended for promotion, was fighting well and with great valor.

Liwen had been out that day. Although many unfamiliar faces walked by him at a leisurely pace throughout the day, he hadn't been the least conspicuous. Many—soldiers first and foremost—had come to Changsha upon hearing of the prosperous conditions prevailing there. Liwen was walking around, surveying the overall atmosphere of the city, though without eliciting the least suspicion toward himself. He observed the situation scrupulously, coming to the conclusion ultimately that "the level of relaxation was extraordinary." Military discipline remained strict, as in the past, though less in fact than in appearance. For example, if a soldier committed an act of some inappropriate behavior in a place within the city where public attention was concentrated, he usually received an excessively heavy punishment. However, incidents that occurred in inconspicuous spots, such as within their own barracks, seem largely to have been ignored.

The soldiers knew this themselves and were particularly shrewd about it. Liwen ventured to a barracks with the confectionery delivery man, and he found that it had been transformed into an enormous gambling den. His timing was just right, for even in the courtyard of the barracks he could see gambling going on here and there.

When the delivery man arrived with the goods that had been ordered, he approached some soldiers whom he recognized and joined in the gambling himself. Indeed, on closer inspection it looked as though many of those involved in the wagering were not soldiers at all.

When the Heavenly King and Eastern King learn of this, thought Liwen, won't it greatly enhance their self-confidence? Yet he was still worried. His opinion had been that the Taipings were better off avoiding a fight at Changsha and heading for Yuezhou, and this view should have been conveyed to the leadership of the Taiping Army by Tan Qi. Were he now to report that the Changsha Army was so relaxed, he worried that his earlier view would seem to have had its basis in fact weakened considerably. Though he was personally witnessing this relaxation, Liwen's opinion did not change.

On the way back to the confectionery factory, Liwen heard his name called in a soft voice, and before he knew it, Tan Qi had approached and was standing next to him.

"Liwen, you can't go back there!" Tan Qi was a short man, and his voice seemed to reach Liwen at shoulder height.

"Why?" asked Liwen, as though tempted, also in a low voice.

"Elder Sister's been caught."

"What? You mean Xinmei?"

"Yes, and it looks like the governor's office has her."

"I think I should go and do something about it. . . . Right, and both the governor and Master Zuo . . ." The newly appointed Governor Zhang Liangji as well as Zuo Zongtang, who was effectively the head of Zhang's staff, both had links to Lin Zexu. They were the richest source for intelligence, and Liwen had been thinking of going to meet them soon. If he gave his father's name, he should have no difficulty meeting these two men in person, inasmuch as his father knew them both.

"Someone should make a deal with them, but not you," said Tan Qi. "These men already know the connection between you and Elder Sister. It's in your family history. They know nothing of your ties to the Taiping Army, but they'll certainly know that you're the son of Lian Weicai."

"What should I do?"

"Come back to my place, for Elder Sister's sake. It doesn't look like she's going to be executed soon. We've made friends with someone who works in the government office, so we'll find out if anything happens there."

"Won't I be captured if I try and return?"

"You'll go back under guard."

"Mr. Yu?" Liwen was afraid that troubles might befall Yu Guangtian, the owner of the confectionery factory, who had been looking after him.

"Mr. Yu is safe. His family's been making sweets in Changsha for five generations, and no one is the least suspicious of him. Everyone does know that there's an extra lodging on the second floor of his place, though, and that it's rented out to a fellow who is the son of Lian Weicai. He's got clout even with the local authorities, so don't worry about him. You, though, have to quietly disappear from sight. Come with me."

Tan Qi turned right onto a narrow alley, and Liwen followed a short distance behind him.

"My place is cramped, but just be patient for a while. Oh, and there's someone else there already." Tan Qi had been speaking in a matter-of-fact, chatty tone of voice.

"Someone else?"

"That's right, just a kid. Chen Picheng."

"Oh, that youngster." The expression of concern for Xinmei on Liwen's face was unconsciously lessened.

"A promising young man" was the expression he had used to get Yang

Xiuqing to let him borrow the services of Chen Picheng as a bodyguard. That year Chen was all of fifteen years old. Liwen was concerned about him after he was separated from his military unit, but Tan Qi reported that Chen seemed to be in good health. Perhaps, upon assessing Liwen's feelings, Tan Qi had come to extract Chen from the Taipings.

"It's great that he's here," said Liwen.

"Yeah, because if you walk around with a kid, no one'll suspect you of anything. That's why I got him," said Tan Qi, laughing.

That evening, in a room at the governor's provisional office, Zuo Zongtang met face to face with Li Xinmei. A secretary who looked to be over seventy years of age sat at a small desk in a corner of the room. He looked just like a referee at a wrestling match. There was no one else present.

"What beguiling coquetry did you use to deceive Lian Weicai's son?" said Zuo Zongtang as soon as he entered the room.

"What?" she responded. "You've made me wait half a day and that's all you want to ask me about?"

"Everyone knows that when you investigate a criminal, you never ask first what you really want to ask," said Zuo. He had learned from subordinates that she was a strong-willed woman, but he was still a little taken aback that she was such a defiant prisoner. Taken aback, but he suppressed the inclination to show surprise in his facial expression. That would have been beneath his dignity.

"What do you want ask about? The Taipings?" said Xinmei, pressing him.

"Today, I just wanted to see you. I know fairly well the tricks you've used to delude men."

"That man's never been deluded."

"What?"

"To be blunt, he's not worth the effort to delude."

"You're proud of it?"

"If you want to think that way, fine. Now that you mention tricks, you gave a pretty skillful performance when you fell into the Xiang River on your visit to the boat of Master Lin."

"What did you say?" Zuo's face visibly altered color.

"Doesn't everyone in Changsha know this story?" Xinmei was challenging him deliberately. She had left the Taiping movement, but she still despised the governmental authorities.

At that moment a low-level staff member entered the room and reported, "Lian Liwen has not yet returned."

Zuo glanced in Xinmei's direction and said, "Someone probably told him that the woman had been arrested."

"Yes. So it would seem," replied the staff man, standing rigidly.

"That's a relief!" said Xinmei, just loud enough to be heard and to be annoying.

"We'll find him soon enough," said Zuo as he stood up. "Lock her up in the Star Tower. I'm going to check this all out piece by piece."

—7—

Even when the main force of the Taiping troops arrived at Changsha, it still lacked the capacity to encircle the city. They might just be able to surround the city, but then they would have to concentrate on the eventuality that the Qing forces would come outside the city walls to engage them in battle.

Xu Guangjin, the new imperial commissioner, had come as far as Xiangtan from Hengzhou, but no further. It was only 30 or so kilometers from Xiangtan to Changsha. In consideration of his soldiers, he did not continue forward—and for that he would later be criticized—but the ten thousand–plus troops under his command brought a sizable amount of pressure to bear on the Taipings, simply by being in the area south of Changsha.

The Taiping military had chosen an area to the west of Changsha as a strategic spot. They tried both east and west, but in the east—the area near Mawangdui—Jiang Zhongyuan's forces had visited a major defeat on them. Naturally, they moved on to pour their strength into the western region. The Xiang River flowed to the west of Changsha, and the two armies vied for control of both sides of the river.

Provincial Military Commander Xiang Rong had shown his mettle in the fighting to that point, but he was a man who simply lacked the capacity to cooperate. He hadn't gotten along with Regional Commander Wang Jinxiu. Xiang had the exceedingly bad habit of paying off personal grudges on the battlefield of war, and with his power of command he sent Wang Jinxiu to the most dangerous site at Shuiluzhou, one of the two islands in the Xiang River nearby. Shuiluzhou came under a ferocious attack by the Taipings, and the one thousand–plus Henan troops under Wang's command were almost completely wiped out. Commander Wang escaped with his life and took refuge within the walls of Changsha.

The Taiping Army crossed the river and took control of the western bank. In an attempt to recapture it, Xiang Rong himself led 3,000 soldiers in a forced river crossing and a relentless attack, but Taiping strategy successfully entrapped them and inflicted a stunning defeat on Xiang Rong's forces.

Furthermore, the effort to retake the western shore was visible from atop the Changsha city wall. From this vantage point, enthusiastic encouragement was shouted down to the masses of troops below. There was, needless to say, little reason to expect that such voices would carry across to the other side of the river, but the scene of action was clearly visible. A Taiping force of roughly three hundred troops had built and guarded a simple rampart near the bank of the river. The Qing Army of 3,000 that came on shore headed in that direction and charged it. In terms of numbers, the Taipings clearly could not expect to protect their base, and they began to implement a simultaneous withdrawal.

"No, don't do it!" screamed Zhang Liangji from atop the city wall.

"What shouldn't they do?" asked one of his staff, with a dubious look on his face.

"It's an ambush. They're setting up an ambush. There's a forest that intersects the road behind them, isn't there?"

"How do you know that?"

"The area around their stronghold is open field. There wouldn't be any road there. Still, the long-haired bandits are all fleeing in the same direction. When an army is put to rout in such a place as that, they scatter in all four directions. They aren't dispersing randomly down there. They're escaping en masse. They're going to lure our forces into a trap."

Zhang Liangji was a civil official, but he loved to read books on military strategy. From such a high observation point, the overall scene was readily apparent to him. As they say, one outside the fray has a better view than the participants.

Zhang was not the only one to see the ambush coming. From a short distance away, Zuo Zongtang too shouted at the top of his voice.

"Pull back! Pull back! They're digging in for an ambush!"

From the woods it became impossible to see what was going on below. Whether the Taipings were laying in wait was unknown, but in observing the manner of their flight, the two men had realized something.

On the ground, none of this was known. When the enemy was escaping, you followed them. Xiang Rong had become indignant. This was a critical moment for him—it could decide whether or not he would be exiled to Xinjiang in the far northwest. The great victory he needed wasn't going to materialize without some daring, even if it was strategically useless.

"Go after them and crush them!" he continued to rail at his men.

At a spot near the forest, a large force of Taiping troops in fact appeared. From the vantage point of the city walls, the way in which they emerged had a spectacular quality about it. It all happened instantaneously. The faint red earth suddenly turned black, just as if it were being dyed. They were witnessing the deployment of the Taiping ambush.

Such a stunning reversal was certainly a rare event. Once the color of the soil had been transformed, the Qing Army of pursuit spun around and raced to the riverbank.

Xiang Rong had been on horseback. He had established a reputation for his equestrian talents ever since the time he had spent in Gansu province. He was famous for his horsemanship among the highest military officials of the Qing Army. He turned his horse around, raised his riding crop, and sped off with the horse at a gallop.

Wu-lan-tai also died on horseback, thought Xiang, as he recalled the scene of the battle death of the colleague with whom he had never gotten along well. Although he hadn't witnessed that event, he had heard it recounted by numerous men who had been there at the time, and hence it floated into his mind as though he had seen it with his own eyes.

He'd had bad luck, thought Xiang, for Manchus like Wu-lan-tai—a man born to a life in the military—were celebrated for their equestrianship. Xiang crossed the river on horseback.

"He can really manipulate the horse's reins fantastically," said Zuo Zongtang, as though spitting out the words.

Nearly all the deaths among the Qing troops in this battle were due to drowning. It was a devastating defeat. Many high-level military officials, such as Assistant Regional Commander Xiao Fengchun and Brigadier Vice-Commander Ji Shengmo, died on the battlefield. This all transpired on the nineteenth day of the ninth lunar month, or October 31, a time when the water of the Xiang River had become especially cold.

The battle over Changsha continued thereafter for an entire month. The Taipings dug tunnels and planted explosive devices, though even when one part of the city wall was destroyed, the Qing troops mended it rapidly, preventing the Taipings from being able to break in with a large force.

"Assemble the blind men!" shouted Zuo Zongtang—a bizarre order.

It was thought that men who had lost their vision had, by contrast, a highly enhanced sense of hearing. Zuo ordered the blind men to put their ears to the ground and try to detect the sounds of tunnels being dug. The tunnel strategy was attempted five times, though not once did it have sufficient destructive power to enable a large force to surge into the city.

"I've heard about it. It's the most famous city wall in the entire realm," sighed the strong-willed Yang Xiuqing as he stared up at the wall before his eyes.

When they attempted the fifth try, Yang said, "Quietly get the entire army ready to move. We may storm the city walls of Changsha, or we may lift the siege and head north. Either way, our forces will be moving."

—8—

The place of Xinmei's confinement was known. When it came to extracting intelligence, Tan Qi was a man of gifted talents. It was in a corner of the Star Tower.

"Somehow, I've got to get her out of there," said Liwen in great haste. For the first time since they had been separated, Liwen realized that Xinmei was irreplaceable to him.

From the information unearthed by Tan Qi, Xinmei was in no immediate danger of being executed for the time being. Zuo Zongtang, it seemed, found her to be a woman after his own heart, and as a result had not treated her at all badly. Were the Taipings, on the other hand, to rush into the city, her life could not be guaranteed. It was standard procedure to execute an important criminal whose case was pending, should a disturbance arise.

Because he was a subordinate attached to the Taiping military, Liwen was not asking the Taipings to stage an assault on the city of Changsha. Before she had been taken into custody, Liwen's view that it would be better to head toward Yuezhou had been communicated to the Taiping military leaders. To ask the army to reverse its position now was not necessarily based on a personal view. With this thought in mind, Liwen calmed his innermost feelings.

"I've mapped out a bit of strategy," Tan Qi whispered to Liwen when they were back in his room.

"Strategy?"

"Yes. We buy off some soldiers and quietly gather up some gunpowder. That's what I'm thinking of using."

"To use the gunpowder on the door of the room in the Star Tower where they've got her?"

"That's it."

"There are a lot of guards there. Buy them off? Can you possibly buy them all off?"

"That would be impossible. But one or two of them is a different story. There's about twenty of them there."

"So, how will you do it?"

"For just a moment, we'll get all twenty of them to evacuate the place." Tan Qi was explaining this strategy, the whole time with a smile on his face.

They were going to plant the gunpowder next to the Star Tower, and in the confusion they would rid the place of all the guards. Perhaps among these guards would be some commendable ones who would refuse to abandon their posts. In that eventuality, Liwen was to scream to them that it was a superior official's order to go help put out the fire. In that instant, they would use the gunpowder to blow the lock off the door to the cell in the Star Tower. Not that much would be needed to remove the lock. To get near the Star Tower, Tan Qi would provide some Taiping soldiers with Qing Army uniforms.

"Thanks," said Liwen, with his head bent. Even Liwen was aware of the embarrassing position he was in. To offer to do such a thing for a single woman at a time like this—Liwen listened to the voice of his own heart reproaching him.

"Everything's set for the eighteenth. That's what we've planned." They were already more than halfway through the tenth lunar month. Three months would have passed at month's end from the time of Xiao Chaogui's arrival at Changsha. The assault on Changsha had been a long one.

There was something beaming in Tan Qi's countenance as he spoke. Liwen felt consoled by the expression on his face.

The appointed day arrived. By the solar calendar, it was the last day of November, the thirtieth. The wind was already brisk and much stronger than ordinarily. The sky was murky and overcast.

Dressed in a government military uniform, Liwen accompanied Tan Qi as they approached the Star Tower. Tan Qi was pulling a cart full of bags of rice. A very short man, Tan Qi's face was well-known to many Qing troops, and thus it was impossible to transform him into a soldier. From behind, Chen Picheng was pushing the cart being pulled by Tan Qi. Having this youngster along served the purpose of getting many of the soldiers to relax their vigilance.

From time to time, Tan Qi greeted soldiers he knew, saying things such as, "How are you? Weather's terrible, isn't it? Supposed to rain tomorrow."

There was a row of willows next to the Star Tower. "Let's rest here," Tan Qi said, "until it's time." And, following Tan Qi's lead, Liwen and Chen Picheng sat down at the base of a willow tree. "When are the explosives going to be set?" asked Liwen, becoming anxious upon seeing how nonchalantly Tan Qi was behaving.

"They're already set."

"Really?"

"We've just got to wait for them to go off," said Tan Qi, smiling as he tapped Liwen on the shoulder.

Tan Qi had kept in continual contact with the Taiping troops outside the city walls, and hence knew of their fifth attempt to use explosives effectively. It was to destroy the wall at a spot near the Star Tower. A time was established, and the Taipings were positioned for an assault on Changsha's city wall.

Shortly after making this explanation with drawings, Tan Qi lay flat down.

"Let's all get down." The appointed time was near. The three men were sprawled out flat on the ground. It seemed like a long time passed, though it was probably no more than five minutes. Then a deafening roar exploded to the surface, shaking the ground.

"Let's go!" The three men raced over to the Star Tower. There was no need for Liwen to address the Tower guards, for just at that moment an actual officer shouted at the top of his voice, "Get over there quick! Pile up those sandbags where the wall was destroyed! What are you dawdling for? We're short-handed as it is!"

They had expected the Taipings to use land mines and had a store of sandbags laid up at various points along the wall. They knew that the most effective repair material was coffins, and they had many of them ready as well. Earth had been packed into the coffins, and these proved to be just the right items to construct a blockade.

Tan Qi let out a hearty laugh as he stood before the door of the cell. "We didn't even need the explosives!"

The door seemed to be locked. The key remained inserted in the lock. In all the confusion, it seemed, they had forgotten to remove it when everyone went running out to the scene of the explosion at the wall.

Tan Qi slowly turned the key and pushed open the heavy door.

This fifth effort to destroy the city wall caused damage along an area 20 meters long, but with a general mobilization, the government forces managed to close it up. The coffins packed full of soil proved extremely efficacious, and even with Taiping artillery pounding there, they were ultimately unable to break through into the city. As a result of this artillery barrage by the Taipings, the Qing forces lost Assistant Regional Commander Zhang Xiezhong in the battle, but barely managed to stem the onslaught of the Taiping military.

The following evening, as had been planned, the Taipings lifted the siege of the city and withdrew. It was a night of fierce winds and rain. A pontoon bridge was laid out across the Xiang River for the Taipings, and the troops on the eastern shore crossed it. The sound of the rain and wind was fierce that night, and served to camouflage the movement of the Taiping forces.

Shi Dakai's soldiers were stationed on the eastern bank. When the first friendly troops arrived, Shi's advance troops quietly began marching toward the north. Qing forces just outside the city wall made no notice of the movements of the several tens of thousands of Taiping soldiers.

"Hey, they're not here. There're no enemy troops out here!" It was dawn of the next day when a sentry posted atop the city wall made this report. Then, the cry of a rooster crowing could be heard.

19

Birth of
a Navy

—1—

Using the wind and rain as cover, the Taiping military forces lifted their siege of Changsha and departed to the northwest in the direction of Ningxiang.

When they learned of the disappearance of the Taipings, the key officials in Changsha were stunned. When they had learned in Guilin that the Taipings had lifted their siege of that city, the important figures on the scene sighed in relief, announced that the incident had come to an end, congratulated each other, and only then did they enter into a feud over who would have the great honor of pursuing the bandit forces. Beijing, though, recognized no great honor whatsoever and censured them for having "loosed the bandits elsewhere."

The imperial commissioner, governor-general, provincial military commander, and others were all stringently punished. If the gods of misfortune and illness had gone somewhere else, that was no cause for happiness. They were also sternly scolded for not mounting an immediate pursuit of the bandits.

"Where'd they go?"

"They probably ran back to where they came from."

"Maybe they're planning an attack on the imperial commissioner."

"We need to dispatch troops quickly."

Xu Guangjin, who was named the new imperial commissioner after Saishang-a was relieved of his post, was within the walled city of Xiangtan to the south of Changsha. Changsha was the provincial capital of Hunan, and Xiangtan was but a county seat. It was small and easy to surround.

This, at least, was what the military leaders in Changsha decided, entirely on their own without corroboration, and they immediately dispatched troops there. Were they to remain quietly where they were, then they could expect to be hit by a bolt of lightning from Beijing to the effect of "What the hell were you doing?" Doing nothing left the major military figures in Changsha at loose ends.

On the twenty-first day of the tenth lunar month, six regional commanders —He-chun, Qin Dingsan, Li Rui, Jing Wendai, Wang Jinxiu, and Chang-lu— departed Changsha toward Xiangtan to the south. Knowing that the Taipings had disappeared, they were eager to find out where the Taipings had gone. Soon, though, this battalion of troops returned, for traces indicating that the Taiping forces had moved toward Xiangtan were nowhere to be found.

Finally, it dawned on them in Changsha that the Taipings might have gone in a northwesterly direction. Zuo Zongtang had elicited from his interrogation of a Taiping male captive, who appeared to be some sort of a leader, the following exchange:

"You people rebel against the gracious heavenly dynasty and act as some sort of outlaws. Why has this come to pass?"

"Because we are starving and on the verge of death. We would rather rise in rebellion than die. We are hungry."

"You lie! I've read documents of your group, and it's clear you intend to seize the realm. Is that not what they say?"

"Yes, but that was only to get off the ground. We certainly entertain no such audacious notions."

"Then what do you intend to do? Will you take Nanjing and then send troops north to Beijing? Wasn't that it?"

"No, no. Nothing could be further from the truth. We have no such strength. You must know that much."

"Yet, you intended, did you not, to take Changsha and make it your base of operations?"

"True. The soil in Hunan province is more fertile than that of Guangxi. We could live in comfort with control over just a small amount of land in Hunan."

"You idiots! You look down your nose in this way at Hunan? The Hunanese people will never allow it. Just look! Has Changsha been taken? It will never fall to you so easily."

"Our allies seem to have become aware of this. Talk has recently emerged concerning attacking and seizing a less difficult base of operations."

"And where would that be?"

"I've only heard the name of a city called Changde."

"What's that? Changde, you say . . ."

Changde was a city fronting onto the Yuan River to the west of Dongting Lake, about 180 kilometers to the northwest of Changsha. Though a large city, it was on a much smaller scale than Changsha.

"To the northwest, then. You plan to head toward Changde via Ningxiang and Yiyang." Zuo believed the words of his captive intuitively.

If Zuo Zongtang had been a Taiping general, would he have set his sights on Changde? The Qing's military defenses were inadequate in that vicinity. With their present troop strength, the Taipings were unable to take Changsha. Xiangtan was smaller than Changsha, but there was an imperial commissioner there with considerable military strength and reinforcements soon to arrive from Changsha. It would be suicidal for the Taiping Army to aim at taking Xiangtan. Changde was of the same scale as Xiangtan and was far from any Qing military base.

"Even among the bandits there must be some sharp characters." This was the conclusion of Zuo's report, which he soon presented to Governor Zhang Liangji.

"Is that right? So, the battalion that headed south went through all that trouble for nothing?" Zhang was extremely stingy when it came to wasting energy. He was now aiming at gathering together some small amount of strength. "It came as a relief, you know. The explanation was that there really was something there," said Zuo Zongtang sarcastically.

"Relief and explanations aside, we did actually lose strength here, and as far as I'm concerned that's a waste, really a waste."

"Strength can be created."

"Yes, but there are limits to troop strength."

"Even the same number of troops, though, when aroused, can fight at two or three times the capacity of their numbers."

"I understand all this, but everything doesn't work according to theory and theory alone. You talk about rousing men to action, but there's got to be a root cause to get them going."

"I've found a fairly good cause," said Zuo.

"Well, let's hear it," urged Zhang Liangji.

"We've learned from a prisoner the place where the bandits buried one of their leaders."

"That could be just what we need," said Zhang, crouching down. The Qing military had learned that the Taipings' Western King, Xiao Chaogui, had died on the battlefield outside the southern gate of Changsha.

Hunan was still hot during the seventh and eighth months of the lunar calendar. A corpse could not be left sitting in a coffin at that time of the year, but had to be temporarily buried. When they withdrew from Changsha, they probably had not had sufficient time to dig up the coffin to carry with them. Xiao Chaogui must have been interred somewhere nearby, thought Zuo Zongtang, and under torture his prisoners revealed where it was: in the vicinity of Old Dragon Pond.

—2—

A memorial service was carried out in Changsha for the government troops who had died in battle. The ceremony itself was not Buddhist in nature. Originally a Daoist rite, a fair number of Buddhist elements had now become mixed into the ceremony. One sensed that they were not so much adapted to circumstances than mixed together arbitrarily.

Zhang Liangji read aloud the funeral address, the draft of which had been written by Zuo Zongtang. Two pillars stood before the funerary podium, and a memorial scroll hung from each. These too were the work of Zuo Zongtang.

> The mountains have cracked, and the trees have fallen,
> The winds are sad, and the clouds melancholy.

Short, but they were sufficient to quiet the people gathered there.

Behind the podium were lined up verses composed for the funeral service by various important citizens of Changsha. The battle was still raging. The men who had fallen in the midst of the fighting seemed to remind these poets of Zhuge Liang (181–234), who had died at Wuzhangyuan. Many were the stanzas that read something to the effect of: "Though yet unable to attain victory with his fellows in battle, he went to his death before them."

Cattle, pigs, and chickens were offered at the altar. One item that caught people's attention among the offerings was a coffin covered with mud. A small, 30-centimeter square box to which mud had clearly been applied on purpose was placed to the side of the coffin. The cover to both coffin and box had been removed.

Here lay the corpse of Xiao Chaogui. It had been dug up from the temporary grave at Old Dragon Pond, laid out on the ground, and decapitated with an auspicious green dragon dagger. The head had then been placed separately in the box beside the coffin into which the remainder of his corpse had been cast.

The highest offering to the government's soldiers who had perished on the field of battle was the remains of this "bandit chief." Although a memorial service, the whole scene was extraordinarily grotesque. Despite that, the people there were clearly moved by the events. The objective was to make commanders and troops alike feel both eerie and proud.

At the time this grotesque ceremony was under way, the Taiping military had already passed through Ningxiang, crossed a pontoon bridge over the

Zi River, and captured the city of Yiyang. Nearby was a Qing garrison force under the command of Assistant Regional Commander Ji Guan.

The occupation of Yiyang had not gone that smoothly, for resistance by Qing forces had been strikingly fierce. Ji Guan had died in the fight, and total government losses numbered as high as seven hundred to eight hundred. After the destruction of Ji Guan's army, the resistance dissipated.

"This is a gift from the Heavenly Father," intoned Eastern King Yang Xiuqing when they entered the walled city of Yiyang. All the Qing's civil and military officials in Yiyang had already taken flight, but well over a thousand private vessels remained on the Zi River. These spoils of war were completely unanticipated.

This made it possible for the Taipings to end the debate they had been engaged in to that point on the line to pursue. There were those among them who had concocted a large, overarching plan to leave the Yangzi River area, take the city of Nanjing, set their sights on the area to the north of the river in Jiangsu or Anhui, and then begin a long and concerted march with the aim of attacking Beijing.

Advocates of a more sober-minded approach were opposed to those in support of a northern expedition. Such a radical plan, they argued, was no different from having resolved to seize the entire realm, but that had to be pondered on the basis of Taiping strength. Before the country could be taken, a base had to be erected, and they suggested making a piece of fertile Hunan province their home.

More supported the latter, more moderate policy. Those who advocated occupation of terrain in Hunan considered Changde a suitable base of operations. The Taiping military had in fact already set off in the direction of Changde. Then well over a thousand boats fell into their possession at Yiyang. Mightn't they use them to sail down the Yangzi River? The possibility of an attack on Nanjing remained. Also, when they spoke with local residents, they learned:

> You won't surprise anybody with that many boats. They had many more at Yuezhou. The big shots over at Yuezhou held back the boats that were trying to get to Changsha via Dongting Lake. Now, well, there's a war going on at Changsha, and the boats that the enemy seized will probably be used by them. No, there's already too many boats over there. It's been three months, so lots of them have accumulated.

Just looking at the hundreds and hundreds of boats before them, it seemed quite possible that they could sail down the Yangzi easily. Now they learned that several times as many vessels had been detained and were being held in Yuezhou. The Taiping leaders held a conference. The opposition between those in favor of a march to the north and those in favor of establishing a base in Hunan emerged, though neither Hong Xiuquan nor Yang Xiuqing expressed a clear opinion.

While the fighting continued, they were increasing their troop strength, and because that troop strength was still insufficient, there was no cause to forbid consideration of the larger plan. This was the objection laid down by those supporting an expedition toward the capital.

"As a final objective," said Luo Dagang—an advocate of moderation—in explaining his own views on the matter, "of course, it is our intention to realize our dream of a Heavenly Kingdom of Great Peace throughout the entire land of China. However, we haven't actually been able to topple Guilin or Changsha. At most we have only between fifty thousand and one hundred thousand troops in our armed forces. Even if county and department seats fall to us, we still lack the capacity to bring down a provincial capital. For now, all we can do is to establish a base at Changde and extend our operations from that point."

Advocates of a base always used the expression "for now." This meant that, were circumstances to change, they were not wedded to this stance. But didn't the discovery of these hundreds of boats at Yiyang suddenly change those circumstances?

"It's still not enough," said Luo Dagang.

Other Taiping leaders had no choice but to listen closely to what Luo had to say, for he had experience as a skiff bandit leading a fleet of vessels on many a rampage. But, he added, "If there are over three thousand more boats at Yuezhou, then I think we may be able to take Wuchang. Waging a battle on the Yangzi would then not be impossible."

At the first such conference, the following resolution was reached: "Is the information on the number of vessels that have accumulated at Yuezhou accurate? We must first ascertain this, and quickly."

It was a Taiping tradition to begin the fighting immediately upon the issuance of a resolution. Yiyang was connected to Yuezhou by the Zi River and Dongting Lake. Many of those in Yiyang had made the trip to Yuezhou.

"Has anyone been to Yuezhou recently?" The Taiping military was seeking out someone who could corroborate the intelligence report.

"There's a timber merchant who just arrived from Yuezhou yesterday."

This man's name was Tang Zhengcai. He had come to Yuezhou at the head of a flotilla of several hundred vessels and gotten caught up in the official ban on passage. Every year Tang traveled to Yuezhou on business. Since his boats had been detained there, he'd had an opportunity to get an overview of the local scene. He had now returned to gather documents demonstrating that he had no ties to the "bandit army" so as to persuade the local officials to lift the ban on passage for him. In spite of this, he had now run right into the bandit army.

"Go with that guy and then report back. Listen to everything you can," said Yang Xiuqing.

—3—

"Hey, Tang, old buddy," said Luo Dagang, staring at his traveling companion, Tang Zhengcai.

"Huh? Old Luo." Tang seemed genuinely surprised. The addition of an "old" by one's name when addressing someone had nothing to do with age, but rather indicated an intimacy with the person so addressed. Tang and Luo spoke to one another in this manner.

"What's this? You two know each other?" said Yang Xiuqing from off to their side. "Well, let's make it short. Find out about what's going on in Yuezhou."

"I never thought I'd find you as a cohort of the long-haired bandits," said Tang to Luo.

"Probably not," said Luo and then went off to introduce Tang to the Taiping leaders.

"He's a fantastic businessman with nerve and steadiness. In the past we often fenced stolen goods through him. On occasion he even went along himself with fleets of our boats and helped us in our work."

"That sort of a fellow, eh?" A smile crept onto one cheek of Yang Xiuqing's face, and then quickly he returned to his original expression. Tang claimed to be a timber merchant, though he evidently was half merchant and half thief. Yang was pondering how Tang might prove useful to them.

"We want to know how many private boats are docked at Yuezhou," said Luo Dagang.

"About five thousand three hundred, and there are also lots of rafts. If I had as many troops as you people do, I'd attack Yuezhou. You've got no other choice but to attack," said Tang frankly.

"Attack, I see. What sort of response would they put up?" asked Luo, fixing his gaze directly into Tang's eyes.

"I'm often amazed that they can put together such a collection of incompetents there. The local officials at Yuezhou are uniformly worthless," continued Tang, completely disregarding Luo's steady gaze in his face.

"There's bound to be a provincial military commander at Yuezhou."

"There's a character by the name of Bo-le-gong-wu, but there's no mistaking him for anything but a coward."

"This isn't the first time I've heard that name." Somewhere he had heard the name Bo-le-gong-wu before. At the time of the Opium War some ten years earlier, as the regional commander in Yichang (in Hubei province) he had been sent to reinforce the army in Guangzhou. He hadn't fought in any great battles, but merely accompanied his army to the field of conflict, and for that he was recognized as having accomplished some sort of meritorious act and was awarded the provincial military command of Gansu province. It was a promotion from regimental to divisional commander.

"He's got only eight hundred troops under his command," said Tang Zhengcai.

Bo-le-gong-wu was the military commander of Hubei province. When the Taiping forces had entered Hunan, he was ordered to proceed with his army from Hubei to Yuezhou in Hunan. Indeed, he only had 800 men under him. It would seem that this divisional commander was actually leading a battalion to terrain outside his jurisdiction.

Then it's just an official trip, thought both Tang and the soldiers. Bo-le-gong-wu was alleged to have said to those on either side of him, "Disposing of the long-haired bandits is up to Guangxi and Hunan. I'll just show my face in the northern part of Hunan, and that ought to be enough to exert some influence." He had no intention whatsoever of waging war.

"Are you absolutely sure?" broke in Yang Xiuqing.

"I was in Yuezhou for three months and pretty much know what was going on there. There's a circuit intendant there by the name of Wang Donghuai who has a bit of backbone, but his father just died and he's returned home to observe the ritual mourning period. Assistant Regional Commander A-er-dong-a is the most military of the military types, but people under him are a feeble lot, and they're all but bereft of any training. Over half of them smoke opium."

"What about the civil officials?"

"There's a prefect and county magistrate there, though both are cowards. If I were prime minister and the country were placed in my trust, I'd put the most capable commander and the strongest army in Yuezhou. It's not the provincial capital, but if Yuezhou is taken, the whole country will be in serious danger," said Tang Zhengcai eloquently.

"You think Yuezhou's such an important site? Really? It's the pivotal point between Hunan and Hubei."

"To my way of thinking, it's not such a big deal if provincial capitals like Guilin or Changsha or Wuchang are occupied. But once Yuezhou is taken, it's all over."

"You mean because of the five thousand boats there?"

"Not only that," said Tang Zhengcai, slowly turning his head from side to side and assuming something of an air before continuing. "The guns and ammunition of the Prince of the Pacified West are all still in Yuezhou right where he left them."

"The Prince of the Pacified West?" Quiet until that point, Shi Dakai pushed himself forward to listen.

"That is true, is it not? Yuezhou was the place the Prince of the Pacified West turned into his base of operations as an impregnable fortress." These words were spoken by Heavenly King Hong Xiuquan himself, who had not said a word until that point. He too had wedged his way into the discussion.

Yang Xiuqing looked at the two men's visages, and for a moment it left him with an unpleasant sensation, but after shutting his eyes momentarily he continued to nod his assent softly. Yang had not received a formal education of any kind and thus did not know who this Prince of the Pacified West was. It was the first time he had heard the name.

"So when the Prince of the Pacified West died, Yuezhou still hadn't been taken by the Qing military. After he died, the government's commanders wanted to return to Yunnan and lost their will to continue the fighting. Until then the Qing forces had progressed only as far as Junshan in the direction of Yuezhou. So, the materiel of the Prince of the Pacified West is . . ." This time it was Wei Changhui who had spoken.

Yang Xiuqing may not have possessed any substantive learning, but he was extremely intelligent and quick-witted. While he had held his eyes shut, he surmised that this "Prince of the Pacified West" whom they were all speaking about was none other than Wu Sangui (1612–1678), the principal player in the great Rebellion of the Three Feudatories (1673–1681) at the beginning of the Qing dynasty.

At the time that the Taipings had risen in rebellion, Yang Xiuqing had done a thorough study of past uprisings in China. Since he was unable to read, he had to rely exclusively on information acquired by listening to others. When he asked for details from the so-called "intellectuals" in the Society of God Worshippers, all he got was spite and anger, so he often badgered the old schoolteacher in Jintian village for stories about wars from the past.

Wu Sangui had originally been a commander in the armies of the Ming dynasty (1368–1644). While he was leading an expedition to the Shanhai Pass at the Great Wall to defend against an attack from the Manchus, Beijing fell to the rebel armies of Li Zicheng (1605?–1645). The year was 1644.

The Ming court was being assaulted on two fronts, from the east by the Manchus and from the west by forces of Li Zicheng. Li Zicheng's forces were the first to bring down the capital city of Beijing. All the high civil and military officials surrendered to Li's armies and thus assumed this posture to prepare for the attack from the Manchus. Li Zicheng had been a day laborer at a post station, and from the perspective of the Ming court he was merely a "roving bandit." He was, however, an ethnic Han Chinese, no different from the Ming imperial court.

Here he intended to build an ethnic Han dynasty and try to defend against the Manchus. At first, Wu Sangui was of the same frame of mind. But when Wu learned that his beloved concubine Chen Yuanyuan, whom he had left in Beijing, had been spirited away with Li Zicheng's armed forces, he exploded in rage. So, he joined forces with the Manchu armies—against whom he had been fighting up to that point—and with their help he attacked Beijing and dealt the forces of Li Zicheng a crushing defeat.

The Manchu armies, who had now entered the walled city of Beijing, made it the capital of their Qing dynasty and eventually came to exert complete control over all Chinese terrain. Wu Sangui was honored as an "elder statesman in the founding of the state" and was effectively enfeoffed as the Prince of Yunnan.

The old schoolteacher in Jintian village spoke eloquently as he described these events. He had a particular aptitude for depicting the nature of the bond that tied Wu Sangui to Chen Yuanyuan.

Yang Xiuqing had not known the name "Prince of the Pacified West," namely the one who had put down the forces of Li Zicheng coming from the west, because in the story told to him by his former schoolteacher, Wu Sangui was known by the name of the province in which he had been set up as a satrap: the "Prince of Yunnan." For his own part, Yang wasn't the least bit interested in tales of generals and their loves. What he continually pestered his teacher for were stories of the rebellion that Wu Sangui subsequently led.

"Yes, yes, that was when the Prince of Yunnan was already an old man. It's regrettable, but you can never take back the years," said the old teacher.

Wu Sangui's rebellion occurred about thirty years after the Manchu seizure and occupation of Beijing. A once young and stalwart military commander was now an old man. The uprising lasted for eight years before Wu Sangui died in his own camp. Just prior to his death, he had ascended the throne with the self-appointed title of "emperor" in the city of Hengzhou in Hunan, though his base of operations had been Yuezhou.

Yang Xiuqing remembered every single detail of the story his teacher had recounted to him. He may not have been literate, but Yang had a phenomenal memory. As he opened his eyes widely, he said, "It would be great to get the weapons left by the Prince of the Pacified West, but we mustn't follow in the tracks of the losses of that old man. It's ridiculous to even contemplate asking the Dalai Lama to divide up the country. We've got to fight this one through to the bitter end, battle by battle."

The people assembled all exchanged glances in genuine admiration for this fellow who knew so much despite having no formal learning at all. While Wu Sangui, the Prince of the Pacified West, was carrying on his uprising against the Qing dynasty, he asked the Dalai Lama of Tibet to make a representation before the Manchu court in Beijing to the effect that, in exchange for a cease-fire, he be given the southwest part of China.

Such an idea was rejected out of hand, but no one there had any idea that Yang Xiuqing possessed such a detailed knowledge of history.

—4—

Wu Sangui's rebellion was suppressed, and 170 years had passed in the interim. One would now almost certainly assume that such old weaponry and ammunition would be of no utility whatsoever to the Taipings, but in that period of 170 years, the techniques and implements of warfare had not developed at all.

"There's so much of it that it's impossible to count," said Tang Zhengcai. Tang was a man in the habit of affixing precise figures, such as the 5,300 boats and 800 troops under the provincial military commander, but this was how he expressed himself on the armaments bequeathed by Wu Sangui.

"Make no doubt about it," judged Yang Xiuqing.

The story of the Prince of the Pacified West lit up the faces of both Hong Xiuquan and Shi Dakai. This information brought by Tang Zhengcai served effectively to get the Taipings to switch their line of approach from "setting up a base" in Hunan to pursuing a long march and wholesale attack. As Yang Xiuqing pointed out, did not the defeat of Wu Sangui provide a negative example to those contemplating the establishment of a base in Hunan or further west?

The Taiping military, then set to advance toward Changde, headed east from Yiyang. Having acquired well over a thousand small vessels, they were able to travel by land and water both. Tang Zhengcai, his dubious past notwithstanding, took over supervision of the groups of boats on the Zi River.

The Taipings took Yiyang on the third day following the lifting of the siege of Changsha, the twenty-second day of the tenth lunar month. Land and water forces of Taiping men allegedly arrived at Linzikou in Xiangyin county on the twenty-sixth.

The Qing court knew full well the strategic importance of Yuezhou. Hubei Governor Chang Dachun set out on his own account from the region of Dongting Lake, put together a flotilla of 500 vessels, loaded them full of stones and earth, and then sank them all. This was aimed at blocking off the river passage as far as Yuezhou.

In this way, he expected to protect Yuezhou, and thinking it would suffice simply to block off the river route, he did not increase the number of troops guarding the point at which it emptied into the lake. They were unable to impede the advancing Taiping forces.

When the Taipings had Changsha surrounded, they were in no position to decide their next course of action. Indeed, there were hopeful observers among them who offered the consoling remark that 500 sunken vessels was no major obstacle at all. There were 500 of them, but they were all small in size. It would have been a disaster had all the sunken ships been large. And, though the boats were submerged, most were in shallow waters. These sunken boats were intended to convince the Taiping forces that they would be unable to cross the area. They were then expected simply to turn around and withdraw. Since the boats were to be sunk, the sails could have been removed from them. Chang Dachun, however, had them all fitted with sails, especially those that lacked them until then. It soon became clear as day that the water route was blocked by this protruding forest. These sails were being used to convince the enemy to surrender. The very idea had to have been the brainchild of someone who made a habit of not working.

"Clear the sunken vessels away!" ordered Yang Xiuqing, who had arrived from the mouth of Dongting Lake, with nothing particularly profound on his mind and as if it were a perfectly normal practice.

Several tens of thousands of nearby villagers were commandeered to remove the blockage. Many among them had assisted in the work of actually sinking the vessels when so ordered by the Hubei governor. The task was completed in a day.

Linzikou, where the Taiping forces massed, was the point at which the Xiang River and the Zi River, having flowed into one another, spilled into Dongting Lake. Some 30 kilometers to the north was a much smaller river, the Miluo, which also flowed into Dongting Lake. A Miluo county seat was located on the shore of this river, between Changsha and Yuezhou, though somewhat closer to Yuezhou.

When the Taipings arrived at Linzikou, Lian Liwen and Li Xinmei were both in the county seat of Miluo. They had separated from Tan Qi and the young Chen Picheng on the trip down the Xiang River, near Xiangyin. Tan and Chen rejoined the Taiping Army.

"There was a fellow by the name of Qu Yuan at the end of the Warring States period over two thousand years ago," said Liwen to Xinmei.

"Why such a complex and old story? How about a story I'll understand?"

"Just about everything flows with great ease into your head."

"Okay, tell your story."

"Qu Yuan's state from that ancient time was one of the warring states, the state of Chu. Government affairs were not being handled well there at the time. He often thought of trying his hand at politics, but scoundrels and villains always got in his way."

"What sort of scoundrels?"

"People who were acting as agents for the powerful state of Qin. So, Qu Yuan was expelled from the capital, and he came to this part of China."

"What a sad story!"

"With his hair disheveled, he is said to have wandered all over this area. His ideals were betrayed. He worked hard for his kingdom, but was never recognized by his king. One day while wandering about these parts, he met an old fisherman."

"What's this about his ideals being betrayed? Sounds like me."

"And the old man spoke to Qu Yuan: 'If the world is so cloudy and filthy, why shouldn't you match it and be just as confused? Try to remain clean and beautiful all by yourself, and you'll truly live a painful life.'"

"This story is really about me. Match the world for its confusion. Whatever happened to this Qu Yuan?"

"For all his efforts, Qu Yuan couldn't live in a state of cloudiness. So, what remained was death alone. It's said that he threw himself into this very Miluo River and drowned."

"I have no intention of dying." Xinmei stood up abruptly and blinked her eyes. Something of an unintentional surprise had crept into her voice.

She then burst out laughing, and in a carefree manner went on. "Are you afraid of something on my behalf?"

"No, no. I'm not afraid for you. You can do fine all by yourself."

"But I'm not by myself," said Xinmei as she sat down in a chair. She then pushed a chair toward Liwen.

"For some reason, I sense this very clearly," said Liwen. In fact, he wanted to say that she had not the least scent of femininity about her at all.

"The place where that fellow committed suicide? How awful! Let's get away from this place now," she said, grabbing Liwen by the arm and shaking him.

The following morning, the two of them left the city of Miluo toward the Miluo River to make travel preparations.

"Let's move quickly. Otherwise, we're likely to run into the war again," said Xinmei.

They would soon find themselves sailing down the Yangzi River, and she wanted to begin a new life in that new place about which she had heard from Liwen, Shanghai. It had become her earnest desire.

Liwen, for his part, was also of a mind that it might soon be a good idea to try something new in a place apart from the Taipings. Without Liwen around to help with all the work of supplies and accounting, the Taipings seemed to be able to take care of things by themselves.

The boat they had hired arrived at the prearranged time.

"Well done! I did it. You know, I almost got dragged off in the direction of

Dongting. I'd never have made it here to get you. Now, you're in charge," said the captain, as he operated the pole to maneuver the vessel.

"Did you say in the direction of Dongting?" asked Liwen.

"Those long-haired bandits are there. They're trying to salvage the boats that the authorities sank there before they came, and they're gathering men together," replied the captain.

"What do you know! Seems they're really moving quickly . . . faster than I thought," said Liwen to Xinmei.

"When you get momentum, you can often go faster than you ever imagined possible. Anyway, could you sing me once more that song you sang yesterday? The old fisherman's tune?"

There was a wind, and the small boat rocked from side to side. Despite the fact that it was she who had had experience plying various and sundry waterways, Xinmei clenched Liwen's sleeve and ducked her head.

"That one, eh?"

Everyone in the world is polluted and I alone am pure. Everyone in the world is drunk and I alone am sober. So grieved Qu Yuan many centuries before. While drinking wine the previous evening, Liwen had sung the song that the old fisherman had sung to Qu Yuan as he departed:

> If the waters of the Canglang River are clean,
> Let us wash the strings of our ceremonial caps in it.
> If the waters of the Canglang River are polluted,
> Let us wash our feet in it.

—5—

In the eyes of the destitute people from Guangxi, Hunan soil seemed rich. The Hunanese, however, were never comfortable with this perception. There had been countless incidents in which such poor immigrants had fled without paying land rent or taxes. The core of the "Enlarged Hunan Army" that joined the Taipings in southern Hunan was comprised of tens of thousands of such abscondees. Once they took flight, having failed to pay rent and taxes, they became fugitives from the authorities. Since apprehension meant certain execution, such people had gathered together to form organizations for self-protection.

During these years, bandit groups of this sort came and went in various parts of the country. The Taiping Heavenly Kingdom was essentially of the same nature, only it had grown considerably in size.

"Well done, I'd say," the boat captain recounted to his passengers. "The other guys went willingly, because they'll get paid. I've heard that the army of the long-haired ones are bandits, but they say those fellows pay for everything. It's strange. When the authorities ordered those boats to be sunk, I not only didn't get wages to help—I didn't even get food."

Small as it might be, when local people learned that a daily wage would be paid, they came rushing in for work. Though the people were exceedingly poor and in search of labor, only rarely did any real work materialize. During the time that Liwen and Xinmei had limpingly made their way across the Miluo River to a village by the name of Taolinsi, the Taiping military had almost completed the effort to clear away the waterborne obstructions to Dongting Lake. Inasmuch as this was a region infested with bandits, the local *tuanlian* defense groups were also quite prominent. Local landlords and others with property that had to be protected trained stalwart young men in personal armies, and the local authorities naturally recognized these new military groupings. In such cases, the landlords paid a daily wage and thus were able to attract men.

The Taipings were going to a place called Tuxinggang, or Saturn Harbor. The landlord there, Wu Shimai, amassed some two thousand *tuanlian* troops to defend his terrain. These were primarily the descendents of fishermen along the shores of Dongting Lake. For whatever reason, the Qing dynastic authorities trusted these fishing people to provide defensive strength. When the Taiping armies approached, Wu Shimai's *tuanlian* took off in flight without so much as a skirmish.

"What?! Everybody ran away? Did you say there wasn't a single bullet fired?" said Bo-le-gong-wu, military commander of Hubei province, who was then in Yuezhou, as he unconsciously rose from his chair upon hearing this news. He had just a short while earlier personally inspected the *tuanlian* troops heading for Tuxinggang.

These *tuanlian* troops were men who ordinarily took boats out on the water and fished for a living, and they were a strong-willed bunch. Compared to the government armies, in which over half of the men were opium smokers, these groups of youths with their bronzed, muscular bodies seemed reliable. In fact, they'd proven completely useless.

So, they all ran away. Our own men are even worse, thought the Manchu commander, a chill running down his back.

News that the Taipings were now heading toward Changde meant that they had changed directions for the east. Yuezhou began to take on the character of a panic.

"This is the end of my brilliant military career," said the military commander to himself.

"Fortunate" would probably have been a better word than "brilliant." Bo-le-gong-wu was a Manchu who belonged to the Plain White Banner. At first he was attached to the Musketeer Guardsmen, a firearm brigade, and in 1813 he was mobilized to Henan and awarded the rank of lieutenant. It was his first military command.

Forty years had since passed. During the Opium War of some ten or more years previous, he had served the army as a regional commander, though without distinction. From his record he might have appeared to be a veteran, but he had absolutely no actual fighting experience.

Later, he was promoted to the position of military commander of Gansu province. The Muslims of Gansu had risen in rebellion, but by the time he proceeded to this assignment, the uprising had already been put down. He had done nothing.

In addition, his "fortune" did not continue forever. When he had first been to Hubei, it was as a regional commander; now as military commander he was the highest military official in the province. Even the most beautiful brocade lasts but for a fleeting moment in time.

He was sent to Yuezhou prefecture, which the Taipings had targeted for an all-out attack.

"Get the old man." In the dead of night, he called for an older man by the name of Lu who had been working by the Manchu's side as a servant straight through for the past thirty years.

"Extraordinary, indeed," said Lu upon arriving. Somehow, he knew why he had been summoned.

"Give me some advice," said the military commander.

"Something you've never confronted before, I would guess." Until that point, old Lu had handled a wide variety of miscellaneous problems for his master, from money to women. Lu was a shrewd and able man, well-trusted in such matters. He had always been much better at dealing with private matters than with public ones. In noting that the present problem appeared to be a first for his master, old Lu had surmised that the council sought by Bo-le-gong-wu involved the troops that had run off.

"The prefectural seat is helpless. The two thousand fishing households will be routed without a fight. Even with a fighting force of sixty thousand, Changsha was unable to land a blow against the long-haired bandits. Unscathed, they're now about to arrive here," said the provincial military commander, his brow knitted. It's the same old story, thought old Lu to himself, and then said, "You shall die for naught."

"That's it. Thrown out of Changsha without a casualty . . ."

"In retrospect, we didn't do such a good job of stopping their ships."

"Why?"

"I have heard that the long-haired bandits have five thousand boats at Yuezhou and that they are on their way here. Perhaps it was a rumor."

"Perhaps . . ." said the military commander, biting his lip. Thinking about what they had done was beginning to torment him.

"What's passed is past. Let's worry about what's to come."

"Good idea. I'm not going to die for naught. Running away is the stuff of a Yu Buyun." During the Opium War, the Zhejiang Provincial Military Commander Yu Buyun (d. 1842) had abandoned Ningbo and fled. He was later executed for his actions.

Bo-le-gong-wu had no wish to repeat this fate. Ten years after Yu's execution, there had been criticism and reflection on the case. Furthermore, while there had been a military commander and a regional commander involved in the defeat and withdrawal, only Yu Buyun was executed insofar as his actions concerned the Opium War.

Yu was put to death by decapitation because he was a Han Chinese. Had the military commander been a Manchu and committed the same offense, his head would probably still be attached to his abdomen. This was just rumor, but even in the ranks of the military a similar discontent was being murmured.

In the court in Beijing, a voice had recently been raised and had reached Bo-le-gong-wu's ears to the effect that: "In military rewards and punishments, we should follow the forms set down by the Kangxi Emperor at the time of the Rebellion of the Three Feudatories."

When the rebellion of Wu Sangui and his collaborators was quelled, the Qing dynasty was only thirty years old. In that brief time, the high Manchu leaders had already become full-fledged aristocrats and their military all but useless. It was the Green Standards Brigade—namely, the Han battalions—who had succeeded in crushing the rebels.

In his distribution of rewards and punishments, the Kangxi Emperor recognized the Han brigades with merits and delivered sanctions against the Manchus, especially the imperial family and those close to them. The Commander Prince Le-er-jin, a general-in-chief, and Labu (Prince Jian) were stripped of their ranks, had their family property confiscated, and suffered imprisonment. These actions were a great inspiration to the morale of the Qing military, and only two years after the Rebellion of the Three Feudatories, the government forces proved themselves able to force the surrender of the rebel forces on the island of Taiwan.

Upon historical reflection, it was ever so clear that this golden age of the Qing military was built upon the assumption of a highly strict attitude taken toward the Manchu military officials. After the beheading of Yu Buyun, to the contrary, morale in the government armies had been dropping, and the court was attentive to this decline.

Predictions within the military ran that, should another war break out, the Manchu commanders would be severely defeated. This too weighed on Bo-le-gong-wu's mind.

"We can't just run away without a fight. We've got to show them something. We'll fight . . . and if it happens, we'll take casualties, and only if necessary will we retreat."

Old Lu understood what the military commander was about to say. It was: We'll put on the show. We'll prepare not just the actors but the entire audience as well.

"Now's the time. Don't be stingy with the money," said the Manchu military commander.

—6—

We have already taken note of the fact that the Taiping Army, having shifted course on its way from Changsha, was heading toward Yiyang via Ningxiang. Ningxiang was to be the hometown of Liu Shaoqi (1898–1969), former number two man in the People's Republic of China until his downfall during the Cultural Revolution, and just 40 kilometers to its south was Shaoshan, the birthplace of Mao Zedong (1893–1976). Less than 20 kilometers to the south of Shaoshan was a place known as Xiangxiang, the ancestral home of Zeng Guofan. Zeng had returned there to take up ritual mourning for his mother on the twenty-third day of the eighth lunar month of that year, corresponding to October 6.

Although Changsha had come under attack by the Taiping Army, with the death of the Western King Xiao Chaogui in the fighting, the main force of the Taiping military had not yet rushed to join them from Chenzhou. Informed by Governor Chang Dachun in Wuchang that the city of Changsha was surrounded, Zeng chose to return home by land rather than risk a water voyage. Had he used the river, his vessel might also have been detained at Yuezhou.

Thirteen years had passed since his last trip home. Zeng was a man of strong passions, and he cried bitterly before the casket of his departed mother.

"Please, be calm," said his younger brother, Zeng Guoquan, pulling him by the sleeve.

"All my strength is gone," he responded. When his duty as a filial son was complete, he went out into the courtyard and stared up into the sky. Bit by bit autumn was already upon him. Zeng was genuinely in despair, though to onlookers his intense despondence seemed to be overdoing it. As he looked into the autumn sky, his eyes finally settled on a spot.

"You cannot remain in a state of sadness forever. The country is full of too many difficulties now," said his younger brother. Zeng Guoquan seemed to have already forgotten his mother's death and to be more anxious about fighting the long-haired bandits.

"Full of difficulties, precisely," said Zeng Guofan, though there was no noticeable strength in his speech.

"Elder brother, you are a vice-minister. Do you not hold a position of one who must be concerned with national crises?"

"I am concerned."

"It does not appear as such. . . . Mother's passing was sad, of course, but . . ." Zeng Guoquan's words broke off as he became increasingly tense.

"Stamping your feet on the ground in anger is no way to prove you're a patriot," reproached Zeng Guofan.

"You're probably right."

"Will you lead troops off to Changsha?"

"If I can, I wish to do so."

"And, if you can't, what'll you do? You'll tell me to join you and stamp our feet together. And that'd be of absolutely no use to anyone."

"True, true. Since I have no troops to command, I shall raise a force, a *tuanlian*, and I'd like you to help me, elder brother."

"Zhu Sunyi had already begun to do so." Zhu Sunyi was the Xiangxiang county magistrate who was then pouring his energies into training a group of stalwart youths. "Yes, but elder brother . . ."

County magistrate was a position that went to one who had passed the highest level of the civil service examinations with a mediocre score. It was not a particularly high post in the Qing Dynasty, one of rank 7A. Zeng Guofan, who had passed the imperial examinations in the top rankings, advanced right past positions like county magistrate. A vice-minister held a rank of 2A, higher even than that of provincial governor at 2B. For all of a county magistrate's efforts, if a high official like Zeng Guofan were to become involved, a much mightier *tuanlian* was likely to be the result. This is what Zeng Guoquan wanted to tell his elder brother.

"Just address the local gentry once, and the strength of the *tuanlian* would be so different," said Zeng Guoquan. His logic was that a *tuanlian* force cost money. It was plenty expensive just feeding a group of young men. For a vice-minister to make an appeal on their behalf—far more than for a county magistrate—would probably lead to a significant increase in donations.

"Yes, that's undoubtedly true," said Zeng Guofan, still staring into space.

"Not just in seeking donations from the rural gentry. If elder brother would take over supervision of the Xiangxiang *tuanlian*, Beijing wouldn't turn its back on you."

"Don't be stupid." Zen Guofan finally returned his gaze to his brother. "What do you mean?" He truly did not know the cause of his brother's consternation.

"You're planning to get money from Beijing too?"

"I estimate just a small amount . . ."

"Let's speak plainly. At present there are between five and six million taels of silver in the national treasury. Since the long-haired bandits rose in rebellion, over ten million taels have been spent to put them down. And it cost that much at a time when it was just a bunch of ragtag rebels. Now they claim between fifty thousand and one hundred thousand members. That's all Beijing has. You understand what I'm saying?" Zeng Guoquan was unable to respond.

"The central government is completely broke. Don't expect a thing from them. If you want to raise a *tuanlian*, you've got to start by raising money. Stamp the ground to your heart's content, but it won't produce a thing."

"I see," said Zeng Guoquan, his head hanging down.

"In any event, keep me apprised of the news from Changsha."

"I shall see to it," said Zeng Guoquan, a glint in his eye. He could hear in his brother's words the great anxiety and melancholy he was feeling for his country. "Hanzhang is on his way here from Yongding county at a gallop, and I believe he was in Changsha. I've heard that he leads a number of troops."

"Really, Hanzhang, eh?"

Li Hanzhang was the younger brother of the famous Li Hongzhang (1823–1901). At this time neither brother held a high official position, though Hongzhang was halfway there, so to speak, as a proxy county magistrate. Li Hanzhang was one of Zeng Guofan's disciples.

"He was just transferred to work for the county magistrate at Yiyang and was on his way to take up his post. This was postponed and he went to Changsha," explained Zeng Guoquan.

"That's very good," mumbled Zeng Guofang.

—7—

The Taipings took Yiyang, and gained control over more than five thousand vessels there. They then decided to head toward Yuezhou, and come out onto the Yangzi River. At that time, there had just been a switch in Yiyang's county magistrate and the position was temporarily vacant.

Though they'd had similar experiences in Guangxi and Hunan, when the Taipings seized a town, the first thing they did was to execute all the high officials appointed by the Qing dynasty. It had become their standard operating procedure. After killing the officials, the pattern called for them to destroy the Confucian temples and the haunts of other idols.

Because of the change in magistrates, there was no one to execute in Yiyang. Li Hongzhang's younger brother, Hanzhang, had originally been appointed Yiyang county magistrate, but this tempestuous lad, en route to assuming his new posting, had entered Changsha, then under Taiping siege, to lead the fight.

The Taipings' mode of operations was already well-known at this time. Provincial Military Commander Bo-le-gong-wu was not the only one in Yiyang seized with terror. Civil officials were just as frightened, for they knew full well of the Taiping policy toward officials.

The walled city of Yuezhou was also the site of Yuezhou prefecture, and the one county over which Yuezhou prefecture had jurisdiction was Baling county. As such, both a county magistrate and a prefect were housed within its walls. A prefect held rank 4B in the civil service ladder, a rather high position. The present Yuezhou prefect was a man by the name of Lian Chang. The Baling county magistrate was one Hu Fanggu. As Tang Zhengcai had told the Taiping leaders, this was a group of complete incompetents.

On the first day of the eleventh lunar month, Xiang Rong finally arrived at Xiangyin from Changsha at the head of a band of troops. The excuse he gave for his tardy departure from Changsha was the necessity of ascertaining exactly where the Taipings were heading. However, Taiping movements were known from early on, and had he moved more rapidly, he would certainly have confronted them—precisely what he feared most.

The Taipings had left Changsha twelve days previously, and Imperial Commissioner Xu Guangjin arrived before the walled city of Changsha from Xiangtan also on the first. The Qing military moved with excruciating slowness.

In Xiangyin, Xiang Rong penned a letter addressed to Yuezhou, which read: "Defend Yuezhou to the death for a day or two. Reinforcements are on their way."

The letter was delivered to Yuezhou the next day, the second. However, there was no one to receive it. The highest civil official, Lian Chang, and the highest military official, Bo-le-gong-wu—prefect and military commander, respectively—had already fled the city through the eastern gate.

"He's away on urgent business," said the prefect's secretary.

"He's quite sick in bed," said old Mr. Lu on behalf of the military commander.

On the morning of the third, County Magistrate Hu Fanggu also beat a hasty retreat from the city. That afternoon, the Taipings began to bring pressure to bear on Yuezhou. Local bandits led an insurrection within the city. The Taipings had established secret contacts with these people, though among the latter were an assortment of pernicious types prepared to take advantage of the chaos and set the town ablaze and plunder what they might.

All of the city gates were opened widely. The Taiping military split into three units, and bit by bit, entered Yuezhou. From time to time the audible clanging of a city bell seemed to indicate some sort of resistance, but it was exceedingly weak. Taiping commanders received no reports of any casualties. The city was taken without spilling a drop of blood.

In one area where the Taipings had not yet tread, a burlesque was being enacted. One shot, two shots, the rather modest reports of a revolver could be heard. Residents of the area shut their doors tight, but there were obviously a few curiosity seekers who were peering outside from between the cracks in the doors or through the windows.

"Hubei Military Commander Bo-le-gong-wu is here! Under his command they'll punish the bandits' forces. Fall back, you rabble," yelled one voice. A third short report rang out.

"Oh . . .," groaned someone aloud.

"What happened, lord military commander? Your wound is deep. Please, let's stop here for now . . . please."

"No. I . . . my life stands in the way of loyalty and sincerity."

"No, it must not be. The way of loyalty and sincerity is truly to plan for a recovery and comeback."

Someone peering out a window saw a scene in which a man was being carried on a rain shutter by two other men away from the scene of action.

"Hey, that's Zhao Yongci." Someone among the rabble had seen through the show. The voice and mode of expression, it seemed to him, were exactly those of Zhao Yongci, a player with a Hunanese itinerant troupe of actors, who was alleged to have left the stage some years before.

The local residents were no fools. They were soon able to see that this burlesque being enacted in an area of Yuezhou was merely a false piece of evidence contrived by the military commander. Both he and old Lu, who, though a commoner by birth, had long lived separated from the common folk, had no esteem whatsoever for the powers of observation of ordinary people. The producer of this little drama had, of course, been old Lu.

Days later, when an investigating official came to the scene, not a soul appeared to corroborate witnessing or even hearing the scene at which the military commander was allegedly wounded. Someone testified to this official that, the day before, the military commander had fled through the eastern gate. He wasn't merely a talentless coward.

Assistant Regional Commander A-er-dong-a died defending the city. After the Taipings departed, Yuezhou reverted once again to Qing military control. Until they later entered the city of Nanjing, even when the Taipings took a city, they usually left it en masse. They had prepared to march forward, without leaving a defensive force behind.

When the Qing armies reentered Yuezhou, for a while they were unable to locate the corpse of A-er-dong-a. Wretched as it clearly was, the provincial military commander, prefect, and county magistrate had all apparently abandoned their city and fled. They were sentenced to death in Beijing. Eventually, the corpse was discovered and his martyrdom became clear to all. His honor was vindicated, and special favors were awarded the surviving members of his family.

His laborious drama complete, Bo-le-gong-wu escaped to Wuchang. He then put on an elaborate disguise and stealthily returned to Beijing, where he hid out in a place known as Huang village under an assumed name.

As far as the Qing court was concerned, his was the worst sort of crime imaginable. Yu Buyun, who had been executed at the time of the Opium War, had abandoned Ningbo and fled, but he never hid and skulked about like Bo-le-gong-wu. For his inability to face up to defeat at the end, Military Commander Bo-le-gong-wu was given the harshest punishment under the law: decapitation and banishment from the city.

Under Qing law, a crime of this sort did not usually implicate others, but it was so heinous that his son Gui-shan, who had risen to the position of vice-director (rank 5B) in the Ministry of Justice, was stripped of his post as well.

Both Prefect Lian Chang and County Magistrate Hu Fanggu were also beheaded. The government felt that, if they did not employ capital punishment in handling this case, then in subsequent encounters with the Taipings, they would be unable to stir civil and military officials alike to action. Once it was understood that simply running away meant execution, officials were far more likely to make every effort possible for themselves and their survivors. Such at least was the expectation of the Qing court.

With the occupation of Yuezhou, the Taipings acquired a large naval force. A new position of commander-in-chief of the navy was created, and the man named to this post was none other than Tang Zhengcai.

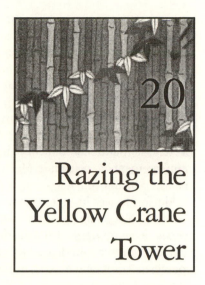

20

Razing the Yellow Crane Tower

The populace outside the city of Wuchang stared at the large number of soldiers. Locals simply hadn't believed that there were so many troops within the city. True, armed men had appeared here and there outside the city, but these were government forces who moved on the orders of their superiors.

"Go! Get out!" screamed the troops as they ran around in circles.

"Destroy it! Set it on fire! Hurry up and get out!"

"Things'll quiet down after noon."

"Just carry out the valuable stuff." The area outside the city was developing all the symptoms of a panic.

This was the uproar Lian Liwen and Li Xinmei heard outside Wuchang as they approached. News of the Taiping sacking of Yuezhou had already reached here.

The Qing Army had fought hard at Changsha, with a huge force at its disposal. One reason for this was that, prior to the arrival of the Taipings, they had not destroyed the homes outside that city. The Taipings took those homes and made them a base of operations from which they made repeated assaults on the city.

At that time, the Jiangnan military commander was a Manchu by the name of Shuang-fu, and he rarely put in appearances at Wuchang. Wuchang was both the capital of Hubei province and the place of residence for the governor-general of the Huguang provinces (Hubei and Hunan). Huguang Governor-General Cheng Yucai was on his way toward Changsha and had not yet returned. Not only that—he had been relieved of his post, and Imperial Commissioner Xu Guangjin had assumed his duties in addition to his own. Furthermore, Hubei Provincial Military Commander Bo-le-gong-wu, the highest military official in Hubei, was off in Yuezhou at the time, and with the fall of that city, it had been reported that his where-abouts were unknown.

The governor of Hubei, Chang Dachun, was a man of good character but lacking in decisiveness. Since no one with any military responsibilities was present, he petitioned the court in Beijing as follows: "A garrison force of reinforcements to remain in Hubei is requested for Jiangnan Military Com-mander Shuang-fu."

Shuang-fu was just the opposite of Chang Dachun. He had plenty of deci-siveness, though his character was far from perfect. As a result, his decisions tended to be arbitrary. "It's a sorry sight indeed," Chang Dachun had memo-rialized, "but the long-haired bandits are closing in, and I would very much appreciate command over an armed force to be stationed here." It was more an entreaty than a memorial. "We are in agreement. It is a time of national emergency, and we must exert ourselves to the fullest to defend Wuchang. To that end, I would like them to be absolutely under my command. Insofar as this is a military matter, all authority must devolve upon me." With these conditions raised by Shuang-fu, Chang Dachun consented.

They proceeded systematically to demolish and burn to the ground each and every private home outside the city of Wuchang, so that the enemy would not take them as bases for further operations against the city. The decision was Shuang-fu's.

Needless to say, the residents of these houses were shocked, and they appealed to the authorities to cease the destruction of their homes. "We shall pool our money and construct earthen walls. We shall contribute our young men as soldiers to help defend the city." They were referring to surrounding the most densely populated area outside the city walls of Wuchang with an earthen wall to keep the enemy at bay.

"It's already too late. There's no time left," said Shuang-fu, shaking his head. This was prior to the fall of Yuezhou. When he learned of that event, he ordered his entire army to take the field and begin disposing of the houses outside the city.

The merciless order went out: "Set the fires this afternoon."

Chaos on a massive scale erupted. Standing directly in the middle of the road, an old woman stared at the sky, beating her breast. People hurried about, trying desperately to save their household property. Some who had tried to resist the soldiers and officials seemed to have already given up. One woman, in a state of apparent absent-mindedness, sat herself down in the doorway of the home in which she had long lived, her eyes streaming with tears.

"These people are losing their homes. Where will they stay tonight and tomorrow? There must be sick people in these homes, and there must be mothers who've just given birth to babies too," said Xinmei, her fists clenched.

"Is there nothing we can do?" said Liwen.

"This wouldn't have happened if the Taipings were not going to attack."

"True, but, Xinmei, you must know that this is beyond anyone's control."

Dust clouds rose from the ground here and there, as groups of soldiers rode around. With large hammers and thick ropes, they carried the necessary implements. Now there was no time to demolish houses politely. With the fires set, they planned to level the area once and for all.

When one dust cloud settled, Xinmei saw a face she knew. "Hey, aren't you Yaxian?" she said.

"Oh, Xinmei, you've come too. You've done a good job. You're with the group that's entered the city, aren't you?" Yaxian did not yet know that Xinmei had left the Taipings and was thinking that she, too, had surreptitiously entered the area with a special task to accomplish.

"No, not me," said Xinmei, shaking her head.

"Really. Well, I'm with the city group. Maybe I'll see you afterward. Rumor has it that if you don't get inside the city walls early, they shut up all the gates tight." Yaxian was a small-framed but chubby young woman, about thirty years old. Her face had dark, elegant features.

"Be careful of your accent," said Xinmei. Yaxian spoke with a strong Guangxi accent, and Xinmei was concerned for her welfare once she had entered the city of Wuchang. Yaxian was in a hurry, apparently oblivious to Liwen, who was standing nearby.

"Rushing to be first?" Liwen asked Xinmei.

Xinmei had lost her faith in the "new world" that the Taiping movement had once promised her. From Liwen she had heard stories of the world developing in Shanghai that was altogether different from anything that had preceded it. She wanted to see that new world in Shanghai—even if only for a day—sometime soon.

"I'm in no particular hurry. Don't you have an acquaintance in Hanyang?" Xinmei responded. She did want to see Shanghai soon, but she had been observing Liwen's feelings too. Liwen still believed that the Taipings would open the door for them to a new world. Wuchang will be the scene of victory or defeat, Liwen had said. Having been unable to bring down a provincial capital—neither Guilin nor Changsha—Wuchang, the capital of Hubei province, was going to offer a major judgment on the capacity of the Taiping military. Unlike Guilin or Changsha, the Taipings could not simply wait and proceed past Wuchang. In order to charge like raging bulls into Nanjing, they had to use the Yangzi River, and it was impossible merely to leave Wuchang as they found it.

Liwen may have wanted to see the place at which they would undergo a major turning point with his own eyes. Xinmei had surmised as much, and said she wouldn't mind stopping here for a short spell.

—2—

This area was known as the Wuhan tri-cities. Divided by the Yangzi River, the provincial capital of Wuchang was on the eastern bank, and Hanyang and Hankou lay on the western bank. Hanyang and Hankou were separated—south and north, respectively—by the Han River. Thus, the three cities seemed to nestle close to one another, though set off from each other by rivers. Everyone referred to them as the Wuhan tri-cities at that time. Now an iron bridge spans the Yangzi, and the whole area is united into one city known as "Wuhan."

There came into the possession of the Taiping military at Yuezhou, weaponry and ammunition that Wu Sangui had stored there 170 years earlier. They transported the materiel to the over five thousand boats that had been detained at Yuezhou. It was as if to say: Here, use these vessels to carry the weaponry.

From Yuezhou, the Taiping forces divided along two routes. The right-route army went over land, following a course virtually identical to the present rail lines. Before reaching Wuchang, they came to the Puqi county seat, which they occupied with little effort, and then proceeded on toward their objective. County Magistrate Zhou Hexiang died in the battle. There were only some four thousand troops in this right-route army, but sturdy men were selected for it, accompanied by a large number of horses.

The left-route army went by water, and advanced as far as Hanyang without encountering any resistance. The principal leaders of the Taiping movement went with this left-route force.

The Qings' armed military strength at Wuchang numbered only 3,000 men, with an additional 1,000 or more militiamen. After Provincial Military Commander Shuang-fu marched these troops all together outside the city gates, and had them demolish and torch the residential houses there, he had every one of them return within the confines of the city walls.

Shuang-fu was obstinate when it came to establishing a secure defense. "We wait for the enemy to become fatigued," he explained his strategic master plan, "and then we begin an all-out attack."

Once the soldiers had withdrawn back into the city, he had all nine city gates into Wuchang bolted fast. Though Hanyang was the prefectural seat, the garrison force there numbered a mere 300. Hubei Surveillance Commissioner Rui-yuan argued that Hanyang needed an increased military presence and suggested a plan for the transfer to Hanyang of part of the force defending Wuchang.

"The provincial capital has laid out a fortified defensive wall. Not one soldier has the leisure to move from his position." Now that Shuang-fu had taken over supreme military command, no one else was welcome to make the least suggestion in military matters.

Taiping troop strength at this time was not accurately known even by the rebel leadership, for with each passing hour it was increasing, like a snowball that grows in size as it rolls forward in the snow. Some said fifty thousand, others eight thousand, and some went as high as one hundred thousand. This number included women, children, and old folks, for in many instances, entire family units would join the Taipings.

From this immense armed force, though, the right-route army numbered only 4,000. The left-route force, heading down the waterways toward Hanyang, numbered well into the tens of thousands. Thus, the 300 troops defending the prefectural seat at Hanyang were effectively helpless. While counting on reinforcements until the bitter end from across the river, not a single troop came to relieve Hanyang's unfortunate fate. Hanyang Prefect Dong Zhenduo died on the battlefield. Assistant Vice-Commander Zhu Han and Assistant Regional Commander Chang-qing, both military officials, shared the fate of the city.

The Taiping military bureaucracy at the time had four military ranks for troop commanders: general, lieutenant general, marshal, and commander. In the attack on Hanyang, Huang Yukun was general, Li Kaifang and Lin Fengxiang were lieutenant generals, and Luo Dagang was but a commander. Hanyang fell on the thirteenth day of the eleventh lunar month, or December 23.

"Kill every last civil official and government soldier, but do not so much as injure a single farmer." This was the Taiping general principle.

Having climbed to the top of Mount Gui north of Hanyang, Commander-in-Chief of the Taiping Navy, Tang Zhengcai, said to Luo Dagang and the other military leaders, "You're all in luck. It is a rare year indeed when Wuchang will be this easy to attack."

Group by group the Taipings came ashore on the western bank. From there they would stage their assault on Wuchang, which lay on the eastern bank of the river. There had been scant rain that year, and the waters of the Yangzi were shallower than usual. Zhongzhou Island could not be seen in an ordinary year, but it was now clear from many points along the river.

"We'll line the boats up into a kind of floating bridge. Let's do that very soon. Since there's not much water in the river now, it'll be easy. From the foothills of Mount Gui, we'll line up the boats in the direction over there of the Yellow Crane Tower. That'll be the best way, in view of the flow of the Yangzi."

Tang Zhengcai was well-acquainted with the local waterways. He even pointed out the spot where the floating bridge was to be strung. (Now, the double-decker Great Wuhan Bridge straddles the Yangzi River precisely at the site where the Taipings built their bridge. The lower deck is a rail line, while the upper deck is for pedestrians and vehicles.)

Six days later, Hankou fell, and as expected, not a single government soldier came to assist from Wuchang. In fact, just before Hanyang fell to the Taipings, the First Route Relief Army under the command of Regional Commanders Wang Jinxiu and Chang-lu arrived outside the city of Wuchang. They had set out with over three thousand men, though by the time they reached Wuchang, over one thousand men had been killed.

Shuang-fu brought this force inside the city as well. He planned to fight with an excellent "fortified defensive wall." Surveillance Commissioner Rui-yuan argued that these allied forces should remain outside the city walls so as to fight in concert with those inside the city, but Shuang-fu turned a deaf ear to all such suggestions. With the First Route Relief Army inside the city gates, the city's defensive forces numbered roughly five thousand.

The Taipings' right-route army reached the city of Wuchang by land at about the same time that the left-route army had—rather quickly—and brought down Hanyang. The right-route army had attacked Puqi along the way and was thus somewhat later than expected. The First Route Relief Army of the Qing military had come via a shorter pathway and arrived earlier, but it was then absorbed into Wuchang. The right-route army, arriving about a day late, found it had no one to engage in battle and set up camps at the prominent strongholds of Mount Hong, Mount Shamao, and elsewhere.

Shuang-fu had seen to it that the homes outside the city were burned to the ground and the land leveled, but he couldn't level the mountains. When the right-route army of the Taipings arrived outside Wuchang, something unusual transpired. Tens of thousands of local residents thronged to the Taiping side.

"If possible, we should like to join the Taiping Army." Not just young men, but women came with these words on their lips as well.

"We've heard tell that there's a women's barracks in the Taiping armed forces and that women can become soldiers just like men. Our bodies have been strengthened by work in the fields, and we have confidence in our physical strength. Please, allow us into the women's barracks." Here was a group of people, their homes destroyed and with nowhere to live, whose hatred for officials and government troops had boiled up all the more.

"Now, pay heed as we take our revenge," screamed a shrill voice, arms raised in the air.

Word of the severity of Taiping military discipline had spread widely in the local area of late. By contrast, the decadence of the government's forces was overwhelming. Stories of the time had it that, when Qing forces on the march passed private homes, people invariably slammed their doors tight, but when the Taiping passed through, not a single door was shut.

Taiping troop strength since coming to this region had risen exponentially. Though local homes had been demolished, the Taiping forces were not in the least inconvenienced. There were a fair number of carpenters among the Taiping forces as well. In a short time, they could build fortifications or set up scaffolding. They constructed bases of this sort outside the range of the firearms within the city. There they prepared to battle against Qing reinforcements should they eventually arrive.

The Qing forces under the command of Xiang Rong began to arrive outside the city of Wuchang one and one-half days following the arrival of the First Route Relief Army. Hanyang had already fallen into Taiping hands by that point, and as such, the Qing forces could not cross to the west bank of the Yangzi River. Furthermore, the Taipings built fortifications outside the range of fire of Wuchang, and set an ambush for the Qing armies.

The floating bridge linking the shores of the Yangzi was put together in one night by lining up the thousands of vessels from Yuezhou. The Yangzi was full of boats, linked one to the next by a metal cable and wooden planks laid across the deck of each boat. The result was exactly the same as a level road. On the western bank of the river, the Taipings could freely move over to the eastern bank now.

—3—

Guiyuan Temple was in the western suburbs of Hanyang, famous for its images of the Buddha's 500 arhats, or disciples, who had attained nirvana. The Taiping Heavenly Kingdom, however, took its guiding principles from Christianity and, as we have seen, had nothing but the fiercest animosity for icons of any sort.

While the old compatriots who had joined the Taiping movement back in Guangxi were unfamiliar with Hubei province, those who had joined the movement after the Taipings entered northern Hunan and Hubei knew the Guiyuan Temple well.

"Guiyuan Temple's the home for idols and icons. They've got five hundred of them there." Upon hearing this story, Luo Dagang took several of his subordinates to take a look at the place.

"Hey, Mr. Lian." At the front gate to the temple, he spotted Lian Liwen standing.

"Mr. Luo, it has been a long time, hasn't it?" Liwen said, smiling. After his severe wound at Suoyi Ford, Liwen had left the military ranks for a time to recuperate. The Taiping defeat there had occurred more than six months earlier.

"How are you feeling? Has your injury healed?" asked Luo Dagang.

"It was through the kindness bestowed on me by this temple that I was able slowly to recover."

"You don't say . . ." said Luo, his expression one of slight puzzlement. He was just at the point of going in and destroying the temple icons, when this comrade-in-arms, with whom he had shared the Taiping appellations of elder and younger brother, now told him that he owed the temple a great debt.

"You've come to demolish it, haven't you?" asked Liwen. "Local people have told me that this temple is famous for the five hundred arhats."

"False rumors have been spreading that the Taiping military murders Buddhist monks, and the temple personnel all fled in haste. I tried to stop them by telling them that it was absolutely not the case. I was told to leave the rest of it up to you, Mr. Lian. That's been a real headache for me. In any event, in their absence they've left the temple in my care."

"That's fine. There are other temples and mortuary shrines in this area. Shall we begin our work at another site?"

Though a sworn brother in the Taiping movement, Luo Dagang had been a leader in the Heaven and Earth secret society prior to joining the movement, and hence was not as fervent in his animosity toward idols.

"Would you drink some tea with me?" asked Liwen.

"That would be nice. It really has been some time since we've seen one another." Luo turned to the new brethren he had acquired since coming to Hubei and said, "This fellow has been a comrade in the movement since the days at Jintian village. He was wounded in battle and is now recuperating. We haven't seen one another in a long time, and we've got countless stories to catch up on."

The celebrated Guiyuan Temple had immense grounds. All the priests and monks had run off, and thus the place was now empty. Even the sextons had fled. The rumor that had intimidated everyone was that anyone found on the grounds of a temple would be slain by the Taipings.

"Do you think those who fled were all cowards?" asked Liwen while they walked around the grounds of the temple.

"No, no, by no means. If you ask me, people probably thought that even if the rumors were largely false, it hardly seemed worth it to them to risk a meaningless death. So they took off."

"Though there probably were some among them whom you'd like to take revenge on."

"You're right on that score. I'd be the very first one to think that way," Luo said, laughing.

The two of them entered a building to the side of the main temple hall. Aside from a scroll hanging there with two large Chinese characters reading "shining everywhere," there was no other decor to the room whatsoever.

"I really would like you not to destroy the five hundred arhats. When anyone thinks of the Wuhan tri-cities, they always think of the Yellow Crane Tower in Wuchang and the statues of the five hundred arhats at the Guiyuan Temple. I understand well the great esteem in which you hold the teachings of the Heavenly Elder Brother Jesus, and it is only natural that you would strike out severely against anyone or anything that violated those teachings. But the arhats are not images of deities," Liwen said, after offering Luo a chair.

"As for those teachings, I am by no means the sole person to determine what they were. What are the thoughts of the Eastern King, to say nothing of the Heavenly King himself, on this matter? Perhaps you, Mr. Lian, should instruct me," said Luo, as he accepted Liwen's offer and sat down.

"I've been away from the Taiping Heavenly Kingdom for some time now, but I still think I've come to understand what it stands for quite well. It has both good and bad points. The massacre at Quanzhou was a particularly sad incident."

"I don't want to hear any more about Quanzhou."

"The Taiping military will at some point have to make amends for what transpired at Quanzhou. And it is in this sense that I ask you not to destroy the five hundred arhats, those five hundred human disciples of the Buddha. Leave the temple itself intact."

"You've taken this temple under your wing, Mr. Lian. We shan't burn it to the ground or any such thing. The armies of the demons have already set too many fires in the outskirts of Wuchang. We've stopped the arson. There are too few places to billet the troops."

"Our allies are men's hearts. If we lose their respect, then everything is over."

"Yes, Mr. Lian, it looks as though things already have turned out well for us. When will you rejoin the army?"

"I think I'll watch from the sidelines for a time."

"An observer of sorts, eh?"

"That's not exactly what I had in mind."

"Shall I inform the Heavenly King and the Eastern King of this wish to watch from the sidelines?"

"I have so much I want to tell them, but wouldn't it be best to wait until after the present battles are finished when the Heavenly King and the Eastern King have time to listen to me?"

"But our victory's a foregone conclusion, you know. I see your point. It serves no interest to discuss matters of the entire realm should we be defeated here. The Heavenly King and the Eastern King should soon be entering Hankou. I must now proceed to Hankou to make the necessary arrangements."

"Shall I make my appearance then? Where will you be making those arrangements?"

"The Heavenly King will be staying at the temple to Guandi and the Eastern King at the Hall of Eternity."

"Huh, separate offices?" said Liwen with a look of despair.

Even before the decision to try to conquer the entire country, the Taiping movement had begun to lose its cohesiveness. Yang Xiuqing seemed to lack the frame of mind merely to assist at the side of Hong Xiuquan.

"In any event, we're now an immense force of over one hundred thousand. We can't be captured because we hold together as one." Luo was speaking in a tone of voice as though he were offering some sort of explanation. Sitting with his old comrade at the Guiyuan Temple, he promised to order his subordinates not to lay hands on the temple for the time being.

"Shall we use it as a storage dump for ammunition?" asked Luo, turning around and looking at the grounds. Were it a strategically important site, it would be protected. By turning the Guiyuan Temple into a powder dump, Luo was trying to find an excuse for protecting it. Without an excuse, he lacked the authority to make a decision of this sort.

In the fighting until that point, Luo Dagang had invariably, it was fair to say, been in the vanguard. As the head of a shock corps, his military exploits had been extraordinary. However, it was only at the time of the taking of Hanyang that he was finally promoted from commander to the rank of marshal. In spite of which, he was still below the ranks of general and lieutenant general.

When the Taiping forces first entered Hunan and later Hubei, chivalrous leaders like Luo of various secret society bands joined them, but they were always seen within the Taiping movement as subsidiary to the original core membership. Huang Yukun, Li Kaifang, and Lin Fengxiang, with whom he had helped bring Hanyang down, all had been original members of the Society of God Worshippers from the start, and all were from Guangxi province.

Though Hong Xiuquan, the Heavenly King, was himself from Hua county in Guangdong province, the Taiping movement originated for the most part in Guangxi, and its core was understandably made up of natives of Guangxi.

Thus, in regard to native place, Guangxi was the main line and Guangdong was secondary.

Luo Dagang came from Jieyang, Guangdong, and hence was out of the mainstream. Despite the ideal of the Society of God Worshippers—"Under the Lord Jehovah all people were equally brothers and sisters"—within the Society these sorts of hierarchical distinctions were beginning to appear.

What a life he's led, thought Liwen as he watched Luo Dagang departing into the distance.

Among the more celebrated sites within the Wuhan cities, Yellow Crane Tower was probably even more famous than Guiyuan Temple. The name "Guiyuan" did not elicit anything like a favorable impression. "Guiyuan" was a Buddhist term that referred to a break with the cycle of birth and death and a "return" (*gui*) to the "original" (*yuan*) state of natural quiescence. Thus, it was intimately tied up with the more mundane idea of "death." It was probably for that reason as well that the temple was never mentioned in poetry or prose.

By comparison, the praises of Yellow Crane Tower inside the city of Wuchang were often sung in Chinese poetry. Most famous among them was a four-line poem, each line seven Chinese characters in length, by the great Li Bo (701–762) of the Tang dynasty, entitled "At Yellow Crane Tower, Parting with Meng Haoran as He Sets Out for Guangling":

> My old friend takes leave of Yellow Crane Tower to the west.
> A hazy mist of flower blossoms in the third month of the year, he
> proceeds downstream to Yangzhou.
> The distant shape of his lone sail filling the blue sky,
> Only the Yangzi River can be seen flowing toward the horizon.

This poem was later included in the illustrious anthology, *Selected Tang Poems*, a work read with great pleasure, even by Japanese, for many generations.

As to how the Yellow Crane Tower acquired its name, one story had it that an eccentric hermit nearby had climbed upon a yellow crane to amuse himself, but a rather more interesting and older local tradition told a different story about the origins of this name.

In the past, there had been a wine shop here to which an old man always came to drink his wine free of charge. When the aforementioned old gentleman got up to leave, he was said to have drawn a yellow crane on the wall of the shop by way of remuneration. This yellow crane attained great notoriety, for whenever someone tapped the wall at that spot, it flew up into the air. An extraordinary event, to say the least, and crowds of customers thronged the wine shop. With thousands and thousands of customers, the owner of the wine shop became extremely rich. Then, about ten years later, the same old man appeared once again, bestrode his crane, and flew off into the sky. Thereafter, the wine merchant built a tower at the site of his shop and named it, appropriately, Yellow Crane Tower.

The Yellow Crane Tower, from which one could look down on the Yangzi River, had burned down any number of times. The edifice standing there at the time of the Taiping attack had been constructed under the guidance of one Shi Yizhi (1682–1763), governor-general of the Huguang provinces, around the year 1736. Records tell that it was a circular three-story structure about 58 meters in height. Though a century had transpired since the reconstruction, it had been repaired and touched up on numerous occasions.

Yellow Crane Tower had been built within the city of Wuchang near the spot where a slightly elevated mound—known as Snake Hill—ran into the Yangzi River. Had this tower not been to commemorate that yellow crane that flew off into the world of the spirits, then it might have been for sending people off on waterborne journeys along the Yangzi. There was no doubt, though, that it had been built with a military objective in mind, as a watchtower.

After the news that the long-haired bandits' attack was at hand, Shuang-fu climbed to the top of the tower to observe the overall situation. He could see clearly that Hanyang had fallen to the Taipings. Fires had broken out in Hankou, and it too would soon fall. Looking down at this devastation with a telescope, Shuang-fu still refused to send a single soldier to help.

"Xiang Rong's army has arrived there. If we open the gates and send troops over, won't he be able to effectuate a pincer attack on the enemy?" suggested Regional Commander Chang-lu.

"Forget it," he responded curtly. He could see clearly from Yellow Crane Tower the floating bridge that the Taiping military at Hanyang had built.

Surveillance Commissioner Rui-yuan then suggested, "If they complete that bridge, that will be extremely disadvantageous to us. We should attack now, before the thing is done." But, Shuang-fu still refused to budge, without offering a word of explanation as to his reasoning.

When circumstances grew to the advantage of the Qing forces, with rain falling and a thick mist collecting, the military commanders saw the great opportunity accorded them and requested that they be allowed to lead an attack, but Shuang-fu still wouldn't allow it.

"Forget it," he again spewed out, in an increasingly gruff tone of voice.

The Taiping forces outside the city were in high spirits. Thousands of local residents had been only too happy to show them about the strategic points in the area. Batteries were built at Changhong Bridge and at Lijia Bridge, both sites selected by local people. In addition to the local geography, the Taipings were also learning a great deal about inside the city walls, such as where the garrison troops were stationed, where military supplies were to be found, the local topography, and the weaknesses of the enemy.

Xiang Rong's forces appeared in an area to the east of Wuchang and took up a position near Changhong Bridge. On the seventeenth day of the eleventh lunar month, Xiang Rong himself arrived at the White Tree range, but he was still too far from Wuchang. He was more than ready for action.

His exile to Xinjiang had already been decided. Were he able now to distinguish himself on the field of battle, his punishment would be rescinded. He had lost out on many fronts because his interpersonal skills had always been so poor. He now held prime responsibility for the reinforcements getting to Wuchang, and he got along well with his assistant, Brigade Vice-Commander Zhang Guoliang.

East Lake, a rather large body of water, lay to the east of Wuchang, and Hong Hill was next to it. The area is now the site of the campus of Wuhan University. The battle between the Taiping forces and the Qing Army under the command of Xiang Rong unfolded primarily in this region. There had been a number of skirmishes around Hong Hill. While allowing such brief encounters to continue, Xiang Rong waited for the additional troops to come and back him up.

"What in the world is Shuang-fu thinking? He hasn't a clue about how to fight a war," said Xiang Rong in vicious tones, in the general direction of the walls of Wuchang, where Shuang-fu had as yet established no communication with him. Although he did not come out and actually say it, in his heart Xiang Rong was cursing Shuang-fu with language drawn from the vocabulary of the Taipings: "That Tatar barbarian doesn't know a damned thing about fighting!"

"Tatar barbarians" was a term—banned during the period of the Qing dynasty—of vitriol used by Han Chinese to ridicule Manchus as uncivilized, barbarous creatures. The only place it was used in public was, needless to say, within the Taiping military.

Shuang-fu was an ethnic Manchu. He had participated in an expedition to Xinjiang and gained success in his professional life in the campaigns against the Zungars in the Pamir Mountains. After serving simultaneously as regional commander in Hebei and Guizhou for one and one-half years, he was appointed to the post of provincial military commander.

Xiang Rong found the whole thing distasteful. He had worked as a regional commander for five full years, before finally being promoted to provincial military commander. Shuang-fu's promotion had been so swift because he was a Manchu—this was responsible for the malice Xiang Rong had for him.

—5—

On the twenty-eighth day of the eleventh lunar month, the largest of the battles unfolded around Hong Hill. It was already January 7 of the new year, 1853, by the solar calendar. Most of the reinforcements from Hunan had by now arrived. They had only been late because the right-route army of the Taipings had seen to it that all the bridges necessary to get there had been destroyed.

Qing military spies reported that among the Taiping forces near Wuchang, were many untrained soldiers who had only recently joined them. Xiang Rong divided his entire army into ten brigades and proceeded to lead an attack on the Taiping encampment at Hong Hill.

Though all nine gates into the city of Wuchang were shut tight, the Taipings, when engaging the forces of Xiang Rong in battle, were always wracked with the fear of not knowing when the gates would be opened for military sorties to go and return. It was also true, as the government spies had observed, that many of the Taiping troops were new. Those who had joined at Yuezhou had only been with the army in the march from Yuezhou to the Wuhan cities. Those who had joined in the suburbs outside Wuchang had not even been involved in a march.

The Taiping forces were compelled to abandon the fifteen bases they had constructed at Hong Hill. From the start of the hostilities, the untrained, new troops were only too ready to run away in the face of a Qing attack. The Taipings retreated, and the Qing forces pursued.

"Come on. Let's do it now," ordered Luo Dagang to his staff members. Any number of times, Luo had led a ragtag band of secret society bandits and faced off against the armed forces of the Qing dynasty. He was used to dealing with the government's armies. He often employed the method of disbanding his bandit forces in all directions to avoid pursuit.

Luo's staff officers all hailed from his days with the secret society bandits, and they knew full well what "it" implied. With smiles adorning their faces, his staff men responded.

"We've been ready for that. Three carts."

"Okay, then . . . So, you'll use one cart each time and do it three times?" Qing forces had not invaded Luo Dagang's fortress. While the two armies were squared off in battle for a period of time, the locations of the Taipings' strong and weak positions became clear to the Qing forces, and naturally

Xiang Rong sent troops against the weak positions.

Many of the troops under Luo Dagang's command were men used to this procedure. Even without the commands of superior officers, they were always prepared for this tactic. Silk, copper coins, a little foreign (primarily Mexican) silver, plated tools of various sorts, clothes as gaudy and ostentatious as possible—these and like items were strewn about the field of battle. Rather than pursue the enemy, the soldiers in the Qing Army immersed themselves completely in vying with one another for this war booty.

With this method, the bandit forces under Luo were able to make their escape to safety. There was a special knack to knowing how to scatter the goods, and several among them knew it well. Those who had experience in such matters did their work with the expected acumen.

Each group was made up of only ten men. They rolled a cart laden with "precious goods" over to the preestablished spot. Silk of various colors was precut in appropriate lengths. One of the essential points was to scatter it about. It had to stand out as conspicuously as possible. For this reason, they often used wardrobe costumes for use in plays. What appeared splashily on the stage would appear just as strikingly spread out on the ground.

There certainly was a knack to luring the enemy in. Once the items were dexterously scattered about, a loud voice screamed, "Hey, there's jewels rolling around over there. Those long-haired bandits took off so fast they left these things behind. Hey, over here, first come, first served. We'll get rich on this stuff!"

As expected, the Qing soldiers ceased their pursuit and in great excitement started grabbing up these spoils of war. The first to take hold of these valuables were the troops at the tail end. Those in the forefront were still in the midst of following the Taipings. Then, these troops too heard someone say, "The rear troops are taking the lion's share of it, you idiots! If you think I'm lying, just double back and look. People that look like beggars are getting rich just like that." At that, they spun around in great disorder and raced back.

Mob psychology is a fascinating phenomenon to behold. In this instance, one officer, brandishing his green dragon dagger in the air, called out, "I'll kill anyone who runs away!" The blandishment had no effect. Had he not been careful, this officer would have been beaten to death. The last thing the men wanted was to be left behind while others were becoming rich.

"Damn it!" Xiang Rong growled, gnashing his teeth. The Taiping strategy became clear as day to him. As a man with considerable military experience, it was the sort of measure he might have expected under the circumstances.

The government forces had no choice but to give up the pursuit. To rally their troops together, they had to retreat.

"Return! Retreat now! Back to camp!" yelled Xiang Rong. Back at his headquarters, Xiang Rong picked up a writing brush and personally wrote his report for Beijing. "We laid siege to the fifteen bases set up by the long-haired bandits at Hong Hill."

Four days later, Xiang Rong again marshaled his troops for battle, sending Zhang Guoliang off to fight on another front. The Taipings confronted the Qing forces and then cut paths to the left and right to avoid further fighting. The Qing forces advanced to a point some fifteen kilometers from Wuchang, but just then torrential rains began to pour. Their gunpowder became damp and could no longer be used in the attack. They were themselves drenched and exhausted.

"What a mess!" said Xiang Rong, shading his eyes from the rain, as he looked out at the city wall before him, hazy in the downpour. Had Qing forces made a coordinated sortie from within the city, it would have been the perfect opportunity to inflict serious damage on the Taipings.

Luo Dagang, who could always be expected to put in an appearance in battles of this nature, was nowhere to be seen. He had taken up another task. The Taipings had tried to extend the siege of Wuchang to twenty days. They had to have a decisive military victory here. More than anything, they wanted to raid and take the city of Wuchang.

Though it had not succeeded at Changsha, burying explosive devices in tunnels around the city seemed to have been their only tactic at this time. The walls of Wuchang were allegedly weaker than those of Changsha, and local folk had specifically indicated the weakest point: near Wenchang Gate.

Luo Dagang took troops under his command who had formerly been coal miners, and had them dig tunnels aimed at Wenchang Gate. Wenchang was the gate opening out to the west of the city.

—6—

The Qing military had also studied the tactics of the Taiping armies. It was well-known that many coal miners had joined the Taipings in southern Hunan. In Wuchang, methods for responding to the tunnel tactic were being considered. All the blind men of Wuchang were gathered together and ordered to listen for subterranean noises. Probing the surface of the ground, they placed empty earthenware jugs there. With these empty items, sounds were easier to distinguish. It was thought at the time that the blind acquired an enhanced sense of hearing to the extent that they had been deprived of their sense of sight. In Changsha as well, the blind had been mobilized to use against the Taipings' tunnel strategy. However, this tactic being pursued by government forces within the city was predicted by the Taiping Army.

Luo Dagang had three tunnels dug in the direction of Wenchang Gate. The middle one, in which the explosives were to be set off, was effectively the main tunnel. To its left and right at a distance of some 15 meters, two wider tunnels were dug out.

He selected cautious, discrete veterans among the miners to dig the main tunnel, and for those on either side he had the men work as conspicuously loudly as they could. If indeed there were men with their ears attentive to subterranean sounds, they were certain to pick up on the sounds of these two tunnels.

During the night of the second day of the twelfth lunar month, one of the blind men heard a loud noise north of Wenchang Gate.

"Here it is! It's here! I heard a sound beneath the earth here! No doubt about it. Right here," he said, thrusting his index finger violently into the surface. "It's right here," he repeated.

Governor Chang Dachun gathered 400 laborers and had them dig at that spot. Then, drawing water from a ditch, they poured it into the hole. Even if explosives had been set at that site, there was no way they could function once they became wet.

Lin Enxi, a circuit intendant in the salt administration, was an activist by inclination. Spending every cent from his own pockets, he hired 800 local braves.

"If it's clear that they're digging a tunnel," Lin proposed to the provincial military commander, "then aren't we well-advised to open up Wenchang Gate and launch an attack on them? Please send me and my men into battle."

"The gate shall not be opened," said Military Commander Shuang-fu, who was no more anxious now than before to open the gate to the city.

Lin Enxi and Rui-yuan were not the only ones favoring a raid against the Taipings. The second son of Governor Chang, Chang Yu, had returned to Hubei, and he too commanded troops and had requested to be allowed to leave the city and engage the enemy in battle. In spite of this, Shuang-fu was adamant. He had adopted an attitude of dogged determination.

Adjutant Chun-ying was drinking heavily by Yellow Crane Tower. Speaking loudly so as to be heard, he said, "What's the commander afraid of? You guys know? He thinks that if he opens the gate, we'll all run away. Ha, ha, we're all cowards. We're just waiting every second for a chance to flee. Fine. The commander obviously doesn't trust us. Why doesn't he dispatch a single soldier out there? Says he's waiting for the enemy to get all tired out. . . . More likely we'll get tired first. Ha, ha! What rotten luck for us to have such a brilliant military commander over us."

Those who heard Chun-ying's shouting were inclined to believe about half of it.

Luo Dagang's strategy worked well. One of the decoy tunnels was discovered and flooded with water. The main tunnel, however, continued to be dug without incident until they reached the foundation of the wall just next to Wenchang Gate. Long fuses were attached to powerful explosives. They were then planted both in the main tunnel and in the other undetected decoy tunnel as well. Prior to lighting the fuse, they carefully checked to see that the explosives were thrust deeply into the tunnels.

The first camp was a children's force of fifty, comprised of a select group of agile fourteen- and fifteen-year-old youths. It was their job to jump off from the point where the explosives broke through, dash up the wall, and hoist the Taiping flag there. They wore the flags wrapped round their mid-sections.

The crash division following the children's force was led by Shi Dakai. Its first camp of 500 moved directly to the north from Wenchang Gate and then split into two bands. The first set fire to Yellow Crane Tower and the second opened Pinghu Gate. At this time, the Taiping forces in Hanyang would be standing by to cross their floating bridge. Setting Yellow Crane Tower ablaze was a signal to Hanyang. The Taiping forces crossed the bridge and entered the city at the already opened Pinghu Gate.

It was dawn of the fourth day of the twelfth lunar month. A thick mist greeted the morning. The mines set by the Taipings exploded into the air with a blast so loud it shattered heaven and earth. Countless scraps and splinters of broken black tiles flew into the sky.

"Look at that! It breaks apart so easily," said Shi Dakai, leaping to his feet.

When they were at the city walls around Changsha, the Taiping camp repeatedly sighed at how mighty the walls were. This had gotten into their heads, and most expected that even if they could break through the walls of Wuchang, they would probably not effect so wide a breach. For that reason, the plan was first to send the children's force because their bodies were smaller in frame. However, everyone now rubbed their eyes in amazement at how readily the walls collapsed.

The explosives had been set in two places, and in an instant, a section of wall roughly 80 meters long was simply blown off. It was beyond their wildest dreams. The resistance of Qing troops within the city was effectively nil. The heavy mist that morning helped the government troops escape. They hurriedly shed their uniforms and blended into the local populace.

"Kill the demons!" shouted the Taiping forces as they rode around inside the walls of the city of Wuchang. At the top of the city wall, the Taiping flag fluttered in the breeze.

Then, Yellow Crane Tower began emitting fire with almost incredible speed. From Hanyang on the opposite bank of the river, the Taiping forces let out a ferocious war cry and thronged to cross over the floating bridge.

"Next we meet Xiang Rong on the battlefield!" said Yang Xiuqing, commander of all Taiping troops, with an agreeable look on his face as he stared up at the blazing Yellow Crane Tower.

—7—

Governor Chang Dachun died by hanging, and over twenty members of his family followed him to their deaths. Only four youths were said to have survived. Chang was sixty years of age.

Provincial Military Commander Shuang-fu died in battle near Wenchang Gate. His wife and three young children cast themselves into the river and drowned. One baby girl was separated from her mother and avoided death.

Provincial Administration Commissioner Liang Xingyuan was in bed with an illness at the time, and when the news reached him that the Taipings had breached the city wall, he arose and penned a note for posterity. The Taiping forces rushed into his quarters.

"I've finished writing. Kill me now," he said as he greeted his impending death calmly.

Surveillance Commissioner Rui-yuan killed his own child, ordered his family members to commit suicide, and then decapitated himself.

Provincial Education Commissioner Feng Peiyuan threw himself down a well.

Circuit Intendant Wang Shoutong died fighting the Taipings in the streets.

Circuit Intendant Wang Donghuai died by hanging.

Wuchang Prefect Ming-shan perished in the same manner, and his entire family was massacred by Taiping soldiers.

Regional Commander Wang Jinxiu slit his own throat atop the city walls.

Regional Commander Chang-lu slit his throat on horseback.

Adjutant Chun-ying fought valiantly to his death.

Assistant Regional Commander Yang Guangjin engaged the Taipings on horseback single-handedly, and when he had spent his last drop of energy, he cut his own throat. His decapitated head fell to the ground, and at just that moment the word escaped his lips: "Splendid!" Sounds of admiration arose among the Taiping ranks. Circuit Intendant Lin Enxi was captured by the Taipings and strongly encouraged to surrender, but he steadfastly refused and was executed. Lin hailed from Haifeng, Guangdong province, and many among the Taipings shared this place of origin. His talents were greatly prized.

The blazing Yellow Crane Tower was clearly visible even from Guiyuan Temple in the western suburbs of Hanyang. Lian Liwen and Li Xinmei nestled closely, staring intently at the fire. The magnificent Yellow Crane Tower looked as though it was wrapped in fire. Here and there in the red blaze were tiny spots where it burned blue and green. Close to its pinnacle the fire changed to a yellowish color.

"I wonder if that's the world-destroying conflagration the Buddhists speak of," muttered Liwen.

"What's that?" asked Xinmei.

"When this world comes to an end, a great fire is supposed to break out and consume everything. Everything."

"Every single thing?"

"The entire universe is supposed to go up in flames."

"When there's a real world-destroying conflagration, I wouldn't be afraid. I'm not alone," said Xinmei, blinking her eyes. Though far off in the distance, the smoke from Wuchang had eventually floated all the way to the area near Guiyuan Temple. Liwen felt a pain in his throat. He shut his eyes, and behind his eyelids he conjured up the image of the scene of carnage being played out in the streets of Wuchang.

"In the old days, an eccentric hermit was said to have climbed up on a yellow-colored crane from over there and sailed to the heavens," said Liwen.

"Aha, so that's why the top of it turns yellow from time to time."

Then unconsciously, Liwen quietly recited a poem entitled "Yellow Crane Tower" by the poet Cui Hao (d. 754) from the Tang dynasty:

> Here long ago a man climbed up on a yellow crane and rode off,
> And now it is all gone save the Yellow Crane Tower.
> The yellow crane flew away, but never returned.
> White clouds hang emptily for eternity.
> Clear streams flow smoothly by the trees at Hanyang,
> And the fragrant grass grows luxuriantly on Parrot Island.
> Dusk, as I gaze toward home from here,
> And a hazy spray by the banks of the Yangzi River makes me
> gloomy.

Lifelessly left behind, Yellow Crane Tower was now disappearing from the earth. The fire continued for several days until it finally consumed the entire edifice. Yellow Crane Tower has never been reconstructed since. At the end of the Qing dynasty, Huguang Governor-General Zhang Zhidong (1839–1909) had a building erected on the site of its remains, but it was smaller in scale and was appropriately not named Yellow Crane Tower but Tocsin Tower. In appearance the structure had an official air, as if to say to onlookers: "People of the country, every time you gaze upon this building, recall the ferocious invasion here and awaken!" Tocsin Tower burned to the ground in 1920.

Now, only the place name, "Yellow Crane," emptily remains.

Hillock of
the Nine
Women

—1—

Tan Qi came with information from time to time. While at Guiyuan Temple in the outskirts of Hanyang, Lian Liwen learned what was going on within the walls of Wuchang on the other side of the river. Tan Qi was his informant.

When the Taipings attacked, the nine gates into Wuchang were shut and bolted tightly. After the city fell, the Taipings again locked the gates. The Qing forces camped in the area of Hong Hill outside the city were waiting for an opportunity to try to recapture Wuchang from Taiping occupation.

Tan Qi's special task was the gathering of information, and thus he had free access to enter and leave the city. His access, though, was limited to Hanyang and Pinghu Gates on the west side of the city, facing the Yangzi River. By securing their floating bridge, the Taiping forces retained control over both Wuchang and Hanyang.

The Qing military amassed its strength in the eastern suburbs of Wuchang. The atmosphere in Hanyang on the west bank of the Yangzi had still not grown overly tense.

"Hanyang's a great place. You can just sit here and drink wine as slowly as you want to," said Tan Qi as he accepted a cup of wine from Liwen at Guiyuan Temple.

"No wine in Wuchang?" inquired Liwen.

"Sure, lots of it," responded Tan Qi, pursing his lips. "But, once things calm down there, you won't be able to drink any kind of alcohol. They seem real anxious over there."

"That's because the Qing forces are camped by Hong Hill."

"There is that, but the sermonizing's begun too. They're nervous primarily about how bad wine is."

"Makes sense," said Liwen, with a forced smile.

"Every day, every single day, it's those lectures on their principles. I wish they'd give it a rest. I really do." Tan then drank down his wine with a look indicating its wonderful taste.

Tan's reference to "those lectures on their principles" meant just that—lectures on the principles and beliefs of the Taiping Heavenly Kingdom. The assembled masses of people in Wuchang were addressed each day on Christianity, the fundamental state-building principle of the Taiping movement. These were religious sermons, pure and simple. Sermons were given in the wards and streets of the city, and drinking wine was no longer the tactful thing to do.

"How many have died?" Liwen asked the question to which he most wanted an answer. A large number of people had died in the process of taking Wuchang, and a wide variety of stories were circulating among the people about it. One tale had it that an army of well over one hundred thousand was reduced to several tens of thousands.

"Everybody's counting in great detail. Luo Dagang says it's probably over ten thousand. Shi Dakai thinks it may have reached twenty thousand." Tan Qi gulped his wine down again. It was a topic that could make the best wine taste bad, but after so long a time, he no longer felt as though it brought pain to his heart.

"That's too many." Perhaps because he had been in Hanyang, where there had been no shortage of bloodshed, Liwen felt pangs of sadness in his heart as he asked for the number of the dead.

"As far as I'm concerned, it's too many," said Tan Qi. There was no trace of defensiveness in his response.

"That's what I'm hearing."

When the Taiping armies burst into the city, a state of panic spread rapidly. The Taiping principle—"Kill every last civil official and government soldier, but do not so much as injure a single farmer"—was repeatedly hammered into the heads of the officers and soldiers of the Taiping Army. There was, however, no reason that local residents would have been familiar with it.

Instead, government propaganda had that: "The long-haired bandits have not the hearts of human beings. They follow the teachings of the barbarians and eat the livers of young children. If these wretches should but once appear, they will murder each and every one of you in a wholesale slaughter." It was a form of coercion to ensure cooperation in times of defensive engagements.

Rumors that the Taiping soldiers killed only officials and government troops while protecting the lives of the general populace had still not spread that far in Hubei. After leaving Hunan province, the Taipings had advanced with such rapidity that complete information about them had not yet arrived when they did. Threats from the government, though, were fierce. People who believed every word of official propaganda that the Taipings would murder them all, considered taking their own lives, especially if they were going to be cut down.

Resident in the Hubei provincial capital of Wuchang were the provincial governor, the provincial administration commissioner, and the provincial military commander; in addition, the Huguang governor-general—who also had responsibilities in Hunan province—resided in Wuchang. By comparison with Hankou and Hanyang, it was an extremely "political" city. The percentage of civil and military official personnel in Wuchang exceeded those in the other cities.

As far as the Taipings were concerned, it was a city in which a large number of persons to be killed lived. They therefore carried out a house-to-house search, which struck terror in the hearts of the ordinary urban residents.

As soon as the Taipings broke through, they liberated everyone held prisoner in the government jails. People had been imprisoned unfairly by the government, though many were the perpetrators of heinous crimes as well. During their house-to-house search, the Taipings assigned those who knew local conditions well to be their guides. Local residents were intimidated by the idea of organized criminals running rampant. These "guides" carried out their searches as they wished, often seizing property for themselves.

"Hmm, just like the authorities said. Even if you survive, there'd be no way to go on in such a world." Such thinking, not the least unreasonable, cropped up here and there.

In a Chinese text of that time known as the *Gazetteer of the Hunan Army*, we find the following reference: "Several tens of thousands of women of the local gentry hanged from girders and cast themselves into the water." This official Qing chronicle was stressing the large number of suicides and made scant mention of Taiping atrocities.

Two days after the occupation, Yang Xiuqing sent out the order to "stop the killing." Even officials and government troops could now no longer be indiscriminately put to death. Such people would now be investigated and punished if the commission of a crime could be established.

On the same day Yang Xiuqing issued another directive: "All residents of Wuchang must pray to the Lord-on-High." The great majority of Wuchang residents had no idea who this "Lord-on-High" was. In the Daoist belief system, there was an expression "Lord-on-High" used, but that didn't seem to be what the Taipings had in mind, for it was known, by virtue of the government's propaganda, that the God of the long-haired bandits was an alien deity.

"He is our Father who art in heaven, and His name is Jehovah," responded the Taipings, realizing that they would have to begin their teachings from the very beginning. These were the "lectures on the principles" of the Taipings, mentioned earlier. Wherever one went into the streets of Wuchang, one ran into people preaching in this fashion, and everyone was compelled to listen to these "lectures on the principles" of the Taipings.

—2—

These "lectures" were held at the Yuema Yard on Chang Street in Wuchang. An elevated speaker's platform had been built there, and at all times there were three lecturers at the podium, instructing the resident populace in the teachings of the Heavenly Father and the Heavenly Elder Brother. There was always one woman among the speakers as well. They took turns lecturing on the way of heaven as well as engaging in dialogue with others on the platform, or what we might now call, a panel discussion.

The audience at these events had not come of its own free will, and hence listeners and lecturers had established no rapport at all. Apparently, the idea of seeing not one but several speakers on the podium was supposed to be an inducement to participate.

After the occupation of the city, while the putrid smells of the dead still wafted about the city, Yang Xiuqing began a registration of the residents of Wuchang. At first, every ten persons were organized into a "barrack," but later this was changed to every twenty-five persons. A "barrack" was the organizational unit for both the civilian and military populace. The distribution of rice, salt, oil, and other items was all handled through these barracks. And, following Taiping practice, women were segregated into barracks exclusively for them.

People assembled by their barrack's unit to listen to the "lectures," and attendance was mandatory. The lecturers spoke with great earnest. Because they were amateurs at sermonizing, their lectures were not expected to go smoothly, but depending on the person, some conveyed the ardor of their feelings to great effect. Some struck sympathetic chords among the populace, while others aroused opposition. Still, though, no one among the assembled audience dared show opposition openly.

The eleventh day of the twelfth lunar month was the eighth day of the Taiping occupation of Wuchang. According to extant records, among those in attendance rounded up that day for the "lectures" in Yuema Yard was one high-pitched voice that rang out, "Those of you gathered here, listen to me and listen closely! This Heavenly Father Lord-on-High is a demon deity of the barbarians, and the Heavenly Elder Brother Jesus is a barbarian imposter. Stop listening to all this gibberish about them!"

That was as far as he got, for the Taiping troops who rushed over to the spot shut him up and made it impossible for him to continue. It was later learned that the man who had spoken up was a government student by the name of Ma from the city of Hanyang. A "government student" was someone who had successfully passed the first level of the civil service examination system. Having accomplished this much, one could then sit for the provincial examinations, which when passed enabled one to become a provincial graduate, the second level of the examination system. Only then had one obtained the necessary credentials to sit for the metropolitan examinations. At the time, there were countless government students in China, though even Hong Xiuquan himself had been unable to enter their ranks. While a government student was still just a student, it was a socially respected status.

After this particular fellow was escorted away, another man leapt to the platform—it was none other than Yang Xiuqing. There were three men and women on the platform, but Yang said something to them, and they hastily stepped down.

"We shall show you all what becomes of those who heap insults on the Heavenly Father and the Heavenly Elder Brother," said Yang. The execution was carried out at that very site. "They say your name is Ma, and I entrust your disposal to a horse." The people assembled quickly comprehended the meaning of Yang's words. The surname Ma literally means "horse," and the site of the Yuema Yard had been an official riding ground. This was an age in which horses incurred the great majority of military outfitting expenses. In addition to stables, there was a large open lot attached to the grounds. Literally, the term Yuema meant to "review" or "inspect" the horses. The troops would be mounted on horseback and undergo "inspection." The inspection of the Hubei division by the provincial military commander also would have transpired on the open lot at Yuema Yard. Perhaps, it was only natural then that the Taipings chose such a convenient open area for their "lectures." Though they herded many people into the area to listen, there was still plenty of room to move.

Five horses were drawn into this open area, forming a circle with their tails brought tightly together. Their heads pointed in five different directions. The government student was then pushed out front. He abdomen was not bound, though ropes were wrapped around his head, and fastened to both his hands and to both his feet. Taiping soldiers then snugly tied each rope to other ropes hanging from the horses' saddles. The rope attached to his head was the longest.

"Dismemberment by five horses"—certainly some among the assembled onlookers were acquainted with this expression. Yet none had ever seen it carried out. Each of the five horses would be attached to the limbs and head of a person, and then with the crack of a riding crop, they would all simultaneously race off in different directions. It was a grotesque form of execution.

These people, who had come against their will to listen to the Taiping "lectures," were now being forced to witness, also against their will, such an execution.

"Who is that man whose eyes are averted?" screamed someone noisily.

Whether one wished to look or not, all had to observe the execution. Those who had turned away did not even know when he was brought to the execution ground, for it was over in a split second. At the snap of the whip, nearly everyone instinctively shut their eyes. Only the very stout of heart could stand the sight of gushing blood. The horse running to the south could be seen by their open, trembling eyes to be dragging something that looked like a head. The sound of people vomiting was palpable.

"The fate of those who heap insults on the Heavenly Father and the Heavenly Elder Brother will be just as you have witnessed it here!" shouted Yang Xiuqing from the podium.

By that evening, people throughout Wuchang learned of the dismemberment by five horses. At the Guiyuan Temple on the outskirts of Hanyang across the river, Liwen and Xinmei learned of it the next day. Yaxian, head of the women's barracks for the Taiping military, came to Hanyang on an errand and described in detail for them the circumstances surrounding the execution. Although Yaxian hadn't been there herself, she had heard of it from an eyewitness. Any resident of Wuchang could have described the execution as well as Yaxian had.

"From now on, they'll all obey Taiping orders submissively," said Yaxian.

"So you think it's good that they obey you submissively," said Xinmei, stunned by the story Yaxian had just told them. Even if I had put up with it and remained in the Taiping camp till now, thought Xinmei, this dismemberment by horses would probably have been enough to make me leave them.

The ideal of the Society of God Worshippers had most certainly never been to force people under threat of terror.

"Yes, but the officials in Wuchang were all going around saying nasty things about the Taipings. The populace believed maybe half of it, so if we didn't do something just a little on the rough side, they'd have ridiculed us." Yaxian's attitude toward the dismemberment by five horses was not at all negative. When it came to belief in the Lord-on-High, Yaxian was the most fervently devoted person in the women's barracks. In essence, her approach was that to protect her religious beliefs, any means necessary, including persecution, were acceptable. After all, had not the enemies of her religious belief, the government of the demons, inflicted on her comrades in the Taiping Heavenly Kingdom torture, punishments, and executions just as heinous as the dismemberment by five horses? Before the Taiping forces had broken through the walls of Wuchang, Yaxian had infiltrated the city and learned the state of anti-Taiping propaganda spread by the Qing government among the populace. To undermine such ferocious propaganda, they felt forced to adopt equally unbending, firm methods.

"Well, probably," said Xinmei in a slightly skeptical tone of voice.

Yaxian responded excitedly, "It was a touch-and-go battle to see who'd crush whom! If we didn't attack and destroy the enemy, they'd have wiped us out."

That I can understand, but . . . it's so suffocating—Xinmei was about to say this, but when she saw the fire burning in Yaxian's eyes, she decided to remain quiet.

—3—

To the north of the Guiyuan Temple was a slightly elevated hillock known as the Ancient Lute Terrace. The multi-storeyed pagoda on it faced Western Moon Lake. The Ancient Lute Terrace was also known as the Bo Ya Terrace. A man by the name of Bo Ya was a celebrated player of the Chinese lute or *qin* during the Spring and Autumn Era in the fifth century B.C. His name had become familiar to the Chinese people through the aphorism, "Bo Ya ceased playing." Bo Ya had a friend by the name of Zhongzi Qi, and Zhongzi Qi listened well, and appreciated Bo Ya's playing of the lute. When Zhongzi Qi passed away, however, Bo Ya ceased playing his lute from that point forward, for only Zhongzi Qi had truly understood the sounds of his lute. With Zhongzi Qi's death, Bo Ya lost all desire to continue playing. In mourning the death of a close friend, Chinese came to use the expression "Bo Ya ceased playing."

The hillock to the north of Guiyuan Temple was the spot, tradition had it, where Bo Ya strummed his lute and Zhongzi Qi listened to his exquisite notes. Xinmei led Yaxian to this hill and put out in a boat on Western Moon Lake behind it. The entire surface of the lake was covered with lotus leaves.

The news Yaxian had brought only made Xinmei's mood gloomier, though Yaxian believed that the actions taken by the Taipings were perfectly acceptable. "It's war," Yaxian had repeatedly said, "and a war in which we win victory or go down to defeat. We have to do whatever's necessary to win."

She's caught up in the fighting, thought Xinmei of Yaxian, and I've left it altogether.

She wondered, though, if her criticism of the present Taiping movement was the reason she had left the field of battle. What had compelled her to break ranks?

I'll consider all this later with Liwen, she thought, keenly aware of her good fortune in not having to ponder these issues alone.

At the same time that Yang Xiuqing ordered the registration of the local resident populace, an "Office for Presenting Tribute" was established. This was an agency that took receipt of the property donated by Wuchang residents. From gold, silver, and copper coins to grain, chicken, ducks, and other foodstuffs, including tea leaves, all were accepted as contributions. People allegedly vied with one another to get into the Office for Presenting Tribute to make their donations.

"Willingly?" inquired Xinmei.

"They said people competed with each other to do so," responded Yaxian.

"They didn't willingly go to the Office for Presenting Tribute, did they?"

"Of course not. You see, the people of Wuchang still don't believe in the Lord God. We've lectured them now any number of times, but it's useless. When they bring some item to the Office for Presenting Tribute, they get a slip of paper. It's that slip of paper that they want."

"A slip of paper? Oh, it's a receipt."

"That's right."

This slip of paper was known as a "certificate." Although all residents of Wuchang had to cut their queues, this was not the only proof that they had passed muster. These certificates were evidence of their cooperation with the Taiping authorities. No one had actually compelled them to cut their queues, but considering the efficacy of these certificates, it was best to see these donations as mandatory.

The items contributed all went immediately into the Sacred Treasury. The cardinal principle of the Taiping Heavenly Kingdom, which prohibited private property, remained strictly adhered to. Immense quantities of contributed goods piled up, and the goods left behind by the government agencies were also considerable. The government's treasuries and storehouses in Wuchang were left virtually untouched for the Taiping military.

In Changsha, Hunan Governor Zhang Liangji and Provincial Administration Commissioner Pan Duo freely distributed property. They increased the bonuses for officers and troops alike and supplied them with sufficient foodstuffs. In Hengzhou, Huguang Governor-General Cheng Yucai thought the whole thing was an abomination.

Cheng had long served in the capacity of a local official, and he was most concerned with allocation of public funds. Even if one intended, without squandering any money, not to reduce government funds as much as possible, one could first perform one's duties successfully. Looking at situations of those who had failed as local officials, it was almost always a case either of men filling their own pockets with money from state coffers, or men using their public authority to overuse public funds. Whether they succeeded or not, reputations often suffered. Cheng understood the situation surrounding state monies well. In a letter to Zhang Liangji and Pan Duo, he had cautioned them: "Is not your manner of using [these state funds] overly lavish?"

Their response effectively said: "Should Changsha fall into bandit hands, all the money in the government's treasuries will likewise fall into the hands of bandits. This being the case, are we not now using bandit money to enhance the defenses of Changsha?"

Cheng Yucai took offense at this "quibbling," though the provincial treasuries fell under the supervision of the provincial administration commissioner who was the highest administrative official in the province, and Cheng had no capacity to intervene beyond that. As governor-general, he had responsibilities over both Hubei and Hunan provinces and feared that the evil contagion in Hunan might spread to Hubei.

He thus wrote a letter to Hubei Governor Chang Dachun: "Zhang and Pan are recklessly spending public funds in Changsha, and I am opposed to this. State funds must always be allocated with the greatest discretion. I earnestly entreat you not to copy Hunan."

Hubei Governor Chang Dachun was a man with a disposition similar to that of Cheng Yucai. When the Taipings had Wuchang surrounded, he took no measures either to increase the wages of his troops or to pay the coolies extra wages. This was not merely a question of public funds, for when it came to foodstuffs, weaponry, ammunition, and any other item made with copper or iron, he was more frugal than frugal. Every last bit of this material remained behind, and all of it passed into the hands of the Taiping Army.

Now the Taipings were equipped for a long overland journey. The Taiping military leaders decided on this course of action precisely because of the immense quantities of materiel and commodities acquired in Wuchang. It was an amount sufficient, it seemed to them, to withstand a lengthy expedition.

Though a long military expedition was decided upon, opinions were divided about the direction—north or east—in which they should head. Those who advocated a northerly policy wanted the Taiping forces to continue moving north, conquer the North China Plain, and then unleash an attack on the capital at Beijing. They wanted to descend in one fell swoop on the heart of the demons' government and bring it to its knees. The people who supported this line of reasoning wanted to continue the momentum from the seizure of Wuchang and effect a blitz style of warfare.

By contrast, others argued that it was dangerous for an army of only about one hundred thousand—including the old and infirm—to advance rapidly and attack the unknown terrain to the north. Better to go downstream on the Yangzi and seize the city of Nanjing. There, after regaining strength, a northern expeditionary army should be sent out. This was the eastern advance strategy. Yaxian had been sent to Hanyang to ask Liwen's views on this and related questions. These were not merely vaguely defined issues, for concrete questions were involved, such as: What would be the reaction among the foreigners in Shanghai?

"As an individual," responded Liwen, "I tend to favor a move toward the north, but hasn't a decision to advance to the east effectively already been decided?"

With the registration of the resident populace, the Taipings numbered some five hundred thousand, including those people incorporated into the barracks' organizations. At the time of the attack on Wuchang, the number had been one hundred thousand. In other words, it had swelled five times. Born in Jintian village, if one thinks of the Taiping Heavenly Kingdom having built its skeleton at Yongan, then one might say that it affixed meat to the bones at Wuchang. And a lot of meat it was—with indeed much fat and superfluous flesh among it.

The core of the Taiping fighting force was the soldiers who hailed from Guangxi. Having been raised in the south, they were exceedingly weak in the face of cold weather. Lightweight equipment for ease of movement was one of the characteristics of the Taiping military. The soldiers in the "barracks" that they temporarily scraped together in Wuchang had no capacity to issue uniforms; people were to wear their ordinary civilian clothes, though the Confucian long gown was forbidden. Many were those who were said to have cut their long gowns in half with a pair of scissors and donned the remains. Could troops from the south with lightweight garb withstand the bitter cold of north China?

Should they proceed north, they would enter the region where the northern dialect of Chinese was spoken. Customs and practices in daily life were also different there. Because of differences in eating practices, the government's forces who came as reinforcements from the north to Changsha had been unable to eat to their satisfaction, and when they arrived many were exhausted from lack of nourishment. The same could happen to the Taipings should they attempt to advance to the north.

To this point, the Taiping forces had always strengthened their deficits in supplies and personnel while on the march. But, going north from Hubei led into Henan and then Hebei province where the land was not the least bit fertile. Many feared they would be unable to replenish supplies readily.

By comparison, the Jiangnan region to the south of the Yangzi River was full of rich farmland. "The Jiangnan provinces are sufficiently rich to satisfy the entire realm"—so ran the Chinese maxim, indicating that this region was the "granary of China." Compared to the north, its topography was closer to that of Guangxi. Even those who had joined the movement in Hunan and Hubei felt no discomfort in the Jiangnan area.

"They wanted to hear your reasons," said Yaxian.

"There aren't that many garrison troops in Henan now. They're all hurriedly giving out orders to amass troops from every direction, but they've only just started to shift position. If you were to proceed north now, I think you could advance with hardly any resistance. If you do go north, do it now, before it's too late," said Liwen, though he didn't think they would adopt his views. Though he was on the grounds of the Guiyuan Temple, he well understood the atmosphere among the Taipings. Supporters of a northern advance were in the minority, as the voices advocating a move to the east overwhelmed them.

Ever since the days back in Guangxi, whenever the conversation turned to an expedition to take the entire Chinese realm, someone would raise a voice calling on them to move on Nanjing. Between Yuezhou and Wuchang, some ten thousand boats had fallen into their possession. Should they advance to the north now, these valuable waterborne commodities would scarcely be used.

"Be that as it may, I shall convey your views, Mr. Lian. You've been able to take a leisurely outing with Elder Sister Li for a bit of time now," said Yaxian, referring to Xinmei. "That's nice, over there at Ancient Lute Terrace and Western Moon Lake . . . well, I'll return now to the dusty theater of worldly affairs."

Yaxian had stayed but a day, before crossing the floating bridge and returning to Wuchang.

As for the reactions of foreigners in Shanghai, Lian Liwen cautioned the Taiping leaders not to entertain excessively high hopes in that department. The Jinshunji, the store managed by Liwen's father, had a business associate in Hankou whose shop was able to garner information in this vein through links it had established by sending tea leaves to foreign merchants in Shanghai.

Because they intended to make Christianity the guiding principle of their state, the Taipings should have been able to win the goodwill of the Westerners. Liwen warned against this kind of optimism within the Taiping camp. "The foreigners in Shanghai are merchants before they're believers in Christianity. Also, almost all of them have ties to the opium trade. Don't ever forget that fact." Through Yaxian, Liwen was able to convey his views to the Taiping leadership.

One of the items in the national policy of the Taiping Heavenly Kingdom was to fight for the complete eradication of opium in China. So strict were they that not only opium smokers, but dealers and even the people who manufactured and sold the apparatus for smoking and handling opium, were all to be executed. In the event that the Taipings were to gain control over the reins of a government in China, they were sure to implement their policies rigorously. Should opium dealing cease to be possible in China, then the number of foreign trading firms in Shanghai would drop by half overnight.

This was a vital question for the Western merchant houses. No matter how many advertised themselves as Christians, with the exception of a few, none considered supporting the Taipings. Foreigners residing in Shanghai enjoyed extraterritoriality and possessed armed self-defense forces. As far as they were concerned, it was perfectly fine that the Chinese government was as weak as it was. If it became too feeble and disorder ensued, business would become impossible to transact. If, on the other hand, the government were powerful and decisive, then it would ban opium.

The present Qing government was just weak enough and yet attentive to domestic threats.

China was now embroiled in a war, and the fact that merchant activity was becoming more and more difficult to pursue was a mortal wound to the foreign business establishments. The Qing war against the Taipings engulfed all of China in the fighting, and it was assumed that the foreigners in Shanghai were allied with the Qing regime.

Liwen grit his teeth and, as if he were giving Yaxian instructions, addressed her in his own words. Still unable to feel at ease, though, he decided to write it down for her.

"Yes, but they all pray to the Heavenly Father and Heavenly Elder Brother, do they not?" Yaxian still didn't seem to understand. There were not many like her among the Taipings, people with pure believing hearts who were moved to action on that basis.

"I'm envious of Yaxian, for some reason. She believes it all—everything," said Xinmei, sighing.

"The Taipings are certain to head for Nanjing. I think we ought to go on after them to Shanghai," said Liwen.

"Is their advance to the east already decided?"

"Almost certainly."

"To move north from here would be really tough. It's still terribly cold there."

As Liwen had said, the atmosphere in Wuchang was to sail with the Yangzi current, take Nanjing, and make it a base of operations. The upper echelons of the Taiping leadership was completely in agreement with this mood.

Preparations to withdraw from the city were secretly under way, so as not to unsettle the local populace. The Taiping forces dispatched troops to Huangzhou and Caidian, both near the city of Wuchang. The prefect and adjutant both fled from Huangzhou, and scarcely any fighting ensued there. The objective of this tactic was to collect more property and boats, a preparatory operation toward the larger strategy of withdrawing from Wuchang.

Within the city of Wuchang, a Barracks for the Sick was constructed. It was an installation to accommodate the ill, a hospital in effect. In Guangdong and Guangxi provinces at the time, the term used for someone who was sick was "capable person," and thus the name of this "hospital" was literally the "barracks for capable people." The reason for this is that the word for "sick" carried a bad omen about it, so a euphemism was adopted in its place.

The Barracks for the Sick was an official Taiping institution. The Christian spirit impelled them to pour their energy into establishing welfare facilities of this sort. The opening of welfare institutions such as this one existed side by side in the Taiping Heavenly Kingdom with gruesome executions such as the dismemberment by five horses. Everyone seemed to have a different understanding of Christianity.

In addition to the Barracks for the Sick, they built a Barracks for the Aged, effectively an old-age home, and a Literary Barracks, a kind of salon for those who wrote poetry. Records also tell of a Boys' Barracks. Wuchang was the first large city occupied by the Taipings, and they used it to experiment in various ways.

Both Heavenly King Hong Xiuquan and Eastern King Yang Xiuqing said at a conference of Taiping leaders that they wanted the city to come back to life. Inasmuch as Hong Xiuquan had come to speak on matters political only in extreme cases, on those rare occasions when he spoke, his words were closely considered by others. This string of health and welfare institutions—the Barracks for the Sick, the Barracks for the Aged, the Literary Barracks, the Boys' Barracks, and others like them—were all based on Hong's concepts.

Yang Xiuqing was a much more practical man. While helping to revive the city of Wuchang, he was secretly attempting to move forward with preparations to abandon it.

The New Year was about to arrive, and at just the right time. The Taipings had devised their own distinctive calendar. According to the Taiping calendar, the New Year would begin on February 3 (1853) of the solar calendar, corresponding to the twenty sixth day of the twelfth lunar month. In their own parlance, the Taipings referred to this year, 1853, as the "*guihao* third year of the Taiping Heavenly Kingdom." It corresponded as well to the third year of the reign of the Xianfeng Emperor in Beijing. In the Chinese sexagenary cycle for dating, which made use of a complex combination of ten Chinese characters for stems and twelve characters for branches, this year was *guichou*." However, in the Cantonese dialect, the pronunciation of the character *chou* was the same as another character that means physically repulsive or deformed. To avoid it, the Taipings elected the character *hao,* which carries exactly the opposite meaning, namely, good or fortuitous. Hence, they called the year, *guihao.*

The Taipings took as one of their missions to fly the banners of the Society of God Worshippers high over the city, and to wipe out the shrine to evil deities and evil religions. At the same time, the omen this bore for the Taipings was a vigorous one indeed. Among the Taiping leaders, there were many like Yang Xiuqing who were completely illiterate. Unable to read, they were dependent on sounds, and if the images associated with sounds were bad ones, Yang often ordered them changed to different, better sounding characters.

For example, the Chinese character *mao*, one of the twelve branches, when pronounced in Cantonese carried the meaning of "deficient" or "lacking." So, they changed it to a character meaning "prosperous." Similarly, another branch character, *hai*, was a homophone for a character meaning "injury." So they changed it to one meaning "open up." From one perspective, they were following a kind of superstition; from another, it was an assault on the Chinese tradition.

As the *guihao* third year approached, a quiet panic arose in the homes of Wuchang. Rumors of "concubine selection" were spreading. Like the emperors throughout Chinese history, Heavenly King Hong Xiuquan was going to create a "outer court." To do so required the selection of beautiful women. It was not just a rumor, as would eventually become clear.

—5—

"Zeng Guofan, vice-minister in the Board of Rites, who is presently in mourning in his native place of Xiangxiang, Hunan province, is hereby ordered to undertake the tasks of organizing and training the local people into a *tuanlian* and investigating the bandits."

This imperial edict from the capital arrived at the Hunanese provincial capital of Changsha, and from there was delivered to Zeng Guofan in Xiangxiang by a messenger sent by Hunan Governor Zhang Guoliang on January 21, 1853—the thirteenth day of the twelfth lunar month. By that time, Wuchang had already fallen to the Taipings. While en route to his native place to take up ritual mourning, Zeng learned that Hubei Governor Chang Dachun, who had rendered him assistance at Wuchang, had died at his post.

Zeng received the imperial edict, but he was in no mood to respond to its dictates with alacrity. He had only been home for some three months or more, whereas the prescribed period for mourning was twenty-seven months.

Possibly, if a full year would have passed, his frame of mind might have measured up to it.

Zeng penned a memorial to the throne, the intent of which described his desire to fulfill his filial duties. Prior to receiving the imperial edict, his younger brother Zeng Guoquan and others were urging him to come to his senses and take action. However, Zeng Guofan turned down their requests.

News of Chang Dachun's death moved Zeng deeply, but when Zeng's disciple, Guo Songtao (1818–1891), came rushing to him, Zeng made up his mind. Guo was also observing a period of mourning at home in Xiangyin, Hunan. Xiangyin was the very place from where the Taipings, having withdrawn from Changsha, set out for Yuezhou via Yiyang. Though no substantive battle had been fought at Xiangyin, Guo Songtao had observed firsthand the Taiping military on the march.

"With my own eyes, I have seen the bandit troops. They trampled my hometown underfoot!" said Guo indignantly. He then continued, "Please bestir yourself. Though you say you are ignorant of matters military, there is not one among that gang of long-haired bandits who can read a single character of a military text. These illiterates brought down the city of Wuchang. With your great talents, sir, we could soon be current in military affairs. You say you wish to fulfill your filial duties, but in the past in times of national crises, it was considered obligatory to serve in a military campaign even during periods of mourning. Who would dare criticize you now that you have received an imperial edict? Please bestir yourself, sir. This is the greatest rebellion since the founding of the dynasty. If you refuse to comply with the imperial edict, your honor will be besmirched. Please consider all these matters carefully."

Tears welled up in Guo's eyes as he urged his teacher to take decisive action.

"Please be so kind as to wait here for just a moment," said Zeng as he rose from his seat. Zeng's younger brother, Guoquan, was there as well. He and Guo Songtao assumed that Zeng Guofan had walked back into his house, quietly deep in thought. Zeng had a habit of virtually excessive contemplation; he was a man who, by his very nature, was effectively addicted to concentrated meditation. Given this circumstance, they imagined that a fair amount of time would pass before he emerged.

Then, unexpectedly, Zeng Guofan returned almost immediately.

"I have set it ablaze," he said, sitting down in a chair.

"What do you mean by 'set it ablaze'?" asked Guo.

"The draft of my memorial."

"Oh . . ." said Guo, his eyes sparkling with joy.

Zeng had referred a moment earlier to the draft of a memorial he had just completed writing that he was going to send to the throne to turn down the imperial edict. By throwing his memorial into the fire, he had clearly decided to accept the imperial edict with humility.

"It was not an easy matter," said Zeng haltingly.

Despite a connotation to the contrary, the Chinese term *bangtong banli*, used in the edict to Zeng, did not carry a meaning of "assisting" the highest officials in the area, namely the governor and governor-general. He was at the same level as those officials and was being instructed to proceed with the matters at hand. This was a special edict, however, and it was no longer a question of similar status, for it carried the commanding authority of the imperial institution. Thus, Zeng now had been given authority stronger than that of the local officialdom.

To be sure, this was no easy matter. Perhaps it was only his imagination, but Zeng seemed to be turning pale.

"Let us make preparations to deal with the business of mourning and then set out as soon as possible for Changsha," he said.

On the fourth day following his receipt of the edict, Zeng Guofan left his native Xiangxiang, and after another four days of travel reached the Hunanese provincial capital of Changsha. After the departure of the Taiping forces, Hunan had been in chaos. The government's military forces demonstrated nearly a total lack of morale, and rebellious groups had begun vigorous activities here and there.

Local residents of the region were in a state of great nervousness. They didn't fear the Taipings in the least, but rather the Qing government's soldiers. During the time spent by the Taipings in Hunan, their soldiers could walk alone wherever they wished. However, Qing soldiers could not do so, for they never knew when someone might smash their heads open with a hoe from behind.

Local residents despised the government's troops. For their part, the latter carried out acts of rape and pillage wherever and whenever they so wished. The worst elements among them were the soldiers from Chaozhou in Guangdong, known as the "Chaozhou mercenaries." Recruited in Guangdong, they formed a poorly trained battalion of hoodlums sent into Guangxi.

The Taiping troops, by contrast, never touched a thing belonging to the local populace and at times helped out with harvests. Needless to say, they had won local support and popularity as a result.

For someone like Zeng Guofan, who to all eyes clearly resembled an official of the government, local folk did not reveal their true thoughts. However, Zeng completely sympathized with what troubled the common people.

"Bringing those troops along from Chaozhou was an enormous mistake," he said upon meeting the provincial governor.

"It was not my doing to bring them here. Someone arbitrarily had them join us. Someone with whom I am not acquainted." The speaker was not the governor but an aide standing at his side.

"Is that right?" Zeng looked the fellow square in the face. The latter stared fixedly, his chin seemingly jutting forward, into the eyes of this high official of the government, this vice-minister in the Board of Rites.

"There is the look of death in your visage," said this fellow. "You are not the kind who can die peaceful at home."

So this is Zuo Zongtang, about whom I have heard such rumors, thought Zeng in an instant. Zeng had often heard in Xiangxiang of things concerning the eccentric Zuo Zongtang, a native of Xiangyin, like Guo. It took no time at all to see that none of the rumors were exaggerated.

—6—

The day Zeng Guofan arrived in Changsha, an incident erupted in Wuchang, then under Taiping occupation. Several Taiping soldiers stepped into the women's barracks. Some of the women let out a scream, for men were not allowed inside. Even if one's own wife were there at the time, it was still forbidden.

In Hunan, the Taipings admitted a large number of recruits from local Heaven and Earth Society groups, and the education given to these newly admitted troops was still, it would appear, far from thorough. The Taiping military officers who rushed to the scene beheaded the offending culprits on the spot, and exposed the severed heads over Hanyang Gate. Taiping military discipline was as relentless as the withering frost and the scorching sunshine.

At the same time, executions were being strictly carried out among the Qing forces encamped on the outskirts of Wuchang. The event of the sort that occurred at the women's barracks was rare among the Taiping soldiers, and thus executions were rare as well. However, violations of military discipline were all too frequent among the Qing troops, and if strict measures were not taken in response, there was a serious fear that military organization itself would collapse entirely.

The Chaozhou mercenaries were the worst behaved of all. Provincial Military Commander Xiang Rong was on the verge of executing all 300 of them—drastic treatment, to be sure. According to a Qing document, the *Annals of Wuchang*, while on the march, they exhausted the limits of lawlessness, plundering property, even stripping the clothes off the backs of people they met along the road. They committed acts of outrage against women, and upon entering a village, would chase the local residents away and then set their homes ablaze. It was cold at this time of year, so they cut down trees as they wished and built fires accordingly. "In the harm they caused, they were no better than bandits," reads this text, and it is a government chronicle. It cites instances of other bandits, but one reads of such cases of violent behavior on the part of the Taipings scarcely at all.

A horrendous gang of hoodlums, the very presence of the Chaozhou mercenaries hindered the military strategy of the Qing forces at numerous points. First and foremost, they played havoc with military discipline, and because of their presence the government was unable to get cooperation from the local populace. In fact, they got just the opposite, being threatened from their rear by local residents. So, not only were they attacking the enemy, but they had to remain vigilant with respect to the local people as well.

"Do me a favor and kill each and every last one of that rabble," decided Xiang Rong.

Whether he would be banished to Xinjiang or pardoned depended on this string of military maneuvers, and as far as Xiang Rong was concerned, his fate hung in the balance. He wouldn't hesitate a moment to kill 300 of such a pack of thugs.

The order went out to the Chaozhou mercenaries to assemble at the Yao Family Ancestral Hall. Thinking there was to be some sort of personnel reshuffling, they all came to the appointed place.

The many ancestral halls to be found throughout China were built by people with the same surname for their common ancestors. They were not limited to wealthy or otherwise illustrious families. Even in Hong Xiuquan's native Hua county, Guangdong province, there was a Hong Family Ancestral Hall, now the "Hong Xiuquan Memorial Hall." Though the family wasn't the least bit influential, the ancestral hall was quite spacious, for on the anniversary of the death of an ancestor, a large number of relatives would assemble at the hall, and it thus had to be sufficiently spacious to accommodate a crowd.

Just as the 300 Chaozhou mercenaries entered the Yao Family Ancestral Hall, a brigade of rifle marksmen laying in wait began firing at them from all directions. Bedlam ensued. In the chaos, over 100 of the mercenaries were killed, and the remaining 200 were able to escape by the skin of their teeth. Those who cheated death on that day surrendered to the Taipings.

This incident took place on the twenty-fourth day of the twelfth lunar month, just two days before the New Year according to the Taiping calendar. Yang Xiuqing was of the view that they should hold grand celebrations to welcome the New Year, now that they held a large city for the first time. Though artificially pumped up, the year-end festivities were full of life. In all the confusion the surrender of the Chaozhou mercenaries was scarcely noticed.

Yang Xiuqing assigned them to work in handling cargo, and they loaded rice onto the boats. While the festivities for the New Year were being prepared, preparations for evacuating the city could not be neglected.

The next day was Taiping New Year's Eve. Concubine selection was carried out on this day. A strict circular went out that day: "The Lecture on Principles for New Year's Eve shall be attended by all girls aged thirteen to sixteen. Absences will not be tolerated. Those who fail to appear shall be beheaded together with their parents."

Horrified families with young women of marriageable age celebrated the notice as they might a wake, and prayed that their daughters would somehow elude the selection process. The site was, of course, the Yuema Yard. No one had an accurate count on the number of girls aged thirteen to sixteen who lived in the city of Wuchang. Some thought the figure might top ten thousand.

In the days before the event, rumors spread like wildfire. "It seems they'll only take a hundred."

"No, I've heard it's to be fifty." In any event, it appeared as though they would select one in a hundred or one in two hundred.

"So, that means our daughter's safe." Some parents were consoled by the odds.

"I know our daughter will be picked. What are we to do?" And some parents were on the verge of hysteria.

Every family worked with undivided attention to ensure that their daughters would not be among those selected by covering their daughters' faces with soot or keeping their hair dry and unkempt.

At the time when the Taipings first occupied the city, Yang Xiuqing had begun a detailed registration of the resident populace, and hence, there was no means of eluding the selection process. The reticulated barracks system did not allow for a single person to fall through the cracks. The threat of beheading also meant that no one would be absent.

At the entrance to Yuema Yard, washbasins full of water were lined up in a long row. Yang Xiuqing had anticipated the efforts of these young girls to make themselves as ugly as possible. He thus had them wash their faces, and even if they had covered their faces with soot, at this stage it would be washed away. And so, sixty young beauties were selected. Yang Xiuqing is said to have presented them to the Heavenly King Hong Xiuquan.

The New Year arrived, and the sounds of exploding firecrackers, their wrappers floating in the air like a snowfall, continued for the entire day through the streets of Wuchang. Residents of the city, in their heart of hearts, were thinking that the true New Year's Day wasn't for another five days hence, but there was no way to avoid following the Taiping calendar. The Taipings had the upper hand in the city of Wuchang, and they retained it with military force.

People set off even more firecrackers than in an ordinary year to demonstrate their submission.

—7—

Xinmei was sullen at the Guiyuan Temple. The sounds of exploding firecrackers in the city streets of Hanyang were audible, but the source of her displeasure was this "concubine selection."

"I wonder what Yaxian could possibly be thinking about it. In the Society of God Worshippers, we taught that men and women were equal. And now what are they doing? Bringing together tens of thousands of young girls against their will and selecting among them after looking at their faces. Yang Xiuqing himself once said that it's the beauty of the heart that suits the will of God. I heard it myself with my own two ears."

Blindly indignant, Xinmei found fault even with Liwen, who found her all the more attractive when she became so angry. Indeed, this was her strength. But Liwen was also extremely upset by the "concubine selection" at Yuema Yard.

"I'm worried about the future," said Liwen.

"You're worried about the future? Do we even have a future?" Xinmei's tone was scathing.

"They're no different from every Chinese emperor in history. Shihuangdi, founding emperor of the Qin dynasty two thousand years ago, is said to have had three thousand women in his harem, and Emperor Yang of the Sui dynasty on the order of twenty thousand. By comparison, sixty is a tiny number."

"It's not a question of numbers. This selection of concubines is an issue of a way of thinking. The Heavenly King has his own wife, doesn't he? At the concubine selection, I hear that Yang Xiuqing made the most beautiful girl in the group his own, and the second most beautiful he presented to the Heavenly King. This is obscene!" She was practically spitting out the words.

"Perhaps I should go meet with them," said Liwen.

He had effectively been confining himself within Guiyuan Temple. Hong Xiuquan, Yang Xiuqing, and the other leaders of the Taiping movement had, after arriving at Hankou, taken and occupied Wuchang. Living on the outskirts of Hanyang, Liwen had met with none of the Taiping leaders, save Luo Dagang. Yaxian had been sent by the leadership to seek out his opinion, but in addition to a view on marching north or east, he now felt as though he had points of view he wanted to articulate.

"Even if we met them, it'd be useless. They'll receive divine retribution and soon be destroyed. This time they've exceeded the limit. The people in the Taiping movement were a pitiable, wretched lot who worked as hard as they could and were pure of heart. I feel so sorry for Yaxian, really. After all the work she's put into it, and now these young princesses, chosen at Yuema Yard for their facial beauty, acquire influence over the Heavenly King and Eastern King as they wish. These young girls certainly didn't become Taiping princesses by their own choice, and to compensate for their ill fate, they'll do as they wish. Believe me, they'll gain considerable clout, and they'll try to use it to influence people. Some will surely try and affect the future of the country. It's not that these girls are such bad people. Whatever opinions people like Yaxian might have, nobody's interested in listening. It's just that nobody wants to hear what a thirty-year-old, slightly chubby woman has to say. Poor Yaxian . . . If you look at her closely, you can see how beautiful she really is, really . . ." Speaking with such pride, at the end, Xinmei seemed to have run out of things to say.

"Xinmei, be calm," Liwen said, his hand on her shoulder, rubbing it lightly.

Yaxian's ill luck did not have to wait till the selected concubines began accruing influence. She ran into it much sooner. On the second day of the Taiping New Year (February 4), as the celebrations were coming to a close, they began loading silver from the government's treasury into their boats. When they put together the amount stored in the provincial administration commissioner's treasury with those in the official treasuries of the salt control circuit, the prefecture, and the county, the total came to 1,600,000 taels.

Pan Duo, the provincial administration commissioner in Changsha, was not engaging in sophistry in the least when he said, "I am using bandit money to enhance our defenses." Upon receipt of the Huguang governor-general's letter, Governor Chang and all those below him refrained from further use of silver from the treasury and expenditures on defense. This all passed into the hands of the Taipings, and it was now being loaded onto their boats. It was to become the military fund for the sacking of Nanjing.

The following day, the artillery and ammunition were loaded aboard ship. Much of the weaponry came from the store left by Wu Sangui nearly two hundred years earlier that had been recovered at Yuezhou. The surrendered Chaozhou mercenaries had just completed loading foodstuffs on boats from the last days of the year. Yang Xiuqing made preparations for a month's military supplies. Food had been stored up in great quantity in Wuchang. When the Taipings left Wuchang, they left behind several hundred bushels of rice in storage. Spades and hoes were loaded in large numbers, to be used for digging tunnels at the time of the attack on Nanjing, as they had been in the past.

The Taiping leaders scheduled the sixth of their New Year, several days hence, to board ship, and the following day, the seventh, to depart Wuchang. In conjunction with the withdrawal, the Taipings had to create a diversion for the Qing armies about to attack them on the outskirts of Wuchang. At the very least, it was necessary to keep to a minimum any Qing interference with their strategic withdrawal.

To that end, they had to open the city gates at the time of their planned departure and launch an attack on the Qing forces to the east. The task before the troops assigned to this assault was onerous. The fate of the Taiping movement effectively lay on their shoulders.

With an immense army of 500,000 boarding boats, the Taipings could not avoid a certain degree of chaos. If those positions were attacked, the Taipings faced the grave danger of sustaining great losses. To guard against precisely such a possibility, they selected their very finest troops to comprise their own attack force. The Taipings' choicest soldiers were not only the most physically robust, but those with the deepest religious fervor. There was a women's contingent among them, and Yaxian was selected to be in charge of it.

The sixth day of the Taiping New Year corresponded to lunar New Year's Day. In various places throughout China, other than the Wuhan cities, it was a day of exploding firecrackers. When the boarding began, women, children, and old people were given priority in getting aboard ship.

At the same time, the attack force opened the gates to the east of the city and launched an assault on the Qing military. The Taiping forces were well aware of the great responsibility resting on their backs. Their ability to draw the Qing forces to them for just a short while longer was tightly linked to whatever bright future the Taiping movement might have.

Before the attack they said a prayer to God. Tears floated into Yaxian's eyes.

"I am so happy," she said, in a voice torn directly from her heart. Her orders were: Fight until tomorrow evening, and afterward we'll gather you up at the Green Mountain ferry crossing. Until that point, Yaxian had not thought much of her own life.

An army of 500,000 going down the Yangzi River—it was a scene of historical splendor, emitting rays of light of great intensity. Thus the hard fight before the troops that would engage the government forces in the outskirts of Wuchang might have been neglected.

As always, the attack force prayed fervently in the name of God. They fought with all their strength, and many lives were lost.

The Qing forces were under the supreme command of Xiang Rong, and under him were Regional Commanders He-chun and Qin Dingsan, and Brigade Vice-Commander Zhang Guoliang, all of whom were officers with military experience. During questioning concerning responsibility for the fall of Wuchang, held five days earlier at the imperial court in Beijing, Imperial

Commissioner Xu Guangjin, who concurrently served as Huguang governor-general, was stripped of his posts, and it was decided that he be apprehended and interrogated. Xiang Rong was appointed imperial commissioner in his stead, and Hunan Governor Zhang Liangji was selected to become the Huguang governor-general.

At the time, Xiang Rong, of course, did not know that he had been named imperial commissioner. He was under the impression that his banishment to Xinjiang might be nullified by his actions to this point. He was working overtime, with a motivation of the sort he had never had previously. The violent group execution of the Chaozhou mercenaries was another indication of a newfound will on his part to act.

Needless to say, the fighting grew bitter. There was a hillock to the north of Hong Hill where the main Qing encampment was based, and on the western bank of East Lake. On the following afternoon, Yaxian was near this nameless hillock with eight of her surviving subordinates.

"I can see them now. Let's go!" she said, shading her eyes with her forearm after climbing the hillock. In the distance, the masts on the Yangzi River were like a dense forest moving slowly to the northeast. She had carried out her job. Yaxian and her eight fellow women fighters were thoroughly exhausted.

"Let's pray," said Yaxian. As she looked out over the Yangzi, she saw that a rifle brigade of the Qing army was making a wide circle around the hillock. Before their prayers were even finished, a barrage of gunfire exploded.

The women's sonorous voices in prayer sounded throughout the area. Though no one was there to witness their deaths, local residents who had been concealing themselves in nearby homes knew they had died when their prayer broke off at the time of the gunfire.

The battle over, the Qing forces began the effort to remove the enemy corpses. This was to be their proof of military victory. However, the remains of the nine women soldiers who should have fallen near the hillock at the bank of East Lake were not there. Their courageous spirit had so inspired the local populace, that the latter had respectfully buried them before the government troops could get their hands on the bodies. The people covered the bodies with a small amount of earth.

Hillock of the Nine Women. Locals called it this, brought offerings there, and burned incense at the site. And so it went for a long period of time. Though known, no one ever divulged that this site was the grave of the Taiping women soldiers, for after the war with the Taipings, the Qing government rigorously tracked down anyone and everyone who had been connected with the Taiping movement.

The area near East Lake was originally desolate terrain, but in 1953 it was turned into a park, now called East Lake Park. It is a place where Wuhan residents go to relax. Separate from this picnic and holiday area and a little further away from the city, a monument to the nine women was erected at the same time that East Lake was turned into a park. Now a tall stone memorial stands without anyone's trepidation.

On the front of the stone monument, the words, composed by the old Chinese Communist Party member Dong Biwu (1885\6–1975), read: "In Remembrance of the Hillock of the Nine Women." The calligraphy is that of Zhang Nanxian. To the left and right, as well as behind the frontal inscription, poems praising the martyrdom of these heroic women are to be found.

A eulogistic poem to an unnamed martyr by Song Qingling (1893–1981), late widow of the great Chinese revolutionary Sun Yat-sen (1866–1925), is inscribed on the right side of the monument, and the characters are the work of He Xiangning (1878\9–1972), widow of the martyred Chinese revolutionary and comrade of Sun Yat-sen, Liao Zhongkai (1877–1925):

> Nine women heroes in Hubei,
> Their brave sacrifice a lesson to posterity.
> The 1911 Revolution and the Taiping Rebellion arising
>   close in time
> Overthrew the imperial system, and we honor them both,
>   new and old.

The stone monument at the Hillock of the Nine Women towers over the hillock bathed in radiant sunlight.

22

Jingkou
Communiqué

—1—

Yu Yisheng, a man sent by the Jinshunji to buy tea leaves in Hunan, came near Wuchang, but when he observed the situation there, he decided to double back to Shanghai. The immense military force of the Taipings had come east down the Yangzi River from the Wuhan cities, and Yu Yisheng retreated to the east himself as if pursued by them. When he came to Jingkou (present-day Zhenjiang), he reported to Lian Weicai, proprietor of the Jinshunji, on his experiences. Lian was in Beijing at the time, so Yu sent his letter of report to the Jinshunji branch in Shanghai, requesting that it be forwarded to Beijing.

The Shanghai branch store of the Jinshunji that received Yu's letter did not forward it but held onto it, because they had word from Lian in Beijing that he would soon be coming their way. When Yu's letter arrived in Shanghai, Lian's plans put him there in about five days.

The government's military forces were in a confused state of escape, and roughly in conjunction with their movement, Yu Yisheng found himself in a clear position to observe the chaos from within. Yu's report accurately assessed the situation from the perspective of the government, as the Taipings were rushing toward Nanjing. "Not so much as a fragment of the prestige of our dynasty's officialdom still exists."

Yu's report began in this manner, and within it one could read the crescendo in the heart of this one merchant, Mr. Yu. The dominant theme was indignation. Any number of times, he had undoubtedly set down his pen and ceased writing when trying to restrain his anger from spewing forth. Thinking that he would write his report in as casual a manner as possible, in bits and pieces of his sentences, his rage as a human being flooded out all the same.

"When you think about it, this prestige probably never existed as such. I can sense quite keenly that the people controlled by these officials live lives of unsurpassed misfortune.

"Having tried to head toward Hankou from Jiujiang via Huangzhou, I found I had no choice but to return to Jiujiang upon learning that the Wuhan tri-cities had fallen into Taiping hands. I was unable to contact our client in Hankou. I hoped to get news somehow of Liwen, but Hankou was in such a state that everything was rushed and hurried, and there was no way for me to accomplish my wish. I believe, however, that Liwen had just arrived there. The Yaoji Tea Firm in Jiujiang notes the following passage in a letter from the Yihe Firm in Hankou: 'A rumor has been heard that Mr. Lian Liwen of the Jinshunji has arrived in Hanyang.'

"Inasmuch as the Taipings strictly forbid their soldiers from all acts of violence against the resident populace, and the fact that they hold fast to this stricture, I do not believe Liwen is in any physical danger. The letter of the Yihe Firm was written in the short period of time following the Taiping entrance into Wuhan and before his communications ceased. After the Taiping troops entered the Wuhan cities, Liwen was in Hanyang without incident, and I feel there is no need for fear on his behalf.

"On the third day of the New Year, the Taipings allegedly left the Wuhan cities along both land and sea routes. The land force was led by commanders Hu Yihuang, Li Kaifang, and Li Fengxiang, with Hu's troops serving as the advance guard. The sea force was apparently under the leadership of Eastern King Yang Xiuqing, Northern King Wei Changhui, and Assistant King Shi Dakai, as well as Qin Rigang and Luo Dagang. Clearly, the sea route seems to be the main force of the Taiping military.

"I have heard as well that the Heavenly King Hong Xiuquan boarded the dragon boat and accompanied the sea force, but no one spoke a word about it. Yang Xiuqing seems fully in charge as the commander-in-chief. It is as if Hong Xiuquan has become so overly renowned that he is solely an object of veneration. Perhaps this was a natural development; perhaps it is the result of the might of the Eastern King surpassing that of the Heavenly King. There are two theories on the matter, differing according to who enunciates a point of view.

"There is also, I am told, a division-of-labor theory by which the Heavenly King controls matters in the religious realm while the Eastern King sees to military affairs. Even when considered in the most favorable light, the

Heavenly King appears to have lost military authority, while the Eastern King appears to be the actual man in power. I do not think, however, that military authority was seized, but that the Heavenly King relinquished it. Or perhaps the Eastern King has acted in such a way that events would take this turn.

"The ordinary people are remarkably well-informed about the Taiping leadership. As far as the government is concerned, the Taipings are an army of bandits, and therefore, reports circulated by the authorities are uniformly of the propagandistic sort that claim the Taipings to be a tyrannical, outrageous band. Nonetheless, the farmers are not so deceived. The truth about the Taiping military has been passed by word of mouth from Guangxi to Hunan and from Hunan to Hubei. Since it involves both their lives and property, ordinary Chinese residents have striven to the best of their abilities to gain as accurate information as possible.

"By contrast, people along the road do not seem informed about the government. Actually, they do not seem interested in learning. Their attitude is one of resignation; all government people are the same in their estimation. They are surprisingly unconcerned about changes in provincial governors, commanding officials, and the like. They do not even know their names. And yet, everyone knows the names of Heavenly King Hong Xiuquan and Eastern King Yang Xiuqing. They know that Hong Xiuquan is a meditative religious figure and Yang Xiuqing is an activist military man.

"As I am sure you are well aware, Lu Jianying, governor-general of the Jiangnan provinces (Jiangxi, Jiangsu, and Anhui), and Qi-shan, governor of Henan, have been ordered by Beijing to mop up the bandit army. Reports have it that both men have been given the oblong official seal of the imperial commissioner, which means that they have accordingly been given the authority to act as arbitrarily as need be. They no longer need to make a request for Beijing's approval each and every time they want to mobilize troops.

"Despite all this, while Qi-shan has proceeded as far as Xinyang, Henan province, he has made no attempt to move his troops any further. Though the Taipings are said to be preparing to advance to the north, everyone sees this merely as an excuse to avoid a war. Attack would be the most efficacious defense. Even a rank amateur can see that the best course of action would be for the Henan Army to move south as quickly as possible.

"Huang Ximing, a member of the Jiangnan governor-general's staff, is an elder cousin of mine, and on many occasions I have engaged him in conversation and offered him the opportunity to discuss these matters. The governor of Henan has come as far as Xinyang, but has not attempted to advance any further. At the same time, the Jiangnan governor-general has headed east from Nanjing in personal command of his troops. The vanguard Nanjing

Defense Army of 3,000 men under the command of En-chang has entered the town of Wurong, Hubei province. En-chang was the regional commander of Shouchun, and the 3,000 troops under his command were untrained and apparently just rounded up.

"The Nanjing defense army was stationed at a place called Rat's Gap near Wurong, preparing for a Taiping advance to the east. According to stories I have picked up from merchants coming from Wurong, they say that their commanders have amassed troops and are about to begin training them, and that locals who have gone over to take a look at these activities have been unable to suppress their spontaneous laughter. The quality of the men recruited for this force is so, so low."

—2—

"During this period, an urgent messenger from Xiang Rong, who had retaken the city of Wuchang, delivered a secret report to the office of the Jiangnan governor-general. Governor-General Lu Jianying had arrived from Jiujiang. "The Jiangnan governor-general did not, in fact, have precise information on the condition of the enemy. Xiang Rong's secret message described how the Taipings had seized several thousand vessels, had sent a waterborne flotilla to the east, and now had immense troop strength. I learned from people en route that the number of boats assembled by Taiping forces at Wuhan exceeded ten thousand. The Yangzi River, or the 'Long River' as it is also known, was despite its name completely filled by this huge flotilla, with a dense forest of masts. As for personal opinions, Xiang Rong had the following to add in his secret message: 'Enemy troop strength is immense. Thus, rather than defend upstream, perhaps we should amass our troops right here and confront the enemy.'

"Upon receipt of this message, the Jiangnan governor-general immediately tried to recall the three thousand troops at Wurong to Jiujiang. As a site for amassing troops at that time, Jiujiang was most appropriate because the governor-general was stationed there.

"Jiujiang sits at a point where the provincial borders of Hubei, Jiangxi, and Anhui all come together. Nor is Jiangsu very far away by the Yangzi waterways. Hence it was surely the more convenient place for gathering troops.

"The original garrison force at Jiujiang numbered less than one thousand men, with some six hundred soldiers from Fujian and two hundred from Zhejiang. However, there were troops in the various surrounding provinces. In the Jiujiang area, there were well over two thousand soldiers under the command of the Jiangnan governor-general. Though they were then on their way to Wurong, as a result of Xiang Rong's message, their advance was halted. Even the three thousand men at Wurong were ordered to retreat as far as Jiujiang. This order, however, arrived too late.

"The Qing forces at Rat's Gap near Wurong, unaware of the enemy's situation, were a miserable lot—the laughingstock of the local populace—as they trained.

"The advance guard of the Taiping military were said to have arrived at Rat's Gap on the evening of the sixth day following their departure from Wuchang. The Qing forces were sound asleep. Taken by surprise, the untrained soldiers fell into complete disorder, and chaos reigned among them. The great majority are said to have been killed that night. Regional Commander En-chang committed suicide by throwing himself into the Yangzi River.

"'Do not so much as injure a single farmer. Kill every last government soldier and civil official.' This Taiping slogan was taken with complete seriousness, as was proven by the battle at Rat's Gap.

"What the Taipings vow, they most certainly will carry out. Rumors are carried from mouth to mouth, and needless to say, it is the soldiers themselves who strike fear in the hearts of their enemies.

"A rumor is never simply a rumor. The corpses of officers and rank-and-file troops are flowing in great numbers, and lower-level soldiers are coming to realize that these rumors are clearly based in fact. When they point at the dead bodies floating past, I am told they say to one another: 'You're going to end up like that, too.' The implied meaning of such an expression is that, when the Taiping Army arrives, they have to flee first and foremost.

"From Wurong to Jiujiang, the Taipings advanced without the least resistance. When the fewer than a thousand troops from Fujian and Zhejiang garrisoned in Jiujiang learned of the appearance of the Taiping military, they dropped their weapons and ran for their lives. They did not even wait to see the enemy soldiers' faces before fleeing. They were gone before the Taipings arrived.

"The armed force stationed in Jiujiang to defend the city was not the only unit to flee. Other soldiers from the immediate vicinity desperately ran for their lives. Jiujiang falls within the jurisdiction of Jiangxi province, and Jiangxi Governor Zhang Fei had advanced with his troops as far as the city of Ruijin. When he learned of the imminent approach of a waterborne Taiping military force, Zhang turned his back on Jiujiang and withdrew to the provincial capital at Nanchang on the pretext that 'the land force of the long-haired bandits has penetrated Jiangxi province, and we must prepare for them.'

"There were Qing forces as well in the town of Hukou, facing Jiujiang across Lake Poyang. However, when they heard of the dangers awaiting in Jiujiang, far from rushing there to attempt to rescue their allies, they shamelessly deserted without looking back. They thought only of getting away with their own skins intact. The troops at Hukou broke into two wings, one fleeing toward Nanchang and one toward Raozhou.

"The Nanchang area was one which the governor of Jiangxi raised a great fuss about: 'The enemy's land force is coming.' However, Raozhou lay con-siderably to the east of Jiujiang, and it was not along the shores of the Yangzi. To a certain extent, it was no more strategic a site than the porcelain center at Jingdezhen, also to the east of Jiujiang. Indeed, it was so secure a region that a Taiping advance there was almost inconceivable. And so they escaped to safer terrain.

"When the Taipings attempted an assault, Jiujiang had already been com-pletely emptied of people. The soldiers fled in a pattern, and the local popu-lace also tried to take refuge somewhere else. The Taiping Army first sent the children's force into the city of Jiujiang.

"Having taken Wurong, the Taipings now occupied Jiujiang without spill-ing a drop of blood in three days' time. As in the past, they burned to the ground the government offices and Buddhist and Daoist temples, seized the foodstuffs and military supplies of the authorities, and remained within the city walls for two days.

"Because Jiangxi and Anhui provinces are production centers of Chinese tea, if it becomes impossible to buy tea in Hunan due to warfare, I have stayed on in Hukou and tried to supplement my purchases in this region. In Lushan, they produce the famous Yunwu tea, for it is an area shut in with clouds (*yun*) and fog (*wu*) near a mountain peak. Such goods of high quality are being produced in greater and greater quantity, while the older teas are already out of stock. One shipper in that region said to me: 'It'd be best if this war came to an end, for if we're surrounded by fighting, I don't know if I can honor my agreements.'

"At any rate the soldiers in Hukou disappeared in a split second, and I have as such decided to take the Yangzi River to Anqing, the capital of Anhui province. I thought it would be a safe bet to assume that, no matter how many government troops had run away, a provincial capital would be guarded at all cost. But the same situation prevailed there as well.

"Between Jiujiang and Anqing there is a point of strategic import called Little Orphan Hill, and for some time past it has been known as the back door into Anqing. Anhui Governor Jiang Wenqing had sent Surveillance Commissioner Zhang Xiyu there with orders to defend the city.

"Zhang Xiyu boarded a ship to go upriver. Whether he actually saw any signs of a Taiping vessel en route or not, he fired one of his big cannons once, and then without so much as turning around, he fled at full speed for the northern bank of the river. Needless to say, the troops under his command followed his lead. They each fired once, a measure designed to avoid the stigma of having raced away without a fight. Such vulgar behavior, though, did not evade condemnation. Zhang Xiyu escaped to Huizhou and Xiuning, but every walled city refused to allow him entrance. More than anger at a commanding officer who had fled in the face of the enemy, people feared the punishment that awaited anyone who entertained the idea of harboring such a person as he. It does look like the end of an era, indeed.

"Having slipped through at Little Orphan Hill, Anqing took shape as the site where they would confront the enemy. The proprietor of an inn recommended that I, too, seek refuge elsewhere: 'You're a traveling man, which must mean you come from a humble station in life. For us local folks, even though we may have run away for a time, everything eventually has got to calm back down. If they shut the city gates in the meantime, it can't help but happen.'

"I am told that there were some ten thousand soldiers in the city of Anqing, though the residents placed no faith in the defensive garrison force. Compared to Changsha and Wuchang, both also provincial seats, Anqing was a smaller city, and its walls were lower. Evidently, they are quite unreliable."

—3—

"Prior to the fall of Jiujiang, Lu Jianying, governor-general of the Jiangnan provinces and imperial commissioner, led a battalion of several hundred troops in retreat toward the outskirts of the walled city of Anqing to the east. The governor-general rode in a palanquin that required the shoulders of four men to carry. The walls of Anqing were not even six meters tall. Anhui Governor Jiang Wenqing had climbed atop the wall, and he appealed to the governor-general as he happened by, 'Won't you kindly honor us by having your military forces stop here at our city of Anqing so that we shall be protected together? I beseech you. It is for the good of the country.'

"But the governor-general merely waived him away. 'The bandit army is huge, far too big to try and defend against them here. Also, I've got orders to protect Wuhu and Jiangning.' He passed by Anqing without so much as slowing down, boarded a boat near the city, and proceeded to the east.

"Among the high officials of the Qing who found themselves along the path of the Taipings' eastern expedition, it seems to me that only Anhui Governor Jiang Wenqing displayed anything like a will to fight. He encouraged high civil and military officials beneath him, and sought to defend Anqing to the death. Despite the fact that, as the governor-general had said, it was impossible to defend against the Taipings there, he devoted his entire energy to that task and heroically fought to the end.

"The governor's intention to fight seemed to present something of a nui-

sance to the other leaders in Anqing. Realizing that they were all going to
become embroiled in the governor's ardor to defend the city, they each began contemplating how to flee from Anqing.

"At the head of the over ten thousand garrison troops in Anqing, was
Regional Commander Wang Pengfei of Langshan. He decided simply to ignore all of those burdensome troops under his command and run away on his
own. Though fleeing in disguise, he feared being recognized and hence killed
as a big shot if he were accompanied by some of his men. The Taiping Army
had issued a manifesto that it would most assuredly kill all government soldiers
and officials. No mercy would be shown, particularly to high-ranking officials.

"Jiang Wenqing decided that he would die in battle, for he never believed
he could successfully defend Anqing. He was concerned with the nearly four
hundred thousand silver taels and the weaponry and reserves of foodstuffs
held in Anqing. He felt that he had no choice but to fight at all cost to try and
prevent that material from falling into the hands of the Taipings, and he ordered that it all be transported outside the city. Apparently he planned to
carry it as far as Luzhou, though having taken this measure, he then ordered
his assistant, Provincial Administration Commissioner Li Benren, to remain
inside the city and defend it to the death.

"However, while the governor was busy preparing things, Li Benren said,
'Government storehouses and reserve supplies of food fall within my jurisdiction, the provincial administration commissioner, and responsibility for
their movement falls to my supervision. Thus, I must be the one to oversee
their transport.' He then departed the city. Perhaps he was thinking to himself, 'What a relief! At least I won't end up sharing the impending fate of that
insane governor.'

"I listened to the advice of the proprietor of the inn and left Anqing. I
crossed the river by boat and proceeded to Niutoushan, and from there I
decided to head toward Wuhu and Nanjing via Chizhou. Li Benren took an
altogether different direction, heading north, and from Tongcheng, he attempted to proceed further north to Shucheng. He left Anqing at essentially
the same time as I did, though his fate was decided only later. Rumors spread
at that time with startling speed, and they usually proved accurate.

"Once they had taken Little Orphan Hill, the Taipings sent their land forces
far around to the north in such a way as to surround the city of Anqing. The
Commodity Transport Battalion that Li Benren had taken control over apparently ran into this Taiping land force. Li and all his subordinates in the
Qing military threw the bundles they were carrying to the ground and fled
for their lives to the north.

"The speed at which the Qing troops and officials beat a retreat was unbelievable. They knew that, were they caught, every one of them would have

been executed. This Taiping standing order tended to militate against sluggish behavior.

"It was Yang Xiuqing, I am told, who espoused this strategy of all-out massacre. Hong Xiuquan was more the sort to act with mercy upon enemy soldiers who fought bravely, but decisions about strategy are now well within Yang's authority. Indeed, this strategy of massacre already has shown a certain positive result, for enemy troops are scattering to the winds before ever engaging the Taipings in battle, and as a result, the terror placed in the minds of government troops and officials has made these victories bloodless.

"Li Benren got as far as Shucheng, and there it seems he was interned. A few days after I departed, the Taipings attacked Anqing. Governor Jiang Wenqing was determined to put up a fight, and a battle of sorts ensued, but in actual fact, the Taipings effectively took the city without the spilling of much blood.

"From the morning of the seventeenth day of the first lunar month [February 24], a southern wind blew up the dust into the air, and the sun was all but completely obscured by the murky clouds of dust. For those who saw this as an opportunity to make their escape, it was a stroke of great luck. The first roar of Taiping artillery was to be their signal to begin their flight, for all hope of being rescued was vain by that point. The northern gate of the city was opened, and the troops crowded about the gate as they fled. People were elbowing and jostling one another, making the exit almost impossible to take advantage of. Since the walls of Anqing were relatively low, I'm told that the younger soldiers climbed onto the walls and jumped over.

"Well, the Taiping military entered the city of Anqing after nightfall. The only remaining troops were those around the governor, and as expected, they alone put up a fierce resistance.

"At first, Governor Jiang Wenqing had been commanding a defensive fight, but the successive desertions of his forces left him without even Regional Commander Wang Pengfei, his principal officer. So, Jiang returned to his office and vowed now to make his last stand. He sat down and tried to write up a detailed report for the emperor on the general pattern of events in this battle to defend Anqing. The Taipings were coming into the city just as he completed his memorial. After entrusting the document to a family member, he left his office with several dozen personal guards and went out to meet a hero's death on the battlefield.

"In the end, only some fourteen went to their deaths that day with Governor Jiang, making it all the more desolate and sad, I would think. And so the provincial capital of Anhui fell. [Note: The present capital of Anhui province is Hefei, but at the time of our story the governor was stationed at the capital in Anqing.] After Wuchang, it was the second provincial capital to come into Taiping hands.

"Those who ran away to stay alive can certainly be forgiven. I'm sure that they had families, and they were largely foot soldiers who had never received the good graces of the government. However, what cannot be pardoned is the plunder many of these escaping soldiers committed at the homes of local residents along the road. The fact that military discipline was not enforced should be the responsibility of the entire leadership of the armed forces and, indeed, of all politicians.

"Regional Commander Wang Pengfei, who also deserted, was captured by Qing troops in Tongcheng.

"Within the four-day period that the Taipings stayed in Anqing, they burned to the ground all temples and government offices within the city walls, and they again proceeded with their march to the east. In this manner, having once occupied a city, they would then soon abandon it to continue with their march. The Taiping troops who attacked Anqing now reboarded vessels and advanced toward the next objective for assault. The final battalion left Anqing on boats on the twenty-second day of the first lunar month. However, Shi Dakai's advance force on that very day had taken Tongling along the Yangzi about one hundred kilometers to the northeast. I was in Wuhu at the time and learned of this event the next day. I soon departed in the direction of Nanjing. Though traveling lightly by myself, I was almost overtaken by the rapid-moving Taiping force, an immense army. They are truly a military to contend with.

"On the day following the departure of the Taipings—the twenty-third—a Qing force of three thousand under the leadership of Regional Commander Ji Shun recaptured Anqing, simply trading places with the Taipings. They were on the march and happened to arrive there on just that day, though scandal-mongering gossips along the Yangzi said to one another, 'Those characters moved along as they wished at their slow pace, and managed with careful planning to arrive after all the Taiping soldiers had left. You think they'd have done so well if they'd have had to face the Taipings?'

"After the recapture of Anqing, they found that the Taipings had removed three hundred thousand taels of silver and one hundred cannons from government storehouses. What Provincial Administration Commissioner Li Benren had claimed to supervise transport out of the city for was in fact only a tiny portion of the whole. His primary concern was to get out of the city as quickly as he possibly could, and thus he hurriedly sent off packages only for show. In any event, it all fell into Taiping hands either way.

"In the prefectural seat of Chizhou, about one hundred kilometers from Anqing, the main force of the Taiping Army had not even tried to come on land. After the government troops and officials had escaped from the city, a small brigade of Taipings landed, simply packed up the war booty, and returned. I'm told that the same scenario transpired in Tongling county.

"The city of Wuhu fell on the twenty-fifth. Shi Dakai, commander of the vanguard force, never disembarked from his ship, as his general Huang Shengcai led the attack. The cities along the Yangzi all fell like ripe persimmons without the Taiping forces ever having to mount an all-out assault.

"There were river battles fought, too. Regional Commander Chen Shengyuan of Fushan, renowned for his bravery, marshaled the military vessels under his command, in the area near Dongliang, downstream from Wuhu and attempted an ambush.

"In matters of warfare, there is a distinction, is there not, between experts and rank amateurs? Regional commanders are supposed to be men who spend twenty or thirty years in the military, studying all facets of warfare and training troops? Well, by comparison, the Taipings have spent only three years raising an army. They are said to have trained military forces prior to that, but even if that were true, it's not that long a period of time. And yet, in these waterborne military encounters, the expert military men of the Qing became entangled in the simple ruses of the amateur Taipings and were completely defeated.

"Through the use of spies, the Taiping military knew that the Qing warships had very little ammunition on board. So, one after another, the Taipings moved vessels laden with mud in front of the Qing armada. The Qing ships shelled and fired with all the power at their disposal on the enemy ships, and eventually they ran out of ammunition and lost the capacity to engage in combat. At that point, Taiping warships with immense quantities of ammunition appeared, and within a matter of moments, decimated the entire Qing force.

"Regional Commander Chen Shengyuan was hit by cannon fire, fell into the Yangzi River, and died.

"Two days later, the Taipings were nearing the seat of Taiping prefecture. Either they would occupy this important city or they would dispatch troops to collect up and transport out the war booty from the city, and set fire to the temples and government offices. However, the Taipings sent no troops into the seat of Taiping prefecture [present-day Dangtu county], a city with precisely the same name as the Taiping Heavenly Kingdom, and rumor has it that they wanted to leave it just as it was.

"Nanjing was already now in severe danger. I left Nanjing, and by the time I arrived at Jingkou, the news was awaiting me that the city of Nanjing had fallen. I do not know how much time it took for them to take the city, but the fact of its collapse to Taiping forces is beyond doubt. . . .

"Without Anhui Governor Jiang Wenqing and Regional Commander Chen Shengyuan, I'm beginning to believe that this country of ours is corrupt beyond redemption."

—4—

Yu Yisheng's long letter generally clarified the overall situation up to the point of the Taiping attack on Nanjing. While engaged in commercial affairs as a purchasing agent for tea leaves, he had also been charged with the important task of contacting Lian Liwen, the son of his boss. As the fighting expanded into the Yangzi delta region, he was forced to retrace his steps, unable to accomplish either of his goals.

Liwen had actually been extremely close to Yu all along. Having traveled east with the Taipings' land route army, he crossed the Yangzi at Hukou, and once entering the area south of the river, he continued in an easterly direction. He was traveling with Li Xinmei, who could keep pace with any man. Yu Yisheng was also moving east, one step ahead of the defeated Qing Army. Liwen was moving as if in pursuit of the Qing forces, between the Qing and the Taipings.

Liwen again hooked up with Tan Qi at Hukou. After their arrival in Wuhu, Tan Qi appeared one morning, transformed.

"What's this?" said Liwen in amazement, pointing at Tan Qi's face.

"What in the world are you trying to imitate?" asked Xinmei, dubiously looking him square in the face.

Because his duties involved a variety of stratagems, Tan Qi had not cut his queue, as had his fellow Taiping soldiers. Now, far from just severing his queue, he had completely shaven the back of his head. His head was now pure blue. Despite Liwen's question, Tan Qi just grinned broadly.

"You look just like a Buddhist priest, is that it?" said Liwen.

"Exactly. I'm entering the Buddhist priesthood," said Tan Qi, half in jest.

"Have you lost your senses?"

The Taiping movement was devoted to Christianity and took an exceedingly severe attitude toward Buddhism. Every time they occupied a city, they made a point of burning Buddhist temples to the ground. They saw it as a blasphemous religion and showed no mercy. As one born into the Taipings, young Tan Qi was a believer in the Lord Jehovah and a faithful disciple of the Heavenly Father and the Heavenly Elder Brother. For that reason, his entrance into the Buddhist priesthood was all but unbelievable.

"You think so?" said Tan Qi, returning the question.

"But, what is it?"

"Mr. Lian, you asked me if I'd lost my mind. No follower of the Society of God Worshippers would believe me for a minute if I should show up in this guise, would they?"

"Of course not."

"So, if I assume this guise, none of the devils will doubt it for a minute, now will they?

"So, that's what it is. But that then means . . ." Liwen then realized that Tan Qi must have again received orders for dangerous work. He would be infiltrating enemy terrain.

"Where are you going?" asked Liwen.

"Nanjing. You know, Liwen, why don't you come along?" Liwen instinctively turned to look at Xinmei. She was anxious to get to Shanghai, where a new world had allegedly come into existence. She had already had more than her fill of both the Taiping movement and the Qing regime.

"Nanjing, eh," said Xinmei. "I've heard about it so many times. We specifically came all the way here, so let's stay a while."

"There's a war going on," said Liwen, looking into Xinmei's face.

"Makes no difference. I have nothing to do with it. If it were my battle, I'd risk my life. But this way, I can observe it more or less at ease." With that said, the three of them proceeded speedily along the route south of the Yangzi.

"Are there a lot of people who've shaved their heads?" asked Liwen.

Yang Xiuqing, unparalleled as he was for his coolness, was responsible for the present operation. He believed in a clear power from the Lord God who dwelt in heaven. He was certain to have set a fair number of men in motion with the disorder in Nanjing and his secret operations. "There really were a lot," responded Tan Qi.

The local authorities had not thought it strange that a large number of Buddhist monks would be entering the city of Nanjing. They regarded it as completely normal. The Taiping military had been razing Buddhist temples, and as a result there were monks throughout the area who had been burned out. The great Chinese poet of the Tang dynasty, Du Mu (803–852), wrote a poem many years before by the name of "Jiangnan Spring." It spoke of Nanjing in the following manner:

> For a thousand miles the oriole sings, crimson against the green,
> Riverside villages, mountain ramparts, wineshop streamers in the
> wind.
> Of the 480 monasteries of the Southern Dynasties
> How many towers and terraces loom in the misty rain?

> [A.C. Graham, *Poems of the Late T'ang*
> (Penguin, 1965), p. 125]

This exceedingly famous poem was known to virtually every Chinese. A thousand years earlier, the number of Buddhist temples in Nanjing had been imponderably huge. The situation had not changed much now. More than anything else, when the subject of Nanjing arose, people tended to remember this poem and the large number of Buddhist temples in the city.

It was probably then only natural that monks whose temples had been burned to the ground would set their sights on making their way to Nanjing, renowned as it was for its large number of temples. Yang Xiuqing's idea was that it would not be at all difficult or awkward to mix in with such a crowd. There was a certain sympathy among the Buddhist monks for those who claimed to be victims of the Taiping armed forces. Yang's notion was to take advantage of this situation and feed his strategy into it.

Before Nanjing fell to the Taipings, even before they encircled the city, a number of unexpected events transpired within the city walls that proved disquieting to the mood of the city. Most of these were the acts of Taiping confederates dressed as Buddhist monks with shaven pates.

All of the eyes in the images of Buddhist figures in certain temples of the city had been bored out. It was possible that some crazy person might have dug out the eyes in the Buddhist figures in a single temple, but in one night, the same thing had transpired in two or three different temples. They were in widely separated sites, too, which clearly meant that this had not been the act of a single person.

Circles were drawn on the gates of private homes. Some were red and others were white circles. On occasion, the Chinese character for "heaven" or the character for "great" was drawn within a circle.

Wild rumors, the product of disquiet, spread through the city. "If the Taipings get into the city, homes with red circles are safe, and people living in homes with white circles will all be murdered."

"'Heaven' means good, but 'great' means no good."

Governor-General Lu Jianying was a man enveloped in superstition. With such a person in charge, it was impossible to bring these rumors under control. To do so would first necessitate the arrest of the governor-general himself.

"The clever official" was how people referred to Lu. It was meant to indicate a man, wise in the ways of the political world, who had succeeded beyond his actual abilities. The secret of Lu Jianying's success was not necessarily based solely on his capacity to make his own way in the real world. He set others' minds at rest. Particularly capable men often tend to make others ill at ease. He was an able enough man, but if he was too able, then the suspicion might arise in others' eyes that in the future, he might become their enemy. In that case he would no longer be an ordinary individual.

Everyone was at ease with him, referring to him knowingly as "that guy . . ." He seriously believed in the miraculous power of the gods and tried to forge a link between it and reality. Perhaps the truth behind his success was the manner in which he enabled others to feel superior to him.

While he was leading troops toward Hubei, it was reported that he invoked something on the order of divine inspiration when he said aloud, "The deity of the frost is aiding our forces." No one had the slightest idea who in the world this "deity of the frost" was.

"Can't you see it? Just look! Standing at the head of the army is a female god, completely naked. She's leading us forward and urging us on!" Lu's subordinates very much wanted to see this naked female deity, but it was, after all, merely a phantom visible only to Lu Jianying.

His idea of the gods was also a confused jumble. "The Guanyin bodhisattva will protect our city," he said, claiming contact with a divine revelation, and he ordered the burning of incense in every home in the city of Nanjing.

It was the custom in funerary ritual of the time to make a doll for each of the four corners of a cemetery with a terrifying expression on its face and weapon in hand to protect the deceased. Originally, someone would impersonate a deity and perform an exorcism, but it seems that this duty was passed on to effigies at a later time. Lu tried to use this as a means of scaring his enemies by ordering these effigies exposed to them.

The Taiping officers and foot soldiers had been inculcated in the denigration of idols, and they reportedly laughed uproariously at the sight of these dolls. Pious as one might have been, not a soul regarded them as anything other than ridiculous.

If one was not a "clever official," one would not succeed. This was a prime symptom of decay in the Qing political world. Perhaps an event of the magnitude of the Taiping Rebellion meant that it would have to be the highest officials in the land who worked on behalf of the people. And yet in emergency times such as the present, the populace that had such leaders over them, as Yu Yisheng had put it, were living lives of unsurpassed misfortune.

—5—

"Divine revelation" in this context probably entailed a bit of craziness on his part. Lu Jianying was conspicuous for speech and behavior that made common sense seem strange. Especially after the annihilation of the Jiangnan defensive force under his command on the way to Hubei, Lu's mental state had become more than a little odd.

In the first place, the very fact of a governor-general personally leading a military force to the front of battle in Hubei was hardly a normal state of affairs. The previous year, the Nan River had burst its banks, and reconstructive work made it difficult to navigate. The shores of the Yellow River were considered the birthplace of Chinese civilization, hence the idea had long become influential in China that the essence of politics was riparian works. Lu Jianying, the "clever official," had absolutely no knowledge of water control. Ordinarily, if one doesn't know, one usually relies on experts, but Lu hit upon a bizarre method of reconstruction through divine inspiration, had his method implemented, and the harm done to the waterways grew larger and larger.

A governor-general was the highest local official position in the Qing bureaucracy. Investigating censors were charged with looking into the administrative records of other officials. An investigating censor carried out an inspection, and the governor-general was indicted for responsibility and received a stiff punishment. And so, this "clever official" volunteered for a military expedition. If his forces were able to suppress the Taipings, the merit for doing so would undoubtedly make good his riparian failures with surplus to spare.

In Lu's mind, the Taiping revolt was on a par with ordinary rural peasant uprisings.

"I'm a governor-general and they're a bunch of peasants. We're on thoroughly different levels." Therefore, he viewed defeat as an impossibility. He truly believed that divine protection was on his side.

Having entrusted civil administration of the Jiangnan provinces to Jiangsu Governor Yang Wending, and matters of military defense to Jiangsu Provincial Administration Commissioner Qi Suzao, Lu set off to the west in high spirits. At Rat's Gap pass near Wurong, however, he lost 3,000 troops, who had been his main support. In a state of utter confusion and chaos, he scurried back to Anqing. There, on top of the city walls, he turned his back on a pleading Jiang Wenqing and pressed on toward Nanjing. With his self-respect seriously wounded, he remained there, shut up in his house, meeting with no one, refusing so much as to cast his gaze toward an official document, and dispensing with all government business.

The leaders of the Nanjing government tried one final time to go and meet with the governor-general in person and request that he head upriver to prevent the onslaught of a Taiping force. Lu did not even get up from his seat, and made no effort to meet with provincial military commanders and field commanders.

This was absolutely outrageous. Jingkou Commander Xiang-hou, Jingkou Vice-Commander-in-Chief Huo Longwu, and Songjiang Provincial Military Commander Fu-zhu-hong-a were the local military leaders. Xiang-hou and Qi Suzao jointly signed an accusatory impeachment to Beijing against the governor-general, which was the proper course of action at the time.

On the eighteenth of the month, Governor-General Lu set off in retreat, and the letter of impeachment from the Nanjing leaders went directly to the capital.

"He is relieved of his position and all concurrent posts," read the determination of Beijing. "In addition, he shall be arrested and interrogated and indicted for his crimes. As for the posts of imperial commissioner and governor-general, they shall be assumed by Commander Xiang-hou."

The court issued this decree on the twenty-seventh of that first month of the lunar year. It was never, however, delivered to Nanjing, for the land-based advance forces of the Taipings arrived outside the walls of Nanjing on the twenty-ninth.

Just one day earlier, the authorities in Nanjing issued a false public announcement that the "long-haired bandits have retreated eight hundred *li*." Lian Liwen and Li Xinmei were together with Tan Qi at the time, now in the guise of a monk, on the grounds of the Baoen Temple in Yuhuatai, to the south of the walled city of Nanjing.

"This is really bad," said Liwen unconsciously. He was looking around at the surrounding terrain, knowing full well that Xinmei and Tan Qi would immediately understand what he meant by "really bad."

"It's true," said Tan Qi. "They've assembled only the scum of the earth here."

"No, only the dregs would ever come here," said Xinmei, a frown on her face.

They were referring to the troops outside the city walls under the command of Provincial Military Commander Fu-zhu-hong-a. They were groups of human low-life who it seemed no military force could ever match for low quality. For all their violent behavior, one could only assume them to be a strong force, but on the battlefield they would prove to be of little utility. Yet, they had all grown scraggy and emaciated, their faces pallid, their hollow eyes staring vacantly. Liwen, Tan Qi, and Xinmei agreed that they were all opium addicts as well.

Just as Xinmei had noted, these troops had hurriedly assembled upon receipt of the news of the Taiping approach, with no respectable people among them. There was no reason to expect that young men with jobs would enlist in this army. Even if they had lost their jobs, men with the capacity to work could usually find day labor and would not resort to the military. Thus only men unable to do an honest day's work were likely to sign up for this service.

For laggard opium smokers beyond the control of their families, this was a prime opportunity to enlist in the army and "be taken care of by the government."

In one contemporaneous account it reads, "Their cowardice was like that of women," though this was a group whose weaknesses would surely have spurred opposition from women at the use of such an expression.

"Nanjing's finished," said Xinmei. Her voice was so loud it made Liwen shudder. Anyone who heard would probably have just nodded in agreement. It was not likely that anyone would become angry or insulted by such a thought.

Yuhuatai was a strategic site in the southern suburbs of the city. Inasmuch as the Taiping land forces were heading toward Nanjing from the south, the very best soldiers available had to be placed here. In spite of this need, these ordinary rank and file troops were lying around, unprepared. It would have been strange if they were not defeated.

Gathering together the matted coverings over the boats in the area, they constructed temporary barracks, but the troops were only there to wait for their meals. Rumor had it that the Jiangning defensive corps that had been defeated in Hubei were laughed at by the local populace as they practiced their military training. The 500 Qing troops at Yuhuatai did not even train. No, these were men who were effectively untrainable.

Fu-zhu-hong-a came to observe Yuhuatai. He shook his head and ordered, "Store the gunpowder and other supplies well so they won't be stolen!" The regular soldiers accompanying him stored a mountain of boxes of ammunition held in Yuhuatai in the storehouse on the temple grounds with the cannons, and then they bolted it shut.

"What in the world are these troops here for?" asked Liwen.

"Don't you know, sir? It's quite clear. There must be five hundred soldiers here, so that's why they brought five hundred men along. It's just a number they have to meet." Tan Qi offered this clear explanation.

The chief priest of the Baoen Temple had a plaintive look on his face: "Are you travelers from the west?"

"Yes, we are," answered Xinmei.

"Have you seen many temples that have been burned down?"

"Yes, many."

"Well, I guess it's to be expected." The chief priest looked around at the temple grounds about him. It was as if he were bidding it farewell for the last time.

—6—

For different reasons altogether, Yuhuatai was later to become a famous place. Following the 1911 Revolution, the new national government established its capital in Nanjing and selected Yuhuatai as the site for its gallows. There was a jail for political offenders and an execution ground, and many revolutionaries met their ends there. There is now a tower and commemorative hall for the martyrs executed there.

In 1853, however, Yuhuatai was home to a Qing military encampment preparing to meet the Taipings, and 500 miserable troops were quartered there. It was already March on the solar calendar, and Jiangnan was well into the spring season.

The advance forces of the Taiping land-based army, under the command of Li Kaifang and Lin Fengxiang, had reached a point known as Shanqiao, southwest of the city of Nanjing. They then hurriedly constructed an encampment of their own. The Qing Army at Yuhuatai stared listlessly at the Taipings. Artillery and ammunition were locked inside the living quarters of the temple priest. Even when the bolt was unlocked, the guards there were not going to haul it out and use it to fight with.

"The cannon is inside there," said the head priest to Liwen and his friends.

"There's going to be a battle. Why aren't they dragging it out?" asked Liwen.

"They say they will, but . . ." A perplexed look came over the face of the priest. "Do you think that bunch of soldiers sprawled out over there could shoot a cannon even once?"

A look over at the Taiping encampment seemed to reveal that they planned an all-out attack. This was something local residents knew as well. They were trying to remain as far removed from the Qing troops as possible.

Stories were circulating. The Taipings had not harmed a single member of the general populace. To the extent that the latter remained unentangled in the fighting, there was no danger. The Taipings thus did not approach Yuhuatai where the government forces camped.

"We too will be leaving the temple. Whether we're here or not, it'll all turn out the same," said the priest.

He had already abandoned all hope of protecting the temple, and he certainly never expected the assembled troops to protect it for him. To avoid the theft of items within the temple, it was wisest to remove them in advance of departure.

"Will you help me remove the Buddhist images?" the priest asked. Liwen helped him carry the Buddhist images and other Buddhist paraphernalia into the inner chamber of the temple. The Qing troops were not likely to steal images of little value, but as the priest put it, "It gets cold here at night." The soldiers were likely to break the wooden images into little pieces and use them as fuel for a bonfire. And were the Taipings to occupy the temple grounds, the Buddhist icons would, needless to say, all be burned. For the time being, the head priest sought refuge together with his statues.

"Will you come along?" asked the priest in a frail voice.

"No, we'd just be a drain on you, and it'd be bizarre for us to go along as your dependents. No, you mustn't get involved with us. We'll take care of ourselves." Liwen spoke as the representative of the group.

"Where will you sleep?"

"We shall impose on your hospitality for a time," said Tan Qi, pointing in the direction of the Baoen Temple grounds.

"It's dangerous, you know, because the barracks are so close by."

"We can get away at a moment's notice."

"I would advise just that, at the earliest possible moment. If you dally long, events may reach an irreversible point."

"Understood. We shan't wait long to leave. We've had to flee on several occasions before. We're rather used to it."

"You can never get used to that. Please be careful." The kindhearted head priest, accompanied by several traveling companions from the temple, set off to the east.

"It'll be fine. The temple won't become a scene of fighting. In warfare you've got to have an opponent, don't you?" Tan Qi laughed as he said this.

He had already apprised the Taipings of the situation at Yuhuatai. "If the Taiping Army attacks, not a single Qing troop is likely to remain at Yuhuatai. They're a force without an iota of fighting spirit. However, we mustn't bombard them as a means of coercion. On the temple grounds are stored large quantities of artillery and ammunition. For our forces to make use of this hardware, it must not be subjected to shellfire. We'll take measures to ensure that the Qing forces do not destroy this materiel."

Tan Qi had seven men working under him. Three were also in monk's guise, and four had the appearance of temple sextons. Their responsibilities were "to keep a watch on the weaponry and ammunition of the Qing military."

He got exactly what he requested without a hitch. On the day following the arrival of the land-based Taiping advance forces at Shanqiao, the main body of the waterborne Taiping military reached the Caohai Pass, putting them within striking distance of Nanjing.

"I think I ought to tell these hired troops that their enemy's on the way," said Tan Qi with a forced smile. The troops were bound to fly in all four directions whether or not they caught sign of the enemy, but they were such a wildly disorderly bunch they probably wouldn't have been able to recognize the enemy.

"Hey! The enemy's already over there!" yelled out one of Tan Qi's subordinates as he came running. They were lazy soldiers, to be sure, but when it came to escaping, they ran with surprising speed. And they disappeared in an instant.

"Take care of the ammunition!" The commanding officer had not forgotten his orders. However, one of Tan Qi's subordinates stuck close to this commanding officer as a precaution.

"Fire! Fire!" Having called out a request for fire, the commander then made a dash for the main temple building. His lieutenant had run away, so he apparently intended to set the blaze himself. From behind, Tan Qi's man approached and said, "There's a flint stone over there." The commanding officer looked in the direction pointed to, and Tan's man pulled out an ax he had been concealing.

—7—

The water of the Yangzi River ordinarily was a light brown color, but on this day near Nanjing, a light green current seemed to be flowing. Assistant King Shi Dakai with the advance waterborne forces, had ordered all of his men to fly green banners on their vessels. The Assistant King's flotilla filled the Yangzi and gave it a greenish coloration. His frontal troops were under the command of Zhang Zipeng. Looking up at the walled citadel of Nanjing before him, Zhang said, "I thought Jinling [Nanjing] was going to be an immense city and I realized it'd be very hard to lay siege to it, but what's this here? If this is all it is, then it's no big deal at all."

He was, of course, saying this for the benefit of instilling courage in the men under his command.

Nanjing was effectively regarded as a second capital of the realm. Compared to the cities the Taipings had encountered to that point—Guilin, Changsha, and Wuchang—Nanjing had a qualitatively different air. The troops couldn't be allowed to entertain any of the fears inspired by such a colossal city. To this end, Zhang Zipeng used the tactic of exaggeration.

The six dynastic houses based in the south during the divisive historical era known as the Northern and Southern Dynasties, had all made Nanjing their capital. The first was the state of Wu. According the famous text, *Chronicle of the Three Kingdoms*, the man who encouraged Sun Quan (182–252) of Wu to place his capital here was none other than Zhuge Liang, who visited Wu as an emissary.

The Yangzi River and Cijin Mountain formed a natural stronghold at Nanjing. A site extremely difficult to attack, the topography was thoroughly uninviting to would-be assailants. And, yet, why was it that the six states that had made Nanjing their capital were all so short-lived?

One explanation offered by historians was that, precisely because Nanjing was such a natural stronghold, the regime that held it perhaps relied overly much on the natural environment. Although we are getting ahead of the story a bit, perhaps we may see why the Taipings also remained settled in Nanjing for such a short period of time.

Within the city of Nanjing, on the day that the surface of the Yangzi turned green, Provincial Administration Commissioner Qi Suzao (1801–1853) vomited blood and died. Rumor had it that he suffered from a surfeit of grief and anger. Qi Suzao could no longer restrain this grieved bitterness even in front of his allies, let alone the bandits, when the latter appeared with a huge army before this second capital of the realm. After the devastating defeat at Wurong, Governor-General Lu Jianying retreated to Nanjing and abandoned everything. How were the internal affairs of the Jiangnan region to be coordinated? By communication with Beijing? What was to be resolved and what would remain undecided? All government matters remained unclear.

The governor of Jiangsu province, who should have assumed responsibility for local affairs, was resident in Suzhou. That meant that the next highest official beneath the governor-general responsible for local government was Provincial Administration Commissioner Qi Suzao. When the governor-general relinquished his bureaucratic duties, they all fell upon Qi's shoulders.

In his rage, he penned a letter of impeachment, signed jointly with Jiangning Commander Xiang-hou, and dispatched it to the court in Beijing. In the process of writing this memorial, he became so excited that he began spitting up blood.

On the day when the Taiping waterborne forces turned the waters of the Yangzi before Nanjing green, Taiping land forces occupied Yuhuatai without the least difficulty. Not a trace remained of the Qing Army there, though large quantities of their weaponry and ammunition had been left behind. It was almost as if the materiel had been politely put aside for them with the message, "Please, be our guests and take what you need."

The Taipings knew this before they began their assault, from detailed reports on the internal operations of the Qing forces delivered by Tan Qi and his men. They had planned to take the enemy's cannons and ammunition and turn them on the city of Nanjing. The syllable "tai" in the place name Yuhuatai, indicated a slightly elevated hill, and from that vantage point it was hard to imagine a better place to bombard Nanjing.

Just before the Taiping occupation of Yuhuatai, several thousand government transport troops reached the Jubao Gate, the southern entry into Nanjing. They were a military escort accompanying the horses and carts laden with military provisions, and had come completely unaware that Nanjing was now becoming enveloped in a war. Unlike the troops at Yuhuatai, though, these were crack troops, discriminatingly selected by the Qing military, with a ferocious fighting spirit.

As the transport troops neared Nanjing, they eventually learned that it was rapidly becoming the scene of serious fighting. They became aware of the presence of the Taiping troops just as the latter were commencing their attacks on Yuhuatai. They tried to engage the Taipings, but because they had been protecting military provisions, they only had weapons sufficient to fight off and pursue local bandits. Even if the Taipings were just "bandits," they had an immense army, and the transport troops had insufficient ammunition to engage them in battle.

"Okay, we are going to enter the city and get ammunition and small arms there," decided the commander of the transport brigade. They reached Jubao Gate and made this request of the man responsible for guarding the gate.

"They're absorbed in taking Yuhuatai and unaware of us. Let's replenish our ammunition and launch a surprise attack on them. If the enemy takes Yuhuatai, we're finished here." The transport brigade commander was one brave soldier.

"Please, just wait. I shall obtain the permission of the governor-general and return momentarily." The officer of the gate galloped off on horseback to the governor-general's office. Inasmuch as the Jiangnan governor-general had abandoned all of his duties, Provincial Administration Commissioner Qi Suzao had to take up those tasks.

"That man's just like a little boy," said Qi, and he ordered weapons and ammunition to be sent rapidly to the Jubao Gate.

Just at that moment, however, Lu Jianying, who had locked himself in his chambers and not ventured out even once since returning to Nanjing, violently threw open his door and emerged. Though he had relinquished all of his duties, the clerks at the governor-general's office had continued throughout in his stead to prepare written documents or deliver oral decisions on important matters. The governor-general had thus far reacted in no way to their actions, but now he stepped in and responded, "Are you all blind or something? That's the enemy at Jubao Gate! No doubt about it, it's a trap! Don't get caught! Rain shells down on them now!" Lu Jianying was screaming in the corridor outside the governor-general's office. In the bureaucratic structure, the orders of a governor-general were absolute.

"Convey my orders to the guards at Jubao Gate!" underscored the governor-general.

Provincial Administration Commissioner Qi Suzao moaned audibly, as if straining his voice from deep in his lungs. He then felt blood about to regurgitate through the back of his throat.

The orders had to be passed along. Anyone responsible for failure to do so would incur the charge of violating a direct order. Once conveyed, the order had to be executed. Severe punishment awaited anyone who failed to carry it out. In one sense, this revealed the inconsistency of the Qing system itself, but in another sense, one had here a public order based on well-organized bureaucratic principles in which one was subservient to strictly enforced laws.

While the commander at Jubao Gate knew full well that those outside were allies, he had no choice but to fire at them. He was an old friend of the commander of the transport brigade. Despite the fact that he knew the man not to be the enemy, an order was an order.

"Fire way off in the distance, and only shoot three times. Whatever you do, don't hit any of the transport troops!" The commander of the gate issued this order with all the resistance he could muster. At the unexpected sound of artillery, the brave transport troops scattered.

When the three firings from within the city concluded, the Taipings began their assault on Nanjing proper from Yuhuatai. Of course, they were not going to stop with three shells. Booming firing continued unabated.

While listening to the dim sound of gunfire in his estranged consciousness, Qi Suzao died in a fit of anger. His tightly clenched fists came pounding down on the table. The whole area was covered in blood.

23

Early Spring in Jinling

—1—

Though Nanjing is an old city, the toponym itself is surprisingly new. During the Spring and Autumn period (722–481 B.C.), it belonged to the state of Wu, while in the Warring States period (403–221 B.C.), it was in the state of Chu. In the fourth century B.C., at the time of King Wei of the state of Chu, the capital Jinling was placed where Nanjing now stands. It was probably then a small walled city. Geomantic observations of the local topography revealed that the area had a royal spirit. Thus, the story went that gold (*jin* in Chinese) was buried there to pacify the spirit.

It was believed at the time that the local deities of the region could bring all manner of spirits to the surface. The royal spirit was the concern of the future king who would emerge. While the king of Chu resided in his royal capital of Ying, in present-day Hubei province, the very idea that a royal spirit dwelt to the east meant that there was always the possibility that another king—namely, one who would rise in rebellion—might appear. Fearing this potentiality, it was the practice in ancient times to bury gold to placate the royal spirit of the earth there so as to calm it down. Hence the name Jinling, or "the tomb in which gold has been buried."

Shihuangdi, first emperor of the Qin dynasty (221–206 B.C.), who brought all of China under unified control, despised any terrain that possessed such a royal spirit about it, and feared that there might be some small efficacy to the burying of gold. He thus ordered his men to cut a pathway straight through the hill known as Jinling and to have a waterway inserted in this ravine. In creating this artificial mountain stream, he severed the mountain in two. The area was subsequently known as Moling.

In the Three Kingdoms period of the third century A.D., Sun Quan of the state of Wu established his capital there and renamed it Jianye, because he was so enthusiastic about the attainment (*jian*) of the great achievement (*ye*) of bringing the realm under his control. The subsequent Jin dynasty (265– 216) changed the name of the city to Jiankang.

From the Tang dynasty (618–906) it bore the name Jiangning. Hongwu, founding emperor of the Ming dynasty (1368–1644), established his imperial capital there and called it Yingtianfu. His son and third emperor of the dynasty, Yongle, moved the capital of the Ming to Beijing and decided to change the name of Yingtianfu to Nanjing. The imperial capital moved to Beijing in 1421, and after the Nanjing area's loss of its position as the capital, it was effectively compensated with the name Nanjing, which means "southern capital." The Qing dynasty retained Beijing as its capital, and since it bore no special relationship to the city of Nanjing, the latter reverted to Jiangning, its name from Tang times. For well over two hundred years, people had grown accustomed to calling it Nanjing, and thus Nanjing continued to exist as the popular name for the city. The peace treaty that followed the Opium War in 1842 is generally known as the Treaty of Nanjing, but in official Qing documents it is the Treaty of Jiangning. Thus, in addition to the official name of Jiangning, this place was known popularly as Nanjing, and the ancient toponym Jinling was also used as a poetic or elegant name.

Nanjing in the Six Dynasties Period (316–589) was said to have been surrounded by a wall ten kilometers long. The waterway dug through the hills on the order of Shihuangdi of the Qin was called the Qinhuai River, and at the time it ran outside the city. Today, it lies within the city limits. The name Qinhuai has become associated with the local red-light district, because rows of brothels were constructed on both sides of the river.

Emperor Hongwu of the Ming intended Nanjing to be his imperial capital, so he had it constructed on a massive scale. The inner city wall alone was some 50 kilometers long, and the outer city wall stretched to over 90 kilometers. Hills and streams were enveloped within the city's walls. These walls differed in height depending on place, but there were points at which it reached 20 meters, giving it a majestic aura of great dignity.

For the great majority of the Taiping soldiers, it was a city the size of which they had never set their eyes on. "Can such a huge city be taken?" thought many of them with a dubious look of discouragement.

"A city like that's no big deal for us," said Zhang Zipeng, commander of the advance forces of the assistant king. He understood full well that he had to encourage his men in this way.

Now that it engulfed hills and waterways, the city of Nanjing formed an irregular shape, unlike Beijing and Chang'an, which were built according to city-planning ideas on level terrain. Of the eighteen gates into the walled city, the traditional perspective was followed of having the main gate be at the center of the southern wall, and that corresponded to Jubao Gate. However, the palaces and government offices constructed during the Ming period were not built facing due north but in an easterly direction, and thus the Zhengyang (Frontal) Gate—which served as an entrance and exit point for the city—was considered, as its named clearly indicated, the main gate of Nanjing.

When Nanjing was no longer the capital in the Qing dynasty, however, Jubao Gate could become the main city gate. Yuhuatai directly faced Jubao Gate. After the fall of the Qing dynasty in 1911, Jubao Gate was renamed Zhonghua (China) Gate, and Zhengyang Gate became Guanghua (China Revived) Gate. These gates were scenes of fierce fighting during the Sino-Japanese War of the late 1930s and early 1940s. In particular, the ferocity of the battle at Yuhuatai remains fresh in local memory.

At the time of the war with the Taiping Army, Yuhuatai fell easily into the hands of the rebels due to the decadence of the government's armed forces. The Taiping soldiers then hauled out the cannons held in the storehouse of the Baoen Temple, and from there, bombarded the inner city.

For their part, the Qing forces rained shells down on the position occupied by the Taipings with cannons that had been placed atop the city ramparts. The Taipings waited for sunset and retreated.

The Taipings' strategy was the same one they had employed at the time of the battle on the Yangzi River, but they had expended a great quantity of ammunition on the Qing Army. In the Yangzi battle, they used boats mired in muddy waters, and at Yuhuatai, they used the Buddhist images.

Outside Jubao Gate was a so-called "temple area." In addition to Baoen Temple, this area boasted Bifeng Temple, Nengren Temple, Tianjie Temple, Xitian Temple, and Zhide Temple. They all, like the Baoen Temple, had places in which to evacuate their principal Buddhist statues, but their staffs had left them unmoved. Among them, the Xitian Temple was particularly famous for its 500 statues of the disciples of the Buddha, and all 500 remained intact.

Unlike images of the Buddha himself, those of his disciples could take whatever shape they wished. Some of them resembled human beings, and there were a total of 500 figures, all but asking to be put to use. At night, the Taipings lined them up here and there along the slope of the hill, and covered them partially with grass and straw. They also outfitted the statues with little props such as flags. Once these preparations were complete, they lit paper lanterns here and there. The lanterns gave off considerable light, to an unnatural extent, giving rise to the fear that the true shape of the 500 images might actually be discovered.

They had created the appearance that soldiers were fanning out in just the right dimness of light. This was not going to be enough to invite an artillery attack by the enemy, for this alone might not be cause for the Qing forces to open fire. When cowardly soldiers become frightened, they tend to try to fire their cannons. They had to be made to believe that an attack was being launched by the army of the 500 disciples of the Buddha. Thus several dozen soldiers were deployed in the hills by Yuhuatai as a suicide corps to shout aloud.

They raised a war cry, and the Qing forces atop the city walls in fear opened fire. The strategy worked stunningly well. Shell fire roared through the night. Only the following morning could they see, with the help of a telescope, that they had been fooled. While they waited for the arrival of their own entire army, the Taipings worked to make the government forces use as much of their ammunition as possible.

After the Taiping waterborne advance forces reached the city of Nanjing, green flags fluttering in the wind, three days would pass before the entire army had arrived and come on land to commence the attack. The main force of the Taipings came on land at a place known as Qilizhou, near Xiaguan. Xiaguan was the port for Nanjing. Vessels plying the waters of the Yangzi set sail from Xiaguan. Before the great bridge spanning the Yangzi River at Nanjing was completed, ferries to Pukou on the far shore of the river also set off from there. It was customary, even if one came by rail from Xuzhou, to get off at Pukou and ferry across to Xiaguan.

If one were to disembark at Xiaguan, the wall along the western side of Nanjing was visible to the east. The gate into the western side of Nanjing, known as Yifeng Gate, was located to the far north. Yifeng Gate was built on Lulong Mountain, and thus the inner city was considerably more elevated than the land outside the city. The outer portion was clearly visible from inside the city as well, making it difficult to launch an attack.

The entire Taiping Army arrived on March 12, or the third day of the second lunar month. That very day, one part of the Taipings attacked Pukou across the river and sent the Qing garrison force under the command of Xuzhou Brigade Commander Feng Jingni to flight. This accomplishment meant that the rear was secure for the assault on Nanjing itself. At the same time that the army arrived, the Taipings once again began their efficacious strategy of planting land mines.

—2—

One condition needs to be added to the statement that Nanjing was located at a strategic position. The army guarding the city was holding Red Gold Mountain in the eastern suburbs of Nanjing. At the time, Red Gold Mountain was commonly known as Bell Mountain, and from its vantage point one could see down into the city of Nanjing.

Atop Red Gold Mountain there is now an observatory and in its foothills is the mausoleum honoring Sun Yat-sen. At the time of the Taiping Rebellion, the Red Gold foothills were home only to the tomb of the founding emperor of the Ming dynasty, Hongwu.

The Qing forces seemed to have no intention of guarding Red Gold Mountain. Unlike Yuhuatai, Red Gold Mountain was immense and guarding it required a considerable commitment of troops. The government's military authorities in Nanjing decided, for no clear reason whatsoever, that they lacked sufficient military strength. The number of personnel needed to protect such a mountain were better used, they felt, on garrison duty within the city walls.

The Nanjing authorities within the city had also invested great energy in defending the inner city. The Manchu Jiangning commander was resident within the city. Insofar as it was the second capital of the realm, there were far more Manchu military men and bureaucrats in Nanjing than in any other provincial capital. When you add their family members, the total number of Manchus there reached some forty thousand. All Manchus belonged to one of the eight banners and were thus known as bannermen. Virtually all resided within the city walls.

In the Ming dynasty, the area at the center of which was the imperial palace was surrounded by a wall of its own. This area was called the inner city. So many Manchus lived there during the Qing period that it came to be known informally as the "Manchu city." The Qing dynasty's policy on ethnicities was effectively a form of apartheid or segregation—racial discrimination. There was no effort at conciliation across ethnic boundaries.

A wide variety of reasons are conceivable for why the city of Nanjing, with its "naturally strategic" placement, fell after only a thirteen-day encirclement—it was only ten days after the entire Taiping Army arrived and the city fell under siege—but later historians have always cited "Han-Manchu discord" as one of the most important.

Red Gold Mountain, which never became the scene of a bloody offensive-defensive battle, lay peacefully to the east of Nanjing. After looking down at Nanjing from his vantage point atop Red Gold mountain, Lian Liwen trudged down to its foothills with great worry in his heart. Li Xinmei had said that she did not want to be seen by any of the Taipings, and had thus confined herself within a local home near the imperial tomb.

Tan Qi had surreptitiously entered the city of Nanjing to direct strategic operations. The sky was cloudy as dark clouds hung low, and it seemed as if rain would break out at any moment.

The rooms of the home where Xinmei waited had small windows and were poorly lit.

"Is it raining out there?" she asked Liwen upon his return.

"Not yet, but it looks like it will soon enough."

"So, do you plan to stay here until Nanjing falls?"

"Yes. I want to watch Nanjing meet its end. I still haven't broken with the Taiping movement."

"It's funny . . . You want to verify what's perfectly plain to see will happen."

"I just want my sense of things put back in order . . . neatly, tidily."

"If you just ignore what you don't like, isn't it better not to look at all?"

"Fine, and then you're better off not watching. Just stay here. No, actually it'd be better if you went on ahead to Shanghai. I'll find you a good guide to show you the way."

"So, no matter what may come to pass, you want to look at this hell?"

"I think I have to."

"You're really still attached to the Taipings. It's better to leave the way things are right now. It won't allow your fond memories of the Taipings—if you see worse things than you've already seen—to be dragged through the mud. I can't sit back silently and watch your precious vision of things be destroyed before my eyes."

"Xinmei, I want you to understand this. If I turn my back on this 'hell' now, I'll probably continue to anguish over it for the rest of my life. That I lacked the courage. Whatever you say, I've got to stay and watch."

"If you say so . . . It does look like rain." Xinmei was looking through a window. Her eyes were teary.

"Will you go ahead to Shanghai?" asked Liwen.

"No, I'll wait here."

"Okay, then . . . I don't think it'll be very long."

"I'm going to keep my eyes shut tightly," she said, closing her eyes.

The word "hell" that came up in their conversation referred to what the Taiping military was probably going to do—commit a gruesome massacre. While the Taipings represented a religious movement, it also had aspects of an ethnic movement. From Hunan to Hubei, the participation by Triad or Heaven and Earth Society members had grown steadily, and the rebellion had gained that sort of coloring characteristic of a secret society. The various Triad affiliates without exception used the slogan, "Destroy the Manchus and revive the Ming dynasty!"

Originally the Taiping movement had not had any thought of reviving the

Ming dynasty. That dynasty had collapsed some two hundred years earlier and had not appreciated the worship of the Christian God. To be sure, the Taipings were a fiercely world-renewing movement, and only now was that goal possible as they were overthrowing the present system. The object being overthrown was, of course, the Manchus' Qing dynasty. The Society of God Worshippers who formed the basis for the Taiping Heavenly Kingdom shared with the Triads only one objective: to destroy the Manchus. When it came to attending to business together, these two qualitatively different groups naturally gravitated toward stressing what they shared.

The "demons" or "devils" of which the supporters of the Taipings frequently spoke referred, in a broad sense, to anyone who did not worship their God. They could not, however, censure those who did not know of the existence of God by saying such people failed to worship Him. "Demons," as the term was commonly used, referred to those who were antagonistic to and oppressive of the worshippers of God—namely, the Qing government, the rulers of the present regime.

That Qing government was capped by the Manchu emperor, and with Manchus in controlling positions, was comprised of Han Chinese who cooperated with them. The constituent elements were, thus, "demons." In a narrow sense, "demons" referred only to the Manchus. In Taiping thought, the ethnic principle of "attack the Manchus" began from this point. And in the process of absorbing members of Triad organizations, they became more and more vehement about it.

"Do not so much as injure a single farmer. Kill every last government soldier and civil official." This fundamental principle of the Taiping movement has come up several times thus far. Since government soldiers and officials were allies of the "demons," they had to be killed. What about Manchu noncombatants, those who were neither soldiers nor bureaucrats? How were the Taipings to treat Manchu women, children, and old people?

All were "demons." They became objects to be exterminated. At least, such was the atmosphere among the Taiping armed forces at the time. Unlike Yuezhou, Wuchang, and Anqing, which the Taipings had thus far occupied, numerous Manchus lived in Nanjing, this second capital of the realm. Some said they numbered thirty thousand, while others put the figure as high as forty thousand. Although the great majority were noncombatants, the Taipings without a doubt planned to kill every one of them.

It was with respect to this expected scene of slaughter that Xinmei and Liwen had employed the expression "hell." Xinmei's mind was now far from the Taipings. Liwen was still attached to the Taiping movement and continued in his efforts to understand it. But he could not condone the wholesale massacre of civilians.

He had spoken at length with Xinmei about all this in the past. Neither could deny the need for a movement of renovation. At present, the great force able to support such a movement was clearly that of the Taipings. That did not necessarily mean, however, that only the road being taken by the Taipings was world-renewing by nature. There were other possible paths.

"Let's go look for it," said Xinmei.

They had lost all hope for the old society. In the Shanghai area a new society was sprouting, and perhaps a way was to be found there.

"All right, it's Shanghai, then . . ." muttered Liwen.

On this they agreed, though Liwen was prepared to start only after he witnessed the unfolding "hell," which Xinmei had no need to see. As far as she was concerned, Liwen's inner self would be severely hurt by the "hell" he was going to observe, and she couldn't bear to watch this transpire. But she was unable to get Liwen to change his mind. Xinmei thought she fully understood what Liwen was thinking about. Indeed, she thought she had to understand him.

—3—

The land mine operation began with the Jinghai Temple in Xiaguan, outside Yifeng Gate. Since they were digging holes below the floors of the temple, the operation was not visible from atop the city walls. There was one problem, though. What to do with the earth they dug up in the process? The Daxiongbao Pavilion on the grounds of the Jinghai Temple was expansive within, but it was soon full of earth.

Quietly, in the middle of the night, they scattered the dirt. They had to get rid of it evenly, too. If all of a sudden a huge mound of earth were to appear out of nowhere, it would no doubt lead to suspicions. The most painstaking problem with this land mine plan, then, was the unearthed soil.

The Qing armed forces should have been able to predict from past experience that the Taipings would plant land mines. They were convinced that the Taipings were digging, though they didn't as yet know where. Once they learned the point where the digging had started, the range of the area over which they needed to remain vigilant would naturally become more limited.

Of course, the Taipings tried as best they could to hide all of their activities. Since there were numerous coal miners from Hunan among them now, that minimized the difficulties involved in digging. Three tunnels for the placement of mines were being dug at Jinghai Temple. If only one of them were to explode, the hole broken through the wall would be too small to get through.

On the day following the arrival of the main force of the army, the Taipings attacked Shuixi Gate and Hanxi Gate, but the main objective of these assaults was to divert the enemy's attention from the Jinghai Temple.

Inside the city, Governor-General Lu Jianying slowly rose and went to the encampment by the Jubao Gate. Jiangning Commander Xiang-hou had taken command of the military camp guarding Yifeng Gate. Eventually, the Qing military began to become aware of the mysterious goings-on at the Jinghai Temple. In the repeated transporting of soil at night and under a variety of camouflage techniques, the comings and goings of numerous people caught their attention.

"They're digging at the Jinghai Temple! No doubt about it!" declared Xiang-hou.

Once the direction in which the digging was proceeding became known, they were able to dig down toward the tunnels from within the city, fill the holes with water, and thus guard against the explosion of land mines. Now that the Jinghai Temple was established as the starting point, the scope of the area to be concerned about was thus restricted.

As they had done in Wuchang and elsewhere, the government forces adopted a countermeasure of relying on the acute sense of hearing of blind men. Blind men placed their ears to the surface of the ground. Things, though, did not proceed smoothly for the Qing Army, for rain soon began to fall, and an intense, pounding rain at that. Keen as their hearing may have been, the sound of the rain falling severely impeded these blind men in their work.

Tan Qi's operation to incite a disturbance inside the city was proceeding rapidly. Outside the city several hundred large, life-size paper dolls were prepared. They were placed astride horses and at night raced in the direction of the southern wall of the city by Jubao Gate. The idea was to feign a military operation under way in the faint light of the nighttime. The sound of horses' hooves broke through the quiet night. The soldiers mounted on these horses were surely officer class. A cavalry several hundred strong was advancing south to the west of the city of Nanjing, turning east at Sanshan Gate toward Jubao Gate.

The majority of the Taiping Army was now ranged between Yuhuatai and just outside Jubao Gate, and further military support was on its way there. This at least was the observation of their movements outside the city as seen from within. They seemed to be placing their emphasis in the south, and perhaps it would be best—reasoned the Qing armed forces—to prepare for the enemy at Jubao Gate and Yuhuatai. Yet their determination to do so did not materialize, precisely because of their anxieties about the operation going on at the Jinghai Temple.

In addition, relations between Xiang-hou at Yifeng Gate and Lu Jianying at Jubao Gate were not good. We have already noted the joint memorial Xiang-hou penned with Provincial Administration Commissioner Qi Suzao, criticizing Governor-General Lu to Beijing in no uncertain terms. It was actually worse than that—they had become bitter enemies, and communications between them, needless to say, lacked even the facade of harmony.

Military movements were dependent on the intuition of the commanding officer of the first line battalion. Snared by the quick galloping of the paper doll cavalry, the Qing Army at the western wall of the city moved to the south. There were a fair number of hills just within the western wall of the city—such as Lion Hill, Dragon Hut Hill, and Cool Hill—and from their peaks much of the action outside the city was visible. Though the government forces had a cannon mounted atop Lion Hill, they had apparently used too many shells when bombarding the Taiping flotilla on the Yangzi, and they now had to be rigidly frugal in the further expenditure of ammunition.

The phlegmatic Qing forces were unable to move at night. However, the feeling now was that they had no choice but to do so, even though they were only half-prepared. The onrush of the cavalry of paper dolls occurred on the night of the ninth day of the second lunar month, and at least achieved the effect of psychologically disconcerting the garrison force within the city.

The three tunnels had reached the area of the foundation of the city wall by that time, and early on the morning of the tenth, the Taipings planned for an explosion to take place. On that very morning, a rare event transpired: Lu Jianying went to visit Xiang-hou at Yifeng Gate.

"The bandits have come around to the south," he said. "You probably saw it last night. A huge cavalry force rode past the Jubao Gate where I was, and I'd like to have further troop strength transferred there."

"The movement of the cavalry," responded Xiang-hou, "was confirmed as well. However, activities at the Jinghai Temple strike us as out of the ordinary. We cannot relax our vigilance one bit. Let's consult the staff officers about the size of the reinforcements."

"The more the better, please," said Lu Jianying. He climbed back into his large sedan chair, carried by four men, and was about to return. Several dozen bodyguards of the governor-general accompanied the sedan chair ringed in felt. Soon after their departure, a land mine exploded. Tiles blown off from the city wall went flying into the sky, and a shower of shards came raining down. The downpour of tile fragments was the signal to storm the city.

"Advance!" and the Taiping Army came rushing in.

"It can't be. There were two explosions. Wait!" By the time the order went out from headquarters, it was too late. The advance forces had already scrambled up what remained of the crumbling wall.

In order to blow as large a hole as possible through the wall, they had dug three separate tunnels. Three land mines had been put in place and had been set off at the same time. They hoped that the hole through the wall would measure at least ten meters. Those with sharp hearing had detected a succession of two separate explosions. There was only a split second between them, and most people heard it as one huge blast. Those who heard two understood it to have been two of the three blasts occurring at the same time, but the third mine failed to fire.

However, Lu Guojin, an explosives expert from Gui county, had serious reservations. The hole in the wall was too small—only about six meters. On his instructions, the order to "wait" had been immediately issued, but in all the confusion it did not reach the ears of the troops pouring into the city.

Lin Fengxiang, the Taiping commander outside Yifeng Gate, was feeling very uneasy, praying that it was just a misfire. All those who knew about army engineering, from Lu Guojin on down, were praying as well. There was a limit to the speed at which the order could be conveyed from the Jinghai Temple to Yifeng Gate.

Had the fire gone out midway along the fuse? Perhaps there was a defect in the mine itself that had prevented it from exploding? Either way was okay. If the explosion was delayed, however, that would be a great tragedy—the worst possible situation.

The third land mine did explode late. Taiping troops at Yifeng Gate had been crowding around trying to break through the wall. A tragic, deafening roar caused the earth to quake, blowing both tiles and soldiers into the air. Many of them lost their lives.

Qing government documents put the number of Taiping troops who died in this explosion from five hundred to six hundred to as many as over one thousand. Even if enemy casualties were, as always, exaggerated, the number of Taiping dead was considerable. Of course, as the Taipings stormed the city, the retreating Qing forces also sustained a large number of casualties.

Because the use of land mines to explode holes in city walls had become the standard Taiping military tactic, the Qing armed forces stationed in Nanjing had encamped at a point somewhat removed from the wall. Regional Commander Cheng Sanguang was the government's man in charge. The Qing troops, who had withdrawn at first, later advanced with great resolution to cut off the ears of the fallen Taiping soldiers. Distinguished military service was determined, it was said at the time, by the number of heads of the enemy one had killed. This gruesome, outdated means of rewarding military prowess was still operative at this time. Since heads tended to be quite heavy and presented difficulty in transportation, ears were used in their stead.

Only a few of those killed in the explosion remained as full corpses. Qing soldiers walked around searching for corpses to which the ears were still attached. The faces of those running around the area angrily with daggers drawn looked just like the tormenting demons from hell itself.

In any event, the hole blown through the wall after the tragic explosion was quite large, though the Taipings were also staggering from this unexpected turn of events.

"Is there going to be another explosion?" said one of the troops by the entry point blown through the wall, as he stood and waited. It was in this interim period that the ear-cutting activities of the government soldiers took place.

"The three land mines have all detonated," someone verified, and again the order to storm the city was given.

The Qing troops had been expecting a Taiping assault momentarily. The hole in the wall had been expanded in the second explosion to twice its size. The ear-cutting was going on amid great excitement.

"Advance! Attack!" went out the war cry, and Qing troops who had been slicing off ears responded by screaming: "Defense Planning Bureau!" And they raced off as fast as their feet would carry them.

The Defense Planning Bureau was the office that awarded "prizes." If they brought the ears they had collected, a monetary prize would be forthcoming. The severed ears would be exchanged for money as quickly as possible, and they would then flee.

These men were not simply going to run away. First they had important business to attend to at the Defense Planning Bureau. They had to hurry there to show off their ears. At least, that was their excuse.

It was a pointless logic. Here was a group of men publicly running away as fast as they could, having scarcely put up any kind of a fight. The Qing force at Yifeng Gate was routed.

"Do not retreat! Do not leave your assigned posts! The enemy is few in number!" screamed Regional Commander Cheng Sanguang in a hoarse voice. But no one who heard him returned.

In actual fact, the number of Taiping troops who broke through the city wall were not many. There had indeed been an explosion, and the wall by Yifeng Gate had been turned into mounds of rubble, perhaps ten meters high, but they still had to scale the wall to reach the hole blown through it. It thus took a fair amount of time for them to get into the city. It would certainly not have been at all difficult to repel a small number of invaders, but such a scenario assumes the will to fight.

Nanjing was an immense city. Once they got past Yifeng Gate, there was nothing resembling a dwelling, save the military camp nearby. The wall that had partially come down in the blast was only the outer wall. A drum tower and a bell tower rose to the east. The Taipings had set their sites on Jinchuan

Gate and Shence Gate on that side of the city. If they could dislodge the Qing troops defending these gates, then they could force open the gates and usher in the Taiping troops waiting outside. To the east of the drum tower was a place known as Shimiao, and there, Governor-General Lu Jianying stood in blank amazement. The four men bearing his palanquin had thrown it to the side of the road and raced away to try and save themselves, without the burden of something as heavy as the palanquin. Their own lives were their first consideration now.

Sedan chair carriers were, in any event, noncombatants, and it was not exceptional at all that they would attempt to flee from a battle scene. What was strange, however, was the fact that nearly all of the governor-general's personal bodyguards had also fled.

Vested with the official business of paying a formal visit to the Jiangning commander to request the transfer of troops, Lu Jianying was wearing his formal uniform as governor-general. His was a civil bureaucratic position, rank 2A, and on the breast of his tunic was embroidered a golden pheasant. The official insignia for rank one was the crane, rank two the golden pheasant, and rank three the peacock. A glance at one's uniform was sufficient to establish the status of its wearer.

By the same token, the Taipings would swoop down en masse on people who at a glance were recognizable as high officials. Hence, even to be at the side of such a person was dangerous. Not anxious to forfeit their own lives, the governor-general's bodyguards had fled.

Under these circumstances, it was unknown why he even bothered with bodyguards. In an effort to maintain his integrity, he had to get together the required number of attendants for a formal visit, and thus Lu Jianying was accompanied by men who appeared to be bodyguards. Since he was all dressed up in formal civil attire, matters of war and the like, he felt, fell outside the realm of his duties at present. Till the very end, two men—both military orderly officers—stood by Lu Jianying's side, one of whom would be killed at the same time as Lu.

The governor-general looked vacantly before him, where a spectacle he did not wish to believe had unfolded. A man who appeared to be a Taiping military commander pointed at the governor-general and said:

"It's the golden pheasant. Since the provincial administration commissioner's already dead, this guy's the governor-general."

Within the walled city of Nanjing, only the rank 2A governor-general and the rank 2B provincial administration commissioner were of the status to wear the embroidered golden pheasant. The Taipings already knew of the death of Provincial Administration Commissioner Qi Suzao.

"It's the great demon! Kill him!" The commander drew his sword, and Lu

Jianying stared without so much as a wink at its gleaming blade in the light. Perhaps it was abject fear that led him to lose consciousness.

He was both governor-general and an imperial commissioner. Though Beijing had decided to relieve him of his posts, he had not been informed of those actions in Nanjing. Lu Jianying died with the belief that he still held both.

The court appointed Jiangning Commander Xiang-hou to replace the cashiered Lu Jianying as imperial commissioner, and thus Xiang-hou took over the position of governor-general as well. Xiang-hou was a military official, and he had evacuated to the rear lines on horseback, though not, to be sure, in a sedan chair. His duties involved staying in contact with, and issuing direct orders to, the troops under his command.

By means of his communications, banner troops were sent from within the city to the field of battle. A brigade of 500 volunteers recruited by the magistrate of Shangyuan county, Liu Tongying, took up arms and confronted the Taiping Army. Though they had received insufficient military training, these volunteers were still a stronger force than the regular government troops.

With the great efforts it took to climb over the mounds of rubble, the Taipings found they were unable to pour troops into the city en masse. They were afraid as well that, if they did not take adequate precautions, the forces that broke through the wall might become isolated. Ever larger numbers of banner troops from within the city were appearing. Under the conditions now prevailing, it would be impossible to break down Jinchuan and Shence Gates.

"Pull out of the city!" The official messenger conveying this order, on Lin Fengxiang's judgment, ran to the commanding officer of the troops that had stormed the wall. These troops themselves agreed that it was a good policy.

Lin then withdrew in orderly fashion. He hadn't had a clear idea of the number of men in the force that had broken through. It was probably only several thousand, and if isolated, they were sure to be massacred.

"We can break back through at any time!" Stating this fact was intended to have a coercive effect on the Qing forces within the city.

After their withdrawal, largely at the behest of the volunteers amassed by Liu Tongying, work began to stop up the gaping hole in the city wall. They collected the tile shards and piled them back up in the wall.

"We had Guilin encircled for a month, and the siege of Changsha went on for a long time too. It's still only been about ten days at Nanjing. It's coming, it's coming. We've got far more ammunition and troops now than we did in those earlier times. There's nothing to worry about at all." Yang Xiuqing was calling on his assembled military leaders to raise fighting morale.

"I heard that you killed the imperial commissioner, right? That's a major achievement in the war," said Yang Xiuqing, offering his personal estimation.

"We were in a great hurry," said the commander of the troops that had stormed the wall, in an apologetic manner, with his head hanging, "and were unable to pull the body out with us, but that is no cause for remorse."

"Ridiculous. No matter how much time you had, the corpse of imperial commissioner shouldn't be brought out. If the corpse of their commanding officer remains inside the city, the demon troops will all remain crestfallen," said Yang.

After the Taiping troops had withdrawn from Nanjing, all indications from the city were that events were unfolding in a manner entirely beneficial to the Taipings, more than even Yang Xiuqing had imagined. The governor-general (and imperial commissioner) was dead. This certainly sent a shock wave through both the government troops and the civilians of the city. Had the Taipings removed the body, then some people inside (even if they knew of the governor-general's death) might deceive others by saying that "his whereabouts are unknown."

Because the body remained behind for all to see, stories began to spread about such things as the condition of his corpse at the time he was placed in the coffin. On that very day, residents of Nanjing learned of the death of the man who had effectively been the "lord" of the city. He had been cut down by "bandits," and the impact of these events on the people was profound.

Everyone was thinking that the bandits had to have been incredibly strong to succeed in taking such actions. Wherever the governor-general's body-guards escaped to, they announced at the top of their lungs, "The governor-general has been murdered by the bandits!" Indeed, they were screaming so loudly and in all directions, that they seemed to be a propaganda squad hired by the Taipings themselves.

Tan Qi and the other "priest-spies" were out vocally spreading the faith, "Hail the Buddha Amitabha. Hail the Buddha Amitabha. There will be killing here. Killing is deplorable. It is forbidden. Please avoid it at all cost. Those many of you guarding the gates will be the first to die. Please, you have but one life."

The priest-spies then set fires everywhere, and they informed the Taipings outside the city when the troops guarding the gates had fled.

—5—

Men from Shandong had always been known for their large physical stature and solid build. They were, needless to say, perfectly suited to military service. According to ancient Chinese texts, China was divided in antiquity into nine *zhou* or "Nine Regions," and the Shandong peninsula was then called

Qingzhou (or the Qing region) in this configuration. From that time forward, "Qingzhou" had become another name for the area of the Shandong peninsula.

Thus it was the Qingzhou soldiers who, together with the Liangzhou soldiers from Gansu province in the northwest, competed for the position as the strongest fighting force in all of China. At the time of the Taiping attack on Nanjing, Qingzhou troops were stationed there and seemed to be reliable.

It seemed the natural order of things that strong soldiers be violent-tempered. No one can now say with certainty why that should have been the case, but the Qingzhou corps began to bicker with the Manchu banner troops. Possibly, the banner troops' sense of special privilege offended the Qingzhou soldiers.

Within the walls of the city of Nanjing, surrounded by a Taiping force numbering in the tens of thousands, some five thousand Manchu banner troops and even fewer Qingzhou troops were now engaged in an armed struggle. With an animosity for one another greater even than what they held for the Taiping soldiers, whom neither side in Nanjing had ever seen before, the two bands of government troops came face to face with one another on a daily basis, only intensifying the hatred. A confrontation that had begun for a trivial matter—over a haughty attitude or vying for the attention of a young woman in a wine shop—had turned into a bloody catastrophe.

This was not something occurring under ordinary circumstances. It was an eventuality that took place within a city encircled by a powerful enemy several men deep. Now that they had to join forces to face the external enemy, serious blood-letting trouble had arisen within the ranks. Under these conditions, it would have been strange if Nanjing had *not* fallen.

Defense of West Gate into Nanjing disappeared not because the troops ran away to save their own necks. The Qingzhou men defending that area had left their assigned posts in order to assist their fellow Qingzhou troops, who had come to blows with the banner troops.

Having verified that the guardian soldiers at West Gate had vanished, the priest-spies sent a signal to those outside the city walls. If these troops disappeared, then a number of soldiers of smaller stature were to scale the wall with rope ladders, and from within, open the gate wide. A surging mass, the Taipings could then storm inside the city.

While they had rushed into the city after exploding a hole through the wall in the early morning hours of the tenth day of the second lunar month, they had been forced to race back outside again. In the evening, however, the guards at Shuixi Gate and Hanxi Gate had fled to safer quarters, and taking advantage of the near vacuum created when the Qingzhou troops sped off to help their comrades, these three gates were thrown open and the Taiping soldiers were able to flood into the city.

It would be inaccurate to say that the Taipings took the city of Nanjing by use of land mines. Nanjing fell for two principal reasons: the fighting morale of the defense forces was low and there was discord between Han Chinese and Manchus. With the three gates flung open, the main force of the Taiping military entered the city on the eleventh day of the month. Defense forces defended against the Taipings outside the city at the northern and eastern gates. Not in their wildest dreams did they suspect that, from their rear, Taiping troops were moving toward them.

"The Taipings have gotten inside!" And with that brief word shouted, the defense forces at the northern and eastern gates rushed to seek refuge inside the Manchu city. That was certainly not unexpected. Their task had been to defend against an enemy assault on the city, and that they had done. However, a break in the defense had occurred at another site. Were they to continue glued to their posts at these gates, they would have been swept away in the Taiping inundation.

No one was at the northern gate, and in the same manner, Taiping soldiers entered the city with rope ladders and opened that gate. The outer city was now entirely in Taiping hands, and the remnants of the Qing forces had all taken refuge in the Manchu city. As noted earlier, there were many bannermen in the inner city.

The Taiping assault on the inner city assumed the form of a war of ethnic or racial revenge. Although such a thing was far removed from the ideals of the Taiping Heavenly Kingdom, no one was in any position to prevent it from happening. Even if there had been one, a voice of reason could never have quelled their burning ethnic consciousness.

"The Tatar barbarians, look at them now! Soon enough we'll pay back an old score from two hundred years ago."

"Chase the bastards out of the central plain of China!"

"That's right. Send them back where they came from once and for all."

"Return them to their old grasslands! They can live off raising sheep. That's what they're best suited for anyway."

"What's all this about sending them back to where they came from? Why such weak-kneed ideas? Don't send them anywhere. Kill them all!"

"Yeah, destroy every last one of this race of Manchu barbarians!"

This exchange occurred among Taiping troops in the outer city. In the language of the Taiping movement, the term "demon" referred specifically to the Manchu ethnicity. It had been newly coined for this purpose. However, among the general Taiping rank and file, an older term remained in use: "Tatar barbarians." A term they had become accustomed to using, it fit the contours of their feelings well. The newer, more technical term, "demon," had a formal, unfamiliar ring to it.

—6—

Nanjing and the area around it fell within the jurisdiction of Jiangning prefecture. The southern portion of the larger walled city fell within Jiangning county, while the northern part belonged to Shangyuan county.

Shangyuan County Magistrate Liu Tongying had put together a force of volunteers whom he led in battle against the Taipings. It was primarily due to the brave fighting of the Shangyuan braves that the band of Taiping soldiers who had initially broken through the wall were forced to retreat. Liu Tongying also took charge of the task of rebuilding Yifeng Gate.

When Liu learned that a huge brigade of Taiping troops, at dawn on the eleventh day of the second lunar month, had penetrated the outer wall of the city via three gates, he wrote in red on the door of the county office, "A notice to bandits: Do no harm to our farmers! I pray that you let me offer myself in their stead."

In front of the office was the Rising Peace Bridge and further to the south was the charming village of Qinhuai. Of course, once the Taiping siege began, the mellifluous sounds of wind and string instruments from this neighborhood died out, and the local aroma of cosmetics no longer floated into the air. It was strange that right near this red-light district was the prefectural school and the examination hall. The former was the highest local school, and the latter was the site at which the civil service examinations were administered.

Provincial-level examinations were performed here. Those who passed the county-level exam, the first rung on the civil service ladder, were government students known as *xiucai* or "men of talent." They then came here to sit for the next level of the examinations. Those who successfully passed this level were known as *juren* or "provincial graduates," and they were then eligible to sit for the metropolitan examination in Beijing. Once they passed this examination and went through the proper formalities, they became *jinshi* or "metropolitan graduates." They constituted the super elite of the system, and their future was completely assured.

The examinations were administered over the course of several days, and during this time the examinees were confined to the examination hall, each in his own room. The examination hall was a kind of jail, honeycombed with solitary confinement cells. The provincial capital had its own examination hall, and once war erupted, it was immediately transformed into a military barracks. It was, after all, a building used only a few days each year, so that it made sense to convert it to other uses.

The Taipings who came into the city through the three opened gates attacked the other gates from inside the city. In fact, there was scarcely any conflict at all, for almost every Qing soldier guarding the gates had run away without a fight.

When Jubao Gate was flung open, the Taiping forces waiting on Yuhuatai dashed across the bridge and rushed into the city. The road extending directly north from the gate ran straight to the Shangyuan county office, with the examination hall on the right and the Jiangning county office on the left. It was the main thoroughfare of the outer city, known as Dagongfang.

Government offices were, for the most part, empty. The examination hall, which right up until the previous evening had been packed with soldiers three or four to each of the cells used to administer examinations, was now vacant.

Arriving at the Shangyuan county office, Jiangning County Magistrate Zhang Xingshu said, "I've come to say good-bye."

"That day has finally come," replied Liu.

"Do you know what you'll do?"

"Just take a look around. I've had no choice but to think about that."

"You put that notice up on the door of the county office. What effect do you think it'll have?"

"I wasn't thinking about its effect. It honestly records my feelings . . . if by some chance we reach a state where words are impossible to utter. When a person is going to die, he wants to express his feelings somehow somewhere."

"Well then, perhaps I shall return and post a large notice on the door of my county office." Magistrate Zhang rose to bid Liu farewell.

"It's no longer possible to go by sedan chair. Let me lend you a horse from our county stable. Please don't feel compelled to return," said Liu.

At that moment a county secretary feverishly rushed into the office. "The bandit army is coming nearer. On the other side of Lufei Alley, the bandits' flag on the military school over . . ." The secretary did not finish what he intended to say, probably because his throat was parched. He was referring to the reserve officer cadet school to the west of the Shangyuan county office, quite near them.

"What about the south?" asked the Jiangning county magistrate. The Jiangning county office was south of the military school.

"I have heard that Jubao Gate was broken through," replied the secretary, swallowing hard, with an expression of great pain on his face.

"Then I shall have to hurry. I shall prevail upon your kindness and borrow a horse." Zhang Xingshu then mounted the horse brought to him by a servant in the office. He raised the riding crop and called out, "Farewell!"

Liu Tongying responded in kind with the standard Chinese term that denoted, "See you again." The two county magistrates in the city of Nanjing exchanged this salutation, all the time thinking that they would probably never see one another again.

Zhang was unable to get back to his own office, because he was surrounded by Taiping soldiers advancing from Jubao Gate. It happened just as he neared Four Elephant Bridge.

"Hey!" screamed a voice loudly, and at that moment Zhang's body became disengaged from the horse, and as if swimming through the air, he fell into the river. He died a martyr's death.

About this time Assistant King Shi Dakai was silently reading the handwritten red notice on the door of the Shangyuan county office. His young eyebrows were twitching.

"Nicely put. He wants to offer himself in place of others. On occasion, you find a decent official in the demon's government. The county magistrate here is one such decent official. Don't kill him!" ordered Shi to his subordinates.

"Shall we take him along with us?" One of his underlings searched the county office and found Liu Tongying in a room far to its rear.

"Please come along with us."

"Where are we going?"

"Wherever the Assistant King is. You're wearing the clothes of the county magistrate of Shangyuan. He said we are to bring you along with civility."

"What's this? The Assistant King? Who is this Assistant King? I've never heard of any 'king' known as the 'assistant king' in our dynasty. The man's a fraud."

"You talk too much. Assistant King Shi Dakai is one of the pillars of the Taiping Heavenly Kingdom."

"Oh, a bandit pillar? That pillar'll be smashed soon enough."

"Shut up! Let's go." Taiping troops to his left and right held Liu's arms as they were about to walk outside together. They had been instructed to treat him politely, so they were not clasping his hands tightly.

Liu Tongying calculated the strength of the men holding his arms and then abruptly twisted his torso and broke free of their grasp. A chase ensued.

"Wait!" yelled the Taiping soldiers following him.

Liu turned the corner at his office building, a place he knew well. His pursuers moved more slowly because they were unfamiliar with the local geography. There was a Dragon King Temple within the county office. The dragon king was the deity of the sea, and many ponds were constructed at sites where one prayed to this figure. On the grounds of the temple in the Shangyuan county office was such a pond, famed for its great depth. It was to this place that Liu was running.

The two county magistrates took their own lives in similar manners. The deaths of these two men seen by many people were passed along by word of mouth to many more. By comparison, the fate by which Jiangning Prefect Wei Xiangda came to his end is less well-known. It seems that, when the city walls were penetrated, Wei—who was not a healthy man to begin with— was taken into custody by the Taipings and died some seven days later. Rumors that he had surrendered and that he had quietly fled to his hometown refused to go away. Few people had actually witnessed his last days.

Probably the death of Zou Minghe was witnessed by the most people. Two years earlier, he had been transferred from his post as prefect of the metropolitan prefecture (effectively, the mayor of Beijing) to governor of Guangxi, and he was subsequently stripped of this position for his responsibility when the Taipings overran Guangxi province. He had then been transferred to serve as manager of the Defense Planning Bureau. This was a position on the order of a director-general of defense headquarters. He was in charge of granting rewards after the examination of services rendered, and thus it was his job to pass along the prizes to the soldiers who had cut off the enemies' ears.

Zou Minghe was captured by the Taipings, dragged out to the Dagongfang, and beheaded in public before a large number of people. On reflection, the Guangxi governorship was the post to which Lin Zexu had been assigned, together with his position as imperial commissioner. He had died of illness on his way to assuming the governorship, and Beijing had assigned the aged Zhou Tianjue to succeed him. Zhou quarreled with everyone with whom he came into contact in Guangxi, and caused annoyances and problems for all concerned. The court ultimately gave his post to Zou Minghe. The thread of fate had been subtlely sewn.

Provincial Military Commander Fu-zhu-hong-a died in battle when he confronted the Taipings en route from Yifeng Gate to bring help to Tongji Gate. Yifeng Gate was the Taipings' first breach point into the city, and there, Regional Commander Cheng Sanguang, Regional Vice-Commanders Fu-er-guo-chun and Shen Ding, and others all met their deaths.

—7—

Liwen and Xinmei were facing one another on a boat floating on Muchou Lake outside Shuixi Gate. They were planning to leave Nanjing the following day.

"I didn't want to see it, and it was all laid out for me . . . The Tatar hags dragged outside the city and burned to death. There were hundreds of them. No, far more." Xinmei had actually witnessed the hell she had so not wanted to see, though it strangely seemed to have calmed her mind.

The Taiping Army had shown the Manchus no mercy at all. The term

"Tatar hags" referred to women of ethnic Manchu stock. For the era in which they lived, the Taipings actually entertained progressive ideas. In an era that privileged men over women, all Taiping institutions were theoretically based on gender equality. The Taiping Heavenly Kingdom, which claimed to be a religious group founded on Christianity, could not, however, suppress its racial antipathies. It was as if they used the anti-Manchu sentiments of the general populace as the energy necessary to build their own authority.

The massacre of Manchus was appalling in the extreme. In his memorial to the throne, Zeng Guofan wrote that a total of over thirty thousand Manchus garrisoned there and their family members were murdered in the Manchu city of Nanjing. Perhaps killing each and every Manchu individually was too troublesome. Large numbers were expelled through Chaoyang Gate and burned to death there. Xinmei was outside the city at the time and witnessed the spectacle intermittently. They also adopted a method of capturing Manchus and drowning them in the river.

"Here's the place where the corpses are finally disposed of. The Han Chinese from the outer city were rounded up for this part of the operation. All they do every day, every single day, is throw corpses into the river." Liwen's voice was without any trace of vigor.

"Revenge will be visited upon them at some point in the future. Isn't that part of the teachings of the Heavenly Father and the Heavenly Elder Brother? It is, isn't it?"

"It's bad, really bad. The people living inside the Manchu city seemed to know that if they lost, they'd all be murdered. So everyone—including women, children, and old people—fought desperately. The Taiping troops certainly had their share of sacrifices as well. They made stepping stones out of the mountain of corpses, . . . the corpses of their own comrades-in-arms. In their minds they were saying to the dead: Excuse me for walking over you, but we will avenge your pain. And they moved on."

"Revenge gives rise to more revenge. It's an endless process."

"There were numerous suicides. I wonder if there's ever been a war with so many suicides. There certainly weren't this many at the time of the Opium War."

"Probably true. When the Taipings say they're going to kill people, they always keep their word. If you're going to be killed, it's much better to die first. If I were to execute a Qing official, he'd be better off dead first."

"I hope this doesn't mean Old Master Zhou died, too."

The expression "Master Zhou" referred to Tang Yifen, who was also known by the pen name Tang Yusheng. He also used the names Qinyin Daoren and

Shanwai Shanren. Together with Fang Xun, Xi Gang, and Dai Xi, he was considered one of the four great painters of the entire Qing era.

"He must have been very old?"

"Seventy-six, I think."

"No matter how old, a retired old man like that just can't die."

"Well, even if Old Master Zhou retired from military service, everyone knows him as a military commander."

"No one thinks of him as a military man. What his name conjures up in everyone's mind are his monochrome paintings of plums."

"That's true enough. His name is synonymous with black-ink plums. That and pine and oak trees."

Because of the achievements of his ancestors, Tang Yifen had been appointed to military posts, and he had served at a high level with various divisions of the Qing Army. His last post was as regional vice-commander in Wenzhou, Zhejiang province, and thus he had been at military rank 2B. He signed paintings "work of a meritorious commander" so frequently that it seemed his military sense of self was still quite strong. Still, among the ordinary people of the time, he was known only as an artist.

Quiet and refined—these were the terms his contemporaries used to evaluate his black-ink plums. Despite his military background, his landscape paintings had a thoroughly delicate quality, and his plums and trees were particularly pleasing.

"Xiang-hou went to confer with him, and it looks like Old Master Zhou related his own views on the situation." No matter how hard he tried, Liwen simply couldn't imagine Tang Yifen's death. He could well understand how the Jiangning commander would listen to the views of his senior colleague, a man who had already retired from the military realm. But, was Tang really aware of his responsibility in this matter?

Though they had been instructed to kill all government soldiers and officials, it still did not seem as though the troops of the Taiping Army had killed this famous seventy-six-year-old artist. Yet the thought kept coming back to Liwen: A person who shouldn't have died has died.

Jiangning Commander Xiang-hou himself died on the field in the bloody battle in the Manchu city. In the chaos, his corpse lay apparently unrecognized. The story that was circulating was that Xiao Youhe, son of the Taiping Western King Xiao Chaogui who had died in the attack on Changsha, had stabbed him to death. As a tale of revenge, the story stirred everyone's heart, but in fact Xiao Youhe was still a little boy at the time, and thus the story fails to fit the facts.

On the day the city fell, Tang Yifen changed into his official uniform, replete with the lion insignia attached to all rank two military men (rank one bore the insignia of a unicorn). The old artist went to his death a military man and a martyr. He went with his only daughter as his traveling companion. She too must have been an older woman. His son, Tang Luming, was also well-known as a painter and was in Nanjing at the time as well. He managed to survive. Tang Luming, who used the pen name Tang Lemin, was fifty-one years of age at the time, and he is said to have lived another twenty years. Left in this wretched circumstance, Tang Yifen's daughter met her death by throwing herself into a deep pond.

Tang was not only known as an artist, for he also won wide acclaim for his poetry. Prior to his suicide, he composed a final poem. Such works of poetry are known in China as a "farewell poem before death." Only a few days following his death, Old Master Zhou's farewell poem was copied in secret and admiringly read by many and sundry.

Liwen tapped the side of the boat. Signs of spring were everywhere to be seen by Muchou Lake. In the Six Dynasties period, the story went, a beautiful woman by the name of Lu Muchou lived near this lake, and thus gave her name to the body of water. Inasmuch as the scenery in the lake's vicinity was soft and tender, it was considered appropriate that its name came from that of a beautiful woman. With this lovely scenery as background, it was all but unthinkable that a horrific scene of gruesome bloodshed was unfolding. But that was the reality.

"There's something going on in Shanghai," said Xinmei, as if instructing herself with a nod of the head. As he looked Xinmei directly in the face, Liwen tapped the side of the boat, reciting a poem quietly. It was the farewell poem of Old Master Zhou, Tang Yifen.

> In the end, life and death are but a moment in time,
> While loyalty and righteousness last for a thousand years.
> I do not willingly dispense with flesh and blood,
> And I've planned well for posterity.
> My hometown—it is to there that my soul must return.
> This last piece of writing—tears are difficult to restrain.
> A simple funeral will be fine,
> For I have amassed countless sins over the course of my life.

24

The Yangzi River Flows to the East

Heavenly King Hong Xiuquan entered the city of Nanjing on the twentieth day of the second lunar month, 1853. A small brigade of Taiping soldiers had broken through on the tenth, only to withdraw. In the early dawn of the eleventh, three gates were thrown open, and a full-fledged assault on the city commenced. Soon thereafter Nanjing fell to the Taiping Army.

The next ten days were a preparatory period. The reeking odor of blood that wafted through the entire city eventually began to dissipate during this period.

On the outside of the door to every home, a piece of paper was hanging inscribed with the Chinese character for "obedient," an indication that the members of a given household were people who had submitted to the Taipings.

Here and there throughout the city, slips of paper—some yellow, others red—had been posted. The yellow ones were bordered in a dragon and phoenix design, official documents of the Taiping Heavenly Kingdom. They were a proclamation, issued in the name of Eastern King Yang Xiuqing, to calm the anxieties of the local populace. In the middle of it ran the following line: "Heaven controls the people by having already produced the pillar of truth. Hence the people are best advised to devote themselves to transformation." Ever since the Manchus had invaded and made havoc of China, it continued in a denunciatory vein, they had ravaged the common people in China and destroyed those who sought to live there. "The Holy Soldiers will by no means use the force of threats, and the masses need harbor no fears in this regard." It was a public proclamation, though the vocabulary was highly dignified and betrayed throughout a profoundly ethnic disposition.

By comparison, what was written on the red papers was short and quite easy to read, almost like a slogan. It read rather like religious propaganda: "The Heavenly King has received a command from the Heavenly Father and the Heavenly Elder Brother to rule the world. In recognition of the Heavenly Father, the people shall submit to the Heavenly King and help pacify the realm, and together we shall receive the blessings of heaven."

Yellow and red papers inundated Nanjing, and from them the residents of the city were able to get a general idea of the atmosphere surrounding the Taiping movement.

Assistant King Shi Dakai had led the attacking army and was thus the first to enter the city. Northern King Wei Changhui rode into Nanjing through Yifeng Gate on the seventeenth. As soon as his mopping up within the city was completed, Shi Dakai was recalled by the Heavenly King. After participating in important meetings, Shi returned to Nanjing about the same time as Wei Changhui.

Hong Xiuquan was at this time aboard a large boat on the Yangzi. The bow of the ship was decorated with the carving of a dragon's head, painted in vivid colors with gold leaf attached. There were over ten cannon emplacements on either side of the ship. It had the dignity of an imperial warship.

Nanjing had fallen. A final meeting was now in session to decide what to do with the city.

The dynasty known as the Taiping Heavenly Kingdom had already been born. Its institutional order had effectively been established back in Yongan, though until now that Taiping Heavenly Kingdom had been an itinerant dynasty.

Eastern King Yang Xiuqing wanted to make Nanjing the Taiping capital. Hong Xiuquan had become, for all intents and purposes, a symbolic existence only, having on his own withdrawn from the actual activities of rulership. Though any meeting to decide on policy would be called in his presence, he would make no effort to advance his own views. Yang's views had become the will of the Taiping movement.

The principal objective for calling this meeting was to make the opinions of the Eastern King well known. The ambiance of the gathering was in no way whatsoever conducive to hearing the views of the other participants. Fervent speeches were delivered at the meeting by men other than Yang, but these were largely what Yang had put them up to.

One of the most eloquent of the speakers at the meeting on the dragon boat was naval commander Tang Zhengcai. Tang had not been with the Taipings from the start. When the Taiping Army was defeated in the attack on Changsha, relinquished the effort to take the city, and moved on to Yiyang, this adventuristic timber merchant just happened to be present on a number of occasions. Through his acquaintance with Luo Dagang when Luo was active as a skiff bandit, Tang had advised the Taiping Army on the assault on Yuezhou, and he thereafter became the Taiping naval commander.

Though a newcomer to the Taiping movement, no one knew more than he about naval affairs and conditions in the region just south of the Yangzi River. The Taiping attack on Nanjing was unimaginable without a naval force. Because he commanded the navy, Tang's role within the Taiping military had become exceedingly important. Accordingly, he had acquired considerable influence.

"We need to proceed north, attack Henan, cross the Yellow River, and seize Beijing." There were those who entertained precisely these views, Shi Dakai among them. However, Shi had a keen sense of fear when it came to lying back and taking advantage of circumstances. They had broken through the encirclement of Yongan, and after a full month in which the army had surrounded Guilin, it had not fallen. Then they had changed course, only to suffer a great defeat at Suoyi Ford. And yet, no one would ever have been able to predict that in a mere ten months following that defeat, a Taiping armed force of immense size would be able to attack Nanjing. It was indeed something even the leadership of the Taiping military had not foreseen.

Now the Taipings were riding high. If they attacked to the north before the momentum was lost, there would have been no difficulty at all in bringing all of China within their domain.

"By raising the Taiping flag we have brought down the demonic government of the Manchus. Is it not our duty now to bring the entire country under our control?" said Shi Dakai at the meeting, voicing his own point of view.

Commander Tang Zhengcai leveled the counter-argument to Shi, "Attack to the north? Do you know what the terrain is like in Henan province? It is part of what's called the Central Plain of China. But it is terribly poor land. I know this because I am a merchant by profession. No one ever thinks of going there to engage in trade unless they're planning to do a lot of it. It's so poor that there's nothing on the land. Do you know why our Taiping military was able to run through Hunan province, head east from Hubei with a huge force, and seize the second capital of the realm? Because the land we passed through was rich and fertile. We had no worries about food. We had not a thought about being torn to shreds in the cold, either. If we move to the north, there will be waiting for us a wide variety of arduous troubles such as we have never known before. Keeping this rich terrain we now have south of the Yangzi is by far more important for us now."

As he was listening to Tang's rebuttal, Shi Dakai realized that he was hearing the views of Yang Xiuqing as well. The self-assured tone of voice in which Tang was speaking led Shi to believe that Tang had strong support behind his position.

From time to time, Tang's line of vision aimed directly at the Eastern King. No doubt about it. Shi abandoned his advocacy of an expedition to the north. He could call for this move until he was blue in the face, but as long as Yang felt differently, Shi's views would never be accepted by the Taiping leadership.

Finally, Yang made his decision:

"There are limits to our strength. Devotion to the Heavenly Father and the Heavenly Elder Brother have certainly afforded us great strength in the past. However, we must consider well our basic capacity. To cross the Yellow River, demolish the demonic government in Beijing, and build a Taiping Heavenly Kingdom throughout the entire terrain of China are, of course, tasks for us to accomplish, but I think we need first to amass greater strength. Not the strength merely to ride the crest of our present momentum, but to create our own momentum. That is what I want us to work toward. To that end we need a base of operations, and we now have that in our hands."

It was a conclusion that enabled Shi Dakai and others who supported a northern expedition to save face. Yang had spoken of a "base of operations," and as the meeting progressed this was converted to a "national capital."

The only elaboration by Hong Xiuquan of something resembling a point of view was to question the name of "capital." Inasmuch as "Nanjing" meant "southern capital," it seemed a little strange to him to have a capital city with the Chinese character for "south" in it. Thus, the name was changed to Heavenly Capital or Tianjing in Chinese, clearly a name much more consonant with a capital for the Taiping Heavenly Kingdom.

—2—

On the day prior to Hong Xiuquan's entrance into Nanjing, Yang Xiuqing entered the city, "To make preparations for welcoming the Heavenly King," as Yang put it, and others thought it was a perfectly appropriate thing to do. Yang, however, had never been the sort of man who devoted his entire energy to formalities of this sort.

Once inside Nanjing, Yang met with Wei Changhui and Shi Dakai, and hurriedly made the necessary arrangements for Hong's arrival the next day. Actually, he said to them, "I entrust all of this to you two kings and expect that you will do a fine job," simply passing the entire task to them, as they sat drinking a cup of tea together.

Yang had far more important business to attend to. He had called a strategy session with his field commanders: Li Kaifang, Lin Fengxiang, Luo Dagang, Wu Ruxiao, and Zeng Lichang.

There would be no northern expedition. To strengthen the base of operations in Nanjing, they needed to seize and occupy the strategically important surrounding cities. The first was Zhenjiang. It directly faced the main entrance to the city of Nanjing and hence was also known as Jingkou or "entry to the capital." They needed also to bring Yangzhou, on the far shore of the Yangzi River, set apart from Zhenjiang, under control. Once these two cities had been occupied, the Taiping would straddle the Yangzi and the defense of Nanjing would become impenetrable.

Even prior to the fall of Nanjing, Yang Xiuqing had been contemplating subsequent military strategies and conveying his designs to Li Kaifang and the other commanders. When Nanjing did fall, these field commanders had begun to implement preparations for the next stage. That strategy would be called the "eastern expedition."

"What's the makeup of the new recruits?" asked Yang.

"Not as bad as you might have thought. There are quite a number of young and vibrant fellows," responded Li Kaifang, who in addition to being a military commander, bore an ostentatious Taiping bureaucratic title with overtones of high status. "But I wonder why they amassed such a bunch of sickly troops there." Yang was referring to the Qing authorities in Nanjing. The government forces as Yuhuatai could only be referred to as a collection of uniformly sickly men.

"It's not that they went out and assembled only such a group of men. Only men of that sort assembled."

"The issue is how the troops were gathered."

Once the Taipings occupied Nanjing, all of the gates to the city were shut tight, and a census was taken. Men and women were separated and placed in platoons with twenty-five persons in each. The men were called "new brothers," and the women were dubbed "new sisters." Those who found enrollment into this barracks system disagreeable were permitted to return to their homes, but this was merely in principle. The sick and the aged were able to remain apart from the barracks, and although healthy young people were not compelled to participate as such, it was in fact extremely difficult to leave the barracks.

Most attractive about the barracks was the fact that once one became a part of the system, all worry of food came to an end. While the Taiping movement professed a belief in gender equality, there was actually a rather considerable difference in the allocation of foodstuffs. Men received a pint of rice per day, while women were in fact allocated only about one-third of a pint.

The residents of Nanjing were in a state of agitation, witnessing all these events before their eyes, as a chorus of voices around the city rang out.

"Nanjing has fallen."

"The governor-general and his commanders have just been killed."

"They were never any match for the Taipings."

"The Taipings' military discipline is incredibly strict."

The people of Nanjing felt pressured by the Taipings' merciless attitude toward their enemies. Should they join the enemy and become allies? They realized they had no choice but to paste pieces of paper bearing the Chinese character for "obedient" on their doors. The young simply entered the barracks.

Those sickly sorts hired by the Qing military were used only in odd jobs by the Taipings. Those in robust health entered the military. Because standing around idly was dealt with on the basis of military discipline, those who did enter the barracks were a nervous lot. At first they received military training, and they frequently became excellent soldiers.

When the census was completed, the gates to the city were opened, though on leaving the city one was not permitted to move goods on shoulder-carrying poles. One could take only what one could carry in one's hands.

The "new army" formed by the new brothers went beyond the city walls to receive basic military training. Yang Xiuqing had devised a plan to move on Zhenjiang and Yangzhou with a battalion primarily comprised of this new army. "Prepared?" asked Yang.

"We can advance at any time," replied Li Kaifang.

"Fine, then leave today, soon."

"Yes, sir."

And thus, on the day prior to the entrance into Nanjing of the Heavenly King, the eastern expeditionary army had already set off. The next day was the twentieth day of the second lunar month, or March 29, 1853, according to the solar calendar.

Accompanied by the principal leaders of the Taiping movement, including the two Taiping kings, Wei Changhui and Shi Dakai, Yang Xiuqing went to greet the dragon boat on the Yangzi River. Li Kaifang and the other commanders then involved in the eastern expedition were absent.

Eastern King Yang Xiuqing appeared in an extraordinarily garish outfit. He was attired in a crimson coat, with a leopard skin hat atop his head with brilliant peacock feathers attached to it.

On the dragon boat, Heavenly King Hong Xiuquan looked at Yang's appearance as though it strained his eyes. "Hmm, so he's got this side to his character too," thought Hong, suddenly stricken with a feeling of panic.

Similar things had happened frequently of late. Though confident that

Hong was a perceptive observer of others, only Yang Xiuqing had managed to avoid comprehension in the eyes of the Heavenly King. Yang had many different aspects to his personality, and the real Yang Xiuqing seemed impossible to grasp. Perhaps he had even more facets to him.

"We are graced by your presence," said Yang. It was a line from a country theatrical performance. It was the only line he could come up with under the current courtly situation.

"Yes . . ." said Hong, producing a strained smile. They had once gone together to see a country play, and Hong now noted that it was becoming the model for Yang's behavior.

Hong Xiuquan was dressed all in yellow. Unlike Yang, he was a reader and hence knew from books what an imperial court looked like. He knew, for instance, that the emperor's color was yellow. He had on a yellow embroidered dragon hat and similar footwear. His palanquin was yellow as well, and its roof was decorated with a crane flying aloft into the heavens.

One scholar who witnessed the scene of the Heavenly King's entrance into Nanjing recounted that his hat resembled that of the Emperor Xuanzong (r. 713–756) of the Tang dynasty as it appeared in the drama, "Pavilion of Long Life." Indeed, there should have been a resemblance, for he had gotten the clothing from the wardrobe of a drama company in Wuchang.

—3—

Having put Nanjing behind him, Lian Liwen decided to stop over in Yangzhou before proceeding to Shanghai. He wanted to show Xinmei, who was familiar only with the southern Chinese provinces of Guangdong and Guangxi, the famous sites of the Yangzi delta.

Many times Liwen had heard the story of some dozen or more years ago concerning the meeting between Wen Han, head clerk of the Jinshunji, and Lin Zexu at the Pingshan Hall in Yangzhou. For one reason or another, Yangzhou had a special allure for Liwen. He had been to the city a number of times in the past, and on those occasions as well he had come—without business to attend to—drawn by the lure of things unseen.

"Is it that great a city?" asked Xinmei, unaware of the particulars of the story behind Liwen's attraction to Yangzhou, because Liwen had pressed her so hard to make this stopover.

"It's a quiet city . . . with beautiful peonies, though it's too early in the season for them now," replied Liwen. Yangzhou was by no means a quiet city. Its leaders had been ready to run away when they heard the news that Nanjing had come under Taiping occupation.

The eastern expeditionary force had divided into two route armies, north and south: the southern route army, dubbed the Jiangnan Army, continued in an easterly direction under the command of Luo Dagang and Wu Ruxiao, with 400 military vessels; the northern route army, dubbed the Jiangbei Army, crossed to the northern bank of the Yangzi and proceeded toward Yangzhou, primarily on land. The objective of the Jiangnan Army was Zhenjiang. Eleven years earlier during the Opium War, the British had seized, occupied, and plundered Zhenjiang. Memories on this score were still fresh in the city. At that time Zhenjiang was hell itself, and no one had any desire to repeat that disaster.

At the news of the approaching Taiping forces, 80 to 90 percent of the resident populace of Zhenjiang took refuge outside the city walls. If this event had been limited to the residents of the city, that would not have presented any problems, but every single official and government soldier also fled, as both knew only too well that they would certainly have been put to death. Reports of this sort concerning the Taipings circulated through many of the cities of the area.

Thus, the Taipings' Jiangnan Army took Zhenjiang without spilling a drop of blood.

At the time of the Opium War, Yangzhou across the river had adopted an altogether different response from Zhenjiang. The wealthiest members of Yangzhou society had amassed a collection of money and paid the British Army off to avoid an invasion. "Gold to redeem the city," people called it.

Jiang Shoumin, a merchant who dealt in art curios, had taken part in the negotiations. Morrison, the British army interpreter, came up with the outrageous figure of U.S. $60,000. Jiang had haggled with him until they settled on a sum of half that amount.

Yangzhou was not attacked by the British armed forces, and Jiang was seen as the benefactor of the city. In fact, from the start the British had no plans to assault Yangzhou, so they got $30,000 for nothing. However, none of this was known at the time. With news of the approaching Taiping Army, the people of Yangzhou again turned their eyes toward Jiang Shoumin. Could Jiang save Yangzhou a second time?

Urban residents of Yangzhou did not rivet their gaze solely in Jiang's direction. Tan Qi appeared in Jiang's art store with two men from the lower Yangzi delta area. Tan Qi was from Guangxi province and, although he was basically able to communicate with people in the area, subtle nuances were another matter. So, just to be certain, he brought along two men from the area who were familiar with the Guangxi dialect.

"Aha. So, there are people even in the Taiping movement who can understand the spoken word. Is that so? Have you known my name for some time?" Jiang spoke with a touch of agitation.

Fame was more important to him than anything else. He donated money to such philanthropic work as the building of temples and the reconstruction of bridges solely because of the fame he accrued in doing so.

He had achieved his greatest renown to date for allegedly saving the people of Yangzhou from the British Army. His next dose of fame awaited, with the opportunity to protect Yangzhou and its residents from the Taipings. In the case of the British, he had gone out and engaged in negotiations, but with the Taipings, they had now come to him. His renown had scaled mountains and forded rivers to reach even the Taiping Army.

Jiang demanded as a condition for handing over money to the Taipings that the latter "pass through the city." Yangzhou would put up no resistance at all. All officials and all government troops would leave the city, and the Taiping Army could then enter the city without spilling blood. The Taipings, though, could not remain inside the city, but the entire army would proceed through and leave. After the Taipings had left the city, the government forces and bureaucrats would return and report to Beijing that they had defended Yangzhou to the last.

"There must be absolutely no murder, no violence, no plundering," underscored Jiang.

"The Taiping Army has done no such thing to this point. You must have heard of the severity of our military discipline," said Tan Qi by way of a guarantee.

Jiang presented the Taipings with a huge quantity of money. It was not, of course, his money alone, but what he had collected from the larger merchants and wealthy families of Yangzhou. The Taipings were to enter the city without incident and leave peacefully. By the same token, the Qing forces outside the city walls were neither to seek reinforcements nor launch an attack. Jiang raced back and forth between the two sides to conclude this agreement. The whole thing was prearranged.

"Do we have any guarantee that, once we enter the city, the Qing Army won't surround and attack us?" asked Tan Qi.

"You have my word. When the British invaded in the twenty-second year of the reign of the Daoguang emperor [1842], with words overflowing with earnestness and devotion, I . . ." Jiang Shoumin spoke eloquently of events eleven years earlier.

"You say your word is a guarantee, but without any substance to it, I can't hold your word ransom."

"Then I shall be your hostage. I, Jiang Shoumin. There is no one in the city of Yangzhou who does not know the name of Jiang Shoumin. I shall remain with the Taiping Army as a corporeal ransom." Jiang's stomach was so tense that he began to tap it lightly.

"You will, eh? If the Qing Army launches an attack on us, we won't hesitate to kill our hostage. It is our practice to keep our promises firmly, but to deal severely with breaches of promise as well. Will that be all right with you?"

"That will be fine," said Jiang decisively.

The populace of Yangzhou, especially the rich upper class, had practically all fled the city. Yangzhou people knew of the reputation of the Taiping Army for strictly keeping to its military discipline. At the same time, stories were also circulating of them showing no mercy toward their enemies. Since the Taipings' wholesale massacre in Nanjing of the "demonic" Manchus—old and young, men and women—had taken place so close to them, there were actually witnesses among the residents of Yangzhou.

No one really knew how far the Taipings went in defining who their enemies were. To err and be considered a Taiping foe meant certain death.

Each person was allotted only one life. In order to be as careful as possible about that one life, many saw the safest solution in temporarily seeking refuge elsewhere. An overwhelming number left Yangzhou. At the same time, government soldiers and officials withdrew from the city. In the tumult of departure, no one even noticed them withdrawing. The authorities did their best to ensure that they would not be noticed. Since they were later going to report that Yangzhou fought the Taipings bitterly, it would not have looked well for their rapid escape to have been too widely noticed.

"Liwen, what will you do?" Tan Qi understood the present circumstances well.

"I plan to leave the city," he replied.

"As you wish."

"The gates to the city will probably be closed, won't they? We're headed for Shanghai. Yangzhou was merely a detour on our way there." In fact, they had earlier planned to go to Shanghai, but another reason for leaving Yangzhou was the fact that Xinmei did not want to run into her former comrades from the Taiping Army.

"In that case, you may precede us there," said Tan Qi.

"Precede?" returned Liwen, having taken from Tan Qi's tone that the Taipings would be following them later.

"Yes. In a few days or so. Perhaps I shall see you there again." Liwen and Xinmei—and a bit later, Tan Qi would follow—left Yangzhou.

They did not see with their own eyes what transpired thereafter. Tan Qi left Yangzhou shortly after seeing the Taipings' unopposed entrance into the city on the twenty-third. Perhaps he would fill them in briefly on the situation in Yangzhou following their departure.

For some time past, Yangzhou had been a center of the salt trade. Throughout the dynasties in China, salt was a state monopoly, used as the basis for the government's fiscal administration. Thus, the highest among the many prominent government officials resident in Yangzhou was the Liang-Huai salt distribution commissioner, rank 3B. Precisely at this time, there was a change in salt distribution commissioners, and two men—the former and the new commissioners—were both present in Yangzhou. The new man was Liu Liangju, and the old one was Dan Minglun.

The next highest official, rank 4B, was the Yangzhou prefect, Zhang Tingrui. Covering a rather wide area of local terrain, Yangzhou prefecture included the city of Yangzhou, which itself fell within Jiangdu county. The Jiangdu county magistrate was one Lu Wuceng. All of these men accepted Jiang Shoumin's proposal and furtively left Yangzhou.

There was more. Upon receiving news that the Taipings had sent troops into Yangzhou, the director-general of the grain transport, Yang Dianbang, organized a relief force and proceeded with it as far as the outskirts of Yangzhou, though he decided to offer tacit approval of the prearrangement concocted by Jiang Shoumin. Had the relief force not been won over, this plan would not have come into being. Yang Dianbang was rank 2A, making him higher than either of the salt distribution commissioners in Yangzhou. He was formally responsible for the government military forces in this setup.

"They're not going to leave right after they get inside, will they? I didn't count on this happening." Yang Dianbang thought that a trap had been set, and he ordered the Qing troops to his rear to advance.

"This is strange," thought Taiping commander Li Kaifang, enraged. "It looks like they're positioning their men to surround the city."

"Was it a scheme to empty out the city?" There was a stern look on the face of deputy commander Lin Fengxiang.

By a scheme to empty out the city, he was referring to the classical strategy of forcing all defensive forces to withdraw from the city, and after the enemy entered, besiege and attack one's foe within. This was a tactic familiar even to common people through storytelling and dramas.

Yet this scheme did give the appearance that there were no troops inside the city, and it did lure the enemy in. In the case of Yangzhou, they were not hiding any soldiers, and thus strictly speaking this was not a "scheme" to empty the city because of the prior arrangement for all troops to depart. It certainly looked like a trap in form, though.

Hostage Jiang Shoumin was led out onto the city walls and publicly whipped by the Taiping troops with him. As far as the Qing military was concerned, though, Jiang was a man of absolutely no consequence at all. For the Taipings to have taken such a person as him hostage was a big mistake. Exposing Jiang atop the walls as a means of forcing the Qing Army to withdraw was overly optimistic under the circumstances. No matter how severely the Taipings might have beaten this hostage, the Qing troops gave no indication that they were about to withdraw a single soldier.

The Taipings imprisoned Jiang in the Zhenshantang, or Hall of Virtue and Goodness. Jiang Shoumin, the man who boasted of being the benefactor of Yangzhou at the time of the Opium War, was now no longer in any position to play such a role. Overcome by despair, he hanged himself inside the Zhenshantang.

Although the Taiping Heavenly Kingdom had placed its capital at Nanjing, this did not imply that the movement had abandoned the idea of a northern expedition. What they had given up on was the idea of an itinerant dynasty that would set its entire army to the north to capture Beijing. Tang Zhengcai had argued that, since the land en route to the capital was poor and unproductive, a military expedition that would simultaneously support a large traveling army was impossible. They had thus decided to dispatch only a portion of their troop strength.

The Jiangbei Army that now occupied Yangzhou was, in fact, to be used for actions to the north. In successive waves, Taiping units entered the city of Yangzhou, causing increased anxiety on the part of the government forces outside the city. For the Taiping Army, Yangzhou was to be the sendoff point for a northern expedition.

What, then, was happening with the Jiangnan Army that had taken Zhenjiang? In addition to securing Zhenjiang, which faced the main entry into and out of the Taipings' Heavenly Capital, the Jiangnan Army had plans to advance further to the east, seize Suzhou, take Shanghai, and eventually bring the province of Zhejiang under its control. However, at this moment, the Jiangnan Army was unable to move forward from Zhenjiang.

A Qing force of over ten thousand under the command of Imperial Commissioner Xiang Rong had circled around to the east of Nanjing. Here the government army was setting up a base from which to attack the city. This spot would later be called the Southern Imperial Barracks; it lay in an area near the imperial tomb of the founding emperor of the Ming dynasty. The Taiping base of operations outside Nanjing was at Zijin Mountain. Observing the unfolding situation, Yang Xiuqing dispatched a messenger to Zhenjiang, calling for reinforcements for the Heavenly Capital. Far from continuing in their eastward march, they were to double back to the west. Luo Dagang sent a battalion to support the Heavenly Capital, and with 3,000 troops under his own command, he held control of Zhenjiang.

In both Yangzhou and Nanjing were a small number of believers in Catholicism, principally a group that proselytized in conjunction with the efforts of a French priest. Yet rumors were circulating that, after the Taipings took each of these cities, the Catholics were persecuted and dozens of them died. French Legation Minister Alphonse de Bourboulon later traveled to the Heavenly Capital to investigate these rumors. He concluded that there was no basis to substantiate any alleged persecution.

There was, however, a basis for these rumors to continue circulating. From the perspective of Chinese Catholics in the lower Yangzi region, there was much that was strange about the beliefs of the Taiping Heavenly Kingdom. They sensed that it did not quite fit together. The Taipings were, needless to say, not favorably disposed to the Chinese Catholics, who, while hiding behind the mask of fraternal relations, put in a word here or there about their own beliefs and prayers.

"The Frenchman's faith is incorrect. It must be properly changed." This was the general Taiping response. They came to the firm belief that these Catholics' errors were quite severe, for they had placed icons, which they called sacred images and which should have been destroyed, into their houses of religious worship.

Incidents cropped up in various places where Catholic churches were demolished and sacred images smashed. The explanation given was that the Taipings had mistaken these images for those of the Buddha or of other deities and smashed them, but clearly members of the Society of God Worshippers would not have mistaken a holy image of Christ being crucified for a Buddhist icon. Apparently the Taipings had developed a strong antipathy for Catholic missionaries or those converted by them.

Bourboulon's report also noted that the Taiping religion was a new religious sect, and were the Taipings to gain control of China, the Catholics whom the French had worked so diligently to convert would no longer be allowed to continue to live freely in that country.

France later adopted a thoroughgoing anti-Taiping stance and tried to bring the other foreign powers around to support this line. When the English were leaning toward recognition of the Taiping Heavenly Kingdom, France was able to pressure them into calling off any such action.

—5—

"They're like a whirlwind, those fellows. They sped off to the north with the gale winds." Zeng Guofan was in Changsha, capital of Hunan province.

The Taipings had been unable to bring down the city of Changsha, and after they had moved on to the north, Zeng entered the city. The whirlwind-like fellows of whom Zeng spoke were not the fighting men of the Taiping Army. He was referring to Zuo Zongtang and Jiang Zhongyuan, whom he had met in Changsha. At that time Zeng had still not had the opportunity to see the Taipings for himself.

This "whirlwind" had gone at the head of an army to reinforce government troops at Wuchang. The defenses around Changsha were inadequate, and although the Taipings did leave, Hunan remained, for all intents and purposes, a nest for adventuristic bands, such as the Triads. The majority of Triads had left Hunan as part of the Taiping Army, but various groups remained, such as those bearing the names of the Skewer Society, the Red-Black Society, the Hall of Loyalty, and the Hall of Righteousness. To supplement his troop strength, Hunan Governor Zhang Liangji decided to invite the Xiangxiang county *tuanlian* to Changsha.

The *tuanlian* were not regular military organizations. They were self-defense volunteer brigades organized by local men of influence who jointly provided funds for the necessary expenses. Zeng Guofan hailed from Xiangxiang county.

"I've come in response to the invitation, but once I leave Xiangxiang expenses are going to be a bit of a problem." Luo Zenan had broken the ice, with apparent difficulty, after meeting Zeng Guofan in Changsha.

Luo (1808–1856) ran a private academy in Xiangxiang and taught the local youngsters there. He was about three years Zeng's senior, though he was a simple-hearted man—the quintessential village schoolmaster. At the request of his county magistrate, Luo had organized a *tuanlian* centered around his own students and begun their military training. To shore up Changsha's deficient military strength, a Xiangxiang *tuanlian* was called together, though the provincial authorities in Changsha were not about to provide the necessary funds.

"*Tuanlian* have been put together without official support till now, so . . ." The reasons this had been possible were twofold: assistance had been made available by locals, and the constituent members of the *tuanlian* were local folks able to supply their own daily necessities. Once they left their local area and traveled to Changsha, though, things could not continue as they had until that point.

"Might the funds be raised some other way?" he asked. Luo had come to seek the advice of the somewhat younger, though highly placed official and fellow countryman, Zeng Guofan. "Let me think about it," replied Zeng, and he in fact did just that.

Why was it that, since the eruption of the Taiping movement, groups had responded to their call to rise in rebellion in many places in China? Zeng knew full well that the political system had fundamentally deteriorated. There had to be other avenues to pursue.

"Laws are not being strictly enforced," he thought. Though war had broken out, those who ran away claimed victory. If you fled and were not punished or if the punishment was light, those who remained and stood their ground in battle were crazy.

About the time that the Taiping Army took Nanjing, Zeng sent a memorial to Beijing, which called for "severe punishments and rigorous laws." The present deadlock, he argued, could never be broken by continuing to apply the same tepid laws in the same tepid manner they had until then. Punishments had to be made stricter, and laws had to be enforced with greater relentlessness. In order to actualize the spirit of Zeng's memorial, he offered a plan for the creation of a Judicial Bureau. Throughout this period, he had been thinking day and night of a way to implement his plan.

While the structure was certainly important, even more critical were the people who would administer it. Although it would be a government office, Zeng knew perfectly well that bureaucrats, once placed in the official realm, were unreliable. The Judicial Bureau was to be an agency created anew for the purpose of enacting "severe punishments and rigorous laws."

"It has to be something brand new. If it is tainted in any way, it won't work," thought Zeng to himself. When he pondered the actual operations of this Judicial Bureau, words to this effect naturally came to mind.

"Yes, yes . . . they are men of learning." This new soliloquy emerged from Zeng's lips. The "they" here referred to the men in Luo Zenan's *tuanlian*.

A *tuanlian* was usually a group of dashing young men from the countryside brimming with self-confidence in their might, with many only a hair's breadth removed from the world of gangsters. But, Luo Zenan's *tuanlian* was different. He had transformed his private academy *in toto* into a *tuanlian*. In place of the schoolmaster, substitutes would lecture at the academy, and these substitutes had served as military officers.

Officers and soldiers took on a relationship of teachers and learners. The officers were the disciples of schoolmaster Luo, and a teacher's words were to be obeyed absolutely. "If this were ever to become a real army," mused Zeng Guofan, as he observed Luo's *tuanlian*, "it would be a new army altogether."

This army was indeed to be the prototype for the Hunan Army created by Zeng Guofan. For Zeng, though, there was a task of graver import than building armies, or actually a prerequisite to the creation of new military forces. That was the establishment of the Judicial Bureau for the enforcement of laws and punishments.

"Fine," he resolved, and soon he left to meet with Luo Zenan. "I have an idea for the Judicial Bureau, and I'm looking for talented men to staff it. I want the leadership of the *tuanlian* turned over to them," he said.

"I am honored to be recognized, but if the leaders are removed, our *tuanlian* will find it difficult to operate," said Luo Zenan, a bit at a loss in a rather hurried conversation. Zeng seemed to have come to pick him out, and Luo knew well what his disciples were like. They were in the *tuanlian* by virtue of the personal bonds they felt to him, and it was highly doubtful that they would follow the command of anyone other than Luo.

"No, you will remain as a *tuanlian* just as you are. That's the best way to proceed. You will go to the Judicial Bureau to handle business matters, and you will of course be reimbursed for your work."

"Thank you. That will help greatly," said Luo frankly. This way, at least, the leaders would have something to fall back on.

"So, do I have your consent?"

"If I might, there's one thing I should like to request."

"What would that be? If I possibly can, I shall be happy to assist you." Zeng was now thinking in the vein of Luo as his fellow, older Xiangxiang native. For Luo, Zeng was the most successful man from their hometown, and his lofty position climbed into the clouds. Both men spoke to one another in highly polite language.

"I would be much honored," said Luo, "if you would be the leader of my *tuanlian*."

"What? Me?"

"Yes. Otherwise, something inopportune might possibly arise."

"Oh, I see." Zeng now understood Luo's point. Luo's *tuanlian* had the quality of a clear line of command and a clear locus of responsibility. These were the greatest lacunae in the Qing military organization. In other words, there was the danger that instructions and orders from a different line of command might be ignored. At present, Luo was the head of the *tuanlian*, and being outside the leadership, Zeng was afraid lest he be unable to take command over the men in the *tuanlian*. Were Zeng to be placed at a position above Luo, there would be no confusion in the line of command.

"So, what sort of work will the Judicial Bureau undertake?" asked Luo.

"It'll be a homicide bureau."

"What's that?"

"It will be a place where people are put to death. It will not be a happy place, not in the least. If we do not, however, take a stand and boldly put these villains to death, the dynasty will be unable to recover. It's an unpleasant business, to be sure, so I need men with sufficient knowledge to understand the significance of the work at hand, and I'd prefer younger men."

Zeng was speaking slowly, staring directly into Luo's eyes.

"I understand." Luo stiffened the expression on his face and bowed deeply.

—6—

Courts convened at the prefectural and county levels. Those who had committed serious offenses were remanded to the provincial level. Death sentence judgments were in principal carried out after receiving final sanction from Beijing. Zeng Guofan's Judicial Bureau was now going to effect death sentences despite there being no contact with prefecture, county, or provincial authorities and without awaiting approval from the capital.

Spies were sent out and informants were encouraged to come forward with information, as Zeng tried to collect as much raw data as possible. Like scales falling from the eyes, things he had hitherto not understood soon became clear.

There were numerous secret societies with massive organizations in Guangdong, Fujian, and Taiwan. There were as well many groups in Hunan province, but aside from the Triads, they were all divided into a countless number of tiny parties. These groups lacked strong structures and easily fell prey to spies and informants.

Zeng Guofan personally interrogated the criminals brought before the Judicial Bureau. People at the time said, "To emerge from Yutangkou is as hard as crawling out of hell." Yutangkou was the name of the site at which the Judicial Bureau met.

Cruel tortures were an everyday occurrence there. In less than six months, over thirty men who were not executed died in prison. Those sentenced to decapitation or clubbing to death were said to number nearly five times as many.

"Why's he still here?" Zeng had personally examined a man by the name of Gao Yongmu, said to be one of the few local Triads. Triad members in the area had almost all joined the Taipings and ordinarily would have entered the city of Nanjing with them. The Judicial Bureau was at present rounding up and investigating people associated with a small party known as the Skewer Society.

Gao said that once the Triad bandits had gone to Nanjing, they had turned around and come back to Hunan. This piece of information perked up Zeng's interest.

"Whatever happens, I'm doomed. Do whatever you want with me! But, your whole world is soon going to come to a crashing halt." Gao Yongmu had assumed a defiant attitude. He had no expectation whatsoever that his life might be spared.

"Shut up!" shouted one of the young officials of the Judicial Bureau beside him. He was a disciple of Luo Zenan.

"I'll shut up if you tell me to shut up, but in return I'll never answer anything you ask me." Gao retorted.

"This is too much," said Zeng, looking at the faces of Gao and the official by turns.

"Yes, well, I'm terribly sorry. This guy talks too much," apologized the young bureaucrat, as he seemed to contract his entire body.

Zeng Guofan, who was of comparable station to a provincial governor or governor-general, yelled from the flanks and got the criminal, whom he had himself attempted to interrogate, to shut up.

"As long as this stupid official's here, I won't shut up even if you kill me!" Gao Yongmu turned the corners of his mouth down as if to accentuate this sentiment. Because of the torture he had to endure, his face was bathed in blood. His hands were tied behind his back, his outer garments stripped off, and moles were exposed over his entire body.

"An obstinate villain," reported the investigating official of Gao Yongmu. "He offered us not one iota of important information."

Maybe there are other ways with guys who betray nothing while they speak right at you, thought Zeng Guofan.

"Get out of here!" he ordered the young official in a severe tone of voice. "Don't you ever say anything while I'm in the middle of questioning someone. Don't you understand that much? Go out into the waiting room and behave yourself!"

"Yes." The young official's face was pallid.

"To hell with you all," railed Gao Yongmu.

There was no longer anyone else in this room at the back of the Judicial Bureau. Zeng rose from his chair and, as he spoke, slowly walked around Gao who had been seated in the room.

"I'm not going to ask you any more questions. I already know whatever it is you're about to say. I see right through everything. You're best off saying nothing further."

This was a psychological strategy on Zeng's part. When told not to speak because everything is already known, people would want to strike back. Zeng had read Gao's character well.

"What do you think you know so well? I'll be damned if you know our overall design. If you did know, you wouldn't be sitting around here so comfortably," said Gao, and then he spit in the direction of Zeng, who had unexpectedly walked up directly in front of him.

"Is that so? And if you knew our overall strategy, you'd just bite off your own tongue and die. Go ahead, do it!" challenged Zeng.

"We don't make empty threats like you. We link hands with our friends and allies. We're going to turn everything on its head. What do you think of that? My friends are everywhere. Everywhere. They're in Shanghai . . . and . . . and . . . they're in Xiamen . . . and . . ." Gao spit again.

"We know that your gang is still hanging around here. We've already begun to round them up." Zeng chose his words carefully so as to make his counterpart angry to the point of distraction.

"Empty threats, empty threats."

"These are no empty threats, I assure you. We know as well of the people making their way to Shanghai."

"What?" Gao's face became slightly flushed. "It's a lie! Who told you that?"

"Perhaps it was a tiger, or perhaps a mole, or . . . no, that's it—lynx silver, Little Qi, and . . ." Zeng had learned only the names of the men responsible for Taiping intelligence and various schemes. One by one he ran off their nicknames in an effort to force a reaction out of Gao.

"It's a lie, a lie! Nothing but lies!" Gao stood up, shouting angrily and recklessly. Compared to the ferocity of his voice, his words carried little weight. It was clear to Zeng that the strength of Gao's voice was only hiding weakness.

"Let's cool your head off," said Zeng, and he lifted a towel that had been sitting in a wash basin, pressed it against Gao's face, and wiped it one time. The blood on his face came off onto the towel.

"We've known for a long time that Little Qi went to Shanghai to make contact with the Small Sword Society." Zeng looked at Gao's bleary-eyed visage. Gao's lips were quivering ever so slightly, as his face momentarily became pale.

—7—

The Xiang River, which flowed nearby Changsha, emptied into Dongting Lake, and the waters of Dongting were linked to the Yangzi. The latter, as if pushing Dongting to the side, flowed on toward Wuchang to the northwest. About 80 kilometers from Wuchang was Jiayu county. Though it belonged to Hubei province, Red Cliff, renowned as the scene of the ancient battle of 208 in *The Chronicle of the Three Kingdoms,* lay within this county.

A bandit by the name of Xiong Kaiyu had risen in revolt there and burned the county magistrate's office. Jiang Zhongyuan, a man with a considerable military record, had been selected in Hubei to serve as provincial surveillance commissioner. Like Zeng Guofan, Jiang had effectively adopted a policy of terror. Liu Lijian, the leader of a local secret society, was captured and was being held by Jiang.

A messenger from Zeng Guofan arrived at Jiang's office with a secret communication: "Be on the lookout for secret society activities in Shanghai. Please contact authorities at the scene at once."

They were able to put out the fires in Hunan and Hubei with the Judicial Bureau's repression. However, should these fires rise up elsewhere and threaten to spread, the fear was that the situation would be beyond repair.

After questioning Gao Yongmu, Zeng learned that the Triads were apparently planning a massive, nationwide uprising. Gao, it seemed, had been sent from Nanjing to make preparations for an uprising in Hunan and then a call for sympathetic rebellions elsewhere.

Zeng learned through his intelligence network that the most influential Triad affiliate in Shanghai was a group known as the Small Sword Society. Adventuristic organizations affiliated with the Triads were, for the most part, based in southern China, even if they claimed a national network. Though centered primarily in Guangdong, Fujian, and Taiwan, from the time Shanghai was opened as a port city, their influence began to move north, and for various reasons Shanghai also became a center of activity. Steadily, the Small Sword Society had increased their influence in Shanghai.

It would be very dangerous, thought Zeng Guofan impatiently, to kindle the flames in Shanghai.

Shanghai was an open port with British and French concession areas. The United States was to gain its own concession a few years later, and it would in subsequent years be combined with the British one into a joint concession. A highly complex social order was emerging there. In the past, China had confined its foreign trade to the south. When Shanghai became a new center for foreign trade, southerners familiar with the business flocked to the city. Secret societies entered Shanghai with them and laid a foundation for themselves there. Although there was a wide variety of these groups, they tended to be secret underground organizations, and this meant that it was often difficult to determine when they had come into being and who their leader might be. Only recently had the name of the Small Sword Society become known as a band of adventurers. Zeng had learned the name through extraordinary intelligence gathering, the results of which had even terrified Gao Yongmu.

Tan Qi had made his way to Shanghai, but he hadn't a clue about how to proceed from there. Though a secret order had come from Eastern King Yang Xiuqing, Tan Qi was still in low spirits. Before leaving Nanjing, Tan had been called to see the Heavenly King Hong Xiuquan. Nanjing had already fallen to them, but Hong was still in his dragon ship on the river. Back in the days when they had been in Jintian village, Hong had often invited Tan to his home, but since Yongan, they had for whatever reason drifted apart.

It wasn't that Tan Qi was intentionally keeping Hong Xiuquan at a distance. The fact was that, while he was the leader of the Taiping Heavenly Kingdom, Hong himself kept his distance from practical matters. Inasmuch as Tan Qi was responsible for intelligence and other operations, he was intricately involved in practical affairs. As time passed, their contacts became less and less substantial. When he was summoned by Hong, Tan Qi was frankly a bit nervous.

"I hear you're going to Shanghai. Is that right?" Hong had already learned that much.

"Yes, that is correct. I have one piece of business to attend to in Yangzhou, and then I'll just continue on to Shanghai," replied Tan Qi.

"The Triads in the Taiping Heavenly Kingdom have been working hard on our behalf. Their discipline has also improved. We have been with them as brethren since our days in Guangxi, and this is the result of our influence on them. You will probably try to contact the Triad affiliate organization in Shanghai, but they will know nothing of the Taiping movement, and I have my fears about this move."

Hong's phrasing of this last sentence was convoluted, to say the least. By his statement that Tan Qi would "probably try to contact" the Triad affiliate, the sense was that the leader of the Taipings had no responsibility or knowledge of this at all. Whether or not to contact the Triads was ultimately his decision. The plan was of Yang Xiuqing's devising, and there was no particular reason why such an important item as contacting potential allies could not be reported to the Heavenly King.

Hong knew this much from reports, and still he was expressing himself in such a twisted manner. Having been so far removed from all of the day-to-day business of the Taiping movement, perhaps the Heavenly King had become, for all intents and purposes, incapable of opposing the will of the Eastern King.

"What I have heard is that the majority of them come from Guangdong, Fujian, and Zhejiang, and that few of them actually are locals," said Tan Qi.

"It makes sense that few are locals. Until recently they were in small rural villages and had never heard of the Taiping Heavenly Kingdom. They knew nothing of our reverence for the Lord God. They've probably never heard of the Heavenly Father or the Heavenly Elder Brother, either."

"That is probably true."

"Many of them have been absorbed into our army, fallen under our influence, and acquired our beliefs. Yet circumstances will be different now. I hear that they have risen in rebellion in Shanghai and it is we who are coming to their aid. It is not they who are taking actions as a part of us. This worries me. I want their character investigated there. From what I have been able to ascertain, the people in this group in Shanghai are mostly opium smokers."

"What? Are such rumors now circulating?" Tan Qi feigned ignorance, but he too had heard such stories.

"Smoking opium is one thing, but I've heard that the leaders of the secret society are actually involved in buying and selling the drug. This is something that cannot be permitted. If we link hands with such people, I fear for the deleterious effects it will have on us, for there are many among us whose religious faith is still not strong."

"Yes, this is true."

"The entire secret society is probably engaged in this loathsome dealing in opium. It's only a rumor. However, if the rumor turns out to be true, to run the risk of decay and work in concert with them is simply unacceptable. Tan Qi, I want you to examine the situation in detail and report to me."

"Of course."

Tan Qi had no choice but to comply with Hong Xiuquan's orders, though he clearly saw the wisdom of it. He now had a dual set of secret orders. He also knew full well, by the time he got to Shanghai, that the largest secret society there, the Small Swords, was deeply involved in the opium business.

He had already established that the leader of the Small Sword Society was a man by the name of Liu. The problem was how to make contact with him. Should he meet with a man introduced to him by a member of the Hunanese Triads? Or should he see Lian Liwen and listen to the advice of Lian's father? Tan Qi sighed as he stood before Shanghai. The Wusong River flowed at his feet. It met the Huangpu River and then drained into the Yangzi.

Traffic on the Yangzi

—1—

Within Shanghai was an old bookstore known as the Siwentang. The owner, Wei Qigang, was an old man, nearly eighty, who rarely showed his face in the shop. From time to time an elegant, middle-aged woman could be seen sitting at a desk, working in the office at the back of the store.

Next door to the Siwentang was the Shanghai office of the Jinshunji. While the headquarters of this company were in Xiamen, a branch had been set up prior to the Opium War in Shanghai. At that time, though, they had built the shop along the bank of the river to facilitate loading cargo onto junks. As a result of the Treaty of Nanjing at the culmination of the Opium War, Shanghai was opened to foreign trade, and the British established their own concession area there. The Shanghai Jinshunji fell within the zone of this concession.

The proprietor of the Jinshunji, Lian Weicai, transferred the Shanghai branch to the Englishman Harry Wade. Wade had come from the Anglo-Chinese College in Malacca and had been able to gain a mastery of the Chinese language. Though he had worked for the British firm of Mays, shortly after Shanghai was opened he became independent and acquired his own store.

Once his riverbank store was in Wade's hands, Lian Weicai built a new Jinshunji shop next door to the Siwentang. On the outside, the Siwentang and the Jinshunji appeared to be separate operations, but inside they were connected. Lian had served as financier for the Siwentang, and Wei Qigang had placed the shop under Lian's care. In addition to his study of the Chinese classics texts, Lian concurred with Wei's not so geriatric ideas of introducing foreign political, economic, scientific, and technological materials to China.

The man in charge of the Jinshunji in Shanghai was Wen Zhang. Just over fifty years of age, he was the son of the late Wen Han, who had served as the head clerk and the real trailblazer for the Shanghai operation.

Lian Weicai had just arrived from Beijing and was reading a letter from his third son, Zhewen, that had just been forwarded from the Liuqiu (Ryūkyū) Hall in Fuzhou. The letter began with the sentence, "I'm now writing this letter from a place not part of the Liuqiu Islands."

"A place not part of the Liuqiu Islands" meant he was in Kagoshima in southern Japan. When he was in the Liuqiu Islands, he wrote clearly to that effect, and the same was true for Nagasaki.

At the end of his business report, Zhewen, true to his calling, suddenly switched subjects and in a more artistic vein wrote, "Eventually, it seems, Japan will be thrown into confusion." What followed from this point in his letter was entirely different in style as well.

Zhewen reported that Commodore Matthew Perry of the United States Navy had come to Japan at the head of a flotilla of four warships, as envoy to Japan, carrying a message from President Millard Fillmore. Lian Weicai already knew this much. In fact, this information was common knowledge among those involved in foreign trade in Shanghai. Commander E.V. Putiatin of the Russian Far East Fleet had similarly planned to sail a battleship to Japan, information known to just about everyone in Shanghai.

"Seems like those of us here in Shanghai can get a better sense of the foreign influences being brought to bear on Japan than Zhewen, who is in Japan," said Lian Weicai.

Wen Zhang was standing before him, having just returned from Wade's shop. Wade had told Wen Zhang that the American fleet under Perry had sailed across the Pacific Ocean. Harry Wade had come to know Wen Zhang over twenty years earlier, at the time that Wen had been sent by the Jinshunji to Malacca while Wade was a student there. Both had sailed on the *Amherst*. Their relationship was thus not simply one of commercial transactions.

Wade informed Wen of all information he managed to acquire. Hence, Wen had learned from Wade that, "The Dutch Factory in Nagasaki had given the shogunal authorities in Edo prior notice of Perry's coming the previous year." The Japanese shogunate had thus had prior knowledge of the visit of Perry's famous Black Ships. Although the accuracy of Dutch intelligence was corroborated by previous experience, the shogunate decided to conceal it entirely. That would give the impression to the ordinary Japanese that the Black Ships had arrived suddenly.

Furthermore, they did not come, as ships had in the past, seeking food or water. Perry was carrying a letter from the president pressing the Japanese to "open their country." It was this event that might lead to an uproar. For some reason, it appeared that Zhewen was unaware of the fact that the Dutch had given the shogunate advance warning.

"Well, since China's already opened up, all manner of stories make their way here," said Wen Zhang, protecting Zhewen.

"I wonder why he wasn't able to elicit the fact that the authorities in Edo already knew."

"Probably because the shogunate keeps things so secretive. They're worried about unsettling the populace."

"But by hiding the fact, I think they ensure that the shock will be huge if it turns out to be true."

"Probably they haven't come up with any kind of policy in response yet."

"Don't you think Liwen would have been able to uncover even the most top secret information? I think he could have."

"You mustn't forget that Zhewen is first and foremost an artist. He's not really well-suited to this sort of business. But in other areas, he exhibits the finest of talents."

"True enough . . . the right man in the right place. Shall I send Liwen back to Japan? I could then recall Zhewen to Shanghai and turn over operations of the Siwentang to him. That would be just the thing."

"Liwen has worked so hard up to this point on the matter of the Society of God Worshippers, it would be hard to continue without having him here in China. Those are my thoughts, but what do you think?" Wen Zhang rarely opposed Lian Weicai's ideas. To that extent, Lian reconsidered his stance quite seriously in the face of Wen's occasional opposition.

"It would be tough."

"According to Liwen's reports, the future of that group in Nanjing is fifty–fifty."

"Maybe forty–sixty," muttered Lian, as he put his hands on the table and looked up at the ceiling overhead.

"That group in Nanjing" referred, of course, to the Taiping Heavenly Kingdom. By their "future" Wen meant whether or not they would succeed in taking full control over China. Wen saw it as an even bet that this possibility would become a reality, though Lian was a bit more severe in his estimations.

—2—

In a room on the second floor, directly above the room in which Lian Weicai and Wen Zhang were having this conversation, Liwen was listening to Tan Qi. Tan had been ordered by Yang Xiuqing to make contact with the secret societies of Shanghai. However, Hong Xiuquan had ordered him to investigate whether members of the Shanghai secret societies were involved in the opium trade. If they—meaning the Small Swords—were connected to opium trafficking, he was absolutely forbidden to forge any sort of alliance with them. This was the wish of the Heavenly King. There were no conditions concerning contacts in Yang Xiuqing's orders.

"You really do have a dilemma," said Liwen.

"Yes, I'm in a fix," said Tan Qi, shaking his head.

It required no special investigation on his part for him to know full well that the Small Sword Society was tied to the opium trade. Everyone was aware of it. It was an open secret, but then again it was, in fact, hardly a secret of any sort whatsoever. In Shanghai it was common knowledge.

"I understand the Heavenly King's feelings on this matter," said Liwen, "and it's not that I don't see Yang Xiuqing's point as well." How could he best advise Tan Qi, he wondered.

If they took the ideals of the Taiping Heavenly Kingdom seriously, then allying with a band of adventurers who were linked with opium dealing ran the risk of contaminating the movement and should probably be rejected. If, however, they attached particular importance to Realpolitik in the here and now—namely, seizing China—then they would want to establish as close ties as possible with preexisting armed bands that might be used to their advantage.

"What a bind," said Tan.

"What's this? You've got a problem, and a tough one to boot, but Tan Qi, you're such a easygoing, optimistic fellow, aren't you?"

"Ha, ha," smiled Tan Qi, scratching his head. "I'm sorry. I'm speaking half in fun, but I'm tired of thinking about it. I came for your advice."

"Well, let's try to put what you've turned up through investigation together with what I know. After we know as much as we can, then we can try to figure out where to go from there."

"Good idea. I've really only undertaken a brief investigation so far, though."

"Then, I guess we can say they fail on the opium question. They certainly don't seem to be the sort of people who would please the Heavenly King."

"There were a huge number of Triads in Hunan, but there were numerous different groupings and that worked well for the Taipings."

"Uh-huh. You can absorb and teach a large number of smaller groups, but that's not the case in Shanghai, is it? The Small Swords are a large organization and have been from the start."

"They're a bunch of hotshots who are very hard to deal with, but do we ignore them completely because of the opium?"

"Because of the great strength they represent? Even if you were to try to ignore them, I don't think you'll be able to. At least if you're interested in taking Shanghai. I don't think the Taiping movement can afford not to take Shanghai."

Since his arrival in Shanghai, Liwen had come to believe that the future of the Taiping Heavenly Kingdom hinged on the city. Having arisen in the remote countryside of Guangxi, the Taipings needed to have a large window from which to observe the outside world. Without good ventilation, things tend to spoil or desiccate easily. Fresh winds tend to restore a nation's nutrients. Shanghai was the means to gain access to just such a wind.

"I think so too," said Tan Qi, who was now in Shanghai for the first time. "We have no future if we fail to take Shanghai. And to take Shanghai, we have no choice but to link up with the Small Swords."

"The story emerged some time ago that the Small Sword Society had a huge organization, but since it's largely concealed from view, I'm sure there are countless cliques below the surface."

"There are lots of them. The Green Turban Society, the White Dragon Party—frightening ones, too. But, whatever the reason may be, there is a large, united group under Liu Lichuan."

"He's an insignificant-looking guy, but somewhere he apparently had the power of attraction. Everyone who's ever met Liu Lichuan says this. He's not a big fellow, well past thirty years of age, but I've heard he still has a childlike face."

"Shall we try and just meet him? We can keep the Eastern King's concern for establishing contacts to ourselves for now."

"I think that'd be a good idea. We've got to try to meet him."

We would now say that Liu Lichuan was a man with a charismatic character. He was not a man of commanding and dignified presence. Just the opposite, in fact. And yet, there were never any objections when people wanted him to be their leader.

Tan Qi discovered through his investigation that Liu was from Xiangshan county, Guangdong, and he had joined the Sanhe (or Three Harmonies) Society, a secret group, in Hong Kong. Xiangshan county was later to become the birthplace of Sun Yat-sen, and it now bears Sun's pen name, Zhongshan county.

The Sanhe Society was less a wing of the Triads than it was closer to an alternate name for the organization. Being a secret organization, it was girded in cryptonymity. The name "Triad" came from the trinity of heaven, earth, and humanity—hence its occasional translation as the Heaven and Earth Society—and the popular name "Sanhe" was said to have originated in the idea of the harmony (*he*) of the three (*san*) elements of heaven's time, earth's productivity, and humanity's unity.

In the early Qing dynasty, during the latter half of the seventeenth century, a movement to "oppose the Qing and revive the Ming"—namely, to overthrow the Manchu's Qing dynasty that had just come into existence in 1644 and restore to power the Han Chinese Ming dynasty that the Manchus had toppled—was begun by Zheng Chenggong (1624–1662), better known by the name Koxinga. Zheng made his base of operations on the island of Taiwan, and borrowing from the dynastic title of the founding emperor of the Ming dynasty, Hongwu, they called themselves at first Hongmen, or the Vast Gate.

Once the anti-Qing nature of the Hongmen began to attract attention, to avoid this name they called themselves the Sandian (or Three Dots) Society. The Chinese term *sandian* meant, literally, "three points," and it alluded surreptitiously to an important element in the Chinese ideograph "Hong." Sanhe was one of the cryptonyms for Hongmen as well.

On many occasions during the Qing period, the White Lotus Sect in north China had risen in rebellion against the government. Though they were crushed on every occasion, White Lotus remnants adopted various political aspects of Hongmen, which they combined with other religious aspects to forge a new group in secret, and this became the Large Sword Society. The branch of this group that spread into central China was known as the Small Sword Society. Although there were no detailed records of these events, they were apparently a ferociously militant group. People from the Sanhe Society in Taiwan, Fujian, and Guangdong had come to the new capital in Shanghai and taken the name Small Sword Society for themselves, but this was different from the aforementioned Small Swords group. Stories of the courageous fighting of the earlier Small Swords had circulated widely in China, and a number of groups emerged that adopted the same name in an effort to share in the good fortune. We know of such groups in Fujian and even in Singapore.

Only ten years had passed since Shanghai was opened to foreign trade as a result of the Treaty of Nanjing. Major foreign commercial enterprises, such as the concerns of Jardine, Matheson and Company as well as Dent and Company, began setting up shops in Shanghai, but they brought their Chinese staff members largely from Hong Kong. People from Shanghai itself were still generally unfamiliar with foreign trade. Not only people hired to work for foreign enterprises, but many of those engaged in business transactions with foreign concerns in Hong Kong and Canton also moved to Shanghai.

Before the Qing government designated the port of Canton as the sole port for foreign trade, Xiamen (or Amoy, as it was frequently referred to) in Fujian province had been an important port for trade. Zheng Chenggong had established a base there as well and carried on marine commercial activities. Once trade was delimited to Canton, many Fujian merchants moved there. The Chinese monopoly trading companies, known as the Cohong of Canton, were run mostly by men who had relocated from Xiamen.

Similarly, when Shanghai become an open port, large numbers of Guangdong and Fujian merchants migrated there. The population of Shanghai at the time was difficult to estimate, but was probably on the order of two hundred thousand to three hundred thousand. Among them, perhaps eighty thousand were from Guangdong and another fifty thousand from Fujian. In other words, over half of the population of Shanghai came originally from these two provinces. The Small Sword Society of Shanghai was comprised principally of Triads from Guangdong and Fujian, and their numbers were by no means small.

—3—

His complexion was not that of a well man. This was Lian Liwen's first impression upon meeting Liu Lichuan. The contours and features of his face were positively boyish, but the dark coloring was what worried Liwen.

"So that's what it is"—whenever Chinese of this period saw someone with Liu's complexion, this expression always came to mind. Liu was an opium smoker.

"So, you're saying there can be no religious images?" asked Liu Lichuan in an unexpectedly gentle tone. He seemed to be interested in the Taiping movement as Liwen was describing it to him.

"That's right. The rules are extremely strict," replied Liwen.

"I've been hearing about Christianity from foreigners, and there's nothing particularly new about it. It is strange, though, that so many people have gathered together because of it."

Because of his long residence in Hong Kong, Liu had known about Christian religious belief. He had been involved in the sugar business with foreign merchants in Hong Kong, and he could speak English, albeit broken English.

"Excuse me for asking, but there's something strange to me as well," said Liwen. "You're so calm and gentle. How did someone like yourself, thrust before the multitudes, become a leader? It is a bit strange, wouldn't you say?"

"Yes, it's funny," laughed Liu with pursed lips like a young girl. "I think it's because I helped people in distress."

After arriving in Shanghai, Liu had become an amateur physician of sorts. Since his prescriptions worked, the sick flocked to his door. He had come to Shanghai on business, never having contemplated becoming a doctor in the least. He examined patients as if he were playacting a role, wrote prescriptions, and handed them to the patients, but never accepted any remuneration whatsoever. His shingle read, "I will not examine anyone who offers compensation."

"Don't you think it's because you've cured so many people? And you don't charge them anything?"

"If I were a doctor, then I'd surely accept compensation. When I was in Hong Kong, I rented a room in the house of a doctor, and I learned from watching him examine and diagnose his patients. If I'm to be conscientious, I can't collect fees."

In a world with so few conscientious people, perhaps Liu's behavior was the secret to his popularity. As commendable as he was, though, Liu was apparently just as talented in his business dealings. Once he set his sites on a goal, he was the perfect tactician.

"And by the same token, I'll fight over the tiniest amount of profit in business. I guess this is only natural, though I quarreled with Mr. Wen Zhang about a great deal. Haven't you heard?" said Liu, as a bashful smile spread across his face.

That smile is certainly part of his attraction, thought Liwen.

It was no easy matter to bring people together from such different places of origin—Guangdong, Fujian, and now here in Shanghai. First and foremost, it had to be a person who frightened no one. There would be no problem with people from the same local place as he, but if he were to vigorously lead people from other places of origin, it would require not just the use of fear, but of mistrust as well. If shunned by people, he could never expect to preserve his leadership position. "Have you had dealings with the Jinshunji?" asked Liwen.

"Only just recently have they begun. You're important customers." Which was as if to say: And, on the basis of Wen Zhang's introduction, I decided to meet with you.

Indeed, it had been as a result of Wen Zhang's introduction to Liu, though as a matter of business, that he decided to come and gauge "if he might be inclined to engage in business with terrain under the control of the Taiping Heavenly Kingdom." Liu's response was greater interest in the Taipings than in business, per se. Tan Qi accompanied Liwen to the meeting as his "servant" and sat there pretending to be little more than a fool, all the while observing with stunning perception.

The two men returned home from Liu's quarters and discussed their report to Nanjing in a room on the second floor of the Jinshunji. Li Xinmei was there as well at the time, but she showed no interest in the two men's topic of conversation. Having come to Shanghai, she met Liwen's father and had a very positive impression. Even more than Liwen, with whom she had a personal relationship, she felt comforted by having Lian Weicai by her side.

"I wonder what he was like as a boy? How much does Liwen resemble him," thought Xinmei, while the conversation between Liwen and Tan Qi never reached her.

Liu Lichuan seemed strongly inclined toward working with the Taipings.

He had a rudimentary knowledge of the religious teachings of Christianity. He was an opium smoker, and he clearly was also engaged in opium transactions. He himself felt that there was no way the opium business could supply large numbers of followers. His philosophy was that life, even if it meant doing evil things, was better than starving to death. It was better to have the Small Sword Society propose the idea of undertaking joint operations. There were certainly decadent elements among the Small Swords, and any work with the Taipings would necessitate pruning such elements away from their organization. To that end, time was of the essence. Under the present circumstances, though, the Taipings could not press their approaches on the Small Swords. For now the Taipings were well-advised to make contacts with the representatives of foreign nations in Shanghai.

Because Liwen could speak English, he decided to lend the Taipings a helping hand in contacting foreigners. Since Xinmei was with them now, Liwen could not say as much to Tan Qi.

"The people in Nanjing should know full well that Shanghai is an open window to the West. This is a prime opportunity to gather information about the West. Aren't the foreigners trying as hard as they can to gather information on the Taiping movement? I'd like that point in particular passed on to Nanjing." Liwen conveyed this wish to Tan Qi, who was soon to return to Nanjing.

Great Britain had sent Shanghai Consul Thomas Taylor Meadows as close as possible to Nanjing to try to get information about the Taiping movement. One of Meadows's missions was to ascertain if what the Taipings advocated was, in fact, Christianity. This much Liwen knew, because Wen Zhang had learned it from Harry Wade, the British businessman.

—4—

Tan Qi left for Nanjing. This meant Liwen was along the communication line to Nanjing, and it was not a solitary line. Information concerning the Taipings was coming in from a variety of routes, and Harry Wade was especially valuable to this end.

Concerns among foreign circles regarding the Taipings were of many and complex sorts. Could the Taiping movement really topple the Qing dynasty and replace it? Would the foreign powers, under those circumstances, be able to preserve the many rights and privileges they had secured through the Treaty of Nanjing and other concessions? Would they be able to continue trading in the most important commodity—opium? What was the genuine nature of the "Christian" religion in which the Taipings professed faith?

What they really wished to know more than anything else was the tendency in the present battle between the Taipings and the Qing regime. All other questions derived from this one. If the Qing government was secure, then all worries about rights won by previous treaties as well as worries about the opium trade were unnecessary.

Meadows traveled from Shanghai, via Suzhou and Changzhou, as far as Danyang and then doubled back. It was, in effect, a scouting party that lasted less than a week. He returned to Shanghai in the middle of April, less than a month after the Taipings had taken Nanjing.

There was no doubt that what the Taipings believed in was Christianity. The Qing Army was exhausted, and troop strength was very low in the various government base areas. This is what Meadows reported. Since he was only an interpreter attached to the consulate, he submitted his report just as a set of observations. The tasks of collecting information, analyzing it, and rendering a judgment fell to the British minister in Shanghai, George Bonham.

One interesting item in Meadows's report was a notice posted by the Qing Army that carried the following sentence: "The British have promised to help us in our assaults on the Taipings with gunboats." He had no recollection of Britain making such a promise to the Qing government. The purpose of such a false notice was apparently to calm people's uneasiness. However, while this was an explicit use of the knowledge of Chinese living along the banks of the Yangzi that the British had especially mighty war vessels, it also described a lack of self-confidence on the part of the Qing government itself. It was common knowledge at the time that soldiers of the sort presently in the Qing Army would never win any battles against the Taipings. For that very reason, Qing officials had been forced to employ the trick of fallacious information in the posted notices.

"I'm going to take a look. There's something amiss about these notices. We've got to erase all misunderstanding. If I go representing the British Empire, that'll be by far the quickest way," said Meadows as he boarded the gunboat *Hermes* bound for Nanjing. "Also, the Taipings present quite a serious problem, which needs to be looked over thoroughly."

The captain of the *Hermes* was E.G. Fishbourne, and Meadows had traveled with him as an interpreter when he engaged in his scouting activities. Minister Bonham's trip to Nanjing had produced no results in terms of making contact with the Taipings.

The Taipings were fired with the idea of establishing their own state. They now boasted that they had a splendid state with a capital city in the former Nanjing, and they claimed that they had recovered it all from the Manchu regime. The language of recovery indicated that they were continuing a historically Sinocentric tradition. Furthermore, this state had no knowledge whatsoever about the customs of international diplomacy.

Bonham was the minister representing Great Britain. As a diplomatic official he had full knowledge of international practices and norms. He had, of course, expected to be received by the Taipings according to said practices.

On April 27, 1853 the *Hermes* arrived at Nanjing. Captain Fishbourne sent a message to the Taiping authorities that read: "We have not come to fight. We have come to talk."

Meadows went ashore and entered the city through Shuixi Gate. He was able to meet with Northern King Wei Changhui and Assistant King Shi Dakai. He began by insisting that Britain was neutral, wanting to make this as clear as possible from the start because of the suspicious notices posted by the Qing forces.

After declaring neutrality, he asked two questions: What was the foreign policy of the Taiping Heavenly Kingdom? Did they plan to raise troops in Shanghai? The Taipings still did not have a clearly defined foreign policy. They did not even understand the notion of diplomacy itself. Wei Changhui and Shi Dakai were able to respond only to the question about an attack on Shanghai: Shanghai was Chinese terrain, and thus at some point the Taipings would become its masters. Naturally, that would require an effort on their part.

"His Excellency, the British Minister Bonham represents the British Empire, and hence he would like to meet the highest-ranking leader of the Taiping Heavenly Kingdom. I would hope that this might be taken care of satisfactorily," said Meadows.

"The highest-ranking leader, you say?" asked the Northern King.

"Yes, of course, the Heavenly King."

"That would be . . ." Wei's voice trailed off and was too indistinct to make out. He looked over at the Assistant King, who evinced something of a dubious look on his face.

"Can't it be done?" Meadows not only had a remarkable talent for the Chinese language, but was thoroughly conversant as well with Chinese customs. Though he still headed only a localized government, Heavenly King Hong Xiuquan claimed to be the leader of a country. It was to be expected that he would have been outfitted with a variety of concomitant powers.

"We shall respond by letter tomorrow," said Wei Changhui.

Meadows thought that Wei could handle foreign affairs nicely. He seemed suited to that sort of work. He was an affable person, talkative. Shi Dakai sat there throughout the conversations, while Wei did almost all of the talking. Perhaps he had wanted to avoid a particular topic, having chosen to talk primarily about religious matters. They hadn't gotten terribly deep into the subject, but he did offer considerable information on the subject. His tactfulness also befit a diplomat.

The next day a letter was delivered from the Taipings to the *Hermes*. "The

Heavenly King is the leader of the country, and thus all those who come seeking an audience must comply with set procedures and rituals."

Minister Bonham refused to accept this letter. It was not yet a matter of Great Britain's recognizing the Taiping Heavenly Kingdom. At the present time, Britain recognized the Qing dynasty as the legitimate government of China. They had only come to observe this regime that was still not well-known and had been established in one part of China only.

His feeling was that a meeting with Hong Xiuquan would entail something on the order of an oral examination. Hong was in no position to be pompously dictating the prescribed procedures and rites to be followed. Bonham was offended. When the disconsolate Taiping messenger was about to return, with the document he carried having been rejected, Meadows handed a letter written in Chinese and said, "Look, read this through carefully. We'd like a careful investigation done of the position we Britishers have in this country."

The document he had passed to the Chinese messenger was a copy of the Treaty of Nanjing. On April 29, a Taiping leader by the name of Lai Hanying came to the *Hermes.*

"There seems to have been something amiss yesterday. That was terribly regrettable. Is it true that Great Britain has allied with no one?" Lai Hanying had come to verify British neutrality.

"Whatever insignificant mistake may have arisen yesterday, the policy of the government of Great Britain has in no way changed. Neutrality is our immutable policy," said Meadows.

"Would it be acceptable to have this verified by his excellency the minister?"

"There is no need," replied Meadows emphatically. It seemed to Meadows that the Taipings were changing for the better at the whim of their leaders. At least he so surmised from Lai Hanying's request for assurances.

"The matter of the Heavenly King aside, you may meet the Eastern King," said Lai.

"Oh, that's very good. Let's make preparations as quickly as possible."

"We shall come about eleven o'clock tomorrow morning."

"And we shall be awaiting your arrival."

"Might we ask the pleasure of the company of his excellency the minister?"

"The minister came here in order that he might meet with leaders of the Taiping Heavenly Kingdom. He shall be aboard the gunboat all day, and can leave at any time."

"I see. Then we shall see you tomorrow," said Lai, and he departed. As he left, Captain Fishbourne presented Lai with a copy of the Bible in English.

—5—

April 30 was set as the day for the meeting between Eastern King Yang Xiuqing and Minister Bonham, but it ultimately did not come off. If a group could be of assistance to the Taipings—be it the Small Sword Society or the British—then Yang Xiuqing, ever the realist, intended to use them. The British knew that Heavenly King Hong Xiuquan had been turned into a puppet within the Taiping camp, and that they were much more likely to get a better understanding of the Taiping movement from a meeting with the Eastern King than from one with the Heavenly King.

The reason that the meeting did not take place, despite both sides' desire for it, was ludicrous, having to do with ritual. Nanjing had just been transformed into the Heavenly Capital. Its beginning was crucial, and Yang Xiuqing thought that it was essential to demonstrate its dignity.

Although far superior to the Heavenly King in real power, Yang was still beneath him in name, and Yang wanted it known to everyone that he was more powerful than the Heavenly King. Yang had tried to use his meeting with Bonham to enhance his own authority, and the ceremony that Yang demanded in meeting with the British minister was not unlike a sovereign's granting an audience to an envoy from a subject state. It set the stage so that Yang alone would stand out. When he learned of the details of this ritual, Bonham was, needless to say, not amused.

The Taipings may have called themselves a country, but Britain had yet to recognize them. Whatever may have been the case with the Heavenly King, who was their leader, this Yang Xiuqing, who called himself the Eastern King, was clearly beneath Hong, and at most comparable to a prime minister. A minister representing a sovereign state was in no position to kneel down before such a person.

"I don't think they get it. What should we do?" asked Bonham.

Meadows replied, "Meeting under this condition is, of course, out of the question. Shall I try to convince them to change this to a meeting of equals or would you prefer just to call it off and return?"

"They don't seem to be convincible. Let's just call it off. How do we go about this?"

"There are two choices. Either directly make a harsh gesture, denouncing them publicly and condemning their discourtesy, and then just leave, or in a more roundabout fashion claim that circumstances have become inconvenient, making a meeting impossible. Which of these shall it be?"

Bonham thought for a moment after Meadows's explanation.

"Let's use the latter. Let's turn them down with euphemistic language."
Bonham was, after all, a diplomat, thinking always of outcomes.

The Taiping Heavenly Kingdom was a regime that would perhaps unite
and take control over China. Though he had not yet analyzed information
received or what he had himself experienced, Bonham thought the possibilities for this were about fifty–fifty. More than the strength of the Taiping Army,
it was the weakness of the Qing military forces that deeply impressed him.

In the future, these were the people with whom he would have to negotiate a whole host of state-to-state issues. Were he to raise his voice and cause
a big confrontation here, he might find some temporary personal satisfaction, but he ran the risk of jeopardizing later negotiations.

"In our euphemistic refusal, shall I reiterate Great Britain's holding to a
strict neutrality?" said Meadows.

"It would probably be most efficacious to go that route. Mortifying as it
is, let's do it," said Bonham softly.

"It was worth it then to have come up the Yangzi River as far as Nanjing."

"Hmm, you think so? I think it was awful. Running aground at Jiangyin
and all that."

"No, but while we were anchored at Xiaguan, a fair number of Qing people
surely saw the *Hermes*. Leaders of the Taipings—Lai Hanying and lots of
others—were shown around the inside of the gunboat. The dignity of a British warship was deeply engraved on their minds." Meadows was speaking to
console Bonham.

"What Meadows says is true," said Captain Fishbourne from the wings.
"I could see the look of intimidation in the eyes of those men who inspected
the ship. Believe me, I saw it. No matter what they might say, in their hearts
they are fearsome of Great Britain. Since it was we who struck that fear in
them, this voyage will by no means have been in vain."

"Well, I hope so," said Bonham, smiling for the first time.

The next day, May 1, the *Hermes* left Nanjing and set sail to the west, in
an effort to display the majesty of the British gunboat to many more people.
After nightfall, the *Hermes* changed directions and returned to where it had
anchored at Xiaguan, near Nanjing.

They had no further business in Nanjing. On May 2, the *Hermes* set sail to
the east for Shanghai. Early that morning, a letter from Yang Xiuqing was
delivered to the *Hermes,* then making preparations for the return trip. It effectively said circumstances had necessitated canceling their meeting, but he
wanted them at least to read what he had to say in this communication.

"You have come from afar to seek investiture. The Heavenly King is greatly
pleased, as too are the Heavenly Father and the Heavenly Elder Brother. You
have already shown submission with a loyal heart. Having thus bowed to this

decree, your leader [i.e., Bonham] and his many brethren have come to the Heavenly Capital voluntarily. You may come and go through the city gates exerting yourselves or perhaps engaging in trade. You shall never be hindered from doing so in any way, and this is in following heaven's will. We shall separately present you with several copies of the Bible. If you wish to seek the true way, you should memorize it."

Listening to Meadows's translation, Bonham became increasingly irritated. He thought he had lowered the curtain on all this with diplomatically euphemistic methods, but now a strongly worded reply seemed necessary. Hurriedly, Bonham addressed a letter to the Eastern King and the leadership of the Taiping Heavenly Kingdom, and he then had Meadows translate it.

It noted that Britain was not a subject land of China, and that furthermore, if British interests in China, as provided for in treaties, were ignored or British persons or property intruded upon, reactive measures would be taken of the sort that transpired some ten or more years earlier (the Opium War). Such retaliatory measures, speaking concretely, would include the occupation of Zhenjiang or Nanjing.

At 4:00 that afternoon the *Hermes* left Nanjing. When the Taipings received Bonham's stern reply, they sent Wei Changhui to try to soothe things over. Wei was best suited for this task, though by the time he arrived at Xiaguan the *Hermes* had already departed. The next day the *Hermes* reached Zhenjiang, and Meadows went ashore. There he met with the Taiping commander at Zhenjiang, Luo Dagang.

When the *Hermes* had sailed from Shanghai to Nanjing, there had been trouble in Zhenjiang. Wu Jianzhang, the circuit intendant of Shanghai as well as superintendent of Jianghaiguan, had purchased American, British, as well as Portuguese boats to escort the *Hermes* from behind up the Yangzi. His purpose was to attack Taiping encampments along the banks of the Yangzi River, and the *Hermes* was put to use as a kind of shield. As one would expect, the Taiping forces at Zhenjiang under the command of Luo Dagang bombarded the Qing navy, and perhaps inadvertently, the *Hermes* as well.

Those aboard the *Hermes* understood the nature of the complications that had produced these results, and on its return, Meadows went ashore for a conciliatory conversation with the Taipings. Luo Dagang expressed the wishes that the British not aid the Qing and that they cease activities in the opium trade. The British, for their part, demanded a promise that their vessels not be fired upon, and Luo agreed to this.

On May 5, the *Hermes* arrived back in Shanghai after thirteen days of travel.

"I'm not overly happy with what has transpired," repeated Bonham, as if trying to persuade himself, "but the trip was certainly not a waste of time." Captain Fishbourne and Meadows echoed this point of view.

—6—

About the time the *Hermes* docked back in Shanghai, some five hundred military vessels sailed east slowly from Nanjing. The Taipings, having occupied Yangzhou, had begun a northern expedition. There were innumerable Taiping boats anchored on the river between Yangzhou and Zhenjiang as well, but by themselves their numbers were insignificant.

The commanders involved in this expedition to the north were all given the rank of marquis within the Taiping movement. Li Kaifang became the Marquis of Barbarian Subjugation; Lin Fengxiang became the Marquis of Barbarian Elimination; and Ji Wenyuan became the Marquis of Barbarian Pacification. In each instance, the "barbarian" referred to was, needless to say, the Manchu regime in Beijing being crushed.

The boats moving east from Nanjing, together with those awaiting them en route, reached a total of roughly a thousand, and onto them poured the Taiping northern expeditionary army in Yangzhou. They then sailed to the west back toward Nanjing. Some of them entered a waterway to a place called Luhe, while certain armies landed at Pukou, across the shore from Nanjing, and proceeded to march to the northwest.

It was a somewhat roundabout manner of attacking Beijing. The shortest route would have been to march directly north from Yangzhou. This more straightforward course was not taken because the Taipings had received reports that a large Qing Army was moving south in this direction.

In fact, Jiangsu Provincial Surveillance Commissioner Zha Wenjing, who oversaw the construction work on the Yellow River dikes at Jiangpu, had passed this information on intentionally. The Taipings did have excellent military spies who intently sought out the nature of conditions in the north, yet they were completely taken in by Zha Wenjing's artificial ploy, which compelled them to take the circuitous route toward the capital.

Zha most certainly did not go out of his way or make a large fuss in disseminating this story of a great Qing military marching south. He whispered around that it was top secret. Secret orders then went out to farming families in the area of Chizhou and Xuzhou that they were to quietly store military provisions. The more stealthily this proceeded, the more verisimilitude it acquired. In actual fact, the idea of a large Qing Army moving south was a complete hoax.

To avoid this large phantom army, the Taipings took the far more circuitous route to the northwest. The impact was the exhaustion of their munitions to dangerous levels, to say nothing of the exhaustion suffered by the Taiping troops themselves. Ultimately, the northern expedition was a catastrophe. From the government's point of view, Zha Wenjing probably provided the most distinguished service in obstructing the advance of this Taiping northern expeditionary force.

Unlike earlier surging Taiping onslaughts, the northern expeditionary army was but one battalion of the larger force. This was another reason for the major defeat they sustained. After leaving Guangxi, the Taipings had become an "itinerant dynastic house." All members moved as a group. When they brought down the city of Wuchang, they left and moved on toward Nanjing without leaving behind a garrison force. This was the Taipings' first case of an expedition conducted by one part of the larger unit. The dynastic house was already lodged at the time in the Heavenly Capital (Nanjing), and thus it had no need to move again. From this point, the nature of Taiping military actions changed.

The Taiping Army took the city of Chuzhou, killed the local magistrate, and launched an assault on Fengyang prefecture in Anhui province. It was May 28, 1853. On that very day, the Shanghai circuit intendant hired foreign vessels for a second time and attacked Zhenjiang, but was defeated and returned to Shanghai.

While the areas of Anhui and Henan along the route taken by the northern expeditionary army were overcome with fear, the cities along the lower Yangzi—Shanghai in particular—that were connected by river transport to the Taiping capital were beside themselves in panic. Disquiet among the foreigners present eventually began to manifest itself as well. In a flurry of activity, they began piling up sandbags for defensive fortifications in the concession areas.

The highest official of the Qing government in Shanghai was Wu Jianzhang. The area belonged administratively to Jiangsu province, and it had developed considerably over the last decade. The provincial governor was resident in the ancient city of Suzhou. At the time Shanghai was still small in scale. The position of county magistrate of Shanghai was well below that of the circuit intendant. Responsibility for all of this concerning Shanghai fell to Wu Jianzhang.

Wu came originally from Guangdong province. As noted above, although Shanghai was part of Jiangsu province, many former residents of Guangdong had moved and settled in the city. This aspect made Wu's work much easier.

Stringent orders from Beijing arrived to make defensive preparations rapidly. A man bursting with ambition, Wu Jianzhang moved ahead vigorously. He was a government official, but he also had experience in foreign trade. He had sent one of his relatives to Hong Kong and had become engaged in business on a large scale there. Liu Lichuan, leader of the Small Sword Society, had occasion to cross paths with him in Hong Kong.

Liu had a particular aptitude for the sugar business, and often would say to others that he had made a lot of money in dealings with Wu Jianzhang, because all of Wu's transactions in sugar passed through Liu's hands.

This then was Wu's forte, to be able to earn money while serving as a high government official. Since he was a merchant himself, he knew the weaknesses of that group.

"The long-haired bandits have taken Nanjing. Have you heard what they're going to do with Nanjing? Every single day, they're dragging merchants out to do physical labor. They're poor farmers and charcoal makers from Guangxi, and they despise businessmen. They look at people who earn money without a drop of sweat forming on their brows as criminals. If Shanghai becomes a second Nanjing, what do you fellows plan to do?"

Having been spoken to in this way by Wu Jianzhang, the rich merchants of Shanghai had no choice but to come up with some money. As superintendent of Jianghaiguan, Wu was also a sort of economic official (in addition to his political role), and his ability to raise funds was indeed extraordinary. On any number of occasions, he leased foreign ships, replete with their crews, outfitted them with cannons, and made plans to bombard areas under Taiping occupation.

When the hired vessels returned from Zhenjiang, Wu Jianzhang summoned his fellow provincial Li Shaoqing. Li was the director of the local Guangdong provincial hall. A provincial hall of this sort was a place for fellow provincials to get together socially, and it operated schools and administered burial sites as well. It was thus more than just a social club. China was a country in which consciousness of common local origins was very strong, and these provincial halls were powerful organizations.

No matter how high an official he might be in Shanghai, when he called upon Li Shaoqing, Wu had to exert every possible fitting courtesy.

"The talk from Beijing is about *tuanlian*. It took a lot of money to lease those foreign boats, so I'd like to ask the provincial hall for one group of *tuanlian*. Under present circumstances, that means a number of people," said Wu. By "present circumstances," he was referring to the extremely dire straits into which Shanghai had fallen. The trade in commodities, which required use of the great waterways of the Yangzi River, had been paralyzed by Taiping military control over Nanjing. Goods that were to be sent inland up the Yangzi remained in Shanghai, while goods that were to flow downriver to Shanghai did not arrive.

The first to lose their livelihood were boatmen, because the boats were not moving. Massive numbers of boatmen crowded into Shanghai, most of them either from Fujian or Guangdong. Not only the transport trades, but business generally had gone completely sour. Every type of business bewailed the harsh times, as more and more men were laid off every day.

The hard times extended as well to the rural villages. Particular misery was visited on farm families involved in raising cotton, as their debts mounted to the sky. Cotton cloth for transport to the interior rose to the ceilings of the Shanghai storehouses. Needless to say, market prices took a nosedive. Textile mills ceased operations. In the auxiliary industry of weaving, not a sound was to be heard. Though cotton was not selling, rents and taxes were mercilessly exacted. The only thing spewed forth from the textile industry, stopped in its tracks, were unemployed workers.

Because of this situation, there was sure to be a rush of people to join a self-defense corps, if only as a means of survival.

"I understand completely. I shall begin immediately to gather the men," said Li Shaoqing. They both knew that present circumstances were such that there was no need for negotiations.

"You may go ahead and choose them. I shall rely on you. Do select men who are young and strong. Also, make sure they have no connections to the Small Swords," added Wu Jianzhang.

—7—

"That's an impossible order. How can we put together a large group of young men who have no links to secret societies? The circuit intendant has got to know this," grumbled Li Xianyun after coming to visit Lian Weicai. Li Xianyun was the director of the Fujian provincial hall. He held the same position vis-à-vis Fujian that Li Shaoqing did for Guangdong.

After Circuit Intendant Wu Jianzhang had summoned his friend Li Shaoqing and asked him to help with the *tuanlian*, he called upon the Fujian representative, Director Li Xianyun. He broached the same subject by asking him to do precisely what he had already requested of his counterpart from Guangdong. That made it impossible for Li Xianyun to turn him down.

As for stalwart young men, the first that came to mind in Shanghai were the boatmen, who were now largely unemployed. But, in one form or another, most of them were connected to secret societies. Much like in the large Japanese businesses today, at the same time one enters the company, one also goes through the motions of entering the union. Work aboard ship was group oriented and dangers were ever present. Boatmen naturally had their own organization, and their leader naturally had acquired considerable influence. This organization, be it the Sanhe Society or, in Shanghai, the Small Swords, was above them.

"So, what will you do?" Lian Weicai asked his friend and fellow provincial.

"There aren't any boatmen who are completely unconnected to the Small Sword Society. These aren't people in prominent positions, are they? Actually, when I go out recruiting, the leaders of the Small Swords won't sign up. They understand that. The authorities hate them," replied Li Xianyun.

"You mean Circuit Intendant Wu Jianzhang."

"Exactly, and that's a problem."

"They're from the same village."

"Weicai, without any wrangling, could you speak to those two? If it comes from you, they'll have to listen."

"No," said Lian, as a quiet smile floated upon his visage, "that will be unimaginably difficult. If I pay a visit to them, they'll probably agree to meet me, and they'll probably listen to what I have to say. But they're no longer individuals."

"What do you mean?"

"They have a large number of people under them, and they no longer possess the freedom to act as such. Even if they were to act as they pleased, the people beneath them wouldn't let it happen. If they try forcibly to get their way, they'll jeopardize their position. That's what they've both become. If you try to move Wu Jianzhang, the authorities as a whole will have to be moved. Try and change Liu Lichuan, and you take on the entire Small Sword Society," Lian explained with great care.

There was an individual feud between Wu Jianzhang and Liu Lichuan. They were from the same hometown, and they had worked together in business. In spite of this, they were on bad terms. Indeed, it was probably more accurate to say that it was because of it that their relations had soured.

As a consequence of his sugar business in Hong Kong going badly, money having been stolen from him, and his being forced into a serious bind accordingly, Liu Lichuan had found himself entangled in legal problems and had come to Shanghai. After all, Wu Jianzhang was in Shanghai. He was a man who had once made Liu a lot of money, and was now working as a high local official there. However, Wu assumed a cold attitude toward Liu, who was now in reduced circumstances. He curtly turned him away at the door.

Wu knew that Liu had come to Shanghai before he appeared at his door. Intermediaries, even some very close to Liu, brought Wu a variety of reports on him. "Liu Lichuan has arrived in Shanghai," went one such intelligence report, "and he's telling everyone from his hometown that Wu Jianzhang owes his present position to 'my support, to the money I earned for him, and the money supplied him by the authorities made him a successful man.'" Wu bristled when he heard this.

To be sure, Liu had been of assistance to Wu in business in Hong Kong. The profits from their business transactions, though, were divided according to prior arrangement. There were countless sugar brokers in Hong Kong other than Liu Lichuan. Wu had hired Liu out of goodwill toward a fellow local. He had literally picked Liu out of a crowd. While Liu surely owed Wu a debt of thanks, he seemed now to be demanding just that from Wu. Things were out of alignment here.

"There isn't much in the sugar business. At that time, sugar was a tiny part of my business. Also, things probably would have gone more smoothly if I'd hired someone else. I don't know what he's all puffed up about. He's going to come see me soon, but I won't do it. So when he comes here, just send him away, and don't stand on ceremony." This was what Wu had said to one of his staff members.

Liu was indignant when Wu refused to see him. The animosities between them had come full circle. If Wu had been so kind to him, even given him work, because of a past friendship, then perhaps he wouldn't have become the leader of the Small Swords. When living became exceedingly difficult, he had relied on the secret societies, and now he had acquired considerable popularity for his playacting at doctor. Perhaps given a bit to bragging about himself, Liu still had the ability to put others at ease.

The time had come in Shanghai for someone to bring together and manage all the secret society elements in the city. There certainly was no shortage of extremely ambitious secret society leaders, but from somewhere among them a voice of opposition was raised.

Actually, Liu Lichuan had been selected as leader of the Small Swords simply because there had been no opposition to him. If he'd had no reputation whatsoever, then there would surely have been some opposition, but Liu had acquired a name for treating sick people for free. He liked to help people. He was not a coercive type of man, and he seemed to be good-natured.

In this way, Liu Lichuan became the leader of the Small Sword Society, and when Wu Jianzhang learned this, he was not pleased. Until then, Liu had been crying through the back streets of the city that it was he who had been Wu's benefactor, but now he took it to the main streets.

As a high-ranking official, Wu was beginning to regard the Small Swords with enmity. Originally, his superiors had been uncomfortable with the secret societies, but were unable to bring them completely under control. Secret societies permeated the breadth of society, and to deal with them was an endless process. Intelligent local officials had been able to get along well with secret society leaders. They had an understanding. In his own way, Wu had worked well with the secret societies when they were split up into countless competing factions. When they came together, it was none other than the despised Liu Lichuan who was sitting in the highest leadership position, and the will to continue the previous arrangement vanished. Thus, when Wu requested help with the *tuanlian*, he added the demand that the men be unconnected to the Small Swords.

Mutual individual misunderstanding had now progressed to an opposition between the government and the Small Sword Society. Even if the two leaders could be reconciled, all those under them would never listen.

This was what Lian Weicai was pointing out.

"Quite a mess, isn't it?" said Li Xianyun, and he returned home.

About this time, the leaders of the Small Swords were gathering at Liu Lichuan's home. Recently government control had become more intrusive. Officials had even become intolerant of something as trivial as gambling. The Small Swords' money-making operations had been frequently raided, and their leaders had to hammer out countermeasures.

"It's terrible that my relations with this ungrateful Wu Jianzhang soured, so everyone's getting dragged into it," said Liu, his head lowered. It was saying precisely things of this sort that probably contributed to the root of his popularity.

"There's no need to talk that way. We're the sort of men who share the same fate. We'll all work for you. That's what I want to talk about today. No one's the least dissatisfied with you," said Pan Kexiang, a young leader of the group.

"That's right," said various voices from all sides. "That's right."

They were planning a strategy to infiltrate members of the Small Sword Society into the *tuanlian*. The Small Swords were saving people who either had had experience raising trouble or whose names might be known, and rather were going to place those who were the most inconspicuous within the *tuanlian*. They were gathering that day to prepare a list of names.

"I'm ready," said Pan Kexiang by way of conclusion. The fierce antigovernment sentiment at that meeting of the Small Sword Society was virtually palpable.

"Quite a surplus of enemies that Wu Jianzhang has made," said Lian Weicai to his son, Liwen, at about this time, shortly after Li Xianyun had left.

26

Love and Hate in the City of Shanghai

—1—

After she reached Shanghai, Xinmei seemed to regain consciousness. Everyday she lightheartedly went out somewhere or other to do this or that. Even if it was only to go sightseeing, she would have occasion to meet people.

"I have business to attend to," she would say, but she would never describe what that business was. Liwen, for his part, never asked. He simply understood.

It was reassuring to her that so many of her fellow provincials were now living in Shanghai. Among those from the province of Guangdong, she felt a strong sense of affinity particularly for the members of the Triad Society, the so-called Hongmen, for her bandit comrades of old had largely been members of the Hongmen.

"It's so easy to absorb the atmosphere of Shanghai," she said, expressing this sentiment.

Yet there was something uneasy at the bottom of her heart. She had joyously lost herself in the Society of God Worshippers, and when she set out to transform the group of men under her command in imitation of that group, there had been a freshness, a vivacity in her life. Now, though, that fever had died down. It was the same thing, that same atmosphere now in Shanghai, she thought, though she worried that the same enthusiasm would also at some point in the future dissipate.

To eradicate her sense of unease, she decided to stay as active as she could. If she remained busily moving about, she would have no time to worry about unnecessary things.

Having seized the city of Shanghai, they would link up with the Taipings in Nanjing and overthrow the Qing government. All those in the Hongmen fold had this on their mind. They also saw that they were creating a world in which there were no swaggering, arrogant officials and in which the poor had no worries.

Although Xinmei despaired of the Taiping movement and had separated herself from it, she had once been a part of it. Something still fascinated her about the Taipings, but there was something equally repugnant to her about them. The Taipings in their present guise repelled her. If they were to correct their ways a bit, she thought, they might improve. Were the Hongmen in Shanghai—that is, the Small Swords—to make contact with the Taipings, then wouldn't the Taipings have to change, even if only a little? Such was Xinmei's hope. And so she rushed around, keeping herself busy, in her hope and unease.

About the time that British Minister George Bonham boarded the *Hermes* to make his visit to the Taipings in Nanjing, a peasant uprising occurred in Qingpu, near Shanghai county. It was a tax resistance movement, as occurred frequently at this time in China. The harvest had been bad, and the peasants were unable to deliver as much produce as they could in an ordinary year.

For the peasants this was a matter of life and death, and under the capable leadership of Zhou Lichun, the uprising burst onto the scene. The Qing government sent in troops to suppress the movement, and under Zhou's command the peasants armed themselves with farming implements and resisted the troops. The government's armies were unable to defeat these peasants and ultimately had no choice but to withdraw.

The Qingpu uprising was left in a half-finished state. The government soldiers had retreated, but they had not acceded to the peasants' demands. Zhou Lichun remained in rebellion and never knew when the enemy might attack again. Yet, since the authorities were busy with a host of other matters, they were not overly concerned with an uprising of a bunch of peasants. The Taipings occupied Nanjing, and Shanghai now had to fortify itself in a variety of ways in response to this occurrence. If the peasants let down their guard, then the government might again send troops in their direction against the Qingpu uprising.

The peasants of Qingpu were nervous. Zhou Lichun prepared against the eventuality of another assault with a number of strategies, such as strengthening the guard. There was no way to turn back now. They had already crossed the all-important line and become an antigovernment movement. This was an issue not only for Qingpu, as Zhou Lichun conceived it, for they might pursue the avenue of expanding the size of the antigovernment movement. To that end, Zhou had set his sights on Shanghai, which was then teeming with men and women out of work.

The strongest organization within Shanghai of an antiestablishment bent was the Small Sword Society, and Zhou naturally was eager to forge contacts with the Small Swords. Xinmei served as the intermediary between Zhou and the Small Swords.

"I'm busy, I'm busy," she said as always, coming out of the Siwentang. She met a young man, Zhou's messenger, at a tea house near the Lesser Southern Gate to the city.

Tea houses were a social gathering place for common folks. One purchased tea leaves and then placed them in a teacup. The hot water was free, and one could drink as many cups as one wished. As the population of the city had recently risen so dramatically, living conditions in Shanghai had declined. Only the privileged few were in any position to invite guests to their homes for conversation, and ordinary people took care of most matters in tea houses.

Zhou Lichun's young messenger announced that he was a teacher in a rural school, and Xinmei, according to plan, was the proprietor of the Siwentang who had come to show the teacher a copy of a textbook.

The bustling tea houses were always packed with people. As the numbers of unemployed in the city rose, the tea houses flourished, for a tiny tea-leaf fee enabled one to sit there all day long. Not only was the hot water served gratis with purchased tea leaves, one could also buy noodles, dumplings, and other small items of food.

They had planned to forge this secret connection under cover of the tumult in such an establishment. They couldn't, though, be negligent of their surroundings. They eyes of the world were upon them, and they would never know if someone were to hear what they were doing.

"When is your cousin's child due?" asked Xinmei.

"She'd like to give birth tomorrow if she could. She's been grumbling about everything that's got to be done in preparation. She'll be in real trouble if her folks don't help her get ready," replied the messenger, with a scowl on his face.

The discussion of "giving birth" meant rising to take action. The peasants in Qingpu, still hanging in the balance, hoped that the Small Sword Society of Shanghai would rise in rebellion as soon as possible.

"I'm sure the birth won't be that late," said Xinmei with a smile.

"It's just that the people in the neighborhood are becoming a little jittery."

"Look at this beautifully printed book. What would you say to using it in your school?" Xinmei removed a single volume from the packaging in which it was wrapped. It was a commentary on the collected sayings of Confucius, printed by the Siwentang. As she turned the pages, she saw that the printing had been done quite sharply indeed.

"I can't make this decision solely on my own. I'll have to take it home and confer with people back there first. I hope that's agreeable."

"By all means take it with you." In fact, sewn into the binding of this innocuous text was a document of communication.

In a corner of the tea house a quarrel had broken out.

"It's that disgusting habit of yours, which you've never corrected. Maybe we should get the authorities to correct it for you."

"Did you say the authorities? This is no time for jokes! The authorities couldn't get anything done now even if they wanted to. They're going to be swept out of power before you know it anyway. They've already started in Nanjing, and Shanghai's not that far behind."

"You think it's safe to go around talking like that?"

"Sure. Who should I be afraid of? The authorities are busy right now making preparation to flee. They've got no time to worry about other people's bad habits."

"Maybe you want the officials to overhear. I don't know."

"What are you talking about? What a coward! It's people like you who shut their mouths in fear of the authorities now."

"Ssh!"

"Hey, I'll scream at you in as loud a voice as I please. The authorities are a lost cause. They say the Small Sword Society will throw the authorities out this fall. Zhou Lichun's going to help them too. Everybody knows that!"

"Go to hell!"

"Oh, are you going to turn me in to the authorities? I beg your pardon."

The two participants in this quarrel did not seem to be drinking to particular excess. Xinmei and the young man with her looked at one another. The Confucian text was hidden away in the young man's bundle, and in this manner they communicated in secret. Still, though, the link between the Small Swords and armed peasants in Qingpu seemed already to have become common knowledge.

"You think someone leaked the information?" whispered Xinmei furtively as they left the tea house.

"Perhaps they just expected that our groups would forge an alliance."

"You think it does seem perfectly natural?"

"Yes," said the young man, as he adjusted the package under his arm.

—2—

"It's going to happen this fall."

"The Small Swords are going to seize the realm this fall."

"I've heard that they're going to do it at the time of the harvest moon."

Shanghai had become an arena of wild rumors. One after another, the wealthier people of the city were fleeing. Some did hire bodyguards, but in times of emergency these bodyguards might just as well become thieves. By the end of summer, respectable store owners had almost all left the city.

"With all this going on, if we don't leave Shanghai, it's probably going to incur suspicion," said Lian Weicai with a forced grin. It was extraordinary at this point to see a merchant of his caliber still holding his ground in Shanghai. The suspicion was that they felt at ease and could thus remain in Shanghai only because of ties with the bandits.

"We'd better leave," and the Lians departed the city.

The seventh month of the lunar calendar was already autumn. By that time, Xinmei's secret maneuverings had already transpired, and the alliance between the Small Sword Society and Zhou Lichun was a fait accompli. Not a single soul doubted for a moment that the uprising of the Small Swords was anything but a matter of timing. Though he had left the city, Lian Weicai had only returned to his former haunts. The commercial house of Wade in the concession area by the river was the Jinshunji's original shop. On the entranceway hung a sign in Chinese characters that read, "Weide [Wade] Company." Most foreign merchants in Shanghai at this time were using Chinese characters for their names. The Jardine, Matheson and Company—champions of the opium trade—were known as "Yihe"; the Dent Company was known as "Deji"; and the Hong Kong and Shanghai Bank was known as "Weifeng." When these concerns had contacts with Chinese, it was always more convenient to use their Chinese names.

"How long do you think you might stay here?" asked Harry Wade, smiling.

"I'm really not sure myself."

"Ha, ha, I guess we'll never know unless we ask Mr. Liu." By Mr. Liu, Wade was of course referring to Liu Lichuan, leader of the Small Sword Society.

"I'll bet if you asked, he wouldn't even be able to tell you himself."

"Shall we ask Mr. Wu? We could then compare the two men's stories, and some sort of general answer would probably emerge," said Wade. The Mr. Wu mentioned here was the circuit intendant of Shanghai (his official bureaucratic title was rather longer), Wu Jianzhang.

"All sorts of speculation is circling about Sanguan these days," said Lian with a smile. Sanguan was Wu Jianzhang's pseudonym. In foreign records of that time, it was often written as "Sam-qua," probably indicating that he was the third of three brothers.

"The Manchu emperor in Beijing and the Heavenly King in Nanjing should probably also listen to each of their stories," said Wade, laughing, twirling the moustache beneath his nose.

After going independent and establishing his own store, Wade's business had progressed smoothly. He had already outrun the Mays Company, at which he had formerly been employed. In sheer quantity of business, he had yet to reach either Jardine Matheson or Dent, but in Shanghai he had already become the leading commercial enterprise from everyone's perspective. Everyone knew that behind Wade stood the Jinshunji.

"I'm beginning to feel ashamed of being in your way for far too long. I'd really like to get things in order as quickly as possible."

"No, no, you're more than welcome. Please, feel free to stay at my home for as long as you'd like."

Wade's words were said in earnest, and were not mere talk. He knew better than anyone that what he had that day he owed to the full support he had enjoyed from Lian Weicai.

"What kind of perspective on these events do the foreigners have?" asked Lian.

"There's a large admixture of hopeful observations. They're all hopeful because they want to carry on an active trade again soon, and they'd like the troubles to be resolved as rapidly as possible."

"So, is there any chance that the foreigners may resort to the use of armed force?"

"As far as I am aware, Great Britain is remaining strictly neutral, an ally to no one. This information was conveyed to me because Minister Bonham recently traveled to Nanjing."

"I understand Britain's posture in this well, for they have no way of knowing what regime may be in power in the next era. What about other countries, though?"

"The United States may be even more neutral than Britain. I heard this from Mr. Oliphant, so it's certainly true."

Ever since the days when Sino-foreign commerce had been confined to Canton, the Oliphant firm had been one of America's most influential. It had also rigorously remained out of the opium trade and thus won considerable trust from the Chinese. Diplomats sent to China by the United States would unhesitatingly solicit Oliphant's opinions on matters concerning China, and whatever Oliphant said was effectively the policy of the United States of America.

"The problem, then, is France."

"Mr. Lian, you know everything there is to know about this matter, and have no particular need to seek my views. In fact, I intend to study many of the facets of this case from you. In this sense, if I were to state my more hopeful observations, I'd like to see the present troubles continue. Ha, ha." Although Lian had not really heard from Wade what the atmosphere was among the foreigners, he had enough raw material to divine it clearly.

Given the opportunity, France, a late-developing country in the area, would want to catch up with Great Britain in trade with China. The French concession area was built along the Huangpu River, just to the north of the Shanghai county seat. It was smaller than that of Britain, though France planned to expand it.

Since there was at present a great difference between the two countries in their quantity of trade with China, to close that gap all at once, France had to do something drastic. While Britain was professing its strict neutrality, France was clearly beginning to adopt a posture of allying with the Qing government. It clarified this attitude with a kind of gamble. It tried to win the gratitude of the Qing government, which ultimately would mean obtaining a great reward. If, on the other hand, the Qing government were to be destroyed, the regime that replaced the Manchus would surely punish the French. Because it was a gamble, the French were naturally aware of the dangers.

"The longer the troubles continue, though, the greater the difficulties in pursuing business ventures. Are you going to be all right?" Lian was asking as an older colleague in the same profession.

"I can continue for about two years not doing anything."

"That's fine. But both warring camps will continue their everyday lives, and they can't very well ignore industry. There's certain to be commercial transactions going on."

"It'll just be difficult to engage in."

"That's for sure. If anything, it'll only become more difficult, but that may be an opportunity to demonstrate real strength."

"It should test real strength, that's true."

"Also, Mr. Wade, you may want to take this opportunity and shift your gaze toward Japan. Admiral Perry has only recently come knocking at Japan's door. It's a kind of sign."

"Japan?" said Wade, folding his arms across his chest in a broad gesture.

—3—

The harvest moon corresponded to the fifteenth day of the eighth lunar month, and the prediction of a Small Swords uprising on that day turned out to be just a little later than the actual event. It would be hard to say that this revolt came as a great shock to anyone. They had been encouraged beforehand in loud and no uncertain terms to rise in revolt. It was not really a matter of whether they would rise up or not, but a matter of when.

Though an uprising was, thus, a foregone conclusion, what was the government to do in the interval before it happened? The Small Sword Society was like a typhoon: the general contours of its coming were known. Shanghai Circuit Intendant Wu Jianzhang and Shanghai County Magistrate Yuan Zude (1811–1853), who represented the authorities locally, met to discuss appropriate countermeasures.

"Rapidly disband all parties and cliques, rectify evil, and follow what is good." So read a proclamation posted everywhere throughout the city. But a notice of this sort had no more value than the paper on which it was printed, and the Small Swords' preparations for an uprising became ever more public knowledge with each passing day.

County Magistrate Yuan was an avidly desperate man. In command of several hundred government soldiers, he captured seventeen members of the Small Swords who had committed acts that were beyond the pale. Yet, shortly thereafter Li Xianyun, director of the Fujian provincial hall in Shanghai, came to Yuan's office to seek a meeting with the magistrate.

"I know that what I'm asking," said Li, in a manner bordering on coercion, "creates a burden for you, but I can no longer discharge the obligations of the directorship. I've decided to resign, though I have no idea what I shall do afterward."

"I didn't want to arrest those fellows," said Magistrate Yuan, "but what they did was simply too outrageous. As Fujian director, you too are going to be in even bigger trouble if you can't bring them under control."

"I have tried to the best of my abilities, and you can see the result. So, I am resigning. Please be very attentive to what follows."

"No, no, no. Now, just wait a moment," said Yuan, panicked.

Men like the managers of the Fujian Hall and the Guangdong Hall played intermediary functions between the people and the government. There was no doubt that, should these halls cease to exist, the government would necessarily come into direct contact with the people, and chaos would ensue. The county government had no capacity whatsoever to interact with the vast, intangible masses of the populace. And the county magistrate knew this better than anyone else.

"Whether I wait or not, I have to resign with those seventeen fellows under arrest," said Li Xianyun. "I wonder who shall succeed me. I hope they appoint somebody good."

"I guess I have no choice but to release them. I have one request. Please be discreet, and don't let them do anything outlandish."

Magistrate Yuan found that he had to mobilize several hundred government troops and discharge the seventeen arrested men that very day. The police functionaries, the first line in maintaining public order, were enormously shocked, to say the least. They had worked so hard to capture the guilty ringleaders, and now they were being released almost immediately.

One police bureau chief by the name of Mao was a man of particularly staunch will. People called him by the nickname "Head Detective Mao." Needless to say, he exploded with rage when he heard of the settlement reached by Magistrate Yuan. He sent the roster of well-known blacklisted secret society leaders to the subbureaus under his jurisdiction and added the note, "If apprehended, execute immediately."

Since, for all intents and purposes the leaders of the Small Swords acted in public, if the police wanted to arrest them, it would not have presented any great difficulty. One officious local police officer did apprehend a certain Small Swords' leader and upon doing so immediately spit out, "If I don't release you, they'll kill you." Blanching, he soon let his prisoner go free.

There was more. The following day it was discovered that Head Detective Mao, covered in blood, had been dumped into a mountain of garbage. He was seriously wounded and on the verge of death, but somehow they were able to save his life. He, though, returned to the countryside, where he continued his convalescence, and never reemerged in Shanghai. After the incident there were no further officials sufficiently bold to risk trying to arrest any members of the Small Sword Society.

The two hall managers, Li Xianyun and Li Shaoqing, suggested to Wu Jianzheng: "The root of the present unrest is the problem of unemployment. If you can get these people jobs, the troubles will surely die down. If they had an income and were organized into the *tuanlian*, then you will probably have killed two birds with one stone. We'll see about raising the necessary funds."

"You have a good point," agreed Wu. "It's best to strike first while the iron is hot."

They decided to solicit from gentry-merchant sources 30,000 pieces of gold annually for administrative expenses. Though it had seemed like a bright idea, the number of members of the Small Sword Society was far more than they had imagined, and 30,000 pieces of gold came to a piddling amount when divided among such an immense number. It was like throwing water on a hot stone. It was far less than the needed amount, hardly an arrangement likely to alter the present state of affairs.

Zhou Lichun and his followers rose in rebellion on the third day of the eighth lunar month. They seized Shanghai's neighboring county of Zhading and issued a proclamation that would "calm the people."

The proclamation noted that "headquarters has received orders from our superiors," but it failed to specify who those superiors were. Eight items were attached at the tail end of the proclamation:

1. Anyone who divulges military secrets will be executed.
2. Anyone who fails to organize into the appropriate units will be executed.
3. Anyone who behaves in an illicit manner with women will be executed.

4. Anyone who spreads fallacious rumors and disconcerts the people will
   be executed.
5. Anyone who obstructs the transport of grain will be executed.
6. Anyone who snoops around about military secrets will be executed.
7. Anyone who keeps provisions to himself will be executed.
8. Anyone who fearfully refuses to come forward will be executed.

The Zhading county offices were destroyed by the rebel forces, and County
Magistrate Feng Han fled for his life. The time that had been long in coming
had arrived.

—4—

"Something red, pure red. Show me whatever you have." Xinmei was shop-
ping in a clothing store.

"Red? For a happy occasion, then," returned the clerk.

The Chinese set a high value on the color red for felicitous events. At the
time of a wedding, for example, people would hang red curtains up everywhere. It was thus perfectly reasonable for the shop clerk to assume Xinmei
would be using whatever she purchased in connection with an auspicious
occasion.

"Anything's fine, as long as it's in red cloth," repeated Xinmei.

"About how much?"

"I believe I said everything you have."

"Yes, you did, but . . ." The clerk seemed displeased as he looked toward
the back of the shop.

Being no exception to the prevailing general rule, the proprietor of
this shop and his entire family had already fled to the suburbs. Leaving
behind orders that the shop must on no account be closed, only the clerk
now remained. Virtually all of the higher-quality merchandise had been
moved to safer quarters, and all that was left to display in the shop was
of a sort that came with apologies. This situation prevailed in most Shanghai shops at the time. Although a trading firm on the level of the Jinshunji
did not display merchandise, as a shop it seemed to offer a wide variety of
goods.

"So, how much do you have here?"

"I'm afraid I have only eighteen bolts of red cloth."

"I'll take it all," she said, turning around and without so much as asking
the price. A cart was stopped in front of the shop. A man who had been
standing at its side came inside shrugging his shoulders.

"Pay him and then carry this out to the cart please," said Xinmei to this man, a stout fellow of about thirty years of age. He had a piercing look in his eye and a large mole on his jaw.

"How much is it?" There was a certain grim quality to his voice.

"Uh . . ." The clerk hesitated momentarily.

"Look, I'm going to pay you whatever you say. But the price better be fair, or things will turn out badly later. So, what is it, how much?" he said, with his lower lip protruding.

"Um, I'll sell that to you at cost. Uh . . . it's right here in the purchase book." The clerk took out the thick purchase book and opened it before the heavyset man. It was at this juncture that the clerk realized the identity of his customer. There was no longer any doubt that the red cloth was being bought for the Small Sword Society.

Someday soon, in due course, Shanghai was going to fall into the hands of the Small Swords—everyone in the city was saying this. The clerk was a man from the countryside who had been in the city now for some six years, and it was apparent to him as well that the Shanghai officialdom was incapable of suppressing an uprising by the Small Swords. Once the Small Swords took control of the city, no one doubted for a moment that those guilty of earlier acts deemed unfavorable to the Small Swords would be visited with merciless retribution.

Thus the clerk brought out the purchase book to explain as clearly as possible that he would not be making an excess profit on the cloth.

"So, you'll get no profit on this deal, will you?" ask Xinmei from the wings.

"No, I'm no longer concerned with making a profit. If I don't take a loss, I shall be plenty satisfied. Yes, uh, indeed, I'm actually quite happy with this exchange." A bead of perspiration rolled down the tip of the clerk's nose.

"Look, business is business. I'm going to add ten pieces of silver to the amount he asked for," said Xinmei to the man shrugging his shoulders.

"Fine, let's do it," he said, and pulled out a pouch full of silver.

Xinmei had not only purchased red cloth from this shop. There were about ten larger clothing stores within Shanghai, and she had gone around to each and every one of them. She had now bought up, for all intents and purposes, all of the red cloth in Shanghai.

Although the shopkeepers were aware of the fact that they were selling to the Small Sword Society, they hadn't the slightest idea of how such an immense quantity of red cloth was to be used. Then, on the fifth day of the eighth lunar month, when the Small Swords rose in rebellion, it all became clear to them.

Xinmei had been buying up red cloth in the city on the fourth, the day before the rising. The fourth was the day after Zhou Lichun and his followers had launched their rebellion in Zhading. At about the same time, a man paid a visit to Lian Liwen's quarters in the firm of Harry Wade. As the owner of the firm, Harry Wade was usually in the business office, and he conveyed the message himself to Liwen in the back.

"Liwen, there's a dreadful character out there who says he's come to see you," said Wade. He was staring wide-eyed with an exaggerated look.

"Who in the world is he?"

"The head of the Small Swords."

"Huh? You mean Liu Lichuan?"

"That's right. The man of the hour, the one and only Liu Lichuan has come to see you. He's waiting in the reception room to the business office. Do you want to see him?"

"Of course, of course."

Liwen proceeded to the office. Liu's complexion had improved dramatically since their last meeting.

"Xinmei has been a great help to us," said the leader of the Small Sword Society out of the blue.

"Is that right? Has she really been of help?"

"She's really quite something. More than anything else, she's a woman of the Hongmen. In any event, will you come into the city tomorrow? Wouldn't you like to see Xinmei after such a long spell? I'll be with her."

"You'll be with her?" Liwen said, his eyes looking directly at Liu.

Liu Lichuan was, without a doubt, the most wanted man by the authorities both in the county and the circuit. Although local law enforcement officers actually dreaded bringing him into custody, he still could not just walk the streets of Shanghai with an air of impunity.

"Right. Tomorrow I'm planning to enter the city," said Liu.

"I see." Liwen did see. The following day the Small Swords would rise in rebellion and take the city of Shanghai.

"It'll be very, very early, before sunrise."

"Where?"

"At the Northern Gate. I'll wait for you there. And please, wear this on your head. That'll be a sign." So saying, Liu handed Liwen a piece of red cloth.

—5—

It was dawn, the fifth day of the eighth lunar month. About six hundred men had gathered outside the Northern Gate of Shanghai, each with a red bandanna wrapped around his head. Each had a sword or spear in hand, though they lacked an equally bloodthirsty mien.

They were receiving advance instructions on the storming of the city.

They were going to rush en masse into Shanghai after battering down the city gate. The Guangdong troops within were actually going to open the Northern Gate for them from inside. It was far better to surge into the city with the gate open. The enemy against whom they should have fought was not supposed to be by the gate. They were instructed that, at the time they broke through the gate, there would be no melee. For that reason, the soldiers of the Small Sword Society waiting their opportunity outside the Northern Gate were not filled with any apparent vengeance.

There were 700 Guangdong troops serving as guards in the northern sector inside the city walls, virtually all of whom had agreed to open the city gate. There were, however, exceptions. Three of the soldiers among them had built up suspicions to the effect, as it passed around locally, that: "I'll bet those guys are government spies. They're probably checking us out and sending off secret reports to the authorities." While the leaders of the Guangdong forces were engaged in private consultations, these three men decided not to report the plan to open the Northern Gate and the collusion with the Small Swords.

The heavy door of the Northern Gate creaked as it opened, and armed soldiers of the Small Swords Army passed through it one after the next. Just at that moment, an unexpected cry was heard, "Who goes there? Who opened the gate? Halt!" It was still dark out and hard to see clearly. Had he known that there were several hundred men coming into the city at that moment, the owner of that voice would surely not have spoken up.

The voice belonged to one of three troops who had not reported on the collusion. He had come running to the gate, sword in hand. It was a rare sight to behold at that time: a soldier of the Qing dynasty with a sense of responsibility. To raise one's voice in the darkness could surely have adverse results. It effectively served to announce one's location.

"I heard there were three spies, and this is one of those dogs. I'll have my revenge now!" said the young Pan Kexiang as he cut down the man who had approached and cried out at them. It was the sole instance of bloodshed as the Small Sword troops poured into the city.

"The county magistrate. I'm going to kill the county magistrate!" barked Pan, splattered by the blood of his victim.

Among the many Small Swords from the two provinces of Guangdong and Fujian, Pan Kexiang was exceptional in that he hailed from Jiangsu province. Although small of frame, he was unmatched for his ferocity. He was always quick to quarrel, and it always seemed to lead to bloodshed. He'd never lost an argument and had nerves of steel.

Pan had originally been a soldier in the private army of Xu Zishan, a gentry-merchant from Shanghai, and he had been arrested because of a fight that broke out with the government's forces and received a severe sentence from County Magistrate Yuan Zude: "Even if this man is killed, he will still have the expression of one who has not died. Do away with him unmercifully! Pull no punches!" Having passed this sentence, the magistrate had Pan put on public display after the administration of 3,000 lashes of the cane and 2,000 whips on the back. Pan's hatred for Magistrate Yuan was, needless to say, of a violent, acute sort. He had become a man who lived solely, it seemed, on anger and hate.

On the fifth day of the eighth lunar month, ceremonies honoring Confucius were to be held customarily early in the morning. That morning, while it was still dark outside, the responsible parties gathered at the Confucian temple to make preparations for the ceremonies. The circuit intendant, the county magistrate, and all the important local officials beneath them were all in attendance to pay their respects.

The man who led the ceremonies was the provincial examiner in the civil service examinations, and major roles were played that day by others in the field of education, including students. When the preparations were complete, and they were waiting only for the presence of the circuit intendant and county magistrate, news of the uprising by the Small Sword Society reached the Confucian temple.

Out of breath, troops and officials came with reports of the unfolding events:

"The Northern Gate's been forced open. We don't know how many the bandits number, but it appears to be a huge army!"

"The troops guarding the gate put up no fight at all."

"Those Guangdong troops defending the gate betrayed us!"

Within fifteen minutes, not a soul remained in the temple. Everyone from the provincial examiner on down made a mad rush to escape. There was no longer any reason to expect the circuit intendant and county magistrate to appear. All were thinking of their families. Ordinary people sent their families to safe places as quickly as possible, while high officials had not done so.

Having surged into Shanghai, the Small Swords Army proceeded directly, under the guidance of their allies within the city, to the Shanghai county offices, which were roughly at the center of the city. Inside sat County Magistrate Yuan Zude, dressed in his ceremonial garb, about to leave for the Confucian temple.

"You, Yuan Zude, hand me the official seal," said Liu Lichuan in a dignified tone of voice.

"No. It is the great seal graciously bestowed upon me by His Majesty the Emperor. Give it to roving bandits like you? The seal stays with me," said the county magistrate.

The main leaders of the Small Sword Society stood waiting behind Liu Lichuan. There was an audible gasp in the room, and then the magistrate continued, "Anyone who tries to take this seal will have to kill me first."

Immediately thereafter, there was a shout. "Aha, I'll kill you all right!" A man jumped forward with sword drawn. It was Pan Kexiang.

"Just who are you?" asked the magistrate instinctively.

"It's me. Have you forgotten already? I haven't forgotten you! Even death wouldn't let me forget you. You told me to kill, so I'm going to kill you. Hmm, that glittering, fine clothing you've got on. It'll make a nice shroud." As he was speaking, Pan approached the magistrate.

There was a look of terror in the magistrate's eyes, and he said, "You, you worthless urchin." He had finally remembered who Pan was.

The sound of the word "urchin" added fuel to the flames burning in Pan's breast.

"Mumble all you want after leaving this world." He then brandished his sword over head and swung it down mightily.

The aim was not to kill but just to wound. For Yuan to die just like that was far too quick, and altogether unacceptable to Pan. After the thousands of strokes of the cane and whip that he had felt on his back, Pan's retribution was not a swift death for Yuan.

The first blow inflicted only a light injury on the county magistrate. The right shoulder of his ceremonial tunic was torn to pieces. It was hot at this time of the year, and the magistrate was wearing only a sleeveless undergarment beneath his tunic. His white skin protruded, stained faintly with his blood.

"Look how pale you are. Here, take a look at me," said Pan, baring one shoulder. Scars from countless strokes of the whip could be seen on his dark-complexioned skin. The magistrate's face seemed to freeze. "You recognize it now, don't you!" Pan raised his sword again. The magistrate's eyes were no longer shut.

Pan let out a scream at the top of his lungs at the same time that he brought down his sword, and then once again raised it. The magistrate's body was plastered against the wall, and thus he was fully at the mercy of his opponent. Pan's method of cutting with his sword was apparently aimed as much as possible at causing pain and agony.

"Stop it, Kexiang! Get him back to life and then expose his body in public, just like he did to you. Take him alive!" Liu Lichuan shouted at Pan from behind, but the words never seemed to reach the ears of Pan Kexiang, who was waving his sword about frantically.

Magistrate Yuan, covered in blood and leaning against the wall, finally fell to the ground, sliding down the wall. And Pan Kexiang again brought down his sword upon him.

"It's done," said Pan, breathing heavily from the shoulders, his bloody sword hanging limply from his hand and his face red from Yuan's blood. Pan stepped down on Yuan's body. His face was distorted and his white teeth bared, though no one could make out whether his expression was that of a laugh or a scream.

"We had no choice with the county magistrate, but the circuit intendant is to be taken alive! Is that clear?!" Liu Lichuan approached Pan Kexiang and spoke loudly, as though Pan were hard of hearing. Pan nodded, his jaw rigid. The sword fell from his hand, making a desolate sound as it hit the stone floor.

—6—

Circuit Intendant Wu Jianzhang did not assume the same pose as the county magistrate. Lifting up his official seal, he shook his head back and forth quietly in a soft, even feminine movement.

"Go back into that rear room and shut the door behind you," ordered Liu Lichuan maliciously.

The other leaders of the Small Swords, then in the circuit intendant's office, had learned from Liu of his relationship with Wu. Though they'd been old buddies involved in common business ventures, when Liu, a decrepit fallen man, went to visit the highly successful Wu, Wu had turned him away at the gate. "He can't be trusted, that man," Wu had said at the time.

Whenever the subject of Circuit Intendant Wu came up, Liu became immediately agitated, and his subordinates in the Small Sword Society realized that he was suppressing his anger. Now, though, he had just witnessed the actions of Pan Kexiang, half crazed by pent up enmity. The fact that no blood was shed in the circuit intendant's office that day was again, it would seem, due to Liu's self-restraint. However, Pan Kexiang's anger at the county magistrate and Liu's at the circuit intendant were of a qualitatively different sort. Pan had been the corporeal victim of several thousand lashes. His entire existence retained the memories of the suffering incurred at that time. Also, prior to the exacting of his punishment, he'd had no contact at all with the county magistrate.

By contrast, Liu Lichuan and Wu Jianzhang had been on friendly terms for a considerable period of time. And indeed, Liu's hatred now was premised on their earlier amicable ties. He had known Wu as a person. "Wu can use a man's talents," offered Liu by way of evaluation.

Though a high government official, Wu was in fact a man well-versed in matters of business, especially trade. In addition, he had close relations with foreigners in China. In his capacity as superintendent of customs on the Yangzi River, Wu had developed considerable contacts with all of the foreigners resident in Shanghai, and his reputation among them was extremely good.

Liu Lichuan had to look toward future developments. He was dealing not solely with his own affairs here. Thousands, indeed tens of thousands, of people depended on him, and that gave him a commensurate sense of responsibility. His personal feelings would have to be suppressed for now.

Liu believed that, by making Shanghai the base of operations for the Small Swords, they could best forge friendly ties with the foreign community. This was first and foremost in his mind. In order to see this top priority through to fruition, there was a possibility that Wu Jianzhang might prove to be of use. Though a slight possibility, to be sure, insofar as it did exist, it had to be taken seriously.

Wu's face had turned pale. He now regretted more than ever his having had Liu summarily turned away earlier. He knew already that the Small Swords had murdered the county magistrate. A messenger had reported that to him soon after it occurred, and he had contemplated an escape. At the time, though, he was fully dressed in his ceremonial garb for attendance at the Confucian temple. He could hardly flee dressed in that fashion, but by the time he changed clothes and then tried to devise an escape, his offices were surrounded.

The story passed along to Wu was that the county magistrate was killed when he refused to hand over his official seal. Wu's seal was going to be taken from him whether he lived or died, so he produced it quite without fanfare. He was thinking that he would have to do everything in his power to go on living. Were he put to death in spite of his efforts, this would be some consolation.

After Wu was brought into the back room staggering, the large rotunda in his office was turned into a meeting of the leaders of the Small Sword Society. It was unclear who had the proper status to preside at such a meeting. Some of the top leaders were then in fact leading their subordinates in a mopping up campaign within the city and thus were not in attendance at the time. Lian Liwen, who had no relationship with the Small Swords, was standing at Liu Lichuan's side and thus happened to attend the meeting. At Liwen's side, Xinmei seemed a fine leader for the Small Swords.

Liu Lichuan leapt up onto a table, raised his arms, and said, "We need to discuss what to do with the circuit intendant."

"There's nothing to talk about. We rose in rebellion against the oppression of the officials. They can't just go on living. Let's be done with them once and for all. We made this appeal to everybody when we began this uprising! Isn't Wu Jianzhang the boss of all the officials in Shanghai? A county magistrate is way below a circuit intendant. It makes no sense to execute a county magistrate and let a circuit intendant live!" The man who made this speech was a major leader by the name of Chen Alin. Chen and a man by the name of Lin Afu were the most prominent rebels from Fujian province in the Small Swords.

As the overall leader, Liu Lichuan stood above the two major groups from Guangdong and Fujian, and insofar as he was himself from Guangdong, he had no choice but to yield to the top leaders from Fujian.

"Alin, I understand full well what you're saying," said Liu. "As everybody here knows, nobody wants to kill this circuit intendant more than me. But, listen to what I have to say. Alin, you've worked at the Skinner establishment, and I'm sure you'll understand. When we set up here in Shanghai, we've got to have good relations with the foreigners. Armies of the Manchu bastards will soon be coming to attack us. Even if they lay siege to the city, we can still get stocks of food and supplies from the foreigners. Alin, you surely know how strong they are. Didn't we look at this closely when we rose in rebellion? Through his capacity in the customs administration, Wu Jianzhang has particularly close ties with the foreigners, and we can use him to get at their strength. Let's not kill him. Let's let him live and put him to work for us." Liu had delivered this speech with great fervor.

Alin had worked as a wagon driver for the concern of the British merchant Skinner. From the look in his eyes, he did understand about the strength of the foreigners: gunboats, merchant vessels, and wealth.

While the Small Swords uprising was counting on help from the Taipings in Nanjing, the foreigners were maintaining a neutral position. They might at least look forward to the possibility of commercial interactions with the foreigners. The first principle of the Small Sword Society was not to act in a hostile manner toward them. Thus, Liu managed to persuade Chen Alin and others that for these reasons they couldn't put Wu Jianzhang to death. "He's right. If we kill Wu Jianzhang, Skinner and the others will be displeased. It's probably the wrong thing to do." Chen finally agreed with Liu.

"You see my point then?"

"Yes. Let's take Wu Jianzhang prisoner now. I don't know if he'll be of any use to us, but we can defer executing him for now."

Chen's acquiescence implied that there were no objections within the Fujian group. Chen nodded his head in assent of Liu's opinion that they not kill Wu. Liu, though, had already thought ahead another step to releasing Wu.

Liu was thinking that he really wanted to repay Wu Jianzhang for his having abandoned Liu at such a painful time. Had Wu helped him out at that time, he'd have done just about anything for Wu out of gratitude. So, thought Liu, they ought to offer Wu, whose fate now hung in the balance, a great,

great favor. Not only should they spare his life, but set him free. Ideally, they could get him to flee Shanghai and engage people outside the city in a plan beneficial to the Small Swords.

One report after another came in to the circuit intendant's office, which had become the base of operations for the Small Sword Society.

Mountains of silver were being kept in the official storehouse. It hadn't yet been counted but would probably be between 300,000 and 400,000 yuan.

"There's no more resistance within the city."

"The head of the Qing garrison forces, Li Dajun, has committed suicide."

Inquiries came, together with the reports, "There are a number of foreigners in the city. What should we do with them?"

"Bring them here. What do you think? We'll treat them well," ordered Liu Lichuan.

—7—

The color red overwhelmed everything within the city of Shanghai. The red cloth that Xinmei had been purchasing was spread throughout the city on the day of the uprising. It had been cut to measurements to make bandannas.

"The bold fighters of the Small Sword Society will wrap their heads in red cloth! That will be the sign!" The aforementioned man with the large mole on his jaw instructed his subordinates to shout out this message throughout the city.

People were racing around trying to find a piece of red cloth to wrap around their heads. Without it, they guessed, they might be mistaken for the enemy. At least if they had a red bandanna on, they were effectively declaring their lack of any intention of turning against the Small Swords. In almost no time at all the Small Swords gained control over the city of Shanghai. The red bandannas attached to people's heads were like a celebration of the birth of a new leader for Shanghai. The psychological effect of this was far greater than they could have imagined.

On the afternoon of the day that the Small Swords occupied Shanghai, American Minister Colonel Humphrey Marshall visited the city to make observations. Among the foreigners in the city at the time of the siege was a group who had come specifically to stay overnight and attend the Confucian ceremonies as observers. They were treated hospitably and escorted out of the city under guard. Before their departure, Liu Lichuan asked them to pass along the message that he would like to invite Marshall to pay a visit.

Liu knew something of Marshall. Because Liu was able to speak English, he had established business contacts with Westerners resident in Shanghai. He had met many of them face to face, but the reason he selected Marshall on this occasion was not solely because of the American minister's high status. He knew that Marshall was on particularly close terms with Wu Jianzhang.

Though Liu had been able to convince Chen Alin of the Fujian group to spare Wu's life, he had not done the same with respect to releasing Wu. However much he tried to persuade Chen and others, their opposition to releasing Wu remained firm, and there was always the danger that his leadership capacity would diminish were he to try and force them to accede to his wishes.

"Liwen, I shall rely on you to bring the American minister here. And when it's time for him to return, I'd like you to see to it that he gets as far as the city gate," asked Liu of Lian Liwen.

"You've given me something of a truly important task here." Liwen sensed something out of the ordinary in Liu's attitude.

"Do you understand? When you send the minister back, there may be one additional person with you. I hope you'll consent to this in advance. Although his appearance will have changed, it is someone you know. We need you to hide this person. Do you understand now?"

"Yes, I do." Liwen actually did grasp Liu's intention. It was brilliantly transparent. From the previous day, Liwen knew that Liu wanted to release the circuit intendant, and now he gleaned that Liu was going to try to use the American minister as a means of achieving that end. Liwen knew as well that Marshall and Wu Jianzhang were close friends.

"However, once the people leave the city they may no longer be under your control. In fact, I'm afraid that may disappoint you," said Liwen.

Wu Jianzhang was a high-level government official. Even if he claimed upon returning to the fold that he had escaped by the skin of his teeth from the clutches of bandits, soon the central government would surely begin to look upon him suspiciously. His superiors would suspect that he had struck some deal with the bandits to effect his release. To dispel these doubts, he couldn't be of the least utility to the bandits. Indeed, he would probably work to take as stern an attitude as possible against the Small Swords.

"I'm taking a long-range view of things," said Liu, full of self-confidence. "If you're worried, that's fine, but I have my own ideas about all this. I know this guy. He's not the sort of person that forgets a kindness done him. He's also very smart. He'll see how things really are around him out there."

"If you really think so, let's give it a try." Liwen now knew why he had been chosen for this task, and it was not simply because he spoke English. Were Wu Jianzhang's escape to become an issue, it would probably mollify the Fujian group's displeasure when they learned that Liwen, the son of Lian

Weicai, was connected. Lian Weicai had acquired a kind of absolute existence among people from Fujian.

When Marshall returned, it had grown very dark outside. After Marshall had completed his courtesy call on the headquarters of the Small Swords, Liu said to him, "I shall entrust your safe passage outside the city to Mr. Lian Liwen. In commemoration of today's events, I should also like to present you with a horse-drawn carriage. We shall provide drivers. Please accept it on our behalf."

On his own judgment Liu had hidden Wu in this carriage to enable him to escape from the city without incident. The Small Swords troops guarding the city gate behaved with extraordinary courtesy toward the American foreign minister, with whom they would have to remain on good terms henceforth. No one thus made any effort to search the carriage.

Wu's escape was known to all within a few days. Two days afterward, two Americans came to observe the Small Swords and were welcomed and later warmly sent on their way back.

The Fujian group was indignant, suspecting that the American minister or perhaps the two Americans had helped Wu Jianzhang escape. They loudly proclaimed that their leader had allowed this important prisoner to escape because they, Liu and Wu, hailed from the same local area.

Chen Alin, representing the Fujian group, paid a visit to Liu's residence.

"Listen, you've got to trust me. I hate Wu Jianzhang more than anyone and would just as soon beat him to death myself. How could I ever purposefully set such a creature free? Believe me!" said Liu as tears flowed from his eyes.

"We in the Fujian group have no doubt that it was the work of the Americans, so a call has been raised to attack the foreign concession area. What do you think?" asked Chen Alin, approaching Liu.

"Do that and it means the destruction of the Small Swords. Don't do it. Look at the overall situation. We've got to swallow our tears and repress this momentary anger for now."

"Ideally, I understand what you're saying. But even if I do, will the younger men in the Fujian group be so understanding? I'll go back and try to persuade them."

"At all cost. The future of the Small Swords depends on it."

"I'll do what I can. Have you heard how much the public funds in the official storehouse came to?"

"Nearly four hundred thousand yuan."

"There's a view that's come up in the Fujian group that wants to divide that money in half with the Guangdong group for each to use as they see fit. What do you think?"

"That would divide the Small Swords in two. I think it'd mean real trouble.

The Small Sword Society is one," said Liu Lichuan, moistening his lips.

"Yes, but in fact the Guangdong group is defending the North Gate and the Fujian group is defending the East Gate. We're already divided in the positions we've taken up. Wouldn't it be more convenient to divide up the military funds in advance?"

"Let's confer on this later." Liu was become exhausted.

Soon after the Small Swords had successfully occupied the city of Shanghai, the groups within the organization—from Fujian and Guangdong—so firmly aligned to that point, began to show signs of a rupture. Distrust was developing within each group toward the other. The rumor was spreading in the Guangdong group that the Fujian band had prepared a boat, transported all of the silver in the official storehouse onto it, and were about to set sail for Taiwan. The basis for this distrust lay actually in the release of Wu Jianzhang.

Having occupied Zhading, Zhou Lichun and the rebels from Qingpu had plans to enter the city of Shanghai. They had sent an advance man, but this messenger returned to Zhading.

"The rivalry between the two groups in Shanghai," he reported, "is quickly reaching a point of crisis. I doubt the Small Swords can go on much longer like this."

"Fujian or Guangdong?" said Zhou Lichun, lost in thought.

What was likely to happen if Zhou arrived with his local rebels just at the point when these two groups were feuding? No, he thought, the realm cannot be divided into thirds. Had Zhou been an ambitious sort, he might have been able to step in as a third force and, circumstances allowing, try to seize control over the Small Swords. However, he was a leader of a peasant movement and was devoid of such aspirations.

"It does seem better not to pursue that any further. If we get caught up in all that mess, it'd probably tear us apart too. I think that we may have misjudged the Small Swords," said Zhou, and he decided not to take his forces to enter the city of Shanghai.

The political authority of the Small Sword Society was riven with discord soon after it came into existence. On the surface it still managed to show signs of great excitement. The feeling that a new age had arrived swelled everyone's head.

Fluttering high above the city ramparts were large green banners on which were written in four large Chinese characters an expression that meant: "If you follow Heaven, you will walk the true way." For the name of their new country, the Small Swords selected "Great Ming," claiming their support for a revival of the Ming dynasty, which the present Qing had conquered over two centuries earlier.

Liu Lichuan assumed the highest position, with the official title, Generalissimo over Political and Religious Affairs Who Has Pacified the Realm. To establish balance, he gave three men from the Fujian group high-sounding military positions beneath him: Li Xianchi became the Great Barbarian-Pacifying General; Chen Alin became General of the Left; and Lin Afu became General of the Right. Pan Kexiang, who had killed the county magistrate, became the Flying Tiger Commander.

There was instability from the start in their regime, but the Small Sword Society's occupation of the city of Shanghai still lasted for nearly one and one-half years.

East and West of the Heavenly Capital

—1—

"What are they going to do next? What'll happen now?" pressed Xinmei repeatedly.

Tan Qi was a bit perplexed by the forcefulness of her reaction. It was just half a year since the Small Sword Society had occupied Shanghai, and three times in that interval Tan Qi had traveled back and forth between Nanjing and Shanghai. On each trip to Shanghai, he brought Xinmei and Liwen up to date on news from Nanjing.

For her part, Xinmei had disowned the Taiping movement and had said she wasn't the least bit interested in hearing about the Taipings, but the subject matter of the conversation let her forget herself. The subject was a controversy going on among the women in Nanjing at that time.

The Taipings strictly segregated men and women. After they had left Guangxi province and set out to conquer the realm, separate men's and women's barracks had been set up. Although there were many entire family groups that had joined the Taiping forces, even husbands and wives were required to live in separate quarters. Anyone who violated this rule, no matter how high his or her status, would be severely punished.

"It is something we shall endure until the realm is ours." This admonition meant that, even after the seizure of Nanjing, men and women would continue to live separately, and discontent was rising within families. The leadership of the Taiping movement ultimately had no choice but to relax this regulation.

The person in charge of the women's barracks was Hong Xuanjiao, the younger sister of Heavenly King Hong Xiuquan and the widow of Western King Xiao Chaogui. Though a woman, she was famous for her ability with a sword, she was able to read and write, and she had already shown stunning leadership capacities. Till this point there had been no wavering in the least about who held the position of the most powerful woman in the Taiping movement.

After the Taipings took Nanjing, however, a remarkably able woman by the name of Fu Shanxiang appeared on the scene. She was able to compose long poems immediately upon being given a title or theme. Chinese poetry had fastidious rules about such things as rhyme, linkage, intonation, and the like, and her impromptu poems fit these rules to perfection. Among the few literary or artistic types within the Taiping leadership, only Assistant King Shi Dakai—and only barely at that—could match her for poetic composition.

Fu Shanxiang was the daughter of Fu Qizheng, who had been a well-known Confucian scholar in Nanjing. Though he was now dead, the literati blood ran plentifully through the veins of her body. Her emergence was a result of the first Taiping examinations. The Taiping movement had been set on destroying the old imperial system, but when it established a capital and set about reorganizing various institutions, it found that it needed officials and could conceive of no other means of selecting them than through a system of examinations much like the civil service examinations of the imperial Chinese state. Since these were Taiping institutions, though, women were afforded the opportunity to sit for these exams, unlike those of the state, which had always been restricted to men.

The person who ranked first in the examinations was known as *zhuangyuan,* or principal graduate, the same title given the person with the highest score on the metropolitan examinations within the Qing system. In the examination carried out in Nanjing on the occasion of Hong Xiuquan's birthday on January 13, there were two principal graduates, for in conjunction with basic Taiping principles men and women had separate examinations.

Fu Shanxiang was the female *zhuangyuan.* She was also a woman of extraordinary beauty. Eastern King Yang Xiuqing had had his eye on Fu, for she assisted Hong Xuanjian in preparing documents for the women's barracks. Yang was illiterate and much less talented in literary matters than she. So he removed her and hired her to be secretary to the office of the Eastern King.

Effective power within the Taiping movement had been moving from the Heavenly King to the Eastern King. It now also appeared as though the effective top female position was going from Hong Xuanjiao to Fu Shanxiang.

"Everybody's feels for Xuanjiao," said Tan Qi. "Whatever anyone says, she's been the commander of the women's barracks through the long expedition from Guangxi all the way to the Heavenly Capital, and her contributions to the cause are immortal. Fu Shanxiang's only redeeming feature is her beauty."

"True, but she can compose poetry, right? I think the fact that she can so easily convert the thoughts in her heart into words is magnificent."

Xinmei had had little contact, to be sure, with poetry in her life, but she still felt herself instinctively drawn to such a talented woman as Fu Shanxiang.

"When it comes to writing poetry, we're all terrible. Xuanjiao has no cause to be any more embarrassed about it than any one of us."

Tan Qi raised his hands overhead in a gesture as if he were brandishing a sword. Xinmei had self-confidence in that area as well. But if she could only compose verse, she thought, what joy that would bring! That was the overwhelming feeling she had whenever she smelled the books at the Siwentang.

"Being beautiful's really an advantage, isn't it?" said Xinmei, with the clear implication to Tan Qi that she herself was not so. He raised his eyebrows and pursed his lips.

"She may be beautiful, but beauty by itself is nothing, nothing at all. I've heard that Fu Shanxiang does this very quietly on the side." Tan Qi extended the thumb and little finger of his right hand before him and bent the other three fingers around. It was an act intended to imitate opium smoking.

"That's very serious . . . even if it's Yang Xiuqing."

Opium consumption was punishable by execution in the Taiping Heavenly Kingdom. No matter how madly in love the Eastern King may have been with Fu Shanxiang, he would surely have to cut off his protection of someone whom he knew to have clearly violated Taiping law.

"The Eastern King's been pushing harder than usual. It's gotten especially bad of late. He's probably put too much stress and strain on himself," said Tan Qi, shaking his head lightly.

"That's a mess, isn't it?" interjected Liwen, who had been silent until then.

Unlike Xinmei, Liwen still harbored high hopes for the Taipings. He tried to put a positive construction on most things, though even in the most favorable light the Taipings were doing many things after their seizure of Nanjing that caused considerable doubt in his mind.

Tan Qi's role had changed, and it wasn't his doing. He was a loyal fighter for the Taiping movement who acted on orders. It was those who gave the orders who had brought about this metamorphosis. At first, Liwen assumed that Tan Qi had just been sent to form a liaison with the Small Swords occupying Shanghai, but that turned out not to be the case at all. On the contrary, it was highly unwise for the Small Swords to know that someone from the Taiping camp had come to them.

The Small Swords were the ones who wanted to link up with the Taipings in Nanjing. It was they who wanted to associate with the much stronger Taiping movement. Though they were maintaining their hold on Shanghai, in fact the fighting strength of the Small Swords was less than five thousand. It was not so much that they were strong, but that the Qing's armed forces were extremely weak, and that was how they kept control over the city. They desperately needed help from a superior force like the Taipings, and they were hoping for an alliance.

For their part, the Taipings were perplexed. Their capacity to send reinforcements to Shanghai was dwindling. They had sent their crack troops on the expedition to the north. One story had it that they were going to dispatch Luo Dagang in Zhenjiang to help out in Shanghai, but the Qing Army under the command of Xiang Rong was pressing in on Nanjing, and the Zhenjiang troops had to return to defend the Taiping capital.

The Taipings were in the midst of an investigation of the Small Sword Society from the point of view of religion to see whether or not they would come to their assistance. Inside Shanghai, the Small Swords were offering incense at the temples as a way of commemorating their military victory. There was no sign that any idols or images had been smashed. It was thus difficult to imagine them as allies of the Society of God Worshippers. Indeed, they shared an opposition to the Qing government, but otherwise there were just too many fundamental differences. At first they proffered that as a reason for hesitating to send relief, and later they pretended that communications were not being handled well.

Why then had Tan Qi come to Shanghai? The answer was business.

—2—

Shortly after the city of Nanjing fell into Taiping hands, circulation of commodities came to a sudden stop, and the resultant economic inactivity was actually one of the reasons that the Small Swords had risen in rebellion in Shanghai. However, movement in certain commodities soon became conspicuously active. Principal among them were raw silk thread and silk cloth. Although also a textile product, cotton cloth did not thrive to the same extent.

"It's not a good sign," said Lian Weicai, upon hearing a report on market conditions.

"Why is that?" asked Liwen of his father.

"Because only luxury items are moving. Isn't that worrisome?" responded Lian Weicai.

"Yes, yes, indeed."

Liwen suddenly realized why his father was so concerned. The fact that luxury items alone were moving meant that somewhere there were people living luxurious lives. By the same token, the fact that ordinary commodities were not circulating meant that they were on the whole in a state of depression.

In the circulation of commodities was reflected the fact that the upper stratum of the Taiping movement had become extravagant in their lifestyles following the seizure of Nanjing. They seemed ever more isolated from the general Taiping populace. At any rate, there was a shortage of silk in Nanjing, a site of silk textile production. But production had not ceased there for a moment.

Once in control of Nanjing, the Taiping leadership established a Textile Agency to encourage the continued production of silk goods. A Nanjing silk merchant by the name of Wu Weitang had offered the proposal to set up the Textile Agency, and when it materialized he became its chief.

The Heavenly King, the Eastern King, and the Northern King all vied with one another over various luxuries. The Heavenly King had taken over the offices of the former Jiangnan governor-general and transformed them into the Heavenly King's Residence, but when it burned down he had a grand palace constructed there for himself. It was a castle town unto itself. Surrounded by walls several kilometers long, the residence of Heavenly King Hong Xiuquan was known locally as the Golden Dragon Pavilion. Yellow (the imperial color) silk was hung over the gates to this residence, and for that alone one could only vaguely imagine the massive quantity of silk required.

Under no circumstances was Eastern King Yang Xiuqing going to be outdone by the Heavenly King. Though the Textile Agency was under his authority, production could not keep up with demand. For that reason, Tan Qi had been sent to Shanghai to purchase silk.

The business offices of the Heavenly King's residence were located in immense three-story structures situated to the east and west on the grounds of the residence. Red and yellow silk was hung over the exterior of their doors, providing shade against the sun. Because the silk was exposed to the rain and wind, new silk coverings replaced the old roughly once a month. Everyone inside wore silk, of course. Not only the leaders, but their family members and close associates all wore silk of various colors.

The former Jiangnan governor-general, the highest official in Nanjing, had always led a completely humble life. "He's a slave of the Manchus, nothing but a serving boy," said the members of the entourages of the Heavenly King and Eastern King. "There are kings here now, and their status is altogether different."

In the shadows, the resident populace of Nanjing frowned furtively and said to one another: "A bunch of country bumpkins born and bred in the mountains, that's what they are. As far as they're concerned, everything's a luxury—they can't tell the difference."

"They can't get used to wearing extravagant clothes. It's just like the wardrobe of some piece of rural theater."

It was, strangely enough, very much like the wardrobe of a rural theatrical performance. Not one member of the Taiping leadership knew a thing about the royal court. Their knowledge of the court all derived from dramas, specifically rural theatrical performances. Their clothing was based entirely on that model and left the people of Nanjing justifiably amused.

And, to be sure, they knew no limits when it came to luxuries for themselves. What the Taiping leaders considered extravagance was the price they paid for creating a sense of majesty about themselves. They had to make a show of their authority to the people of Nanjing, and to that end a bedraggled appearance simply would not do. They were profoundly aware of their own humble origins and worked avidly to embellish their external appearance.

"It really is a mess," said Liwen, drawing a deep breath after hearing Tan Qi's story.

"I remember you once told me the story of the states of Wu and Yue," said Tan Qi. "It was about how easy it is to share hard work and how hard to share joy. When I heard it, I thought it was a bunch of nonsense, but now I understand what it's really about, and it's so true."

Kou Jian, king of the state of Yue in ancient China, had been able to destroy his old foe Fu Chai, king of the state of Wu, with the counsel of the famed minister Fan Li. Thus gaining control over the south of China, the state of Yue ushered in a golden age, and yet for some reason Fan Li turned his back on it all and left Yue. The year was 472 B.C.

At the time Fan Li's thinking was, "We should be able to share our troubles, but it is so difficult to share the peace." A long time before, Liwen had recounted this famous story to Tan Qi. Tan Qi had known tales of Wu and Yue from plays and stories, but he could never understand the psychology behind Fan Li's decision to leave Yue. Once the hard times were over and the easy times had begun, why had he then seen the need to leave?

Looking at the internal affairs of the Taiping movement after the occupation of Nanjing, Tan Qi finally seemed to comprehend.

"The Eastern King and the Northern King haven't been getting along well, have they?" asked Liwen.

From the very start, Eastern King Yang Xiuqing and Northern King Wei Changhui had simply not gotten along by nature. At the time of the Taiping Army's painfully long march, they had joined forces and fought side by side, but when luxuries became plentiful following the seizure of Nanjing, suspicion and doubts between the two men bubbled to the surface everywhere. Liwen had foreseen this eventuality when he left Nanjing shortly after the Taiping occupation.

"There's no reason to expect they would, is there?" said Tan Qi, winking. "They never hit it off, and now this mysterious woman is caught up in it."

"Woman?"

"One of our people Hou Qianfang's involved? It's an embarrassing story, really. It makes me ill to have to tell it."

Hou Qianfang was the name of a spy working for Yang Xiuqing. He worked with Tan Qi, made his way surreptitiously into Nanjing before the Taiping attack on the city, and was involved in several maneuvers. He had forged links with a number of people in Nanjing Triad groups, and he managed to investigate the disposition of troops as well as the sites of the munition and supply depots. He had performed meritoriously in the shadows for the Taipings in their seizure of the city.

"Hou was different from us. The fellow had lots of money. In his contacts in the Triads, he was always going over to the river." Brothels were lined up on both sides of the river, and when one spoke of "the river" in Nanjing it carried the meaning of what we might now call the pleasure quarters.

According to Tan Qi, Hou Qianfang was on intimate terms with a woman there by the name of Hong Luan. Hong Luan was one of the most famous prostitutes, if not the most famous, of the entire river area. Hou was under Yang Xiuqing's orders. His work with the Triads included payoff tactics, and so he carried a great deal of funds with him. This enabled him to live in such opulence and on such intimate terms with a woman of Hong Luan's reputation.

"That's I job I wouldn't mind having."

"True enough. Everybody was envious of him. But the Eastern King used him only as an errand boy. No one else could have gotten away with such a setup. It was a special relationship. Hou's younger sister was a stunning beauty, and she was becoming the Eastern King's mistress. They called her Lady Hou. She was pretty well known herself. He was assigned the great job he had because of his younger sister. At least, that's the rumor."

"What happened next?" interjected Liwen. His tone was one of indignation. It then dawned on him that she had died in battle at Wuchang, one of the nine women soldiers of the Taiping forces.

"When we took Nanjing, the Northern King demanded that the number one prostitute of the river area join him and he seized her. Hou Qianfang was beside himself, as you can imagine. So, he decided to enlist the help of the Eastern King. He convinced Yang that Hong Luan, who really was an extraordinary beauty and was now in the residence of the Northern King, was well worth looking at." Sensing Xinmei's resentment, Tan Qi picked the words of his story carefully.

At Hou Qianfang's instigation, Yang Xiuqing sent a messenger to Wei

Changhui's residence: "Please turn over Hong Luan, the prostitute of whom so much has been said."

To this, Wei shouted back, "And then might you turn over your Lady Hou to me?"

This response enraged the Eastern King, and Wei Changhui knew full well how frightening an enraged Yang Xiuqing could be. Troops were mobilized at the Eastern King's residence, and rumors began spreading that he was going to launch an attack on the Northern King's residence. Wei Changhui realized sooner than anyone that this was by no means an empty threat.

He really can get crazy, thought Wei, gnashing his teeth patiently, and then he's dangerous and there's no way to deal with him. "I'll turn over Hong Luan," he told the messenger. An express courier was sent from the Northern King's residence, and the Eastern King cancelled his emergency battle formations.

"Hong Luan went to the residence of the Eastern King," said Tan Qi, as he concluded his story, "and ended up not returning to the Northern King's residence."

"It still goes on. Really it does," said Xinmei. While she listened to the story, she was unconsciously clenching her fists. When she suddenly felt the pain in her hands, she slowly unbent her fingers.

Liwen struggled to stifle a sigh. What had happened, he wondered, to the enthusiasm at the time they first raised troops in Jintian village? If they forget that, he thought, the Taiping movement would dissipate like a dream.

—3—

They were not only squabbling over women. They were fighting over goods too. There wasn't enough silk to go around.

"Somehow we're short-handed. We're working day and night, but we just can't meet the demand. If we only had some more people." Wu Weitang, head of the Textile Agency, had said the same thing when he placed his orders. He was only able to deliver on fifty to seventy percent of the orders he received from the residences of the Heavenly King, the Eastern King, the Northern King, and the Assistant King.

"Go ahead and quietly add some people to your staff," the influential Eastern King had said, and Wu increased his staff at the Textile Agency.

"The examination at the city gates is too strict for stocking material," said Wu on another occasion, when he brought this complaint to the Eastern King.

"Anyone holding a document bearing the seal of the head of the Textile Agency has free access in and out of the city gates." So ran the text of a notice issued by Yang Xiuqing to the corps of guards at the gates.

Wu Weitang was no ordinary man. He was an officially sponsored merchant of the Qing government. The job of a person of such status involved winning others over by any means at his disposal. He had the old bureaucrats of the Qing dynasty in the palm of his hand, and thus he could treat the simple-hearted Taipings who had no immunity on their own as he wished.

Wu harbored ambitions of greatness. He had tried to render distinguished service of the sort that would be recorded in history. Though just a merchant, he was extremely ambitious—so ambitious that in ordinary times he would have been fabulously wealthy and probably played a major role in the business world. But his ambition was even greater than this, and in that regard opportunity had knocked at his door.

People close to the Qing sensed calamity in the Taiping occupation of Nanjing. Wu Weitang looked for a way to turn this perilous situation into a blessing. "They're not long for this world," he thought to himself, and by "they" he meant the Taipings.

Murder, theft, plunder—the sort of behavior one ordinarily associated in Chinese history with the military—these things were altogether absent among the Taiping troops. The rumor that they were a nearly miraculous band of saints and wise men had been spreading for some time among the common people, who quietly had high hopes for them.

Had they in fact been a band of saints and wise men, then they probably would have been able to gain popular support and undermine the Qing. However, Wu Weitang had seen the reverse side of the situation. Perhaps he only saw the reverse side. The competition among the Taiping leaders over luxury items was corroding the infrastructure of the movement like germs. One of the people responsible for procuring goods for a king's residence had gone so far as to send a bribe to Wu Weitang to get even more silk from the Textile Agency. If the supply system worked smoothly, it was to the merit of this man in charge of procurement and worthy of his being promoted. Whether or not it proceeded apace, though, it would be seen in comparison to the other kings' residences. This competition reigned not just in the upper echelons of the Taiping movement, but was just as ferocious in the lower ranks.

There were earthly desires mixed in with this competition as well. An assortment of stratagems were employed, and they were all completely transparent to Wu Weitang. In the midst of this kind of depravity and with the Qing military surrounding them, it must have seemed clear to Wu that the life span of the Taiping regime would not be long.

With the Taipings collapsing, if he were to lend a hand in that collapse, it would be extraordinarily meritorious service. In fact, it was Wu's secret ambition to play the foremost part in the destruction of the Taiping Heavenly Kingdom.

Having become head of the Textile Agency, Wu received from Eastern King Yang Xiuqing the authority to hire men as he saw fit. They were the staff of the Textile Agency. Once he affixed his official stamp to someone's documents, indicating that they belonged to his agency, they became off limits to other agencies.

Although the Taiping ideal of equality between the sexes may seem to have been favorable to women, there were instances in which it was a particularly heavy burden for them as well. Women had to perform work together with men. For women of the upper classes, unused to labor as they were, physical labor made for considerable pain. The leadership of the women's barracks approached many families and took the women out to join the labor forces.

"Why don't you come work at the Textile Agency? That way you won't have to tote sandbags or dig any canals." This was Wu Weitang's way of enticing the richest and most famous of Nanjing's families when he visited them. As far as they were concerned, he wasn't asking for anything special.

"That would certainly be welcome. I'm very grateful." This was their usual response, for it was in fact a blessing of sorts.

"I have to send the Eastern King a fairly good-sized bribe to get him to overlook my employment of staff at the Textile Agency," added Wu. It was unnecessary for Wu to speak of superfluous matters, though bit by bit an enormous amount of money was rolling into his pocket.

"This is an act of mercy, because this is a dangerous bridge for me to cross. You just persevere for a little while longer," he said softly, with a meaningful wink.

After the collapse of the Taiping movement, having braved these dangers, Wu would act to protect these people after the return of Qing control. Only people with close ties to the Qing system were employed by him as members of the staff of the Textile Agency, thus avoiding compulsory manual labor.

"You must have saved up a lot of money by now, haven't you?" said a man abruptly one day as he casually paid a call on the head of the Textile Agency. "How about spreading a little of it around to places where there isn't any, okay?"

"Uh, uh, Mr. Zhang," said Wu Weitang, staring ahead of him in amazement.

The man before him was Zhang Jigeng. Zhang was a leader of the self-defense corps, known as *tuanlian*, that were being created with government sponsorship. After the Taiping occupation of Nanjing, he had stealthily escaped the city, but managed to sneak back inside. Had he been caught, he would doubtless have been executed by the Taiping government.

Zhang had been a powerful man in Nanjing, and Wu knew him well. Though he came from a minor gentry family, he had contacts with gangsters and was a pretentious swaggerer in his own right. He now looked bedraggled, dressed in the outfit of a laborer in the Textile Agency, which was needless to say a disguise.

"What do you think? Should I inform on you?" said Zhang.

"No, no, that's crazy. I expected that you'd return, Mr. Zhang."

"Is that so?"

"Yes, I really did, because there's no time when someone like you is needed more than the present."

"I've got lots of plans. If I can put away some war funds, great things can be done."

"Great things, you say. I'd like to help as much as I can."

"As much as you can, you say?"

"There's a lot more money than the silk merchants association gave to the *tuanlian* in the past. Think about it."

"Is that so?" said Zhang, his white teeth gleaming.

While this exchange was transpiring, the two men each sensed the same echo: What a distinguished honor to bring the Taipings down! And what a prize the government in Beijing would give!

Each thought they actually heard the beating of the other's heart. Wu Weitang and Zhang Jigeng established a bond closer than anything they had ever shared before.

For a time the rumor was spreading in Shanghai that, as a result of fighting between Heavenly King Hong Xiuquan and Eastern King Yang Xiuqing in Nanjing, the Heavenly King had died. Although it soon became clear that this report was in error, it was by no means completely without foundation. Where's there's smoke, there's fire.

What kind of kindling had caused this fire to spark? A gloomy mood fell over Liwen as he heard Tan Qi's response.

From the days back in Jintian village, Yang Xiuqing had always wanted to outshine Hong Xiuquan. This Liwen had seen for himself. But the charismatic quality that Hong possessed as the creator of this religious body had always enabled him to prevail. It seemed that Yang was using Hong, expanding the power of the Taipings as a group, and later waiting for just the right moment to make his move and seize control.

At the time of the occupation of Nanjing, the effective power of the Taiping movement was virtually all in Yang's hands. All that remained was the movement's highest position. In practical terms, he was already there, but it had yet to be publicly recognized. Yang wanted the real power, but he wanted the name that went with the highest seat in the Taiping order as well.

"The Heavenly Father's Descent to Earth." Yang Xiuqing was the only person within the Taiping camp who claimed, through divine inspiration or spirit possession, to have the ability to convey the words of the Lord God Jehovah to the people. Even Hong Xiuquan, who it was said had once ascended to heaven and heard God himself speak, lacked such a capacity.

After the Taipings had taken Nanjing, Yang had thought of using the Heavenly Father's Descent to Earth, which had hitherto been used as a weapon to forge unity among the Taiping fighting men, now against the Heavenly King himself. The opportunity seemed to present itself at the time of the troubles concerning the women.

A problem had cropped up in Hong Xuiquan's attitude toward the treatment of women officials in his residence. Contradictions were developing around the issue of male-female equality. Hong Xiuquan had treated as subordinates two older women: Yang Changmei, the younger sister of Yang Xuiqing's father, and Shi Dinglan, a relative of Assistant King Shi Dakai. As far as the women were concerned, there was no cause for them to be treated as servants by Hong.

"I'm ready to take a rest. I'm getting too old for this, but the Heavenly King won't permit it. He's too stiff, too hard-boiled. If he's got any faults at all, it's blowing up at us." Listening to his aunt express her discontent, Yang Xiuqing hit upon a way to transform in one fell swoop this attitude of Hong's.

For some time, he had thought that he could use the Heavenly Father's Descent to Earth to confront the Heavenly King. He would have Jehovah reprimand Hong Xiuquan. Yang Xiuqing was the sort of man who, once this idea dawned upon him, began immediately to make the necessary preparations to see it through to fruition.

A Heavenly Father's Descent to Earth was carried out on December 24, 1853, precisely on Christmas Eve. Rebukes issued forth from the Heavenly Father Jehovah toward Hong Xiuquan, who was down on his knees.

"Be magnanimous toward the female officials."

"Be attentive to the education of the young master."

Then an order was conveyed. "For these faults, you shall be punished with forty lashes of the cane."

Northern King Wei Changhui stepped forward and said, "I shall take the Heavenly Father's place and take the lashes on myself."

"Never!" said the voice of Yang Xiuqing with the words of Jehovah.

Yang quickly surveyed the atmosphere surrounding this event and decided that it was still too soon. Not just Wei Changhui, but others who wished to incur the punishment of Jehovah in place of the Heavenly King seemed to come forward one after the next in succession.

The Heavenly Father's Descent to Earth, calculated to send the Heavenly King's authority into decline, was in fact having the opposite effect of strengthening the people's devotion to Hong Xiuquan. There was as well the possibility that it would impair the Eastern King's authority.

Several dozen members of the Taiping leadership were present, and all seemed as though they were in tears—tears for the ordeal visited upon the Heavenly King. Open sobbing was soon destined to join simple tears, and then lamentations would surely follow. Wailing that would unhinge heaven and earth was certain to enhance the power and influence of Hong Xiuquan and make it all the more difficult ever to displace him.

"Today, I shall pardon you," Yang Xiuqing was forced to say. "Be careful in the future." The people assembled there heaved a sigh of relief upon hearing Jehovah's forgiveness.

As a result of this incident, Yang Xiuqing learned something about Hong Xiuquan's strength, and Hong became aware of Yang's assault on his position. It didn't end there.

Hong ended the matter on the surface by ordering this female relative and meritorious official to take a period of rest. Nonetheless, no one among the Taiping leadership believed that the matter was really resolved.

Yang's younger brother, Yang Fuqing, broached the subject of proceeding quickly to the city of Anqing after the matter ended. The western expeditionary force of the Taiping Army from Nanjing had gone up the Yangzi River and reached Anqing, and Assistant King Shi Dakai had been in command.

"Why go to Anqing?" Yang Fuqing was asked by someone close to him. Looking around, he was reported to have replied, "Troubles are coming here soon."

Yang Fuqing sensed that his brother's high-handed manner of doing things was eliciting a strong reaction. The devine possession incident had superficially calmed down, but everyone could readily surmise that the Heavenly King was surely contemplating retaliation.

Thinking that he could well do without this particular entanglement, Yang Fuqing had tried to leave Nanjing. He had sought refuge under the shelter of Shi Dakai because he thought he could trust him personally and because Shi was removed from the center of political squabbles in Nanjing.

"The atmosphere in the Heavenly Capital is suffocating. Please, find a place for me here," said Yang Fuqing, his head lowered deeply as he stood before Shi Dakai.

Shi thought of this bad turn of events. As if digesting the import of the event, he carefully considered the meaning of the fact that the younger brother of the Eastern King had taken refuge with him. Though he tried to suppress it, a sigh nonetheless escaped his lips.

In Shanghai Liwen reported to his father on the state of affairs in Nanjing as he had heard them from Tan Qi. He then asked, "Is there nothing that we can do with the strength at our disposal?"

His father, Lian Weicai, folded his arms and replied, "It's going to be very, very hard. There may yet be a way to defend against cataclysm with the might of the Assistant King. But it certainly does seem that once they entered the city of Nanjing, that whole group of leaders simply changed altogether."

—5—

Zeng Guofan had been assiduously building ships.

"Ships. We need ships. Without them, we're helpless. Fighting a war without ships is like going to your death. Ships are the first thing in battle." This was the theme he had been striking of late.

The boats used by the Taiping forces in Hubei and Hunan had enabled them to carry off everything. Indeed, their flotilla had effectively brought down the city of Nanjing.

Because they had scarcely any ships of quality left, Zeng Guofan had established shipyards in Xiangtan and Hengzhou in Hunan province, and he was having ships built there around the clock. Orders brought by post horse messenger from Beijing only urged them on.

The northern expeditionary force of the Taipings had arrived at Tianjin. Taiping forces under the command of Li Kaifang and Lin Fengxiang had defeated the Qing Army under Sheng-bao, who had replaced No-er-jing-e as imperial commissioner, and killed the Tianjin county magistrate Xie Zicheng. Nearby Beijing was in a state of terror, and the wealthy were beginning to seek refuge elsewhere.

The western expeditionary army was advancing to the west from Anqing, having defeated an army under the command of Jiang Zhongyuan at Tianjiazhen and Banbishan, and having occupied Hankou and Hanyang. Prefect Yu Shunqing and Magistrate Liu Honggeng both died in the fighting.

Across the Yangzi River in the walled city of Wuchang, Hunan-Hubei Governor-General Wu Wenrong (1792–1854) and Hubei Governor Chong-lun (1792–1875) had been quarreling with one another in the face of the enemy. Chong-lun proposed the creation of a base outside the city walls from which to prepare for an enemy assault. Thus far, some people who had said they were just leaving the city temporarily had actually abandoned it altogether. Countless high officials of the Qing dynasty had already fled, with the excuse that they were going to go out and engage the enemy. The governor-general had seen through to the secret intentions of the governor.

"Our fate is tied to this city," said Governor-General Wu sternly as he thrust his dagger into the surface of the desk before him. "If this city falls, we fall with it. If it continues to exist, so shall we. The discussion of this matter is resolved here and now. If there's anyone who says they're going to leave the city, I will draw his blood with this blade!"

Chong-lun repeatedly protested that simply holding the city was no strategy, but he was outdone by Wu Wenrong's unbending stance. In his heart, though, Chong-lun was burning with indignation.

To be sure, there were self-righteous aspects to Wu Wenrong. In the middle of a war, to pull out a dagger and wave it overhead as a way to force one's point of view was probably open to criticism. Yet, had he not done so, Wuchang would have easily fallen into Taiping hands.

For some reason, the Taiping Army lifted its siege of Wuchang, departed from occupied Hankou and Hanyang, and retreated to Huangzhou. One explanation put forward was that they withdrew to await reinforcements. It was unsafe, or so it seemed, to have one's supply lines extended to their maximum length while waiting for reinforcements to arrive at the Wuhan tricities. If, however, the Qing military leadership had escaped from Wuchang, that would probably have strengthened Taiping self-confidence and led to a continuation of their encampment.

For his part, Wu Wenrong thought that by their holding firm to the defense of Wuchang, they had forced the bandits to retreat in fear. On the other hand, Chong-lun asserted that while they had remained shut up within the city walls, shrinking in the shadows, they had lost an opportunity to annihilate the enemy, for bandit forces were already on the decline, and had they gone out and engaged them in battle, they could have crushed them.

Although his real intention was, in fact, to run away, with the Taiping Army in retreat, he was able to speak so boastfully. Chong-lun was not merely speaking his mind, for he committed his ideas to paper and submitted them in the form of a memorial to Beijing.

"We just sat there in vain, while the opportunity to destroy the bandits was lost." This was, in effect, the report submitted by Chong-lun, a Manchu official.

Wu Wenrong had been transferred to his present position from the post of governor-general of Yunnan and Guizhou provinces. For some time past, he had anguished over the fact that morale among the Qing's troops had not improved, and to the court he had accused Manchu military officials of incompetence. Chong-lun's accusations on this occasion were calculated to pay him back.

The following was received from Beijing: "Pursue and attack the bandits immediately!"

The actual situation at the war front was not known in Beijing. At the imperial court, there had been a great fear that the northern expeditionary army of the Taipings would come upon them with the momentum of raging waves. More than anything else, they seemed to be giving priority to restraining the northern expeditionary army by moving the front further to the south. In the extreme event, whatever the outcome of the fighting, the court wanted the Qing forces to pursue the fighting fiercely in the south. This, it seemed, was all that Beijing really wanted.

"We are building warships with all of our strength," read a report Zeng Guofan sent to the court. "In a short while, we shall be able to organize a navy of our own. If we engage them in battle before this has been accomplished, it is quite clear that it will be to our disadvantage. We must take a longer view than what the immediate war situation confronts us with."

The court in Beijing, though, had time only to consider the immediate situation.

Jiang Zhongyuan had almost been killed because of the court's impatience. Jiang marched to the east at the head of his army of Hunan volunteers. The Taipings left Hankou and Hanyang on November 6, 1853, and shortly thereafter Jiang's forces entered the Wuhan tri-cities. From there he reported that reinforcements were late.

At this time, the jealousy that high-level Manchu officials felt for powerful, influential Han Chinese became one notch stronger. In but a year, this mere intellectual with no office to speak of—Jiang Zhongyuan—had advanced in rank from a county magistracy to a provincial governorship. This was not merely a double or triple promotion. It was historically unprecedented. No one else in the entire history of the Qing dynasty had risen with such speed. In addition, Jiang had no connections at all with powerful men to gain access to the central government.

The large number of meritorious acts in battle, such as at Suoyi Ford, had enabled his phenomenal record of promotions. Oddly, it was common knowledge at this time that, while promotions gained through personal connections were acceptable, those gained through genuine ability seemed highly suspect.

As Li Jiaduan's successor, Jiang Zhongyuan had just recently been appointed to the post of Anhui governor. Because his reinforcements arrived late at Wuhan, though, he was punished by a "reduction in rank while remaining in office."

Hubei Governor Chong-lun arrived just as Jiang, at the head of an army of 2,000 troops, was about to set out from Hankou.

"Our troop strength in Wuchang is weak. Why not leave half your soldiers here?" proposed Chong-lun.

"Half of them? You mean one thousand men?"

"Oh, you mean there are only two thousand Hunan volunteers?"

"That's right, and it took a great deal of trouble to assemble those two thousand men."

"Well, I guess there's no alternative. We'll take one thousand of them," said Chong-lun coercively.

Jiang Zhongyuan looked up into the sky. Now, thought Jiang, nodding in assent, he could go attack the long-haired bandits.

He wanted to proceed to battle with no further delays. Had he rejected Chong-lun's proposal, it would certainly have delayed his departure for several days. Having sent his younger brother, Jiang Zhongyi, ahead to Hunan to continue raising troops, it was best, in his estimation, to hold positions that could then be further supplemented with new recruits.

Jiang set out from Hankou five days after the Taiping withdrawal. He fell ill at Lu'an in Anhui province and remained there for a time, and finally entered the temporary capital at Luzhou on December 10. The Anhui provincial capital had been Anqing, but a Taiping Army under the command of Shi Dakai had already seized it and held control there.

—6—

The occurrence of the Heavenly Father's Descent to Earth took place in Nanjing after Jiang Zhongyuan had already entered the city of Luzhou. Around this time, Taiping forces had also retreated from Yangzhou, and Imperial Commissioner Qi-shan entered Yangzhou, which had been emptied out.

Hunan-Hubei Governor-General Wu Wenrong amassed his troops at Huangzhou, and because of Chong-lun's attacks on him to the court, he had no choice but to send them into battle. Zeng Guofan had sent word ahead to wait at least until the navy was organized, but Wu Wenrong did not wait. The mood would not allow the assault to be postponed.

It was the ninth day of the twelfth lunar month by the time Wu Wenrong had raised his troops at Huangzhou. It was already early in 1854 according to the solar calendar—January 7 to be precise. Historical records indicate that Jiang Zhongyuan, ignoring his own illness, arrived in Luzhou three days later.

It looked like a suicidal mission at the time for both of them. Ultimately, it didn't turn out that way, but there were clear signs that both Jiang and Wu were fully aware of the fact that nothing but death awaited them. Jiang left half of his armed forces at Lu'an, it too being an important site. Depositing these troops under his direct command was an extraordinary thing to do, for he was undoubtedly trying to preserve the Hunan braves as best he could.

Once in Luzhou prefecture, Jiang lost all hope, for no preparations whatsoever had been made to face the Taiping Army. Luzhou Prefect Hu Yuanwei was a man so obese that it seemed painful for him to walk. Because of his illness, Jiang Zhongyuan's nerves were so on edge that he was even unhappy about how Hu had managed to become so fat.

"There're no troops here and no military provisions either. The city's completely wasting away. Despite that, the prefect is fat as a pig. How in the world can anyone have grown so huge?"

Jiang was usually partial to a little humor, but the words he used about Hu Yuanwei went well beyond humor. Anger had appeared in Jiang's eyes. Perhaps he would have been able to hide it with a little effort had he been healthier, but his illness made him unable to conceal his true feelings. Jiang's stinging language plunged deeply into Hu's breast.

"He's wearing the face of a provincial governor," thought Hu Yuanwei. Keeping his own face clear of emotion, Hu was submerged in profound indignation. Until the previous year, he had been at a much higher rank than Jiang. Several years had passed since his promotion to prefect. There had been a large disparity in rank between a prefect and an examination student with no post at all. Had he come requesting a personal interview, Hu would probably have just refused him out of hand.

"He's like a savage beast that suddenly rises from nowhere in wartime," thought Hu. He was being scathingly attacked by a man whom in the past he would have rejected without so much as a second thought. Hu was deeply resentful.

"I'll inspect the braves of the local militia," said Jiang, as he proceeded to make a surprise examination of the troops.

A man by the name of Liu Mou was supposed to take command of 500 troops, but when counted they numbered but 150 men. On the register, pay and provisions for 500 had been allocated.

"Execute him. That's an illegality worthy of death." Jiang's voice had become shriller since his illness.

Provincial Administration Commissioner Liu Yuzhen was stunned, and tried to calm him down. "Could you postpone the execution for now? The bandits will be coming here very soon."

"Precisely because the bandits are on their way here is why we have to exact a heavy punishment."

"If we execute him, the militia probably will stop obeying orders, and we'll be in no position to fight," said Liu earnestly.

"In no position to fight . . ." said Jiang, swallowing the words he intended to say next: "I doubt they were ever ready to put up a fight." The gentle Liu Yuzhen was one of the people responsible for their laggard military preparations. Looking at Liu's face, Jiang abandoned the idea of execution.

It seemed hopeless at this point. The day after Jiang Zhongyuan's arrival, the city of Luzhou was thrown into a state of war, though not in a battle with the Taipings. The Hunan militiamen with whom Jiang had come were attacked by local militia troops and had counterattacked, while the residents of the city all locked their doors tightly.

The Taiping troops involved in the Luzhou campaign were led by commanders Hu Yihuang (the "Marquis to Guard Heaven"), Zeng Tianyang, and Zeng Jinqian. According to the records of the Qing dynasty, the Taipings were at a troop strength of 100,000 men, but this was probably an inflated report. In fact, 30,000 to 50,000 seems closer to reality.

Jiang's sickness derived from overwork. A high fever still afflicted him, and no medicine seemed to bring it down. Aside from the illness that wracked his body, he appeared around this time to have been overcome by what would now be called a manic-depressive psychosis. One could sense something abnormal in the excessive sarcasm hurled at Prefect Hu Yuanwei, and the abuse unleashed at the man responsible for the local militia.

The execution order for Liu Mou, commander of the local braves, was canceled, but he was thrown in prison. This action angered the Anhui militiamen and caused them to attack the Hunan braves under Jiang's command. This was something that Prefect Hu, ridiculed as incompetent and grossly obese before everyone, was privately hoping for. "The Manchus invaded and conquered China over two hundred years ago," he thought, "and the time has come somehow or other to replace them." If the next rulers of China turned out to be the Taipings, then the quicker the switch took place, the better. "They'll be doing us a favor," thought Hu.

He would offer up the city to them and surrender. There was no greater present he could give than to surrender. In fact, there may have been no higher act of merit than Luzhou's abandonment of all resistance to the Taipings. In the very midst of the fiercest fighting, to open the city gate and invite the enemy in was the most desirable thing he could do.

On the evening of the day he had been the butt of Jiang's insults, Hu Yuanwei sent a trusted underling out of the city to establish contact with the Taiping military and convey his wish to collaborate. Fierce internal discord was erupting within the city both while the collaborators were at home and when they went to welcome the enemy. Had either the discontent or the collusion been absent, Luzhou would probably have fallen either way, but what really hastened the city's collapse was Jiang Zhongyuan's frenzied arrangements.

Local Taiping forces made use of the miners' brigade and aimed at blowing up the city walls with numerous land mines. On January 14, the wall at the Shuixi Gate into Luzhou was badly damaged, and Taiping troops surged in from that point. Because of Jiang's secret contacts with the Taipings, they knew the places that pursued resistance within the city and places prepared to surrender. The assault was successful.

Luzhou was by no means an isolated, unsupported fortress. Shu-xing-a, governor-general of Shaanxi and Gansu provinces, was camped with 15,000 troops under his command at Gangziji on the outskirts of Luzhou. Jiangnan Governor-General He-chun was rushing to the scene with reinforcements from Xuzhou. Yuan Jiasan (1806–1863), who had been serving in Beijing as a supervising censor (a secretary for the emperor), was in the northern part of Anhui province at just this time, and he observed the troops of the local *tuanlian*; they were ordered to go to the assistance of Luzhou. Yuan Jiasan had no biological sons, and had taken a relative by the name of Yuan Baoqing as his adoptive son. Yuan Baoqing would also have no sons and would adopt as heir a nephew by the name of Yuan Shikai (1859–1916), the man who was destined to play such an important role in the last years of the Qing dynasty. Yuan Jiasan was thus the grandfather of the man destined for such a major place in modern Chinese history.

Qing reinforcements had arrived, but the Taipings' troop strength out-numbered them. Luzhou fell. Jiang Zhongyuan, it was said, fought this battle from his sickbed. The day was thick with fog and mist. Resigned to the fact that he was now going to meet his end, Jiang attempted to commit suicide with his dagger, but the reduced strength caused by his illness prevented him from dying.

"What are you doing?" said one of the Hunan braves. "We must plan our recovery." Wresting the dagger from Jiang's hand, he lifted Jiang's bloody body onto his back and ran outside. He was young and quite strong. Holding Jiang's sickly body firmly, he ran off impetuously.

"Don't be an idiot! There's no way we can escape!" Jiang was yelling from atop the young man's back, but the latter didn't seem to hear Jiang's words. Jiang knew they were running toward the Jindou Gate.

"Hmm," he thought, "there's a pond over there." In his weakened state, Jiang was wondering how he might get off this fellow's back. He saw in front of him the nape of the young man's neck. When he noticed that they were approaching the pond, he abruptly bit the young man on the back of his neck.

For a moment the strength in the young man's arms was diminished as he screamed in pain. Jiang jumped to the ground nimbly, and with his last spurt of energy leapt in the direction of the pond. It was an old pond known for its depth that Jiang threw himself into. He was forty-two years of age.

Liu Yuzhen, the Anhui administration commissioner, Li Benren, the former Anhui administration commissioner who still lived in the province, and Chen Yuanyan, soon to be a prefect, all died in the fighting. County

Magistrates Zou Hanxun and Hu Ziyong, Adjutants Song An and Dai Wenlan, and most of the leaders of the city of Luzhou died in their sleep. And yet, on the list of those who died at their posts, the name of Hu Yuanwei was conspicuously absent.

—7—

Although Luzhou was officially a prefectural seat, it was for all intents and purposes, the provincial seat as well. Anqing, the capital of Anhui province, had been occupied by the forces of Shi Dakai. Within Anhui, Luzhou was situated in an important place for communications, far further to the north than Anqing. It had become an important base site for the Taipings to send support to the northern expeditionary force, which had begun to send back stories of hard-fought battles.

The commander of the Taiping forces that led the attack on Luzhou was Zeng Tianxiang, holder of various posts in the Taiping hierarchy. After Zeng and his troops occupied Luzhou, they set out to return to Huangzhou. He was given the nickname of Flying Commander, for one moment he was nearby and the next he was actively at work at a point far removed. Before he appeared at Luzhou, he had been in Jiangxi province and had gained fame for bringing down the city of Jingdezhen, well-known for its ceramics. The potters in Jingdezhen at the time had been in secret communication with Zeng's army, and together they routed the Qing forces.

One might associate the name Flying Commander with a dashing young warrior, but in fact, Zeng Tianyang had already surpassed the milestone of fifty years of age when the rebellion first began back in Jintian village. Within the Taiping armed forces, he might just as well have been called the Old Warhorse.

Shi Zhenxiang (a cousin of Shi Dakai), who had pulled back from Wuhan, took over general command of the Taiping Army at Huangzhou. Thus, the leaders of the forces under him were Wei Jun, Wei Yide, Shi Fengkui, Shi Zhenlun, Huang Zaixing, and Lin Shaozhang. Add to this group the forces of the Flying Commander Zeng Tianxiang, and Taiping overall troop strength there numbered 40,000.

Governor-General Wu Wenrong, who had left Wuchang to confront the Taipings because of the accusations leveled against him by Chong-lun, arrived on New Year's Day at Ducheng, a town some ten kilometers from Huangzhou. Because it was far too small a place to accommodate his 7,000 troops, he perforce pitched camp for most of his men in the open field.

In frequent memorials to the court in Beijing, Zeng Guofan had urged a postponement of further military actions until the navy was in working order. By saving their strength, he argued, their subsequent blows would be that much stronger. However, scarcely anyone in Beijing understood a thing about either military strategy or tactics.

At sixty-two years of age and braving the severe cold weather at that time, Wu Wenrong set out for the front. The thirteen barracks at Ducheng appeared to be buried in snow, and indeed some men did freeze to death. Wu was also prepared to die.

All manner of sights and sounds from the past floated rapidly through his mind. Looking up into a sky hazy from the snow, he thought back over the events of his career: that grand day in 1819 when he became a metropolitan graduate by virtue of passing the highest level of the civil service examinations; and that day in 1838 when he personally tested the provincial graduates of the entire realm as the assistant examining official at the metropolitan examinations. One of the young men who passed that year and became a metropolitan graduate was Zeng Guofan, now in Hunan province.

Wu wondered what role his birth and place in the world had played on behalf of others. He hadn't lived his entire life absorbed in the vapid world of the bureaucracy—or had he? He certainly must have helped the Ryūkū Islands, he thought. While serving as the governor-general of Fujian and Zhejiang provinces, Shang Yu of the Ryūkūs came to propose that the tribute-trade be changed from once every four years to every other year. One of the reasons given for this request was the fact that the Ryūkū Islands were lacking in medical supplies and one replenishment in four years left them much in need. This was a matter of human life, and Wu Wenrong set to work enthusiastically at the court in Beijing so that tribute-trade might be allowed every other year. In addition, he selected four provincial graduates from the Ryūkūs and enabled them to study at the National University in the capital. This sort of work characterized his years as governor-general of Fujian and Zhejiang.

"The bandits are surrounding Ducheng even as we speak. They seem to be encircling us at a considerable distance. I am trying to destroy the circle they are forming around us!" Wu was brought back to reality from his reminiscences by the faltering voice of one of his staff men making a report. Wu kept his composure.

At last the time of my death has arrived, he thought, accepting this reality with extraordinary peace of mind. Death was something he understood. It was just the manner in which he would die that he could never imagine.

"It's snowing, but the pond outside the encampment hasn't frozen," said Wu Wenrong. The staff man stared ahead blankly, stupefied.

On all four sides, the Taiping Army had surrounded 7,000 Qing soldiers. The 7,000 troops of the Qing Army at Ducheng were annihilated. In the midst of the confused fighting, any number of men witnessed the sight of Wu Wenrong throwing himself into the pond outside his camp. Although this event was reported to Wuchang as it had occurred, Chong-lun in Wuchang reported the following to the imperial court in Beijing: "Our national forces at Ducheng fell to the strategies of the bandits and were demolished. The whereabouts of Governor-General Wu Wenrong remain unknown."

Taiping forces under the command of Shi Zhenxiang and Zeng Tianyang destroyed the Qing troops at Ducheng, and once again moved to occupied Hankou and Hanyang for the third time. It took place on the fourth day following the death of Wu Wenrong, February 16, 1854.

Zeng Guofan, who was in Hengzhou, Hunan province at the time, finally rose to his feet. The navy had been organized. At least the form of a naval force had taken shape in great haste. For his part, Zeng was still not completely satisfied with it.

High-speed vessels ("quick crabs"): 40
Large-scale armed vessels ("tall dragons"): 50
Sampans: 150
Converted vessels (from private to military): 120
Baggage vessels (hired privately): 100+

The naval militia assembled numbered in excess of five thousand men and was divided into ten brigades. The army division was also over five thousand men. The Xiang Army (a force of Hunan volunteers) was born here. This was also, some argue, the birth of warlordism in modern Chinese history.

The order given by Zeng for the Xiang Army to begin marching went out on the ninth day following the fall of Hankou and Hanyang for the third time. The fight to the death between the Taipings and the Xiang Army had begun.

There had been an urgent appeal from Beijing, and requests for assistance had come any number of times from Wuchang. Furthermore, these requests had been made in the name of Wu Wenrong, though Governor-General Wu had died some time previously. The despicable Chong-lun had purposely used the name of the dead governor-general. Inasmuch as Wu had been the assistant examining official at the time Zeng Guofan became a metropolitan graduate, Chong-lun was trying to appeal to this old tie.

After the fall of Hankou and Hanyang, Wuchang across the river held its ground for six months before also falling to the Taipings. At the time it collapsed, Chong-lun had run off, fleeing to the north.

Zeng Guofan later sent to the court in Beijing vitriolic memorials of impeachment. Although he wrote a large number of such memorials, the vehemence of the language was unusual even for him.

Though everyone in the army knew that Wu Wenrong had died a martyr's death, Chong-lun reported that Wu's whereabouts were unknown and insinuated that he may have deserted. In response, Zeng Guofan stated in no uncertain terms: "Not only was he [Wu] ignored in his lifetime, but he was being slandered again after his death." Zeng denounced this as pernicious fraudulence, for at the time that Chong-lun had forged the documents using the name of Governor-General Wu Wenrong, Ducheng had already fallen.

"He was obsessed with jealousy, making false accusations concerning another man's duty. In truth, I do not know of what substance his heart is made." This last line was the strongest language Zeng used.

On the day prior to the fall of Wuchang, Chong-lun said, "I have been relieved of my duties and called back to Beijing." Then, he promptly left the city. No such order had ever emanated from the capital.

Chong-lun fled as far as Shaanxi province, where he became severely ill. On his sickbed, he heard the news that Wu Wenrong had been enshrined in the Temple of Luminous Fidelity in the capital for "facing the battle array, sacrificing his own life, and not neglecting a higher duty," and the special privilege of being given a hereditary post of commandant of the cavalry was awarded to a descendant of his.

At the same time, Chong-lun learned that a decision had been reached concerning himself. "Arrest him and escort him back to the capital, where he shall be placed before the Ministry of Justice." Chong-lun well knew that he would not evade the death penalty under interrogation there. However, before he could be escorted back to Beijing under guard, he succumbed to his illness in Shaanxi.

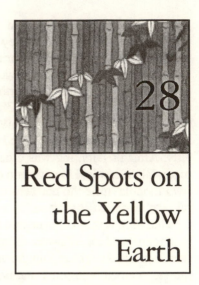

28

Red Spots on
the Yellow
Earth

—1—

Beijing was in an uproar. The long-haired bandits had already approached as far as Tianjin. From the perspective of the Qing court, the Taipings' northern expeditionary army was perpetrating an act of high treason. This Taiping Army was coming to attack with a crescendo of violent force, having departed Yangzhou, and in just over a month, arriving at the Yellow River.

Yet after they reached the banks of the Yellow River, the troops of the northern expeditionary army wasted too much precious time. After the Qing precipitously withdrew its vessels along the Yellow River, the Taipings were in a bind as to how they would cross the river.

The Yellow River is not now what it was then. At that time, the waters of the Yellow River flowed swiftly near the city of Shangqiu, which lies far to the south of where the river now courses. The Taiping forces initially planned to ford the river at that spot, but inasmuch as they had no boats, they continued to move to the west in search of a place to cross over.

In the process, they attacked the city of Kaifeng, once a strategic point, the capital of the Northern Song dynasty (960–1126). The battle at Kaifeng was, for all intents and purposes, superfluous, for the decision to cross the Yellow River had already been made.

Unable to overrun Kaifeng, which was stubbornly defended by Provincial Administration Commissioner Shen Zhaoyun, Surveillance Commissioner Lin Yangzu, and others, the Taipings lifted their siege, advanced to the west, passed by Zhengzhou, and in Gongxian, near the city of Luoyang, they were finally able to secure boats and successfully forded the Yellow River. Successfully only to a point, for they had so few vessels that they were unable to cross en masse. The great majority of the 20,000 Taiping soldiers completed the crossing, but it took a full week's time.

After the leaders of the northern expeditionary force—Li Kaifang, Lin Fengxiang, Ji Wenyuan, and Zhu Xikun among them—crossed the river, they laid siege to the prefectural city of Huaiqing (present-day Qingyang county). Though the siege lasted for sixty days, they were unable to take the city. After the fighting was over, it was perfectly clear that it had been a colossal diversion. However, no one would have initially imagined that after two months' time the northern expeditionary army would have proved unable to bring the city down.

Huaiqing was at the center of the Qing's munitions industry. Gunpowder, handguns, and the like were all produced here, and it was for this reason that the Taipings sought to capture it. Victory would enable them to seize the gunpowder and weaponry and not allow it to pass into Qing hands. Government forces naturally fought back with great stubbornness.

The northern expeditionary army of the Taipings was supposed to fight on as far as Beijing with lightning speed. The more time it took this force to move toward its goal, the more time Qing armies had to adopt a number of different tactics. After abandoning their assault on Huaiqing, the Taipings entered Shanxi province. It was already the eighth lunar month of 1853, precisely the same time that the Small Sword Society in Shanghai had moved to occupy the county seat.

Eventually, the northern expeditionary force moved on from Shanxi to Zhili, present-day Hebei province. As the Chinese characters of the word Zhili imply, it was terrain "directly under the control" of the imperial court in Beijing. Now the northern expeditionary army of the Taiping rebels had attacked the imperial capital of the Qing dynasty.

On the first day of the ninth lunar month, the Taipings captured Baixiang, a prefectural seat about 70 kilometers south of the city of Shijiazhuang. By the solar calendar it was October 3, 1853, already well into autumn. Thereafter, in succession, Zhaozhou, Luancheng, Gaozhou, and Shenzhou all fell into Taiping hands. From Shenzhou—present-day Shenxian—only about 220 kilometers remained before reaching Beijing.

Accused of responsibility for these developments, Zhili Governor-General No-er-jing-e was stripped of his position and replaced by Gui-liang. At the time of the Opium War, Zhili Governor-General Qi-shan had transferred to Guangdong; picking up where Qi-shan had left off, No-er-jing-e had held this post over the course of fourteen calendar years. The governor-general of Zhili was the most important bureaucratic office in the land, for he not only had jurisdiction over Zhili province, but over neighboring Shandong, Shanxi, and Henan provinces as well. Later in the Qing period, Zeng Guofan, Li Hongzhang, and others effectively became "prime ministers" in this post.

On October 11 (the ninth day of the ninth lunar month, the day of the Chrysanthemum Festival), the Qing court finally appointed Prince Hui (Mian-yu) of the imperial family to the position of general-in-chief. Prince Hui was an uncle of the Xianfeng Emperor. At the same time, the court made a Mongol prince by the name of Seng-ge-lin-qin (d. 1865) the grand military consultant, and the two men were to lead the government's troops. Together with Sheng-bao (d. 1863), who had been appointed imperial commissioner, these three men acquired the highest responsibility for defense against the Taiping forces that had begun to bring pressure to bear on the capital.

Next, Prince Gong (Yi-xin, 1833–1898) was sent to inspect the defenses. Prince Gong was a younger brother of the Xianfeng Emperor, who was the fourth of eight brothers. Because his three elder brothers had predeceased him, at present Xianfeng had four younger brothers. However, from his youth, Xianfeng had been raised solely with the sixth brother, Prince Gong, and as such the two of them were on extremely close terms.

This younger brother—in whom the emperor placed the same trust he would in a confidante—appeared in public. This was due to the gravity of the situation. When the news was heard that Prince Gong was out on horseback, the populace in Beijing was thrown into further unease.

The governor-general of Zhili resided at the provincial capital, which was then in Baoding. Imperial Commissioner Sheng-bao entered the walled city of Baoding on the eleventh day of the ninth lunar month (October 13). At that time, Grand Military Consultant Seng-ge-lin-qin had advanced his troops as far as Zhuozhou, which lay precisely between Beijing and Baoding.

One part of the Taipings' northern expeditionary force advanced to Zhangdeng, some 30 kilometers to the south of Baoding.

The Qing authorities were going to fight just as stubbornly. On the charge that he had permitted the bandit army to invade the imperial capital of the Son of Heaven, Zhili Governor-General No-er-jing-e was sentenced to execution. (Later, though, the death sentence was rescinded, because it was said that he was a man of ordinarily diligent abilities, and he performed military service for two years before being released). One could not allow oneself the luxury of absent-mindedness. Seng-ge-lin-qin built a large encampment at Zhuozhou. It was in fact a protective barrier for Beijing. He was resolved not to move so much as one single step to the north from that position.

Appropriately, the finest select troops were stationed in the capital. Brigades of imperial guards were effectively put in place: a scouting brigade, a firearms brigade, a two-winged (left and right) vanguard brigade, and a policing brigade. These formed the foundations for the encampment at Zhuozhou. They were further augmented by 2,000 intrepid Mongol soldiers. The grand military consultant of the Zhuozhou encampment was himself a Mongol prince of the blood, and this tended to enhance the morale of these reinforcements. From Dongsanmeng in Mongolia, cavalry forces continued to move south in rapid succession.

There had been over ten thousand troops at the encampment of the imperial commissioner, but suddenly some six thousand Mongol soldiers arrived, as well as cavalry and artillery forces.

The Qing Army that the Taipings had hitherto confronted was rather different now. Qing armed forces in Guangxi, Hunan, Hubei, and elsewhere, had been far from the imperial capital. Even if defeated on the battlefield, they could deceive the authorities or gloss over the facts. A rout, for example, was often reported as a "change of course."

Such deception was utterly useless when the fighting transpired in Zhili.

—2—

"The gleaming Na-ku-ni-su sword." It was the name of a precious sword given by the Xianfeng Emperor to Seng-ge-lin-qin when the latter was appointed grand military consultant. Seng-ge-lin-qin was in effect being told to use it to decapitate the bandits and then return it to the court. As such, its presentation to him was no state secret, but a loan of sorts.

"Is that what this is, then?" asked Lian Chengwen as he stared at the precious sword placed before him on the table.

"Is that really it?" asked his wife, Cailan, peeping in from the side, her shoulders hunched.

"Yes, this is the real thing. That Mongol commander will have to fabricate his own bogus one now. Ha, ha . . . ," laughed Xiling.

She was still in Beijing. Even after Lian Weicai had left Shanghai, she remained in the capital. The waters of Beijing seemed to agree with her.

Lian Weicai's second son, Chengwen, and his wife had recently arrived in the capital. "I return south with Chengwen when he does," she had said, adamantly insisting on remaining where she was. "It is wonderful to be able to meet with people from Guiping again and here in the capital," she told Chengwen.

Since she had then been in Guiping, Xiling knew of the early years of the Taiping movement. She even knew the leaders themselves. They were now on their way north, fighting their way to Beijing. She would see them in the capital. Or so at least Xiling had imagined the scene unfolding. The membrane separating imagination from reality in her case was extraordinarily thin.

She prayed for success in the Taipings' northern march, though there was nothing she could really do on behalf of the northern expeditionary army. She informed them as rapidly and accurately as she could of conditions prevailing in Beijing, and she hoped that by doing so she had been able to be of some service.

"Stop, stop please. It's too dangerous." Chengwen tried to put a halt to it. Chengwen well knew that, on account of his father, Xiling was being extremely cautious. The Qing dynasty was desperate, and it would take merciless measures in dealing with the Taipings.

"I'm prepared." Xiling was afraid of nothing. She had long been of the mind that death was preferable to boredom.

"The news from Beijing is that the Taipings themselves are calling in the spies they've placed there. You're just duplicating their efforts, so please put an end to it."

"I can do things that Taiping spies cannot do," she said. It was she who had stolen the illustrious sword given by the emperor himself from the residence of the grand military consultant. Chengwen didn't know whom she had relied on to accomplish this feat. He had a few ideas on the matter, but had decided not to pose the question. In any event, she had risked her life by stealing it.

The hand-guard on the sword was made of gold, and the hilt had rubies inlaid on a white jade background. The pommel was surrounded with turquoise. The scabbard was ebony with tortoise shell and cowry inlaid in the form of Arabic writing.

"By the hilt it indicates that it was made during the reign of the Qianlong Emperor, but the sword was a tribute gift of Muslims coming from lands to the west," explained Xiling.

When emissaries of the lands to the west of China came to bear tribute to the Chinese court, they often included precious swords among the items presented. This occurred on many occasions during the reign of Qianlong, and on one such occasion when Nepal brought tribute to the Chinese capital, the emperor was presented with this sword. At such times, the Chinese characters for "made in the Qianlong reign" were ordinarily inscribed on the sword.

"It certainly looks sharp," said Xiling, as she nonchalantly lifted the sword, placed one hand on the hilt, and unsheathed it. The blade was etched with a stunning floral design full of gold.

"Chengwen, were you thinking what I'd do with such a sword if I'd stolen it?" asked Xiling.

"Yes, I was," replied the thirty-seven-year-old Chengwen honestly. Since she knew about his childhood, he felt compelled to answer honestly.

"I'm happy with this. It's very satisfying, and that's all," she said. Doubtless it had cost a lot of money to steal this sword, and at any rate, she'd risked her life.

"The grand military consultant must be beside himself."

Having lost this invaluable sword lent him by the emperor, Seng-ge-lin-qin had no choice but to atone for it with his life. This might bode ill for the Taipings, for Seng-ge-lin-qin would surely fight them now with great intensity and desperation. A sense of apprehension suddenly came over Chengwen. Xiling was the sort of person who did not so much as try to see the consequences of her actions.

"True enough," she said, "and it serves him right. He may seem brave, but while he's riding astride his horse, in his heart he'll be worrying about the sword that was stolen from him."

"Xiling, if you're satisfied by this whole business, then why don't we set off for the south? Shanghai's a very interesting place, you know." Chengwen was trying to draw her out.

"That's what they say," she said, and after a moment she turned her gaze back on the blade of the gleaming Na-ku-ni-su sword. "Beijing is becoming a very lonely place."

At the news of the Taipings' northern advance, officials and those with any amount of money fled from the capital. The rumor that the Taipings massacred all officials had even spread to north China. It was the national capital, and as such, Beijing was home to numerous bureaucrats, high and low alike, though the Taipings were said not to make such distinctions. Thus, even those at the level of gatekeepers at the yamen offices had escaped for their lives. And those with a small amount of wealth feared depredation.

High officials at the court couldn't simply run off by themselves, but first placed their families outside the city of Beijing. Some 30,000 households, it was said, resettled outside the city walls. In the northern sector of the city lived 18,000 households, but after the Taipings entered Zhili province, 10,000 of them moved away, leaving but 8,000.

Indeed, it had become desolate, deserted. Several of the people with whom Xiling would ordinarily come into contact had left, and she had become lonesome. She returned the sword to its sheath and sighed ever so slightly.

"The name of the sword . . ." she said, turning it over on the table. "In the language of the western regions, I am told, *na-ku* means 'good' and *ni-su* carries the connotation of 'omen.' The sword of good omens. Yet, good omens for whom?"

—3—

It was gradually becoming clear that the sixty-day siege of Huaiqing had been a defeat for the Taiping forces. Not only had it afforded the Qing authorities time to devise countermeasures, but the Taipings brought on themselves that great enemy of the winter in north China.

Realizing what had happened only after they arrived in Zhili, the Taipings were not particular about the seizure of territory. Some cities that they assaulted fell, but where there was severe resistance, they decided to pass through without trying to maintain an occupation. For example, they attacked the city of Shunde in Zhili, but the defense of the city was so intense that the Taipings concluded that it would be best to move on, leave Shunde, and to occupy Renxian instead.

Meanwhile, time passed and they fell behind schedule. Winter's frost was marching double time and heading for the plains of Zhili. Many of the troops in the northern expeditionary army came from the warmer provinces of Guangxi, Hunan, and Hubei, while few were from the provinces of Jiangsu and Anhui. In either case, they had all been raised in areas that never experienced truly frigid winters. Not only were they physically unfamiliar with such weather, they did not even know how to prepare themselves for the cold.

Taiping leaders knew secondhand of the severity of Zhili winters. The order for the northern expedition went out at the beginning of the third lunar month, and at the time of the troops' departure, they received the following instructions: "It is advisable that the fighting be completed before the onset of winter."

The Taipings also knew full well that a large, secure encampment was to be established around Zhuozhou and that it would be extremely difficult to overrun and destroy it. From early on in the operation, Taiping intelligence activities had been completely trustworthy.

Government troop strength was continually increasing along a line from present-day Zhuoxian to Gu'an, with the Yongding River to their backs. It was not simply that the Qing forces were putting up a defense. Imperial Commissioner Sheng-bao had assaulted the Taiping forces at Shenzhou along four routes, led by military commanders Mian-xun, Gui-ling, Shan-lu, and Xi-ling-ga (a banner commander-in-chief). Such a ferocious attack by the Qing Army was something the Taipings had never experienced.

"We're going to really be hurt badly if we follow past practices now," said Li Kaifang at a meeting of the Taiping leadership. He had underscored this point on numerous occasions to the generals of the northern expeditionary forces.

"Yes, their response this time is altogether different from anything we've seen to this point." Whenever one crossed swords with an opponent, the strength of the opponent was measured by their response.

"A direct attack on Beijing will be exceedingly difficult," said war veteran Lin Fengxiang, who also felt it would be impossible to overrun the defense line along the Yongding River.

"Let's move around to the east," put forth Ji Wenyuan.

"You mean toward Tianjin. It'll be difficult to take Beijing by winter. But Tianjin's another story," said Li Kaifang weakly.

The northern expeditionary army headed to the east, as it had been dislodged from Shenzhou in a fierce attack by Qing forces under the command of Sheng-bao. The Taipings moved on to seize Xianxian and Jiaohexian.

"They may have hurt us this last time," said Li, "but we're going to repay the favor."

When the Taipings occupied Jiaohexian, Lin Fengxiang executed County Magistrate Kong Qinggui on the spot. Two days later, on the twenty-fifth day of the ninth lunar month, they attacked and claimed Cangzhou, and murdered Department Magistrate Shen Ruchao. On the twenty-seventh, the northern expeditionary force proceeded north from Cangzhou as far as Jinghai county. They were now but a stone's throw away from Tianjin. But, it was the twenty-ninth of October according to the solar calendar.

Li Kaifang continued north with his troops to Duliu and Yangliuqing. Yangliuqing was a tiny town, though the area was well-known for woodblock prints and the reproduction of books and paintings.

By the time winter arrived, the northern expeditionary army had begun its effort to take Tianjin, and the Qing armies had no choice but to desperately defend that city. Qing forces repeatedly attacked Duliu and were victorious after a battle on the twelfth day of the eleventh lunar month. However, a battle on the twenty-third day of the same month saw the Taiping forces win a major victory over the government. Dong-jian, a Mongol banner vice-commander-in-chief, and Xie Zicheng, the Tianjin county magistrate, were both killed by the Taipings in the fighting.

As such a bloody battle unfolded in the environs of Tianjin, the Heavenly Father's Descent to Earth was enacted in the Heavenly Capital of Nanjing, and germs of internal dissension within the Taiping movement were gradually coming to the surface. Just then the new year dawned.

Early in the first month of the fourth year of the Xianfeng reign (1854), the Qing Army was continuing their relentless assault on Taiping forces in the Tianjin area.

"There's an enemy out there more intractable than the Mongol cavalry," said Li Kaifang, grinding his teeth. "No matter how brave our troops and commanders are, compared to the enemy, we're all like children." By this reference to the ferocity of the "enemy" compared to the Mongol cavalry, Li specifically meant the cold of north China.

Even if the Taipings were able to break through the walls surrounding Tianjin, it was still doubtful if that would be enough to keep themselves warm. Still, though, the strongest military forces of the Qing government were obstructing the advance of the northern expeditionary army. The majority of Qing forces were comprised of a battalion transferred from Mongolia, youngsters inured to the cold and who would never, in any event, complain about it.

"The cold is going to lower troop morale. I can see that now," said Lin Fengxiang, with no other option now available.

Day by day the number of those freezing to death was on the rise.

"We've got to do something." The Taiping leaders were becoming impatient. Had it not been so cold, they could have trampled right over Tianjin, and then used the new momentum to advance and occupy Beijing.

"It's because of that river then. If it hadn't been for that waterway . . . oh, how I regret it now," Ji Wenyuan, rarely one to complain, said repeatedly with disappointment. When they had been moving northward from Cangzhou, the Taipings had an opportunity to attack Tianjin directly, but the river that ringed Tianjin was overflowing at the time, and the Taiping forces had halted their advance. The weather had not looked favorably upon the Taipings.

"Don't say that!" warned Li Kaifang with a frown. "It doesn't help us resolve the present situation at all."

Indeed, how were they to escape the present predicament? Retreat further south—it was the only way to avoid the frigid weather. There was Tianjin before their eyes. Jinghai and Duliu, where the northern expeditionary army had made camp, were both part of Tianjin prefecture.

"It's a total defeat for us, completely."

Li Kaifang finally decided to abandon camp and move south. The northern expeditionary army began to move toward the southwest from Jinghai county on February 5, 1854, corresponding to the eighth day of the new lunar year. It had been snowing incessantly on the Zhili plain.

"How many of our troops will fall by the roadside and be buried in the snow?" muttered Li Kaifang, his head between his hands, as they were leaving Jinghai.

The day prior to the northern expeditionary forces' retreat southward, reinforcements for Tianjin in the north set out. Huang Shengcai, Chen Shibao, Xu Zongyang, Huang Yiyun, and Zeng Lichang were appointed commanders of these reinforcements.

As the northern expeditionary forces moved south, they came under attack by the Qing Army. Even greater than the number of those lost in the fighting, though, were the number of Taiping dead due to the cold.

On the eleventh day of the second lunar month, Li Kaifeng and his men entered Foucheng, a city in southern Zhili near the border with Shandong province. There, enduring a siege by the Qing forces, they awaited the arrival of the reinforcements sent to assist them, while painful fighting continued.

—4—

"It says that Chengwen and his wife are coming to Shanghai, together with Xiling," said Lian Weicai, as he folded a letter he had just finished reading.

"What route are they taking?" asked Liwen.

"By ship."

"That's a safe way to come." Any land route was likely run into fighting between the Qing Army and the Taipings' northern expeditionary force and reinforcements to it. To become enveloped in the conflict would be extremely dangerous.

"They said they'll take a boat if the ice thaws on the frozen river." For the three months of winter, vessels did not leave Tianjin due to the frozen conditions.

"Xiling can be a very curious creature. The land route will not suffice for her. She gave up that idea."

"Chengwen and his wife were probably worn down by her into agreeing."

"A full report from younger brother Zhewen hasn't arrived."

"Hmm. I'm expecting it. He should be in Kagoshima by now, not the Ryūkyū [Liuqiu] Islands, but are reports about Edo that hard to get one's hands on?"

"The ruling Shimazu clan of Kagoshima has been working hard to have fast-sailing ships ready throughout the Inland Sea of Japan, and to get its hands as rapidly as possible on news from the capital in Edo."

"I wonder if Zhewen just did a bad job of getting hold of information?"

"He's been introducing us to speedy sources of information, such as a young man by the name of Ōkubo from the Ryūkyū Hall, but will that do?"

"Maybe he's just painting his pictures?" said Lian Weicai with a wry smile.

They had learned from Zhewen that Commodore Perry of the United States of America had returned to Japan this New Year's Day. In the sixth month of the previous year, Perry had sailed into Uraga Bay. He was conveying a message from President Millard Fillmore, and after agreeing to extend the date of his return by a year, he set off for Hong Kong by way of the Ryūkyū Islands.

That year, Japan was to be pressed for a response. Lian Weicai was deeply concerned with the sort of resolution Japan would attempt to make. Further prolongation was impossible. Just after Perry departed the previous year, the Shōgun Tokugawa Ieyoshi died, and about the time that the shogunate requested an extension from Perry in Hong Kong, it was firmly rejected.

Lian anticipated that Japan would have no choice but to conclude a peace treaty, though what he really wanted to know was the content of such a treaty.

"It says that he arrived in Kanagawa Bay on the sixteenth of the first month of the year, so the treaty should already be in the making," said Lian Weicai.

"The shogunate probably won't make a public announcement of it."

"True, but the Shimazus are important vassals and they should know its contents."

"Possibly Zhewen himself already knows and has written us a letter. My guess is that it just hasn't arrived yet."

"It's already the seventh of the third lunar month."

Lian Weicai's words were meant to convey two meanings. Some fifty days had passed since Perry's arrival in Kanagawa Bay. Four o'clock that very afternoon was the time limit that Shanghai British Consul Rutherford Alcock had expressed in an ultimatum to move the Qing military encampment adjacent to the foreign concession area. It was April 4, 1854.

The very next day was the Qingming Festival. It was the custom in China on Qingming day to visit the graves of one's ancestors and tidy them up. The long winter had passed, and at last spring-like weather was in the air. To visit graves meant, of course, going out of the city. Having been confined to their homes until then, people made something of an excursion of it on a beautiful spring day. It was ordinarily a happy, lighthearted event for most, though because of the war raging that year, there was little joy to be found.

The area on the outskirts of the city where Qingming observers were to go was presently where 20,000 Qing troops were stationed for their assault on Shanghai. From time to time, Qing soldiers entered the foreign concession quarter of the city, and Rutherford Alcock leveled a firm protestation before them.

To be sure, the Qing military had its own objections once inside the concession area. The land itself was, after all, Chinese terrain. Why should the entrance of Qing troops there be seen as something improper?

At that moment in time, the walled city of Shanghai was under occupation by the rebel band known as the Small Sword Society. The authorities had to recapture the city. If the work of retaking the city continued at the present dilatory pace, the imperial court might threaten them with capital punishment—no empty threat.

The leaders of the government's forces were burning with impatience. Why had they been unable to take back Shanghai? It was because they had been unable to secure a hermetic siege of the city. That in turn was due to the foreign concession area. The rebels within Shanghai had been receiving unlimited quantities of supplies from the concession area. Since those within the concession area had no business ventures more desirable at present, they continued to do business by supplying commodities to the Small Swords under siege.

Shanghai was a city of some three hundred thousand residents, though after the occupation by the Small Swords there had been successive waves of refugees fleeing the city, which reduced the population to several tens of thousands.

Worried about an insufficient number of combatants, the Small Swords pressed residents into military service, and this only increased the flow of refugees.

The troop strength of the Small Swords within the city of Shanghai was said to be no more than several thousand. The 20,000 Qing troops had become disheartened in conducting their siege of the city. To their way of thinking, the concession area was standing in their way.

British merchants had even been selling the Small Swords weaponry and ammunition. On the surface they claimed to be observing "strict neutrality," though commerce was an altogether different matter.

"How can you sell guns and bullets only to the rebels and not to the authorities? That's not neutrality at all." This criticism from the French was delivered to both the British and the Americans.

"The buying or selling of a commodity is merely a commercial transaction, pure and simple," they replied to such criticism.

The Qing armed forces sent government merchants to purchase military supplies from the foreigners, but they could not agree on a price. Relying on the authority of their superiors, these official merchants haggled ferociously over prices, though it did no good. As a result, such commercial negotiations were more likely than not going to collapse.

The negotiations in which the government was going to attempt to get its official merchants to buy cannons stocked in the concession area had already failed once. There had been an incident in which official merchants, with the assistance of government troops, under cover of night, had tried by force to transport the cannons out of the city and had been stiffly repelled by a force of foreign volunteers from the concession area.

This incident had taken place after troops repeatedly gained entrance into the concession area from the Qing's military base adjacent to it. It was a form of harassment. That Qing base was close to the racetrack in the concession, and government forces purposefully carried out marksmanship practice in the direction of the racetrack.

There was another incident in which a British couple, riding near the racetrack in a sedan chair, had been assaulted by Qing troops. The soldiers had plunged their lances inside the sedan chair, and the woman barely escaped with her life, while her husband sustained wounds.

As the marksmanship practice was being carried out in the direction of the concession area with ever greater conspicuousness, it resulted finally in the ultimatum from Consul Alcock. Would the Qing forces really abandon their position and move elsewhere? Lian Weicai had been observing them all morning, but he'd seen no movement of this sort from the Qing encampment. "Today's not a day to go outside," he said. "What a waste it'd be to get hit by a stray bullet."

A Chinese servant from the Wade Company came in and said, "Mr. Tan Qi has arrived."

Tan Qi had been in the Heavenly Capital (Nanjing) for some time and had surreptitiously reentered Shanghai.

—5—

"Zhang Jigeng's been caught, and Wu Weitang has run away. Their revolt against the Taipings has failed. I hear also that the laborers are going to be stocking up on silk from now on," said Tan Qi, relaying information from the Heavenly Capital.

Following their occupation of Nanjing, the Taipings had put into place strict control over the local residents. First they divided the families into units and then divided them into male and female barracks. They similarly demanded of all, men or women, that they perform service to society. Those who were ardently religious—no matter how unselfish they may have been— were despised for this by the local populace. Needless to say, the discontent of that social stratum that had never worked before in their lives was by far the strongest.

Wu Weitang, chief of the Taipings' Textile Agency, had been an official Qing government merchant. Because of his ability to satisfy the luxury demands of the Taiping leadership, Wu had been appointed to such a responsible post in the Taiping regime. In his own mind, he looked condescendingly at the declining state of "these country bumpkins" whom he was now serving.

Wu had been given, on the basis of a special order directly from Yang Xiuqing, freedom of access into and out of the gates of Nanjing with a document bearing the seal of the head of the Textile Agency. Furthermore, because he was registered at the Textile Agency, Wu was able to avoid the labor service demanded by the Taiping government. Many people had come to rely on Wu Weitang, and those lucky people had often lived happy lives as well under the Qing dynasty.

When people of this sort looked about them, they were wont to say, "A bunch of wild monkeys from Guangxi"—nothing but deprecation for the Taiping movement. They seemed to have hallucinations that all the people of Nanjing despised the organization of life under the Taipings, who had created circumstances not unlike purgatory.

In fact, the poor people, who lived and worked from day to day and made up the great majority of the populace of Nanjing, found that under the Taiping regime they had work, their livelihood was secure, and their circumstances had actually improved. From the perspective of Wu Weitang and his cohorts, however, such people were not part of humanity.

The place was overflowing with discontent, grumbling, and resentment; were someone to light a fire, the surface would surely explode into flames. Judging the circumstances surrounding him as such, Wu Weitang won over Zhang Jigeng—a man of considerable influence who had worked for the Qing authorities—to help create the *tuanlian,* and together they planned a revolt against the Taipings.

Working on this premise that "everyone hated the Taipings," they moved with great audacity and with undue carelessness. With Wu Weitang's seal affixed to a document, one could come and go at Nanjing at will, and that made contacts outside the city rather easy. Wu used his seal as head of the Textile Agency not simply for passage through Nanjing's gates, making contact with rebel confederates on the outside, but also to enable those people who had become disgusted with Taiping politics to flee from their control. Of course, he collected a fee—and not a small one—from those who wished to escape.

"There seem to be an awful lot of people who come and go here . . . with papers bearing the seal of the head of the Textile Agency," noticed the man in charge of guarding the city gate.

When Taiping leader Huang Yukun learned of this development, he quietly investigated. A follow-up investigation of Zhang Jigeng, who was acting without the least bit of wariness, was immediately implemented by the Taiping authorities.

When the Qing Army attacked in an effort to recover Nanjing, it was Zhang's job to get specialists in strategy within the city to act in concert with the government's forces. The Taipings inferred this, and pausing momentarily, were able to haul in all the culprits involved. Wu Weitang, who had a merchant's extraordinary sense of smell, took off as fast as his feet would carry him, but Zhang and the others were captured.

"Were they executed?" asked Lian Weicai.

"They hadn't been at the time I left the Heavenly Capital. But they've probably been put to death by now. Since they all confessed everything, they couldn't be allowed to go on living."

"Aren't you supposed to be buying silk now?"

"Nothing escapes your purview, sir. Exactly. Wu Weitang is apparently on his way to Shanghai right now."

"Won't he be killed as soon as he's spotted?"

"No, we're tracking his movements. It's easier to follow the movements of an opposing force if it's kept off guard."

"So, you've already found him?"

"I think you may be clairvoyant, sir. That's correct. He's been spotted in the main Qing military encampment. He was involved to a point in the recent attempt to steal cannons."

"Is that right? That group? Well, thanks to that a great event is about to unfold," said Lian Weicai.

"One way or another, we're setting the Qing Army on him."

"They've lost the leadership of Ji-er-hang-a, so they're getting into deeper and deeper trouble," said Lian, shaking his head. Ji-er-hang-a was the provincial surveillance commissioner of Jiangsu and the superior of Wu Jianzhang, the Shanghai circuit intendant. He also held military control over a force of troops.

The Qing armed camp just to the west of the racetrack involved in the incident described earlier was known as the Northern Camp and was under the command of Regional Commander Hu Songlin, though Hu was unable to control the riffraff under him.

The attempt to remove the cannons from the warehouse of a British merchant was a reprisal aimed at the rupture in commercial negotiations, an action geared toward increasing Qing firepower. There was, however, an act of pure theft in which Qing troops attempted to seize lumber from the building of the Britisher Bowman and to dispose of it through sale. Bowman shot his pistol at them, two Qing soldiers were wounded, and a number were later captured by foreign volunteers in the Concession Area.

The foreign volunteers had been organized on April 12 of the previous year, 1853, and had now seen a full year pass. Britain, the United States, and France were the three countries participating in the joint force. French forces, though, did not join the volunteer force raised to confront the Qing's Northern Camp. France held only the French Concession Area, which was quite small, and had eyes on expanding its terrain. To negotiate such an eventuality, the French would perforce have to deal with the Qing authorities, the present rulers of China.

The feeling in Shanghai was that the French were trying to score points with the Qing court. They were clearly giving assistance to the Qing forces in the war between the Small Sword Society and the government in Shanghai. They thus protested against the violation of neutrality evidenced by the British merchants' sale of weaponry and ammunition to the Small Swords.

Although the Small Swords claimed to be acting in concert with the Taipings, the French had demonstrated no good feelings toward the Taipings from the very start. The Taipings, for their part, had no fondness for Catholics from anywhere. Inasmuch as Catholics placed statues and images in their chapels, from the perspective of Taiping ideals, they were not true Christians. Just as they had destroyed the icons in Buddhist, Daoist, and Confucian temples, so too did Taiping soldiers smash the images and statues of Christ and Mary in

Catholic houses of worship. Being a Catholic country, it was not at all surprising that France eyed the Taipings with hostility.

Were the Taipings to succeed and become masters of China, in the judgment of the French, there would be no future for Catholicism in this country. France thus looked forward to the defeat of the Taiping movement. Accordingly, it boycotted the call to join the foreign volunteers, who were screaming about illegalities committed by the Qing military. To strike a blow at the Qing forces was beneficial to the Small Swords and served as well the cause of the Taipings, who supported the Small Swords.

France was not merely standing on the sidelines, but had actually begun to contemplate actively assisting the Qing forces.

"Wu Weitang fled the Heavenly Capital and is now in the French Concession in Shanghai. He seems to come and go regularly at the Qing encampment too," said Tan Qi.

No wonder the Qing is acting so boldly, thought Lian Weicai, as if he could read their intentions.

Wu Weitang probably reported to the leaders of the Qing armed forces that the foreigners would not try to confront the government's troops, and France was at least not opposed to this. If that were in fact the case, then the Qing would not try to stop the penetration of government soldiers into the foreign concessions.

Unable to recover the city of Shanghai, the Qing military leaders had been influenced by Wu Weitang in their strong antipathy for the foreign concessions—areas they wanted back but were at a loss to recover.

"It would be best if these were all faits accomplis. What are you afraid of?" Wu Weitang was working hard to recover from the losses incurred in Nanjing.

Ji-er-hang-a had in any event not firmly curbed his men from encroaching on the concessions. He tried to take stock of the situation after repeated small infringements. A fierce protestation had arrived from the British consul. And a deadline was in place.

"The foreigners' volunteer corps numbers only a few hundred men. We have some ten thousand men here. What is there to be afraid of?" said Wu Weitang on more than one occasion.

"True, true . . . but France is not part of it," said Ji-er-hang-a with his arms still folded tightly.

"The Northern Camp here lies outside the concessions. Whether we move or remain here is entirely up to us. To be intimidated by the foreigners, break camp, and flee would surely incur the censure of the imperial court in Beijing."

"That's for certain. The deadline has been set for four o'clock this afternoon, and things will remain as they are now." There would be no changes in the Northern Camp of the Qing forces.

—6—

Though they were within the walls of Shanghai, the Small Swords had intimate knowledge of activities going on outside. Even their highest leaders, such as Liu Lichuan, had on occasion disguised themselves and ventured outside the city, so that intelligence came in not only from spies, as the leaders themselves had observed their surroundings with their own eyes. The discord between the Qing forces and the English and Americans inside the concessions was soon known inside Shanghai, as was the ultimatum and its accompanying deadline. "It's not just a threat. If the red-heads say they'll do something, they always do it. There's a strict rule among merchants that if something's been contracted, it must be carried out. There'll definitely be conflict. And the Manchu forces aren't going to pull back, because they probably take their counterparts for granted." Having had occasion to cross swords with merchants himself, Liu Lichuan predicted a confrontation between the foreign volunteer corps and the Qing Army.

The Qing Army's rejection of the foreigners' demands and its refusal to move its encampment were made known to the Small Swords by spies concealed within the government's forces.

A debate broke out among the Small Swords about what sort of action they should pursue should such a conflict come to pass. A conclusion was soon reached: Set out and vigorously attack the Qing military. Though such a conclusion hardly required debate, the meeting dragged on and on over the question of who should lead the assault troops.

As noted earlier, from the beginning of its occupation of Shanghai, a rivalry between Guangdong and Fujian cliques within the Small Sword Society had come to the surface. The fact that the Small Swords had not split apart was due to their continual temporizing and patching over of genuine problems. If they came apart at the seams, it would be a total loss for both cliques, as both would collapse together.

"So then, who do we go with?" Liu Lichuan was troubled. The Guangdong clique was larger in terms of numbers, but Liu belonged to it himself and that made it especially hard for him to pick it. By the same token, if he selected a commander from the Fujian clique, he would probably find himself under severe pressure from the majority Guangdong group.

Zhou Lichun's daughter, Zhou Xiuying, had spoken up several times during the course of the meeting. "When's our turn going to come? We're on loan to you, remember." Her first remarks were off the subject at hand, but Liu Lichuan responded to her in the affirmative.

"That's right. We owe you."

Zhou Lichun had led a peasant resistance movement in Qingpu, near Shanghai. He and his forces had occupied the Zhading county seat and responded to the call of the Small Swords to rise in rebellion together. The Small Swords had successfully taken the city of Shanghai only two days later, but in that time Zhou Lichun's peasant army met with great difficulties. It was this debt to which Liu Lichuan was referring.

When Zhou Lichun heard that, following the Small Swords' seizure of Shanghai, the city had erupted in an ugly fight between two cliques—one from Guangdong and the other from Fujian—over the spoils of war, he lost hope and did not enter the city. In his place, he sent his daughter Xiuying to observe the situation. She was a strong-minded young woman, capable of the task assigned her by her father. Zhou Lichun had made appearances in Shanghai from time to time, though it seems that he did this principally for the purpose of advising his daughter.

Perhaps it would be best, thought Liu Lichuan, to pick a commander from a third party, as long as the Guangdong and Fujian cliques were feuding. Zhou Lichun did represent the local area. Choosing Zhou would probably settle the matter well.

"How about having Zhou Lichun, the man who has struggled so hard in Qingpu, perform these duties for us?" suggested Liu.

The meeting that had been boisterous and noisy until then fell silent. Since he had not selected either of the rival sides, neither expressed any active opposition at that point. After a moment, a voice spoke up. "Lichun's a good choice, but he doesn't seem to have been around much lately."

"Hey, I'm here," said Zhou Xiuying, responding to the voice as she jumped to her feet. "My father's been amassing troops outside the city, and I'm going to move out with the few troops under my command and link up with his forces. The time's already been set, though it's not going to be that easy for him to do."

People were reminded of the dashing figure of Zhou Lichun from the early days of the rebellion by this young woman, Zhou Xiuying, standing before them. The Small Sword Society had expressed its heartfelt thanks to Zhou Lichun for his brave deeds and dubbed his daughter the "woman general." This appellation indicated that she had sufficient status to command troops in the field.

"So, let's rely on our companions in Qingpu." Liu concluded the meeting by naming the place, not the man.

The time of the confrontation between the foreign volunteer corps and the Qing military was set for 4:00 p.m. The Small Swords had adopted the extremely simple strategy of waiting until hostilities broke out between the two sides and then attacking the Qing forces. Times and places were supplied.

Both Liu Lichuan of the Small Swords and Lian Weicai in Wade's Company in the concessions may have foreseen the conflict, but neither of the two armed forces involved did. The British and Americans lined up three gunboats on the Huangpu River: the British vessels *Grecian* and *Encounter,* and the American vessel *Plymouth*. Army battalions landed to supplement the volunteers.

The commanding officer of the volunteer corps was British Vice-Consul Wade, who was also a reserve lieutenant-commander in the British Navy. Captain John Kelly of the American warship *Plymouth* commanded the American forces. Altogether, though, the American and British forces numbered only a grand total of 380 men. The British had one field gun, and the Americans had one cannon and two short-range field pieces.

Since it was the Qing forces who were making demonstrations of their prowess, the leaders of the British and American forces anticipated that they might just have to tuck their collective tail between their legs and beat a hasty retreat.

The Qing Army had been inspired by Wu Weitang. It was he who had told them that the French were not participating. What could the joint British-American army of only some three hundred or so do? Would they strike fear in the hearts of the Qing forces and attack?

The joint Anglo-American force sounded their war drums and marched ahead toward Park Lane—present-day Nanjing Road.

—7—

There were 2,000 troops at the Qing Army's Northern Camp. Cannons were lined up as well. It was unclear just how many cannons the government forces had, because they were in the habit of frequently deploying inoperable cannons as well as dummy cannons to threaten the enemy. They assumed that their foes would either run away or double back upon seeing the array of artillery. That would certainly have been a strange military encounter.

The Anglo-American forces linked up on shore and began joint activities as of 3:00 that afternoon. By the time of the ultimatum at 4:00 p.m., the Anglo-American forces had already advanced to the front of the Northern Camp. War drums beat loudly, as military standards fluttered in the wind. They marched toward the eastern edge of the racetrack, and there the foreign volunteer corps split into two arms. The American battalion turned left, following the course of the racetrack, and there they stood directly before the Qing's Northern Camp. They had assumed a position in which the Americans would attack from the front, while the British battalion would launch an attack from the wing.

Even at this time, Lieutenant-Commander Wade, the British vice-consul, and Captain Kelly, as well as Consul Alcock, who was in the rear, all expected that the Qing forces would abandon their encampment and depart. For its part, the Qing military forces similarly thought that the foreign troops would sooner or later simply make an about-face and withdraw—a vainly optimistic observation.

"Load guns!" ordered Captain Kelly. There being no change in the other side's position by 4:00, an artillery attack remained the only option.

An American by the name of Wetmore who participated in the battle confessed that he was exultant when they began to march, but that gradually he became uneasy, and when they appeared before the enemy he became completely despondent and lost all hope. The American forces took up a position in a nearby graveyard. The troops chose the tallest of the many grave mounds to lay in waiting.

"Fire!" It was 4:00. Captain Kelly gave the order as he stared at his watch.

At the same time over in the British battalion, Lieutenant-Commander Wade gave the order to commence firing.

Continuous explosions sounded in the Northern Camp of the Qing military. They were followed by gunfire. In order to hit his mark, Wetmore placed his gun on his shoulder, staring straight before him, his eyes blinking, and all the time wondering what in the world was going to happen.

This battle came to be known as the "Battle of the Muddy Flat." The area was known in English at the time as the Muddy Flat, and when it rained, the place indeed became a quagmire. When this battle erupted, the weather was fine, and the earth was dry. On deserted land where no grass was growing, the surface was a monochrome yellow.

The reason Wetmore's eyes were blinking, as he forgot even to squeeze the trigger, was that before he knew it, the brilliant yellow before him began to mix with red. From yellow to red. The color of the earth was changing before his eyes.

Gradually, Wetmore and the others assembled there began to realize what it was. The men who had worn pieces of red material around their foreheads had appeared on the battlefield from somewhere.

"It's the Small Swords!"

In the bombardment a moment before, the Qing forces at the Northern Camp had been thrown into a bit of confusion, but now they lost all fighting spirit at the sight of these men with the red bandannas. Soldiers of the Qing Army had been focused solely on the foreigners' corps before them. Their commanders kept repeating, as if it were a Buddhist prayer formula: "The enemy's few in number. Not even a tenth as many as we are. They're nothing to be afraid of. We can beat them easily. Don't get rattled!"

Though they had expected the enemy simply to turn around and take off, they were to a certain extent prepared, in a worst case scenario, for the eventuality of a shelling. Should that have come to pass, they still knew that it would not come before 4:00. Not for one moment, though, had they suspected an attack by shock troops of the Small Sword Society.

There were 20,000 Qing troops surrounding the city of Shanghai. If one of the gates to the city had been opened, an urgent message to that effect should have arrived from an allied force. There was no such report.

Disgusted by the internal discord within the city of Shanghai, Zhou Lichun remained in hiding outside the city walls, and many of his subordinates were with him. His daughter Xiuying furtively departed the city with a handful of men, rallied her father's subordinates, and launched an attack against the Qing encampment.

The red bandanna around the forehead had become the Small Swords' uniform ever since they had forced their way into Shanghai. It was they who were dying the yellow surface of the soil with dots of red. They were not just men either, for women were mixed among them, and they were led by a woman on this occasion.

"Burn it down! Attack!" reverberated a serene voice near the Northern Camp.

According to Wetmore's account, the reason a smaller number of troops was able to gain the upper hand and defeat a larger number was the direct result of the unanticipated cooperation of the Small Sword Society. However, at another point in his account, Wetmore notes that since the foreign volunteer corps made a desperate attempt to attack, the opposing commanding officer may have given the order to retreat.

The number of warriors with red bandannas who took the field at that time is unknown, but it was surely an immense number, for the earth seemed to have been dyed red. The number of foreigners killed was listed as two, with fifteen wounded. The Qing Army suffered 300 deaths, its barracks were burned to the ground, and two cannons that it abandoned were destroyed.

Wetmore noted that most of those killed and wounded among the foreign volunteers were not the result of the Qing attack but that of mistaken friendly fire.

—8—

"It certainly ended quickly. I was hoping to go and inspect the scene afterward, but now I can't." Tan Qi was regretful that this battle had come to a close so rapidly and so simply.

"What happened to Wu Weitang?" asked Lian Liwen after a moment's pause.

"The Qing forces probably thought they were tricked by him. But he's surely linked to some element of the Qing Army by the power of money. He's got to be," replied Tan Qi.

"At least, it is true that France criticized the actions of both the British and the Americans. With that we may be able to recover some sense of trust," offered Lian Weicai by way of conjecture.

After being tied up with the foreign volunteers on the battlefield, Harry Wade eventually returned. He and the British vice-consul of the same surname had both commanded the troops at the front lines, while Rutherford Alcock remained in the rear.

"Mr. Lian, I'd really like to know what will become of the consul," said Wade.

"Nobody really knows what happened out there. In the battle today, it was completely and totally unexpected, but a huge force of the Small Swords just appeared on the field," replied Lian Weicai.

"Perhaps the Small Swords have actually been able to get their hands on assistance from the Taipings."

"Mr. Alcock should have foreseen that."

"The Qing Army is so terribly weak, they just buried their heads in their hands when the unexpected came to life."

"Harry, what would you like to see happen?"

"Either way's fine with me, because once the war comes to an end, business should resume on a large scale. However, those who deal in opium probably wouldn't like to see the Taipings win, because if the Taipings do win, they'll probably enact a ban on opium. There was even grumbling among those who participated in the foreign volunteers' actions today. As far as they were concerned, to attack the Qing Army was stupid. It was effectively helping the Taipings, who are enemies of the opium trade. See what I mean?"

The only thing Harry Wade—a man who had nothing to do with transactions concerning opium—wanted was peace.

"But, since the Qing forces entered the concession area and fired on it, they had to be driven away," said Liwen.

"Ji-er-hang-a came to apologize, expressing his regrets. He promised never again to impinge on the concessions and declared that they would not reconstruct the Northern Camp. He hoped that there would be friendship in the future. He also stressed as firmly as he could that, as far as the United States and Great Britain were concerned, acting in amity toward the Chinese government's military forces would be to their benefit. I served as the interpreter and heard the surveillance commissioner as he spoke. I felt at the time that what he was saying was inspired by someone else. They weren't really his own words, you know, but seemed to me to have been implanted in him by someone else, and he was just repeating them over and over again, like a parrot." This was the way Wade recounted his impressions.

At that point a servant came to call Wade away. It seemed much remained still to be settled from the day's affairs. The night was becoming late, and Tan Qi yawned as he said, "No doubt about it. The person who 'implanted' those words in him was Wu Weitang. I'm going to look for him and stick to him like glue."

"You're probably exhausted. You just arrived from Nanjing. Why not take today off and relax?" said Lian Weicai.

Ordinarily nothing changed in spite of the fact that a war had occurred. People still looked forward to a period of relaxation as if nothing had happened.

"If they don't take Shanghai, things are going to go badly," mumbled Lian Weicai to himself.

"Father, would you like to convey that advice to the people in the Heavenly Capital?" asked Liwen.

Lian Weicai shook his head from side to side. Given the prevailing conditions he had heard of in the Heavenly Capital, he was hardly of a mind to do so. "They haven't been attentive, have they?"

"No. Right now, they're conducting a two-sided operation. From the west, Zeng Guofan is coming at the head of a force of Hunan volunteers. This will be the first time the Taipings will face this army of his. Since the west is upstream, if the Taiping troops don't put up a good fight, their cause may be lost. Because of the severe cold, the northern expeditionary army couldn't even take Tianjin, let along Beijing. Reinforcements have now been sent to the north. In the west and the north, they're going to have their hands full. And I don't think they've been attentive to events in Shanghai to the east. From what I've seen, though, the east is by far the most crucial theater. Do you know what I mean, Liwen?"

"Sure. Shanghai is open to the entire world."

"If they can focus their attention on the world at large, I think they'll be able to grow stronger, but they have to be attentive to this on their own. It's not something you can teach them."

"Certainly."

"What's happened with Xinmei?"

"She's gone to stay at a friend's home."

Lian Weicai asked nothing further, though he likely knew her whereabouts. Liwen of course knew. Xinmei was supposed to have slipped into the city of Shanghai on the previous day. She had left saying: "I've heard it's Xiuying's turn. I've got to help her."

Liwen had arranged with someone to inform him if anything came up. No news had yet arrived at this late time, so Xinmei was undoubtedly safe.

29

Secret
Messenger
of the
Heavenly King

—1—

It was now the time of Qingming festival two years later, 1856. This year the Qingming festival fell on a day corresponding to April 4. Shanghai had recovered its animated spirit.

Over a year had passed since the destruction of the Small Sword Society. Everyone in Shanghai vividly remembered the events of that time, for they had taken place on the lunar New Year's Day. No one knew if it had been gunfire or the explosion of firecrackers. In fact, both had gone off at the same time.

Jiangsu Governor Ji-er-hang-a finally achieved his goal. He was able to conquer the Small Swords, who had occupied the city of Shanghai for nearly a year and a half. The French military took part in the attack on Shanghai at that time. French Admiral Laguerre actively joined the assault against the Small Swords. The French had already been cooperating with the Qing strategy of a military blockade and had frequently complained to Great Britain and the United States, who continued to funnel supplies to the Small Swords, that they were not acting in compliance with strict neutrality. At the same time, the French went to war on the side of the Manchu government and posted casualties of nine dead and thirty-six wounded. When Qing forces retook the city of Shanghai, they engaged in wholesale plunder and slaughter.

"Poor Xiuying." Xinmei was moved to tears whenever she recalled the day the Small Swords were annihilated. The entire leadership of the Small Sword Society from Liu Lichuan on down had been massacred. Among them had been Deng Lichun's daughter, Xiuying.

Even under blockade, and as a result having reached the utmost poverty, the Small Swords still entertained the hope that the Taiping Army would come to their rescue. Both the Taiping northern expeditionary force and reinforcements sent to assist it were on the verge of crisis. Furthermore, the battles fought in the west between the Taipings and the Hunan Army under Zeng Guofan had been particularly severe. Though they were able to reoccupy Wuchang, which they had relinquished, they were unable to hold it for more than four months before the Qing Army recaptured it once again. While the Small Swords were in their final days, the Taiping military was devoting all of its energies on the western front to taking Wuchang a third time.

"It's all because there was a Guangdong faction and a Fujian faction," said Lian Liwen, "and when they came together, it led to incessant internal squabbles. Had they really cooperated, the Small Swords would probably have been able to continue their control over a walled county seat."

"But, now, after such a long period of time, nothing can be said that will change things. They waited and waited, but the Taiping forces just never came."

"That was some time ago. More than a year has passed since then. The whole atmosphere in Shanghai has unbelievably turned for the better. Isn't it better that people are happy again?"

"I just feel sorry for people like Xiuying who were murdered," said Xinmei, her eyes clouding over.

Liwen peered out the window. Ten schooners were anchored in the Huangpu River. The people of Shanghai all knew full well that they were opium mother vessels. Though business on the whole was in a slump, the trade in opium seemed to be growing.

Harry Wade's investigation indicated that, in the year following the demise of the Small Sword Society, opium unloaded in Shanghai exceeded thirty thousand chests. A single chest of opium weighed one picul, or about 60 kilograms. In other words, thirty thousand chests were in excess of 1,800 tons of opium.

Even according to the Treaty of Nanjing, which concluded the Opium War, the opium trade was not supposed to become legal. Great Britain wanted to avoid an open declaration legalizing traffic in opium within the text of the treaty. In 1844, two years after this treaty was signed, the United States concluded a treaty with the Qing government at Wangxia that was in general accord with the Treaty of Nanjing. In the Sino-American treaty it was stipulated that: "Citizens of the United States of America who engage in trading opium or other prohibited items will be extended no protection whatsoever by the government of the United States."

This difference merely recounts how much more idealistic American politicians of the time were than their British counterparts. Though opium was not mentioned in the Treaty of Nanjing, trade in the drug was flourishing.

Among the opium ships on the waters of the Huangpu River, four belonged to merchants from the United States.

The figure of thirty thousand chests applied only to Shanghai. Guangzhou was the center of the opium trade, posting a figure no smaller than this one. Particularly Guangzhou in China's south had a long history with respect to opium transactions, and thus the quantity of opium bought and sold there certainly was on a par with that of Shanghai.

"Wade's been doing his part," said Liwen. Harry Wade was a citizen of Great Britain, but he himself had sworn not to lay so much as a finger on the drug.

"And aren't we going to help him as much as we can?" Xinmei was unconsciously looking out the window.

Foreign merchandise other than opium had not been selling at all well on Chinese markets. Despite the talk of Sino-foreign trade, basically it was foreigners selling opium to the Chinese for tea leaves and raw silk thread. Since the Wade Company was not going to touch opium, all that was left to buy and sell were tea leaves and raw silk thread. Tea leaves were brought to Shanghai along the Yangzi River. However, the Yangzi was now a battleground between the Taipings and the Qing forces. Fearful of the dangers involved, merchants had refrained from transporting such merchandise by water routes.

To the extent that tea leaves could be transported to Shanghai by land, the quantities were smaller and there were difficulties getting one's hands on it. By the same token, of course, its market value had risen accordingly. If the article was to be had, it could command quite a high price.

With all the strength available to his company, the Jinshunji, Lian Weicai gained control over tea leaves transported over land and supplied them to the Wade Company. Overland routes were by no means secure—not in the least. After Zeng Guofan had entered the city of Nanchang, tea production sites throughout the provinces of Hunan and Jiangxi had increasingly fallen within the war zone.

War was not the only problem, for there was also the danger of being overrun by bandits while transporting the product. Avoiding this danger necessitated advance negotiations with the leaders of local secret societies. Xinmei had herself led a group of bandits affiliated with the Triads, so that she was known in this realm. Lian Weicai also had many friends and acquaintances among the older underworld bosses.

During this period, even the large commercial enterprises, such as Jardine Matheson and Dent, which had already become financial combines, were effectively unable to lay their hands on tea leaves. Staff members at these large concerns were all wondering how it was that only Wade was receiving shipments of tea leaves. They decided that they would go that very day to Wade's storehouses and take copious notes on the goods received by him.

—2—

Nineteen days after Shanghai had been retaken by Qing forces, Dongguang-lian in Zhili province fell under Qing attack, and one of the leaders of the Taiping northern expeditionary army, Lin Fengxiang, was taken prisoner. Dongguanglian was a town in Zhili along the Grand Canal but close to the provincial border with Shandong. Lin had dug a deep cave for himself nearby and hidden there.

The Taipings were very fond of children. Innocent youngsters were often inspired by the ideals of the Taiping movement and became indefatigable Taiping soldiers. While camped in an area for a time, Taiping troops often gathered the young people together and put them through various drills.

Grand Military Consultant Seng-ge-lin-qin tied up members of a youth brigade trained by the Taipings, and tried to extract from them the spot where Lin Fengxiang was hiding by simultaneously torturing and flattering them. One of the youngsters confessed, "The Barbarian-Pacifying Lord has been seriously wounded and is hiding in a cave."

"Who is this Barbarian-Pacifying Lord?! Keep that idiocy to yourself!" screamed the Qing commander who was carrying out the interrogation, as a look of joy crept over his face.

Many different reports had been conveyed to Shanghai concerning the death of Lin Fengxiang. The most reliable one of the lot seemed to be that he was gravely wounded, and when captured by Qing forces, he quickly swallowed the poison he always carried on his person and died. There was also a story going around that he had been executed by crucifixion while under armed guard on his way to Beijing.

"That one's a lie. No one in Beijing has seen him," said Liwen, discounting the Beijing theory. The execution of a rebel as an object lesson would have been carried out before the general public, and not one of the reports coming out of the capital had mentioned Lin's execution.

In his report to the throne, Seng-ge-lin-qin noted that Lin Fengxiang was already gasping for breath when dragged in before him for interrogation: "He was immediately taken out and executed." Distrust was immediately cast on the report, coming as it did from a high official. There was far too much about the situation that might prove offensive to his status. He had to have couched his report in a manner that would be most advantageous to himself.

There was much more merit to be won for taking a prisoner alive than for him to already be dying. For a prisoner to die as a result of taking poison, even if captured alive, there was always the danger that one would be criticized as responsible for not keeping the prisoner vigilantly under guard. Lin was near death from his wounds at the time of his being apprehended. Had they just left him be, he would soon have died on his own, and they would not have been able to execute him as a warning to others. For that reason, he was taken out while still alive and quickly put to death. This was the way in which Liwen reconstructed what had transpired, as he argued for the strong possibility of the suicide by poison theory.

Li Kaifang, the man who ever since the initial uprising in Jintian village had always stood in the forefront of the Taiping Army, and together with Lin Fengxiang was hailed as a courageous commander in the field, was captured on May 31 at Fengguantun, the last base of operations for the Taipings' northern expeditionary force. Li was taken under guard back to Beijing, and there his execution was carried out. Many were on hand to observe it.

It thus seemed as if the prospects for the Taiping movement were steadily deteriorating, though that was not necessarily the case. The Taipings had attached a great deal of importance to the western expeditionary army. The upper echelons in the Heavenly Capital had to be protected at all cost.

While the northern expeditionary forces were being destroyed, Taiping commanders Qin Rigang, Wei Zhijun, and Chen Yucheng again attacked Wuchang and for the third time occupied that city.

"So, it was Picheng," said Xinmei happily. Chen Yucheng was the name that Chen Picheng, who for a time Xinmei had raised as a young boy, had now taken. He was still only seventeen or eighteen.

Chen Yucheng and the forces under his command had seized a number of county seats in Hebei province, such as Dean and Yunmeng. In the period from December 1855 through March of the following year, Assistant King Shi Dakai had in succession occupied the three prefectures of Ruizhou, Linjiang, and Ji'an in Jiangxi province.

The Taipings' western expeditionary army had never won a series of victories in battle. As in the case of the Luzhou prefectural seat, they usually occupied a place and then were forced to withdraw because local men of influence within the occupied site had linked up with the Qing armed forces. From an overall perspective, though, they were in a superior position. Although the northern expeditionary army had been obliterated, the various forces involved in the western expedition continued to post battle victories against their opponents in the Hunan Army. The Qing forces under the command of Imperial Commissioner Xiang Rong established a military base, known popularly as the Jiangnan Encampment, on the outskirts of Nanjing. Troops were amassed here in an effort to bring pressure to bear on the Taiping capital. Though it was later to be transferred, another imperial commissioner, Qin-shan, built a similar military base of operations on the outskirts of nearby Yangzhou. It was known as the Jiangbei Encampment.

The two Qing camps, Jiangnan and Jiangbei, were not actively aimed at attacking the Taiping military, but, in a word, to compel the respect of the rebels for the government's armed forces. A great number of troops were brought to these camps, and they were well-stocked with ammunition and supplies. Here were full-fledged military encampments set up by the enemy right in front of the eyes and nose of the Taiping capital. The Taiping Army had to do something, but both camps were tightly guarded.

A report arrived saying that the Taipings were in the midst of an assault on the Jiangbei Encampment.

"Since Picheng's in Zhenjiang, he's certainly involved in this strategy," said Xinmei, though the nature of her expression was difficult to ascertain. Though Chen Yucheng had changed his name, Xinmei still referred to him by his former name. It was one thing for the brilliant and gallant Picheng to distinguish himself on the battlefield, but she was worried that he might risk his life by venturing into especially dangerous areas. As usual, it was Tan Qi who brought the news of the attack on the Jiangbei Encampment to Shanghai.

"Let there be no doubt about it, the Jiangbei Encampment is going to sustain a crushing defeat, but, um . . ." said Tan Qi, prevaricating.

In actual fact, on the day prior to the Qingming festival, the imperial commissioner at the Jiangbei Encampment, Jiangning Commander Tuo-ming-a, and former Zhili Provincial Military Commander Chen Jinshou were unable to withstand a ferocious assault by the Taipings, abandoned their camp, and fled to a place called Sanchahe.

Qin Rigang was in charge of the attack on the Jiangbei Encampment. Under his command were two new leaders within the Taiping movement, Chen Yucheng and Li Xiuqing.

—3—

Tan Qi's reason for equivocating in his report was that, in spite of the military achievements posted by the western expeditionary army and the attack on the Jiangbei Encampment, internal dissension in the Heavenly Capital had grown severe. It remained an undercurrent, but the general populace was unaware of it. All sorts of things were clear to people like Tan Qi, who were involved in undercover work, that never appeared on the surface. "It's not good that the Heavenly King never goes outside," said Tan Qi, shutting his eyes and shaking his head. "And I can scarcely understand him when he speaks."

"He's been listening to wild rumors. The man's been completely emasculated. Isn't there also the theory that in addition to supplying the Heavenly King with beautiful girls, the Eastern King has well-laid plans for the future?" said Xinmei.

Following Eastern King Yang Xiuqing's last divine visitation, the "Heavenly Father's Descent to Earth," Heavenly King Hong Xiuquan had locked himself up inside his palace grounds and had not since ventured outside. Local residents quietly murmured among themselves that they hadn't seen the Heavenly King for some time and wondered if he would ever come out again. Particularly worried were those former members of the Society of God Worshippers who had worked together with Hong Qiuquan ever since their days back in Guangxi province.

Might the Heavenly King already be dead? Unconfirmed reports had made their way to the Qing military. The rumor was floating about the Heavenly Capital that Hong was surrounded by hosts of beautiful women, and that he was perfectly satisfied with such a life, and had thus lost any desire to ever go out again.

"We've become aware of it recently," said Tan Qi, explaining that particular theory, "but that story was actually begun by Qing military sources. My investigation leads me to believe that it was done on purpose."

If they were able through deleterious rumors to discredit the authority of the Heavenly King, this would certainly strike a blow at the Taiping movement, which was held together by its common religious faith.

"Not likely, but perhaps true," said Xinmei, as she offered a sharp argument to the conspiracy theory.

"I agree," said Tan Qi. He had only seen them on occasion, but Tan Qi tried to envisage one or another of the faces of the beauties from the Heavenly King's residence.

"Might the rumor you mentioned a while ago have originated not with the Qing Army but with the Eastern King?" said Liwen.

"Both sources are conceivable," said Tan Qi. He was a specialist in the area of plots, with insight far beyond that of ordinary people.

"The stories just might have flowed into one another," said Liwen. He was concerned that factional strife might be carried out with weaponry. Rumors flowed fast and furiously, but the basis of this rumor seemed to have taken shape in the fact that the Heavenly King, in his opposition to the Eastern King, had won over Northern King Wei Changhui and Assistant King Shi Dakai.

"With the Heavenly King remaining in seclusion, such wild rumors only breed further exaggeration." Liwen was genuinely irritated. It was not a major ordeal for the man to stick his head out in public, and the situation would so greatly improve if he did.

"It's a mess," said Tan Qi, his elbows resting on the table and his head in his hands. "I think the trouble for me is that I just know too much. There have just been so many secret messengers sent by the Heavenly King to the front lines."

"To the front lines?"

That really was a problem. One could only imagine that these messengers of the Heavenly King were sent to see the highest commanders at the front lines. That meant Wei Changhui and Shi Dakai. Rumors were seeming less and less to be simply rumors.

"Yes. Should I report this information to the Eastern King or not? It really puts me in a bind."

"Isn't the Eastern King aware of what's going on?"

"You'd expect him to be, but for some reason I don't think he is, especially since he is the source of the rumor we were just talking about."

"What'll happen if you inform him?" asked Liwen.

"He'll probably attack the residence of the Heavenly King with a vengeance. Either that or he may use the tactic of a Heavenly Father's Descent to Earth again."

"I've heard enough," shouted Xinmei in a shrill voice.

"I have no plans to inform the Eastern King. None whatsoever," said Tan Qi, shrugging his shoulders slightly.

This was no way to improve matters. As for the Heavenly King's secret messengers, Tan Qi was the person to look into this and perhaps confirm the story.

"You don't want to say anything that'll make it like the Small Swords," said Liwen.

A much greater reason for the failure of the Small Sword Society than the lack of support from the Taipings was seen as their internal factional strife. The Guangdong and Fujian cliques had gotten along well through the occupation of Shanghai. While sharing an objective, no matter how many different cliques there may be, all compromise on the items they must and make concessions to the others. The Taiping movement was no different in this regard.

After the occupation of Nanjing, a wide variety of problems seemed to have surfaced for a time among the Taipings.

"It's the nature of the Eastern King," said Tan Qi, sighing. These few words communicated directly to Liwen. Liwen had been observing the Taiping movement from its earliest days in Jintian village, and he understood the importance of Tan Qi's words and sighs together.

The beginning of Hong Xiuquan's decline could be traced back to his departure from Thistle Mountain in the early days when he traveled to Guangzhou to help secure the release of Feng Yunshan from custody. Without its religious founder and his right-hand men, the Society of God Worshippers fell for a time into the hands of Yang Xiuqing. Had it been a political society, Yang Xiuqing might have seized complete control over the organization, but inasmuch as the Society of God Worshippers was a religious group, that did not come to pass. Yang still lacked self-confidence when it came to matters of a religious nature. He greeted Hong and Feng upon their return and managed to muscle his way in among these two leaders.

With the order of Hong Xiuquan, Yang Xiuqing, and then Feng Yunshan, the unexpected death of Feng on the battlefield severely shook up the Taiping leadership. Yang could no longer bear to remain in another's shadow. Perhaps this is true of many men, but Yang Xiuqing's nature was that of a man of uncommon strong-mindedness.

—4—

"Has the event of last year left any kind of trail?" asked Liwen.

"Just as expected," responded Tan Qi angrily. By the "event of last year," Liwen was referring to the incident that took place in the Heavenly Capital just after the Anglo-American foreigners' brigade in Shanghai came into conflict with the Qing military, and found the Small Swords joining the battle that had led to the Battle of the Muddy Flat. For all intents and purposes, Eastern King Yang Xiuqing had reached the epitome of arrogance. While the Heavenly King refused ever to appear in public, the Eastern King rarely stepped outside his residential quarters. He seemed to think that never showing one's face to the populace was a means used by people who had acquired a certain authority. Though the Eastern King did occasionally step outside, at such times as many as a thousand of his retainers dressed resplendently were kept close at hand, with grandiloquent bombast surpassing all manner of great pageants and processionals.

Back in the era of Jintian village, the leaders of the Society of God Worshippers ate and slept in the same quarters and had feelings for one another that went beyond kinship. Whatever came up, they would gather in one room to deliberate in an atmosphere of a free exchange of opinions.

After the occupation of Nanjing, they began to break up. Each of the members of the Taiping leadership had his own separate official residence, and it would have been a wonder, indeed, if factions had not developed from this breakdown. The core element of each of the factions was the kindred bond felt for the central personality of a given clique. This only made the various kings haughtier and further distanced them from each other. They were like foxes assuming the authority of tigers, little men with delusions of grandeur. Having come from the backwoods of Guangxi, they lacked the cultivation to restrain themselves. They manifested their haughtiness in no uncertain terms.

"You remained seated when we happened to pass by. Shouldn't you have gotten up and made some sort of salutation!" screamed the cousin of Yang Xiuqing's father at Qin Rigang's stableman. "Two hundred lashes!" said this cousin on the spot, indicating the punishment for this stableman. This much still did not placate him, though, for the stableman was then taken to the home of Huang Yukun.

Huang was from Guiping in Guangxi province, and had been with the Society of God Worshippers from the early days. He had some education and gained access to the local magistrate's offices, where he worked in the capacity of a scribe. As a result, he had a basic knowledge of the law. After Feng Yunshan was taken prisoner, Huang's advice played a major role in the success of the movement to gain Feng's release. Furthermore, his daughter married Assistant King Shi Dakai. The Taipings appointed him to a high ceremonial post, and he served simultaneously on the board of punishments of the Heavenly Dynasty.

The poor stableman was taken to Huang's home because Huang ran the jail. "Well, two hundred lashes, you say" said Huang approvingly. "They've already been administered, then, and there'll be no further punishment."

Yang's cousin was indignant when he brought the matter to Yang Xiuqing's attention, "We brought this stableman to the home of Huang Yukun so that we might carry out the punishment and awaken people to the power of the Eastern King. In spite of that, there was no further punishment for this rude man. Was not your authority slighted by this? To leave matters as they are would impinge on your authority. It would be good for you to take a stringent measure."

Yang Xiuqing listened to his cousin and then responded, "I understand your point, and I shall adopt a mercilessly harsh line of action." When everyone throws themselves at my feet, thought Yang Xiuqing, the realm will be mine.

Using the Heavenly Father's Descent to Earth as his weapon, Yang had actually tried to attack the Heavenly King with the rod about six months earlier. At that time, all the Taiping leaders from the Northern King on down had stepped forward and offered themselves as recipients of the flogging in place of the Heavenly King. A little too early yet, Yang had thought, judging from this response. The Heavenly Father then pardoned him and withdrew the punishment of the cane.

According to the traditional Chinese conception of "abdication," Yang had thought that he might seize from Hong Xiuquan the position of leader of the Taiping Heavenly Kingdom. He wondered how much resistance there would be were he actually to carry this out. So, he tried it via the Heavenly Father's Descent to Earth.

Those who had rendered devoted and earnest service on behalf of the Heavenly King still knew much, and Yang Xiuqing thought that the timing was premature. He was certainly not going to wait comfortably for the appropriate moment to arrive, but rather Yang was working hard to enhance his personal authority.

Yang was a firm believer in power. The Society of God Worshippers was itself one source of power, and simply for that reason he joined it. Years later, when Li Xiuqing was captured by the Qing forces, he claimed in his deposition that Yang Xiuqing seemed to possess no belief in the Christian God.

Yang's efforts were bent on demonstrating to others the power he possessed. There were those now who were trying to get his cousin to treat with magnanimity this man who had acted disrespectfully. Were he to deal a crushing blow to the man, the word would spread through the Taiping movement that one better be overcome with fear before the person of the Eastern King. Thereafter, everyone would be prostrate before him.

His cousin was bristling with anger. Yang's plan of action was by no means emotional but well-conceived. He ordered Shi Dakai to arrest Huang Yukun. He was ordering Shi to arrest the father of his wife, Shi's own father-in-law. By so doing, Yang was testing Shi, the most popular of all the Taiping kings.

Huang, though, angrily offered up his resignation. Qin Rigang, who was the master of the stableman in question, as well as Chen Chengrong, who was involved in the actual handling of political administration, resigned their posts as expressions of protest. For his own part, Eastern King Yang Xiuqing had gone too far to retreat now. When he had tried to have the Heavenly King whipped, he had been able to back down by using the Heavenly Father's Descent to Earth as a cover. On this occasion, though, he could not do so.

Yang's plan was to try to do what was excessive, and then observe the aftereffects. Huang Yukun received 300 lashes of the cane; Qin Rigang also received 300 lashes; Chen Chengrong received 200; and the stableman was executed by having his limbs sliced off.

Qin Rigang was already an elder statesman who had performed glorious military service for the Taipings and had just been invested as the King of Yan. Both Huang Yukun and Chen Chengrong had received high honors and titles as well.

Even the kings among the highest leadership of the Taiping movement were now subject to this manner of cruel punishment for neglecting courtesies before a relative of the Eastern King. It was a great shock. Everyone held their breath, with people throughout the capital breathing furtively. And Yang Xiuqing was satisfied.

Not a single voice was raised in protest. For Yang this meant that everyone had thrown themselves at his feet. He was unconcerned with what sort of ill feelings they might harbor within. Those who were prostrate recognized his strength, and that was just fine. From the very start, Yang had never relied on affecting people's minds.

Huang Yukun was stripped of his honorary rank and demoted to foot soldier. Shortly thereafter, there was a proposal from Shi Dakai. "I would like to use Huang Yukun in the office of documents in the residence of the Assistant King. Please take measures to see that this is carried out."

Yang Xiuqing permitted it. "Fine. He's probably learned his lesson by now, and he's not that young."

Soon Huang's position was returned to him and he was, as before, put in charge of the jailhouse of the Heavenly Dynasty.

Yang seemed to have felt that everyone now fully understood from this display the power in his hands. The matter was over and it had been a great success, as he saw it. However, Yang did not know what had transpired before Huang returned to his post.

Stripped of his position and demoted to the rank-and-file, Huang Yukun had been placed in the office of Luo Bifen, a high-ranking Taiping official. Ashamed and angry, Huang ran away from camp in the middle of the night and attempted to commit suicide by drowning. Luo Bifen was personally close to Huang, and had been very concerned about his friend. He quietly kept an eye on him.

Luo was aware of Huang's departure soon after it occurred. He followed Huang and ultimately saved him from drowning. Luo kept this matter in total secrecy. According to the religious principles of Christianity, suicide was considered a grave sin among the Taipings. Were it learned that Huang had attempted suicide, he would have been beheaded.

Yang Xiuqing seemed to have been unaware of Huang's shame and indignation. Though he had been subject himself to humiliation back in Guangxi, Yang had been able to explain to himself that it was a result of his own insufficient strength. It was only natural that his counterpart who possessed power would choose to embarrass him, and although it made him uncomfortable, it did not cause him to bear resentment.

Someone who believes in power and power alone cannot understand what goes on in the crevices of the minds of those who experience anger and resentment.

"Two years have passed," said Tan Qi, "and he's far bolder now than ever before. The Eastern King can read any situation with such agility and alacrity, and it seems he hasn't been at all aware of it."

—5—

In the classification of teas, selection and discrimination were tedious work in which one could not relax one's attention. If through contemplation, it was argued, one acquired the ability to distinguish teas, then one had truly come of age. The eye remembered what the teas looked like as one bounced them back and forth between the hands. This was work for the eyes and the hands, with no need for the intrusion of the mind.

When he wanted to give his brain a rest, or when he wanted to put some sort of idea into shape, or perhaps when he hoped that a new idea altogether might come to him, Lian Weicai would place a large pile of tea leaves before him and proceed to sift through them for quality.

"There was more when I was in Shanghai," he muttered to himself at first. The main office of his store, the Jinshunji, was located in Xiamen (Amoy), Fujian province, and that was the location of his principal residence as well. And yet, over the past few years, he could count the number of days—they were so few—that he had actually spent in Xiamen. The core of his business was now in Shanghai.

As much as possible, he now tried to entrust business affairs to the younger men, while he would remain out of sight. He was already sixty-eight years of age, nearing the round number of seventy. He was now perplexed about what he should do with the organization of the Jinshunji. Though he had retreated from the front lines of work as much as he could, he was still the centerpiece of operations. In fact, he had too much power. Though the company had branches at many sites, they were able to coordinate their activities well primarily because of his presence.

He wondered what would happen after his death. Should the Jinshunji continue with the same organization that it had until this point? Or should the various branches take shape as independent concerns? He was still unable to decide. Had one of his sons excelled and shown particular powers of leadership, then things would probably have been fine as they were. However, each of his four sons had different natures, and not one of them towered above the others. That would ordinarily mean turning to his eldest son, Lian Tongwen, but Tongwen probably didn't have the necessary leadership skills. Tongwen had a certain coarse side, and Weicai felt he couldn't entrust the Jinshunji to him in good conscience.

"The only thing left to do is to reorganize," Weicai said to himself as he continued sorting through the tea leaves. As he was pondering organizational matters in his head, his reference point was Western examples. No matter how large commercial organizations were in China, they never completely broke away from the family. Even in the famous thirteen *hong* or guilds of the earlier Canton System of Sino-Western trade, the largest was the Yihe (or Delightful Harmony) *hong*, run by a five-family group. It was simply inconceivable that the Yihe *hong* could exist apart from this style of organization.

The East India Company of Great Britain, by contrast, had no relationship to any specific families. Playing the role of advance guard in the British push eastward, the East India Company was in the process of ceasing its activities.

British companies in Shanghai now bore the names of individuals, whether it was the Wade Company that Lian Weicai had supported or those of Jardine Matheson, Dent, or Butterfield, but their ties to specific families were still not at all as firm as was the case in China.

Having long done business with the British, Lian Weicai knew that elemental to the structure of their companies was the idea of "shares." Later this concept would be translated into the term *kabu* in Japan and *gufen* in China. At the time that Weicai was considering it, though, China as yet had no commonly recognized term comparable to "share."

Since Weicai knew English, he was thinking about the term in its original language. In the midst of difficult negotiations, British merchants had often said, "We'll have to consult with our shareholders." Lian had sought an explanation so as to acquire as much information as he could. What a fascinating organization, he had often thought to himself. Whether he maintained the Jinshunji in its present form or divided it up, he still thought that perhaps this Western organization should be studied and actively emulated.

Lian Weicai's fingers were sifting through the tea leaves when suddenly they stopped short. Between his thumb and index finger, he pinched a tea leaf that looked as if it were coated with a thin powder. From that point forward he had to concentrate entirely on the functions of his eyes, fingers, and mind, which were to that point carrying on in different realms. Just then an important item popped into his head. He needed to study this all thoroughly before adopting a foreign organizational form.

"Will the company reach the generation of my grandchildren?" he said, gathering his thoughts. He was addressing himself.

He began to move his fingers again. The dried tea leaves were falling from his fingers, having been crushed into a powder as he rubbed them.

His eldest grandson was fifteen, the eldest son of Tongwen now living in Taiwan.

"He studies harder than I did as a boy and his prospects look far better than mine." Weicai recalled this sentence in a letter from Tongwen. When he had read this letter out loud, his wife Lian Wan had laughed and said, "He'd be in big trouble if he couldn't do any better than Tongwen. A child who hated to study as much as Tongwen would be hard to find anywhere."

Perhaps Weicai ought to send this grandson to Great Britain to study. Not a bad idea, thought Weicai, standing up. It was his nature to move toward executing an idea as soon as he hit upon it. He would soon write a letter to Tongwen in Taiwan, and it would be best to consult Harry Wade about where to study in Britain.

Yes, he thought, and Ruxing too. Ruxing was Xiling's daughter and the same age as Tongwen's son. Perhaps it would be best for her to breathe the air of a foreign country as well. But he still had to convince Xiling about sending Ruxing overseas.

Having returned from Beijing, Xiling then departed Shanghai for Hong Kong before returning again to Shanghai. Her daughter had remained in Shanghai throughout. Lian Weicai paid a visit to Xiling's home.

"Why don't you send Ruxing abroad to pursue her education? Tongwen's son is planning to go to Britain," he said, not beating around the bush. It was so abrupt that the expression on Xiling's face belied a certain unease.

"Did the idea just pop into your head?"

"Yes, it did."

"And you were thinking of her happiness?"

"Of course I was."

"Should her happiness be decided by ideas of this sort?"

"Call it inspiration, if you will." Lian Weicai's response had a calming effect, for it no longer appeared as though he had simply taken a random thought and translated it into words.

"Okay, I see what you're saying, and it makes sense, but not Great Britain," said Xiling.

Lian Weicai silently nodded assent.

"If Ruxing goes somewhere, I'm going with her."

"I was thinking the same thing," said Lian, with a forced smile.

"Can we really do it?"

"Sure, you can."

"But, shouldn't we leave soon?"

"Of course. As soon as we decide on a destination, I'll make all the necessary contacts in advance."

"I have one thing I have to do in the interim."

"One thing? Where?"

"At the Heavenly Capital."

"Do you absolutely have to go there?"

"Absolutely. A secret messenger from the Heavenly King himself came to see me."

"A secret messenger from the Heavenly King?" Lian cut himself short.

One could never be stunned by any occurrence that concerned Xiling, and it was virtually impossible to compel her to abandon an idea once she had set her mind on it. Realizing he had no alternative, Lian awkwardly laughed hoarsely.

—6—

Above the number two man in the Taiping organization, Yang Xiuqing, stood only Hong Xiuquan, about whose activities in the Heavenly King's Residence no one knew a thing. Immediately below Yang was Northern King Wei Changhui.

To claw one's way upward, one had no choice but to kick others downward. Yang Xiuqing showed scarcely any fear of his superior, Hong Xiuquan. The basis of all Yang's judgments was power and power alone, and he discerned in Hong nothing that bore the least resemblance to power.

They had carried out actions in tandem for a long period of time. Yang had always tried to understand Hong as well as he could. On two points only, Yang recognized that Hong surpassed him: Hong could read and write, and he had a certain knowledge of Christianity.

"The Heavenly King is compiling a book. As a result, he is terribly busy." Such was the excuse offered by the female attendants at the Residence of the Heavenly King to people who wished to have an audience with him.

To be sure, Hong was writing every day, engrossed, it was said, in religious work. Hong was a man of considerable solemnity. He believed in all seriousness that he had come into the world to instruct the souls of the ordinary masses of people.

"I'm happy he's engaged with his writing. I can hardly wait to read it," said Yang for surface appearances, but with an undertone at Hong's expense. Yang never dreamed that there might be "power" in such things as religious books.

Although Yang was illiterate, he did enjoy listening to others read to him. There were occasionally interesting works of history, though Yang found little else equally absorbing. It was actually painful for him to sit quietly and listen to sentences from books with no interest for him whatsoever. How much more boring would it be to write such stuff? This was not the sort of work for a clever man.

As long as Hong worked day and night solely on his religious writings and showed no concern for day-to-day politics, Yang had not the least fear of him. The ones he needed to be wary of were those below him. In addition to Wei Changhui, Shi Dakai and Qin Rigang were objects of his vigilance. What he feared was that these men together might amass great strength and begin to exert pressure on those above them. Yang thus did all he could to prevent these men from preserving their strength.

The one Yang most distrusted was Wei Changhui. They had been acquaintances since the days back in Jintian village, and he knew full well that Wei was very different on the surface and beneath it. After the occupation of Nanjing, Yang had taken over control of personnel matters and appointed Wei to be commander of the army in the Taiping capital. Had he placed this dangerous person outside the city, Wei might establish himself locally or collect his troop strength and launch an attack against the capital. For that reason, he kept Wei within sight.

Shi Dakai and Qin Rigang had commanded forces in the western expedition and as such had often left the capital. Yang had taken measures to ensure that neither of them would ever acquire too much power. For example, when Shi Dakai had been stationed at Anqing, the local people had come to admire him greatly; sensing the danger inherent in this development, Yang sent Qin Rigang to replace Shi. Shi was called back to the Heavenly Capital, but in a form whereby he was transferred so as to be under the authority of Wei Changhui, commander of the capital forces.

The power of the number three man, Wei Changhui, had to be curtailed as much as possible. Ironically, the more Yang Xiuqing sought to extend his own authority, the more Wei Changhui's authority grew. In order to heighten his own dignified status, for example, Yang decided not to handle items of various importance from the front directly.

Eventually, Yang Xiuqing became the Taiping sovereign in both name and fact and had no time for piddling details. He decided to receive only important reports from the office one step beneath him, and that was the Residence of the Northern King. There reports from the front were scrutinized, and it was established which were sufficiently important to pass on to the Residence of the Eastern King.

By this system, the Eastern King's Residence was certainly seen as far superior to the Northern King's Residence. This was clear to all. However, it was the Residence of the Northern King, in fact, that effectively took control of all practical matters.

Which reports would be sent on to the Residence of the Eastern King was the sole provenance of the Residence of the Northern King. Everyone sought the good graces of the latter, and people tended to collect at that spot. It was in this sense that Wei Changhui's power grew ever stronger. The principal objective in recalling the popular Shi Dakai, then in Anqing, to the Heavenly Capital, was to gain control over the increasingly mighty Northern King's Residence by entrusting to Shi Dakai half of the practical duties that Wei Changhui monopolized in the city.

The western front of the fighting was reaching a critical point, and it seemed rather unnatural that Wei Changhui continued to remain in the Heavenly Capital. Yang once ordered Wei to oversee the war in Hubei, but his order was countermanded when Wei was unable to gain permission from the Heavenly King.

Qin Rigang was stationed in Anqing as Shi Dakai's replacement, and he increased his troop strength there to 2,000 soldiers. Unhappy about this development, Yang decided to replace him with Luo Dagang, and to incorporate a portion of Qin's increased military forces into that of the Eastern King's Residence. Finally, Yang moved to dispatch Wei Changhui to Jiangxi province.

Though Yang might find himself in a difficult situation if Wei did leave the Heavenly Capital and amass a force of troops, Wei would still be a source of trouble for Yang if Wei remained in the city and continued to acquire real power. So, after calculating in a fashion distinctive to Yang, he decided to send Wei out. If Wei Changhui remained in the capital, the Northern King's Residence might become the center of a plot against the forces of Yang Xiuqing and his allies. Communications from the front were all forwarded to the Heavenly Capital, where Wei held control over them, and that set of circumstances did not make Yang happy.

He could not leave Wei in such a position of continual contact with the commanders at the front for long. Although Wei might enhance his troop strength once outside the confines of the city, he would have to fight the enemy too. Zeng Guofan, commander of the Hunan Army, was making his base camp around this time in Nanchang, capital of Jiangxi province. While sensing a danger in Wei Changhui's being at the center of the communications network in the city, Yang did not at all think it unsafe that Hong Xiuquan be in the very same place.

Not much he can do, thought Yang, making light of Hong.

"The Heavenly King has dispatched a secret messenger." When he heard this piece of information from one of his spying subordinates, Yang's face broke out in an expression of disaster.

"Where'd he go? Hubei? Jiangxi?" Shi Dakai was in Hubei, and Wei Changhui was in Jiangxi.

"No. He went to Shanghai."

"What? Shanghai?"

"Do you happen to recall a woman by the name of Xiling from the Xishi Monastery in Guiping?"

"Yes, she had some tie to the Jinshunji. Mixed blood, a beautiful woman. But much older than us."

"We think she may have been called to the Heavenly Capital to manage the affairs of the harem of the Heavenly King's Residence."

Yang laughed uproariously. Two years earlier, Yang had enabled several older women to leave the Heavenly King's Residence by virtue of one of his Heavenly Father's Descents to Earth. A battle among the women in the Heavenly King's harem, which was full of stunningly beautiful women, had become serious, and Hong Xiuquan found himself in an extremely awkward position.

"If it's really Xiling, then she's certainly no child. She's an old friend, and I think she's got just the qualities needed to settle the battling there. Looks like the Heavenly King knew just how good a situation he had," said Yang, laughing away his fears.

At just this time, Lian Weicai stood with arms folded in a room of the Wade Company in Shanghai. "It seems as though somehow news of a secret messenger from the Heavenly King has gotten out."

"You mean that secret messenger who was sent to Xiling? It appears to have been craftily worked out so that that item was purposefully released," said Lian Liwen.

"It was a desperate measure taken to camouflage the real messengers sent to Jiangxi and Hubei. The Heavenly Capital is in danger." A half-written letter lay on the table in front of Lian Weicai. It was addressed to his eldest son Tongwen in Taiwan.

—7—

News of the destruction of the Qing's Southern Imperial Barracks reached Shanghai at the end of June that year, 1856. The Southern Imperial Barracks had been erected just after the Taiping Army occupied Nanjing. Xiang Rong had built them after arriving in pursuit of the Taiping forces.

Nanjing, popularly considered the dynasty's secondary capital, had been taken by the rebels almost without resistance, and having failed to prevent that meant virtually certain death. Xiang Rong had to demonstrate that he would retake the city, and soon. The very existence of the Southern Imperial Barracks symbolized this effort.

At first, the story circulated that Imperial Commissioner Xiang Rong had been killed in the fighting. Later, though, it was learned that this report was incorrect. Though severely wounded, Xiang Rong had fled to Jurong and then retreated further to Danyang. His death occurred in Danyang on August 9, 1856, fifty days after the collapse of the Southern Imperial Barracks.

The Taipings depicted the result of this battle as the "Heavenly Capital Lifts the Siege." Strictly speaking, there had been no encirclement or siege of the Taiping capital. Taiping troops and personnel had been able to come and go freely at Nanjing. It was merely that the Qing military had established a powerful base of operations close to the Heavenly Capital.

If you have a boil above your eye, you are certainly well-advised to lance it with alacrity. Defense of the Southern Imperial Barracks was unexpectedly firm. It was a base for guarding rather than attacking. The significance of the Southern Imperial Barracks lay in the fact that it actually existed, and it seemed only natural that great effort would have gone into defending it.

"Why not attack Nanjing as quickly as possible?" Such was the stringent pressure for action from the court in Beijing. If, however, the Qing Army at the Southern Imperial Barracks tried to go on the offensive, the troops of the

Taipings' western expeditionary army would undoubtedly to a man return to help in the defense of their capital. The Qing Army of assault on Nanjing might accordingly find itself the victim of a reverse encirclement and be completely exterminated.

They explained the facts to the imperial court. "Because the Southern Imperial Barracks is close to Nanjing, the long-haired bandits cannot send large military forces out to other locales." Thus, the import of the Southern Imperial Barracks was its presence. In the final analysis, it was crushed by the Taiping armed forces. For the Taipings, the Southern Imperial Barracks was like a dagger about to be plunged into their throat—at some point it had to be destroyed. When they moved to destroy it, the Taipings would have to employ a strategy whereby their entire population would go into battle.

Eastern King Yang Xiuqing sent out an armed force under his command from the Tongji Gate of the city. Assistant King Shi Dakai divided his men into two units and devised a pincer operation against the Southern Imperial Barracks. Qin Rigang attacked the Qing encampment at Zijin Mountain to the east of the Heavenly Capital, and both Li Xiucheng and Chen Yucheng were part of this last operation.

The headquarters of the Southern Imperial Barracks was at Xiaoling, the grave site of one of the emperors of the Ming dynasty and near to the grave of its founder. Close to what would later become Sun Yat-sen's mausoleum was an area for stationing troops of the Southern Imperial Barracks.

The man who supervised the overland transport of tea leaves and who thus frequently traversed the area near Nanjing reported on conditions at that time to Lian Weicai. "Morale is completely different between the two groups. They have pulled together all the strength they possibly can, for they have to destroy the Southern Imperial Barracks. If they fail to do so, the Taipings will lose all desire to go on living. There is no halfheartedness about them. It is the Qing Army, in fact, that is noncommittal. The longer there is no attack against them, the more they become nonchalant about things."

"I see, pulled all their strength together . . ."

After this man departed, Liwen arrived and reported, "She entered the Heavenly King's Residence apparently healthy before the war at the Southern Imperial Barracks began."

"The battle at the Southern Imperial Barracks looked to be quite a remarkable event."

"Yes, indeed. The festivities have apparently already begun throughout the Heavenly Capital. Immense quantities of guns, revolvers, and ammunition, as well as mountains of food and provisions were left behind. I'm told that everyone is watching as it's all transported inside the city walls." Liwen had sources for his intelligence.

"Victory always excites people, and the Heavenly Capital seems now to be caught up in this excitement."

"It does look as though people are in high spirits."

"Afterward, relaxation will probably come."

"There's no sign of that at present. Shi Dakai left for Wuchang. Wei Changhui has been fighting hard in Jiangxi, so much so that Zeng Guofan in Nanchang has had no room to move whatsoever."

"No, he won't fail to come. People's attention lapses. They wouldn't be human beings otherwise. There'll certainly be some people in Nanjing not taking part in the festivities."

"You mean people who can't get excited by what has happened?"

"That's right. There are just too many things that still have to be done. They can't get excited over something like the Southern Imperial Barracks. Who's going to move first, the Heavenly King or the Eastern King? It would be very interesting if it weren't so injudicious to say so."

"Who would it be better to move first?"

"As far as I'm concerned, I'd have the Heavenly King do so, but it'd be best not to assist either side. At least, for now."

Lian Weicai was watching his son's face before him, the area by his ear. A map was stuck to the wall behind it. It was a map of the world. He stood up from his chair and slowly walked over to the wall.

"This is Paris, France," he said, pointing to a spot on the map.

"Huh?" The subject having changed so abruptly, Liwen was taken aback.

"The world's fair was opened there last year."

"I've heard that."

"Zhewen mentioned in a letter that Japan participated in it, but not as Japan. Both the shogunate in Edo and the Shimazu family from Satsuma sent their own representatives. Apparently, everyone thought there were two Japans."

"Yes, that's what happened." Liwen could not help but feel that his father wanted to say something.

"Wouldn't two Japans mean domestic controversy? This problem will have to be resolved sometime soon. I don't think we can very well choose our own ally from among the two."

"Of course not."

"If Japan is this way, then the same may apply in the struggle within the Heavenly Capital."

"Though Japan is on the other side of the sea, the Heavenly Capital is right here in the middle of our own China. It's right here."

"When something destined occurs and we have no particular relationship with it, we have no choice but to quietly sit and watch it take place. But it's a different matter if it concerns us."

"Yes, indeed."

Liwen now thought he understood what it was his father was trying to say. Were Eastern King Yang Xiuqing to rise in rebellion, he might bring pressure to bear on Heavenly King Hong Xiuquan to abdicate. Or the Heavenly King might strike first and purge the Eastern King. If Liwen remained in Shanghai, both men's movements would be detectable.

Lian Weicai moved his finger to the space occupied by Japan on the map on the wall. "Japan is changing tremendously, and all we can do is stare at her." He had learned of the contents of the peace treaty between the United States and Japan signed the previous year in Japan. News of a young man by the name of Yoshida Shūin (1830–1859), who had tried to stow away to the United States and was then caught by the shogunal authorities, was conveyed to him in a letter from Zhewen.

"Last year the Japanese built a naval training institute in Nagasaki, and they have assembled the brightest young men from the entire country at this school."

"In Nagasaki?"

It was a place name close to Liwen's heart. He walked over to the wall and stood next to his father, focusing his gaze on the map, which was made in Great Britain.

"We have no such institute in our country. What's more, how many of our young men would risk violating a national prohibition and try to make their way overseas, like this Yoshida fellow?"

The answer came in a murmur and was not anticipated.

"It's not that they don't exist. They simply don't know. And more than anything else, we've got to make them aware. The very first thing for us to do . . . is to inform them of these needs."

Although Liwen responded in an agitated manner, as he spoke he became aware that he had to bring his emotions under control.

30

The Arrow
Is in the
Bow

—1—

From the perspective of the Qing court, the Taipings were a band of rebels who, because they cut their queues and grew their hair, had earned the name, "long-haired bandits." Also, because of their place of origin, they were known as the "Ao bandits." At the time that Zeng Guofan set out with the Hunan Army, the armed corps of volunteers he had organized, he issued an official proclamation concerning "Conquest of the Ao Bandits." "Ao" was a term denoting the Chinese provinces of Guangdong and Guangxi.

Surprisingly, there was no mention whatsoever in this proclamation of loyalty to sovereign and love of country. What Zeng stressed instead was the brutality of the Taiping forces, their rejection of Confucian ritual propriety of several thousand years in China, and their destruction of Confucian temples. The Taipings therefore had to be crushed, in his view.

The reason he had not mentioned loyalty and patriotism was to avoid the possibility of stirring up a hornet's nest. Who was this sovereign due loyalty? The Qing emperor, a Manchu whose people had invaded China from the northeast. And the "country" owed patriotism was none other than the Manchu regime in Beijing. Both sovereign and country held sway over and oppressed the Han people, who comprised the great majority of the population of China.

Ordinary Han Chinese despised the Manchus and their regime, and the Taiping rebels struck a deep chord of delight among the populace at large. Zeng Guofan feared that the Taipings' movement might arouse the sympathies of the general Han population, and thus in his proclamation, he chose to raise the issues of the Taipings' lack of respect for and destructiveness of traditional Han Chinese culture, their belief in the foreign religion of Christianity, and their transgressions of moral principles. The proclamation should have been effective among China's literati class, which was firmly conservative and antiforeign.

Once the proclamation was issued, he left Hengzhou. Now, two and one-half years had transpired, and in that time much that he regretted had come to pass. He could never forget the humiliation he had sustained at Jinggang shortly after his departure. Jinggang was a town, then under Taiping occupation, along the Xiang River between Changsha and Lake Dongting. Because of Taiping pressure, the Hunan provincial capital at Changsha was isolated both from Xiangtan upriver and Jinggang downriver.

"Let's take Xiangtan back first," argued Peng Yulin, a member of Zeng's staff whom he treated with every courtesy.

They had no choice but to advance toward Wuchang, umbilicus of the nation, if even just one step, and to that end Zeng wanted to continue moving to the north. To trace the Xiang River back upriver to the south and recapture Xiangtan thus assumed the form of a retreat.

"If we're to retake it, we're better off focusing on Jinggang," said Zeng, offering his views.

"If we attack Jinggang downriver, bandit reinforcements are sure to come soon thereafter from Xiangtan upriver," responded Peng. "I really think we should move south, and I'll lead the advance forces."

Peng Yulin marched south downstream along the route from which he had come together with Chu Ruhang, Xia Luan, and Yang Zaifu, all commanders of the Hunan Army's naval forces. Ta-qi-bu commanded the land forces. It was April 27, about three weeks after the Battle of the Muddy Flat in Shanghai.

The following day, Zeng followed with the remainder of his troops, though his feeling about the whole operation had significantly changed. Since he had originally wanted to continue their march to the north, a change of heart on his part was probably the suitable expression for the present action.

The problem was that by marching north and attacking Jinggang, they would ensure that enemy reinforcements from Xiangtan in the south would come rushing to the fight. Yet because Peng Yulin and the others headed south, the enemy in Xiangtan was in no position to assist Jinggang. Jinggang could expect no reinforcements and had to brace itself for the impending storm. Zeng did not follow the strategy plans decided at the war council. It was an effort to move first against the enemy. However, Zeng was defeated in this preemptive attack on Jinggang.

Although raised in a riverside district, Zeng was unaware of the dangers of the water. That year the snow from the Luoxiao, Xuefeng, and Nanling mountain ranges had thawed earlier than in normal years, and the waters of the Xiang River were swelling, its current becoming furious. Furthermore, by only observing its surface movement, its real strength remained unknown.

Zeng planned to attack Jinggang with an armada of forty vessels. The Taiping forces at Jinggang were under the command of Shi Zhenxiang. Zeng's armada set sail for the wharf at Jinggang to come on shore, but the current was too strong and the ships would not proceed as planned. They were unable to dock, swept along in the swift current right past Jinggang.

The Taipings at Jinggang readied small vessels in an attempt to ambush Zeng's forces at the water's edge. Zeng's ships, however, miscalculated and passed by in front of them. The small Taiping flotilla then all began to row in pursuit of Zeng's forces. From the start, the battle scenario resembled a chase after a defeated enemy. Those pursuing from upstream, needless to say, had an overwhelming advantage.

The incendiary arrows and other weapons that the Taiping prepared for their defense suddenly became offensive weaponry. Deluged with these burning arrows, Zeng's armada was instantaneously engulfed in flames. The troops rushed to shore and then scrambled to flee. They dispersed and scattered.

Fixing the flag in the ground, Zeng screamed at the top of his voice, "Do not run away! The enemy is few in numbers. They have no reinforcements. Attack! Those who flee will be beheaded! Those who run ahead of the flag will die!" Once his troops had scattered, though, there was no returning.

"All my energies for the past six months, a life's ambition, all gone right here." Disconsolate, Zeng Guofan threw himself into the Xiang River at the Jinggang shore. His secretary Zhang Shoulin rushed to rescue him and managed to save him from the brink of death.

A thorough wreck, Zeng went to rest at the Gaofeng Temple outside the southern gate of Changsha, though even there the jarring noises of the outside world intruded. At the Gaofeng Temple, Zeng composed his will, his determination unchanged. Then came the startling news of a victory at Xiangtan.

The Taiping forces at Xiangtan were under the command of Lin Shaozhang, but for some reason there was disunity in the ranks. A dispute arose between the "elder brothers" (those who had joined the Taipings back in Guangxi province) and the "younger brothers" (those who joined after the Taiping Army entered Hunan), apparently leaving several hundred dead.

Although the Hunan Army had lost a high-level officer, Assistant Brigade Commander Zhang Wanbang, they recaptured Xiangtan and won complete victory. Zeng now saw some hope in the future and abandoned plans for ending his own life. His men had been able to retake Xiangtan, he realized, because of dissension among the bandit forces, and the bandit army was no longer the unified monolith that reports had always made it out to be. Here is clearly our chance to seize victory, he thought.

Having endured criticism and abuse, Zeng was now waiting for the next opportunity. Some six months later, the Hunan Army wrested Wuchang from the Taipings' grasp.

At the court in Beijing, saddened by a succession of news of defeats, the Xianfeng Emperor and his ministers could not conceal their elation at the happy news of the recapture of Wuchang. The decision was made to appoint Zeng Guofan governor of Hubei. Zeng declined. Under ordinary circumstances, there would also be instructions requiring the appointment, but not on this occasion. Separate instructions read: "Honor him with treatment befitting a vice-minister in the Ministry of War."

Vice-minister in the Ministry of War was comparable to an undersecretary in a department of defense. Zeng had been vice-minister in the Ministry of Rites (something like an undersecretary of education) before he had resigned to take up a period of mourning, and thus this new conferral was certainly no promotion. Nor was he to become an actual vice-minister, but just to receive the same treatment accorded a vice-minister.

One of the men on his staff spoke up. "There's something not quite right here. It would be better under the circumstances to accept the position of Hubei governor."

A governor was the highest provincial official, with powers of decision-making in military as well as political affairs. A governor had troops under his control, and he served as the representative of the emperor in his own province.

"It's fine. I'm still in mourning now. But if I were to become governor of Hubei, wouldn't an expedition to the east be rather irregular? I'm sure the emperor will have considered this option," said Zeng, and he then began calming the disconcertedness around him.

By an expedition to the east, Zeng meant an attack on Nanjing, base of operations of the Taiping movement. To get to Nanjing, he would have to pass through the provinces of Jiangxi, Anhui, and Jiangsu, and with the title of Hubei governor alone, such an expedition certainly would be irregular.

—2—

"This is fine, fine," said Zeng, not just to persuade those around him, but for himself as well.

The Hunan Army under his command was not a national army but a corps of volunteers. While he served as commander of this "private" force, Zeng was not, for the time being, in government service and enjoyed a free hand.

A variety of rumors later circulated about this, and they were greatly displeasing to him.

Zeng's appointment as Hubei governor was not called off so that he could pursue a military expedition to the east. Grand Minister of State Qi Junzao (1793–1866) memorialized the throne about Zeng as follows: "He is an ordinary man [i.e., not an official], a commoner. He once stood up and called out, and over ten thousand men responded to his call. This may not be a blessing for our nation." Rumor had it that because of this memorial, Zeng's appointment to the Hubei governorship was abandoned.

This exchange took place deep in the recesses of the imperial court, making it impossible for Zeng Guofan, who was off in Wuchang, to verify the accuracy of the rumor. It did, though, seem to reflect the truth. Zeng had indeed become a "commoner" during the period of his resignation to take up mourning, and the Hunan Army that he had put together was a regular force.

The recovery of Wuchang, linchpin of the Chinese empire, was certainly a welcome and joyous event, but because it had been the work of the Hunan Army, it was not the result of a strong state structure. The problem was that despite the fact that the emperor had a host of agents serving him throughout the realm—governors, governor-generals, and provincial military commanders, among others—the recapture of Wuchang had been achieved through the brilliant work of a corps of men led by a mere commoner.

"If you distinguish yourself on the battlefield, it gives rise to envy and slander. This has always been the case. The best way to overcome envy and slander is by performing more meritorious deeds on the field of war," said Zeng, burning with the desire to set off on an eastern expedition.

After the recovery of Wuchang, morale in the Hunan Army was high. Having lost Wuchang and retreated, the Taiping forces established a fortified military base in Tianjiazhen near the provincial border between Hubei and Jiangxi. Tianjiazhen was a town on the north shore of the Yangzi River; across the shore to the south was Mount Banbi. The Taipings were connecting thick iron chains between Tianjiazhen and Mount Banbi and tethering floating wooden rafts to them, all as a means of blockading the Yangzi River.

A suicide squad in the Hunan Army succeeded in destroying the iron chains and breaking through the rows of rafts. Taiping commander Qin Rigang, who was defending Tianjiazhen, set fire to his military base and retreated to Jiujiang, but before he knew it he was confronting a fierce attack by the Hunan Army. Commander Peng Yulin then reduced over five hundred Taiping military vessels to ashes. As to why he had destroyed these ships when it appeared that they might prove useful to the Hunan Army, Peng explained his actions. "Above all else, the Hunan Army must be an army of benevolence and justice. If there is decay in the minds of our officers and men, we cease to be a military force." His point was that, if he had allowed the 500 ships to remain intact, plunder by troops of the Hunan Army was sure to begin. Once they had acquired a taste for plunder, the men's minds would decay.

"The heart of the Hunan Army," added Peng, "is far more important than the five hundred ships."

Using their momentum, the Hunan Army followed the Yangzi downstream, advancing their forces toward Jiujiang, where the Taipings had built their new base. Taiping forces there were strongly defended, and the Hunan Army was unable to draw them out. So, Zeng Guofan left Jiujiang, advanced to the east, and attacked Hukou.

As the Chinese ideographs of its name indicated, Hukou lay at the entranceway to Lake Poyang from the Yangzi River. The Taipings had prepared the area by placing generals Shi Dakai and Luo Gagang there. The navy was organized into vessels large and small, with the larger ships storing military supplies, weaponry, and troops, while the smaller ships, with their greater mobility and speed, were outfitted for battle. Ferocious seaborne battles were fought one after the next, with neither side yielding to the other.

On January 29, 1855, a naval battle began at Baijiazhou near Hukou, and the outlook for the Taiping forces looked rather poor. With 120 smaller, agile vessels, the Hunan Army commenced a furious assault on the Taipings. Unable to withstand the attack, Taiping warships turned around, or at least they seemed to be doing so.

"The bandits are escaping!"

"Don't let them get away! Chase them!"

The momentum now on their side, the Hunan forces pursued the Taiping flotilla. In fact, though, the whole thing was an elaborate Taiping stratagem. The light 120 vessels of the Hunan forces were enticed into Lake Poyang. Waiting eagerly for them there, the Taipings blocked passage between the lake and the river and set out on the water rafts, on which cannons had been mounted.

The small vessels that came onto Lake Poyang found all exits closed off to them, while the larger vessels of the Hunan Army remained afloat on the Yangzi River. For the first time, the navy was faced with the opportunity to effectively demonstrate the functions of large and small ships simultaneously. Having now split into two groups based on the size of the vessels, their military strength was reduced far more than their numbers indicated. The larger vessels, unable to fight by themselves, relied on the fighting capacity of the smaller ones, while the smaller vessels relied on the larger ones for replenishment of military supplies and ammunition.

Zeng Guofan was aboard one of the ships on the Yangzi. The Hunan Army's flotilla on the Yangzi fell easy prey to a nocturnal attack from the Taipings' armada of small boats, with Shi Dakai himself at the lead. Ships set afire, ships seized, ships in flight—the river was lit up brightly. Hurriedly, Zeng jumped aboard a small boat and escaped to the Hunan Army base on land. Even the Hunan land forces were making plans to flee. Both seaborne and land forces of the Hunan Army escaped to the west.

"We shall fight to the death! We'll show them the stuff the Hunan Army is made of!" Zeng was about to lead a raid all by himself on horseback directly into the forces of the Taiping Army, when he was restrained by Luo Zenan.

The Taipings sent a large force in pursuit of the Hunan Army, which had broken up and was in full retreat. On April 3, the Taiping Army occupied Wuchang for the third time. Tao Enpei, who had been appointed to the position of governor of Hubei province after Zeng Guofang had turned down the position, died in the fighting at this time.

Once they returned to Hunan, would they ever be able to recover this lost ground? Or might they try and persist by establishing a base of operations near the Taiping base? After serious deliberation, Zeng decided to follow the latter course. He selected Nanchang, the provincial capital of Jiangxi, as a base to lead attacks on Jiujiang and Hukou and to put pressure on Nanjing.

For more than a year thereafter, Zeng found himself holed up in Nanchang. He passed his days in bitterness and anxiety. Only the news of the setback inflicted on the northern expedition force of the Taiping Army consoled him.

The seventh lunar month of 1856 was about to come to an end. A force under the command of Taiping Northern King Wei Changhui was building a camp before the city of Nanchang, where Zeng was still living. The base was located in the vicinity of Tangtouling and Wanshougong, to the southwest of Nanchang.

Assistant King Shi Dakai was in Wuchang. The Southern Imperial Barracks of the government's army had been destroyed. A confirmed report had just arrived saying that Imperial Commissioner Xiang Rong had died in Danyang. The smile disappeared from Zeng Guofan's face.

"We must not allow our spirits to fall," said Peng Yulin as encouragement to Zeng. "It's important that we keep our minds open and bear up under this burden. Waiting is also a part of war! Never forget that our victory at Xiangtan was by no means something I attained alone."

The great victory at Xiangtan had been the result of internecine strife between factions of the Taiping armed forces. If they endured and waited, Peng was saying, the enemy's weaknesses would again manifest themselves in some form. Far from being gloomy about the turn of events, they should open their minds and await the next chance to strike.

"Many thanks for this admonition," said Zeng Guofan. "I've actually been telling myself the same thing. An opportunity will surely come." As a diversion,

Zeng picked up a brush and drew Chinese characters in the air. The opportunity arrived unexpectedly soon. When Peng Yulin was about to leave, an officer entered his quarters. An officer in the Hunan Army was more a scholar than a military man.

"There's something strange about the appearance of the rebel camp at Tangtouling," he reported, in a tone altogether lacking in self-confidence. "Perhaps it's a ruse."

"Why do you say 'strange'?"

"There's no sign of people there. I've verified this over and over again. We asked farmers in the area, and they said that suddenly last night the rebel troops began to move."

"What's this? Are you saying that Wei Changhui has broken camp and cleared out?" Peng shifted his gaze to Zeng Guofan, as if to say, "This is it!"

"Yes. Perhaps it's a deception," said the man, with intense seriousness.

"There's something to this," said Zeng, as he stood up and drew in his chin. "Let's check it out closely."

—3—

"The enemy camp is in chaos."

Zeng Guofan had not gone to bed expecting such happy news. Though still in Nanchang himself, he always had scouts and spies observing the inner goings-on of the Taipings in Nanjing. He also learned from such reports that hostilities had arisen among the Taiping leaders and grown more severe with each passing day. Zeng analyzed the reports, trying as hard as he could to eschew all subjective content.

Zeng anticipated that when the internal dissension among the Taipings became serious, Northern King Wei Changhui was sure to make some sort of move. Wei's departure at the head of his troops in front of Nanchang was nothing short of a harbinger of this internal discord.

"We've received a report that a suspicious-looking woman entered the rebel camp to the north several days ago," said Peng Yulin, "Perhaps there may be a link of some sort between that and the rebels' retreat."

Peng was forty years of age, some five years Zeng's junior. From Hengyang in Hunan province, Peng had never sought an official career in government. When the rebellion of Li Yuanfa erupted in Hunan, Peng had volunteered and participated in its suppression. Similarly, when the Taipings entered Hunan from Guangxi, he had used his own money to raise a force of volunteer braves. His career closely resembled that of Jiang Zhongyuan, who had died in battle at Nanchang.

When Zeng Guofan was organizing the Hunan Army, he sought the assistance of Peng Yulin. Zeng greatly admired him as a man with no personal ambition and no desire to advance in the world.

"Yes, a navy is particularly important," said Peng, at the time he agreed to take part in the establishment of the Hunan Army, "and I too shall work hard to see it come into existence. I just have one condition."

"What sort of a condition would that be? If it's within my power, I shall grant it."

"It's quite simple. In the future, I want no bureaucratic positions. That's all."

Zeng had silently nodded in response to Peng's request. From Peng's words, Zeng was able to read something further of the nonverbal message being conveyed. It was as if Peng had said, "The Qing is a Manchu dynasty, and I am too proud to serve as an official in its government. However, as a responsible literatus, I simply cannot allow my local area to fall into anarchy. For this reason alone, I shall work with you."

Although there was an immense difference in status between them, Zeng could never think of Peng as his inferior. The victory at Xiangtan and breaking through the iron chains across the Yangzi at Tianjiazhen were both due to Peng's leadership. Still, he did not boast of these accomplishments, repeating only that victory had been due to discord within the enemy camp.

It was Peng Yulin who most often stressed this dissension, and at times this irritated Zeng Guofan. Does that mean that we wouldn't have won had there been no such discord within the enemy camp? wondered Zeng. Yet momentum was clearly on the side of the Taipings now that they had gained control over Wuchang, destroyed the Southern Imperial Barracks, and effectively sealed Zeng up in Nanchang.

"Do you really think there is some link?" That a woman could have had some relation to the major shifts within the realm was unimaginable in Zeng's consciousness.

"Women often effect movements among these bandits," said Peng.

"Those people are neither men nor women. They've lost all sense of human morality."

"The story had been circulating more and more that bandit Hong detests bandit Yang. Hatred is hatred, isn't it? Bandit Yang is very strong now, but at present he's not ready to make a move. Once he does, though, Hong may try to use women to make Yang act carelessly."

"It's not impossible, but let's focus on the situation in Nanjing till this point. It seems that contacts with those in Nanjing have not been proceeding smoothly of late." When Zeng spoke of those in Nanjing, he was referring to the intelligence agents he had sent there.

"They've become extraordinarily wary recently, particularly after the destruction of the Southern Imperial Barracks. And not only in Nanjing, but along the roads as well."

"If communications had been better, I would know a great deal more now," said Zeng, as he assessed the actual facts about Wei Changhui's departure.

At this time, Lian Weicai in Shanghai had reached an even more precise judgment. On the second story of the Wade Company, he said, relating his own views on the matter to his son Lian Liwen: "They're being extremely careful, but more toward the Heavenly King than toward the Qing Army."

"I agree entirely," said Liwen, nodding his head.

"It's been since the razing of the Southern Imperial Barracks. It looks to me as though the Eastern King has decided that the right moment for him to act has at long last arrived. The reason he hasn't made his move until now was the existence of the Southern Imperial Barracks, but with that now gone, there's no longer any reason to hesitate."

"Perhaps this is an omen of one of his Ten Thousand Years," said Liwen.

"It's an infantile story, but that is something the Eastern King uses."

By "one of his Ten Thousand Years," Liwen was referring to Yang Xiuqing's frequent use of the Heavenly Father's Descent to Earth. It was the greatest weapon at his disposal to enhance his own public position. The Heavenly Father Jehovah had at one point taken possession of Yang's body and directed the following comments toward Heavenly King Hong Xiuquan: "You and Yang Xiuqing are both my sons, and together you have performed meritorious service. Then why do you earn ten thousand years and Yang but nine thousand?"

Within the Taiping movement, the cheer of "ten thousand years" (comparable to "long live the king!") was directed only at the Heavenly King, while the Eastern King, Southern King, Western King, Northern King, and Assistant King each received greetings of progressively one thousand years less. Accordingly, Yang Xiuqing got "nine thousand years," and his son was called "Qiansui" or "one thousand years."

Heavenly King Hong Xiuquan fell prostrate before this divine revelation and had no choice but to respond, "Yes, of course, the Eastern King has accomplished great things in beating back the rivers and mountains. We should indeed address him as 'ten thousand years,' too."

"Then, I ask you, why do you call the Eastern King's heir only one thousand years?" The inquiries of the Heavenly Father continued through the mouth of Yang Xiuqing.

"Since the Eastern King is now to be called ten thousand years, then his heir shall also be ten thousand years, for it shall be passed on for generations."

"Yes, this is true. Fine, I am satisfied with this. And now I shall return to heaven."

By this declaration, the Heavenly King and the Eastern King were now on equal status as to this title among the Taipings. There were earlier instances of such behavior in Chinese history, such as when Cao Cao (155–220) and his son Cao Pi (187–226) usurped the throne from Emperor Xian of the Later Han dynasty in the early third century and when Sima Zhao (211–265) of the Jin dynasty forced the transfer to him of the imperial institution from the Wei dynasty in the middle of that century. Yang had effectively entered the palace with his sword at his side and proceeded to the step of adding the Nine Imperial Gifts, nine items—such as chariots and horses, robes of state, certain bows and arrows, and the like—that the emperor alone could confer on his subjects.

"He's added the Nine Imperial Gifts," said Liwen.

"No, no. Yang Xiuqing is no man of learning. What he did was much more flagrant, far beyond the Nine Imperial Gifts," said Lian Weicai, frowning. The Nine Imperial Gifts were imperially conferred items otherwise not permitted to imperial subjects, but they were always one rank beneath that of the emperor himself. Yang Xiuqing had acquired the appellation of "ten thousand" just like the Heavenly King, and it was this, according to Lian Weicai, that made Yang's action a more blatant move toward forced abdication than just the Nine Imperial Gifts.

"There will surely be an abdication," said Liwen.

His father responded, "Yang Xiuqing may be planning one, but I wonder if the Heavenly King is aware of it."

"Even if he isn't, he'll be forced into it. He'll have no choice."

"When you look over the actions of the Heavenly King to this point, there is a certain indecisiveness to him. However, when it comes to defending his terrain and his very life, I doubt he'll be as slow to react as he's been in the past. He's not that irresolute a man."

"I'm sure he'll make a move. Xiling did go to Nanchang."

"It'll be before the Eastern King's birthday. The Eastern King is clearly thinking about seizing power on that day. The Heavenly King must be aware of this, so if he makes a move, it should be before then."

Hong Xiuquan had ascended to the position of Heavenly King on his own birthday. Perhaps the Eastern King would follow suit. The seventeenth day of the eighth lunar month was Yang's birthday. The affair over "ten thousand years" had taken place on the twenty-second day of the seventh month. There was still time, but Hong would have to take action quickly.

Hong Xiuquan had permitted Yang the title of "ten thousand years" so easily, because he seemed to be so slow-witted, incapable of posing any sort of threat. When he handed over this privilege, he even had an expression of apparent happiness on his face. In fact, however, Hong was burning with rage inside.

Far from Nanjing in Shanghai, Lian Weicai grasped almost exactly the Heavenly King's intentions and the timing of his decision to act, but Yang Xiuqing failed to see this. Caught up in the maelstrom, he couldn't make out the circumstances surrounding him, for the Eastern King had been too indulgent in his perceptions of the Heavenly King, and the performance by the Heavenly King blurred Yang's judgment.

With his life on the line, the Heavenly King threw himself into his act. Xiling, one of the secret messengers of the Heavenly King, conveyed the following message to Wei Changhui. The same instructions were sent to Assistant King Shi Dakai in Wuchang: "If we don't liquidate the Eastern King, that snake in our midst, the ideals of the Taiping Heavenly Kingdom will never see fruition. Send the Northern King with his troops to visit heavenly retribution upon the Eastern King and his entourage!"

September 1 corresponded to the third day of the eighth lunar month in 1856, though at the time the Taipings used neither the lunar nor the solar calendar, but one of their own devising.

"Late tonight," reported Xiling, who had just returned from Nanchang to the Heavenly Capital and headed for the Residence of the Heavenly King, to Hong Xiuquan.

Rumor had it that Hong was infatuated with beautiful women, and in fact he had a strong tendency in that direction, but this was now part of his act. By camouflaging his true intentions within this apparent affection for attractive women, he could keep Yang Xiuqing at bay.

Access to the Residence of the Heavenly King was not the least bit guarded when it came to women. Some sort of problem had arisen concerning the women at his residence, and Xiling acted in such a way, as she approached the building, as to give the impression that the Heavenly King had sought the services of an experienced woman of mixed blood to resolve it.

"This shouldn't go beyond us," Xiling swore many to silence, but in such a way as to effectively ask them to spread the word. "But the Heavenly King is awash in troubles and animosities with the women around him. It's gotten to the point where he can't just ignore it any longer. He's asked me to take care of it for him. Please don't tell this to anyone."

The inner recesses of the Heavenly King's Residence were a particularly secret place about which no one knew anything. An occurrence there would arouse people's curiosity all the more. Inquisitive eyes inclined in the direction of Hong's Residence would not likely be able to look elsewhere. Heavenly King Hong Xiuquan's subterfuge was succeeding.

"Tonight?" whispered Hong, expressionless. It had become his habit not to show any emotion on his face.

"You won't change your mind, will you?" repeated Xiling.

"The arrow is in the bow, and an arrow fixed to the bowstring cannot but be shot." This was Hong Xiuquan speaking, the man said to be flawed in matters requiring decision-making. His determination to eliminate Yang Xiuqing was not going to be shaken. He understood clearly now that Yang was looking forward to his birthday, preparing formally to accept the title of "ten thousand years" and to ascend to the Great Treasure (as the Taipings called their most exalted position).

These matters were, of course, top secret even at the Eastern King's Residence, though Eastern King Yang Xiuqing did seek advice from several of his trusted friends. One of them, Hu Yihuang, revealed the plan to the Heavenly King.

On one occasion prior to the Jintian uprising, Hong Xiuquan and Feng Yunshan were hiding in the hills of Pingnan, and Hu Yihuang offered them shelter. Through the cracks and crevices in the surrounding Qing Army, he made contact with Jintian village, and Yang Xiuqing's reinforcements eventually located them on the verge of disaster. Since then he had been one of the top leaders in the Taiping movement, though gradually he had grown closer to Yang Xiuqing and was seen as a confidante of the Eastern King. Hu's wife was a female official in the Eastern King's Residence. She ran all the housekeeping affairs at Yang's quarters, an indication of the depth of Yang's trust in Hu.

Stealthily, this same Hu Yihuang now came to the Residence of the Heavenly King and reported, "As it presently stands, your life, let alone your rank of ten thousand years, is in grave danger. Please take action quickly. It matters little what happens to me. I would throw away my life to protect yours. It is far more dangerous now than when we were back in the mountains of Pingnan."

"I thank you. From my heart, I thank you." Hong had no doubt about Yang's plans to usurp his position. From Hong's facial expression, it was clear that Hu understood this.

Hong did wonder why Hu had come to report secretly on Yang's activities, but he did not ask Hu about it—he was able to surmise the answer. Perhaps he recalled their relationship from the days in Pingnan. Branded in his memory even more, though, was the stunningly beautiful visage of Hu's wife, whom he had met once also in the Pingnan hills. It had already been recounted to him that Hu's wife worked by Yang's side in the Eastern King's Residence.

"We shall soon begin," muttered Hong Xiuquan, as always expressionless, after listening to Xiling's report.

The Residence of the Eastern King knew nothing of these plans. News of the destruction of the Qing Southern Imperial Barracks and the death of Imperial Commissioner Xiang Rong had arrived at Yang's quarters, and the joyous atmosphere there bordered on giddiness.

"A propitious day is near, and perhaps a little too late," said Hu to Yang. He was praising Yang for work done. Yang became even more arrogant when receiving praise. In a chair reserved for trusted friends, Yang offered an extremely simple response, attempting to hide neither joy nor anger.

"True enough, it was too late. But it's because of the events in the north and the Southern Imperial Barracks . . . it was a long time coming." By "events in the north," Yang was referring to the failure of the Taipings' northern expedition, in which many of his own followers had been among the leadership of the forces.

Though his own troops had met with defeat in the northern expedition, in the interim they had been replenished in the Heavenly Capital. In their large numbers he brazenly showed off the fact that his power and authority exceeded that of the Heavenly King himself.

"We shall be like the shade of a great tree when they come to us"—and they did flock to the Residence of the Eastern King.

As it presently stood, there were three cliques within the Taiping military forces. Of the Taiping kings, Southern King Feng Yunshan and Western King Xiao Chaogui were both dead, and Heavenly King Hong Xiuquan was hidden deep in the recesses of his official residence, far from political and military affairs. Thus, only the Eastern, Northern, and Assistant Kings still had troops directly under their commands. The Eastern King was hard at work within the Heavenly Capital, having sent the Northern and Assistant Kings to outlying areas. He anticipated that a struggle between the soldiers of these two cliques would reduce their strength.

At just that time, though, there was a string of rebellions led by Triad groups in Guangdong, and with the downfall of the Small Sword Society, which had absorbed many Triads, forces from the Guangdong Triads streamed into the army of Shi Dakai in neighboring Guangxi province. This was one of the reasons Yang Xiuqing had transferred Shi's army to Wuchang and relieved him with Wei Changhui. Yang feared Shi Dakai's popularity.

As for seizing the position of Heavenly King, Yang was most concerned about Shi Dakai's movements. Most of the best intelligence agents under the command of the Eastern King had been sent to Wuchang to keep a sharp eye on Shi's activities. Yang had treated Wei Changhui with utter contempt. While he would always just rub his hands together and say flattering things to Wei's face, Wei's reputation within the Taiping movement remained, as always, an unsavory one.

It was not reported to the Eastern King, though, that Northern King Wei Changhui had boarded his 3,000 troops onto 200 or more vessels and was heading toward the Heavenly Capital. This was because he was moving both secretly and swiftly.

—5—

The 200 boats under the command of the Northern King dispersed and reached shore at various points outside Nanjing. For several dozen vessels to dock at an embattled site like Nanjing was not the least bit extraordinary. Replenishing stores of provisions and weapons went on continually there.

It was late in the night when the army of the Northern King split up to enter Nanjing through various city gates. Hu Yihuang from the Residence of the Eastern King had contacted the guards at each gate. "Small military units will be entering the capital for relief. See that they get through."

Having entered the city separately, the troops of the Northern King quietly began to reassemble. The leaders of this coup met in a private home near the Heavenly King's Residence. In the forefront of the anti-Yang group, Qin Rigang proposed that they attack the Eastern King's Residence immediately. Hu and his men, who had been inside Nanjing, also laid out a plan for a surprise raid to take place without a moment's delay. There was no doubt that the possibility increased that they would be discovered the longer they postponed moving into action. Nonetheless, Wei Changhui frowned and said, narrowing his eyes, "We move after I meet with Hong Xiuquan."

"Time is of the essence now," said Hu. "We cannot allow for delays."

"I received my orders to execute the Eastern King from a messenger of the Heavenly King. The messenger's credentials looked valid enough, and I trusted them and returned to the capital. However, I want to verify this plan with the Heavenly King just to make sure."

Wei Changhui was not about to give ground on this matter. If he didn't give his consent, his troops wouldn't budge. Hu shrugged his shoulders and sighed.

"Okay, okay. I'll go with you, or a doctor can accompany you. Mr. Wei can go as his assistant. How about it?" said Xiling.

Though security may not have been that strict, anyone who entered or exited the Residence of the Heavenly King had to be prepared for the watchful gaze of the Eastern King's spies. These "doctors," of which there were a few, were surgeons in the Taiping government, and Xiling knew one of them well. If such a doctor were to flash his card, his duties gave him free access to the Residence of the Heavenly King, and Xiling knew this.

As far as Northern King Wei Changhui was concerned, he was dealing with an order from the Heavenly King, and he was prepared to risk his life to liquidate the Eastern King. However, if the Heavenly King were later to claim no knowledge of the plan, Wei would suddenly find himself a rebel who had willfully murdered the Eastern King. The ever careful Wei Changhui thus wanted to reconfirm the intentions of the Heavenly King.

A vague sense of fear was recognizable in Heavenly King Hong Xiuquan's eyes. Though he made a habit of concealing his emotions, a strong passion was about to emerge somewhere. "The Eastern King thinks he will turn the Taiping Heavenly Kingdom into a possession of his own. He had no reverence for the Heavenly Father Jehovah and the Heavenly Elder Brother Jesus Christ. If I am hounded into relinquishing the position of Heavenly King, not only will the Taiping Heavenly Kingdom be seized by Yang Xiuqing. The Taiping Heavenly Kingdom will itself cease to exist. It will become something entirely different, nothing at all like the Taiping Heavenly Kingdom. It will become but a dynasty of the Yang house. Execute Yang and his brothers! Beyond them, there is no need to commit unnecessary butchery." Such were the words of the Heavenly King.

"I understand. I have my orders," said Wei Changhui, and he withdrew. The intentions of the Heavenly King were reconfirmed, though Wei wondered if the executions could be limited to just Yang and his brothers. This was war, after all.

If they attacked the Eastern King's Residence, Yang's troops there would surely accept the fight and return fire. A battle, a handful of death, and the matter ending there was unacceptable.

"Unnecessary butchery?" The words escaped Wei Changhui's mouth unconsciously.

"By 'the Eastern King and his brothers,' he means if at all possible. The Heavenly King wants as few deaths as possible," said Xiling.

"Oh, I see," said Wei, with a cynical smile unseen in the surrounding darkness, resolving in his mind all the while to kill as many as possible.

The military forces at the Eastern King's Residence were all the enemy. If they were allowed to go on living, they might later rise to avenge the murder of Yang Xiuqing. The more people in Yang's quarters that Wei killed himself, the greater the personal safety he would later enjoy.

Upon returning to the headquarters of his forces, Wei issued the following orders: "This will be a life-or-death struggle. All restraint is useless. Take not the least consideration. There will probably be men there who fought shoulder to shoulder with you in the past, but you must show no mercy. On the contrary, just vengeance. Kill, kill, kill them all! Every one of them. If there's a piece of white cloth on their left arm, take it as a sign, and kill all of those without a piece of white cloth on their left arms. Men and women, old and young—all of them."

—6—

Hong Xiuquan had wanted to add one further demand in addition to the point that no one aside from Yang Xiuqing and his brothers was to be killed, but he had been unable to utter these words before Wei Changhui had said that they must move immediately. Although resolved to eliminate the Eastern King, Hong wanted it done by Wei Changhui and Shi Dakai.

He did not want Yang executed solely because the Eastern King was on the verge of wresting the position of Heavenly King for himself. Yang lacked religious faith and deceived people with his Heavenly Father's Descent to Earth. It was necessary to bring this issue of religious belief to the surface. The Taiping Heavenly Kingdom was a regime founded on its faith in Christianity. Hong Xiuquan believed firmly that the basis of the state lay in these religious principles. In matters religious, Yang Xiuqing had been a dubious figure since their days in Jintian village.

Spirit possession of the Heavenly Father's Descent to Earth sort was all playacting, though Yang always seemed to avoid discussing questions of religious faith.

The man has no religious faith, thought Hong, nor does he seem to have any intention of studying religious matters. As far as he's concerned, religion is merely a way of gaining secular power. Can we allow someone like that to seize control over the Taiping Heavenly Kingdom? I must eradicate this apostate Yang Xiuqing on behalf of our faith and to preserve the true Taiping Heavenly Kingdom.

After convincing himself with thoughts of this sort, Hong made the decision to liquidate Yang, with none of his more usual indecisiveness apparent. The entirety of the Taiping movement denied the very existence of Yang Xiuqing. In this construction of the case, the Northern King Wei Changhui and the Assistant King Shi Dakai would have to be the two men who carried out the execution of the Eastern King.

Hong had thought of issuing the order to postpone the action until the Assistant King arrived from Wuchang, but Wei then spoke up, "We shall act tonight. If we put it off until tomorrow morning, Yang Xiuqing may become aware of us. About myself, I care nothing, but I shall not be able to guarantee the safety of the Heavenly King. There is no alternative to moving into action right now."

It was certainly a reasonable argument. The Northern King's troops were already deployed for the coup, and everyone would discover them by the following morning. Despite Hong's thought that they wait for Shi Dakai's return, Wei was counseling that this could not be done. There was something of a slight to the Heavenly King in this advice, though Hong thought better of it and later decided not to articulate his wishes in the form of an order.

Hong did regret that he hadn't earlier sent a messenger to Shi Dakai, who was far from the capital in Wuchang. In fact, Wuchang was further from Nanjing than Nanchang, where Wei Changhui had been. Furthermore, while Shi had fought furiously and continuously in Wuchang, Wei had penned Zeng Guofan into Nanchang.

Wei Changhui had been able to leave the front with comparative ease, while it was much more difficult for Shi Dakai to do the same. Hong Xiuquan's lack of military knowledge meant that he hadn't considered this difference.

"You're an important person right here, so please stay put," said Wei Changhui to Xiling as he left the Residence of the Heavenly King.

"But . . . isn't there anything that I can do?" Her curiosity was extraordinary. In her mind she concocted the following scenario: I'm a woman and everyone knows me since the days back in Xishi Monastery in Guiping. For that reason, Yang Xiuqing will probably be off guard around me, and it wouldn't be at all hard for me to get close to him. I'd move in close with a concealed dagger and stab him in the chest . . .

But Wei Changhui was shaking his head:

"It's too dangerous. Anyway, you're too important."

After Wei departed, Xiling ruminated over his words and unconsciously began shaking from the very core of her body. She then realized that what was "dangerous" was the fact that Wei Changhui planned not only to kill a few people, as instructed by Hong Xiuquan, but was contemplating a massacre on a much larger scale.

What in the world had he meant by "too important"? Aside from the Heavenly King's entourage, the only person who could testify that Wei Changhui had received the order to execute Yang Xiuqing directly from the Heavenly King himself was Xiling. And if the Heavenly King were to claim no memory of such an order, those in his entourage would surely feign ignorance and say that they had heard no such order ever issued.

Xiling would have no choice but to attest to the fact of what she had seen and heard in full. Those who had known her since the old days in Guiping knew that she feared absolutely no one. She was coming to the realization that she was "important" because she was a witness. The death of so important a person would pose problems. Such was the extent of the massacre Wei had designed.

"I'm going outside," said Xiling to the leaders in the Heavenly King's Residence. "Please let me go."

"No. The orders of the Heavenly King are that no one can leave this place tonight." They were united in this response to her request.

"Fine, then please allow me to see the Heavenly King."

"He has already entered the inner chambers. Once he withdraws from here, he sees no one."

"But it's an emergency."

"No." She could sense both a coldness and an eerie tension to their response.

While he'd given the order to execute the Eastern King, Hong Xiuquan now wanted to remain as aloof as possible from the action.

I've, no, no, *we've* misjudged Hong Xiuquan, Xiling thought.

—7—

At this time a ghastly slaughter was spreading through the Eastern King's Residence in Nanjing. As cunning as a fox, people used say of Yang Xiuqing. A fox is known as an extremely careful animal. Even when a stream freezes over, as long as he can hear the sound of the water flowing below the ice, a fox will not attempt to cross. Though praised for being so careful, at this time Yang had relaxed his vigilance.

After wresting the title of "ten thousand years" from the Heavenly King, Yang gained a great sense of self-confidence, feeling that he now controlled the Taiping Heavenly Kingdom. Self-confidence has a way of becoming overconfidence on occasion—the result of vanity. What allowed Yang to relax his otherwise strict wariness was this vanity.

After meeting with the Heavenly King, Wei Changhui stationed his men around the Residence of the Eastern King. This too was done in a leisurely manner. They moved in small groups so as not to be conspicuous, and the guards at the Eastern King's quarters were inattentive to their activities because the Eastern King's own subordinates were careless. Followers of the Northern King were placed not only at the Residence of the Eastern King but at strategic points throughout the city of Nanjing.

If Yang Xiuqing slips through our fingers tonight, thought the Northern King, who was now the more vigilant one, everything will be ruined.

First to break into the Residence of the Eastern King were the soldiers of Qin Rigang.

"I should like to lead the advance guard inside," said Qin to Wei Changhui. "I believe you know my reasons."

Two years before, as described earlier, Qin's groom had apparently committed an act of discourtesy to a relative of Yang Xiuqing, and the whole question of punishment arose. At the time, Qin himself received 300 lashes of the whip, and he had not forgotten the humiliation.

"Mark my words. I shall kill Yang Xiuqing and that stupid old man with my own hand. Find them and bring them to me alive," Qin said for emphasis to his men before the raid began. The "stupid old man" was the elderly cousin of Yang's father, the culprit who had raised such a fuss when Qin's groom failed to greet him properly.

"That stupid bastard living off Yang's authority. Some fox!" said Qin, bracing himself.

The advance forces were, of course, crack fighters. Before they knew what had happened, the unobservant guards at the Eastern King's Residence had been cut down. With his newfound arrogance, Yang Xiuqing frequently summoned high-level leaders of the Taiping movement to his quarters in order to show off his majestic import. Qin Rigang had himself often been to the Eastern King's Residence and was more than familiar with the surroundings. Qin was thus able to guide the elite advance corps once inside. Knowing the location of Yang's bedroom, Qin drew his dagger and rushed straight in that direction.

"It's an enemy attack!"

"No, they say they're troops sent by the Heavenly King!"

"Quick, assemble the soldiers!"

"Ring the tocsin!"

In the noise and confusion within the Residence of the Eastern King, Qin Rigang broke into Yang's bedroom. Yang was naked. A woman wearing red silk was crouching at his side. He snatched the silk garment from her and tried to wrap it around himself.

"It won't do any good, you naked snake!" said Qin Rigang, glistening blade in hand, as he thrust its back edge at Yang's wrist.

"You bastard!" Yang scowled at Qin and quickly looked in either direction. The lights in his bedroom were burning brightly.

"You had my groom drawn and quartered, his limbs ripped to shreds. Now you're going to come to the same end," said Qin, as he slowly approached Yang.

Till the bitter end, Yang was thinking about an escape. Extinguishing the lights and running away flashed through his mind, but five different lamps were set up in the room. "Just wait a second, I, I . . ." said Yang, in a voice close to a scream.

"I expected to hear that voice."

Qin lifted his dagger before Yang, who was both stark naked and unarmed. When he brought it down on Yang, Qin seemed insane.

"Now you'll feel my vengeance!" Each time he lifted and brought down his blade, he screamed the same thing. Qin was so drenched in the blood of his victim that he appeared to have been dyed red, as if the flames of the light in the Eastern King's bedroom licked out at him.

"The old man has been brought here. This is he, is it not?" One of Qin's men came in with an elderly man and sent him staggering into a sea of blood.

"No doubt about this one. It's him. For my own sake, I'm going to avenge the groom who was torn limb from limb," said Qin, with a crazed look in his eye.

The fear in the old man's eyes suddenly disappeared and his demeanor changed, as he took on the same crazed look as Qin. His lips trembled ever so slightly and formed an uncanny, eerie smile.

There was a spray of blood.

"Is it over with?" Wei Changhui entered the room. He wasn't even wearing a sword.

"It's over," replied Qin Rigang in a scratchy voice.

"The attack has been successful. We have carried out the Heavenly King's orders. Now remnants of the enemy forces are being mopped up, and order should soon be restored," said Wei, indifferently gazing at the corpses at his feet.

"Now what shall we do?" Qin just managed to ask this question.

"I shall go to the Heavenly King's Residence to apologize."

"What are you going to apologize for?"

"The Heavenly King said not to kill people, but several thousand have been executed."

"They put up resistance. It was a fight, and if we hadn't killed them, they'd have killed us."

"The Heavenly King will not understand this. But this is my problem. I shall receive the proper punishment. I go now for that purpose."

"That sort of thing . . ."

"Let me handle it. Um, circulate the story around the city that on the orders of the Heavenly King, traitor Yang Xiuqing has been killed."

"We shall divide into groups and carry this out."

Gunfire continued throughout the night. Resistance from the Eastern King's Residence had long ceased, but Wei Changhui ordered his men to continue firing away. Amid the shots into the night sky, one could hear voices spreading the word.

"The Nine Thousand Years has been killed!"

"Praise! Praise!" responded other voices to this shout. "Praise" was a well-established cheer within the Taiping movement. It was unclear if this cheer was coming from the soldiers who had executed the coup or from ordinary citizens of the city.

31

The Collapse of the Finest Pagoda in the Realm

—1—

Xiling thought it was strange. "We came upon fierce resistance and had no choice but to reluctantly kill large numbers of people. I now manfully accept my punishment. Do not spare the whip." So offered Wei Changhui to the Heavenly King. But Xiling knew Wei Changhui well, and he was not the sort of man who would ever be likely to say such things.

There was one more strange thing as well, and that was the fact that Hong Xiuquan—who should have known Wei Changhui even better than she—did not seem to think that Wei's offer was the least bit odd.

It was a tragedy that could have been avoided. Even after the tragedy had occurred, Xiling was initially not remorseful. At that time, she had stated clearly to the Heavenly King. "Don't you think it strange what the Northern King has just informed you of?"

"Strange?" responded the Heavenly King, not seeming to grasp her point. "In what way?"

"Isn't he being far too commendable in his behavior? It's not like Wei Changhui. And what is this request for a flogging?"

"Miss Xiling, after you left Guiping, the Northern King frequently read and studied the holy scriptures. He is different now from what he was back then," said the Heavenly King.

"Is that right?" said Xiling dubiously.

When an important matter of state came up, women who held the rank of "female edict proclaimers" would stand in front of the Heavenly King's Residence and read out the proclamation. Later, they would post notices at prescribed spots in the Heavenly Capital. This was the Taiping practice. On this occasion, the notice read: "Because of the crime of having murdered many innocent persons, Northern King Wei Changhui shall be punished with four hundred lashes."

Within one hour of this announcement, everyone within the Heavenly Capital knew it, and the responses were many and varied.

"Just like the Heavenly King. It's a fair judgment."

"The Eastern King's tyranny just couldn't go on, and in crushing it the Northern King went too far."

"Exactly, and excesses must be punished."

"True enough, but I'm worried about whether the Northern King will accept this judgment or not."

"He's a subject of the Taiping Heavenly Kingdom and thus has no choice but to abide by what is proclaimed by edict."

"Many of the Eastern King's followers are still in the Heavenly Capital. Perhaps this is a way to mollify those whose master was slain."

"It ought to satisfy them."

"No, I don't think it'll end here. I wonder if it's just beginning."

"We will always have faith in the words of the Heavenly King."

These were some of the voices in the city, though scarcely anyone saw that this was a trap set by the Northern King. Xiling's look of dubiousness indicated that she had been able to see through this ruse. Following the execution of the Eastern King, the Heavenly King issued an edict that proclaimed: "The conspiracy of the Eastern King has been uncovered by heaven, and the remnants of his group are uniformly pardoned. They are all to be acquitted."

For a long time, no rain had fallen on the Heavenly Capital. The atmosphere was extremely dry, and there was worry of a bad harvest because of the drought. However, during the evening of the very day that the Northern King executed the Eastern King, a great shower came down on the city in torrents. The Northern King's proposal had been accepted at that time, and he was to receive a flogging.

"The blood that has flowed," he said to his attendants, "will now be washed away. This whole matter will end with my flogging. It is the will of God." The words of the Northern King spread rapidly in the form of a rumor throughout the capital. Virtually all of the troops at the Residence of the Eastern King had been killed in the Northern King's wholesale massacre, though troops directly under Yang Xiuqing's command still resided in dispersed locales within the city. It was for them that the Heavenly King had issued his amnesty order. The former subordinates of the Eastern King were ordered to observe the flogging of Wei Changhui and Qin Rigang.

"They are saying that this will be our payoff."

"Even if the Northern King's back were broken and his blood spilled, our comrades are never coming back to life." With comments of this sort, the former adherents of the Eastern King made their way to the punishment site. There were some five thousand of them.

They were accommodated in the two "morning halls." These morning halls were buildings erected so that people with no special status might observe when important ceremonies were carried out on the open grounds. They were much like outdoor bleachers with a roof overhead. The buildings allowed for large numbers of people, and the ground was clearly visible to all.

The flogging began. There was certainly no collusion here. The man executing the sentence wielded the whip with all his might. Wei Changhui and Qin Rigang took their beatings prone with their limbs stretched out. Every time the whip came down, their voices sounded with pain. The whole event gradually unfolded as the skin on their backs tore open and blood oozed from the wounds. At the two hundredth lash, the whipper himself looked exhausted.

The tragedy really began only after this. A corps of the Northern King's troops, most of whom were part of the force that had returned to the capital from Nanchang with Wei Changhui, quietly surrounded the morning halls. As the flogging was being administered, those in attendance were calling out the numbers. When it reached 350, that was a signal for a second massacre to commence.

Taiping rules forbade the people from carrying their weapons into the morning halls, because terrorists might slip in among those in attendance at important national observances. The troops of the Eastern King knew this regulation well and unquestioningly deposited their weapons at the entranceway.

"If they didn't enforce this rule," uttered a soldier when he handed over his guns, "someone might aim a shot at the head of the Northern King."

"They made this rule for people like you," said his comrade, laughing in response.

The 5,000 soldiers inside the morning halls were completely unarmed.

"Three hundred and fifty!" rang out a high-pitched shout from the audience, already a bit hoarse. Just at the moment that this exaggeratedly long, drawn-out voice ceased, a war cry was raised: "Kill! Kill!" Troops under the command of the Northern King rushed at the disarmed men of the Eastern King. The latter were empty-handed and trapped inside the confines of the morning halls. All preparations were in order so that this grotesque massacre would proceed without a hitch.

Troops of the Northern King's army wore white armbands as a signal to one another, and screaming in voices even they could not understand, they swarmed into the morning halls. Although following orders, they all knew that this was morally unjustified murder. They raised their voices to shouts to purge themselves of nagging consciences.

A person nearby later remembered hearing cries. The word "slaughter" is more appropriate for what transpired on this day than "massacre." In addition to the troops that had raided the halls, soldiers of the Northern King were surrounding the buildings two abreast. The Eastern King's men had to fight without weapons.

"Kill me!" one seriously wounded man begged of his butchers.

On the ground before them, the four hundredth lash was completed.

—2—

"I don't have much of a taste for such things," said Xiling, in response to an invitation from a female official at the Heavenly King's Residence to go witness the flogging.

She felt uneasy in the pit of her stomach. If some sort of calamity were to transpire, someone would come and explain it later. This time, though, her uneasiness felt like the real thing.

"It's as if something bad is about to occur," she was saying to everyone.

"'Something bad?' In what way?" asked the female official, opening her eyes widely.

"In what way? I'm not really sure. But if something does happen, I wouldn't be at all surprised. Just look at all the people that have come to see this bloody horror."

The scene outside Guangzhou at the time of the Opium War flashed through Xiling's mind. In the fifteen years that had passed since then, that scene rarely entered her thoughts. She didn't want to recall it and simply repressed the memory. But it didn't disappear, and at times like the present she was reminded of it.

"I've seen horror myself," said the female official.

She was from the city of Wuchang. When the Taiping Army occupied her city, they assembled all the young women and picked out the more beautiful ones. After smearing her face with soot, she went to the selection site, but washbasins had been placed at the entryway and she'd had to wash her face. When she saw this, she lost all hope of escape. In the past she had pride in her beauty, even boasted about it, but standing before the washbasin, she only cursed her own good looks. Separated from her parents and abducted from Wuchang, she had no choice but to come with the Taipings to Nanjing. The "horror" of which she spoke was this scene by the washbasins.

"How old are you?" asked Xiling of this sweet young woman. Xiling had heard stories of the fortunes of these female officials, but she hadn't known their ages.

"I was sixteen then," she replied, as if after the selection in Wuchang, she was no longer herself and her age had frozen at that point in time.

"If that hadn't happened, the Assistant King wouldn't be having such difficulties now," said Xiling.

Assistant King Shi Dakai was in the midst of a desperate fight over the city of Wuchang. While the undisciplined Qing forces had lost the people's support through acts of pillage in villages nearby, the Taiping military had still not won over the local populace completely. To be sure, the Taipings committed no wanton acts of rape or theft, but by picking out the beautiful young women and abducting the young men, they created immeasurably bad blood deep in the hearts of the older men and women of Wuchang. The able-bodied young men were drafted into military service, which may actually have enhanced their future prospects. For all of its boasting about strict military discipline and selfless public service based on religious faith, the Taiping Army selected women on the basis of their beauty and wrenched them away from their fathers and brothers.

It was this behavior that seriously damaged the views concerning the Taiping movement held by the people of Wuchang. Had they actually gained the complete trust of the local populace, the battle for Wuchang would certainly have been much easier. Xiling stared fixedly into the face of the young woman official before her eyes.

"What's your name?" she asked.

"Yu Cairong."

"The horror I witnessed doesn't compare to yours. Cheer up. For women like us who've seen the bloodshed and horrors that we have, there's no other way to go on living than to just keep on confronting the world as it appears."

"You're probably right."

While Xiling was carrying on this exchange with Yu Cairong, an officer came rushing into the Heavenly King's Residence. "I have an urgent communication. Here you are." Though short of breath, this officer showed the agent at the door his transit pass, which permitted direct access to the Heavenly King.

"One person to enter," said the doorman, granting permission. He recognized the other man as an official within the Heavenly King's Residence. The officer then trotted further inside.

"He's in an awful hurry. What in the world happened?" asked the doorman of the attendant to the officer who had brought the message after his boss had left him.

"The troops of the Eastern King who had gone to observe the punishment of the Northern King were massacred inside the morning halls. It's terrible," said the attendant, a scowl across his face.

"Massacred?"

"That's right, and it's going on right this minute."

"When they entered the morning halls, they'd all have to have been empty-handed, right?"

"Of course. They were completely unarmed. The whole thing was planned in advance. I thought it was strange that the Northern King was asking to be punished. It seemed much too sweet and tender for him."

The voice of the attendant in the hallway was clearly audible to Xiling, who was in an anteroom separated by only a bamboo screen.

A massacre, thought Xiling, feeling as if she couldn't breathe. Yu Cairong turned pale, her red lips looking more vivid than ever.

"So that's what happened," muttered Xiling to herself. She'd had a foreboding that something bad had come to pass, but she could never have imagined anything as horrific as the mass murder of all the former subordinates of the Eastern King.

Xiling felt dizzy. From time to time, she felt a spasm of dizziness, perhaps on account of her age. This paroxysm may have been due to her physical condition, but it was more likely due to the words she had just heard from this attendant.

"Is there something wrong?" asked Yu Cairong, apparently worried, when Xiling appeared to be staggering.

"No, just a bit. When women reach my age, such things do happen. If I can just rest for a moment, I'll be fine." Xiling sat down on a chair with an upright back on which she could lean. Nonetheless, she felt as though she just couldn't sit still. She fidgeted in the chair, and then after about fifteen minutes, she stood up and began walking.

"Is everything all right?" asked Yu Cairong from behind Xiling's back.

"Thank you for being concerned. There's really nothing the matter." As she answered, Xiling passed by the officer in the hallway who had moments before brought the news. He had delivered his message directly to the Heavenly King and was now returning.

As she entered the courtyard, a cool breeze blew in from somewhere. Xiling paused there to take a breath, and before long the figure of Heavenly King Hong Xiuquan clad in a yellow garment appeared in the passageway at the other side of the courtyard. It was not far from her, and his expression was clearly visible.

For a moment, Xiling stopped breathing altogether. He was smiling! No doubt about it, the Heavenly King had a smile on his face. What's more, it was a broad, satisfied smile.

Had the Heavenly King and the Northern King conspired, she wondered, to carry out this massacre and annihilate the forces of the Eastern King?

Clouds of suspicion were rising and gradually expanding. Xiling had been castigating herself until that point for allowing doubts to creep into her thoughts. Now, though, she had witnessed this beaming smile across the face of the Heavenly King just after he had received this ghoulish report. Even if he wasn't in collusion with the Northern King, he certainly had been happy about the results.

When the Northern King requested punishment, the Heavenly King probably surmised what his intentions were. This possibility, Xiling thought, was now sufficient to be entertained. The Heavenly King turned in the passageway and disappeared. A man followed after him, and what he said to the Heavenly King was clearly audible: "That's right. No one can believe it, other than those close to him. Do you see what I mean?"

Upon receiving secret orders from the Heavenly King, Shi Dakai hurriedly boarded a ship from Lujiagang. Shi had, needless to say, become disgusted by the despotic behavior of the Eastern King, though he was nonetheless alarmed to be ordered back to the Heavenly Capital with his troops. Shi Dakai was a young commander, only twenty-six years of age, and an idealist as well. He was strong-willed and stout-hearted, to be sure, but he also seemed to be somewhat of a dreamer.

Weren't these guys the same people, he wondered en route, whom we've shared so much hardship with? I'm sure we'll square everything after we speak.

Shi was accompanied by only a handful of subordinates. He was by nature the sort of man who avoided as much as possible the spilling of blood among comrades. Furthermore, it was exceedingly dangerous at this point to pull a large number of troops away from the Wuchang front where the war continued and head eastward. If such a conspicuous movement became evident, it might elicit an attack from the government's forces.

As his boat sailed down the Yangzi River, Shi repeated, "We'll talk about it. I'm not going back to fight with friends."

Zhang Suimou, a member of Shi's staff, had gone ahead to gather as much information in the Heavenly Capital as he could in advance. The reports he collected, though, were exclusively and overwhelmingly bad:

—Eastern King Yang Xiuqing has already been killed, and there are a huge number of corpses at his residence.
—Afterward, 5,000 of the Eastern King's followers were murdered in a sneak attack.

—The Northern King has been insanely carrying on a relentless search for all remnants of the Eastern King's party. He's leaving no stone unturned, and the people in the Heavenly Capital are completely panic-stricken.

—Anyone with the least connection to the Eastern King or his people is trembling in fear and is in hiding. Anybody who offers such people shelter will be killed as soon as they are discovered.

—The news is not at all good.

"Why don't you put off entering the capital for a bit so we can investigate the situation some more," suggested Zhang to Shi Dakai.

Another of Shi's staff men, Zeng Jinqian, agreed entirely. "The Northern King is a far more dangerous man than we thought. The incident at the morning halls is inconceivable for any normal person."

"That incident hasn't been verified yet." Shi still couldn't believe the information he had heard of the massacre. It was circulating largely as a rumor more than as fact, and he thought that it couldn't have been as dreadful as the stories Zhang related about it.

"No, they are confirmed now."

"Perhaps such an incident did in fact occur. Still, I think the numbers of people involved must have been exaggerated."

"It was about five thousand people, but even if it had been ten, even just a single person, it would have been unacceptable."

"If it's all true, then I've really got to go there. I appreciate your concern on my part, but I never did get along at all well with the Eastern King, and the Northern King should know that. I'm not worried about myself," said Shi. He then entered the Heavenly Capital and headed first for the Residence of the Heavenly King.

"This is really and truly terrible," said Hong Xiuquan when he confronted Shi Dakai. "As bad as the Eastern King behaved, what the Northern King did was even worse."

From the wharf, Shi had passed through the city gate with his flag raised and made his way directly to the Heavenly King's Residence. He rode in a sedan chair with bamboo screens, which made it difficult to observe conditions in the city.

"Then it's just as rumor has it."

"I don't know what rumor you've heard, but it's worse than unimaginable. Old people and young, men and women, anyone with the least connection to the Eastern King was shown no mercy."

"Does it continue as we speak?"

"Yes," said the Heavenly King. "You have arrived too late."

"Aren't you supposed to be the leader of the Taiping Heavenly Kingdom?" Shi Dakai wanted to say. "Couldn't you stop this massacre with your power and influence?" But he restrained himself.

"I am sorry. I shall proceed to the headquarters of the Northern King. I would like to speak with him," said Shi with his head bowed.

"Try to be understanding when you speak to him, but . . . do be careful," said Hong, shaking his head slightly from side to side. There were dark rings around his eyes.

"I shall express myself sincerely and try to prevail upon him."

"But, uh, Dakai," said Hong, using his name from their days back in Jintian village. Shi Dakai much preferred that name to the more official "Assistant King." It carried a feeling of warmth with it.

"Yes?"

"It's a question of learning. These fellows with no learning are becoming a major problem. Originally I too believed that there was no relationship between religious faith and learning. I now deeply understand that learning is essential to the possession of religious belief. The Eastern King was illiterate. Although the Northern King can read, the level of his learning is very low. No, it effectively does not exist. Within the Taiping movement, you alone have a depth of learning, and I am relying upon you."

"I am much obliged." Shi left the Heavenly King's audience room and, accompanied by Zhang Suimou, who was waiting for him in an antechamber, was about to leave the Heavenly King's Residence.

"Dakai," a woman's voice called to him, and he spun around. From the shadows of a pillar in the corridor appeared Xiling. He knew her face from their days together back in Guiping.

"When did you get here?" he asked her.

"I want to die."

"What? What in the world are you talking about?"

"Xiuquan asked me to go summon Wei Changhui from Nanchang. Then Changhui came here and the killing has known no end."

"It does seem to have been terrible."

"Xiuquan called Changhui here and he too is responsible, but I was stupid to be his willing messenger, ignorant of what the result would be."

"There's no responsibility in being a messenger."

"I'm not the Heavenly King's servant. I could have refused his request. But I did just as he asked, and look what's happened now. I'm twenty years your senior."

"I'm going to go talk to the Northern King. We've got to quell this bickering once and for all. I'm on my way to his headquarters now."

"Wouldn't it be better to stop right now? Even if the Heavenly King had not so ordered, Changhui would probably have murdered Yang Xiuqing. Changhui can't seem to stand people like you who are higher in rank than he is. I think it would be dangerous for you."

"I'm below the Northern King in status."

"But you're much more popular within the Taiping movement, and that's why it's dangerous. I think that even more than Xiuquan, you now stand in the Northern King's way."

"Still, I can't leave things as they now stand. I'm going to talk with him." Shi bit the edges of his lips and then quickly departed.

"If it looks dangerous, get out as quickly as possible," said Xiling, as the young Shi Dakai sped off.

Wei Changhui's expression changed to anger: "Are you trying to preach to me?"

"This is not about preaching. I just want to talk with you. This string of incidents has to be stopped," said Shi Dakai, averting his counterpart's line of vision. There was an eerie gleam in Wei Changhui's eyes, and Shi wondered if he might just be insane. If Wei was mad, then talking to him was useless.

"What string of incidents?" said Wei, as froth formed on the edges of his lips. "There were no incidents. They were put to death for crimes. It was an execution."

"I agree that the Eastern King—no, Yang Xiuqing committed crimes, and it's perfectly proper to execute a criminal. But what crimes did all his subordinates commit? When they left Guangxi and entered Hunan, the number of followers rose dramatically, and then they proceeded into Hubei province. Aren't we the leaders who organize the troops into units? They don't just pick whomever they want to be attached to. They just happened to have been assigned to Yang Xiuqing's command, and by chance several thousand of them were stationed at the Eastern King's Residence. What possible crimes could they have committed?"

Shi had become agitated. He tried to argue amicably for further executions to cease, but his words had inadvertently become quite sharp.

"Shut up, you little boy!" screamed Wei Changhui.

It seemed to Shi that Wei had now dropped all pretense. Wei had been an affable man, in fact unctuously flattering. There had scarcely been a situation to that point in which he had a bad thing to say. However, beneath the smile on his face, an insidious man was hiding. He had killed Yang Xiuqing and practically liquidated his entire entourage of followers. No need for pretense now.

"You seem angry. Perhaps I have spoken inappropriately. If I say any more today, it probably won't get our discussion any further along. I shall shut up, as you put it, and return. However, I shall be back, and I would like to sit down and have a quiet, deliberate conversation with you at that time." Shi Dakai rose from his chair, bowed, and repeated: "I shall be back."

"If you can, do come back," said Wei Changhui spitefully.

Aha, thought Shi, all the more keenly as he left the Northern King's Residence, is it anger that stirs this man?

An affluent landlord, Wei Changhui had acquired the position of Student by Purchase through a monetary contribution. This position carried a status of no more than a student in the National University. Even if one did not study at the National University, one could acquire just the title of such a position through purchase. For a set amount of money, one could even buy fairly respectable bureaucratic posts. Though a wealthy man, Wei Changhui was not overly rich and was happy with the post of Student by Purchase. Over his door hung a placard reading, "Court Gentleman for Promoted Service," the equivalent of a rank 9A in the Chinese bureaucracy. A Student by Purchase was not an official post at all, making this placard a misrepresentation. He had struggled ever so hard to pass the civil service examinations so as to become an official, but at some point Wei had grown indignant with the process, been castigated by Police Chief Wang Ji, and subsequently thrown in prison. He pulled his money together and was released, but this proved to be the motive force driving Wei into joining the Taipings.

He swore revenge to himself that he would kill all those men who had rebuked him. Yang Xiuqing had often thrown his weight around among those beneath him, and Wei had been humiliated by him. Wei withstood it at the time, but he never forgot his anger. In fact, the malice had consumed him completely. And when he dropped his pretense, one found a ferocious, scary man standing there.

As Shi left the Northern King's Residence and walked toward the sedan chair, a voice whispered to him. "Ride in the palanquin as far as the turn at the next corner, where you should get out quickly. By that tree there. Then seek refuge along the perpendicular alley over there. Your life is in danger. I'm Tan Qi."

Before he had given his name at the very end, Shi Dakai already knew the man to be Tan Qi, and he had no reason in the least to doubt what Tan Qi had said.

"Mr. Zhang, this applies to you too. I just explained the gist of the situation to the palanquin bearers." When the voice finished, a human figure moved nimbly behind the tree.

A large tree was in fact standing at the corner of the road. Zhang Suimou, who had been walking beside the sedan chair, was crouched there.

"Here," he whispered, and leapt to the side street. Shi Dakai jumped from the sedan chair and followed Zhang.

"Come in this door." It was the back door to a private home, and all that he could see was the face of Tan Qi sticking out. Shi and Zhang were quickly sucked inside.

About five minutes passed, and Tan Qi, Shi Dakai, and Zhang Suimou went up to the second floor. There was something that looked like a balcony in the front where large earthenware vessels full of salted vegetables were lined up. The three men hid behind them and looked down into the street below. They could see the palanquin bearers surrounded by troops from the Northern King's Residence.

"The Five Thousand Years," a reference to Shi Dakai, "remembered some important business he had to attend to, so he and Mr. Zhang said they were going to take a shortcut through the alley. Yes, and they got out right over there, and, uh, this chair is completely empty," responded the palanquin bearers, flustered. Tan Qi had prepared them with this little speech while they were waiting with the sedan chair.

"What? It's empty?" The commander of the troops kicked the sedan chair, causing it to turn over on its side. The bamboo screens fell to the ground, and it became clear that there was indeed no one inside.

"What alley?" said the commander with a staff in his hand, banging it on the ground.

"Yes, from here you won't be able to see it, but over there by that large tree," he replied as he fell on his backside.

"Okay, let's go after them." There were about twenty soldiers, and troops from the Northern King's Residence followed their commander, who rode off in the opposite direction.

"It's too dangerous here," said Shi Dakai, squinting.

"You're right, it is. I thought you had decided midway not to go into the Northern King's Residence, but I was late," said Tan Qi.

"Thank you. This is all so unbelievable, completely unbelievable."

"The Heavenly Capital is no longer in secure shape. Things have gotten way out of hand."

"Such as what?"

"If you return to the Assistant King's Residence, you will be going to your death."

"My family's there."

"We can only rely on heaven for the fate of your family. For now, think only about how they can flee the Heavenly Capital. The Northern King has the whole city under martial law."

"Has a trap been set?

"Let's head for the Lesser Southern Gate, where the Northern King has few or no troops at all. He'll soon have troops posted there, so if we're to flee, now would be the best time," urged Tan Qi.

—5—

When all is said and done, the source of such madness is power. If you have it, everybody obeys whatever you say, and all bow their head before you. Anyone who sets his sights on such a position of dominance cannot help but lose his balance. When former friends remembered Wei Changhui, they always recalled a humble figure smiling, a man with little authority, though when this man began to approach a position of power, he became exceedingly ruthless.

When he learned that Shi Dakai had fled, that very night Wei Changhui surrounded the Assistant King's Residence and murdered Shi's young wife and infant son. Not only relations of Shi's were killed. The important men under his command were at the front in Wuchang, but some of them had remained at the Assistant King's Residence, and they and their families were also murdered at that time.

For the present, Shi Dakai had left Wuhu for Ningguo. Troops under his command were stationed there. The news then reached him that his entire family had been murdered.

"If only Luo Dagang had been there . . ." The words escaped Shi's lips unconsciously.

The power structure of the Taiping movement was built on a subtle balance. Shi Dakai got along well with Luo Dagang. Luo was a leader of a Triad group and a military commander with considerable fighting experience. When Shi had been in Nanchang, he had incorporated into his forces Triad members who had moved north from Guangdong to increase his personnel strength. For that reason, relations with Luo Dagang had been good. Luo had been killed the previous year in fighting. Shi's forces had been allied with Luo's, and they proceeded to inflict a great defeat on the Hunan Army of Zeng Guofan at Jiujiang. Because the two men worked so closely, there had been no opportunity for Wei Changhui to take advantage of.

At this point there was nothing Shi could do. He moved on from Ningguo toward Anqing. A huge army under his command was amassing there. He had sent out a written appeal to all units of the Taiping armed forces in many different locales.

"We shall surround his military forces and strip them from his sides."

The Taiping troops formerly under Eastern King Yang Xiuqing's command, needless to say, responded to this call. Their commander had been murdered by Wei Changhui, their allies had been perfidiously attacked in the capital, and one by one their remnants had been hunted down and slaughtered.

Troops outside the capital that had belonged to the Eastern King were agitated, having lost their focus. They even lost the will to amass allied forces from scattered locales. It was to them that Shi Dakai's call went out.

The Eastern King and the Assistant King had not been particularly close; indeed, there had been a latent rivalry between them, but circumstances had now changed completely. They now had a foe in common—Northern King Wei Changhui—and not just any foe, but a mortal enemy. Troops of the now deceased Luo Dagang were certain to join forces with those of Shi Dakai, who had always gotten along well with Luo. Loyal King Li Xiucheng had an army in Tongcheng, and the majority of them joined forces with Shi Dakai's men. Li Xiucheng had begun to gain prominence within the Taiping movement through the good offices of Yang Xiuqing, and Li's army was effectively a quasi-Eastern King force, although he was regarded as neutral.

Shi Dakai put together 100,000 troops.

At the same time, knowing that Shi had fled the Heavenly Capital, Wei Changhui offered his ally in the coup, Qin Rigang, a force of 15,000 to pursue Shi. The plan was to attack before Shi could muster his army from various sites. Qin's army attacked a small force under the command of the Assistant King at a place known as Xiliangshan, close to Wuhu, though it did not try to advance further, for fears were on the rise back in the Heavenly Capital, where Wei Changhui's popularity had hit bottom after his murderous spree.

The Eastern King had certainly not been in good favor. People had frowned at his arbitrary behavior, for even a high Taiping leader such Qin Rigang had been entangled in an incident where a neglect of courtesies to one of the Eastern King's relatives led to his suffering a humiliating punishment. For that reason, Qin had cooperated in the Northern King's coup and personally killed both Yang Xiuqing, whom he so despised, and his relative.

Revenge had been taken. The execution of Yang Xiuqing was, additionally, carried out in response to a secret directive from the Heavenly King. Thus loyalty and honor were on the side of the coup. Afterward, though, Wei Changhui's ways had become grisly in the extreme. It was as if he were hiding his excesses behind the claims of the tyrannical behavior of the murdered Yang Xiuqing. Dead he was, and Yang's unpopularity was forgotten.

The great villainy of Wei Changhui now rose to the surface. There had been no edict from the Heavenly King to pursue and attack Shi Dakai. Wei Changhui had ordered it. Shi had earlier enjoyed a fine reputation, and as he became the central figure in the tragedy of the Heavenly Capital, his popularity was gradually on the rise. When he left the capital and passed through various centers of Taiping influence, Qin began to realize that he had been ordered to attack Shi Dakai's forces by a man who was just as evil as the man the coup had rid them of. The realization sent him deep into thought.

Meanwhile, news reached them that Shi had been amalgamating forces from various locales. Soon their number would exceed that of Qin's army.

"Let's go fight the Qing armies," said Qin, as he changed his fighting objectives. Whatever discord may have erupted within the Taiping camp, the first enemy remained the armies of the Qing dynasty. The calculation was that to the extent that they would attack Qing forces in the area, they would not rouse the antipathy of the Taiping forces aligned with Shi Dakai.

Li Hongzhang, at the time a compiler in the Hanlin Academy at court, had recently returned to his home in Anhui province, raised an army, and achieved a measure of military success in the recapture of Chaoxian.

The activities of Qin Rigang in attacking various Qing forces in the area effectively cleared the path for Shi Dakai's forces to advance on the Heavenly Capital. Wei Changhui was desperate. A secret messenger from Shi Dakai had already entered the capital and demanded of Heavenly King Hong Xiuquan "the execution of Wei Changhui and Qin Rigang." And the following condition was added, "Should this not be carried out, I shall attack the Heavenly Capital at the head of an armed force, and with all the power at my disposal, execute them myself."

The arrival of Shi Dakai was not imminent.

"If he does nothing and leaves things as they are," said Xiling, shaking her head, in the courtyard of the Heavenly King's Residence, "the Taiping Heavenly Kingdom will be finished."

"Perhaps he'll return to Wuchang. He's completely given up." Yu Cairong's expression became animated at such an expectation.

—6—

"The finest pagoda in the realm." Or so people referred to the pagoda at the Great Baoen Temple outside the Jibao Gate south of the Heavenly Capital. Records list its height as the equivalent of roughly 100 meters. The *Encyclopedia Britannica* gives it as 260 feet under actual observation, or some 80 meters. Undoubtedly, the former figure of 100 meters includes the height of the land on which the pagoda was built. Even if it was only 80 meters, that makes it considerably taller than either the Great Goose Pagoda in Xi'an or the Liuhe Pagoda in Qiantang.

It was not merely a famous sight in the Jiangnan region of the country—it was seen as the very symbol of China itself. At the time of the Opium War, a draft of the "Treaty of Nanjing," which was signed aboard the British ves-

sel *Cornwall,* was drawn up by members of the Chinese and British delega-
tions beneath the Great Baoen Temple pagoda. People who traveled to China
from abroad at that time would always go to see it. It was comparable to the
great Buddha at the Tōdai Temple in Japan.

This greatest of pagodas in all of China is now destroyed, the work of an
order issued by Northern King Wei Changhui. Explosives were set off, but
only the inside of the pagoda was gutted, as the exterior remained intact.

"Climb to the top of the pagoda," ordered Wei Changhui, "and start tearing it down from there."

He wanted to demolish it, so that when Shi Dakai's forces neared the city
they would be unable to use this immense structure as a base for their attack.
When the Qing Army had earlier been under Taiping assault, it never even
considered leveling the pagoda. Because the Taiping movement was based
in Christianity and saw Buddhism as a heterodox faith, there was no resistance to speak of when it came to destroying the pagoda. It was, though, a
symbol of China at the time and a work of art.

As they watched the pagoda being torn down, the residents of Nanjing
quietly sighed. It was not merely a question of religious devotion. This great
tower was everyone's pride and joy. It was now being ripped to shreds, blown
up, shelled—slowly it was disappearing before their eyes.

The pagoda had originally been constructed in compliance with an edict
of the Yongle Emperor (r. 1403–1425) of the Ming dynasty. Construction
began in 1412, lasted a period of nineteen years, and was completed in 1431.
It was a magnificent edifice, octagonal in shape and nine stories tall.

Yongle had the Great Baoen Temple built as a memorial to his mother.
History books tell us that his mother was the Empress Ma, the legal wife of
the founding emperor of the Ming dynasty, Hongwu. In fact, however, his
mother was said to be a princess in the imperial harem who came originally
from Korea. When the Yongle Emperor was born, the story goes, Empress
Ma immediately took the infant away from his biological mother and had
her put to death. Only after he had grown up did Yongle reportedly learn the
truth of his origins. The veracity of this tale has yet to be proven. Perhaps
because of the Great Bao'en pagoda's immensity and beauty, this story of its
connection to the emperor's mother was concocted to accompany it.

The pagoda's exterior was covered entirely in layers of white lapis tiles.
They were porcelain and thus were white with a distinctive charm. The tiles
of the roof on the ninth story were of five-colored lapis. The roof tiles gave
off a brilliant hue, while the tower itself was a pure white. The interior was
made of multicolored lapis layers. From beneath the surface, even more than
the surface, it appeared to be wearing a stunning suit of clothes, giving one a
sense of refined, courtly elegance.

The pagoda was constructed on a site said to have been the place where Sun Qian, well-known from the Three Kingdoms period, had built the King Asoka Pagoda in the third century.

"Although Buddhism is a demonic religion from India," said Hong Xiuquan to his aides, "to destroy that pagoda would seem to be overdoing it." At the time Hong's two older brothers were always by his side.

Hong Xiuquan's original name was said to have been Hong Renkun. He was the last of three brothers, the eldest of whom was Renfa and the middle brother was Renda. Eastern King Yang Xiuqing had tried to keep the Heavenly King and his brothers as far away from affairs of state as possible, and indeed he had succeeded in doing so. Yang had at his disposal the absolute weapon of divine possession—the Heavenly Father's Descent to Earth—and both Renfa and Renda feared immediate punishment if they acted out of hand. Living with such a fear, the Hong brothers went about their business outside the framework of Taiping politics.

With Yang's death, there would be no divine visitations, and the elder brothers of the Heavenly King no longer had reason to fear anyone. The Eastern King's tyranny and subsequent execution were followed by the tyranny of the Northern King, and in certain quarters Hong Xiuquan had become discredited by all this. "We're your relatives," his two completely commonplace brothers had tried to convince him, "and you've got to rely on your real brothers now."

When he learned that Wei was having the pagoda demolished in preparation for an assault from the armies of Shi Dakai, Hong Renfa reported the matter to the Heavenly King.

"No, it cannot go on," said the Heavenly King. "If he destroys that tower, punishment will be meted out. Wei Changhui's despotic behavior has gone on long enough. Retribution will soon be delivered, and it will be I who deliver it."

The Heavenly King's words reached Wei Changhui's ears that very day. The foolish Hong Renfa was so pleased by what his younger brother had said that he spoke of it within the Heavenly King's Residence. Among those who worked as cooks and handymen within Hong Xiuquan's residence were spies for the Northern King.

"Is that right? He plans to mete out punishment?" said Wei Changhui with a smile on his face. "After I've destroyed that pagoda, we'll have several other tasks to attend to as well." By these "tasks," he was referring to attacking the Heavenly King's Residence, murdering the Heavenly King himself, and taking control over the Taiping movement.

Maybe we should even change the name of our country as well, he thought to himself.

Wei learned of the demands made by Shi Dakai through a secret emissary. It seemed that the two brothers of the Heavenly King mistakenly thought that their brother's residence was sealed tightly and assumed that whatever was said within its walls would never escape to the outside world. So they felt at ease to say whatever they pleased.

"The blue-eyed woman who was at the Xishi Monastery said something very apt. She said that we may regret the fact that Hong Xiuquan has no troops directly under his command, but all troops in the Heavenly Capital will surely obey the orders of the Heavenly King. That's exactly right, if he issues orders. It's an edict that man can't oppose."

Hong Renfa had walked into the galley, speaking in a loud voice. He liked the kitchen area of the grounds.

Xiling had not gone out of her way to urge Hong Xiuquan on. She had merely recounted the facts as she knew them: "The Northern King does not have that many troops at his disposal. Qin Rigang left the capital with a force of fifteen thousand. Despite the Northern King's persistent search, remnants of the Eastern King's party remain waiting undercover within the Heavenly Capital for an opportunity to take their revenge."

The Heavenly King was aware that circumstances had taken a turn for the better as far as he was concerned. A secret edict was sent to the commander of a brigade of Taipings near the Heavenly Capital in the middle of the tenth lunar month of that year (1856).

A young cousin of the Eastern King by the name of Yang Fuqing was then in Jiangxi province, while a relative of Shi Dakai by the name of Shi Zhenji was even closer in Zhenjiang. Both of these men, needless to say, burned with hatred for the Northern King. Taiping forces in the environs of the Heavenly Capital began to move toward the capital, and this information leaked out to Wei Changhui.

—7—

The Northern King now realized that he was trapped. He had to recall Qin Rigang, who, although having departed the Heavenly Capital at the head of a large force of men, had not attacked Shi Dakai but fought only against Qing armies. Yet for all the messengers sent out, Qin hadn't tried to return to the capital.

Qin knew only too well the state of affairs there. Were he to return now, he would certainly find himself in an unpalatable situation. Rumor had it that Qin had taken shelter in the war front and planned to wait there until the storm passed.

"That bastard has no intention of returning to the capital," said Wei, spitting out the words, though he realized that if he were Qin, he probably wouldn't return to the capital either.

He understood well what was going on in Qin's mind. Granted, it was virtually impossible to predict, but Qin's 15,000 troops had to attack the Heavenly King's Residence as soon as possible.

When will it be? wondered Wei, as he folded his arms, looking up at the half-destroyed pagoda.

"We have collected together as many explosives as we could find. The base should be blown out from under it in one or two tries," said the man in charge of demolition, reporting to Wei Changhui.

"Good. On the day that the pagoda comes crashing to the ground, we'll invade the Heavenly King's Residence." It was early in the eleventh lunar month.

From dawn to dusk, Wei stared at the finest pagoda in the realm. Explosives were detonated several times. They were having a great deal of trouble with the foundation of the tower, but in fact on the fifth explosion, the pagoda finally disappeared completely.

Resistance from the Heavenly King's Residence was ferocious, far exceeding Wei Changhui's expectations. There were many "female officials" there, and women from Guangxi province were famed for not binding their feet and for being particularly strong. They went into armed battle. Dressed as men, they were nonetheless reputed to be more courageous than Jiangnan men.

Not only was the resistance of the Heavenly King's Residence beyond Wei's expectations. The fighting morale of the troops under the Northern King's command was exceedingly laggard. Whenever he took his eyes off them, his troops fled in every direction.

The climate had changed since the attack on the Eastern King's Residence. The Northern King's subordinates had for a long time gnashed their teeth, enduring the tyranny of the Eastern King. Morale was extremely high when they attacked Yang Xiuqing's residence. It was the day they had long been waiting for, and everyone was in high spirits.

When it came to attacking the Heavenly King's Residence, the same morale was nowhere to be found. Hong Xiuquan dwelt well inside the recesses of his residence, never showing himself to those on the outside. The general impression was that, though he had been kept under control by the Eastern King and did occupy the highest position in the movement, now many things could unfortunately not remain the same.

Since they were attacking a sovereign who was neither a tyrant nor an inhuman brute, it was no surprise that their assault lacked great clout. After the raid on the Eastern King's Residence, many of the soldiers had a penitent sense that it all seemed excessive.

They laid siege to the Heavenly King's Residence for an entire day but were unable to break inside. Wei rested his troops and the next day launched his attack anew. Before noon on that day, a battle cry arose unexpectedly, and from behind Wei Changhui's troops surrounding the Heavenly King's Residence, a military force of unknown lineage began an attack of their own.

"The Zhenjiang force shouldn't have arrived yet," said Wei, inquiring into reports from outside the city. At the earliest it wouldn't be there until the next day.

"It's Fu Xuexian!" reported a messenger as he dashed in.

"Are those guys still there?" said Wei, biting his lower lip. For several days he and his men had been out searching for remnants of the Eastern King's party, but the whereabouts of this formidable Taiping leader, Fu Xuexian, remained unknown. No reports placed him outside the Heavenly Capital.

"How many men?" asked Wei Changhui.

"I don't know, but there are a lot. Two thousand, perhaps as many as three thousand," said the messenger, blinking.

"Don't make wild guesses!" shouted Wei.

The messenger departed at full speed. He saw in Wei's eye the possibility that he would be killed, and fled for his life. As Wei's messenger, he clearly enjoyed Wei's confidence, but by the same token it was highly unlikely that he would now ever return again. As the greatest pagoda in all China was being destroyed, Fu Xuexian had quietly amassed the remnants of the Eastern King's men. In addition, he welcomed the participation of unaffiliated troops. Although there were people who had observed Fu's movements, no one had tried to communicate that information to Wei Changhui. This was proof positive that Wei had completely lost all popular support.

The door of the Heavenly King's Residence opened, and a force of bodyguards came out fighting. Wei's forces numbered only some two thousand men, and they were arrayed in a pincer operation. No one rushed to Wei's aid. He was there alone, sitting cross-legged in the area in front of the Heavenly King's Residence, in blank amazement. What took place before his eyes at that point was completely unbelievable to him.

"What? There's that northern bandit over there!" screamed a voice. Normally agile, Wei Changhui had now lost even the will to flee the scene.

He was arrested and dismembered. First he was beheaded, and then the rest of his body was torn to pieces.

"Send the head to Dakai," said Hong Xiuquan.

The original Taiping kings of the four directions—north, south, east, and west—were now all dead. The Taiping state now had only Assistant King Shi Dakai to rely upon. Nothing was more efficacious in the effort to gain Shi's favor than presenting him with Wei's decapitated head. The headless torso of Wei Changhui was chopped up into small pieces of flesh and suspended from various places within the city. Beside them signs were set up indicating, "This is the flesh of the northern traitor. Just observe. Do not remove."

Xiling now wanted to return to Shanghai, for she had seen the whole situation to which events had now come.

"You've seen one more gruesome spectacle," she said softly to Yu Cairong, placing her hand on Yu's cheek. Yu Cairong nodded.

"I'll get you out of here," said Xiling. "Wuchang's still in a state of war, so let's head for Shanghai."

"Can you really get me out of here?"

"Yes. I've spoken with the Heavenly King himself, and he's allowed it."

"Really?" Yu's eyes glistened, and she seemed very happy. "It's just like a dream. The Heavenly King really did give us permission?"

"He and I are old friends. If I make a special request, he usually will consent." Xiling did not, however, explain to Yu Cairong just how she managed to persuade Hong Xiuquan. What she had said to him was: "I think a dangerous time is coming for the Heavenly Capital. I pray that this will not come to pass, but we must be prepared for such an eventuality. Whether all of your heirs are placed in the Heavenly Capital remains in doubt. Those children already born are too dear to be sent away. However, a child yet to be born . . . I can take to Shanghai with Yu Cairong, because she is carrying your child."

Hong Xiuquan listened closely, licked his lips, and then nodded affirmatively. As for Yu Cairong's pregnancy, Xiling had said the first thing that popped into her head. She was only thinking of how she could best get Cairong out of this incarceration.

Part of the military force that had killed Wei Changhui was sent immediately to capture Qin Rigang. His 15,000-man army summarily handed over its own commanding officer.

"Such is the authority of the Heavenly King's edict," said Hong Renfa in a jovial tone of voice, as he stood by his brother's side. "It is all powerful."

The decapitated heads of Wei Changhui and Qin Rigang were placed in brine and sent to Shi Dakai, who was then in Anqing. At the same time, a proclamation reached him there: "Return to the capital and assist us in the governance of the Taiping Heavenly Kingdom."

On the day of Shi's departure from Anqing back to Nanjing, Xiling and Yu Cairong left the Taiping capital and boarded a ship heading downriver.

32

Victory and Defeat

—1—

After the uprising of the Small Sword Society was crushed, Shanghai was again tranquil. For all the efforts of the Small Swords to join forces with the Taipings, the Taipings made no attempt to reciprocate. The principal reason for this was the fact that the physical constitution of the Small Sword Society did not sit well with the leaders of the Taiping movement. There were a good number of both opium smokers and opium dealers among the members of the Small Swords.

"Taiping strength has reached its limit on account of this fastidiousness on their part," Lian Liwen had observed.

"The very fact of this fastidiousness," replied his father, Lian Weicai, "has enabled them to get as far as they have. Without it, they'd have been no different from ordinary bandits."

This debate over Taiping purity aside, Weicai saw the Taipings' lack of serious attention to Shanghai as evidence of the immaturity of their policies.

"Shanghai is a window through which the outside world is observable," Weicai had frequently made a point of saying.

The Taipings' formidable enemies were to the west. From the perspective of the Heavenly Capital (Nanjing), the west was upstream. Defending against the Hunan Army, the volunteers organized by Zeng Guofan, had become the greatest task before the Taiping forces. Because Wuchang had to be held at all cost, the Taipings sent their best forces to the west.

"Life or death depends on this, so they've got to turn their attention to the west," said Liwen.

"Of course," responded his father impatiently, "but they can't just focus on the west. If they're attacked by the Hunan Army from upriver, depending on circumstances they might have to abandon Nanjing altogether and retreat to Shanghai. Shanghai has the vitality to breathe new life into the Taiping movement."

"No doubt about it, they're much too attached to Nanjing. They've built palaces there and established a base of operations, so they'll cling to it till the bitter end."

"And for that reason, the situation in Shanghai has taken a turn for the better for the British."

Weicai said "the British," but he meant the entire foreign community there. As of July 1854, consuls of the three countries that had treaties with China— Britain, the United States, and France—had renegotiated land regulations in Shanghai and had gained the recognition of the Qing court's circuit intendant in Shanghai. The new municipal organization included a city council, the core of which was made up of people from the foreign concessions in Shanghai. The circuit intendant of Shanghai at the time was Wu Jianzhang. At the time of the rebellion of the Small Sword Society, he had been taken prisoner and was subsequently saved by the American Minister, Colonel Humphrey Marshall. In fact, it is perfectly clear that the leader of the Small Swords, Liu Lichuan, purposefully created the conditions enabling him to escape.

Wu Jianzhang was in a delicate position.

"Why don't you collect a tax from the vessels that come into Shanghai?" This was the complaint placed before Wu by British Consul Rutherford Alcock (1809–1897). Ships and cargo entering the port of Shanghai had been subject to a customs duty, but the maritime customs office had been destroyed during the Small Swords' rebellion, and it had not been restored.

The British consul led the way by paying customs fees on its own vessels. However, because the French consul did not regard the Chinese as fitting counterparts, he took the attitude that there was no need to pay. The American consul announced that he intended to follow the French lead if other vessels did not pay customs fees.

Alcock complained that honest men were making fools of themselves. Having been saved by foreigners, Wu Jianzhang was, needless to say, in a weak position with respect to them. He tried to revive the maritime customs office within the concessions, but he ran into opposition from the foreigners, who argued that it would become the object for an attack by the Small Swords, and Wu abandoned the idea altogether.

Still, customs duties had to be levied. Complaints of this sort raised by Alcock were forthcoming. It was impossible for Wu either way, collecting them or not. The circuit intendant's office now found itself in extreme poverty, and Wu simply couldn't continue without collecting this levy.

"Leave it up to us." Under such pressure from certain members of the foreign community, Wu Jianzhang did just that. A new maritime customs office was established, with a member of the British Consulate's staff in charge, nominally appointed by the Qing government as Inspector General of the Chinese Imperial Maritime Customs.

Wu Jianzhang was reprimanded by Beijing for this, and when it was learned that he had engaged in joint trading operations with foreigners, he was further censured. Additional doubt was cast on him for his behavior with respect to the Taipings, and he was eventually exiled to Chinese Turkestan. Wu received his punishment, but the capacity to collect customs fees, once lost, would never return.

A Committee for the Management of Customs comprised of one member from each of the three countries that had treaties with China functioned reasonably well. They were all experts in the field. Maritime customs officials of the Qing government had studied insufficiently just what was entailed in customs duties, and as a result they had had no end of trouble. "This way will certainly be better for business," said Lian Weicai with a forced smile.

As a merchant involved in trade, it was much easier to deal with a maritime customs agency run by foreigners. Still, though, for the Chinese people, the loss of one part of national sovereignty was a bitter price to pay. The system came into existence in Shanghai in the same year as the land regulations, 1854. It was officially ratified with the signing of the Treaty of Tianjin four years later and applied as well to the other open Chinese ports.

"We have to train specialists of our own in maritime customs," said Liwen. "It's been dreadful for us to this point. I think everyone would agree with that."

"True enough. If we train people in every relevant area, one day soon we'll have to get control of customs back. It's too bad for now, but soon they'll be going overseas to study . . . to study abroad." Weicai had begun to think in earnest about sending his sons overseas to study.

The system of the customs inspectorate run by foreigners (as determined by the British) was not even abolished as a result of the 1911 Revolution, which toppled the Qing dynasty. When the Pacific War erupted in 1941, Japan dismissed the British Inspector General of Customs, but in its place a Japanese Inspector General was established. With Japan's defeat in the war, things came full circle, and at long last in 1949 the system of the Inspector General of Customs was abolished.

—2—

Just before the internal dissension erupted into fighting within the Taiping camp, Lian Weicai received a disturbing letter from Wen Zhang, who had gone to Hong Kong. It read in part: "The British seem to think that the fact that the Qing government lacks the capacity to fight the Taipings is a golden opportunity for them to secure concessions from the Chinese . . ."

Clearly, the concessions referred to here implied an anxious desire to get involved in the fighting. As they followed the news of trouble among the Taipings, a report arrived that the *Arrow* Incident had transpired in Guangzhou (Canton) on October 8, 1856. By that time, internal strife among the Taipings had already exploded in Nanjing.

Although it was already October, Guangdong province was still very hot.

"They're pirates there. Pirates!" A man, his face bathed in perspiration, came flying into the naval patrol guard room. "It was a month ago, at Shangchuan Island. I'll never forget that face. He'll get away!" The sailors in the guard room at the time didn't fully understand why the man was so agitated and what he had said at first. "Sit down and speak slowly!" they said to him. With the back of his hand, he wiped away the saliva that was foaming in the corners of his mouth and sat down quietly in a chair.

When he got over the excitement and sat down, he explained himself so the other sailors could understand. One month earlier, this fellow said that he had been attacked by pirates at Shangchuan Island and that they had plundered all of his possessions. What property he'd had didn't seem to amount to much, but for him it was irreplaceable. Other people had been visited by pillagers at the same time, and they had notified the authorities.

"So, then, you're saying that one of the pirates was there at that time?" asked Brigade Commander Liang Guoding as he emerged from another room. The man had been speaking in a high-pitched voice that carried into the adjoining room.

"That is correct."

"That was at Haizhu Island, right?"

"Yes. It's connected to this. We've got to hurry. They'll get away. Please, please catch them this time."

"Fine. Let's go inspect the situation right now," said the brigade commander.

Haizhu Island was on the Pearl River, near Haizhu Park in present-day Guangzhou. Liang Guoding was a rare commodity in the Qing navy at the time—an activist officer. Boarding a patrol vessel himself, he rushed to the scene. The ship indicated by the man who had reported the incident was a lorcha bearing the name of *Arrow*.

A lorcha ship was defined as "a sailing vessel that combined Eastern and Western shipbuilding principles." In mast and sail, it was effectively the same as a Chinese junk, but the body was built according to European fashion. Since what first caught the eye was the mast and the sail, from a distance everyone took it to be a Chinese junk. As one got closer to it, though, at least those familiar with ships could see that it was different in form and shape from a junk.

Accompanied by three county-level officials and sixty sailors, Liang Guoding searched the *Arrow.*

"Oh, so it's you guys," said one of the officials connected to the county police when he recognized the faces of the notorious pirates. "Liang Mingtai, Liang Jianfu, . . ." He even knew their names.

There were some fourteen sailors on board the *Arrow,* but they were all Chinese. The master was an Irishman by the name of Thomas Kennedy, and at the time of the raid on his ship, he happened to have been away visiting a friend on a nearby vessel. When Master Kennedy returned, the raid was over, and the fourteen sailors were about to be taken away.

"What will I be able to do if you take them all away?" protested Kennedy.

"Okay, we'll leave two behind." Although branded as pirates, they had become friendly with him as honest seamen. Leaving behind two men about whom there had never been anything suspicious, Liang Guoding finally departed with twelve men under arrest.

Kennedy appealed to British Consul Harry Smith Parkes (1828–1885) in Guangzhou. Parkes, who would later become minister to Japan and forge close ties there, was twenty-eight years of age at this time, a young man burning with ambition. He had just been promoted from vice-consul in Xiamen to consul in Guangzhou.

When Lian Weicai first received news of the *Arrow* Incident, he unconsciously muttered, "No, it'll be bad. Parkes is there. They hit that youngster at a bad time." Parkes had been orphaned at an early age. The wife of the missionary Karl Gützlaff (1803–1851), who was active in China at the time of the Opium War, was Parkes's cousin, and as a result he came to be with her in Guangdong when he was fourteen years old. He became a dependent in the Gützlaff household, studied the Chinese language with Robert Morrison II, and became an expert in the field of Chinese relations. He was, in effect, the local upstart.

His predecessor, Rutherford Alcock, had come to the diplomatic corps from a novel background as a military doctor, though he had received a standard medical education and belonged to the elite stratum of British society. From the perspective of conservative British sensibilities, Parkes had to have been seen as a sort of collateral diplomat. As far as he was concerned, he saw the diplomatic profession as a way to get ahead in the world and post successes to be proud of. From the connection to Gützlaff, Lian Weicai had gotten to know this young man and his overwhelming ambition.

To be successful in diplomatic ventures on behalf of Great Britain meant winning diplomatic and commercial concessions from the Qing dynasty, and that necessitated appeals to military action. An excuse for commencing hostilities—Parkes was always looking for it. Parkes must have been delighted when Kennedy screamed foul at the *Arrow*'s coming under investigation.

Parkes immediately demanded that Brigade Commander Liang Guoding personally hand over the arrested sailors to the British Consulate. It was not a call for their release, but for their transfer. The essence of Parkes's demand was that the *Arrow* was a British vessel and hence that Qing police and judicatory powers did not extend to it.

Liang Guoding rejected the demand: "The *Arrow* was constructed in China, owned by Chinese, and manned solely by Chinese crewmen."

At that time, the ship was registered in Hong Kong as a British vessel as a means of transporting—illegally—opium and salt (which was a government monopoly). Flying a British flag, it was off limits to Chinese official inspections. Because the British flag was an effective charm for openly being able to smuggle contraband, ship registry papers were not so easy to get one's hands on. The *Arrow*'s papers were in the hands of a Chinese who had bought them for $1,000.

The Chinese authorities deeply resented the fact that smugglers could evade the law and carry on their business in this way with no control over the spread of opium. Righteous-minded officials like Liang Guoding conceived of this as an opportunity to try to unmask contraband-smuggling vessels. However, the British also were thinking about this "opportunity," and the man in charge on the scene was the ever ambitious Harry Parkes.

"It doesn't look like things will go well," said Lian Weicai with a sigh. "I certainly hope my premonitions turn out to be wrong."

—3—

> Petty bandits running rampant, becoming inured to gnawing at
>   human flesh,
> Attacked and completely destroyed an entire family in its prime.
> Late at night, looking tentatively at the top of the city wall,
> The large number of inauspicious stars everywhere hover like a
>   ring overhead.

Shi Dakai composed this poem when he heard that his entire family had been murdered by Northern King Wei Changhui. His wife, young children, and other family members—over ten persons in all—were killed, among them his aged mother. In his diary, he noted: "I am so terribly sad. My head reels."

A village known as Hanjiacun was located near the walled city of Taihu in Anhui province. With widespread disorder and banditry running rampant, this village too had been visited with plunder and massacre. Afterward, Shi Dakai's Taiping military force entered the city, and the bandits fled for their lives.

"I've found one little girl," said a guard, as he approached Shi Dakai with the girl in hand.

"Just one person?" asked Shi.

"Yes, just one."

"Is that so," said Shi, as tears welled up and flowed from his eyes.

The local bandits had attacked the small village of Hanjiacun and massacred its inhabitants. Only this small child, hiding in an area of high grass, had been spared.

"What's your name?" asked Shi.

Sobbing, she replied in a clear voice, "My name is Han Baoying."

"How old are you?"

"I'll be fourteen."

"Oh, so you're going to be fourteen? I thought you were a little younger than that."

Shi stared at her face. She was a small child and gave the impression of being younger than her years. At that time in history, fourteen was already old enough for marriage.

Tears continued to flow from her eyes, and from time to time she cried audibly.

"We're the same, you know? Our entire families have been killed, and only we've survived. I know what you're going through. I've cried those same tears you're now crying. But you can't go on crying forever. I'm going to take revenge for you."

"Revenge?" she said, raising her tear-soaked face and staring directly into Shi's gaze.

"That's right—revenge." Shi mobilized his vanguard troops and 1,000 men from his company and ordered them to comb the hills.

The Taipings had frequently confronted bandit forces, but the principal enemy of the Taiping movements remained the demonic Qing Army. As long as such bandit forces did not resist or get in the way, the Taipings ordinarily just left them alone. The search presently under way was out of the ordinary.

The bandits who had attacked Hanjiacun and committed such atrocities numbered only between one hundred and two hundred. The Taiping troops sent on the search mission returned with every last one of them bound together.

"Baoying, you were able to observe what was going on from the marshes, so you'll probably remember their faces. Point them out to me from that group," said Shi Dakai, and one by one Han Baoying looked over the faces of the captured bandits.

"That man there. And that one too . . ." They'd murdered her father, mother, elder brother, and his wife, and although only a child of fourteen, Baoying seethed with enmity. The dozen or more men pointed out by Baoying were killed on the spot. Another group of the killers were put to work digging graves for the murdered villagers. When the burial was completed, the remaining bandits were permitted to leave.

"Why did you allow them to go?" asked Zhang Suimou. "Those dozen or so may have killed Baoying's entire family, but the others certainly committed all manner of atrocity."

"There'll be no more massacres here." Shi Dakai looked up into the night sky.

"Okay, I understand. It was no good with the Northern King, and the Eastern King too committed massacres like this one, right? You're different from the Northern and Eastern Kings in that way, and it's because of that difference that we entrust you with our lives."

"You've all been through so much."

"What shall we do with Baoying?"

"We can't just leave this young girl, a lonely orphan. I think she can be useful to us, because she can read and write."

"Not only that. She surprised me. She can compose poetry."

"I'm going to adopt her. After all, I lost three daughters."

Of Shi Dakai's three daughters, one died in infancy and two were murdered by Wei Changhui. Thereafter, Han Baoying was known among the troops of the Assistant King as "Siguniang" or "fourth daughter." Although Shi's biological daughters had been younger than Baoying, the name "fourth daughter" carried the nuance that she was carrying on for the three who had departed.

Shi Dakai was at this time twenty-six years old himself, which made her more on the order of a younger sister than an adopted daughter. Shi became visibly more cheerful with Baoying by his side, for they shared the experience of having lost their families.

With the decapitated head of Wei Changhui having been sent to Shi Dakai by the Heavenly King, Shi regrouped his forces and returned to the Heavenly Capital at the beginning of the eleventh lunar month of the year. The residents of the Heavenly Capital, thrown into abject melancholy by the internal dissension of the men in power who washed blood with blood, truly hoped that a new era was now upon them. Rumors of the events in Hanjiacun soon began spreading throughout the Heavenly Capital, and people began saying to one another just what Zhang Suimou had said.

"This is different from the Eastern and Northern Kings."

The populace was sick to death of the savage means that their cold-blooded leaders had used until then. Noting the difference between Shi and the Eastern and Northern Kings was their way of expressing relief. "I think it's because he's an educated man."

"They say he tried not to destroy images of Confucius and the Buddhist mortuary tablets."

"He understands human feelings."

Indeed, Shi Dakai had some education, and compared to the other Taiping leaders, he was less radical and more dependable. He had come from a landlord family, but this is only a comparative assessment. Perhaps the fact that he joined the rebellion despite his landlord background was proof that he was never at ease with his own upbringing. He had not joined the Taiping movement out of personal financial distress, but rather as a man of ideals. He had felt compelled to throw himself into the action. His insides had been burning with indignation, which had to have something severe as its root cause.

The inhabitants of the Heavenly Capital had learned by bitter experience of that severity. Largely because of his training, Shi could maintain an outside appearance of calm and make people think he was in fact a man at ease. People's expectations, one might say, caused there to be a huge discrepancy between reality and appearance.

Shi had both an extraordinary determination and a talent for action. Of this, there was no doubt whatsoever. However, people looked to him for something more, something beyond these qualities. A sense of hopeful anticipation was produced by the psychology of awaiting the return of a hero. The sun rose and set on him, and Heavenly King Hong Xiuquan, needless to say, was none too happy with this turn of events.

"The Taiping Heavenly Kingdom has its Heavenly King! What is this recent rise in popularity of Shi Dakai among the common people? Clearly, Shi Dakai and the people close to him have been deliberately stirring up agitation." Members of the Heavenly King's entourage had been speaking to him in this manner. With all the discord caused by the Eastern and Northern Kings, the Heavenly King's distrust of his own leaders was only confirmed.

The only people he could rely on were blood relatives. His two elder brothers, Hong Renda and Hong Renfa, both actively took advantage of this feeling on the part of the Heavenly King, and new factions were soon formed.

There were the pro–Shi Dakai faction and the anti–Shi Dakai faction. Shi himself had earned the prestige and confidence of the general populace, and he was sustained by it. Those who opposed him—centered around Hong Renda and Hong Renfa—might be called the entourage party or the kin clique.

And signs began to emerge that political strife, the likes of which the local population had no wish to see erupt for a second time, was again intensifying.

—4—

At about this time, gunfire roared intermittently in Guangdong. Ever since the end of the Opium War, one issue that continued to smolder just beneath the surface in Guangdong concerned the right of foreigners to enter the walled city of Guangzhou. According to the Treaty of Nanjing, foreigners should have been allowed to enter cities designated as open ports. In fact, foreigners came and went as they pleased in Shanghai, but this had not transpired in Guangzhou.

Why had foreigners, who by treaty stipulations possessed the right to "enter the city," not been allowed into Guangzhou? The Chinese authorities claimed that the residents of Guangzhou were violent and impetuous, making it impossible to guarantee the safety of foreigners there.

If there were a danger to life and limb, they couldn't compel their own nationals to enter Guangzhou. Diplomats from the three signatories to the treaty accepted the situation at the time, in which entrance of their nationals into the city would be rejected, but with the understanding that in the near future, "entrance" would be permitted.

In actual fact, the area in which foreign concerns were constructed outside the city walls was not terribly safe. This was by no means simply because Guangdong people had a habit of being "violent and impetuous." The Westerners were every bit as violent themselves. On one occasion in 1846, some Westerners found a fruit seller's street hawking noisy and bothersome, so they kicked over his stall and tied him up inside a trading house. When nearby Chinese residents learned of this, they gathered to try to set fire to the factory, but Qing troops intervened and put down the trouble.

Inasmuch as half of the responsibility for not being able to exercise a right recognized in the treaty lay with the foreigners themselves, foreign consuls refrained from taking an overly hard-line stance on this issue. Prior to the Opium War, foreigners' residence and trading were recognized as a special privilege bequeathed by the beneficence of the Qing government, and thus the foreigners assumed a humble attitude for their part. As foreigners hastily gained legal rights with the Treaty of Nanjing, they became starkly arrogant, and trouble arose on successive occasions.

George Bonham, the British minister to China in 1849, mentioned the subject of "entrance" into the city of Guangzhou to Xu Guangjin, the governor-general of Guangdong and Guangxi, in a conversation in Humen (near Guangzhou). At the time, Bonham stated that under present conditions, the issue was a difficult one and would not be addressed for a while. Though he had tabled the issue, he by no means intended to give up the matter and bring it to a close.

He used Gützlaff, whose brilliance in Chinese extended to dialects, as his interpreter. Still, though, the Chinese understood the statement of the British minister to mean that they were relinquishing their right of "entrance." This was due to the vagueness of portions of Bonham's statement, and he was reprimanded for it by Prime Minister Palmerston.

In addition to the issue of entering the city of Guangzhou, there remained another unresolved issue: the face-to-face negotiations within the city of Guangzhou between the Anglo-American plenipotentiary and the highest local Chinese official, the governor-general of Guangdong and Guangxi. The fact that there were so many difficult, unresolved problems meant that it required a great diplomatic feat to settle them. Naturally, the ever ambitious Parkes was all wound up over the *Arrow* Incident.

In the age of imperialism, the diplomats of the Western powers saw their chief aim to be the protection and extension of their countries' interests, while friendly relations with the host country came second. Parkes later rose from the post of minister to Japan to become minister to China, and he died in Beijing. He may have attained his desires, but he never reached any level of intimacy with either the Japanese or the Chinese people. When he was minister to Japan, Parkes worked to keep strict enforcement of the unequal treaties with Japan, throughout his stay remaining opposed to any treaty revisions.

With the departure of Bonham, the positions of minister to China and governor of Hong Kong were filled with the arrival of John Bowring (1792–1872). Bowring was already at this time sixty-four years of age. At age forty-three he had become a member of the British House of Commons, but more than as a politician, he was known in the literary world as the editor-in-chief of the *Westminster Review* and as the editor of the collected writings of Jeremy Bentham. Although he had little experience as a diplomat, he adopted a hard line with the Chinese, and in this sense he made for a fine combination with the young Harry Parkes.

"It's gotten to the point where it would be strange if war didn't break out," said Lian Weicai when he learned of the *Arrow* Incident.

The Qing court turned to Ye Mingchen (1807–1859) to handle matters on its behalf. Ye had moved from governor of Guangdong to the governor-generalship of Guangdong and Guangxi. While he was a civil official, he had experience in military action, having posted impressive results in crushing local bandits. In response to Parkes's demands, Ye Mingchen said, "Among the sailors taken away by the authorities, two were recognized as pirates, and one was seen as highly suspicious. I shall order an official under my jurisdiction to escort the remaining nine by ship."

Parkes rejected the offer. "If you do not repatriate all members of the crew, this will be unacceptable to us."

The thinking behind this reply was that the *Arrow* was a British vessel, and thus the right to investigate and judge anything and everything on it belonged to Great Britain. Even if there had been pirates on board, establishing that fact ultimately fell to Britain. For that reason, the British were now pressing for the return of all members of the ship's crew.

On the morning of October 20, in compliance with instructions from Bowring, Parkes gave Ye a forty-eight-hour ultimatum: "A written public apology and a guarantee of respect for the flag of Great Britain."

The British were protesting the fact that a Chinese official had hauled down the British flag flying on the *Arrow*. The Qing authorities refuted the claim, saying that the *Arrow* had never flown the British flag. Master Kennedy testified to Parkes that the *Arrow* had been flying the British flag, and Parkes used that evidence as the basis for his claim of the insult done to it.

The Chinese sailors taken into custody, however, testified that the British flag was being held in storage on ship and had never been hoisted aloft. Ye Mingchen based his rebuttal on this evidence.

At the time of the incident, Kennedy had been only some 50 meters away from the *Arrow* on an inspection of a vessel known as the *Dart*. The master of the *Dart* also recounted that he had seen a man wearing an official's cap pull down the flag.

A member of the crew of the Portuguese ship number 83, the same distance as the *Dart* from the *Arrow* at the time, related that the *Arrow* had not been flying the British flag. Furthermore, an English-language newspaper published at the scene ran a story claiming that the *Arrow* had been docked there for six days, but it had not once raised any flag at all.

Historians consider all this argumentation futile, unending.

Governor-General Ye Mingchen claimed, in response to Parkes's demands, that the British flag had not been pulled down. "Henceforth, Chinese forces will not take into custody sailors aboard foreign lorchas without cause. However, the British must purchase registration papers for Chinese vessels and not exacerbate the difficulties involved in distinguishing Chinese and foreign ships." He had not complied with the British demands.

As a reprisal, the British seized a large Chinese junk, which they apparently thought was a Guangdong troop ship. It was, however, a privately owned merchant vessel.

On the twenty-first, Bowring issued an ultimatum for compliance with British demands within twenty-four hours. Ye Mingchen sent a letter in reply, but it did not accede to the demands of the ultimatum.

Rear Admiral Sir Michael Seymour of the East India Squadron took action on the twenty-third by destroying the Qing fortress near Guangzhou and sending armed troops into the foreign merchants sector. On the twenty-seventh British military forces bombarded the offices of the governor-general, and on the twenty-ninth they raided those offices, only to vacate them soon thereafter. It was a demonstration of their capacity to seize and occupy such sites at will.

"The military and the populace shall cooperate and exterminate the disgusting British barbarians!" While issuing these instructions, Governor-General Ye sent none of the forces under his command into battle.

"Even street urchins who act rowdily calm down after a time," Ye told the members of his staff.

—5—

"Not a particularly clever plan of response," replied Wen Zhang, when he heard from the governor-general of the countermeasures taken. There was no response that could have had a rapid effect on the situation at hand.

"Is there really nothing?" he was asked again.

"If I must say, you'd need to train one hundred men like myself—if possible, one thousand—and then a plan of action might naturally emerge, but that takes time," Wen Zhang answered.

Wen Zhang informed Lian Weicai by letter of his exchange with the governor-general.

"I wonder if Ye Mingchen really understood what Wen Zhang was saying to him," said Lian, shaking his head as he showed the letter to his son, Liwen.

"I wonder."

"Well, the fact that he sought Wen Zhang's advice is progress. A governor-general, someone who's risen to the highest civil rank, has asked guidance from an ordinary merchant."

"He was at a complete loss," said Liwen.

As a young man, Wen Zhang had studied at the Anglo-Chinese College in Malacca, and he had acquired a rich experience living overseas. His daughter, Cailan, married Lian Weicai's second son Chengwen. Wen Zhang had long been active in the Jinshunji as Lian Weicai's right-hand man. The Anglo-Chinese College was founded by Robert Morrison (1782–1834). Inasmuch as Consul Harry Parkes had learned his Chinese from Morrison's son, Wen Zhang and he were effectively pupils of the two Morrisons, respectively.

Ye Mingchen may have known of this connection and perhaps hoped for some influence with Parkes through Wen Zhang. What Wen Zhang wanted to say was that, if they were to increase the number of people like himself who were knowledgeable of the affairs of foreign lands, then that would constitute a force for progress, and in foreign affairs the best possible counteractions would be hammered out and executed.

The most effective method that struck Wen Zhang even now was to stop Great Britain's use of military force in Guangzhou. If Parliament would not recognize the exercise of force, then the East India Squadron would have no future course of action. They would have to go to London to lobby Parliament.

At the time of the Opium War, the measure sanctioning expenditures for the necessary military outlay only passed Parliament by nine votes. Opium merchants such as Jardine returned to London from Guangzhou and worked hard at lobbying in Parliament to support a military invasion. He was ultimately successful by a 271–262 vote. We'll never know what might have transpired had the Qing government lobbied in the halls of Parliament. Although such a method was at their disposal, it was well beyond Wen Zhang and two or three others like him to do anything about it. They needed the strength of large numbers of people to see their plan to fruition, and before that they had to train such people. And that would take time.

"Educating human talent requires time. Before that, though, the court in Beijing must be made to understand the need for such human talent. And that will require far more time. No, no matter how much time we devote to that task, it'd probably be a waste of time."

The speaker was sitting in a room of the Hong Kong branch of the Jinshunji, facing Wen Zhang. It was Hong Ren'gan, thirty-five years of age. He hailed from Hua county in Guangdong province, a clear indication that he was related to Hong Xiuquan. In each generation, the Hongs of Hua county had one character of their given names in common. Hong Xiuquan had originally been Hong Renkun, and his elder brothers were Hong Renfa and Hong Renda. Every member of their generation bore the character "ren" in his name. Hong Ren'gan was a cousin of the Heavenly King.

"You have so few hopes?"

"Not 'so few.' None at all."

"Is all hope gone?"

"Well, there's still one possible way for China to be restored to life."

"What way is that?"

"To change governments. The Qing dynasty's already beyond all hope, so we need to invest our hopes in a different government. Even my cousin's Taiping Heavenly Kingdom would do. It's certainly preferable to the Qing."

"Then, why haven't you joined the Taipings?" asked Wen Zhang.

Only recently had Wen Zhang gotten to know Hong Ren'gan. Hong had come to borrow an English-language book entitled *Astronomy and Agricul-*

ture. He had studied both astronomy and mathematics in exchange for teaching Chinese to a British missionary in Hong Kong. The missionary told him that if he wanted to know more about the relationship between astronomy and agriculture, there were undoubtedly interesting books at the home of a Mr. Wen of the Jinshunji. Hong proceeded to Wen Zhang's home just prior to the outbreak of the *Arrow* Incident.

Wen Zhang had a fondness for collecting English-language books. He enjoyed literature, but collecting books went beyond the scope of his personal interests. The criterion for entry into his collection was rather if the work contained information that might be useful for China some day. For that reason, *Astronomy and Agriculture* did indeed appear in his library.

Hong Ren'gan was a man whose interests ran to odd tastes. That was the extent of what Wen Zhang knew of this man, other than the fact that he was a cousin of Hong Xiuquan.

"When my elder cousin began the Society of God Worshippers, I helped him a bit," said Hong Ren'gan.

"Did you go to Jintian village?"

"No, it was before then. Back when we studied the Bible in Hua county. We got along very well, but I wasn't informed before he began raising an army."

Before he raised an army in Jintian village, Hong Xiuquan summoned the members of his family in Hua county, just those in his immediate family. He apparently did not want at that time to cause problems for the other branches of the Hong lineage. When he put together an army, though, trouble did visit other branches of Hongs, and rebel relatives who became involved in this act of high treason came under sharp repression. Hongs who sensed the dangers to their lives decided to depart Hua county quickly and escape the trouble.

Intending to join the Taipings, Hong Ren'gan headed toward Guangxi province, but the Taipings were then at Yongan and he had no way to get there. So he returned as far as Xunzhou, only to find that he could no longer go back to his home in Hua county. He proceeded to Hong Kong.

When the Taipings occupied Nanjing, made it their Heavenly Capital, and gave it the appearance of a state, Hong Ren'gan tried to enter Nanjing via Shanghai. After struggling to make his way to Shanghai, he found Qing troops before him and could proceed no further.

"I heard all manner of things about conditions in Nanjing when I was in Shanghai. Realizing that it was essentially impossible to get there, I headed back for Hong Kong."

From Hong Ren'gan's manner of speech, it would seem as though the presence of Qing troops along the route from Shanghai to the Heavenly Capital was not the only reason he did not go there. He knew full well of Eastern King Yang Xiuqing's seizure of power and Heavenly King's figurehead status. Even if he had made it into the Heavenly Capital, it was highly doubtful that, as the cousin of the Heavenly King, he would have been assigned a position commensurate with his talents.

"Was that a year ago? It was probably wiser to return," said Wen Zhang.

"I thought so, too."

"But now, haven't things changed considerably?"

"True, conditions in the Heavenly Capital are changing, but as far as I'm concerned, I'm not at all sure they're changing for the better."

"In what sense do you mean?"

"People far less capable than either the Eastern King or the Northern King now hold control over political power in the Heavenly Capital. I'm their cousin too, but there's no one in their family aside from the Heavenly King." Hong Ren'gan was, of course, referring to the Heavenly King's two brothers, Hong Renfa and Hong Renda.

"Doesn't that make it all the more incumbent on you to go there? Shi Dakai may return."

"I've heard no report on that as yet, but he's probably on his way back right now. Renfa and Renda probably won't get along too well with Shi. Until that rivalry calms down, I plan to keep away from the Heavenly Capital. At least, that's my plan of action for now," said Hong Ren'gan with a smile on his face.

—6—

The Qing armies recovered the city of Wuchang on December 19, 1856. The capture of Wuchang had been but a question of time. When Shi Dakai's forces at the Hubei provincial frontier returned to the Heavenly Capital, there were no significant Taiping forces to reinforce Wuchang. The Taiping commander holding the city was Wei Jun, younger brother of Wei Changhui. After his execution, Wei Changhui's decapitated head had been sent to Shi Dakai, a fact now well-known to Wei Jun, who was nervous about his own future and not in the best frame of mind to be paying close attention to defensive measures.

The Qing forces surrounding Wuchang continued to increase in number. The man who took charge of the army on this front was Hubei Governor Hu Linyi. A native of Hunan province, Hu had attained the metropolitan degree in 1836, one class ahead of Zeng Guofan. While serving as a prefect in Guizhou, Hu Linyi had successfully quelled a local uprising and thus gained considerable military experience.

The Qing Army had broken the iron chain of defense that the Taipings had laid out across the surface of the Yangzi River, burned the Taipings' military vessels, and effectively stripped Wuchang bare. Wei Jun and the others inside the city gave up all thought of defending Wuchang and thought only of how to escape. Also inside the city walls was the Heavenly King's cousin, Hong Renzheng.

"We'll open all seven city gates at the same time," decided Wei Jun.

They had no choice but to open at least one gate to escape, but in order to confuse the enemy, he opted for the tactic of opening them all. In the loss of Wuchang, Taiping forces sustained over ten thousand casualties, but Wei Jun, Hong Renzheng, and others among the leadership escaped without injury. Spiritually, the Taipings had seriously deteriorated. After Wei Jun left the city, he headed in the direction of Jiangxi, without returning to the Heavenly Capital.

Those close to the Heavenly King were attacking Shi Dakai. "Responsibility for the fall of Wuchang also lies with Assistant King Shi Dakai. He was the highest commander of the Wuchang front army and he willfully left his post."

With the new year, Hong Renfa was invested as the Tranquility King and Hong Renda as the Blessing King. It was becoming ever clearer that Heavenly King Hong Xiuquan was moving toward a government by his closest relatives.

The young Shi Dakai was disconsolate. Wherever he thought of taking some sort of action, he found his way impeded. Now fifteen years old, Han Baoying (Shi's "fourth daughter") turned to her adoptive father, the twenty-seven-year-old Shi Dakai, and said, "Father, I really can't see beyond this, but you are going to be caught in a trap laid by the Hongs. In fact, it's already happening. How much longer will you remain here? You no longer have a family to worry about, just like me."

She frequently encouraged him in such language to leave the Heavenly Capital. There was nothing of interest there any longer. The only person left to care for this lonely orphan, Han Baoying, was a similarly lonely "orphan," Shi Dakai.

"A family to worry about? Didn't someone just join my new family? You."

"Your new family. Just the two of us can make a quiet life in the mountains and forests."

"So, all of our hard work to this point will be for naught. My wish is to create on this earth a new kingdom for all troubled people to inhabit."

"Must you be inside the Heavenly Capital for that wish to come to fruition? Must the center of that kingdom be here?"

"We are amalgamating our strength."

"No. You are killing each other. Isn't it true? Father, the family is being exterminated. Why do you retain these lingering connections to the soil where your mother's blood was spilt? I simply do not understand. The land here seems to carry a curse."

Baoying's facial expression as she pressed Shi Dakai to withdraw from the Heavenly Capital acquired a ghostly air.

"Cursed?" said Shi, holding his head in both hands.

"Any terrain over which Taiping forces have passed is cursed. You surely know of the scheme under way to try and blame you, Father, for the fall of Wuchang. Why, after all, did Wuchang fall? Was it really your responsibility?"

"Indeed, I was returning to the Heavenly Capital from Hubei, in compliance with a request from the Heavenly King."

"So, responsibility then lies with the Heavenly King. The reason Wei Jun didn't fight to defend Wuchang was almost certainly that his elder brother had been killed in the Heavenly Capital, and it was the Heavenly King who killed his brother. That too, then, makes it the responsibility of the Heavenly King."

"People make mistakes."

"I understand, but the Heavenly King has made so many—too many. At least, I can't believe that with the creation of a new kingdom on earth he would make an appropriate ruler."

"But is there anyone else?"

"Yes, there is."

"There is? Who? You can't have met very many people since coming to the Heavenly Capital."

"It's you, Father. With you, a fantastic state more marvelous than even the Taiping Heavenly Kingdom will be formed. I believe that it is your duty, Father. Why must you remain indefinitely with this decrepit state?"

"Decrepit, is it?"

"Yes, it is. What are the Tranquility King and the Blessing King doing? Shouldn't you know, Father? Not a single resident of the Heavenly Capital believes any longer in the Heavenly King."

"That's really overstating it. You don't know what the devils in the Qing regime are up to now. The populace is much better off by comparison here now."

"The era of the devil's government is long past. We common people are now full to the brim with hope. That is the era in which we now live. Since they have lost hope in the Heavenly King, the people harbor great expectations in you, Father, and you must respond to them. These are the hopes and expectations of four hundred million people. However, if you stay in the Heavenly Capital, nothing will be accomplished. Father, you must leave here and take up the work that God commands you to."

Though just a fifteen-year-old child, Baoying was an eloquent orator. There was no connection between her words and her charming face. It was as if a sorceress were announcing God's message through her. To Shi Dakai, it seemed as though she were possessed, and he thus listened closely to what she had to say. He tried to listen submissively, not as if they were her words but as though she were the vehicle for the transmission of those words.

"I heard it often back home," continued Baoying. "A peddler from Wuchang told stories of the young commander who spoke of the way of God to the common people at Yuemachang and who advocated a new kingdom. They say that everyone listened to the stories of this young commander. This same peddler told other stories as well, such as how in Wuchang one named Xuan Fei gathered together all the young women of the town to select the most beautiful. They say everyone hated that story. No one understood it. In the Taiping movement, good and bad—like oil and water—do not mix, but float apart, for it can be no other way. The people entrusted their last hopes to the good of the Taiping Heavenly Kingdom. To be more specific, they looked to none other than the young commander who spoke to them at Yuemachang. This young commander, of course, is Shi Dakai. It is you, Father. On your shoulders rests the hopes and wishes of four hundred million. Will you try to relinquish their hold and break free of them?"

"Think about my position here for a moment."

"If you take action, Father, how many of them will follow you?"

"Maybe two hundred thousand," said Shi Dakai, staring intently at his feet.

—7—

Shi Dakai left the Heavenly Capital in command of an immense army of 200,000 in May 1857. Only half a year had passed since he had returned to the Heavenly Capital from Anqing to serve as a counselor in political affairs.

Affiliate forces in various locales directly under the command of the Assistant King joined Shi's "expeditionary force," and Shi appealed to friendly forces outside his direct line of command. Chen Yucheng and Li Xiucheng were in the midst of fighting in northern Anhui province and could not respond to Shi's call. Chen gathered together large numbers of starving people in Anhui, organized them into a military force of several hundred thousand, attacked eastern Hubei province, destroyed the Qing forces there, and posted major military gains. Shi Dakai was accompanied by virtually all of the troops and military leaders from the Heavenly Capital, and the new forces were supplemented by those of Chen Yucheng. In a word, the Taiping movement was in a serious predicament following the departure of Shi Dakai.

Jurong, a site only 40 kilometers to the southeast of the Heavenly Capital, fell to the Qing Army on July 16 of that year. Provincial Military Commander Zhang Guoliang captured it, and Qing forces proceeded west from Jurong as far as Chunhua, just a few kilometers south of the Heavenly

Capital. The Southern Imperial Barracks were reconstituted, and a sense of crisis gripped the Heavenly Capital.

The Heavenly King's two elder brothers, the Tranquility King and the Blessing King, used their positions to accept bribes. Not a soul in the Heavenly Capital was uninformed of the fact that they were stuffing their own pockets. They had acted obediently and submissively until then, because they feared the Eastern King's powers and his "Heavenly Father's Descent to Earth." Once Yang Xiuqing was dead, they feared the emergence of a second Yang, and in Shi Dakai they envisioned such a possibility.

Hong Xiuquan's two elder brothers were in their late forties and had acquired a cunning commensurate with their age. They had thus been successful in banishing the twenty-seven-year-old Shi Dakai. There was no one else they feared, so they could now carry on their graft in the open without a worry. People frowned at their arrogant behavior, and eventually news of it came to the attention of the Heavenly King.

"We must pay close attention to my two elder brothers. I'm wondering just what we can say," counseled Hong to Meng De'en, the man he most trusted apart from blood relatives.

Meng De'en had originally borne the name Shangsheng, but in Taiping, usage the Chinese character for "Shang" was reserved for the Lord Jehovah. Meng, therefore, avoided it and adopted the name De'en. A participant in the movement since the days of the Society of God Worshippers, Meng had joined the insurgent forces at Jintian village, but being a man of delicate condition, Meng found himself assigned to watch over the Heavenly King's person. In the Heavenly Capital, he had been administrator general of the Institute for Women—meaning that he supervised the women's quarters, a function that in the imperial Chinese system would have been carried out by eunuchs. Since there were, of course, no eunuchs in the Taiping movement, a man who resembled them in nature and physique was assigned this responsibility. As the emperor invested much confidence in eunuchs under the old system, Heavenly King Hong Xiuquan too placed great trust in this eunuch-like figure of Meng De'en.

There was no fear whatsoever now that the Taiping movement would be taken over by a ferocious general steeled in many battles, such as Yang Xiuqing. Always wearing an ashen mien, as if he felt ill, Meng was soon on his sickbed. This was the man whom the Heavenly King trusted.

"You must remain unsparing on the surface," replied Meng De'en.

"Unsparing?"

"They must be stripped of their respective 'kingships.'"

"Their kingships?" Hong was trying to say that he thought such a measure was too ironhanded.

"At present, not only every civil and military official, but the populace throughout the Heavenly Capital despises the two kings. What's more, it is entirely possible that the hatred for them will become transformed into hatred for your majesty, the Heavenly King. Should someone create an artifice of that sort, the ignorant masses are likely to believe it. You must take action to prevent the spread of public enmity for the person of the Heavenly King. By the same token, if you give careful instructions to the two of them to forebear a bit, perhaps you may be able to obtain their consent. Something on this order must be done to keep the Taiping Heavenly Kingdom alive for eternity."

"I see your point. Honest counsel that is concerned with my person is always welcome, indeed. I shall remove my brothers' kingships."

Eventually, the Tranquility King and the Blessing King lost their kingships, and they were demoted, respectively, to lower Taiping ranks of nobility. Just as Meng De'en had said, by stripping the kingships from his brothers, Hong Xiuquan prevented the spread of the fires of public indignation from turning on him.

Political affairs in the Taiping movement were now being managed by Meng De'en, Chen Yucheng, and Li Xiucheng. Meng and Chen became "premiers," and Li became a "vice-premier," though Meng was the man in charge. Meng remained a eunuch-like retainer, and the two former kings receded, on the surface, to the background. Li Xiucheng tried to resist the influence of these two kings, maneuvered for the return of Shi Dakai, and caused the displeasure of Hong Xiuquan. Chen Yucheng was still very young, not fully twenty years of age at the time he was appointed "premier." He had joined the Taiping movement at age fourteen.

"In both character and talent, he's extraordinary," said Lian Liwen with a sigh, sitting in the Shanghai office of the Jinshunji. He had known Chen well when he was still known as Chen Picheng. "Unfortunately, he's still much too young. But, for all his youth, just wait till he gets to be Shi Dakai's age."

"It's so pathetic, to be assigned such a major role at the most difficult of times." Into Xinmei's head floated the image of Chen when he was about fifteen years old.

More than a full year following the *Arrow* Incident, the British launched a full-scale military operation in Guangdong. The expeditionary force had finally arrived. It had been delayed because deliberations in Parliament over sending such a force had gone through a stormy voyage.

Lord Derby in the House of Lords laid a motion on the table that criticized British official actions in China, but his motion was voted down. In the House of Commons, though, Richard Cobden's proposed motion passed by a margin of sixteen votes. His motion argued that, because the government's report could not demonstrate good reason for Britain's taking such a violent course of action, an investigator needed to be selected. Such a person was to look into whether or not the bombardment of the governor-general's offices and occupation of the Chinese battery—the "violent course of action"—were in fact appropriate. Although not critical of the actions, strictly speaking, this proposal did amount to voting down an immediate dispatching of an expeditionary force.

Prime Minister Palmerston dissolved the House of Commons. In the elections held forty days later, hard-liners won a majority of the seats, and the sending of an expeditionary force to China was approved.

Wen Zhang, who was an avid reader of British newspapers, wrote to Lian Weicai in Shanghai: "Had they been able to keep the pressure on members of the British Parliament, they would have been able to stave off an expedition." But the means of restraining a British expedition lay elsewhere, and Wen Zhang was unaware of it at the time. Later, when related governmental documents became public, this became clear.

In his report to Prime Minister Palmerston, John Bowring, the Hong Kong governor-general and minister to China, included the following sentence: "The vessel [namely, the *Arrow*] was not under our protection at the time, but the Chinese do not know this. We must never, under any condition, reveal this fact to them."

The fact that the *Arrow* was not at that time under the protection of Great Britain meant that the ship's registry papers had expired. Registration was good for one year at a time, and the certificate of registration had been sold, as noted earlier, for $1,000. Renewals, though, only cost a fee of ten dollars. The renewal process was so simple, it had been overlooked. The *Arrow* had been registered on September 27, 1855, and the renewal procedure had not been started by the time the incident surrounding it arose on October 8, 1856. Therefore, legally, the *Arrow* was not a British vessel at that time.

Aside from the diplomatic efforts of which Wen Zhang had spoken, they could not neglect to carry out an investigation of the basic facts of the case, but the Qing authorities never investigated if the vessel had British registry or not.

Lord Elgin (1811–1863), who was appointed British plenipotentiary, arrived in Hong Kong in July 1857 at the head of an expeditionary force, and he awaited the arrival of the French plenipotentiary, Baron Gros (1793–1870). In February of the previous year, a French priest by the name of August Chapdelaine violated Chinese law, entered Xilin county in Guangxi, stirred up believers, and was executed for the crime of plotting rebellion. The French held the Qing government responsible for this incident and decided to send a military force to seek an indemnity.

Baron Gros arrived in Hong Kong three months after Elgin. In December 1857, a joint Anglo-French force—made up of 5,600 troops, largely British —attacked Guangzhou. Guangzhou fell on the 29th, and Governor-General Ye Mingchen was taken prisoner and hauled off to Calcutta. The joint Anglo-French force then tried to move north.

Just as the Qing government was finally gaining the upper hand in the fighting with the Taipings, it found itself faced with the dire circumstance of the northern movement of this foreign armed force. Two days prior to the fall of Guangzhou, government armies under the command of Imperial Commissioner He-chun and Hunan Provincial Military Commander Zhang Guoliang took Zhenjiang, which provided access to the east of the Heavenly Capital. The Taiping force defending Zhenjiang was led by Wu Ruxiao, but Li Xiucheng came to his rescue and Wu was able to return to the Heavenly Capital.

About this time, Chen Yucheng won a great victory over a Qing force led by Vice-Commander-in-Chief Duo-long-a and Regional Vice-Commander Bao Chao near the city of Taihu in Anhui province. Over three thousand men were slain in the fighting. But in Guazhou, on the other side of the river from Zhenjiang, a Qing force led by Imperial Commissioner De-xing-a and Naval Commander Chen Guotai attacked the Taipings and recaptured the city.

One victory, one defeat—the free-for-all continued. Having departed the Heavenly Capital, Shi Dakai's army began to lose heart about this time while besieging the strategic site of Jishui in Jiangxi.

33

Elegy for the Heavenly Capital

—1—

Five years had passed since Assistant King Shi Dakai departed the Heavenly Capital at the head of a large force of men. It was 1862, the first year in the reign of the Tongzhi Emperor. In the system of the Qing dynasty, each emperor had only one title for his entire reign, and thus the first year of a reign implied that in the previous year, an emperor had died and a crown prince had acceded to the throne.

The Xianfeng Emperor had been only twenty-six at the time of his death, which occurred on the seventeenth day of the seventh lunar month at his summer palace in Rehe. His empress had borne him no sons, and thus the six-year-old Daichun, son of Princess Yi of the Yehonala Manchu clan, took the throne as the Tongzhi Emperor. Later the empress of the Xianfeng Emperor would become known as the Eastern Empress Dowager, while Tongzhi's birth mother (Princess Yi) would become known as the Western Empress Dowager. The era of the latter, known to history simply as the "Empress Dowager," in the early twentieth century commenced in this way.

The first year of the Tongzhi reign began with the personnel matter of awarding to Governor-General Zeng Guofan the position of assistant grand secretary. The event was officially announced on New Year's day. It was in recognition of the great deeds accomplished by Zeng on behalf of the Qing dynasty.

With Shi Dakai's flight from the capital, the Taiping movement had lost all four kings of the directions—north, south, east, and west—as well as the Assistant King. Its two principal supports now were Li Xiucheng and Chen

Yucheng. Although even Zhenjiang—known among the Taipings as the entry to the capital because of its relationship to the Heavenly Capital—was now lost, it was because of new leadership of these two men that the Taiping movement was able, barely, to escape destruction. In addition, its military forces were reconstituted.

In the intervening years, the Qing government had sustained serious damage as a result of the Second Opium War, occasioned because of the *Arrow* Incident. Joint Anglo-French forces had taken Dagu and forced the Qing court into signing the Treaty of Tianjin. It had no choice but to capitulate.

The Anglo-French forces attacked as far as the environs of Beijing and struck terror in the heart of the dynastic authorities. It seemed as if this might offer the Taipings something of a breathing spell, but such was not at all the case. The Hunan Army under Zeng Guofan never anticipated any assistance or reinforcements from the government's armed forces.

News that the Anglo-French forces were pressing in on the capital actually stirred up the soldiers of the Hunan Army. When foreign troops had attacked Dagu, Jiujiang, which was under Taiping control, was attacked by Qing forces. Lin Qirong, the commander in charge of the Taiping garrison at Jiujiang, and his 17,000–man army were killed to a man. And the bloody war continued.

Within half a year following the attack on Jiujiang, Li Xiucheng retook Yangzhou three times, fought together with Chen Yucheng against the Qing forces at Sanhe, and wiped out 6,000 men of the Hunan Army. At this time, Li Xubin of the Qing Army, who had once captured the city of Jiujiang, committed suicide. As a result of this victory, the siege at Anqing, the Taipings' largest base on the western front, gradually lifted.

Hong Ren'gan, who had been in Hong Kong, entered the Heavenly Capital in April of 1859. He was a distant cousin of the Heavenly King Hong Xiuquan. The Heavenly King's two elder brothers, Renfa and Renda, were men of disreputable character and were appropriately dismissed from their posts by the Heavenly King. Hong Ren'gan, however, was quite a talented and capable man. From his early days back in his hometown in Hua county, Hong Xiuquan had known of his cousin's abilities, and thus much anticipation greeted Ren'gan's arrival at the Heavenly Capital. Despite the decline of the Heavenly King's two brothers, Hong Xiuquan still believed that he could trust only blood relatives.

Hong Ren'gan was named the Shield King and acquired supervisory control over Taiping political affairs. Later, Chen Yucheng was made the Heroic King and Li Xiucheng the Loyal King. The Taiping movement eventually recovered from the chaos caused by internal dissension.

Taiping armies captured Hangzhou and Suzhou in 1860, but the attack on Shanghai was not successful. A foreign brigade under the command of

Frederick Townsend Ward was formed, and because it was armed with modern, Western-style guns, it was known as the "Foreign Rifle Company." This company was unlike the foreign volunteer corps formed in 1853. The earlier corps advocated an armed neutrality in the defense of Shanghai. At the Battle of the Muddy Flat in April 1854 and on other occasions, this volunteer corps fought against the Qing armies. Ward's Foreign Rifle Company, by contrast, was openly an ally of the Qing government in its war against the Taipings.

It was much easier for the foreigners to get the weak-kneed Qing government to sign the Treaty of Tianjin. Since that treaty accorded them all manner of special privileges, it was well within their interest to see the Qing dynasty stay in existence. The major trading item for every country with respect to China was opium. The Taipings claimed they would eradicate opium, and where they held sway, they were enforcing a ban with severe penalties. If the Taiping rebels were to replace the Qing dynasty and take over the reins of power, the opium trade was likely to be dealt a fatal blow. Furthermore, the Taipings were openly and clearly proclaiming that they would abrogate the unequal treaties signed by the Qing before them. From armed neutrality, the foreigners' volunteer corps had switched to reinforcing the Qing military.

In August 1860, the joint Anglo-French forces, having pressed for ratification of the Treaty of Tianjin, again attacked the city of Tianjin, occupied Beijing, and destroyed the Yuanmingyuan or Summer Palace. The Qing court was compelled to sign the humiliating Treaty of Beijing.

Heading south in February of 1861, Admiral James Hope of the British fleet crossed the Yangzi River to Nanjing to enter into negotiations with the Taipings. The Taipings agreed not to attack Shanghai for one year and not to interfere in commerce along the Yangzi. However, in September of the same year, the Taipings lost their important base of operations at Anqing. Heavenly King Hong Xiuquan dismissed Hong Ren'gan and Chen Yucheng for responsibility in the fall of Anqing, and he reappointed his two problematic brothers, Hong Renfa and Hong Renda. Renfa was made the Faithful King and Renda the Valorous King, and Taiping politics began once again to show signs of internal chaos.

The time limit on the treaty expired in January 1862, and the Taipings attempted to attack Shanghai, but the Foreign Rifle Company at the core of the defensive forces there remained firm, and the city did not fall to the rebels. An Anglo-French expeditionary army was assembling in Shanghai at this time. British Admiral Hope, French Vice-Admiral August Leopold Protet, and British Generals Sir Charles Staveley and Sir John Michel arrived in Shanghai from Tianjin in command of the Ninety-Ninth Regiment and Gunners.

Li Hongzhang, a man who hailed from Hefei, Anhui province, was building his own military force on the model of Zeng Guofan. Hefei was near the Huai River, and Li's force came to be known as the Huai or Anhui Army. Seven thousand troops of the army were transported by British vessels to Shanghai at the beginning of May, when the fighting at Shanghai was particularly bitter.

Ward's Foreign Rifle Company was officially recognized at that time by the Qing government. Although started as a foreigners' brigade, unemployed Chinese eventually joined it and received Western-style military training under a Filipino assistant, V. Macanana. About half the Company were Chinese soldiers.

Ward was an American, and when he was arrested on suspicion of instigating the desertion of British sailors, the British turned him over to the American consul. He had hoped to win over British sailors to build up the Foreign Rifle Company. The American consul had to place Ward on trial, but there was a loophole for him. If he abandoned his American citizenship, he would not have to stand trial, and the matter would end there. So Ward renounced his citizenship, saying to himself that he was a Chinese citizen. He had married the daughter of Yang Fang, a Shanghai financier. If there was little hope of personal advancement as an American, he thought, then he would make his way as a Chinese military commander.

Jiangsu Governor Xue Huan dubbed Ward's Foreign Rifle Company the "Ever Victorious Army." Eventually the Ever Victorious Army effectively became the experimental corps for Li Hongzhang's Anhui Army and was absorbed into it, but at this time it still had its bizarre, invigorated quality as a band of daredevils.

The Taipings' attack in and around Shanghai was a series of fierce battles: at Gaoqiao in February, at Qibao twice in April, at Taicang and Jiading in May, and at Qingpu in June. The Taiping leader Ji Qingyuan died in the Gaoqiao battle; Admiral Hope was severely wounded and Admiral Protet killed at Qibao; and Qing Prefect Li Qingchen died in the line of duty at Taicang. When the joint Anglo-French forces under the command of General Staveley, who were defending Jiading, learned of the impending attack by the Taipings, they set fire to the city and retreated without a fight. At the battle of Qingpu, Admiral Hope boarded a vessel known as the *Balkan* and took command of the forces on his own, but could not defend against the ferocious Taiping assault, and the Taipings recaptured Qingpu. Vice-Commander of the Ever Victorious Army Edward Forrester was taken prisoner at this time. Three months later, he was released in exchange for weaponry and ammunition.

The Taipings were gaining the upper hand in the fighting surrounding Shanghai.

—2—

It was just about this time that the new building of the Jinshunji in Shanghai was completed. Xiling had gone with her daughter Ruxing to the United States and now returned to Shanghai after a four-year stay. Ruxing remained at the American university where she was studying.

A banquet was held in celebration of the completion of the building and to welcome Xiling home. Lian Weicai was now seventy-four years of age. Liwen was forty-two. He traveled from the Ryūkyū Islands, passing Satsuma in southern Japan, then boarded a British vessel from Nagasaki, and worked for a time with a British commercial concern in Yokohama. He arrived back in Shanghai just one week after Xiling.

Aside from the eldest son Chengwen, who was in Taiwan, the three other brothers of the Lian household were all now gathered in Shanghai. Weicai's wife, Lian Yuan, had been living in Shanghai for the past few years.

"Rather than stay here in my old home," Lian Yuan had said, "I'd like to live in a new one. For whatever reason, the children and grandchildren of the Lian family seem to have set down deep roots in Shanghai." And, with no apparent lingering affection for the city of Xiamen in which she had lived for so long, Lian Yuan just quite naturally moved to Shanghai.

Everyone had great fun listening to Xiling's stories of her travels in the United States. For the level of knowledge in China at that time, the Lian family had acquired considerable first-hand information on foreign lands, and thus Xiling's stories were interesting in and of themselves. Even the stories of her failures bore a clarity distinctively hers.

"Since whenever we were together, we always spoke Chinese, her English wasn't progressing as it should. So I decided to put her in a boarding house. I haven't spoken Chinese at all for the past four years. Well, I may have spoken to myself a few times." Xiling's capacity to tell stories had, in fact, improved in proportion to the few times over the past four years in which she had used her Chinese.

"I see that the Taiping movement is still active. They're really bearing up well." Her manner of speech was masking an apparent indifference, though she had known the leaders of the Society of God Worshippers ever since their early days in Jintian village. She certainly retained some fond memories.

Xinmei was making a gloomy face. She had left the Taiping movement and had tried to sever all interest in it. Although her heart jumped at the brave fight put up by Li Xiucheng around Shanghai, she repressed it, and Liwen was well aware of it. Indeed, Liwen knew only too well the reason for the melancholy look on her face now. A report that Chen Yucheng had been killed had only just arrived. He was only twenty-six years old at the time of his death, the same age as the Xianfeng Emperor, who had died the previous year, though no two youthful lives could have been more different.

When Heroic King Chen Yucheng had been fourteen years old, Yang Xiuqing asked Liwen to watch after him for a while. When Xinmei, dressed in the disguise of a farmer's wife, went into the closely watched city of Yongan to make contact with her confederates, she took the young Chen with her. Going with a young child in tow seemed less out of the ordinary. The youngster feigned as though he were about to cry, calling out, "Mama, mama." That voice from twelve years earlier was still fresh in Xinmei's memory.

When she had praised his acting, he replied, "What do you mean acting? I really felt like I was escaping with my mother." Xinmei had been moved to tears.

This young man, who along with Li Xiucheng provided the backbone of the Taiping Heavenly Kingdom, grew into the Heroic King Chen Yucheng. After he had lost Anqing and suffered demotion for it, Chen had become rather impatient. Besieged at Luzhou, he escaped and made his way to Shouzhou, where he was captured. It was Miao Peilin who enticed him there on the pretext that Shouzhou was well-stocked with food and able-bodied men.

Miao Peilin was half bandit and half mercenary leader for local landlords. He effectively was balancing two sets of scales—the Qing dynasty and the Taipings—on his shoulders. After Anqing was captured by Qing forces, Miao examined the gradations on his scales and calculated a way to get himself back into the good graces of the government. It was at this point that he concocted a plan to lure Chen Yucheng and deliver him to the authorities as proof of his own allegiance.

The bravest of Taiping commanders, Chen Yucheng was but a lad of twenty-six, and he was unable to see through the trap set by Miao Peilin. Miao was harboring an ulterior motive while pretending to be loyal to the Taiping movement. Shouzhou fell within his sphere of influence. Because it was clearly disadvantageous for him to fight at the besieged city of Luzhou, Chen Yucheng rushed to get away. There had been a way to return to the Heavenly Capital at that time, and had he done so, he probably would not have been ensnared in Miao's web.

Xinmei pondered the matter. He just didn't want to go back to the Heavenly Capital, because, say what you will, the Heavenly King is the evil one. His distribution of honors and awards is chaotic. He trusts no one but his own blood relatives, and they're all repugnant. Had there been an atmosphere in the Heavenly Capital conducive to encouraging his speedy return, then he'd have surely chosen to go back. Had the Assistant King been in the Heavenly Capital at the time, then the Taipings would have put his 200,000-man army into action. In that case, Shanghai would have fallen quickly. As she thought of all this, Xinmei unconsciously clenched her fist. Liwen softly stroked her tightened hand.

Nineteen days following the capture of Heroic King Chen Yucheng, he was put to death at a place known as Yanjin in Henan province. From his arrest until his execution, Chen retained a dignified pose. The word that reached Shanghai was: A splendid end, so fitting for the most heroic figure in the entire Taiping movement.

Every time she heard this story, it tugged at Xinmei's heartstrings. Liwen changed the topic. "The situation's gotten critical in Japan. About the time I set out to return, the discontent among conservatives was growing tremendously."

"Is it just that they instinctively reject contact with foreign countries?" asked his father, Lian Weicai.

"There are many psychological aspects to it, but the fact that living conditions have become very difficult seems to me to have made people's lives most tumultuous."

"Have prices been rising?"

"They're rising, as you'd expect. Japan's been a closed country for a long time. It's been self-sufficient. They've been producing within their means only what they themselves consume, and if someone were suddenly to buy up a large amount of a commodity, the whole system would be thrown into disarray. Take tea leaves, for example: The more foreigners have gone there to buy them, the more the price on them has skyrocketed."

"Even if the price on limited commodities like tea leaves and marine produce goes up, they're only a small part of a much larger structure," said Lian Weicai.

Western countries at that time were not only trying to buy commodities from Japan, like tea leaves, that were consumed at home. But, because their seaborne vessels had superior transport capacity, they were engaged in business buying up Japanese produce needed in China and then transporting and selling it to the Chinese. Maritime products such as abalone, sea cucumber, and shark fin were the principal items of these Western merchants. The shogunate adopted a protective policy toward such commodities, prohibited their domestic consumption, and assigned them entirely to be exported to China from Nagasaki. These had never been eaten in Japan before, so although their market price soared, it would have had no effect in the kitchen budgets of common people.

"It's rare that commodity prices rise in only one small part of the overall structure. For whatever reason, prices on other commodities are going up too. Because it's structural."

"That much I understand. They have an agitating effect. The price of tea leaves rises, and as a result transport charges on tea also rise. Then labor costs will have to go up too. Everything is stimulated in this way and it leads to trouble."

"The Japanese are proposing a deferment of the two open ports and two open cities promised in treaties with the foreigners. The two ports are Hyōgo and Niigata, and the two cities are Edo and Osaka. The reason they're giving for this is that the tremendous rise in prices is having a deleterious effect on the people's daily lives and discontent with trade is on the increase. These really are important reasons, but a far stronger reason is the basic conservatism or exclusionary instincts of those people who are upset."

"I've heard that it's because of all the sand bars at Niigata and the difficulty of anchoring there."

"Exactly, but the main reason the shogunate wants to postpone the opening of Hyōgo is because it's so close to Kyoto. The imperial court and its entourage are in Kyoto, and the extreme conservatives are especially strong there. People sympathetic to that strain of thought have recently been gathering in Kyoto. That's been a source of agitation, too."

"No matter how much they agitate, though, they can't swim against the tides of history." Lian Weicai's words were in reference not only to Japan, but applied to China as well.

—3—

It so happened that when Lian Liwen was in Japan, Kazunomiya was married to Shōgun Iemochi. The shogun was the actual ruler of Japan, and foreign nations often referred to him as the "emperor" or the "great sovereign" (*taikun* in Japanese, origin of the word "tycoon"). With the sharp rise of Japanese nationalism, though, the emperor—who was the nominal ruler—began to reemerge from obscurity in a major way.

The shogunal authorities began perforce to consider a merger of imperial court and military government (shogunate) and welcomed Kazunomiya to Edo. This event too, inspired the conservatives, as the nationalist antiforeign tide became all the stronger.

The "tides of history" of which Lian Weicai had spoken would sweep away whatever reactionary or antiforeign movement stood in their way. Even the shogunate realized that it would be exceedingly difficult to maintain its closed-door policy, and it allowed the construction and seaborne passage of formerly banned large vessels. Although aimed at deferring the opening of the two ports and two cities, the shogunate sent Takeuchi Yasunori and others to London and began publishing the *Official Batavia News* to inform them of events overseas. Eventually, Enomoto Takeaki (1836–1908) and others were sent to study in Holland, and little by little, Japan's closed-door policy was relaxed.

About ten days earlier, a vessel by the name of *Senzaimaru* arrived in Shanghai from Japan. Perhaps this was one manifestation of what Lian meant by the "tides of history."

"What's the purpose of the ship that's just arrived from Japan?" asked Chengwen.

"They say they've come to observe trading conditions," replied Liwen, "and I suppose we can take them at their word."

Although the negotiations over postponing the opening of ports continued, the shogunate knew full well that, given the overall global situation, this was only a temporizing measure. Before long, commercial interaction with foreign countries would grow to major proportions, and they foresaw that to remain in the present state, passive and unchanged, would be highly disadvantageous. In order to move ahead actively, they first had to observe how it was done.

The shogunate had purchased the *Armistice,* a British sailing vessel, and renamed it *Senzaimaru.* With Numa Heirokurō, a investigative official in the Nagasaki Hall, in charge, Nedate Sukeshichirō, a lower-ranking shogunal official, merchants, attendants, and others, altogether fifty-one men who made up the Japanese group of trade observers, had boarded this vessel bound for Shanghai.

The *Senzaimaru* reached Shanghai on the sixth day of the fifth lunar month, or June 2, 1862. Just at that time, Loyal King Li Xiucheng led an attack on British forces under the command of Major Montgomerie near Songjiang and obtained 400 rifles and 36 boxes of gunpowder. In the written records left by those aboard the *Senzaimaru,* we find accounts of seeing the horizon in the west ablaze the night before and hearing gunfire the next day.

They arrived in Shanghai right in the middle of war, but the hustle and bustle of the international port there was not to be extinguished in the conflagrations of the battles. Takasugi Shinsaku (1839–1867), a Japanese aboard the *Senzaimaru* from the domain of Chōshū, described the scene in Shanghai in his *Daily Record of the Voyage* as follows:

> European countries have docked merchant vessels and warships by the thousands here. The forest of masts is about to bury the mouth of the port. On land, the mounds of dust outside the foreign commercial establishments are almost as high as a castle rampart. I cannot draw with brush and paper their enormity or formidableness.

"All sorts of rumors are floating around in public," said Chengwen.

"All nonsense," replied Liwen, laughing.

By public rumors, Chengwen was referring to stories such as the one that the Qing government had requested military reinforcements from Japan to put down the Taiping rebels, and that the *Senzaimaru* was the detachment to arrive.

"I've been over to the Hongji," said Zhewen.

Hongji was the name of the inn in which the passengers aboard the *Senzaimaru* stayed. It was operated by Chinese, but was a Western-style hotel with primarily European guests residing there. The Japanese had entrusted the Dutch with handling their cargo, and the Dutch in turn selected the Hongji, which was only three doors down from the Dutch Consulate. Zhewen was able to speak Japanese, but he purposefully pretended not to be able to and went there ostensibly trying to sell his paintings.

"I engaged them in brush conversations," he said, referring to the means Chinese and Japanese had long used to carry on a "discussion" on paper in literary Chinese, "and there's some remarkable calligraphy in it. I asked about conditions in Japan, but they embellished a lot."

Zhewen had lived for a considerable period of time in Japan and was quite knowledgeable about the state of affairs there. From his perspective, much of the introduction Japanese gave of their country in brush conversations was exaggerated. From inside his paintbox, Zhewen pulled out the roll of paper used in the brush conversations.

"I could bind this and have a whole book made out of it. There's no reason they'd expect me to know Japanese, and so they spoke among themselves about lots of things without reservation when they were standing right in front of me. After I got home, I recalled what they had said and wrote it down here. I think this could be really important material," he said.

"Really? Let me read some of it." Chengwen placed it before him, spread out one page at a time and read.

"This Takasugi Shinsaku has some fascinating ideas. Godai Saisuke's also extraordinary, but what's all this about being a sailor?" said Chengwen after reading it.

"He decided to assume the role of a sailor, but it's not at all who he is. He's a retainer from the domain of Satsuma. I could tell by his accent. The translators among the Japanese, Shū Kōjūrō and Sai Zentarō, and one of the merchants from Nagasaki were a bit worried that someone might by chance recognize his face," said Zhewen. Since he himself had lived in Nagasaki for a fairly long period of time, Zhewen wondered if his own face might be recognized.

Tan Qi then arrived at the place where this discussion was transpiring. He had been a member of the staff of Li Xiucheng, responsible for intelligence, and was now living in Shanghai with an air of nonchalance. He was a frequent guest at the Jinshunji.

"The Taipings have decided to withdraw their troops from the environs of Shanghai," he began, upon entering the room.

"Withdraw their troops?" said Liwen, unconsciously half rising to his feet.

Tan Qi stared directly at Liwen and nodded affirmatively.

—4—

"Three edicts in one day," said Tan Qi, as tears came to his eyes. He was clearly upset.

The Heavenly Capital was surrounded by forces of the Qing military. Heavenly King Hong Xiuquan inside the capital had ordered Loyal King Li Xiucheng, then engaged in battles near Shanghai, to return with his men and participate in the effort to break the siege of the Heavenly Capital.

Shanghai was on the verge of capitulating, but Li had no choice but to withdraw his forces. Had it been within his power, Li Xiucheng would have continued to concentrate all of his strength in the battle at Shanghai and ignore the orders from Hong Xiuquan. The withdrawal edict was issued three times in one day, a manifestation of the Heavenly King's strong views on the matter, and equivalent to saying that he did not want to hear Li Xiucheng's views.

"We've got no choice," Li Xiucheng had said. His staff members swallowed and awaited further explanation. Did he mean that they had no choice but to follow the orders of the Heavenly King? Or did he mean that they had no choice but to ignore those orders and leave the Taiping movement like Shi Dakai?

"Let's be on our way back to the Heavenly Capital," he had said with his eyes shut tightly, and then reportedly sped off at a rapid pace. He could sense his staff members' feelings on the matter.

"He must have known Shi Dakai's feelings," said Liwen, sighing.

After he broke with the Taipings, Shi Dakai wandered from place to place in Sichuan and Guizhou at the head of a large military force. It wasn't simple movement, either, because he was being pursued by the Qing Army. As far as he was concerned, Shi only wanted a base of operations anywhere, but fierce Qing attacks would not allow that to happen.

Even he seemed to be thinking that leaving the Taipings had been a mistake, and the Taiping leadership certainly recognized that much. Li Xiucheng was not about to choose the same path that others had taken to failure. He reasoned as follows as to why the stringent order had been issued three times in a single day: The Heavenly Capital is the national capital of the Taiping Heavenly Kingdom. Even if we take Shanghai, if the Heavenly Capital is lost, the Taiping movement will itself disintegrate. Thus breaking the siege at the Heavenly Capital is a far more important operation right now than the attack on Shanghai.

"Yes, indeed. The Heavenly Capital has been a famous city since the era of the Three Kingdoms, and hasn't it been able to withstand sieges lasting one or even two full years? The government forces began their siege of the

Heavenly Capital just recently. By comparison, just a little more push and Shanghai would probably have fallen. It was a major miscalculation on the part of the Heavenly King to summon Li Xiucheng back." Liwen had had the closest relations with the Taiping movement and had been most excited about it until now, as was apparent from the changed tone of his voice.

"Everyone thinks so," replied Zhewen agreeably.

"The Heavenly King's failed," said Chengwen.

"He's failed because of those brothers of his," said Zhewen. "They're not men of courage or spirit, so as soon as the Heavenly Capital was surrounded, they became frightened and anxious, always making a big fuss about reinforcements, reinforcements."

"The Heavenly King hasn't just failed. He's been a failure from the very start. And because of it, he used Renfa and Renda in the first place," said Xinmei, relating her own merciless views on the subject.

"That may be overstating it, Xinmei," said Lian Weicai in a tranquil voice. "If the Heavenly King had been a failure from the start, whose power and influence are responsible for taking half of the entire realm?"

"Everybody's," she replied quickly, but her tone of voice had softened considerably.

"Yes, but who was able to bring all of their power and influence together? Was it because Yang Xiuqing was so brilliant?"

Xinmei shook her head negatively to Lian's question. The one person she had hated most of all the Taiping leaders was Eastern King Yang Xiuqing. It was he who had issued the order for the massacre at Quanzhou, a human annihilation, and that had been the motive for her breaking with the Taiping movement.

"How about Wei Changhui?" Xinmei also shook her head at this suggestion. She had had no particular fondness for Northern King Wei Changhui. He evoked a physiological abhorrence in her.

"Feng Yunshan and Xiao Chaogui died early on. To take the Heavenly Capital by storm, there was no one else who brought everyone's strength together. Am I wrong? Li Xiucheng's status was still too low, and Chen Yucheng was only a child at the time." Lian Weicai spoke as if he were instructing.

One had to admit that the Heavenly King's accomplishments were formidable. However, he also had his failings. One could not simply assume a one-sided or emotional view on this subject. This was what Lian had left unsaid.

"Is it possible to get the Heavenly King to think better of his decision?" said Tan Qi, looking at Lian with an expression that asked for help.

"Go back, ask the Loyal King, and see what happens. Say that the appointed time for the capitulation of Shanghai can't be far away and could he make such a promise to the Heavenly King," said Lian.

"Even a promise . . ." Tan Qi stopped on that word. He sensed the need for a pause. Every officer and soldier in the Taiping Army had a response to it. On the battlefield, one faced an opponent, and there was no reason for there to be firm promises.

"If the Anhui Army and the Ever Victorious Army remain as they are at present," Tan Qi began again. Well-versed on intelligence, Tan Qi did not believe that the enemy's strength would remain the same as it presently appeared to be. He was advancing a hypothesis in which he himself did not believe.

"Li Hongzhang is the most capable man in the Qing camp. From what I've seen, he's far more talented than even Zeng Guofan. It would be strange to expect him not to replenish the Anhui Army. I'm sure you've got continuous reports about Anhui Army training and the like." Lian enunciated each word slowly. Tan Qi lowered his head dispiritedly.

"This Ward fellow in the Ever Victorious Army is a thoroughgoing American villain, but we can't look down our noses at the rest of his group. Ward lives off the bounties and prices he collects. A group of Shanghai merchants put a price of thir;ty-thousand taels of silver on the recapture of Songjiang, and he set off to try as hard as he could to win it. He's a professional. In his mind, it's all business. As you may know, to succeed in business, he once tried to hire some British sailors and was arrested for instigating their desertion. His enthusiasm to get the job done is frightening. Still, though, this Ever Victorious Army certainly has taken a strange name. They say Xue Huan gave it to them. Do you know how it got the name?"

Lian Weicai had explained to his family members the history of the name Ever Victorious Army. The name had been used over 700 years earlier. In the era when the Liao dynasty of the Khitan people controlled Beijing, a man by the name of Guo Yaoshi (early twelfth century), who came from the state of Bohai, a state conquered by the Liao, organized a corps of troops that was dubbed the Ever Victorious Army. They defended the city of Yanjing, as Beijing was then known, on behalf of the Liao, and when attacked by the armies of the Song dynasty, they were defeated. When the Jin forces of the Jurchen people attacked from the east, they were defeated by the Jin, and as the advance forces for the Jin they served in the assault on the Song capital at Kaifeng. Whether or not they knew that it was the name of a foreign military force that changed loyalties any number of times, once again the same name was attached to a foreign fighting force.

They were not, however, to be dismissed lightly. That was for sure. They were contracted to win wars, and if they won, they earned a certain amount of money for their efforts. They were not only entrepreneurial about it; they were avid about their work.

Just like the Hunan Army, the Anhui Army was this sort of workmanlike force of soldiers. There was no reason to expect that they could promise a date by which Shanghai would fall. At least, Li Xiucheng was not likely to make any such promise.

"If it were you, Mr. Lian, what would you do?" asked Tan Qi.

"If I were in a position to give orders to the Taipings, I would have the entire army rush out of the Heavenly Capital and head back toward Shanghai. Then Shanghai would be sure to fall. I'd make Shanghai the new capital, create a sphere of management along the seacoast, and then it just might be possible to build a state through trade and commerce. But I don't expect the Heavenly King has any such plans. It's just a dream of mine," responded Lian Weicai.

—5—

Although he didn't put it into words, in his heart Lian Weicai was thinking that the end of the Taiping Heavenly Kingdom was near at hand. If I were only twenty years younger, he mused to himself. Twenty years before, China was right in the midst of the Opium War, a time when he was on the move and full of vigor. At age seventy-four now, he had reached a sense of maturity.

"If we'd just had another ten men like Lin Zexu." This was Lian's favorite phrase, implying high-level officials with extraordinary abilities in both political and military affairs and of upright character. Had there been ten political figures comparable to Lin Zexu, he implied, China might have been saved.

Because of his age, Lian Weicai was now no longer as active as he had been. He sensed that the Taiping movement was but one political authority in China, but not China itself. To be sure, it was far better than the decadent Qing government, but to leave everything in the hands of the Taipings would have been highly destabilizing.

While they destroyed and burned Confucian plaques and images, murdered high-level bureaucrats, and renounced the government's status system, the Taipings seemed to be adopting a posture directly opposed to the Qing. Soon after rising in rebellion, they set up the five kings—north, south, east, west, and assistant—and made these positions hereditary. This already posed a contradiction, for they seemed to be recreating their own status system. They advocated gender equality, and yet the selection of beautiful women at Wuchang had greatly disappointed Lian Weicai. If the Taiping movement was in fact doomed, then it could surely count severe internal dissension as the primary cause—dissension rooted in power struggles and many interests surrounding that power.

While they killed members of the specially privileged classes of landlords and high-level officials in many places, the Taipings themselves created their own privileged class. Distinctions in titles based on privilege were even more cumbersome than those in the regulations of the Qing. For example, the dynasty made taboo only those Chinese characters that represented the posthumous names of emperors. The Taipings, by contrast, had far, far more taboo characters. There were, for example, minute distinctions, based on privilege—distinctions virtually impossible to remember—in the names of officials' wives.

The Chinese character for "fire" is an extremely ordinary ideograph, but it could not be used, because it appears in the Chinese transcription for Jehovah, the Heavenly Father. To express the word for "fire," the Taipings had to use a lexically similar word. They became fastidious about these seemingly extraneous matters and effectively bewildered everyone. There was nothing for even able, intelligent political figures to do.

It all seems so cruel, thought Lian with an air of indifference. He had no other means than that at his disposal. In their positions around Shanghai, the Taiping forces began to retreat on orders from Li Xiucheng on June 19, 1862, while the *Senzaimaru* was still docked in Shanghai.

"Jinling [Nanjing] is in a critical situation, for the fall of the city appears imminent." Hibino Teruhiro, a retainer from Takasu domain in Japan and a passenger aboard the *Senzaimaru,* made this observation in his account of the trip to Shanghai.

While leaving an attack force behind, the Taipings withdrew without a fight. In everyone's eyes, though, it appeared that they were pulling back because of exhaustion and lack of provisions and ammunition. The event was a great psychological boon for the Qing side.

With those three edicts issued in a single day, not only was Li Xiucheng called back to assemble a force to break the siege at the Heavenly Capital. Attendant King Li Shixian in command of a force at the front in Zhejiang had the same order issued to him, and all at once he withdrew with his men. Li Xiucheng opened a strategy session at Suzhou, and he later made frequent trips between the Heavenly Capital and Suzhou. His headquarters in Suzhou was at a garden still famous today and visited by many tourists.

With the withdrawal of forces from both the Shanghai and Zhejiang fronts, guerrilla brigades were left in place. In the accounts of Japanese aboard the *Senzaimaru,* one finds records of fighting after Li Xiucheng's retreat. Furthermore, Ward of the Ever Victorious Army was severely wounded in a battle with Taiping troops at a place known as Ziqi in Zhejiang province. He subsequently died on August 22 of that year, 1862. The Qing court awarded the post of regional vice-commander to Ward, a military post just below regional commander, with a 2B rank. He left behind 60,000 British pounds, an immense sum of money at the time. He had risen from a common sailor, and in his thirty-seven years of full-fledged adventure, he became a rich man. He met his end working as a mercenary, but it was a dramatic career.

With Ward's death the Ever Victorious Army was reorganized. Personnel were reduced, and Major Charles Gordon (1833–1885) of the British Army was appointed its commander. The former band of fortune hunters were incorporated into a regular army unit, and it in turn became a model for the Anhui Army. With this qualitative change, the Ever Victorious Army, now on a par with Qing armed forces, continued the fighting against the Taipings.

The armies ordered to break the siege around the Heavenly Capital surrounded the nearby Qing base area at Yuhuatai. Li Xiucheng led an army said to have thirteen kings and 600,000 men, but it actually numbered some 100,000 troops at most. The Qing forces at Yuhuatai were under the command of Zeng Guoquan (1824–1890), younger brother of Zeng Guofan. Guoquan now held the important post of Jiangsu provincial administration commissioner, and just at this time the governorship of Jiangsu had passed to Li Hongzhang. As a ferocious battle aimed at Yuhuatai was unfolding, Regional Vice-Commander Zhu Lingui died on the battlefield, and Zeng Guoquan was seriously wounded. Unlike the government's regular military units, the Hunan Army was still extremely strong.

People at the time referred to this battle as the showdown in which neither the two Lis nor the two Zengs would give in to the other. The two Lis referred to Loyal King Li Xiucheng and Attendant King Li Shixian of the Taipings, while the two Zengs referred to Zeng Guoquan, in charge of this operation, and his younger brother Zeng Zhen'gan. The battle ensued for forty-six days, at which point Taiping military provisions ran out and clothing resupplies were difficult to come by. It was late November and would soon become cold, and then they would be unable to continue the fight with only thin clothing on their backs. Li Xiucheng finally decided to give in, lift the siege at Yuhuatai, and return to the Heavenly Capital.

Hong Xiuquan stripped Li of his title and ordered him to advance north across the Yangzi River. The use of punishments and rewards was, of course, essential, but the spirit of devotion could no longer be felt in the Heavenly King's actions, as he had gradually divorced himself from the minds of his troops. The Heavenly King entrusted all political matters to his brother Renfa and all military affairs to his brother Renda. Their incompetence was well-known to all, but the Heavenly King still placed the fate of the Taiping movement in their hands.

Supplies for Li Xiucheng's forces north of the Yangzi were not forthcoming in full because of the incapacity of the military authorities. Stark simple orders to seize necessary military provisions on the scene were issued, but far from being able to confiscate supplies on the scene, the men shared what little military provisions they had with the local starving people. Because the war had gone on for such a long time, numerous farmers had abandoned their land, become itinerant in search of work, and shown up in the cities.

In June 1863 the Heavenly King called Li Xiucheng back to the Heavenly Capital. His brothers' incompetence had gone so far that even he, Heavenly King Hong Xiuquan, could no longer bear it.

—6—

In February 1963, Suzhou, where Li Xiucheng made his base of operations, fell into Qing hands. In March of 1864, Taiping armies lost Hangzhou, and in May of the same year, Qing forces recaptured Changzhou. The military unit that attacked Suzhou was made up principally of the Ever Victorious Army under Gordon. The Anhui Army participated in the assault, but it was like a group of trainees studying through observation the model military operation of the Ever Victorious Army. Known for its waterways, Suzhou had streams and rivers running in every direction. All communications going outside the city were entrusted to these waterways. In the attack planned for Suzhou, Gordon was attentive to them and concentrated his energy on intercepting traffic along those waterways. He first consolidated the assault on the Taiping artillery used to protect the waterways, and then he implemented a psychological tactic.

Because of the politics within the Heavenly King's entourage, many among the Taiping military forces lost the will to act, which had an undermining effect on the movement. The man who implemented the psychological stratagem was Cheng Xueqi. Cheng came from a peasant family in Anhui province and had originally joined the Taiping movement. While in camp in Anqing, he surrendered to the Qing Army. Because he had intimate knowledge of the internal conditions of the Taiping military at Anqing, Li Hongzhang employed him, and he distinguished himself in the attack on Anqing. Cheng became a regular military official in the Qing armed forces and subsequently advanced to the rank of regional vice-commander.

Needless to say, former close colleagues of Cheng's were among the Taiping leaders at Suzhou, and secretly he met with one of them, Vigorous King Wang Anjun.

"For those of you in the Taiping movement, if you're not a member of Hong's family, you'll get nowhere. You know that when Li Xiucheng was engaged in battle, he borrowed one hundred thousand taels from Hong Xiuquan. He's fighting for the Taiping movement, but in a sense it's a war for the Heavenly King. Nonetheless, Li Xiucheng had to fight at his own expense, and since he didn't have any money, he had to borrow it from the Heavenly King. He signed a written statement to the effect that if he fails to return the money on a certain day, he'll be punished. Is this the kind of man you'd die for? If you surrender as I did, you'll be appointed to a regular bureaucratic post like mine. It's been three years since I submitted, and look at me. I've risen to the position of regional vice-commander, rank 3A."

This was Cheng Xueqi's pitch, and his words had a persuasive power. What he was saying was largely factual, as well.

"You're not at all envious of me? You're not at all interested?" said Cheng, exhorting Wang to surrender.

"It's not that I'm not interested. It's just that Emulating King Tan Shaoguang now has command control over Suzhou. He's a very obstinate man," said Wang quietly.

"What about the others?"

"They're sensible fellows. They're always talking about it obliquely. Just yesterday Wu Guiwen said that all land does not belong solely to the Taipings. I think he's tempted in a way to surrender."

"Wu Guiwen? Isn't he one of the Taiping kings? All these kings, how stupid! Gao Yongkuan may be interested. What king is he?"

"He's the Tribute King."

"Isn't the whole thing ridiculous?"

From the original five kings, the Taiping kingships now came in mass production and of inferior quality. The explosion began after Hong Ren'gan arrived from Hong Kong and was enfeoffed as the Shield King. He had not been part of the movement back in Jintian village and had performed not a single military deed. It was perfectly natural, then, that if such a man as he were made a king, those with military credits to their records would feel discontent. Then, rapidly, Chen Yucheng became the Heroic King and Li Xiucheng the Loyal King. Later, kings were born one after the next until there were more kingships than one could count.

Despite being called kings, there was no material gain to be had from such a title. As Cheng Xueqi had put it, it really was fairly ridiculous. Compared to titles like the Tribute King, a post of rank 3A in the Qing military had far greater importance.

"It'd be best if obstinate Tan Shaoguang were killed, wouldn't it?"

"Probably would. Wu Guiwen and Gao Yongkuan would probably be sympathetic, and the Peaceful King wouldn't be a problem either."

"The Peaceful King? Who's that?"

"Zhou Wenjia."

"What? That fellow's a king too?"

"Listen, though—there's a condition."

A plan of group treachery by leaders of the Taipings at the Suzhou encampment was being concocted here. Wang Anjun and the others would first deal with Tan Shaoguang, and then they would open the city gates of Suzhou and not resist as the Qing armies came pouring inside. The arrangement was that the Qing forces were going to receive their surrender and treat them the same as they had Cheng Xueqi at the time of his surrender.

The more hard-line Tan Shaoguang was stabbed to death at a meeting by Vigorous King Wang Anjun and Commander Wang Youwei. In addition to these two men, six others surrendered: Wu Guiwen, Zhou Wenjia, Gao Yongkuan, Fan Qifa, Zhang Dazhou, and Wang Huaiwu. Thus, Suzhou fell into the hands of the Qing forces without difficulty.

"What shall I do with those eight men?" asked Chen Xueqi of Li Hongzhang, the man with highest responsibility.

"It's been decided, hasn't it? Is there a single one of them who could be useful to this world?" said Li Hongzhang sullenly.

"I understand," said Cheng, blinking with a sour expression on his face. The pathetic eight men who had surrendered were all put to death.

Casualties among the troops of the Ever Victorious Army under the command of Gordon at the Suzhou front were extremely high. For that reason, it was Gordon who had enthusiastically encouraged acts of betrayal within the ranks of the Taipings.

"We must keep our promises," said Gordon, enraged at the murder of the eight surrendered commanders, and he clashed vehemently with Li Hongzheng. Unlike Ward, Gordon came from a noble family in Scotland and became a military man after graduating from the Army Military Academy. He had a very strict view of contractual obligations. He had been reared to believe that it was only a shameless person who broke a promise. About two months earlier, the Taiping forces at Suzhou complied with a request in a document personally written by Gordon and repatriated the American Henry A. Burgevine—who briefly commanded the Ever Victorious Army, following Ward's death—and other interned wounded men who were his subordinates. Gordon considered this the appropriate code of a gentleman, and his opponents were gentlemen. Li Hongzhang had said he would be merciful and then had the men executed. It was a stab in the back.

"The man has no shame!" Charles Gordon, a major in a land of gentlemen, could not decide how to respond to Li Hongzhang's contemptible action. The idea of looking Li in the face nauseated him, so he wrote Li a stern letter:

> For three years Suzhou was under the control of the Taipings, and it fell because of the surrender of eight Taiping commanders. The promises made concerning their surrender, which had to be kept in the name of humanity, you chose to violate. You must leave Suzhou and relinquish your post as

governor of Jiangsu. You can leave the governor's seal with me. The imperial court in Beijing is waiting to punish you. If you choose to do otherwise, the cities thus far occupied by the Ever Victorious Army will all be turned over to the Taipings.

Gordon also assembled the officers of the Ever Victorious Army and said to them, "If the Qing court fails to mete out a punishment for Li Hongzhang, I intend for our Ever Victorious Army no longer to be under his command and for control to pass to a British military commander."

Li Hongzhang had not foreseen that Gordon would become this enraged. Weren't those guys rebels, guilty of high treason? he thought. And whether we let them live or kill them, the court gave me complete freedom to act as I saw fit—and after I went and recommended him for promotion to regional commander!

A regional commander was a post comparable to general. Ward was treated as a regional vice-commander, a post more or less the equivalent of a brigadier general. A regional commander was above a regional vice-commander. Gordon had only just turned thirty, still much younger than Ward. In the British military ranks, he was still a major. Unhappy with this situation, he verbally abused Li Hongzhang—"Get out of here!" or "Why don't you quit your post!"—who was the governor of Jiangsu, the highest commanding officer in the area. This was something Li Hongzhang simply could not understand.

With the Ever Victorious Army as its mainstay, Li's forces had taken the cities of Fushan, Taicang, and Kunshan. Qing armies retained control over Changshu too, though without the reinforcements rushed there by the Ever Victorious Army, it would probably have been stormed and seized by the Taipings.

From Gordon's unusual manner of displaying his anger, he seemed to have no choice but to actually relinquish control of these cities to the Taipings. Li had to placate Gordon, who had withdrawn to command headquarters in Kunshan. Over the next two months, Gordon didn't budge from Kunshan. Li relied on Robert Hart (1835–1911), the inspector general of the Chinese Imperial Maritime Customs, to persuade Gordon.

"It's impossible for the Qing court to punish Li Hongzhang, the highest-ranking commanding officer on the eastern front, in the middle of a war against the Taipings."

"Rumors among the people are rife that the Ever Victorious Army is going to capitulate to the Taipings."

"Li Hongzhang may reorganize the Ever Victorious Army, and in that case our British influence over the Chinese government will decrease dramatically."

In this way, Hart tried to get Gordon to rejoin the fight. Hart was two years Gordon's junior, but he already had a certain talent at captivating people. He would later become a diplomatic advisor to the Qing government and demonstrate his skills in foreign diplomacy. Furthermore, by appealing to "our British influence," Hart was able to convince Gordon to return to the fight against the Taipings.

On February 2, 1864, Gordon met with Li Hongzhang and proposed a strategy in the war against the Taipings. It was to attack Yixing from Wuxi, cut off Taiping supply lines, and thus break the Taipings' communications between the provinces of Zhejiang and Jiangsu.

—7—

The Taipings' Heavenly Capital, the city of Nanjing, fell to government forces on July 19, 1864. It was the third year of the Tongzhi reign period of the Qing dynasty. On that day, Lian Liwen was aboard a British merchant vessel on the Yangzi River. At his side, Tan Qi was observing the Heavenly Capital through a telescope. The fact that death had not yet overtaken Tan Qi was due to Lian Weicai's good judgment. He had wanted to return to the Heavenly Capital, but Lian detained him, effectively imprisoning him in Shanghai. Tan Qi had come to Shanghai this final time to report the news of the death of Heavenly King Hong Xiuquan. Hong was fifty-two years of age (by Chinese counting) at the time, and he had lain on his deathbed for some three weeks. Tan Qi had not been allowed deep into the recesses of the Residence of the Heavenly King, but he learned that it was illness that took Hong. He only heard from the doctor the general circumstances surrounding Hong's final hours.

"Bring the usual stuff," Hong Xiuquan had reportedly said to the doctor. Strangely, while his body had grown debilitated, his voice remained unchanged.

"The usual stuff," he pressed. According to the doctor, the "usual stuff" referred to the poisonous drugs that would enable him to die without any pain. When the doctor hesitated, Hong next ordered one of the women attendants: "In the drawer at the top of the shelf over there you'll find it wrapped in red paper. It's got the character for 'long life' written on it in gold. Bring it here."

One could not disobey an order, and a female attendant would not have known what the "usual stuff" actually was. She reverently placed it in a tray and put the tray on a small table beside the sickbed. The Heavenly King gulped down a crystal glass of water and then looked at the record-keeper. He ordered him to take down the words that would follow—an edict to be directed at all the people in the Heavenly Capital: "People of the Taiping Heavenly Kingdom, it is best for you to be at ease. Henceforth I shall ascend into the Heavenly Hall. I shall have the Heavenly Father and the Heavenly Elder Brother dispatch heavenly soldiers to protect our Heavenly Capital firmly."

After speaking, he swallowed the medicine wrapped in red paper. This occurred on June 1, some forty-eight days earlier.

"Doesn't look like heavenly soldiers will be coming down from the sky," said Liwen. The moment after he looked into the sky the sound of an earth-shattering explosion burst in his ears.

"The tunnels reached the Taiping Gate." Tan Qi took the telescope from his eye and checked to see if, in fact, the Taiping Gate had been blown off. Then he closed his eyes.

The commanding officer of the Qing forces involved in the assault on the Heavenly Capital was Zeng Guofan's younger brother, Zeng Guoquan, then governor of Zhejiang province. He had an even more violent temper than his older brother. In the attack he used a massive amount of force, and in one day three regional commanders (Chen Wansheng, Wang Shaoyi, and Guo Pengcheng), one regional vice-commander (Xiong Zixi), two assistant regional commanders, and two brigade commanders all died on the battlefield. Given casualty figures such as these among the high-level military men, the number of rank-and-file killed was also phenomenally high.

Jiangsu Governor Li Hongzhang saw that his subordinates were exhausted and needed to rest, and thus he didn't participate in the operation at the Heavenly Capital. Zeng Guofan sent a number of memorials to the throne, urging Li Hongzhang to join the attack at Nanjing.

"We have yet to recapture Changxing and Huzhou. When the fighting is over at those two places, I shall reorganize the troops and send them to Nanjing." This was Li's excuse, and as before he made no move at all toward Nanjing.

It was not that he feared the battle there. Li Hongzhang knew only too well what sort of a man Zeng Guoquan was. Zeng would want all merit accruing to the capture of the Taipings' national capital to fall to him alone. Over the course of the past two years, he had led attack after attack against Nanjing, and when at this final stage he had sought reinforcements from Li Hongzhang, the mortification was too profound for tears. He spread out his elbows and called out "I'm the one who'll bring this place down!" as if he were surrounding it. Li Hongzhang knew full well that Zeng Guoquan was this sort of fellow.

Better not to send troops to Nanjing, thought Li, because if I do it, Zeng Guoquan will resent it.

Zeng Guofan didn't move from Anqing. Because he seemed so important, he feared that he might fall under suspicion by the court. He had already received an unsigned letter from Peng Yulin: "The southeast half-piece of jade has no master. Does the teacher have such intentions?"

Although unsigned, the author's identity was apparent from the calligraphy. The meaning was clear: No one controlled the southeastern sector of China, and mightn't the "teacher" (meaning Zeng Guofan) have the desire to become its master, set himself up there, and call himself emperor? Peng Yulin was not in government service and had joined the Hunan Army under that condition.

"After the fall of Nanjing, Zeng Guofan may take charge of the Hunan Army, march north, attack Beijing, destroy the Qing dynasty, and make himself emperor of China." Zeng Guofan learned that false rumors of this sort were circulating. It was dangerous for him to win too much acclaim, and thus he turned over the assault on Nanjing to his younger brother. Guoquan was a relative, though, so it was not overly desirable for his accomplishments to be too great either. So he sought out Li Hongzhang's help in taking Nanjing.

Li was thinking about himself and decided not to move from the Jiangsu front. Since Zuo Zongtang had cleaned most of the Taipings out of Zhejiang province, perhaps he would join the assault on Nanjing. In great haste, Zeng Guoquan repeated the same unwarranted strategy, while the excavated underground tunnels finally reached to beneath the city walls. By setting powerful explosives, that day he finally succeeded in breaking through.

The explosives seem to have been laid out laterally over a considerable distance. Tiles, sand, and earth flew up into the air and then fell once again to the ground. A hole five to six meters wide had been blown in the city wall, and troops of the Hunan Army could be seen rushing in its direction.

"It'll soon be over," whispered Tan Qi.

"Aren't there only about ten thousand of them inside the city?" The reference was to the number of Taiping troops remaining inside the Heavenly Capital. The main force of the Taiping armies had left the city to fight against the Qing armies surrounding it. Though following a plan to break the siege, their own communication lines had been cut.

"Only about half of them can really offer any sort of a fight," said Tan Qi. Crack troops had been sent to take part in breaking the siege.

"I wonder what might have happened if they had accepted the Loyal King's proposal."

"They're having a hard time of it here, but so are their counterparts."

Loyal King Li Xiucheng's proposal entailed a choice of two possibilities: evacuate everyone from the Heavenly Capital, establish communication links with Taiping forces outside the city, and look for a new national capital; or resist the Qing as an itinerant state, as they had during the period when they struggled to find their way from Jintian village to Nanjing. The Heavenly King had rejected the proposal. Nanjing was selected as the place to establish the Heavenly Capital, and they had been living for the past eleven years in palaces erected there. The Heavenly King was not about to discard the city now.

"It's been a contest of endurance."

"They've probably already won."

"What way public sentiment will go will probably also be a contest."

"They'll win that one too," said Tan Qi promptly.

The Heavenly Capital just then began to erupt in flames. First the Residence of the Heavenly King and then the principal buildings of the Taiping movement looked as if someone had piled up twigs over which oil had been spread and torched them.

"They've set it on fire," said Liwen, shading his face with his hand. The duty fell to him to report to his father that the Taiping Heavenly Kingdom was destroyed. Several days later, he had to enter the Heavenly Kingdom, now just Nanjing. He expected to find much that would be difficult to bear.

Not a single soldier or officer in the Taiping Army was said to have surrendered at the time of the collapse of the Heavenly Capital. Several thousand palace women reportedly committed suicide. Hong Xiuquan's son, Junior Lord Hong Tiangui, acceded to the Taiping throne shortly after the death of the Heavenly King. He was protected by Loyal King Li Xiucheng and ushered out of the Heavenly Capital in the confusion of the night. Li Xiucheng, though, was captured and executed, and eventually so too was the Junior Lord captured and executed at Nanchang. He was sixteen years of age.

Hong Ren'gan, Hong Renfa, Hong Renda, and others of the entire Hong family in the Taiping movement were killed. Attendant King Li Shixian, however, escaped from Fujian into Guangdong. Resistance in the south finally came to an end when Accompanying King Tan Tiyuan was captured escaping from Jiaying, Guangdong in February 1866.

Taiping forces north of the Yangzi River were under the command of Obeying King Lai Wenguang, and they continued their antigovernment activities as the Nian rebels.

The final Taiping military force was the western Nian Army under the command of Zhang Zongyu. This group was surrounded by Qing forces near the Yellow River and wiped out. Nothing, though, was ever learned of the whereabouts of Zhang Zongyu himself.

In the middle of August 1868, Japan underwent a restoration of imperial rule, the capital was moved from Kyoto to Edo, and the Meiji period began.

CHIN Shunchin is a leading writer of historical fiction in Japan, where he is a household name. His novels and stories are distinguished by recurrent themes he has developed concerning China, Chinese history, and Chinese people living in Japan. He is the recipient of a number of distinguished Japanese literary awards and prizes.

Joshua A. Fogel is professor of history at the University of California, Santa Barbara. His latest books are *The Nanjing Massacre in History and Historiography* (2000) and a forthcoming volume on Chinese views of Japan in the Ming-Qing period. Professor Fogel also translated CHIN Shunchin's mystery *Murder in a Peking Studio* (1986).